*Congo Love Song*

The John Hope Franklin Series in African American History and Culture
*Waldo E. Martin Jr. and Patricia Sullivan, editors*

# Congo Love Song

*African American Culture and
the Crisis of the Colonial State*

IRA DWORKIN

The University of North Carolina Press
*Chapel Hill*

© 2017 The University of North Carolina Press
All rights reserved
Set in Adobe Text Pro by Westchester Publishing Services

Library of Congress Cataloging-in-Publication Data
Name: Dworkin, Ira, 1972– author.
Title: Congo love song : African American culture and the crisis of the colonial state / Ira Dworkin.
Other titles: John Hope Franklin series in African American history and culture.
Description: Chapel Hill : University of North Carolina Press, 2017. | Series: The John Hope Franklin series in African American history and culture | Includes bibliographical references and index.
Identifiers: LCCN 2016046557 | ISBN 9781469632711 (pbk : alk. paper) | ISBN 9781469632728 (ebook)
Subjects: LCSH: African Americans—Relations with Africans. | African Americans—Intellectual life—19th century. | African Americans—Intellectual life—20th century. | Anti-imperialist movements. | Black nationalism. | Africa.
Classification: LCC E185.625 .D95 2017 | DDC 305.896/073—dc23 LC record available at https://lccn.loc.gov/2016046557

Cover illustration: William Sheppard with Chief Maxamalinge, former prince and son of Nyimi Kot aMbweeky II (king of the Kuba, 1892–96), c. 1900. Box 4, WHSPA, Courtesy of Presbyterian Historical Society, Philadelphia, Pennsylvania.

Portions of Chapter Five were previously published in "'In the Country of My Forefathers': Pauline E. Hopkins, William H. Sheppard, Lucy Gantt Sheppard, and African American Routes," *Atlantic Studies* 5, no. 1 (April 2008): 101–20, available online at http://www.tandfonline.com/doi/abs/10.1080/14788810701878291. Used here with permission.

Portions of Chapter Seven were previously published in "'Near the Congo': Langston Hughes and the Geopolitics of Internationalist Poetry," *American Literary History* 24, no. 4 (Winter 2012): 631–57. Used here with permission.

A full list of copyright credits can be found on pages 417–18.

*For Ramona and Gwendolyn*

# Contents

*Acknowledgments*, xi

*Abbreviations Used in the Text*, xvii

Introduction, 1
  *James Weldon Johnson's Transnational Vaudeville*

PART I  The Nineteenth-Century Routes of Black Transnationalism, 17

*Chapter 1*  George Washington Williams's Stern Duty of History, 19

*Chapter 2*  William Henry Sheppard's Country of My Forefathers, 49

*Chapter 3*  Booker T. Washington's African at Home, 78

PART II  The Twentieth-Century Cultures of the American Congo, 107

*Chapter 4*  Missionary Cultures, 109
  *The American Presbyterian Congo Mission, Althea Brown Edmiston, and the Languages of the Congo*

*Chapter 5*  Literary Cultures, 139
  *The Black Press, Pauline E. Hopkins, and the Rewriting of Africa*

*Chapter 6*  Visual Cultures, 163
  *Hampton Institute, William Sheppard's Kuba Collection, and African American Art*

PART III  The Congo in Modern African American Poetics and Politics, 201

*Chapter 7*  Near the Congo, 203
  *Langston Hughes and the Geopolitics of Internationalist Poetry*

*Chapter 8*  Another Black Magazine with a Lumumba Poem, 224
  *Patrice Lumumba and African American Poetry*

*Chapter 9* The Chickens Coming Home to Roost, 257
  *Malcolm X, the Congo, and Modern Black Nationalism*

Conclusion, 288

*Appendix,* 295
  Malcolm X on the Congo, February 14, 1965, Detroit

*Notes,* 299

*Bibliography,* 363

*Credits,* 417

*Index,* 419

*A section of color plates follows page 172.*

# Maps, Figures, and Plates

*Map*

1. Democratic Republic of the Congo, xx

*Figures*

I.1  James Weldon Johnson and J. Rosamond Johnson, "Marie Cahill's Congo Love Song" cover (1903), 6

2.1  APCM missionaries from Luebo and Ibanche stations (c. 1909), 50

2.2  APCM missionaries at Luebo (c. 1902), 51

2.3  British consular officials with Sheppards and unidentified Kuba porters (c. 1908–9), 57

2.4  Compagnie du Kasai officials and William Sheppard entering the courthouse in Kinshasa (1909), 57

2.5  William Morrison, William Sheppard, Chief Niakai, and unidentified witnesses at trial in Kinshasa (1909), 59

2.6  "Maxamalinge" William Lapsley Sheppard (c. 1903–4), 69

2.7  Université Presbyterienne Sheppard et Lapsley du Congo (UPRECO), Ndesha (2006), 77

4.1  William Henry Sheppard, "Maxamalinge" William Lapsley Sheppard, Lucy Sheppard, Althea Edmiston, and Joseph E. Phipps (c. 1903–4), 110

4.2  Edmiston family (c. 1907), 114

4.3  William Sheppard playing the banjo, 117

4.4  "Do bana coba" from W. E. B. Du Bois, *The Souls of Black Folk* (1903), 119

6.1  Curiosity room, Hampton Institute (c. 1904–5), 168

6.2  Unidentified artist (Bushong), *ndop* statue of Kuba King Shyaam aMbul aNgoong (late eighteenth century), 170

6.3  Kuba textiles from William Sheppard's collection, *Presbyterian Pioneers in Congo* (1917), 173

6.4  Domestic science students at Hampton Institute (c. 1920s), 178

6.5  *Southern Workman* cover (June 1928), 179

6.6  John Biggers, *Country Preacher* (1943), 188

6.7  John Biggers, *Africa* (1942), 188

6.8  John Biggers, *Three Quilters* (1952), 190

6.9  Founder's Day presentation of John Biggers's bust of Samuel Chapman Armstrong, Hampton Institute (1949), 196

7.1  E. A. Harleston, "Voice of Congo," illustration from *Crisis* (March 1917), 212

8.1  *The Black Panther* cover (January 16, 1971), 233

8.2  Ted Joans, "LUMUMBA LIVES!" (1961), 239

8.3  Lewis Michaux's National Memorial African Bookstore in Harlem (1961), 249

9.1  Malcolm X with Patrice Lumumba picture in background (*La Vie Africaine* 1965), 263

*Plates*

1. Unidentified artists (Shoowa), raffia cut-pile cloth (undated), collected by William Sheppard (acquisition 11.152)

2. Unidentified artists (Shoowa), raffia cut-pile cloth (undated), collected by William Sheppard (acquisition 11.174)

3. Palmer Hayden, *Fétiche et Fleurs* (c. 1926–33)

4. Malvin Gray Johnson, *Negro Masks* (1932)

5. John Biggers, *Quilting Party* (1980–81)

6. John Biggers, *Starry Crown* (1987)

7. John Biggers, *House of the Turtle* (1991)

8. John Biggers, *Tree House* (1991)

9. James Phillips, *The Soul and Spirit of John Biggers* (1995)

10. Faith Ringgold, *Breakfast in Bed, Windows of the Wedding Series #2* (1974)

## Acknowledgments

It feels impossible to begin to thank the countless friends, colleagues, students, teachers, relatives, librarians, strangers, and others who have contributed to the making of this book. I am honored to share the kindness of their teaching, mentoring, feeding, reading, invitations, questions, answers, camaraderie, and solidarity, and I hope that this book represents that spirit. Acknowledgments such as these are necessarily insufficient and incomplete.

Before I went to college, Houston Baker was the first person to show me what literature and scholarship could be, and I still have no idea what I did to deserve his continued generosity. He opened up the possibilities of the wider world that animates what I write about in this book—African American communities that, through periods of colonial crisis, continually insisted on the importance of the Congo. From the Graduate Center of the City University of New York (CUNY), I remain indebted to Michele Wallace for mentoring me; she made this work possible by teaching me how to read and see and listen. The generosity of James de Jongh and Tuzyline Jita Allan has set a standard to which I continuously aspire. Robert Reid-Pharr long ago shared insights that continue to resonate. A fellowship at the Center for Place, Culture and Politics provided crucial intellectual and material support, and my gratitude for the vision of founding director Neil Smith is equaled by my sadness at his passing.

On this road, a group of friends and colleagues were around the project at its inception and have listened to me talk about it for years, including Moustafa Bayoumi, Gabrielle Civil, Samba Diallo, Chris Iannini, Geoffrey Jacques, Stacy Morgan, Cara Murray, Wilmetta Toliver-Diallo, Tisha Ulmer, and Michelle Wilkinson. For places to stay, I thank Andrew Draper, Rodd McLeod, and Marina Phillips. In more recent years, I have been fortunate to have Ebony Coletu, Chris Iannini, Geoffrey Jacques, Stacy Morgan, Hanan Sabea, John Schaeffer, Julia Seibert, and Andrew Zimmerman read various pieces of this work. With the sudden passing of Barbara Harlow, this book and I both lost a beloved fellow traveler on the road from Cairo to Texas.

I could not have written this book without the support I received from the programs in Africana Studies and American Studies at the University of Miami; the faculty of letters at the Université de Kinshasa; the department of English and the program in Africana Studies at Gettysburg College; and the department of English and Comparative Literature and the Center for American Studies and Research at the American University in Cairo. Every day I am reminded of the particular privilege to finish this book in the company of so many wonderful students and colleagues in the English department at Texas A&M. At these stops, the research assistance of Hunter Williams-Carey, Nioni Masela, Larice Toko, Mushira Sabry, Shannon Callahan, Sheehan Kane, Nermine Sergius, Amanda Rico, Amilcar Flores, and Isabella Agostino helped to pave my way. Felicien Kalonda from Université de Kinshasa assisted with the translations of Tshiluba spirituals.

I am thankful for a Publication Support Grant from the Melbern G. Glasscock Center for Humanities, Texas A&M University; a Travel Grant from the John Hope Franklin Research Center for African and African American History and Culture, Rare Book, Manuscript, and Special Collections Library, Duke University; a Fulbright U.S. Scholarship from the Bureau of Educational and Cultural Affairs, U.S. Department of State; and a Postdoctoral Fellowship from the programs in Africana Studies and American Studies, University of Miami in Florida. I am grateful for additional support from the department of English, Texas A&M University.

Librarians and archivists are among the heroes of this project, and I need to thank Donzella Maupin, Andreese Scott, and Cynthia Poston at Hampton University Archives; the late Beth M. Howse at Fisk University Franklin Library Special Collections; Jennifer Thompson at Duke University Rare Book, Manuscript, and Special Collections Library; Robert Heath at Stillman College William H. Sheppard Library; Bonnie Coles at the Library of Congress; Ralph Raunft at the Miami University Center for the Study of the History of Art Education in Ohio; Mathilde Leduc-Grimaldi at the Royal Museum for Central Africa in Tervuren; and Père Godefroid Mombula at Scolasticat Père Nkongolo Bibliothèque Père Francois Bontinck in Kinshasa. Additional thanks to colleagues and collections including the African Archives in Brussels; American University in Cairo; Brooklyn College; Emory University Manuscript, Archives, and Rare Book Library; Gettysburg College; Howard University Moorland-Spingarn Research Center; l'Institut Émile Vandervelde in Brussels; Luther Seminary; Presbyterian Historical Society in Philadelphia and the former Presbyterian Historical Society in Montreat, North Carolina; Princeton Theological Seminary; Saint Pierre Canisius Library at Kimwenza in Kinshasa; Sanford Museum in Florida; Schomburg Center for Research in Black Culture; Syracuse University; Texas A&M University; Tuskegee University Archives and Museums; University of Massachusetts, Amherst, Special Collections and Archives; University of Miami; University of Pennsylvania Van Pelt Library; University of Texas, Austin; and

Yale University Beinecke Rare Book and Manuscript Library. I remain grateful to Joshua Walker for a visit he made to the African Archives in Brussels on my behalf.

For kind assistance with images and text that I am privileged to reproduce here, I thank Emilie Algenio, Kathleen E. Bethel, David A. Brown, Ronald Chrisman, Laura Corsiglia, Melvin Edwards, Stephanie Elmquist, Berlinda Fontenot-Jamerson, Rebecca Hankins, Bruce Herbert, Fredrika Newton, Grace Matthews, Faith Ringgold, Kem Schultz, Vanessa Thaxton-Ward, and Elizabeth Vass Wilkerson. Cecilia Smith of Texas A&M University created a beautiful map that will, I hope, help make the Democratic Republic of the Congo visible. I especially want to recognize the unnamed Kuba artists, images of whose work are reproduced here; following consultation with colleagues, I have made a donation in their honor to a university in the Kasai.

During two stays in the Democratic Republic of Congo in 2005–6 and 2009, Athanase Malekani Kapele and his family were, and remain, very much my own. At the University of Kinshasa, thanks are also due to Ferdinand B. Ngwaba, Albin Majambo Kalonda, Thierry Nlandu, Jacob Sabakinu Kivilu, Mukash Kalel, Omar Mvele, N'zinga Luyinduladio, Paul Serufuri Hakiza, and Elie P. Ngoma Binda. I was also fortunate to teach a great group of graduate students, especially Daniel Kahozi, Seketula Kithima, Nioni Masela, Raymond Sangabau, Larice Toko, and the late Kambale Kabila Mututolo. Also in Kinshasa, I appreciate the various forms of support and fellowship I received from Patrick G. Cannon, Yolanda Covington-Ward, Christopher Davis, Filip De Boeck, Bertine Diangana-Kinkela, Chris Diomi, Alain Mesa, Ditumbule Minion, Brigitte Mputo, Pauline Mushiya Tite, Anicet Musikingala, Veronique Ombur, David Shapiro, Walt Shepard, Larry Sthreshley, Katya Thomas, Cécile Voka, and the late Annie Kalonji Meta. During two trips to Kasai Occidental, Etienne Bote-Tshiek, Denis Kabamba, Bernard Kabibu, Mulumba Mukundi, Etienne Mutshipayi Petumpenyi, Kabuika Ntambala, Ntambue Kazadi, Blaise Kwete, Simon Ntumba Tshitenga, Tshisungu Daniel, and Albert Tshitenga Elo Lungenyi generously shared the history of the region with me. Over the course of these same trips, Farris Goodrum, Kathy Humphrey, E.A. Manier, Katrina Manier, Katy Manier, Phyllis McAndrew, Jimmy Shafe, Sarah Stranahan, and Elizabeth Vass Wilkerson shared family histories of the American Presbyterian Congo Mission with a welcome and graciousness that I do not take for granted. Farris, Phyllis, Sarah, and Elizabeth also assisted with Tshiluba translations.

This work is significantly better than it would otherwise be thanks to the opportunities I have had to share it with audiences at the Modern Language Association; American Studies Association; Institute for Research on the African Diaspora in the Americas and the Caribbean (IRADAC) at CUNY; Collegium for African American Research; Belgian Association of Africanists; American Literature Association; Middle States African Studies Association; American University in Beirut; University of Miami; Washington College; Université Libre de Bruxelles; Université Catholique de Louvain, Louvain-la-Neuve; Université Pédagogique Nationale in Kinshasa; Université Presbytérienne Sheppard et Lapsley du Congo, Ndesha; Institut National des Arts, Kinshasa; Centre Culturel Français de Kinshasa; Orientale American Studies International School (OASIS) at Università di Napoli (L'Orientale); Alexandria University; Cairo University; Helwan University; and Menoufiya University.

For supporting me and sharing so many different things in so many different ways, special mentions are due to Edmund Abaka, Hisham Aidi, May Alhassen, Susan Andrade, Jonathan Arac, Paul Austerlitz, Sophia Azeb, Robert Benedetto, Nandini Bhattacharya, Paola Boi, Melba Joyce Boyd, John Bryant, James Campbell, Victoria Chevalier, James W. Cook, Brian Cooper, Eric Covey, George Cunningham, Christopher De Santis, Jane Desmond, Mvemba Dizolele, Sherman K. Edmiston, Brent Edwards, Brian Edwards, Marian Eide, Laura Estill, M. Giulia Fabi, Keith Feldman, Terri Francis, Lea Fridman, Kevin Gaines, Tamara Giles-Vernick, Sylvia Grider, John Cullen Gruesser, Donna Akiba Sullivan Harper, Juliette Harris, Salah Hassan, Bruce Haynes, Nancy Henderson-James, Cheryl Higashida, Lucia Hodgson, Sharon Holland, Jessica Howell, Mary Lou Hultgren, Michel Huysseune, Rashidah Ismaili, Maura Ives, Donatella Izzo, Lawrence Jackson, Shona Jackson, Bogumil Jewsiewicki, Emily Johansen, Konstantina Karageorgos, Jeff Kerr-Richie, Daniel Kilbride, Rosamond King, Alisha Knight, Nadine Knight, Amor Kohli, Pierre Lannoy, Robert Levine, Bernth Lindfors, the late Richard Long, Alex Lubin, Melani McAlister, David McWhirter, Giorgio Mariani, Wendell Marsh, Christopher Miller, Alan Nadel, Mary Ann O'Farrell, Jeffrey Ogbar, Larry Oliver, Ranen Omer-Sherman, Donald Pease, Pierre Petit, Charlotte Pierce-Baker, Vijay Prashad, Vanita Reddy, Larry Reynolds, Anne Rice, John Carlos Rowe, Heather Russell, Susan Russell, Ray Sapirstein, the late Alastair Scougal, Amritjit Singh, Joseph Slaughter, John David Smith, Dianne Stewart, the late Jon-Christian Suggs, Gordon Thompson, Lindsey Tucker, Mikko Tuhkanen, Johnny Van Hove, Jean-Luc Vellut, Hanna Wallinger, Jennifer Wenzel, Richard Yarborough, and the late Jim Zwick.

In addition, I have had the good fortune to discuss the work of the Lucy Sheppard Arts Club in Tuscaloosa with member Martha J. Hall-Cammon. Yvonne Seon spoke to me in great detail about meeting Patrice Lumumba during his only visit to the United States in 1960, and her life in the newly independent Congo. Nyimi Kot aMbweeky III, king of the Kuba, invited me into his office on two occasions to share his singular perspective on the history of his people. And in Cairo, Juliana Lumumba gave generously of her time and her family's story.

My six years in Egypt were rich, thanks in large part to many colleagues. In addition to those already named, I must also acknowledge Tahia Abdel Nasser, Ferial Ghazoul, Walid El Hamamsy, Amy Austin Holmes, Areeg Ibrahim, Osama Madany, Ana Menendez, Mona Misbah, Amy Motlagh, Omneya Mohallal, Somaya Sami Sabry, Sherene Seikaly, Ola Shanab, Heba Sharobeem, Mounira Soliman, and Mark Westmoreland. My students have taught me so much about why we do what we do as academics and have shown in word and deed the possibilities of a changed world. Of the many brilliant students for whom I am grateful, special thanks are due to Asmaa Abdallah, Heba Ahmed, Nermine Sergius, Sarah Mostafa Yousri, and Zainab Magdy for creating a community among themselves that remains my collaborative ideal.

At the University of North Carolina Press, I have great confidence in the support of Mark Simpson-Vos, Lucas Church, Jessica Newman, their colleagues, and the press's readers. I consider myself fortunate to have my work in their hands. It is a unique privilege to be included in the John Hope Franklin Series in African American History and Culture, a series whose namesake directly shaped my understanding of George Washington Williams as he has the world's understanding of African American history. Sherri Barnes prepared the index.

There is a final, and most profound, absence of words for my debt to my families: Dworkins, Arnolds, Moshinskys, Stracks, Sebastians, and Wrays. My mom Harriet Arnold and my dad Gus Dworkin made sure I always had everything I needed, including books. They took me to the library and the bookstore. My father would have enjoyed holding this book in his hands and I am sad that he did not live long enough to do so. For Jenna, my love and gratitude are eternal. This book is dedicated to Ramona and Gwendolyn, because Ramona asked.

## Abbreviations Used in the Text

| | |
|---|---|
| ACS | American Colonization Society |
| AIA | International African Association (Association Internationale Africaine) |
| AMA | American Missionary Association |
| AME | African Methodist Episcopal Church |
| ANC | African National Congress |
| APCM | American Presbyterian Congo Mission |
| CAO | Committee of African Organisations (U.K.) |
| C.K. | Compagnie du Kasai |
| CRA | Congo Reform Association |
| ECFM | Executive Committee of Foreign Missions of the Presbyterian Church (U.S.) |
| HBCUs | Historically Black Colleges and Universities |
| IMPROKA | Imprimerie Protestante du Kasai |
| LCA | Liberation Committee for Africa |
| MoMA | Museum of Modern Art (New York) |
| MMI | Muslim Mosque Inc. |
| MNC | Mouvement National Congolais |
| NAACP | National Association for the Advancement of Colored People |
| NoI | Nation of Islam |
| OAAU | Organization of Afro-American Unity |
| OAU | Organization of African Unity |
| PCUS | Presbyterian Church (U.S.), Southern |
| PCUSA | Presbyterian Church (U.S.A.), Northern |
| RAM | Revolutionary Action Movement |
| RMCA | Royal Museum for Central Africa |
| SNCC | Student Nonviolent Coordinating Committee |
| TSU | Texas Southern University |

| | |
|---|---|
| U.N. | United Nations |
| UNESCO | United Nations Educational, Scientific and Cultural Organization |
| UNIA | Universal Negro Improvement Association |
| UPRECO | Université Presbyterienne Sheppard et Lapsley du Congo |
| USIA | United States Information Agency |
| WPA | Works Progress Administration |
| ZNP | Zanzibar Nationalist Party |

*Congo Love Song*

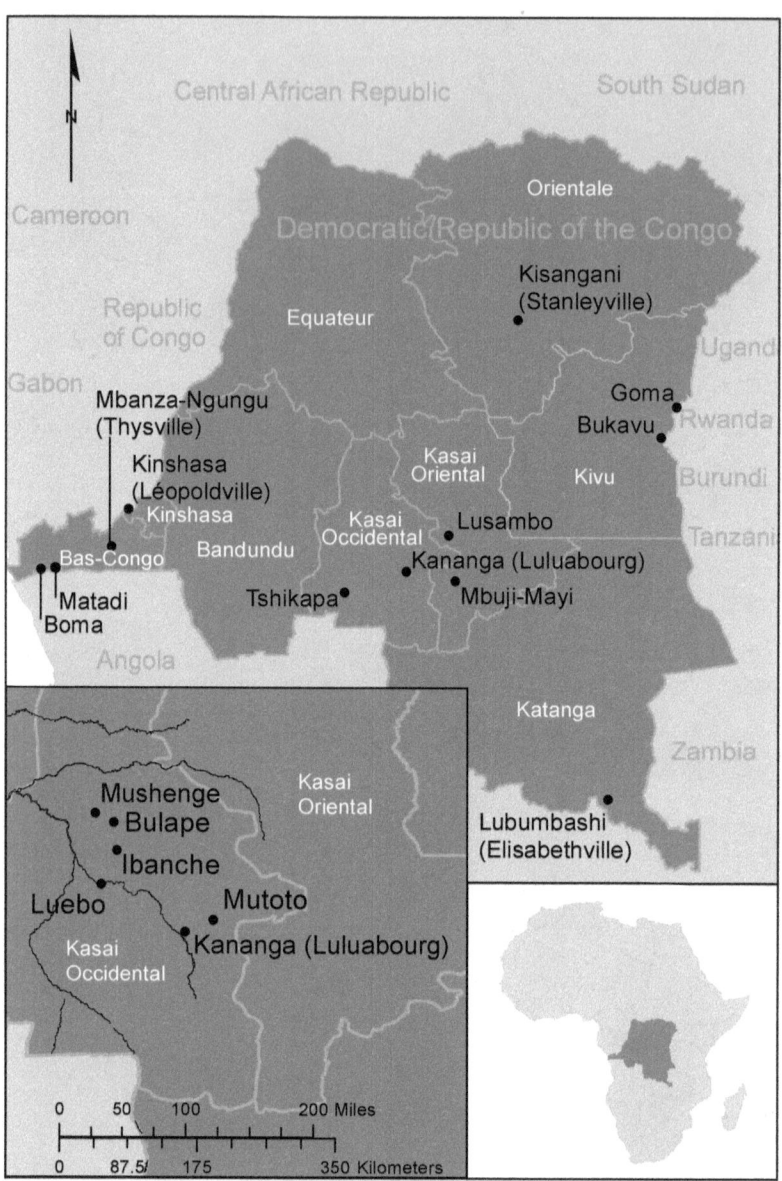

*Map 1* This map reflects the most common provincial borders for the period 1966–2015 (excluding the 1988 division of Kivu). The colonial names of major cities are provided parenthetically. (Cecilia Smith. *Democratic Republic of the Congo*. RDC_data_2013. Democratic Republic of the Congo: Direction Inventaire et Aménagement Forestiers, Direction Gestion Forestière, and World Resources Institute, 2013. Using *ArcGIS for Desktop*. Edition 10.3. Redlands, CA: Esri, 2014.)

# Introduction
## *James Weldon Johnson's Transnational Vaudeville*

'Way down where the Congo is a-flowing,
'Way down where the bamboo is a-growing
Down where tropic breezes are a-blowing
There once lived a little Zulu maid;
Each night, very silently canoeing
Up stream, came a Kaffir chief a-wooing
He came for the maiden's hand a-suing
Singing as along the banks they strayed:

CHORUS:
"As long as the Congo flows to the sea,
As long as a leaf grows on the bamboo tree,
My love and devotion will be deep as the ocean;
Won't you take a notion, for to love-a but me?"

The Maiden, though his gentle words believing,
Told him that she thought he was deceiving,
This set his poor Kaffir heart a-grieving,
Yet he never changed his ardent theme;
One night, to her father's kraal he traced her,
And there in his lusty arms embraced her,
Then in his canoe he gently placed her,
Singing as they floated down the stream:

[CHORUS]

This maid, in the wilds of Umbagooda,
Down where this bold Kaffir chieftain wooed her,
May have been perhaps, a trifle cruder
Than girls on the Hudson or the Seine;
Yet, though she was but a little Zulu,
She did just what other artful maids do,
And showed there were tricks of love that she knew;
For she kept him singing this refrain:

[CHORUS]

—"Congo Love Song" (1903), lyrics by James Weldon Johnson

They told you and me we came from the Congo. Isn't that what they told you? I mean, isn't that what they taught us in school? So we came from the Congo. We're savages and cannibals and all that kind of stuff from the Congo; they've been teaching me all my life I'm from the Congo. I love the Congo. That's my country. And that's my people that your airplanes are killing over there.

—Malcolm X, Audubon Ballroom, New York City, December 13, 1964

Expressions of love for the Congo take a range of forms within African American culture. In the first years of the twentieth century, James Weldon Johnson wrote the lyrics to the hugely popular "Congo Love Song," which invokes the fictitious "wilds of Umbagooda" in a manner that may seem commonplace among the era's representations of Africa. On first glance, Johnson's song might appear to reproduce the kinds of stock representations that are the subject of Malcolm X's brilliant commentary on the role played by primitivist images of the Congo not only in the debasement of African Americans, but also as a justification for U.S. colonial violence. However, such an approach would miss the critical contexts that are at the center of this book, which demonstrates that throughout the colonial era African American connections to Africa have included, at their core, modern political engagement. More specifically, I argue in *Congo Love Song* that this engagement, which was routinely routed through the Congo as a uniquely visible and troubling site of imperialist crisis, has shaped African American culture throughout the colonial era.

Johnson's pastoral image appeared at a time when African Americans were playing a major role in an emerging international campaign against the brutal colonial regime of King Leopold II of Belgium. Whereas Malcolm X undermined a caricatured image of the Congo by tying it to U.S. state violence, Johnson wrote earnestly about a romance between a Kaffir "chieftain" and a Zulu "maid"—a version of the "Jungle boys and girls in love" of Countee Cullen's Harlem Renaissance poem "Heritage"—at a time when "it was innovative to imply that both blacks and whites experienced the same romantic emotions in the same way."[1] While romance was also the theme of black vaudevillian Ernest Hogan's "My Little Jungle Queen: A Congo Love Song" three years earlier, its white lyricist James O'Dea employs crude dialect that is absent from the published version of Johnson's song. After Hogan's African American vocalist marries his "sweet Congo girl," the song culminates with his crowning, a trope of royal welcome and return whose frequency points to the breadth of cultural productions that imagine the Congo as a representative homeland.[2] Johnson's use of language that suggests southern Africa ("Kaffir," "Zulu," "kraal"), rather than central Africa, seems to render the "Congo" a synecdoche for the African continent. Yet his comparison of the Zulu woman to Paris and New York women deliberately expands the song's geographic parameters in a way that, as Amy Kaplan writes of W. E. B. Du Bois's *Darkwater*, "discursively produces new aggregates of social space that can be policed, contested, and transformed." Johnson himself later explained that the Zulu are a national group whose "bravery and prowess in battle" resulted in arguments that they "are not really Negroes," a canard which "Congo Love Song" effectively disputes.[3] Indeed, by 1920, Johnson explicitly recognized the exploitation of Black workers in South Africa to be part of the same colonial system as the Belgian Congo.[4] So while African women "May have been perhaps, a trifle cruder" than their counterparts in France or the United States, Johnson ultimately accentuates similarities (including female knowledge of the "tricks of love") between the Congo and the cosmopolitan capitals of the West that contest and transform popular portrayals of "savages and cannibals."

Read in the context of colonialism, Johnson emerges less as a foil for Malcolm X's political engagement than as his intellectual fellow traveler. Whereas Malcolm X knowingly embraced the postindependence Congo in an explicit act of political solidarity, Johnson used music to challenge this same tradition of misrepresentation. For his part, Malcolm X explicitly acknowledges the political possibilities of seemingly primitivist representations by noting their simultaneity with a love for the Congo and identification with its people. Ranging from the early years of Leopold's involvement in the Congo through a half century as the Belgian Congo and the early years of independence as the Republic of the Congo and Democratic Republic of the Congo (or Congo-Kinshasa to distinguish it from its northern neighbor, a former French colony commonly known as Congo-Brazzaville to invoke its capital city), my book *Congo Love Song* aims to make the political geography of cultural work like "Congo Love Song" visible so that it is understood as part of a wider culture of African American engagement with the colonial state that extends beyond romantic configurations of a homeland and heritable notions of ancestry.[5] Several African American travelers, notably historian George Washington Williams and missionary William Henry Sheppard, helped inform the world—including James Weldon Johnson and his audience—about the Congo in the late nineteenth and early twentieth centuries. In its function as an affirmative counterpoint to colonial ideologies, "Congo Love Song" is exemplary of the relationship between African American popular culture and imperialism at a time when the Congo was a charged political site, not a generic marker for an entire continent. To put it differently, "Congo Love Song" is not the same thing as "Umbagooda Love Song."

Such an international context would have been consistent with Johnson's worldview from a young age: his mother was from the Bahamas and he traveled to Nassau as a child. After graduating from Atlanta University, he became the principal of the largest African American school in Jacksonville, Florida, started a newspaper, trained as a lawyer, and passed the bar. Meanwhile, he was also pursuing a career as a lyricist, composing "Lift Every Voice and Sing," which was later adopted as the "Negro National Anthem," with his younger brother J. Rosamond Johnson, who wrote the music to "Congo Love Song."[6] In 1898–99, the Johnson brothers collaborated on a musical, *Tolosa*, which James described as "a comic opera satirizing the new American imperialism" of the Spanish-American War and the annexation of Hawai'i.[7] By the time "Congo Love Song" appeared, James's oeuvre had an established level of gravitas, being the work of an antiimperialist artist devoted to racial uplift and on the threshold of a distinguished career in international relations. In 1906, he was appointed to serve as U.S. consul in Puerto Caballo, Venezuela, a post that began a period of diplomatic service that continued until the 1913 inauguration of Woodrow Wilson brought with it the removal of African Americans from consular posts. James Weldon Johnson spent the years 1914 to 1923 as a contributing editor to the *New York Age*, where he published more than 2,000 essays, including many critical commentaries on American imperialism.[8] His career suggests a geographical sophistication that recognizes, as he does explicitly in later speeches, the historical specificity of terms like "Congo," "Zulu," and "Kaffir." Even his use of a seemingly derogatory term is an act of anticolonial redefinition, evident when, in a later ethnographic essay, he cites the "Kaffir" for their "constructive imagination far beyond that of any other races of Africa" and their military success against the British army.[9]

The international human rights campaign with regard to the Congo—one in which African Americans played a leading role—was inescapable at a time when the black press was reporting that "the situation in the Congo had become scandalous."[10] The audience, which helped "Congo Love Song" earn $13,000 in royalties and made it arguably the most popular song in the United States, was not insulated from contemporary news of the campaign of the Congo Reform Association (CRA). By 1905, with the international movement well underway, the Johnsons heard "Congo Love Song" at the Olympia theater in Paris. In Europe and the United States, audiences were listening to

"Congo Love Song" as part of a popular musical repertoire, while also reading regular reports in the black press, among other sources, about the colonial brutality of Leopold's administration.[11] For those familiar with these accounts, Johnson's song not only describes African "civilization," but also erases the nonfictional colonial apparatus that European powers and the United States authorized at the 1884–85 Berlin Conference, which German Chancellor Otto von Bismarck hosted to settle conflicting European colonial claims in Africa. Johnson's invocation of a romantic precolonial Congo featuring a traditional chief functions as a counterpoint to commonplace images of the Congo as alternately an imaginary site of "savages and cannibals" and an actual site of colonial violence.

In the late nineteenth-century United States, which historian Rayford Logan famously characterized as the "nadir" of racist segregation, disfranchisement, and terror, violence in central Africa was understood well enough that journalist and activist Ida B. Wells could describe, without any additional explanation, the lynching of two colleagues in Memphis as "a scene of shocking savagery which would have disgraced the Congo."[12] Her 1895 reference is general enough to include both the perceived savagery of the Congolese people and the actual savagery of the colonial regime. As in the case of Wells's or Malcolm X's characterizations, invocations of the Congo were often used to make explicit commentaries on domestic racism. In a 1925 article on lynching, for example, Johnson cited a sympathetic speech by Georgia governor Hugh M. Dorsey: "both God and man would justly condemn Georgia more severely than man and God have condemned Belgium and Leopold for the Congo atrocities."[13] While the performance of "Congo Love Song" could potentially undermine the sincerity of the written lyrics, the musical arrangement complemented Johnson's self-described attempt to "bring a higher degree of artistry to Negro songs, especially with regard to the text."[14] For Johnson, the American musical form complements the African setting of "Congo Love Song" in ways that render it a domestic parable, which parallels the elegiac poetry that later memorialized Patrice Lumumba through brilliant literary innovations that have come to define the Black Arts movement.

Johnson's decision to name the "Congo" in his title, as elusive as his lyrical representation may be, stands in stark contrast to Joseph Conrad's contemporary novella *Heart of Darkness* (1899), which never even uses the word "Congo" yet remains its most lasting English literary representation. Even the cover of the published music attributes "Congo Love Song" to popular singer Marie Cahill, whose nearly full-body portrait is framed by a tropical landscape intended to represent the Congo. (See Figure I-1.) Like other compositions by the Johnsons, this song, explains Noelle Morrissette, "entered the publishing world as sound and text and as a commodity that rendered them

*Figure I.1* James Weldon Johnson and J. Rosamond Johnson, "Marie Cahill's Congo Love Song" (1903), sheet music cover page. Although the writing team of "Cole and Johnson Bros." is noted on the cover page, their frequent collaborator Bob Cole is not credited at the top of this sheet music. (Beinecke Rare Book and Manuscript Library, Courtesy of Yale University.)

both physically present (in the title page's acknowledgment of the composers' names) and absent (in the transferring of vocal presence to the popular performer inscribed on the page)."[15] This tension between the songwriters and the performer is mediated by the prominence of the song's title on the cover page of the sheet music, which ensures the visibility of the "Congo." The pastoral cover image presents the Congo without African people; the only person whose image appears is Cahill. Still, Johnson's lyrics narrate a romance between two Africans that provides an alternative discourse about the Congo that may not explicitly confront colonialism but nonetheless is embedded within the political challenge that African American activists, artists, and intellectuals were posing to the racist logic of the colonial regime of King Leopold II of Belgium.

A popular song provides a particularly useful entrance into this conversation because, as Eric Sundquist argues, it expands our "understanding of the literary text, not to mention the conflicting traditions of which it may be a part" in a way that helps us to appreciate the diverse career of James Weldon

Johnson as a poet, novelist, autobiographer, essayist, anthologist, songwriter, attorney, educator, diplomat, and civil rights worker as the terrain and context for "Congo Love Song."[16] Furthermore, thanks to scholarship by David Chinitz, Geoffrey Jacques, and Michael North among others, the influence of the Johnsons—along with their frequent collaborator Bob Cole, and peers like Hogan, George Walker, and Bert Williams—on white modernists like T. S. Eliot is increasingly well understood and finds parallel in Patricia Leighten's argument about the political context for engagements with African art by visual modernists like Picasso who were aware of the ongoing crisis in the Congo.[17] This Congo is a real place, not solely a discursive one, and its history tethers African American transnationalism to long-standing political traditions, a connection that Mark Sanders finds absent from twenty-first century analyses that do not "account fully for the historical practice of transcontinental, transcultural, or comparative scholarship in African American studies and its links to activism."[18]

Popular music reaches communities of listeners, like the "forgotten readers" of Elizabeth McHenry's masterful study of African American literary societies, in ways that can highlight the relationships between the literary and the nonfictional worlds, and between the "Congo" of Johnson's "Love Song," and the "Congo" of African American political discourse. McHenry points to the importance of locating meaning within the social processes of readership.[19] Such dynamic discursive communities across time and place provide context for reading the cultural trope of the "Congo" as a product of the political work undertaken by African Americans in response to imperialism. "Modern black political culture," Paul Gilroy asserts in *The Black Atlantic: Modernity and Double Consciousness*, "has always been more interested in the relationship of identity to roots and rootedness than in seeing identity as a process of movement and mediation that is more appropriately approached via the homonym routes."[20] Following Gilroy, a study of the Congo reveals the sustained ways that these routes engage with Africa, as well as Europe, and the histories and cultures of colonialism, anticolonialism, postcolonialism, and neocolonialism.

Williams and Sheppard, prolific writers in their own right, arrived in the Congo in 1890, the same year as Conrad, albeit with very different aims. They were intrigued by this new country which was initially claimed by King Leopold II of Belgium in 1877 under the supposedly philanthropic guise of the International African Association (AIA), which promised tariff-free trade for European companies, unrestricted access for Christian missionaries, and the abolition of slavery. However, the AIA was a fraud designed to provide Leopold absolute control of what Adam Hochschild measures as "one thirteenth of the African continent, more than seventy-six times the size of Belgium itself."²¹ In the United States, Leopold's rapacious efforts were supported by Henry Shelton Sanford, who took the opportunity provided by the Senate's 1877 rejection of his appointment as ambassador to Belgium to parlay his political connections—his diplomatic career included a Civil War–era ministerial post in Brussels—into a job with Leopold as an AIA lobbyist. From the start, Sanford saw the Congo State as a forum for white supremacy: "nearly 5,000,000 of our people are of African race—descendants of slaves. . . . The idea of this people, by the aid of the descendants of those who held them as slaves, returning to civilize and regenerate their parent country—to extirpate the slave trade and introduce into that fertile region the cultures which they were sold from their homes to toil at across the ocean—is certainly attractive, and one worthy of earnest promotion in the United States."²² On behalf of Leopold, Sanford recruited explorer Henry Morton Stanley, who quickly became the king's most important ally, to undertake a five-year expedition to the Congo, during which he dubiously claimed to have signed nearly 500 treaties with African chiefs ceding land to Leopold, his trip's financier. Stanley's initial plan, as early as December 1878, to have fifteen African American men, between the ages of 22 and 27, work in the Congo never materialized.²³

The imperial involvement of the United States is rooted in the country's intensifying commitment to white supremacy at the end of Radical Reconstruction, which coincided with the establishment of the AIA. For his part, Sanford and his ally Senator John Tyler Morgan of Alabama—who spearheaded a unanimous January 1884 resolution to investigate the potential for American commerce "in the Valley of the Congo River in Africa"—saw an opportunity to redirect African American attention away from domestic political participation.²⁴ In April, the Senate approved diplomatic relations with the AIA, which was crucial in establishing its international standing as equivalent to that of a nation-state. With the Berlin Conference opening in November, President Chester A. Arthur appointed John A. Kasson, Sanford, and Stanley to represent U.S. interests in Berlin, which predictably led to preliminary U.S. approval of the General Act at the close of the conference in February 1885, which formalized Leopold's absentee claims on the Congo, whose people, Loso K. Boya reminds us, "are still grappling with the fallouts."²⁵

As the "King-Sovereign" of the AIA, Leopold renamed his African dominion l'État Indépendant du Congo in May 1885, the irony of which raised the ire of Williams, who recognized it as "an absolute monarchy, an oppressive and cruel Government, an exclusive Belgian colony."²⁶ In his 1890 report to President Benjamin Harrison, Williams assesses the regime in no uncertain terms and uses the occasion to envision a truly independent Congo that, by most accounts, remains unrealized more than a century later. In the two decades immediately following Williams's prescient criticism, Leopold implemented an unconscionably brutal regime in the Congo that, according to historian Isidore Ndaywel è Nziem, likely led to the deaths of 10 million people.[27] Williams published his analysis of the burgeoning colonial system in 1890, at a time when "The structural realisation of European hegemony on the ground was only beginning to be effected."[28] Williams and Sheppard witnessed the rapid expansion of rubber production, the state implementation of a system of forced labor, and the intensifying military enforcement of that system. When villages failed to meet rubber collection quotas, workers were beaten, female hostages held for ransom, and entire towns slaughtered. As the state's export income increased more than a hundredfold—from 150,000 francs in 1890 to more than 18,000,000 francs in 1901—due primarily to rubber, the colonial Force Publique increased its military presence in the Congo from 1,487 troops in 1889 to 19,028 troops in 1898.[29] With the Force Publique, Leopold created a military infrastructure that "conflated military and policing functions." Under that regime, "control of the military units was strongly decentralized to serve the needs of the territorial administrators, who used the army for civilian tasks as well as to suppress dissent," a role the military continues to serve and, Jason Stearns points out, which is the basis for many ongoing crises throughout central Africa.[30]

The most infamous of Belgium's many misdeeds was their requirement that the hands of victims be severed to account for the military's bullet allocation: one hand per bullet expended.[31] This torture, which included victims who were still alive, was brought to international attention by an 1899 investigation by Sheppard, who cofounded the American Presbyterian Congo Mission (APCM) with Samuel Lapsley, the son of Senator Morgan's law partner. Sheppard's report, which was distributed internationally, became foundational to the CRA, which, in 1903, the year "Congo Love Song" was published, began its full-fledged campaign for regime change by establishing alliances between social reformers, trading companies, European governments, and Protestant missionaries who saw their own access to the Congo being limited. Political pressure, the decimation of the wild rubber supply, and widespread African resistance ranging from mass flight from state-controlled rubber regions to the assassinations of several state agents compelled Leopold to transfer titular control of the Congo State to Belgium in 1908. One year after the Belgian Congo was born, Leopold died. Unfortunately, neither the change in title nor Leopold's death ended the ongoing exploitation extensively documented by Jules Marchal. Belgium not only continued a similar system under the guise of taxation, but it also expanded many of its practices to the rapidly developing mining regions of the country, laying the foundation for an economic system that continues to provide resources to the United States, Belgium, China, and elsewhere in the twenty-first century, at incalculable human cost.

Sheppard was not the first African American missionary to travel to the Congo; by 1886, the American Baptist Foreign Mission Society had African Americans serving in the western Congo (the ancient Kongo).[32] Though Sheppard proved to be a unique force in the reform movement, he is only the most famous representative of a broader class of African Americans who had varying forms of involvement with the Congo. In addition to his service to the Presbyterian Church, his articles and speeches about the Congo circulated widely through the *Southern Workman*, the official publication of Hampton Institute in Virginia where he was a student in the early 1880s. Through twenty years of service in central Africa, Sheppard not only recruited an extraordinary cohort of ten African Americans to the mission, but his writings and speeches motivated people internationally to support the emerging Congo reform movement. Following the success of the CRA in exposing Leopold's crimes, Sheppard and his colleagues were targeted by the colonial state and the Force Publique, which went so far as to attack an APCM mission station. Sheppard maintained his staunch resistance, which culminated in 1909 in libel charges for criticizing the concessionary Compagnie du Kasai's mistreatment of its workers. Despite his vindication in a trial watched internationally, Sheppard was forced to retire by a Nashville-based mission board that was—like the Belgian authorities at whose discretion their stations operated—increasingly uncomfortable with its African American pioneers whose presence in leadership positions threatened their shared commitment to the colonial racial order.

After leaving the mission field in 1910, Sheppard was widely recognized for his accomplishments and remained an important conduit for information about the Congo. Pioneering social scientist St. Clair Drake, for example, recalls Sheppard visiting his home and church in their mutual hometown of Staunton, Virginia.[33] Print culture extended his reach even farther. In May 1915, the *Crisis*, a magazine that began publication in 1910 as the official organ of National Association for the Advancement of Colored People (NAACP), named him one of their "Men of the Month" (a feature that also honored women) for his activist work in the Congo and his subsequent "notably constructive social uplift work" in Louisville, Kentucky.[34] By way of context, in the same issue of the *Crisis*, the premier national African American magazine, editor Du Bois criticized white fascination with a clichéd "Africa" in an article about Vachel Lindsay's popular poem, "The Congo (A Study of the Negro Race)." Lindsay unselfconsciously claimed to be interested in "the Africa of the romantic Negro's imagination, a scrap of black grand opera, if not the actual Africa," despite citing as models Conrad and Stanley, writers who both traveled to the Congo. Within the pages of Du Bois's *Crisis*, Sheppard offered a counternarrative to what Lindsay could only imagine as poetic license.[35] In 1916, Du Bois more directly explained the stakes of his criticism: "Mr. Lindsay knows little of the Negro, and that little is dangerous."[36] Du Bois knew that Sheppard's experience contradicted Lindsay's presumption about the "romantic" and the "actual." In practice, firsthand accounts and highly politicized African encounters by figures like Sheppard helped to shape ideas about the Congo ranging from Johnson's song to Du Bois's emerging analysis of imperialism.

In the same month that the Sheppard profile appeared in the *Crisis*, Du Bois published "The African Roots of the War" in the *Atlantic Monthly*:

> It all began, singularly enough, like the present war, with Belgium. Many of us remember Stanley's great solution of the puzzle of Central Africa when he traced the mighty Congo sixteen hundred miles from Nyangwe to the sea. Suddenly the world knew that here lay the key to the riches of Central Africa. It stirred uneasily, but Leopold of Belgium was first on his feet, and the result was the Congo Free State—God save the mark! But the Congo Free State, with all its magniloquent heralding of Peace, Christianity, and Commerce, degenerating into murder, mutilation and downright robbery, differed only in degree and concentration from the tale of all Africa in this rape of a continent already furiously mangled by the slave trade. That sinister traffic, on which the British Empire and the American Republic were largely built, cost black Africa no less than 100,000,000 souls, the wreckage of its political and social life, and left the continent in precisely that state of helplessness which invites aggression and exploitation. "Color" became in the world's thought synonymous with inferiority, "Negro" lost its capitalization, and Africa was another name for bestiality and barbarism.
>
> Thus the world began to invest in color prejudice. The "Color Line" began to pay dividends. For indeed, while the exploration of the valley of the Congo was the occasion of the scramble for Africa, the cause lay deeper.[37]

David Levering Lewis calls the essay, which anticipated Lenin's thesis on imperialism by two years, "one of the analytical triumphs of the early twentieth century."[38] Du Bois's position represented a shift from that of the late 1890s, when he expressed interest to Belgian consul general Paul Hagemans in "commercial intercourse between the Congo Free State and the Negroes of the West Indies and of the United States," which is an important reminder that internationalist radicalism in the late nineteenth and early twentieth centuries was a process rather than a fully formed entity.[39] As Du Bois was reflecting on the career of Sheppard, he placed the Congo at the center of his analysis of global capital's dependence on colonialism.

In 1919, as national field secretary of the NAACP, James Weldon Johnson organized a conference—"Africa in the World Democracy"—inspired by Du Bois's Africa thesis. The conference was held at Carnegie Hall in New York City as part of the association's annual meeting, and Johnson invited Du Bois and Sheppard to be featured speakers. In his remarks, Sheppard included an account of hand severing, a lasting image that starkly contrasts with Johnson's own "Congo Love Song." Still, even in such company, the song remained popular enough that it was performed at a 1931 party where Du Bois, Mary McLeod Bethune, Walter White, and others honored Johnson on his retirement from the NAACP.[40] The coexistence of the song and political programs, under the direction of Johnson and the umbrella of the NAACP, represents the vibrant cultural milieu they share and the important role of the Congo as part of a long history of African American cultural production that this book maps.

Adam Hochschild's *King Leopold's Ghost: A Story of Greed, Terror, and Heroism in Colonial Africa*, which duly features Williams and Sheppard, has brought their stories along with the history of European colonialism in the Congo to a remarkably wide audience. Even U.S. president George W. Bush claims to have read the book to which Hochschild—who has proven to be an indispensable commentator on both the Congo and American empire— responded sharply by noting that, if so, his actions in Iraq demonstrated that he had not learned its lessons.[41] Moving beyond the heroes and villains whose stories *King Leopold's Ghost* valuably recovers, my book focuses on the ongoing "transatlantic 'bridges'" that connected African American communities to the Congo. As historian James T. Campbell argues in his expert multisite study *Songs of Zion: The African Methodist Episcopal Church in the United States and South Africa*, such linkages "were not that unusual." He continues, "The borders that define historical inquiry were not the borders of lived experience for the historical actors themselves. Long after the decline of the transatlantic slave trade, black life continued to be shaped by a constant traffic between Africa and the New World."[42] As one of many lanes of the "constant traffic" of transatlantic exchange, the Congo is not exceptional. Rather, its case pointedly reveals that an appreciation for African American discourse about Africa must maintain a historical grounding in particular locales, whether the Congo, Ethiopia, Egypt, South Africa, or elsewhere. It is not sufficient to discuss African American ideas about Africa in broadly conceptual terms, despite the valuable scholarship that has been done under this rubric. While the travels of Williams and Sheppard have some basis in what Gilroy terms "identity," their careers suggest a relationship to Africa that is not primarily romantic or imaginative. A study of the Congo reveals how cultural discourses about Africa are deeply grounded in the historical routes of colonialism, and "histories," Stuart Hall reminds us, "have their real, material and symbolic effects."[43] In response to shifting crises, of which the Congo has had more than its share, these routes have been mainstays within African American culture at least since Leopold II established the AIA in 1877.

Given these origins, *Congo Love Song* insists that the colonial state is an object of examination. Such early confrontations follow Ifeoma Kiddoe Nwankwo's brilliant observation regarding "the pivotal importance of nineteenth-century texts in the development and public articulation not just of Black or African Diasporan identity, but also of ideas about the significance of transnational engagement for those identities." In *Black Cosmopolitanism: Racial Consciousness and Transnational Identity in the Nineteenth-Century Americas,* Nwankwo finds transnationalism inadequate for a study rooted in an earlier hemispheric tradition of slave narratives and antebellum writings, because "it foregrounds geographical-national boundaries and presumes them to be salient."[44] *Congo Love Song* aims to mark the African American confrontations with colonialism that emerge from these rich antecedent traditions to critique the "geographical-national boundaries" of identity, while consistently paying attention to the political actions of nation-states in the colonial era. As a result, transnationalism remains a particularly useful rubric for opening up colonialism as a field of inquiry with the capacity to approach the African experience as rigorously as it does the American.

*Congo Love Song* presents a broadly inclusive analytical model that understands colonial discourse as part of a continuum that includes, but is not bound by, the nation-state. Patience Kabamba recognizes that "the very social relations and struggles that engender state formations may also take non–state forms. The state form is always contingent, and each state is a historically particular distillation of more elementary social relations and conflicts."[45] Kabamba's perspective allows for a deeper understanding of what Nwankwo identifies as a "substitute national identity" that is based in a cosmopolitanism that emerged from African Americans' exclusion and that "may include people in places they have never visited, and with whom they have never had contact, because the connection they imagine is based on the common experiences of slavery and discrimination and African heritage, rather than shared terrain or face to face encounters."[46] *Congo Love Song* extends this terrain to argue that since the late nineteenth century, African American conceptions of the nation-state are not only matters of national identity, but also include confrontations with often contradictory forms of colonial disidentification. For instance, Pauline Hopkins's "cosmopolitanism was," as Gretchen Murphy notes, "bound up in the era's conflicted narratives of global expansion and civilization," which centers imperialism as formative to the construction of diasporic identities.[47] Figures like Johnson and Hopkins, who never traveled to Africa, remain central to this story's entangled network of Congo connections that includes often unacknowledged "face to face encounters," even if it is not limited by them.

In its careful attention to the internationalism at the heart of African American culture, *Congo Love Song* parallels some of the most important developments within the field of American studies; much of the field has committed itself to dismantling the fiction of American exceptionalism and to locating the United States on a map with the rest of the world. Kaplan and Donald Pease's groundbreaking 1993 anthology *Cultures of United States Imperialism* begins with Kaplan's essay, "'Left Alone with America': The Absence of Empire in the Study of American Culture," which uses the fact that Perry Miller wrote *Errand into the Wilderness* on the Congo River to interrogate the notion of an autonomous American identity that elides the nation's racial history. Unacknowledged in Miller's account is the fact that his "apparently random and quixotic arrival in Africa could only have been made possible by the longstanding economic, political, and cultural involvement of the United States in European colonialism, of which the Congo is a major case in point." African American writings about the Congo, such as Williams's open letter, recognize precisely what Miller elides, namely "the multiple histories of continental and overseas expansion, conquest, conflict, and resistance which have shaped the cultures of the United States and the cultures of those it has dominated within and beyond its geopolitical boundaries."[48] The outstanding challenge is how to move from an acknowledgment of the existence of transatlantic networks to the kind of "careful, multilocational history" that Houston A. Baker Jr. advocates in *Turning South Again: Re-Thinking Modernism/Re-Reading Booker T.* In *Congo Love Song* I aim to expand our understanding of the geographical and chronological circulation of people, ideas, texts, songs, visual culture, and other media as a way of rethinking the political contours of African diaspora cultures by including within our analysis what Gerald Horne identifies most precisely as "the African American Diaspora."[49]

If we take literally Kaplan's assertion that, "The field of American studies was conceived on the banks of the Congo," we can begin to interrogate the Congo as not only a weighty trope for Miller and others but also as a geopolitical place at the heart of a transnational American studies.[50] The goal of such a project is to restore the political context to cultural discourses in ways that consider modern Africa and avoid the pitfalls Jemima Pierre points out in *The Predicament of Blackness*, whereby "the 'Africa' part of this cultural continuum exists in the (traditional) *past*, rendering continental phenomena static and bounded."⁵¹ Kaplan concludes her essay with a critique of Eleanor Coppola's documentary about the making of *Apocalypse Now*, *Hearts of Darkness*, which, by failing to acknowledge the film's production in the Philippines under the Marcos regime, "takes the viewer to 'the beginning of time,' indeed, as the productive political context of U.S. imperial culture fades from view, we are left alone with America."⁵² My work aims to excavate the "productive political context" of the Congo as a visible site of American and African American engagement and counterengagement, that locates colonialism, in all of its political minutiae, at the heart of American culture from these early postbellum encounters through the Cold War and early years of postcolonialism.

The first section of the book looks at "The Nineteenth-Century Routes of Black Transnationalism" by examining the connections of African American Congo activists to Historically Black Colleges and Universities (HBCUs) during the Leopoldian era. Chapter 1, "George Washington Williams's Stern Duty of History," begins with Williams's efforts to enlist African American students to travel with him to the Congo and ends with a series of open letters—to Leopold, President Harrison, and railroad magnate Collis P. Huntington—that inspired opposition to Leopold's regime that continued well after Williams's untimely death in 1891. Chapter 2, "William Henry Sheppard's Country of My Forefathers," examines the work of a former Hampton student whose 1899 eyewitness report on the brutal practice of hand severing became a foundational document for CRA activists and who, for decades, educated audiences from Hampton to Tuskegee to New York City to Louisville about the Congo. Chapter 3, "Booker T. Washington's African at Home," examines Washington's service as vice president of the CRA to consider a dynamic U.S. relationship with Africa as a critical contact zone for emerging ideas about race, ideology, and empire in American culture.

The second section, "The Twentieth-Century Cultures of the American Congo," looks broadly at the influence of Sheppard and the APCM on African American musical, religious, literary, and visual cultures. Chapter 4, "Missionary Cultures: The American Presbyterian Congo Mission, Althea Brown Edmiston, and the Languages of the Congo," examines the work of the Fisk University graduate who mediated the hegemony of colonial language policy by writing the first dictionary and grammar of the Bushong language of the Kuba and by working with her colleagues to translate African American spirituals into Tshiluba. Chapter 5, "Literary Cultures: The Black Press, Pauline E. Hopkins, and the Rewriting of Africa," begins the process of tracing the influence of travelers like Sheppard on emergent transnational print culture, including more conventionally fictionalized literary work like the novel *Of One Blood*, which must be read in the context of networks of intellectuals, writers, and activists that were cultivated by the black press, literary societies, civic organizations, HBCUs, and religious institutions. Chapter 6, "Visual Cultures: Hampton Institute, William Sheppard's Kuba Collection, and African American Art" considers the influence of Sheppard's collection of Kuba art, whose provenance and circulation link it directly to the reform movement, on the aesthetic vocabulary of twentieth-century African American artists such as John Biggers.

The third section, "The Congo in Modern African American Poetics and Politics," examines the political dimensions of African American literature and culture from the Harlem Renaissance through the late twentieth century in order to argue that the colonial politics of the Congo are embedded within signal moments in modern African American history and culture. Chapter 7, "Near the Congo: Langston Hughes and the Geopolitics of Internationalist Poetry," explores the ways that the poet's seminal work "The Negro Speaks of Rivers" engages a discrete and familiar geopolitical space rather than a generic "Africa." Chapter 8, "Another Black Magazine with a Lumumba Poem: Patrice Lumumba and African American Poetry," further charts this literary movement to examine verse by Ted Joans, Jayne Cortez, and Raymond Patterson as part of a genre of elegiac meditation on the Congo in post-1960 African American literature. My book concludes with "The Chickens Coming Home To Roost: Malcolm X, the Congo, and Modern Black Nationalism" and a figure whose proximity to the international Congo crisis of 1964 hints at something more than rhetorical posturing, and whose frequent commentary on the subject, in many of his most important forums during the final year of his life, locates the trajectory of African American involvement in the Congo at the center of his political vision and organizational praxis, and, by extension, at the heart of modern Black nationalism.

African American readers and writers consistently responded to imperialism in the Congo. At a moment of crisis, Malcolm X articulated his identification with the Congo in language and with tactics that may not have been available to Johnson or Williams or Sheppard. Yet there is always a response, even if its shape shifts. These discourses—circulating throughout HBCUs and the black press, among missionaries, historians, activists, novelists, poets, and artists—resonated on decidedly political registers which may not be transparently evident in the lyrics of "Congo Love Song," especially if readers prefer to think about identity in broad terms rather than to consider more precisely the historical contours of the colonial state. "Congo Love Song," like Malcolm X's identification with the Congo, is part of a long-standing African American engagement, a relationship that belies simplistic presumptions about the romantic African American attachment to Africa and locates opposition to colonialism at the heart of diasporic understandings of Africa.

PART I

# The Nineteenth-Century Routes of Black Transnationalism

*Chapter 1*
# George Washington Williams's Stern Duty of History

On December 12, 1889, the eminent African American historian George Washington Williams eagerly visited the campus of Hampton Normal and Agricultural Institute.[1] He had returned less than two weeks earlier from an antislavery conference in Brussels, where he also had a personal meeting with King Leopold II of Belgium, the sovereign ruler of l'État Indépendant du Congo. Williams parlayed his royal audience, which he had actively sought since 1884, into a commission from the Belgian Commercial Companies to recruit educated black Americans to work in the Congo State. Soon thereafter, he traveled to Hampton with a letter of introduction to founder and principal Samuel Chapman Armstrong from trustee Collis P. Huntington, a railroad magnate with whom Williams had discussed his planned Congo expedition.[2]

Williams left Hampton believing his visit to the Virginia campus was successful in recruiting students to accompany him to the Congo. A few days afterward, on December 16, he sent Armstrong the names of ten male students who expressed interest in going to the Congo with him. Four of them were seniors (from a class with 29 male students), who did not want to leave before graduation. However, three of the others—stone roofers F. H. Meann and James F. Aldrich, and blacksmith Alejandro Santa Cruz of Cienfuegos, Cuba—were, according to Williams, willing to travel immediately.[3] Armstrong, however, sent Huntington a letter on the same day, telling a different story. He acknowledges that his students "are much interested, & Col. Williams has done a great deal by eloquent talks and private discussions to widen their interest," but contends that, at present, "Our pupils are not developed enough to stand the test in Africa." Although Armstrong knew that former students like Ackrel E. White and Samuel T. Miller had worked successfully in Africa, he confided in Huntington that he would do his best to discourage others from traveling.[4]

For his part, Williams was encouraged. In a follow-up letter the next day, he thanked Armstrong for his hospitality and asked how much the students' transportation from Hampton to New York would cost; apparently Williams had begun making their travel arrangements. While giving attention to such logistics, Williams remained a historian, never losing sight of the precise significance of the proposed voyage: "Please say to the boys that I shall not require them to sail until the first of January, 1890, 269 years after the first slaves landed at Jamestown, and 344 years from the time the Spaniards began the slave-trade to this Continent."[5] Hampton's campus is located at the former Old Point Comfort—the very spot where "20. and Odd Negroes" of likely Ndongo origin from the Kongo Kingdom arrived on a Portuguese ship from Luanda, Angola, for Jamestown.[6] His Congo trip, Williams suggested, was much more than a commercial venture; it was an opportunity to make history and, in a sense, reverse the Middle Passage voyages of the transatlantic slave trade. As Jason Young proposes that "New World slaves *remembered* Africa intentionally and deliberately," Williams drew on similar remembrances as a way of "creating new and vibrant cultures informed by memories of Africa."[7] In a December 18 letter to Huntington, Williams was wholly motivated; he described his intention to allow "recruited agents" to visit their families before they set sail on January 1.[8] Yet on December 19, Armstrong definitively nixed the plan, responding that none "of the boys are likely to go," offering a series of explanations and excuses, while noting that Williams made a "deep impression" and asking him to keep in touch from Africa. Armstrong concludes with the hope that, "We should I think [find] a company of six or ten first rate [men] ere long."[9]

Williams's followup letter to Armstrong, dated December 21, responded with "a new tact" requesting that four male seniors pursue a specific curriculum (French, math, and African studies) in preparation for a summer departure. For Williams, this was the beginning of a much larger "endeavor to secure places for educated American Negroes in the East African and South African Companies. I want the American Negro to be the educated and enlightened leader and civilizer in Africa."[10] On December 23, two days after sending this letter to Armstrong, Williams met with President Benjamin Harrison, who solicited Williams's advice regarding ratification of the Berlin Act (which the U.S. delegation signed at the 1884–85 conference, but which had not yet received Congressional approval). While Williams was in Washington, Senator John Sherman of Ohio, chair of the Senate Foreign Relations Committee, also sought his counsel on the Berlin Act. Then, on Christmas 1889, Williams set sail for Europe.[11] When he arrived in Brussels, he had additional meetings with Leopold and his aides, as well as with Albert Thys, who, a few months earlier, commissioned Williams to recruit forty African American workers for the Belgian Commercial Companies. The *New York Times* reported on his success: "The proposition to settle in the Upper Congo country a colony of negroes [sic] from the United States meets with much favor here [in Brussels]. It is thought this would greatly facilitate the peaceful introduction of the ideas and methods of industry and commerce of civilized countries. King Leopold and all the Belgian merchants concerned in

African trade favor the scheme." In a January 19, 1890, address to the American Colonization Society, Edward Wilmot Blyden alluded to Williams's recruitment drive in noting, quite favorably, that Belgium's "philanthropic monarch has despatched an agent to this country to invite the co-operation in his great work of qualified freedmen."[12]

Williams continued to work with Armstrong to lay a firmer foundation for future recruitment efforts. On January 21, 1890, Williams sent a letter to Armstrong proposing a curriculum that would include reading Henry Morton Stanley's *The Congo and the Founding of Its Free State: A Story of Work and Exploration* (1885) "and other Congo literature that may be available."[13] Williams even requested two specific graduating seniors as members of the smaller three-man cohort he was now seeking: Jackson M. Muncy of Henderson, Kentucky, and James Robert Spurgeon of Richmond, Virginia. Even after Williams set sail to Africa from Liverpool on January 30, 1890, his recruiting efforts at Hampton continued to reverberate and make news beyond the Virginia campus. In the March 2, 1890, *New York Tribune*, Thys expressed his disappointment that Williams had not recruited any clerks, engineers, or mechanics, but found consolation in Williams's proposal that "recruits should be sent to the chief industrial schools of the Southern United States" for "special studies, especially French, African geography, etc." The students would be selected by examination to "give us the services of the best men, especially prepared for our work." Apparently, Thys was convinced: "Since the return of Colonel Williams, the companies have carefully considered this plan, and have now adopted it in every detail, exactly as it was laid before them."[14]

While Williams was in Europe preparing for his trip to the Congo and for the future recruitment of Hampton students, Armstrong was explaining the proposal to readers of Hampton's widely circulated monthly journal, the *Southern Workman*: "An invitation to become citizens and employe[e]s of the Congo Free State has been extended to the students of Hampton Institute, by Col G. W. Williams, who comes from Brussels with authority from the 'Companies of the Congo,' under King Leopold of Belgium, to contract with twenty-four colored men of the United States as clerks and mechanics, engineers, carpenters, etc., in the service of the Companies." Armstrong describes how Williams "quite stirred our young men by his eloquent appeals to embrace this 'first opportunity ever offered to American colored men to go to Africa, not because they are not wanted here, but because they are wanted there: to stand on equal footing with European white colonists as pioneers of civilization and destroyers of the slave trade.'" Williams's offer forced Hampton to take a position regarding African American enterprises in Africa. The process of emigration should be selective, albeit voluntary. Although "quite a large number of the Hampton students apparently felt strongly inclined to go," in the end Armstrong resolved "that they should finish their school course before undertaking such very stern realities of life." As a result, "even the few who took the preliminary examination and were accepted" were withdrawn from consideration. Armstrong felt, "The graduates out in the field with more age and experience of life would be generally fitter material for such an enterprise, with its severe tests of morals and character. Yet in most cases, the best fitted of these would be least likely to be free from engagements which they could not honorably drop to start for Africa on a week's notice."[15] Armstrong used the visit from Williams as an opportunity to clarify Hampton's attitude about alumni working in Africa, which sought to balance the missionary ideology it promoted with the emigrationist agenda it opposed. Furthermore, Armstrong's words, here and elsewhere, indicate tension over whether or not Hampton's best and brightest should represent the school at home or abroad.

In his *Southern Workman* summary of Williams's visit, Armstrong cautioned against equating the lack of any recruits with failure: "we doubt not that what they have heard has sown seed which will be fruitful of greater interest in Africa, not unlikely to result in sending some representatives of Hampton to take worthy part in what is one of the most interesting enterprises of the age."[16] Almost immediately, Armstrong was proven correct in his prediction when former Hampton student William H. Sheppard sailed from New York as a cofounder of the APCM in February 1890. Sheppard's career, like Williams's speech, was covered in the *Southern Workman* and other periodicals, which drew African American attention to the Congo. Such networks, including the exemplary cases of those based around Hampton, deeply embedded the Congo within the literature and thought of the period. Their impact, Armstrong astutely notes, must be measured broadly in the "greater interest in Africa" that they inspired including, in Sheppard's case, the successful recruitment of African American missionaries.

When Williams arrived on Hampton's campus, the question of what role African Americans might play in the Congo was already being actively debated. A December 1889 *Southern Workman* editorial, likely written by Armstrong prior to Williams's campus visit, recognized "A tide of Negro emigration may some time set strongly from America to Liberia or the Congo Free State, and Afric Americans may take heroic part in some enterprise like that proposed by Mr. Huntington against the abomination of the slave trade. But only those fit to stay will do any good by going. To work for the improvement of the race here is for the interest of Africa and America."[17] Again, in referencing the "fit," Armstrong anticipates a conflict between sending abroad those Hampton students who have the most to offer at home. To reconcile this paradox, the editorial argues that the development of Hampton is directly beneficial to Africa, making a fundamental philosophical assertion about the relationship of HBCUs to the continent, which Armstrong's acolyte Booker T. Washington tried to put into practice even more fully at Tuskegee Institute in Alabama.

The same December 1889 issue of the *Southern Workman* also includes a review of Huntington's broadside attack on the slave trade in Africa, *A Few Words to Americans*. While Huntington self-interestedly argues that a commercial railroad system was needed to abolish slavery in Africa, the *Southern Workman* acknowledges a special role for Hampton students and alumni in the campaign:

> It is not wholly a white man's mission. Not the least of the inspiration of those who are at work in America, for the Negro, is our belief, that some among our pupils may be enrolled, as some already have been, in the crusade for Africa. The challenge to their Christian manhood and womanhood which comes to them from across the sea is, beyond doubt, a powerful factor in their education. It never does or can weaken the work at home.
>
> Every one who goes leaves behind him a legacy which makes good, ten times over, the force which he takes away. The reaction of the Negro race in America, of the few—it need be a [*sic*] only a few—who may join themselves to Africa, would be of untold value to their self-respect and breadth of interest and view.[18]

According to the *Southern Workman*, African American involvement in Africa should be promoted not only as a service to people abroad, but also because it benefits "the work at home." As in the editorial, Armstrong sees his international and domestic commitments as complementary.

The meaning of the white man's supposed mission to civilize Africa was transformed by the participation of African Americans, even if "only a few." Williams's mission was not only a symbol and a model, but also one that reverberated internationally in the works of writers, politicians, and business leaders. The roles that African American intellectuals like Williams, HBCUs like Hampton, and periodicals like the *Southern Workman* played in the transformation of colonialism in the Congo is one side of this book. The other side is a consideration of its "legacy" on "the work at home"—how the "greater interest" sown by Williams, and African American involvement in the Congo more broadly, informed the religious, political, visual, musical, and literary cultures of the United States and Europe.

A Preliminary Consideration

Williams's visit to Hampton was consistent with the transatlantic vision he articulated throughout the many incarnations of his career. As early as 1874, at the age of twenty-four, in his first sermon as pastor of Boston's Twelfth Baptist Church, Williams preached of Africa: "My heart loves that land, and my soul is proud of it. It has been the dream of my youth that that country would be saved by the colored people of this country."[19] Williams resigned as pastor of Twelfth Baptist in 1875 and, ever a renaissance man, tried his hand as a newspaper editor in Washington, D.C. After eight issues, his newspaper closed, and in 1876, he accepted an appointment as pastor of Union Baptist Church in Cincinnati, where he became active in the city's Republican Party. In 1879, at the age of thirty, after one previous unsuccessful bid for office, Williams became the first African American elected to the Ohio House of Representatives. Two years later, he chose not to run for reelection, deciding to devote himself to his historical studies and spending most of the 1880s as a lecturer and writer. During a period, as Gerald Horne explains, of "deepening engagement with the international community by the formerly enslaved," Williams's increasing focus on the African diaspora reflected these developments.[20]

One of Williams's earliest historical publications was his July 4, 1876, Avondale, Ohio, oration *Centennial: The American Negro, from 1776 to 1876*, which demonstrates an interest in using African diaspora history—in this instance Haiti—to understand contemporary political formations:

> It will ever be the glory of the black man's government in Hayti that he built it on the ruins of slavery, and ratified its benign and humane principles with his own blood.
>
> Neither France nor England can glory in that they freed St. Domingo; but the negro [sic] can boast that he threw off his own yoke, drove his oppressors from the island, conquered the skilled soldiery of England and France, and built his own government upon the rock of human justice and equal rights—a government that has stood during the present century, and will stand through the ages to come![21]

In this address on the centennial of the Declaration of Independence, Williams lauds the agency of the Haitian people. Such diasporic celebration of black self-determination and infrastructural achievement is illustrative of Williams's belief that independent statehood represents the zenith of modern history.

Indeed, the title of the book for which Williams remains best known, *History of the Negro Race in America, from 1619–1880: Negroes as Slaves, as*

*Soldiers, and as Citizens*, fits the historical processes that Williams outlines in his 1876 speech and in his longer historical works. In the movement toward emancipation, "soldiers" assumes the central position, connecting "slaves" and "citizens." Since Williams was studying law while working on his two-volume opus *History of the Negro Race in America*, he knowingly situated his historical project "to record the truth, the whole truth, and nothing but the truth" as sworn testimony with legal standing.[22] This dramatic flourish, which he repeated eight years later in his report to President Harrison, boldly exercises African American citizenship rights and connects his legal and political work to his historical studies.[23]

The relationship between Africa and America provided the bedrock for Williams's *History of the Negro Race in America*, which is generally considered the first scholarly historical survey of African Americans; its subtitle announced: "Together with a Preliminary Consideration of the Unity of the Human Family, an Historical Sketch of Africa, and an Account of the Negro Governments of Sierra Leone and Liberia." Published by G. P. Putnam's Sons in December 1881, the book, which garnered widespread attention, including more than 300 newspaper and magazine reviews, opens with an eleven-chapter section on Africa.[24] Williams describes, for example, the "series of brilliant conquests" by "The Ashantee Empire" to evoke the military strength of Africa without directly challenging the arrogance of Western "civilization": "It is a fact that all uncivilized races are warlike. The tribes of Africa are a vast standing army."[25] According to historian Wilson Jeremiah Moses, the "warlike ideal of the virile barbarian," which Williams celebrates, was popular among African American intellectuals seeking a legacy other than that of victimization.[26] Military potential represented an essential ingredient in Williams's advocacy for full recognition of black citizenship within the United States: "The Negro empires to which we have called attention are an argument against the theory that he is without government; and his career as a soldier would not disgrace the uniform of an American soldier."[27] The more recent valor of black soldiers became the subject of Williams's other major historical tome, *A History of the Negro Troops in the War of Rebellion*, published in 1887. Williams, himself a Civil War veteran, believed that the contributions of African American soldiers made the strongest possible case for full citizenship.[28] His interest in the establishment of the Congo State and his fierce defense of its independence are part of a historical narrative of black statecraft that remains alert to the present and future threat of colonialism.

The emphasis that Williams places on military agency, citizenship, and independence connects his earliest civic and political work to his well-known historical writings. *History of the Negro Race in America* marks the independent black republics of Sierra Leone and Liberia as important sites for African Americans to serve as consular representatives of the U.S. government and, on their return to the United States, to shape "attitudes and opinions toward the continent."[29] For instance, instead of going to the Congo with Williams after graduating as the valedictorian of his Hampton class in 1890, Spurgeon went to Yale Law School and in 1898 was appointed by President William McKinley to the legation at Liberia, where he served as secretary and chargé d'affaires. After leaving his government post, Spurgeon served as the director of the New York and Liberia Steamship Company, practiced law, and was active in Democratic party politics.[30] As one of the "seeds" that Williams sowed, Spurgeon's distinguished career took root in Liberia rather than the Congo, marking the far reach of this tree's many branches.

Williams saw the founding of Liberia as a product of the antebellum era: "The circumstances that led to the founding of the Negro republic in the wilds of Africa perished in the fires of civil war."[31] As early as 1875, Williams expressed trepidation regarding U.S. intervention in Africa and wrote critically of an Americo-Liberian leadership whose policies are "at once cruel and unchristian. If we interfere, let us interfere in behalf of a different policy than that adopted by the Colored Americans in Liberia—a government wholesome and beneficent in its influence upon the long abused natives of Africa."[32] With increasing encroachment from colonial governments, Williams shifted his position a few years later, describing Liberia as a model of "a black government in Africa," where "the cause of religion, education, and republican government are in safe hands, and on a sure foundation."[33] For Williams, effective black leadership in Liberia provided evidence of the potential for black civic participation in the United States and elsewhere in Africa.

Williams's writings on Liberia, an independent republic that once was a dependent state, explain his enthusiasm regarding the Congo. Like Stanley, with whom he would later feud, Williams saw U.S. support for the founding of Liberia as a precedent for recognition of Leopold's Congo regime. As the rapid expansion of European territorial claims during the 1880s tempered the hopes that Williams held for Liberia, contemporaneous developments in the Congo State rendered it an ideal site for him and others to transfer their aspirations.[34] As a historian and a political intellectual, Williams maintained a staunch commitment to independent black statehood, be it Haiti, Liberia, or the widely misunderstood system of governance being implemented in Leopold's Congo.

## States Will Be Founded

Soon after Williams published his *History of the Negro Race in America*, he actively tried to get involved with the development of the Congo. His 1889–90 recruiting drive was the culmination of a longer historical trajectory dating back to 1884 when Williams "was actively aiding King Leopold in his African enterprise. The idea then was to employ a large force of American negroes [sic] to go to Africa as ordinary laborers, to open up roads, build trading stations, etc."[35] Williams was involved in high-level discussions; at the White House, President Chester A. Arthur introduced him to Leopold's American agent, Henry Sanford, who, along with Alabama senator Morgan, led the U.S. campaign for diplomatic recognition of the Congo a year before the Berlin Conference gave European sanction to Leopold's supposedly philanthropic dominion.[36]

As early as late 1883, nearly a year before the November 1884 start of the Berlin conference, Williams reportedly began writing "a series of articles" challenging "Portugal's claim to the Congo."[37] Williams's interest in the Congo achieved public prominence with an oration he delivered in Washington, D.C., on April 16, 1884, addressing the importance of the "Valley of the Congo" as a source of "honest pride" to black Americans on the occasion of the district's Emancipation Day, a major celebration that, according to one report, drew 50,000 people.[38] By making this connection, Williams linked the situation in modern Africa to the transatlantic slave trade: "Africa is yet going to pay this nation dollar for dollar of the three billions spent in prosecuting the war; and America is going to compensate Africa for stealing her children by placing the means of civilization in her waiting and willing hands."[39] While the notion of "Africa"—whether the continent or the diaspora—owing America a debt (presumably, given the context, for the U.S. Civil War) may be confounding, Williams's sound argument in favor of reparations for the slave trade recognizes the intertwined transatlantic histories that formed the foundation for an economic and political relationship between the United States and Africa, even if he constructs a false reciprocity based on his understandably mistaken belief that the Congolese state had the rights and responsibilities of an independent entity.

In this address, Williams further lauded Congress for its approval six days earlier of diplomatic relations with the Congo State: "Thanks to his Excellency President Arthur for his message on the Congo, and loud huzzas for the United States Senate for recognizing the International African Association."[40] Despite the shadiness of the actual arrangements (as part of Leopold's efforts to secure complete control, the "International African Association" had been stealthily supplanted by the "International Association of the Congo"), the currency of Williams's oration was extraordinary.[41] On April 10, an executive session of the Senate recognized the AIA as "a friendly Government."[42] On April 12, President Arthur forwarded the resolution to Secretary of State Frederic T. Frelinghuysen, who on April 22, less than a week after Williams's address, officially made the United States "the first country in the world to recognize King Leopold's claims to the Congo."[43] Following U.S. recognition, the *New York Globe* reported on a Washington banquet where Williams and Richard Greener discussed how "the ultimate redemption of the dark continent would be effected by the voluntary efforts of the educated race-loving colored people here." Ultimately, Williams asserted, "all the young men who are now being educated at the best colleges here will regard it as an honor as well as a labor of love to engage in the work of propagandism in Africa."[44] In the same issue, an editorial supported U.S. recognition of the International Association as a necessary counterbalance to European imperialism: "England must not dominate, France must not control, Portugal must not be sovereign on the Congo River. Let this key and gate-way to equatorial Africa be free and open to all nations alike. Let it be international ground."[45] The following month, the *Globe* saw fit to reprint the conclusion of Williams's speech, including his commentary on the Congo.[46]

As Williams was turning his attention to the Congo in 1884, his words were consistent with his 1874 sermon, his 1876 address, and *History of the Negro Race in America* in advocating both progressive civilization and independent black republics: "Africa is sure to be the scene of the world's greatest civilization. She will be quickened in every nerve and fibre by the power of commerce; and Christian civilization will give tone to her sluggish moral pulse. Africa will be regenerated; tribes will be converted; states will be founded; arts and letters will flourish; peace will reign in her mountains and smile in her valleys; ships and cables, journals and literature, science and discovery, will bind her to the civilized world in bonds of eternal friendship."[47] Williams uses the passive voice—"states will be founded"—to emphasize the result he anticipates, rather than the process through which it might be accomplished. To the extent that the Congo is a site for the projection of romantic aspirations, it is a prominent topic in U.S. political discourse during the very week that Williams spoke. Williams envisions a full-fledged African renaissance emerging from the establishment of the Congo State. Even if he was, like many observers, hoodwinked by Leopold's machinations, his initial optimism was rooted in an academic engagement with modern African politics, rather than the kind of romantic racial allegiance he criticizes in *The History of Negro Race in America*, where he declares that he writes, "Not as the blind panegyrist of my race, nor as the partisan apologist, but from a love for *'the truth of history.'*"[48]

Williams immediately acted on his enthusiasm. During the summer of 1884, he made his first trip to Europe, which included his first attempt to meet with Leopold. Although a meeting with the king did not take place at that time, there was interest in his proposal to employ African Americans in the

Congo. At the beginning of June, likely before Williams even broached the subject, Count Paul de Borchgrave of Leopold's cabinet wrote to Sanford about the possibility of hiring African Americans.[49] On August 19, Count Charles de Lalaing, Leopold's cabinet attaché, forwarded a letter from Williams to Stanley, suggesting a meeting: "of course his pretensions to serve us with a commission of Colonel constitute a demand which we cannot [countenance] but perhaps it would not be a bad place to get a few american [sic] blacks in our service."[50] Two weeks later, Borchgrave wrote to Stanley to request additional information regarding "the monthly pay to give to the Negroes he offers to recruit for us at New Orleans," so that he could compare the wages with those of laborers from East Africa, West Africa, and China.[51] On the same day, probably as a result of a meeting with Leopold, Borchgrave sent Sanford two letters—one from Williams and one from Stanley. According to Borchgrave, Leopold was intrigued by Williams's proposal, and asked Sanford if he thought black Americans from New Orleans could be employed "comme travailleurs, laboureurs et porteurs" (as workers, laborers, and porters).[52] The regime seriously considered Williams's proposal even if they ultimately decided against it because of concerns about salary and a lurking fear that African American dissatisfaction could lead to instability.[53]

Remarkably, Williams was involved in all of these extensive deliberations before the formal establishment of the Congo State at the Berlin Conference. Early recognition of Leopold's dominion gave the United States a special relationship with and, activists would later argue, responsibility to the Congo. Stanley was duly appreciative: "The recognition of the United States was the birth unto new life of the Association, seriously menaced as its existence was by opposing interests and ambitions; and the following of this example by the European Powers has affirmed and secured its place among Sovereign States."[54] The United States was Belgium's strongest ally in Berlin. While the delegation of Kasson, Sanford, and Stanley predictably approved the General Act at the Berlin Conference in February 1885, incoming president Grover Cleveland refused to submit it for Senate ratification out of fear that such a claim of jurisdiction would threaten the standing of the Monroe Doctrine, which was instituted in 1823 to curtail European intrusion in the Americas.[55] Stanley, on the other hand, adopted Sanford's rationale and made the case for U.S. involvement on racial grounds: "It was an act well worthy of the Great Republic, not only as taking the lead in publicly recognising and supporting the great work of African civilisation in history, and in promoting the extension of commerce, but of significant import, in view of its interest for the future weal of the 7,000,000 people of African descent within its borders."[56] U.S. racial politics were unavoidable in debates regarding foreign policy. Stanley, Sanford, and Williams all believed that African Americans had a special role to play in the Congo, even if they ultimately disagreed as to what that role should be.

After the Berlin Conference closed on February 26, 1885, Williams continued to lecture and write about the Congo. He was scheduled to give a speech on the Congo at the Fifteenth Street Presbyterian Church in Washington, as part of a lecture series that included Frederick Douglass, on March 2, 1885, the same day as his bizarre nomination by outgoing president Arthur to replace John Mercer Langston as consul to Haiti.[57] Williams never assumed the position in Haiti, but remained active in international affairs. The following year, he spoke at the Cuban Embassy, presumably on the topic of emancipation. Meanwhile, in 1886 and 1887, he busied himself researching a historical study of Reconstruction and writing a novel, all while continuing to lecture on the Congo.[58]

In June 1888, Williams's work on behalf of the Congo took him to London as a delegate to the Centenary Conference on the Protestant Missions of the World. In his address at Exeter Hall, Williams spoke about abolishing the slave trade and "putting down the liquor traffic on the Congo" River.[59] His international exposure increased lecturing opportunities in the United States, and the Congo was a regular topic. James B. Pond, the country's premier lecture manager, who was also employed by Stanley and Mark Twain, advertised Williams's expertise on the Congo and, in 1889, booked a Memorial Day lecture on the Congo State at the First Baptist Church in Worcester, Massachusetts.[60]

For the fall of 1889, S. S. McClure of the Associated Literary Press hired Williams to cover an antislavery conference in Brussels, providing the media credentials that, along with Williams's own persistence, finally got him a personal audience with Leopold. During this trip, Williams's affiliation with McClure enabled his dispatches, including the Leopold interview, to reach a substantial audience through their publication in the *New York Tribune* and other newspapers.[61] One of Williams's articles favorably noted: "King Leopold expressed his admiration for America in the most flattering terms.... He is as modest as he is wise."[62] During the interview, Leopold explained his involvement in the Congo as "a Christian duty to the poor African," a wholly altruistic undertaking without financial reward. Williams left the interview claiming that Leopold was "one of the noblest sovereigns in the world."[63] It was on the heels of this meeting, with a commission to recruit black American employees for the Belgian Commercial Companies, that Williams headed to Hampton Institute, making what would prove to be his last sojourn in the country where he was born and whose history he chronicled.

## The Opening of Africa

By the time Williams left Hampton with the names of recruits (if not formal commitments) and returned to Brussels in January 1890, it had become clear to Belgian officials that he was not going to be the cog for which they had hoped. Despite its admiring portrait of Leopold, Williams's November 1889 *New York Tribune* article, "The Opening of Africa," expressed misgivings about Stanley's role in the Congo enterprise. To start, Williams questioned Stanley's national loyalties based on his route during the 1887–90 Emin Pasha "rescue" mission: "In looking over my map I am rather puzzled to learn that Mr. Stanley contemplates making his exit from the Dark Continent through German rather than through British territory."[64] Even more serious, however, is Williams's accusation that Stanley was in cahoots with the notorious slave trader Tippu Tip. By 1890, as he prepared to visit Congo, Williams's optimism was evaporating, and he soon emerged as a major critic of a colonial state whose establishment he had recently championed. This transformation reveals a dynamic relationship with Africa that is the product of an ongoing engagement with colonial politics.

The response of Leopold and other officials to Williams's nascent criticism of Stanley was swift as they actively tried to discourage him from traveling to the Congo. Williams later explained to President Benjamin Harrison that Leopold had insisted "that all necessary information would be furnished me in *Brussels*. In reply I told His Majesty that I was going to the Congo *now*."[65] Such resolve was needed since Leopold was trying to sabotage Williams's plans. Leopold refused him passage on government steamships, forcing him to rely on missionary and non-Belgian commercial vessels. When Belgian officials failed to prevent Williams's expedition, they maneuvered to preemptively discredit it. The Belgian ambassador to the United States started rumors, which Stanley later parroted, that Williams was a tool of Huntington's business interests.[66]

Williams began his investigations while en route to Congo: "I found among my fellow voyagers several British Government officials, and have already begun my work by enquiring into the treatment bestowed upon the natives by Europeans." Even at this early stage, he knew he was facing powerful opposition and feared for his life: "I have reason to believe that I may be assassinated or poisoned. However, I shall take every precaution to preserve my life and shall do my duty to history and humanity with unflagging zeal and dauntless courage."[67] Once Williams arrived in the Congo State in late March, his understanding of the regime's misdeeds and his fear for his personal safety intensified. In April, he wrote to Huntington, "I can now understand why the Belgians did not wish me to visit the Congo; and know a dozen excellent reasons why my coming is, in the Providence of God, the best thing that could happen for the poor native and the misguided Belgian." While Williams may have held a somewhat inflated sense of his own role in the Congo, he believed he was in legitimate "danger of assassination or poison," going so far as to make arrangements for the safekeeping of his diaries and his personal effects in the event of his death.[68] Although there were previous occasions when the United States provided military protection to agents in the Congo, Williams received no response to a letter he sent to Massachusetts Senator George F. Hoar requesting a "man of war" to "save me from embarrassment and from assassination."[69] Despite his personal fears, however, he remained focused on the victims of "twelve years of Belgian occupation," arguing forcefully, "The dogs get bones, but these poor Africans get *only* rice and rotten fish."[70]

Williams's diminishing optimism regarding Leopold's Congo regime corresponded with changes taking place on the ground when he arrived in the Congo. The year 1890 marked a "fundamental turning point" when "the system of exploitation which was to keep the state solvent, was then developed." Prior to 1890, the rubber industry and tax system that brought about the most depraved violence were still in their infancy. In 1890, Leopold declared the Congo a "régime domanial," whereby the colonial government was "declared proprietor of all vacant land."[71] With the state holding a land monopoly, rubber replaced ivory as the most valuable export, jumping from 100 metric tons in 1890 to 1,300 in 1896 and 6,000 in 1901, leading to the development of a brutal system of forced labor that provoked international abolitionist organizations to call for humanitarian intervention.[72]

The critiques Williams developed while touring Africa in 1890 proved remarkably precocious. In the wake of this changing colonial economy, Williams wrote three passionately critical tracts about Leopold's regime, which circulated widely in the United States and Europe. Hochschild believes Williams's pamphlets were printed and distributed in conjunction with "a Dutch trading company, the Nieuwe Afrikaansche Handels Vennootschap [NAHV], which had trading posts in the Congo and owned the steamboat, the *Holland*, on which Williams traveled."[73] If Hochschild is correct, it was Leopold's refusal to allow him passage on state steamers that helped Williams make the contacts he used to distribute his pamphlets. The *Open Letter to His Serene Majesty Leopold II, King of the Belgians and Sovereign of the Independent State of Congo* and the equally indignant *Report on the Proposed Congo Railway, by Colonel the Honorable Geo. W. Williams of the United States of America*, ostensibly written for Huntington, were distributed in a single volume. Williams penned both of these tracts at Stanley Falls in July 1890. Several months later in October 1890, while in Luanda, Williams wrote *A*

*Report upon the Congo-State and Country to the President of the Republic of the United States of America, by Colonel the Honorable Geo. W. Williams* to fulfill President Harrison's request.

While Williams's three Congo tracts were clearly intended as public statements, they spoke to distinct constituencies. As his report to President Harrison detailed the complicity of the United States in the establishment of a brutal regime, his *Open Letter* was unflinching in its comments about its declared addressee. Williams made it very clear that, like other colonial regimes, Leopold's "personal Government" had no legitimate standing: "The world may not be surprised to learn that your flag floats over territory to which your Majesty has no legal or just claim, since other European Powers have doubtful claims to the territory which they occupy upon the African Continent; but all honest people will be shocked to known [sic] by what grovelling means this fraud was consummated."[74] While Belgium may be the worst offender, it was not alone in its crimes against Africa. Williams challenges the fundamental legitimacy of European colonial claims in Africa, at a time when challenges on such broad terms were rare.

The *Open Letter* asserts that the theft of land was foremost among Leopold's transgressions: "Your Majesty's Government has sequestered their land, burned their towns, stolen their property, enslaved their women and children, and committed other crimes too numerous to mention in detail." Williams's criticism was based on the protection of African land rights, a position that was not typical, even among Leopold's opponents. Leopold, Williams drolly commented, was wrong to establish military posts in "territory to which your Majesty has no more legal claim, than I have to be Commander-in-Chief of the Belgian army." In the conclusion, Williams was precise as to where ultimate responsibility rested: "All the crimes perpetrated in the Congo have been done in *your* name, and *you* must answer at the bar of Public Sentiment for the misgovernment of a people, whose lives and fortunes were entrusted to you by the august Conference of Berlin, 1884–1885."[75] At a time when many other critics focused on his violations of commercial treaties, Williams impeaches Leopold for his crimes against African people.

### A Shudder among the Simple Folk

Williams ascertains multiple layers of culpability for the Congo atrocities. Leopold, who never set foot in the Congo, could not have succeeded in grabbing power without the help of many accomplices. Prominent among them was Stanley, who claimed to have signed treaties with Africans, "Of their own free will, without coercion, but for substantial considerations, reserving only a few easy conditions, they had transferred their rights of sovereignty and of ownership to the Association" of Leopold.[76] Williams, however, used his *Open Letter* to accuse Stanley of supervising the cruel manipulation of people into signing away their land by convincing them of the supernatural powers of white people to start fires (using a lens and a cigar) and survive gunshots (using a cap gun).[77]

In *Open Letter*, Williams used his concluding charge on the infeasibility of the Congo Railway to make broader accusations against the railroad's most prominent booster: "HENRY M. STANLEY's name produces a shudder among this simple folk when mentioned; they remember his broken promises, his copious profanity, his hot temper, his heavy blows, his severe and rigorous measures, by which they were mulcted of their lands."[78] Significantly, while most opponents of Stanley based their denunciation on his own shameless accounts or those of his white officers, Williams drew on interviews with Congolese men and women for his criticism. As Hochschild observes, "Of the hundreds of Europeans and Americans who traveled to the Congo in the state's early years, Williams is the only one on record as questioning Africans about their personal experience of Stanley."[79] At a time when African voices were excluded from conversations about colonialism (there were no African representatives at the Berlin Conference), Williams gave credence to their stories. As an activist, Williams's method was similar to his work as a historian noted for his use of traditionally marginalized voices. For instance, Williams conducted interviews with black soldiers, which, according to his biographer John Hope Franklin, "surely mark Williams as one of the pioneer investigators in the field of oral history."[80] Williams approached Stanley and the Congo in a similar manner. Unlike most of his white contemporaries, Williams considered Africans to be authoritative commentators. His methods of research and analysis enabled him to reach his conclusions, unique in their time, about the Congo, and to establish a prototypical anticolonial discourse that is grounded in the voices of its resisting victims.

*Report on the Proposed Congo Railway* extended the Stanley criticism that Williams introduced in *Open Letter*. In many respects, Williams writes an explicit corrective to Stanley's bestseller *The Congo and the Founding of Its Free State*. He criticizes Stanley's statistics on the population and density of the Congo. He also resurveys Stanley's projected railway route and presents his own estimates of the construction time and costs which proved much closer to the actual figures.[81] Ultimately, Williams challenges the book's standing as the dominant English-language narrative of central Africa and, fundamentally, its author's expertise: "I know of no work, dealing along with the commerce of Africa, more unreliable and misleading than Mr. STANLEY's, 'The Congo Free State.'" Although a few months earlier Williams recommended that Armstrong include Stanley's book in the Hampton curriculum, he now dismissed it as a "two volume advertisement" and its author as someone inclined to "flights of imagination."[82] Williams understood the devastation Stanley wreaked in Africa and the political significance of his support for European imperialism as crimes far more severe than creative embellishment.

Recognizing that Stanley's authorship functioned as an instrument of Leopold's colonial rule, Williams believed that his own job as a historian and a writer include responsibilities which Stanley had abdicated: "It is not an agreeabl[e] task to have to say these things of a man whose valour, perseverance, sufferings, and triumphs [sic] have sent a thril[l] of admiration throughout the civilised world; but it is the stern duty of history to prevent error from being canonized instead of the truth, which must be written with an iron pen."[83] Such sentiments—his "love for *'the truth of history'*"—were characteristic of Williams's philosophy.[84] In an 1884 address, Williams asserts with regard to the Civil War: "However repulsive the task may be, we owe it to the truth of history to bring our best literary workmanship to the dissection of the problem back of and underneath the later war."[85] As had generations of African American writers before him, Williams grasped the sacred responsibility of "literary workmanship," particularly within a discourse dominated by Stanley. In the opening African chapters of *History of the Negro Race in America*, Williams notes "the noble life-work of Dr. David Livingstone, and the thrilling narrative of Mr. Henry M. Stanley," pinpointing the fundamental difference between Livingstone's project and Stanley's.[86] Whereas the less sullied Livingstone was a man of action, Stanley was a raconteur whose first African expedition, his 1872 search for Livingstone, was organized and funded by the *New York Herald*.[87] In his description of Stanley's *Through the Dark Continent*, Williams makes clear that the explorer's greatest accomplishments are as a storyteller: "How many times we have read this marvellous [sic] narrative of Stanley's march through the Dark Continent, we do not know; but we do know that every time we have read it with tears and emotion, have blessed the noble Stanley, and thanked God for the grand character of his black followers! There is no romance equal to these two volumes."[88] Whatever kind of critique is visible in his characterization, Williams understood that Stanley was "the veriest romancer" who belonged squarely in the literary realm.[89]

Williams was not the only person to recognize that Stanley's importance and influence derived at least as much from what he wrote about his travels as it did from his work during those travels. Stanley himself understood as much as early as his August 1872 address to the Royal Geographic Society, where he effectively affirms Williams's characterization of him as a storyteller: "I consider myself in the light of a troubadour." After coming to international prominence for supposedly tracking down Livingstone, Stanley faced a skeptical geographic establishment that was embarrassed by the success of a person who "quite simply lacked the credentials of either the gentleman or the scientist."[90] Stanley and his family were vehemently committed to this image. In *Autobiography of Sir Henry Morton Stanley*, a misleadingly titled posthumous collection of Stanley's writings, Dorothy Tennant Stanley insisted on the primacy of her late husband's identity as a writer, rather than an imperial profiteer who "would never take the slightest personal advantage of the commercial opportunities incident to the opening of the new countries, on the Congo, or in Uganda. *I desire to emphasise the fact that such property as he had came almost entirely from his books and his lectures.*"[91] Stanley's standing as an author and his concomitant commercial interests took primacy over his status as a colonial agent. His widow echoed Stanley's own assertions that insisted he was a writer and a troubadour, not an imperialist. However, Stanley's career demonstrates the deep entanglements of literary work and imperialism. Leopold understood the import of literary work to the consolidation of empire as well; his editorial markings remain visible in the margins of the manuscript of Stanley's *The Congo and the Founding of Its Free State*.[92] The book consummated the five years of work Stanley did as "Leopold's man in the Congo," and was only the beginning of a royal propaganda machine that targeted African American Congo reform activists for decades to come.[93]

Williams was acutely aware of his own vulnerability and sought the protection of the U.S. government and, in at least one instance, quite literally the U.S. flag, which he asked Huntington to send him for his tent.[94] Stanley, by contrast, goes out of his way to suggest his indifference to such questions of nationalism. During his second African expedition, when his British assistants nervously ask him if they can "make a small British flag to hoist above our tent, and over our canoe," he agrees: "This is not an American Government or a British Government Expedition, and I have neither the power nor the disposition to withhold my sanction to your request."[95] Stanley's journalistic commission, jointly sponsored by the *New York Herald* and the London *Daily Telegraph*, positioned him as a uniquely Anglo-American literary subject, whose mercenary sense of national identity enabled him to serve at least four governments, sometimes more than one simultaneously, over the course of his career.[96]

Despite his consistent support of Leopold, Stanley's work is based less in conflicts between the European powers than in the differences between Africans and Europeans, blacks and whites. As V. Y. Mudimbe explains, in many European representations of Africa, "The African has become not only the Other who is everyone else except me, but rather the key which, in its abnormal differences, specifies the identity of the Same."[97] Stanley's encounter with and representation of Africa constructs the "Same" as neither British nor American, but rather as not-African, a sort-of transnational white subject. His allegiances were literary, financial, and ultimately racial, leading Felix Driver to point out, "The sheer variety of the political claims on Stanley suggests that, rather than representing the interests of any empire in particular, he was a pioneer of the new imperialism in general. Like Kurtz in *Heart of Darkness*, 'all Europe contributed' to his making."[98] This European nationalism finds a parallel in the postbellum United States, where the political reconciliation of the Civil War's white factions was used to construct a new form of white national identity.

Williams's discursive interventions are rendered all the more significant by Stanley's extraordinary efforts to maintain a contractual monopoly on central African travel writing by requiring his officers to sign contracts agreeing not to publish anything about the excursion until at least six months after Stanley issued his own version of events.[99] Even more remarkably, the Congo—or at least *The Congo*—is responsible for making Stanley a U.S. citizen, which he only sought "to protect his book royalties" against the commercial threat of "a pirated edition of his book on *The Congo and the Founding of Its Free State*."[100] After his death in May 1904, it became more difficult to control that narrative due, in part, to the increasing prominence of the Congo reform movement. In a July commemoration, British journalist Sidney Low recognized Congo reform as a threat to Stanley's legacy: "It was no fault of Stanley's if the work has been badly carried on by his successors, and if the Congo State, under a régime of Belgian officials, not always carefully selected, has not, so far, fulfilled the promise of its inception. So long as Stanley was in Africa, no disaster occurred; there was no plundering of the natives, and no savage reprisals."[101] Low absurdly sought to disclaim violent actions—like his vengeful mass murders on Bumbire Island—that Stanley bragged about for most of his life.[102] In 1909, a year after Leopold transferred control of the Congo to the Belgian government, Dorothy Stanley reprinted Low's commentary in her late husband's posthumous "autobiography," thereby acknowledging that Williams was right about the horrors of the Congo and only wrong in holding Stanley responsible.

Williams understood what Driver terms "the new imperialism" in a way that allowed him to recognize multiple levels of responsibility within an empire that was, in the end, still a function of state power and moneyed interests. His opposition to Leopold's regime took aim at a transnational array of targets, and was prototypical of the diverse international movement that soon developed around the issue of the Congo State. Williams challenged Stanley's monopoly by following the identical routes that he detailed, interviewing African people about their experiences, and questioning his findings. His revision of Stanley's bestseller is important for appreciating Williams as a literary figure. Furthermore, the international response he evoked further codifies the importance of his writings. Franklin notes the magnitude of the contemporary response to Williams's Congo writings: "What was remarkable about the incident was the furor raised by a relatively brief statement by a relatively obscure black American about the conduct of one of the most important and most powerful men in the world."[103] Indeed Williams's words traveled fast; his three reports on the Congo made their way to Europe more quickly than their author did.

While Williams was still in Africa, his writings were beginning to attract attention. In October 1890, one of his patrons, William Mackinnon of the Imperial British East Africa Company, showed Stanley a copy of Williams's *Open Letter*. Even a transatlantic trek for a six-month American lecture tour organized by Pond could not help Stanley escape Williams's reports. On January 2, 1891, Leonard Wilson, whom Leopold hired as a secretary on Stanley's recommendation, sent Williams's pamphlets to Stanley in New York City as "commanded by His Majesty the King." In his cover letter, Wilson describes Williams as "a coloured native of America, and who, failing in his endeavors to obtain an entrance into His Majesty's service, resorts to this means of revenge." He then mentions U.S. Ambassador Edwin H. Terrell's aspersions "that the author of the enclosed is that kind of character known as a 'blackguard,' and that, consequently no reliance can be placed upon his statements."[104] This continues the racist pattern of discrediting Williams at the highest levels of the international diplomatic community.

In April 1891, at the close of Stanley's U.S. tour, the *New York Herald* ran a story about Williams's exposé of the Congo State under the descriptive heading, "Stanley the Bugbear of Congo Land. The Administration of the African Free State Declared by an American Citizen to be Barbarous. Investigation Demanded. King Leopold of Belgium Arraigned in an Open Letter by Colonel George W. Williams for Countenancing a Corrupt Government." The article consists of excerpts from the *Open Letter* followed by an interview with Stanley, several of whose African expeditions the *Herald* had financed. Stanley "stopped to talk about Colonel Williams' letter at some length," acknowledging that Mackinnon, who told him "that Williams had applied to him for permission to visit the territory of the East Africa Company with a similar purpose," had shown it to him in October. Williams's words chased Stanley, who was unable to escape them when a reporter literally put them in front of him just as Mackinnon and Leopold had. In the same interview, Stanley recalls meeting Williams in 1884 and being impressed enough to recommend him to Leopold. Rather than disputing Williams's most serious charge of brutality, which was prominent in the excerpt reprinted by the *Herald*, Stanley emphasized the illegitimacy of Williams's undertaking based on a relative technicality: "the statement that Williams had charge of the surveys of the Congo Railroad is absolutely false."[105] Stanley then accused Williams of blackmail, based on his association with railway investor Huntington. Huntington, however, defended Leopold, and aligned himself more closely with Mackinnon and Stanley than with Williams.

After Williams's criticism became public, Huntington reached out to Stanley in January 1891 while they were both in New York. Huntington offered his assistance, in general terms, "to do something to advance your interest in this country," explaining it as not only a tribute to Mackinnon, but also to Leopold, "the man who has done so much, at such great cost to himself, to open up Equatorial Africa so as to make it possible to drive out the slave trader and spread commerce and civilization over a country that has been so long cursed, not only by the native African but by the most wicked from all the nations of the Earth who have been hovering around the borders of that dark land carrying with them the worst vices and none of the virtues known to civilization."[106] Huntington's praise of Leopold is without equivocation, and appears to be an attempt to appease Stanley in the wake of Williams's reports. Despite Stanley's fears of betrayal, Huntington was, in 1890–91, as consistent in his defense of Leopold as Williams was uncompromising in his condemnation.[107] Throughout their correspondence, Williams remained gracious toward Huntington even while he was unflinchingly critical of Stanley and Leopold.

"I Shall Attack the Congo State from an Hundred Platforms in Europe"

On June 1, 1891, Williams arrived in England from Egypt, where he spent a few months convalescing from an illness at the end of his African tour. Later that week, Stanley accused Mackinnon, who had provided for Williams's transportation, of doing a disservice to both Stanley and Leopold. Stanley recalls his October 1890 encounter with Mackinnon:

> in the smoke room of Ismayi House where after receiving Huntingdon's [*sic*] letter, you were about to assist a notorious blackmailer in the person of the slanderous negro [*sic*] George Williams (colonel).
>
> Of course you had not read the letter through, and had not reflected that by assisting G. Williams with a loan, advance, or courtesies you would be countenancing slander against one whom I know you esteem and honor as a man, and a noble benefactor to his age. There is no doubt

of it, but that if you had known the full extent of Williams' villainies you would have tossed Huntingdon's letter into the fire to avoid a thought even of the man whom you were asked to serve.[108]

In his June 6, 1891, letter, Stanley does not mention Williams's current whereabouts; however, the timing suggests some connection to Williams's arrival on the scene, since the incident would otherwise have been old news.[109] At the very least, it reveals the lasting impression of Williams's Congo writings on powerful figures in the United States, England, and throughout Europe.

Williams's writings inspired a concerted effort to discredit their author. At the same time that Stanley was dealing with Williams in the United States and England, Leopold was personally responding to the same "scandalous and utterly unfounded charges" in Belgium. In April 1891, Leopold warned Lord Hussey Vivian, the British ambassador at Brussels, to be wary of Williams. Vivian dutifully reported Leopold's allegations to the British foreign secretary, but added, "Colonel Williams may be all the King says he is, but I suspect there is a good deal of disagreeable truth in his pamphlets."[110] In his communication with Vivian, Leopold apparently made personal attacks on Williams, whose writings, after circulating in England for at least six months, were gaining increased traction throughout Europe.

Disparaging attacks on Williams like those from Stanley and Leopold became commonplace when news of his exposés hit the Belgian press with the publication of "Un colonel noir" in *Mouvement Géographique* in June 1891. By the middle of the month, Franklin points out, "virtually every newspaper in Brussels and several in Paris had plunged into the melee." Many newspapers resorted to personal attacks. *Journal de Bruxelles* characterized Williams as "unbalanced" in what Franklin politely deems "a highly imaginative biographical sketch."[111] However, several other Belgian publications, including *La Réforme, Courrier de Bruxelles, Le Jour,* and *Flandre Libérale*, took the allegations seriously and called on the government to respond. Although some members of the Belgian Parliament defended Leopold by slandering Williams, the legislature found his *Open Letter* to be credible enough for them to formally investigate. On June 18, 1891, the Belgian legislature held hearings on Williams's allegations. Although parliamentary deputies predictably recycled Stanley's blackmail accusation, the legislature agreed to an official investigation into conditions in the Congo. In July 1891, Edmond Van Eetvelde and Camille Janssen, the Administrators-General of the Congo State, released a forty-five page report in direct response to the twelve allegations outlined by Williams in his *Open Letter*: inadequate resources, corrupt soldiers, violations of work contracts, racist courts, cruelty to prisoners, female prostitution, unfair trade practices, mistreatment of Africans, waging wars, trading in slaves, illegal territorial expansion, and misrepresentation of the railroad project. The report was hardly disinterested. One of its signatories, Janssen, was singled out by Williams in the same pamphlet for his racist refusal to prosecute his guilty white servant for thefts for which innocent black workers had already been punished.[112]

In the final months of his life, Williams's reports on the Congo continued to attract international attention from media, governments, and Stanley and Leopold themselves. Even in personal correspondence, Williams called out Huntington, his primary benefactor, for deeming Leopold "a friend of humanity." Despite his own serious illness and lack of financial means, Williams insisted that "I shall tell the whole truth!"[113] In February 1891, while convalescing in Cairo, Williams sought to ensure the publication of his "six journals full of valuable information" about the Congo, asking Huntington to write an introduction pleading "for justice and humane treatment of the natives."[114] After arriving in England in early June 1891, Mackinnon quickly became frustrated with Williams's persistent agitation. After corresponding with him several times, Williams sent Mackinnon "a most intemperate letter from Cairo denouncing in unmeasured terms everything that Stanley has done & everything the King of the Belgians has attempted to do." Mackinnon fears what Williams intends to do on behalf of the Congo: "I dare say we shall hear a great deal more about him soon as he appears determined at all hazards to rouse what he calls public sentiment in London. I doubt if he will find this an easy business in the way in which he attempts it."[115] The following month, as Williams's health continued to decline, Francis W. Fox visited Williams at a hydropathy center in Lancashire where "the Doctor had told him he would not probably be alive for more than two months." Still, Williams was actively "trying to get Harper Bros. of New York and London to publish two books on Africa giving an account of his journey," which he saw as his final testament.[116] These accounts of the final months of Williams's life reveal a staunch commitment to exposing the crimes of Leopold's Congo to the largest possible audience, despite the opposition of many powerful figures, including patrons on whom he depended for sustenance.

Although there is no corroboration beyond motive of the assassination plot that Williams expected, his death was close at hand. He died on August 2, 1891, at the age of forty-one, two months after arriving in England. He was buried in a grave in Blackpool, England, that was unmarked until 1975 when his heroic biographer Franklin personally paid for a tombstone to be erected in his memory. His death in Europe well before his political voice on the Congo had the chance to fully blossom certainly looks like the kind of conspiracy he consistently feared. Williams told his correspondents during the final weeks of his life that he was writing "what he regarded as his final statement on Leopold's rule in Africa."[117] At the very least, his untimely death, "coupled with the fact that the king-sovereign took care to discredit him in advance, saved the Congo government from what might have been," in the words of historian Sylvanus J. S. Cookey, "an embarrassingly formidable opponent."[118] In a lengthy letter to Huntington in December 1890, Williams was insistent: "I have not said one tenth of what I have to say and *will say*; and can establish every charge against the King's Government by credible witnesses! I shall attack the Congo State from an hundred platforms in Europe, and if the King wishes to refute my charges let him undertake the task, and I will place 46 white men on their oath as to the truthfulness of my assertions; and will produce official records in evidence!!"[119] Indeed, the *New York Tribune* obituary remembered Williams not as the author of *History of the Negro Race in America*, but as "a colored lawyer from America, who some time ago visited the Upper Congo country, and who wrote letters to King Leopold of Belgium severely criticising the methods of the Congo Free State officials and also those of Henry M. Stanley."[120]

## One of the Foulest Crimes of Modern Diplomatic History!

By early 1891, Williams's pamphlets were receiving coverage in the American press. In April, the *Cleveland Gazette* reported, "Hon. George W. Williams, at one time a member of the Ohio assembly from Cincinnati, has published what are proving to be sensational letters and pamphlets. They expose the sad state of things on the Congo in Africa. The natives are being cruelly and outrageously treated by dishonest agents and immoral whites. He has written many startling facts, and investigations by foreign countries, resulting in a change for the better."[121] He is credited, as a writer, for inspiring international reform while he consistently attended to the role of the United States in the establishment of the Congo State. In *Report upon the Congo-State and Country to the President*, a follow-up to his December 1889 meeting, Williams outlined the importance of U.S. recognition of the AIA after its initial rebuff by nearly all European governments. Williams parroted the assertions of Stanley on this point, asserting in his Worcester address that recognition by the United States "infused new life into the association."[122] Whereas this was a compliment for Stanley, it was a point of criticism and a matter of accountability for Williams. With recognition, he contended, came culpability for the formation of l'État Indépendent du Congo, the installation of Leopold as head of state, and the ensuing misdeeds. Leopold's seizure of power not only violated international law but also betrayed the trust of the United States. The secretary of state, Williams stressed, "never permitted his Government to become a party to a scheme of seizing and dividing the Congo-country among certain European Powers, one of the foulest crimes of modern diplomatic history!"[123] He asserted that Leopold conned the U.S. government, which should inspire prideful indignation if not moral outrage on behalf on the people of the Congo.

Ever the historian, Williams looked back in order to understand the responsibility of the United States antecedent to the Berlin Conference. Politically, he appreciated its position in a complex transatlantic web: "Although America has no commercial interests in the Congo it was the Government of the Republic of the United States which introduced this African Government into the sisterhood of States. It was the American Republic which stood sponsor to this young State, which has disappointed the most glowing hopes of its most ardent friends and most zealous promoters." By 1890, Williams, who once supported U.S. recognition of the Congo State, determined that the United States, as the first country to establish diplomatic relations with Belgium's African regime, was blameworthy for the "Congo atrocities." More importantly, "The people of the United States of America have a just right to know *the truth*, the *whole truth* and *nothing but the truth*," as in *History of the Negro Race in America*, "respecting the Independent State of Congo, an absolute monarchy, an oppressive and cruel Government, an exclusive Belgian colony, now tottering to its fall." Williams went beyond his criticism of the current system to articulate a radical vision for the future: "when a new Government shall rise upon the ruins of the old, it will be simple, not complicated; local, not European; international, not national; just, not cruel; and, casting its shield alike over black and white, trader and missionary, endure for centuries."[124] Although it took another seventy years for the people of the Congo to gain independence and achieve, even fleetingly, some form of "local, not European" government, Williams was unwilling to compromise his principles and made it clear that the crisis could not be solved simply through the liberalization of colonial rule.

Throughout his public report to President Harrison, Williams effectively balances principled jeremiads with pragmatic arguments, for example, about free trade, which appealed to business leaders who were irate about the import and export duties from which Belgium and its concessionaires were exempt.[125] His multilayered argument insisted that Christian missionary work be combined "with practical missionary work, or industrialism," language that echoes the Hampton–Tuskegee ideal.[126] In his *Report on the Proposed Congo Railway*, Williams makes a strong case for a revision of colonial labor practices: "Africa needs the blessing of a practical labor system which, while it addresses itself to the soul, will not ignore the body, its earthly temple; and, while inculcating spiritual truths, will not fail to teach the native the primal lesson of human history: *For in the sweat of thy face shalt thou eat thy bread*."¹²⁷ By employing terms such as "blessing," "soul," "temple," and "spiritual" to make an argument about labor practices and political economy, Williams offered a cautionary note on narrowly religious missionary work. His suggestions, not surprisingly, were similar to those expressed to him by Huntington: "The Christian residents should follow agricultural pursuits, or be medical men, or better still, combine the two avocations. They would soon be able to raise up around them a group of native teachers and assistants, while engaged in their secular calling, . . . would be carrying out in a most effectual manner the highest and foremost work of the Christian missionary."¹²⁸ Huntington's interest in colonial labor helps explain why Williams chose to promote his plans for the Congo at Hampton, a school that promoted secular industrial education. Although Williams corresponded with an official from the American Missionary Association about the prospect of recruiting from their schools (including Fisk and Talladega), a working relationship never developed. Williams used secular uplift rather than religious civilization to frame his work in the Congo, advocating for the application of the Hampton–Tuskegee model of education in Africa. Like his domestic colleagues, Williams believed that Christian ethics could be promoted through industrial education.¹²⁹

Within his pragmatic framework, African American agents are the best equipped for the task, a position that Williams had advocated in one form or another since 1884. His experience in the Congo, however, made him rethink the role for African Americans that he had in mind when he agreed to recruit students from Hampton for the Belgian Commercial Companies. Williams realized that his original strategy at Hampton had been premature, and he presented President Harrison with a long-range plan that included a more limited niche for African Americans: "Emigration cannot be invited to the Congo for a quarter of a century, and then only educated blacks from the Southern United States, who have health, courage, morals and means. They must come only in small companies, not as laborers, but as landed proprietors. One hundred families in ten years would be quite enough and not for twenty five years yet. *White labor can never hope to get a foot-hold here*."¹³⁰ In Williams's writings, there is a shifting model of African American involvement, which is developed in different ways during the next two decades by two former Hampton students—Sheppard and Washington. Williams anticipated that a future educated elite was going to uplift Africa, a point he rearticulated throughout his career and which was a variation on Du Bois's "talented tenth" thesis.¹³¹ Williams came to consider his Hampton recruitment plan to be something best cultivated methodically over the course of a generation.

## Whenever the Natives Refuse to Feed These Vampires

Williams's engagement with and revision of Stanley's writings about the Congo has precedent in African American letters. In *Figures in Black: Words, Signs, and the "Racial" Self*, Henry Louis Gates Jr. suggests that Phillis Wheatley and Thomas Jefferson's textual exchange represents a founding moment of "the Afro-American literary tradition [that] was generated as a response to eighteenth- and nineteenth-century allegations that persons of African descent did not, and could not, create literature."[132] At that pivotal moment, Wheatley did much more than respond to Jefferson. Her expert verse necessitated Jefferson's elaboration of ideas that, more than two centuries later, remain central to any discussion of the racial ideology of the nation's founders. Under much different circumstances, Williams did something similar by revising Stanley's exploration narratives, which were among the most popular literature of its day. If, as Gates posits, African American letters is "a literature often inextricably bound in a dialogue with its potentially harshest critics," European traditions likewise need to be understood as the products of their critics, including those international sources that Franklin spent decades compiling.[133] Williams's forceful commentaries, like Wheatley's poetry, elicited strong responses from powerful men. Williams's writings could not be ignored by the state or by Stanley. The international reaction to Williams suggests that African American writers were not only reacting to what people were saying about them, but were also themselves being reacted to, in many cases, by the same figures. The resulting conversation represents one major contribution of African Americans to a developing transnational discourse about Leopold's Congo reign.

Where the dominant literature is also "inextricably bound in a dialogue," it demands what Edward Said, in *Culture and Imperialism*, calls a "contrapuntal" reading built on "a simultaneous awareness both of the metropolitan history that is narrated and of those other histories against which (and together with which) the dominating discourse acts."[134] Following Said, Williams's voice should be read as a part of an African American intellectual tradition that is shaped by colonialism in the Congo while simultaneously shaping the "dominating discourse." In this case, and in the case of Sheppard, the European colonial archive must be seen as a product of its African American critics. Though based among African American individuals and institutions, the cultural and political discourse that this book maps reached the upper echelons of European and American power. Within less than two years, Williams, the most prominent African American historian of his century, reached an audience that included King Leopold II, Henry Stanley, Collis

Huntington, President Harrison, William Mackinnon, and Samuel Armstrong, along with countless other American, Belgian, and British leaders.

The erasure of Williams from metropolitan history was deliberate. Émile Banning, one of Leopold's senior advisors, wrote extensively in his *Mémoires politiques et diplomatiques: Comment fut fondé le Congo belge* of a June 1891 meeting to strategize "mesures à prendre pour combattre l'effet produit par le pamphlet Williams, dont la presse parisienne surtout fait un vrai scandale" (measures to be taken to combat the impact of Williams's pamphlet, which the Paris press has made into a real scandal). At the meeting, several high-ranking colonial administrators devised a plan for "un exposé à la fois historique et statistique, qui serait publié dans un numéro spécial du Bulletin officiel, et envoyé dans toute l'Europe et aux Etats-unis comme antidote du pamphlet qui ne serait d'ailleurs pas même nommé" (an exposé that is both historical and statistical, that will be published in a special issue of the official Bulletin, and sent throughout Europe and to the United States as an antidote to the pamphlet that will not be mentioned by name).[135] Belgian officials strategically decided to counter Williams without ever acknowledging him (*qui ne serait d'ailleurs pas même nommé*), rendering his opposition and writings invisible, as they have remained throughout much of the historical record. Despite the methodical ways in which Banning and his colleagues tried to erase Williams, the 1985 publication of Franklin's brilliant and groundbreaking biography has made that increasingly difficult to sustain. In particular, Franklin's inclusion of Williams's three Congo reports as appendixes to the biography has enabled the metropolitan culture of the Leopoldian era to be read contrapuntally.

One of the most encouraging instances of the intervention of Williams into metropolitan discourse about the Congo is his inclusion in 1988 in Robert Kimbrough's third edition of his Norton Critical Edition of Joseph Conrad's *Heart of Darkness*, which has been, for several generations, the most prominent literary text of the period and one which Said himself has written about extensively. Conrad's seventy-six-page novella is complemented by more than forty pages by or about Williams including excerpts from all three pamphlets.[136] Williams has posthumously transformed the way we read Conrad's short novel, much as he did Stanley's popular accounts. However, literary posterity has been kinder to Conrad than to Stanley. Conrad, whose *Heart of Darkness* remains a dominant image of the Congo, was there at the same time as Williams. Williams, however, published his scathing reports on the administration of the Congo before he left Africa whereas Conrad did not write his novella for another decade, and later refused an invitation to join the CRA.[137]

Williams appreciated the literary conventions of his era, describing, in his letter to Leopold, "black Zanzibar soldiers," who are responsible for feeding white officials: "These piratical, buccaneering posts compel the natives to furnish them with fish, goats, fowls, and vegetables at the mouths of their muskets; and whenever the natives refuse to feed these vampires, they report to the main station and white officers come with an expeditionary force and burn away the homes of the natives."[138] In portraying the Congo, Williams invokes the vampire, which, according to Stanford M. Lyman, "provides the Gothic sociology of capitalism with demonological symbol: corporate enterprise's world-roaming drive for its life-sustaining substance, abject labor power."[139] In an era of European vampire novels, Williams describes the exploitation of the Congolese people in language that was also an allegory popular among Africans seeking to explain colonialism.[140] A decade later, *Heart of Darkness* would echo the imagery used by Williams, though Conrad's text finds its tragedy less in the mistreatment of the Congolese people than in the degradation of colonizers like Kurtz. Despite Conrad's personal experiences in the Congo, *Heart of Darkness* remains a literary construction based at least as much on accounts published in the British press as on firsthand experience.[141] The popular uses to which the novel has been put within the media have contributed to a "paradox" according to Kevin Dunn: "While Westerners are generally uninformed about Congolese history and politics, they feel they know it well because of the powerful images of it encountered everyday."[142]

The canonization of Williams's writings as auxiliaries to *Heart of Darkness* has increased his visibility by association with a text that has been reinvigorated, thanks in large part to novelist Chinua Achebe's 1977 essay, "An Image of Africa: Racism in Conrad's *Heart of Darkness*," a touchstone for postcolonial studies. Williams, however, remains overlooked. Despite citing the 1988 Norton edition of *Heart of Darkness*, Peter Edgerly Firchow still claims *Heart of Darkness* as "the very first and only important English work, either fictional or documentary" to expose the brutality of Leopold's state.[143] Even Driver's excellent *Geography Militant*, which cites the same edition of *Heart of Darkness* in which Williams is well represented, tells a tale of opposition to Stanley without mentioning Williams. Although Williams is slightly less well represented in Paul B. Armstrong's 2006 fourth and 2016 fifth Norton Critical Editions of *Heart of Darkness*, his letter to Leopold remains and will hopefully inform future scholarship.[144]

Among African Americans, Williams was well remembered. While in Europe in 1894, Charles Spencer Smith, a "protégé" of Henry McNeal Turner, "was anxious to learn if there is a favorable opening in the Congo for colored

Americans."[145] After being turned down by the director general of the Congo Railroad in Antwerp, Smith alluded to "many conflicting reports concerning the management of this railroad" and "remembered that the great colored historian, Hon. George W. Williams, visited the Congo several years ago, but his report was never published, he having died in England, *en route* to America."[146] Smith's error regarding the publication of the report makes his recollection of Williams all the more remarkable since it indicates that his criticisms circulated beyond those who actually read his writings. Smith refers to two distinct positions held by Williams, who, on one hand, offered the most radical critique of Leopold's regime and, on the other, sought constructive engagement through his Hampton recruitment efforts. While these may seem contradictory, the failure of his recruitment efforts, which foreclosed the possibility of a permanent or otherwise long-term appointment in the Congo, arguably freed him of the sorts of obligations that might have necessitated a different set of political positions such as those that encumbered Blyden.[147]

Beyond his influence on figures like Smith and Spurgeon, Williams makes important contributions to some of the most urgent discourses in contemporary thought and suggests ways that a transnational contextualization of African American writings can enrich understandings of the long history of African American contributions, as Ann duCille points out, to "the study of power relations between colonizer and colonized."[148] George Washington Williams and many other names can be added to duCille's list, which includes Du Bois, Crummell, Hopkins, and Cooper. Their writings, which are antecedents to postcolonial criticism, help to reinscribe the centrality of transnational conversations about colonialism within African American culture since the nineteenth century.

*Chapter 2*
# William Henry Sheppard's Country of My Forefathers

On December 9, 1889, three days before George Washington Williams traveled to Hampton Institute to recruit students for his Congo expedition, William Henry Sheppard, a twenty-four-year-old Virginian who attended Hampton, was appointed to serve as a missionary. At a time when many African Americans had a regnant desire to go to Africa, Sheppard, a graduate of Stillman Institute in Alabama (then known as Tuscaloosa Theological Institute), distinctively pursued his dream. Trailing Williams by a few months, Sheppard left New York for Liverpool on February 26, 1890, arriving in Africa on May 9.[1] Soon after landing in the port of Boma, he carved his name on a tree, where, a few years later, Charles Spencer Smith saw it: "Among the hundreds of names that I see is that of Rev. S. P. Shephard [sic], a colored man from America, who is laboring as a missionary among the Kassia [sic] people in the Upper Congo, under the auspices of the Board of Missions of the Southern Presbyterian Church. He has outstripped many others in the height of the point where he carved his name, and I found myself humorously ejaculating, 'Well, old fellow, if you never write your name anywhere else, you have certainly written it here. Bravo!' "[2] Smith's encounter with Sheppard in Boma, coupled with his awareness of Williams in Europe, is evidence of the height and visibility of the African American presence in the Congo, which Sheppard served to codify during his two decades as a missionary.

Sheppard's arrival in the Congo was the culmination of several years of lobbying the Presbyterian Church (U.S.) (PCUS) to establish an African mission. The Executive Committee of Foreign Missions (ECFM) of the Southern church initially proposed that they contact their Northern counterparts, the Presbyterian Church (U.S.A.), about establishing a "joint mission" in the Congo. The Northern Presbyterians declined the invitation, and the Southern Presbyterians rejected Sheppard's proposal in October 1889.[3] The committee reversed itself in November after Samuel Norvell Lapsley, whose father was a well-connected white Alabama judge and former law partner of Senator Morgan, volunteered to serve and was assisted in his arrangements by Morgan and Henry Sanford.[4] In March 1892, Samuel Lapsley died, leaving the American Presbyterian Congo Mission (APCM) under the effective direction of an African American man, the very situation that his appointment was designed to avoid. While church authorities spent years struggling to

*Figure 2.1* APCM missionaries from Luebo and Ibanche stations (c. 1909). Seated: Bertha Morrison, Lucy Sheppard, William Sheppard, Althea Brown Edmiston with Sherman Kuetu Edmiston on lap, Alonzo Edmiston, William Morrison, Bessie Martin; Standing: Lachlan Cumming Vass II, Lucius DeYampert, Henry Hawkins, Llewellyn Coppedge, Adolphus Rochester, James McClung Sieg, Motte Martin, William Scott. (Box 3, WHSPA. Courtesy of Presbyterian Historical Society, Philadelphia, Pennsylvania.)

recruit whites (of varying qualifications and racial attitudes) to the majority-black APCM, Sheppard served for nearly two decades as the senior member of a segregated Southern church's racially integrated mission. (See Figure 2.1.)

Though officially a representative of the PCUS, Sheppard was devoutly independent and maintained as close ties to Hampton as he did to his religious sponsors. Immediately after his arrival in the Congo, he wrote to Armstrong that he was "trying to start a school on Prof. B. T. Washington's (Tuskegee) plan." Much like Williams, he told Armstrong that he "would certainly be glad to have companions from Hampton."[5] For the rest of his life, Sheppard was featured frequently as both subject and author in the *Southern Workman*. During leaves of absence and after his retirement, Sheppard returned to Hampton nurturing that community's awareness of and interest in the Congo. Much of the effectiveness of the APCM in recruiting blacks to serve in Africa was due to Sheppard's writings and speeches at colleges and churches. During his 1893–94 furlough, his first recruit was his fiancée, Lucy Gantt. The couple got engaged prior to his 1890 departure, and they married in Jacksonville, Florida, in February 1894 (the same year James Weldon Johnson became head of the city's largest African American school). Lucy was a graduate

*Figure 2.2* APCM missionaries at Luebo (c. 1902). Seated: Joseph Phipps, Lillian Thomas, Maria Fearing, William Morrison; Standing: Henry Hawkins, Lachlan Cumming Vass II, William Sheppard. (Vass Family Papers, RG 476, box 8, subseries 2 "Photographic Materials, 1893–1951." Courtesy of Vass Family and Presbyterian Historical Society, Philadelphia, Pennsylvania.)

of Talladega College in Alabama and had been a soprano vocalist with Frederick Loudin's Original Fisk Jubilee Singers.[6] Lucy returned with William to the Congo in 1894 along with two other Talladega graduates, Lillian Thomas and Maria Fearing, and one Stillman graduate, Henry Hawkins.[7] (See Figure 2.2.)

At Talladega, Fearing, who was fifty-six years old in 1894, had been a dorm mother and roommate to Lucy Gantt, who was the school's youngest student when she entered at the age of eleven. Fearing's "long cherished desire to be a missionary to Africa, was so deeply stirred and quickened by a visit and address from Mr. Sheppard, that she at once wrote to the Committee [ECFM] in Nashville, offering her services."[8] (This report from the Presbyterian *Missionary* unfortunately minimizes Lucy Gantt's obvious recruiting role given her close connection to Fearing and the Talladega community.) Fearing's commitment was so strong that after being refused a salaried position because of her age, she sold her house to Judge Lapsley and used the proceeds to finance her passage and work in the Congo on a volunteer basis, without a missionary appointment. Four months later, she was granted a food allowance, and within one year, she became a full-fledged employee of the APCM. "After she had been there about two years, our Executive Committee, having heard how she had mastered the native language and of her ever-increasing efficiency in the work of the Mission, appointed her as a regular missionary under their care, at half the salary of a single worker. A few months later her salary was increased to the same amount as that paid to each individual missionary."[9] The sacrifices made by Fearing, who served on the APCM until the age of eighty and lived to be ninety-nine years old, expose a gap between the enthusiasm of African Americans and their reluctant acceptance by the ECFM.

William and Lucy Sheppard were able to use their personal relationships and reputations to tap into existing interest in Africa. The influence of William Sheppard's speeches and publications, while not easily quantifiable, extended well beyond those like Fearing, who joined the mission, and Smith, who traveled to Africa by other means. The Sheppards' recruitment efforts, like those of Williams, were successful in having "sown seed which will be fruitful of greater interest in Africa."[10] In these ways, the Sheppards' work for the APCM resonated in the United States, as well as in the Congo, and among many people who never traveled abroad themselves. The resulting story reveals the transatlantic networks through which information and ideas about modern Africa circulated.

In addition to the success of the Sheppards in recruiting black missionaries, William's work in the Congo was lauded by his white colleagues. In an October 1890 letter to the *Missionary*, an official PCUS organ, Lapsley writes that William Sheppard:

> has won the esteem of all the missionaries as a true man and a gentleman, while with the natives he is, according to Dr. [Aaron] Sims [of the American Baptist Missionary Union], the most popular man that ever came to this station. He has the constitution needed, and the gift of getting on in Africa. While I was away he devoted much time to hunting on the river, and has actually brought home twelve "hippos," to the great delight of the blacks and admiration of Europeans.
>
> Dr. Sims, who has known and treated almost every important worker on the Upper Congo, says: "You have a treasure in him; the very best companion you could have on your trip."[11]

One year later, Lapsley reported: "Sheppard seems to have been as great a favorite there [at Wissmann Falls on the Kasai River] as at Kintame, for I find that numbers of the Bakuba trading here now, or a month ago at Kapunda, had learned to like 'Shoppity,' or 'SHOPPIT MONINE,' *the great Sheppard*."[12]

Throughout his travels, Sheppard was continually well received and known for a litany of talents. The posthumously published *Life and Letters of Samuel Norvell Lapsley* describes Sheppard as "a most handy fellow," "a thorough river-man," and a skilled hunter.[13] He is consistently lauded for providing food for people, which suggests that from the start, he imagined a balanced mission that emphasized service and development, alongside religion. Nor was there any talk of the kind of emigration planned by white supremacists like Morgan.

After the death of Lapsley, the *Missionary* continued to extol Sheppard in terms that highlight his linguistic facility: "Mr. Sheppard seems to have learned the language of the people rapidly. Mr. [George] Adamson [an APCM missionary from Scotland] writes us that when Mr. Sheppard preaches to the people at Luebo, they listen with close attention and he says Mr. Sheppard is 'gifted.' "[14] A few months later, Arthur Rowbotham, a missionary from England, wrote of his senior colleague: "Bro. Sheppard is just a whole team in himself. He has the natives well in hand, and they like him, too. He has a good way with him in being friendly with the carriers, and yet having them do as he says."[15] De Witt Snyder, who served from 1892 until 1901, noted the value of Sheppard's return from furlough in 1894: "Since the arrival of Mr. Sheppard we have acquired a deeper hold of the language, his knowledge of the Bakuba dialect being a wonderful assistance in getting at obscure meanings."[16] William M. Morrison, who later authored the church's Tshiluba dictionary and grammar, was likewise taken with Sheppard's linguistic expertise: "Mr. Sheppard seemed providentially the man to go to open the mission. He has been there, is known along the road, and speaks the language."[17] In a dispatch to the *Missionary*, Morrison described the presence of Sheppard as a form of divine intervention: "I have faith to believe that the door of the [Kuba] tribe is now open, and God has used Mr. Sheppard as the human means with his unusual tact and wisdom, in the management of the natives."[18] Collectively, these communiqués suggest that Sheppard developed a unique relationship to the Congo. As Morrison succinctly summarized, "There is no man in all this country who had the influence over this people [Kuba] that Sheppard has."[19] Lapsley, Adamson, Rowbotham, Snyder, and Morrison, the APCM's first five white male missionaries, all praised William Sheppard, stressing his particular rapport with the Congolese people as an instrument of missionary work. This same influence enabled Sheppard to document the brutality of the colonial regime.

On September 14, 1899, Sheppard set out in search of the camp of the Zappo Zaps, a reputedly warlike group working for the Belgians. From its start, his investigation held an aura of danger: "We may suffer at their hands, but we are going as near as possible, near enough to smell them."[20] Despite such peril, Sheppard was able to collect valuable data in the aftermath of a massacre, most graphically evidence of the state practice of hand severing, and to conduct an interview with Zappo Zap Chief M'lumba N'kusa about what happened. The most brutal and lasting image from the report Sheppard wrote was of a pile of 81 hands burning on a fire, which became a prominent symbol of Leopold's depraved regime as "people overseas began to associate the Congo with severed hands."[21] Sheppard writes, "M'lumba N'Cusa [N'kusa] explained that they always cut off the right hand to give to the state on their return." His account points to the misdeeds of the colonial government, even when they are carried out by its African subjects. Sheppard acknowledges as much when he tells the chief: "The state has sent you and you have to go by your instructions." He carefully phrased his questions to emphasize the culpability of the state. For instance, in order to discern the extent of the violence, Sheppard asks, "To what villages did the state send you?" In terms of ammunition, he reports that they have "8 state rifles" and a large box of state gunpowder.[22] None of this violence could be attributed to African savagery—all of it was perpetrated by the colonial state. As a result, his report, which received media coverage in the United States and Europe, established the APCM as a formidable opponent of Leopold's regime.[23]

Samuel H. Chester, secretary of the ECFM, promptly, if halfheartedly, expressed appreciation for "the courageous and prudent conduct of those members of the Mission by whom the investigation was made" (presumably, first and foremost, the unnamed William Sheppard). However, such political activism made church leadership in the United States feel nervous. In its letter to the APCM, Chester used the occasion "to remind the Mission as to the necessity of the utmost caution, in making representations regarding these matters to those in authority, or in publishing them to the world, to observe all proper deference to 'the powers that be,' and to avoid anything that might give any color to a charge of doing or saying things inconsistent with its purely spiritual and non-political character."[24]

If Chester's January 1900 memo reached the editors of the *Missionary*, it was either disregarded or received too late for their February 1900 issue, which features "Atrocities in the Congo Free State," an article that unequivocally lauds Sheppard's investigation: "Again Mr. Sheppard has given evidence of his heroic mold and his worthiness to be our representative."[25] In the same issue, Morrison echoes Sheppard's criticism of the state with some added religious fervor: "We do not blame the Zappo Zaps primarily, for they are only kept by the State to the number of several thousand and used as tools, but we do blame all the white Belgian officials from the highest to the lowest, who are implicated directly or indirectly in such outrages upon an innocent people, and we are praying that if they do not repent the Lord of justice will mete out to them swift and sure punishment."²⁶ By April, Sheppard's chronicle of the brutality of Leopold's administrators and their agents reached Hampton, whose *Southern Workman* asserted that his report "cannot fail to stir the hearts of the civilized nations of the world and cause them to demand a thorough investigation into the practices of the State authorities by whose orders, apparently, these bloody deeds are being committed."²⁷ Sheppard's investigation led to a broad condemnation of Leopold's regime, rather than a scapegoating of his underlings.

Sheppard's activism established the oppositional reputation of the APCM, and gave an African American face to the emerging international campaign against the colonial regime. His report was foundational to the Congo Reform Association (CRA), which was established in 1903 by Liverpool shipping company employee E. D. Morel to organize opposition to Leopold's system of rule. By January 1904, Belgian Ambassador Baron Ludovic Moncheur was aggressively lobbying Sheppard, who refused his advances. In August, Sheppard repeated his criticism at a church lecture in Warm Springs, Virginia, which Moncheur attended, an event that has entered the annals of local lore.²⁸ By October, Sheppard was even more prominently in the public eye with his report being cited at the Universal Peace Congress in Boston.²⁹ Later that month, Booker T. Washington mentioned Sheppard in an article in *Outlook*. That same month, William Morrison, who corresponded with Morel and other leading figures of the movement, sent a copy of Sheppard's report to Mark Twain, who used it in *King Leopold's Soliloquy* (1905).³⁰ These networks enabled Sheppard's 1899 report to reach diverse audiences, independent of its author and often without attribution. The repeated image of hand severing became the dominant trope of colonial brutality in the Congo and remains a physical marker of the ongoing international circulation and influence of Sheppard's report.

So Meager That They Cannot Live upon It

The emergence of Sheppard's activism coincided with the founding of the APCM's quarterly magazine, the *Kassai Herald*, which was published at Luebo station and distributed in both the Congo and the United States. The magazine, which was edited by Hawkins from 1904 to 1907, quickly became an important forum for writings by black missionaries.³¹ Though its pages were dominated by articles describing the religious, medical, and educational work of the APCM, the January 1908 issue featured William Sheppard's "From the Bakuba Country," which reported: "There are armed sentries of chartered trading companies, who force the men and women to spend most of their days and nights in the forests making rubber, and the price they receive is so meager that they cannot live upon it."[32] Sheppard's description of the role of "chartered trading companies" was easily recognized as a reference to the Compagnie du Kasai (C.K.). C.K. Director Gustave Dryepondt responded vehemently, if unconvincingly, that his company "does not use armed sentries at all, and is not a chartered C[ompan]y," and asked the *Kassai Herald* to publish a rebuttal to Sheppard's charges.[33] Morrison, the editor at the time, refused the request and defended Sheppard's reputation: "It would seem that if you had been desirous of really knowing the truth about the situation in this region, you would have instituted an impartial investigation, without presuming, as the tone of your letter implies, that Dr. Sheppard only ignorantly or maliciously maligned your company. If you were pained and astonished that Dr. Sheppard should write such things, I must say that I am equally astonished and pained that you should so hastily conclude that a man of Dr. Sheppard's long residence in Congo and his well-known integrity should write a serious article of this kind without knowing what he was doing."[34]

By the time Sheppard's article appeared, the C.K. had already mounted a public relations campaign to defend itself. Sheppard's attorney later reflected that the trial was the product of the C.K.'s increased alarm after his client led British Consul Wilfred Thesiger on a fact-finding tour of the Kasai.[35] (See Figures 2.3 and 2.4.) Sheppard was being targeted for his activism beyond what he wrote, which represents a far cry from Moncheur's 1904 claim "that Sheppard is only a tool in the hands of Morrison" and "does not have the moral courage to protest."[36] The C.K. filed suit, arguing that Sheppard's article libelously mischaracterized the company's relationship to the state as "chartered" or concessionary. While this may seem like a minor technical point, the company's hollow claim to autonomy demonstrates how deeply scrutinized its relationship with the state was, and, by extension, how private entities—whether businesses or missions—struggled to project independent identities. The culprit was the entire colonial infrastructure, not some renegade capitalist failing to abide an otherwise legitimate set of rules. On February 23, 1909, the Belgian government, which took control of the Congo from Leopold the previous year, issued a summons for Sheppard and Morrison, but the charges against Morrison were dropped before trial. The trial was to be held before a court in Leopoldville (Kinshasa), hundreds of miles from the nearest APCM station across seasonally unnavigable waterways. Regardless of its outcome, the proceedings presented obstacles that, seemingly by design, would preoccupy and displace two of the state's harshest critics for a period of several months.

While the allegedly libelous article never named the C.K., and the case for the defense could have been narrowly argued on those grounds, Sheppard

*Figure 2.3* British Consul Wilfred G. Thesiger (tall with necktie and left hand on hip at center) with Lucy Sheppard (to Thesiger's right), William Sheppard (to her right, leaning on rifle), likely British Vice Consul Jack Proby Armstrong (holding a cane standing to Thesiger's immediate left), and unidentified Kuba porters (c. 1908–9). (Box 3, WHSPA, Courtesy of Presbyterian Historical Society, Philadelphia, Pennsylvania.)

*Figure 2.4* Compagnie du Kasai officials and William Sheppard (dark jacket in rear) entering the courthouse in Kinshasa (September 20, 1909). (Box 3, WHSPA, Courtesy of Presbyterian Historical Society, Philadelphia, Pennsylvania.)

and the APCM made at least four strategic decisions to ensure its political substance. First, Sheppard maintained that the case was about the treatment of the Congolese people by the state, not the treatment of the missionaries. This point came to the forefront when, after the publication of his article, he was challenged in an interview with a Belgian colonial official: "Je lui ai demandé alors sur quoi il pouvait baser ses affirmations de son article. Il m'a répondu que c'était des Bakubas venus de fort loin qui lui avaient raconté cela!!!" (I asked him what he could base his claims in his article on. He responded to me that it was some Bakuba who came from afar who had told him that!!!)[37] Sheppard's response indicates he did not hesitate to validate the accounts of the Congolese people, as shocking as that seemed to his interlocutor. Sheppard personally recruited twenty Congolese witnesses to travel with him to Leopoldville, which reveals that he understood their experiences to be the substance of the case. (See Figure 2.5.) Even his one-time codefendant Morrison was less keen on Congolese testimony, explaining to a white colleague: "Sheppard has been trying to persuade some Bakuba to go, but with no avail as yet. We shall try to take along a few Baluba. I was almost in favor of taking no witnesses at all; just telling them that when they had the trial in a place where we could get the witnesses, and all we wanted, we would be ready, and not before that time. Others thought that we might take what we could get. I am almost afraid that the few we shall get will do us no special amount of good, whereas if we went with none, and made no effort to prove anything under the circumstances, we would perhaps come out better."[38] Unfortunately, the twenty witnesses who traveled to Kinshasa did not testify, so their stories never made it into the official record. Still, Sheppard's insistent recognition of the importance of Congolese testimony affirmed his unique respect for the Congolese people and distinguished him from Morrison. Sheppard's efforts, like those of Williams who alone asked "Africans about their personal experience of Stanley," represent a unique African Americans commitment to documenting the voices of African victims of European imperialism.[39]

Second, Sheppard elected as his attorney Émile Vandervelde, a leading member of the socialist Parti Ouvrier Belge. In his opening speech to the court, Vandervelde made his political priorities clear:

> I agreed immediately to defend them, I say, because I saw the enormous masses of the natives of the Kasai, for whose protection these men had raised themselves up. I agreed to defend them because this lawsuit actually is not between the Company Kasai and Mr. Sheppard, but between the Company Kasai and the natives who live in the territory exploited by this company for over ten years.

*Figure 2.5* William Morrison (far left), William Sheppard (far right), Kuba Chief Niakai (center with anklets), and unidentified witnesses at the William Sheppard trial in Kinshasa (1909). (Box 3, WHSPA, Courtesy of Presbyterian Historical Society, Philadelphia, Pennsylvania.)

> In every circumstance, on every occasion, I have struggled for the rights of the natives of the Congo, and in doing so, I believe that I have defended the nation better than those who try to keep covered-up the mess, the existence of which is no longer contested.⁴⁰

Vandervelde problematically suggests that his defense of Sheppard can help to restore the integrity of the Belgian state. Still, by hiring a prominent leader of the Belgian opposition as counsel, the APCM chose to politicize the case in a manner that was explicitly critical of colonial rule. Vandervelde's position on the Congo was not a simple party line; at trial, his opposing counsel was Gaston Vandermeeren, a fellow party member.⁴¹

Third, the church appealed to the U.S. consul for assistance, drawing the government into the conflict at the precise moment when the APCM's adversarial relationship with Belgium was at its peak. The Department of State advocated on Sheppard's behalf, and both Consul William Handley and Vice Consul Milton Beckwith Kirk attended the trial.⁴² In this fleeting moment, the APCM forced the U.S. government to choose sides between an African American man and the colonial regime of a friendly European government. Other governments were drawn in as well; British Consul Thesiger attempted to submit an affidavit on behalf of Sheppard and his deputy Jack Proby Armstrong attended the trial. British and U.S. support for Sheppard represented a public rejection of the old colonial infrastructure of the new Belgian Congo.

Fourth, they undertook a larger publicity campaign that drew the attention of some of the best-known Congo activists in the world and effectively reinvigorated the CRA at a time when many veterans of the reform movement were confounded, if not entirely satisfied, by the transfer from Leopold to Belgium. Arthur Conan Doyle made several references to the trial in his 1909 tome *The Crime of the Congo*, which itself reflected an important resurgence of international Congo activism after the 1904 peak of the CRA. In its pages, Doyle lauds "these lion-hearted missionaries," Sheppard and Morrison, "for telling the truth about the scoundrels."[43]

On October 4, 1909, Judge Charles Louis Gianpetri handed down his verdict. Sheppard was acquitted and the C.K., which was suing for 80,000 francs, was ordered to pay court costs of 42 francs. The court ruled that the prosecution failed to prove malicious intent or damages. In addressing the veracity of Sheppard's accusations, Judge Gianpetri cited Thesiger's 1905 Commission of Inquiry as corroborating evidence of brutality and misrule.[44] The decision, all twenty-nine pages of which the U.S. consulate translated into English, completely vindicates Sheppard. Although Morrison was dropped from the suit, he sent an excited letter to Morel: "Throw up your hat! Sheppard & I acquitted."[45]

Although Morrison remains an important figure in the history of Congo reform and he supported Sheppard throughout the trial, his prominence came, all too frequently, at the expense of Sheppard, which exposed some tension between the two colleagues.[46] Soon after the resolution of the court proceedings, Morrison successfully sought Sheppard's removal from the APCM on the grounds that he committed adultery with African women several years earlier while Lucy was on leave. (Publicly, his retirement was attributed to health.) William Sheppard privately confessed his indiscretions to Presbyterian authorities in the United States and quietly served a one-year suspension from the church. Whether Morrison's charges were motivated by jealousy or not, their timing is, at best, peculiar, and had the predictable effect of removing the strongest immediate challenger to his own international prominence in the field of Congo reform and weakening the standing of the APCM in the field. Within a span of two years, Morrison levied similar charges against the three senior male missionaries at the time, all of them black, effectively ending the APCM's remarkable history of black appointments.[47] In the wake of his meeting with Sheppard, Chester decided to bar African Americans from the mission field:

> In view of all the experience of the past few years, I am confident that our Committee will deem it wise to send out white re-inforcements to Africa for the present.

> We do not think it necessary or wise to make any public proclamation of this policy, but we think it will probably be necessary to set upon it until we receive further light in a quiet and unostentatious way.[48]

Morrison's charges not only dramatically changed the complexion of the mission, but also removed experienced political allies from the field. While several black missionaries continued to serve on the APCM, the PCUS appointed only one black person in the fifty years following Sheppard's trial, and in that case it was a woman who married a recently widowed missionary.[49] That appointment, like the dismissals, is one of the mechanisms the church used to police the sexual behavior of its African American missionaries. During that same period, the APCM became less outspoken politically and increasingly aligned with the colonial state. The final departure of the Sheppards from the APCM serves as a reminder of the ways that, as Amy Kaplan explains, "putatively domestic conflicts are not simply contained at home but how they both emerge in response to international struggles and spill over national boundaries to be reenacted, challenged, or transformed."[50] The history of the APCM and more generally the American response to imperialism in the Congo, though occurring largely outside the borders of the United States, remains deeply embedded within its racial geography and sexual politics.

## Always Have White Help at the Head

Even before Sheppard returned to the United States, his career was informed by a domestic landscape that included not only Hampton, but also the white supremacist policies of the PCUS. With the APCM staffed by a group of educated African Americans, there was an intensive push by church officials to maintain white leadership. For instance, despite his appreciation of Sheppard's language skills, De Witt Snyder wrote in 1894 of the need to "always have white help at the head. I don't think our colored brethren are capable of doing good work by themselves."[51] Snyder's opinion was consistent with church policy. The *Missionary*'s appeals for white missionaries reflected U.S. racial politics. In September 1895, Chester requested "Help Needed for Africa" in the form of "four additional white men, one of these to be stationed at Matadi, one at Lukunga, one at Leopoldville, and one at Luebo. On account of 'The State,' with which we have relations of many kinds, it is desirable to have white men at all these points to represent the business interests of the mission. Outside of this, our policy is to reinforce the mission chiefly with colored men. More of these are offering than we are able to send, but at present no white man is offering for the African work. . . .

Dr. and Mrs. Snyder ought to be brought home at once, to recuperate their strength but they *will not* come till their places are supplied."[52] In retrospect, Chester's candor draws attention to the centrality of race to the mission, despite later attempts to whitewash such discrimination.[53] Under the guise of its "business interests," racial hierarchy took precedence over the physical health of its members.

As the Snyders' health deteriorated, Chester became more desperate. The following month, he again pleaded, "On account of relations with 'The State,' and for other reasons, it is absolutely necessary that we have one white man, and very desirable that we have a least two, in our mission work on the Congo. Dr. Snyder, the only white man now connected with that work, will be compelled to come home for rest very soon, in order to save his own life and that of his noble and devoted wife." The Presbyterian Church was even willing to waive the basic medical and religious credentials for appointment as long as the candidate was white.[54] In an October 18, 1895, letter, De Witt's "noble and devoted wife" May made the appeal herself: "My dear husband is now longing for at least one white male helper, but his constant reply to my question, 'Do you really think they mean to send any more white missionaries here?' is, 'This is the Lord's work. He knows our need. He will take care of it.'"[55] Although De Witt Snyder believed that divine intervention would ensure a white volunteer, his wife and the *Missionary* continued to help out as well.

In November 1895, in response to Chester's racist pleas for white missionaries, the Presbyterian Mission Board appointed twenty-two-year-old Samuel Phillips Verner to the APCM without any seminary education and despite serious questions about his mental health.[56] His family connections to the political elite of Southern white supremacy—including Morgan and Benjamin Tillman—were no doubt reassuring for an appointment that enabled the APCM to maintain white leadership while the sickly Snyders took "a much-needed furlough."[57] Soon after arriving in the Congo, Verner began to criticize his black colleagues "for paying exaggerated attention to the 'social consequences' of their work."[58]

Verner's time on the mission was a disaster and his legacy even worse. After two years, when he was "ordered to return home," ostensibly for health reasons, he was accompanied by Kondola and Kassongo, two African boys whom he purchased and then tried to "rent" to the Smithsonian in Washington, which foretold of Verner's future career.[59] In 1903, Verner signed a contract with W. J. McGee, formerly of the Smithsonian, to bring eighteen Congolese people for an exhibit at the 1904 St. Louis Fair. William and Lucy Sheppard, who were leaving Africa on furlough, traveled on the same transatlantic steamship as Verner and the nine Congolese young men he was bringing to St. Louis for exhibition. Lumbango, Latuna, Kalamma, Shamba, Malengu, Lumo, Bomushubba, Ota Benga, and Kondola ranged in age from early teens to early twenties; Kondola traveled from the United States to the Congo and back to the United States as "Verner's assistant." (Kassongo tragically died in a stampede at a Booker T. Washington speech in Birmingham in 1902.) While William Sheppard and Verner were reportedly "cordial" during the transatlantic trek, a passing acquaintance, at the very least, between the Sheppards and the Congolese travelers seems unavoidable.[60] Lumbango and Latuna, at least, were Kuba, and Latuna led the resistance at the fair, which included refusing to perform for spectators, protesting clothing and accommodations, attacking "a photographer who would not compensate them for having their pictures taken," and organizing "a military unit modeled on one that Native Americans had begun."[61] Ota Benga accompanied Verner on a return trip to the Congo, but, unlike the others, did not remain in Africa. Instead, he came back to the United States with Verner and, in 1906, was displayed at the Bronx Zoo and the American Museum of Natural History in New York. A protest organized by black clergy secured his release, and Ota Benga relocated to Lynchburg, Virginia, where, through his friendship with the poet Anne Spencer and her family, he met the many distinguished visitors who passed through her home. Ultimately, Ota Benga's life ended tragically. On March 20, 1916, he used a gun to commit suicide. His burial site was unmarked until 2005.[62]

Although Verner was no longer a missionary when he met Ota Benga, his APCM service, which was a direct result of the church's racial policies, was the basis for his St. Louis Fair commission. Even after Verner was diagnosed with brain fever and spent six months in a sanitarium in 1899, Phillips Verner Bradford and Harvey Blume explain, "the church and he continued to have uses for each other domestically."[63] Contrary to some accounts, there are many indications that Verner continued his affiliation with the PCUS after his 1899 resignation from the APCM. First, after leaving the APCM, Verner joined the faculty at Stillman Institute, the PCUS seminary for black theology students, which was run by his uncle. Second, when Verner traveled to the Congo on his St. Louis Fair expedition, he was accompanied by Alonzo Edmiston, a Stillman graduate who was appointed to the APCM in 1903.[64] Third, according to a January 1904 letter from Belgian Ambassador Moncheur, the Presbyterian Church was planning to reappoint Verner; later that year, Moncheur granted Verner a commercial concession.[65] Fourth, Verner, who actively solicited the Smithsonian to house his curio collection as early as 1896, organized a 1905–6 expedition with Frederick Starr that removed more than 4,000 Congolese art objects, many from areas around APCM stations in the Kasai, for the American Museum of Natural History.[66]

Finally, Verner's book, *Pioneering in Central Africa*, was published under the auspices of the PCUS in 1903 (more than a decade before the publication of Sheppard's similarly titled tome), which closely ties his religion to white supremacy: "Africa must be made a stronghold of Caucasian power, of Christianity, of European and American civilization rather than the cess-pool of Asiatic vice and corruption."[67] That publication challenges the claims that "There is no evidence that other members of that staff were mainly interested in Caucasian and capitalistic power at the expense of the human rights of the Africans."[68] While Verner is sometimes dismissed as the rogue member of a nonracist mission, his ill-fated appointment was the direct result of the church's racial hiring policies. At every turn, the PCUS continued to support Verner before, during, and after the St. Louis Fair fiasco. It was not until 1907 that the ECFM definitively decided to disavow Verner for publicly defending an embattled Leopold while the PCUS General Assembly was calling for an investigation into his Congo abuses.[69]

These racist ideas were sometimes implicitly challenged by the leadership of Sheppard and other black men on the mission. Sheppard served as either chair or president of the APCM in 1897, 1899, 1903, and 1909. In 1899, Hawkins was secretary, and in 1907 Alonzo Edmiston was chair.[70] The roles of African Americans in the field did not always accommodate the official policies of the PCUS or the racist beliefs of some of its white missionaries. The common perception that the APCM was able to "pioneer a new kind of relationship between the races" may be appealing; however, it should not be taken as a parable of antiracism since, as historian Barbara J. Fields reminds us, "Racial prejudice is sufficiently fluid and at home with contrariety to be able to precede and survive dramatic instances of interracial unity in action."[71]

The exceptionalist notion that the APCM operated both geographically and ideologically outside of the United States ignores one of its most significant characteristics—namely its adherence to the racial practice of the American church that it represented. Sheppard's work in Africa is only one part of what makes him so interesting. The broader networks through which he maintained deep personal, institutional, cultural, and textual connections with people in the United States before, during, and after his missionary service are integral to appreciating the breadth of his career as a transnational African American subject. While there is relatively minimal attention to Sheppard's American career in either William Phipps's or Pagan Kennedy's biographies, both authors autobiographically establish their own personal proximity to Sheppard. When Kennedy was introduced to Sheppard by *Ota*

*Benga*, which was cowritten by Samuel Phillips Verner's grandson, she felt an immediate personal, yet inexplicable, attraction to her subject. A visit to her grandmother in a Virginia nursing home revealed the connection: her grandmother's first cousin, Robert Dabney Bedinger, served on the APCM.[72] Phipps, who published his book in the same month as Kennedy, also had "a personal reason for my interest in writing the biography": he and Sheppard were both born in Staunton, Virginia.[73]

Such gestures are indicative of a desire of white American writers to claim Sheppard's story as their own, much as Morrison did following his libel trial. The apparent ease with which Sheppard gets incorporated as an American subject is ironic because both biographies focus, almost exclusively, on his career in the Congo, not as a Hampton product or a Louisville minister or an NAACP activist. The transatlantic connections that Kennedy and Phipps use to preface their biographies are reminders that the tentacles of the APCM are deeply entwined in American history, culture, and communities. Yet both Kennedy and Phipps neglect what their introductions intuit—Sheppard's story is a profoundly American one. The biographers' personal accounts, along with the tragic conclusion of Ota Benga's life, the history of Hampton, and the domestic careers of the Sheppards, suggest that the story of the Congo is not confined to one side of the Atlantic Ocean, but extends deeply into the fabric of the lives of black and white Americans.

## They Knew Me Better Than I Knew Myself

In some sense, Kennedy and Phipps seem to be following the path paved by Sheppard. One year after Ota Benga's suicide, the same church that Sheppard continued to faithfully serve after it removed him from the Congo published his only full-length book, *Presbyterian Pioneers in Congo*. Though published in 1917, it deals almost entirely with the years 1890 to 1893 and seems strangely anachronistic. As a result, *Presbyterian Pioneers in Congo*, whose plural subject in its title conceals its autobiographical character, effectively erases the two best-known episodes in the entire history of the APCM: Sheppard's 1899 report on maiming by the colonial Force Publique and his 1909 libel trial for an article on the rubber collection practices of the C.K. In both instances, Sheppard gained international attention for his writings. His autobiography effectively reasserts and extends his identity as an author, while simultaneously eliding his most significant earlier literary accomplishments. The book enables the PCUS to depoliticize the APCM by recovering and promoting a seemingly less radical moment from its past.

On the other hand, by highlighting African American contributions, *Presbyterian Pioneers in Congo* offers an implicit commentary on the Presbyterian

Church's more recent history of racial exclusion. While the book, which details Sheppard's quest to establish mission stations in unchartered areas, fits many of the literary parameters of the popular exploration narrative, its unusually belated publication violates a core tenet of the genre by diminishing its perceived currency. Within this context, the book is self-consciously retrospective, which draws attention to the shifting racial history of the APCM. Sheppard acknowledges at the outset, "I shall dwell but lightly upon my American life of twenty-five years; speaking more in detail of my African life of twenty years." In the book, however, he actually covers only a fragment of the latter. A brief concluding chapter, "His Kingdom Coming in Congo," includes a picture of "Lukusa, later called 'Dick,' the first convert in the Kasai region, and the first member of the Luebo Presbyterian Church, received April 1895."[74] The date of Dick's conversion, by then more than twenty years past, is the latest mentioned in the book, which Chester identifies in his introduction as "an expansion of autobiographical and historical lectures delivered by its author."[75]

A discussion of the trial or the years when Sheppard was the de facto head of the mission would not fit the story that Chester and the church wanted to see in print at a time when the APCM's racial policies were clear: black missionaries need not apply. In the introduction, Chester commended Sheppard's authorial humility "in telling his story up to the time of Mr. Lapsley's death, he always keeps Mr. Lapsley to the front and himself in the background."[76] Chester interpreted *Presbyterian Pioneers in Congo* as an exemplar of black obsequiousness at a time when his activism and trial were important parts of his lore. The book constructs a sort of nostalgia for a naive missionary culture, before it found itself in direct political conflict with the colonial state. From Sheppard's perspective, his foregrounding of his fellow pioneer also can be read as a critique of his subservient position on the mission, especially for the many readers who were presumably familiar with his activism from other sources. In *Presbyterian Pioneers in Congo*, Lapsley dies of a fever while Sheppard was preparing to enter the "Forbidden Land" of the Kuba.[77] Lapsley's death facilitates Sheppard's emergence. Newly independent of his white comrade, Sheppard travels to the "Forbidden Land," where his reception by the Kuba becomes the literal crowning moment of the book and his career. Through his writings, Sheppard could partly reclaim a lost era of opportunity and collaboration.

On his arrival in the hidden Kuba capital of Mushenge, Nyimi Kot aMbweeky II, king of the Kuba (1892–96), recognized Sheppard as a reincarnation of an ancient king: "'The foreigner who is at Bixibing,' said they, 'who has come these long trails and who speaks our language is a Makuba, one of the early settlers who died, and whose spirit went to a foreign country and now he has returned.'" Sheppard denied any Kuba lineage, asserting, "I have heard distinctly all that you have said, but I am not a Makuba; I have never been here before." Sheppard's next line, a boldfaced subhead, is ironically telling: "They Knew Me Better Than I Knew Myself." Despite his claims of disbelief, he took unmistakable pride in the association. Sheppard repeatedly made a show of his denial of the king's assertions, even demonstrating his linguistic facility by translating the king's phrases into English for his readers: "I leaned from my seat toward King Lukenga and getting his attention said briefly, 'I understand, king, that your people believe me to be a Makuba who once lived here.' The king replied with a smile, 'N'Gaxa Mi' (It is true). 'I want to acknowledge to you,' said I, 'that I am not a Makuba and I have never been here before.' The king leaned over the arm of his great chair and said with satisfaction, 'You don't know it, but you are "Muana Mi" (one of the family).'"[78] Here Sheppard initiates a conversation about his ancestry, which indicates that his denials should not be taken for disinterest. Indeed, versions of Sheppard's narrative of return begin in one of his first communiqués after his arrival "in the country of my forefathers" and recur throughout his oeuvre.[79] His repeated disavowals of this genealogy only enhance the story's momentum. As a black American encounter with Africa, Sheppard's narrative complicates the racial paradigm that is foundational to Western accounts of Africa. By subverting conventional tropes of sameness and difference, his book provides an archetypal African American narrative of African travel as return which appears throughout the era in works as diverse as Smith's *Glimpses of Africa*, which describes its author's "long-cherished desire to make a personal visit to the land of my forefathers," and Ernest Hogan's performance of "My Little Jungle Queen."[80]

Sheppard's narrative about his reception by the Kuba had long appealed to the Presbyterian press and its readers even while he ostensibly critiques such a possibility. The story, James T. Campbell writes, "would be retailed endlessly in years to come, becoming one of the classic tales of nineteenth-century mission Christianity."[81] In 1893, the *Missionary* saw fit to publish two separate third-person accounts. In the first, the article proclaims:

What an interesting visit our missionary, Mr. Sheppard, had to King Lukenga and his people! He was the first foreigner that ever succeeded in getting to them. Other men had tried to make them a visit, but had always been kept back; but Mr. Sheppard, under the good hand of God, made his way to the great town where the king lives, and was most kindly received by the king and his people. There had been an old story among these people that the spirit of a dead king, who had ruled over the tribe, went to a foreign land and so, when the people saw Mr. Sheppard, they said that the spirit of the dead king was in him. In this way they explained Mr. Sheppard's skill in finding his way along the forest paths to the town where Lukenga reigned. You see that God uses even the strange superstitions of the heathen to open the way for his Gospel.[82]

In this version, the *Missionary* attributed Sheppard's reception to Kuba superstition. Two months later, the *Missionary* retold the narrative of Sheppard as part of a longer unsigned article, which included additional details such as the name of the deceased king: "'It is all well,' said Toenz[a]ida; 'and now you need not try to hide it; you are Po Pay M'Cobba, who reigned before my father. He died, and his spirit went to a foreign land. When your mother gave birth to you, that spirit was in you.'"[83] Given his feelings about "the country of my forefathers," his reception was certainly consistent with a broader sense of homecoming that predated his trip to Mushenge, which suggests the conscious development of a narrative of return.

Although Sheppard claimed to reject the lore of his ancestry, the accolades of his colleagues confirmed his distinct affinity for central Africa. In addition, there are other ways that *Presbyterian Pioneers in Congo* enacts Sheppard's personal identification with the people of the Congo. In the dedication "To the Southern Presbyterian Church/Which took me as a half-clad, barefoot boy and trained me for the ministry of Christ," Sheppard sets up a personal relationship to the church that mirrored that of the church's Congolese subjects.[84] He uses the same language to describe his condition prior to his religious awakening that he uses for his prospective acolytes among the "very scantily clad" and "half-clad natives."[85] This is another way of intimating that he is Congolese. Their near nakedness represents what historian Matthew Frye Jacobson describes as a "tendency to define 'natives' as a kind of 'wilderness in human form'—so 'natural' as to be less than human."[86] Indeed in Atlanta in 1906, newspapers used the headline "Half-Clad Negro" to incite white supremacist violence against a perceived threat.[87] Nakedness was read as an absence of civilization, a situation in need of missionary repair. In anticipation of a military attack on their residence, Fearing instructed her students to wear their full wardrobe in layers: "Now children, if you must run, and your lives are spared, you will have your clothes."[88] For weddings, Sheppard showed striking empathy in lending his clothes to the grooms.[89] Sheppard cast his lot with the Congolese, representing his once "half-clad, barefoot" self as both a subject and an agent of Christian conversion. That civilizationist ideology is visually represented in photographs of his son Maxamalinge William Lapsley Sheppard, including one distinguished, according to the album caption, as "Our baby in his big shoes" in contrast to the bare feet of his older companion, whose body is obscured behind Max and whose head is partly

*Figure 2.6* "Maxamalinge" William Lapsley Sheppard wearing shoes, captioned "Our baby in his big shoes" (c. 1903–4). (Box 5, WHSVA [2015], Courtesy of Hampton University Archives, Hampton, Virginia.)

cut off in the photo. (See Figure 2.6.) (William Sheppard named his son for his friend Chief Maxamalinge, a former Kuba prince who lost his title after his father Kot aMbweeky II was deposed by Mishaape in 1896.)

William Sheppard's use of nakedness and clothing as metaphors of the possibility of immediate "civilization" suggests that it is not an allegory of the long history of Africans in the Americas, but rather an indication of the superficiality of presumptively "racial" difference. Within American racial discourse, Africa functions as an implicit measure of African American achievement under the supposed civilizing influence of the United States. For instance, Rebecca Harding Davis, author of *Life in the Iron Mills*, celebrated Lucy Gantt Sheppard's missionary work, but insistently claimed that "It has taken centuries of such civilization as they have had here [in the United States] to produce" the Sheppards.[90] In 1910, Theodore Roosevelt defended both slavery and colonialism by making a similar argument regarding "the progress the American negro [sic] has made." Sheppard refuses this logic by associating himself with the Congolese, and demonstrating a much more rapid development of "civilization" among the Congolese than Davis ascribes. Sheppard further diverged from Roosevelt's lauding of "white influence" by attributing the highest levels of civilization to the remote Kuba.[91] When asked after a Hampton lecture in 1893, "Do the Bakuba attribute their superiority

Country of My Forefathers 69

to the outside influence of any other people?," Sheppard responded with an unequivocal "no."[92] By answering without explanation, Sheppard boldly challenged the presumptions implied by the question. In this forum, he allowed for some radical speculation: "'What has made the Bakuba so superior do you think?' 'I don't know. Perhaps they got their civilization from the Egyptians—or the Egyptians theirs from the Bakuba (!)'"[93]

He, in effect, asserted that all of the accomplishments of the Kuba were completely products of African culture. When Sheppard entered the kingdom of the Kuba, he immediately felt a profound respect for their "apparent superiority in physique, manners, dress and dialect." Over time, his original impression of the Kuba was borne out: "They were the finest looking race I had seen in Africa, dignified, graceful, courageous, honest, with an open, smiling countenance and really hospitable."[94] These markers of civilization were complemented by the absence of idol worship and their artistic accomplishments, which are discussed further in chapter 6.[95] Overall the brightness and vitality of Sheppard's landscape contrasted with archetypal renderings of Africa as a place of absolute darkness: "The moon shines nowhere more brightly and beautifully than on Lukenga's plain. And the beauty is enhanced by the thousands of majestic palms, and the singing of birds with voices like the mocking bird and the nightingale. I have sat in front of my house moonlight nights until 12 and 1 o'clock."[96] In Sheppard's account unlike Conrad's, there is barely any darkness in Africa.

*Presbyterian Pioneers in Congo* shrewdly revises the purported darkness of the African landscape, a central trope of canonical exploration narratives. Like Williams, Sheppard consciously treads paths once passed by Stanley. As in Williams's accounts, Stanley was a well-known symbol of repressive state practices. Lapsley explains, "the Congo natives here learned the important lesson of discrimination between the missionary and other white men. Since Stanley, the State officials, and even the white settlement here, is called *Bula Matari* (Stanley's native name; it means breaker-of-rocks, from his road-making achievements!) White man is *mundila*; the missionary is *mundila-nzambi*, 'God's white man'; or, sometimes *nganga-nzambi*, 'God's medicine man.'"[97] Even with his extremely generous etymology of "Bula Matari" that omits Stanley's reputation for violence, Lapsley realized that, in order to be effective, the APCM needed to separate itself from Stanley's legacy.

As Sheppard literally followed Stanley's footsteps, he saw firsthand the shameful legacy of his fellow Royal Geographic Society member: "We found a road had been made by Mr. Stanley and saw some of Stanley's heavy iron wagon wheels lying by the roadside; also sun-bleached skeletons of native carriers here and there who by sickness, hunger or fatigue, had laid themselves down to die, without fellow or friend." From Sheppard's point of view,

Stanley's "road-making achievements" were far less auspicious, and this graphic account set the stage for Sheppard's revisionist intervention. Soon after passing the horrific trail of bones, Sheppard encountered another Stanley inheritance in the possession of Bakete Chief N'Galiama: "a white handkerchief with W. M. Stanley's [sic] name on it. We asked the old chief to give it to us, but he refused; then we tried to buy it, but he would not part with the handkerchief of the great explorer. The religious work with these people was not very hopeful. They were reserved, hard to reach, and clung to their idols of wood."[98] Stanley's only legacy is a handkerchief that Sheppard considers a commodity and N'Galiama considers an idol. Still, Sheppard's desire to possess the handkerchief represents his interest in occupying, if not supplanting, Stanley's mantle. Even Sheppard's typographical mistake, the replacement of his own first initial for Stanley's, can be read as his anxiousness to supersede Stanley. N'Galiama's refusal to sell the handkerchief reflected the corruption of the Bakete people's potential as missionary subjects; soon thereafter Sheppard turned his attention to the Kuba. In effect, Stanley's demons needed to be exorcised for either Sheppard or Christianity to make inroads in the Congo.

*Presbyterian Pioneers in Congo* represents Sheppard's textual revision of Stanley's prevalence at a time when the experiences of Sheppard and other African Americans were overshadowed by Vachel Lindsay's popular poem "The Congo (A Study of the Negro Race)." Certainly *Presbyterian Pioneers in Congo*, which found enough of an audience to require multiple printings during Sheppard's lifetime, can be read as a response to Lindsay and his ilk. While there are clear possibilities for reading *Presbyterian Pioneers in Congo* in dialogue with contemporary works about the Congo, Sheppard's own speeches and writings simultaneous to the book publication reveal an entirely different representation of his role in the Congo, one which emphasizes, rather than erases, his political work. Those speeches and writings that challenged the colonial regime in the Congo found voice as part of an African American discursive tradition that has roots in Historically Black Colleges and Universities (HBCUs) and in relationships that Sheppard had been cultivating since the early 1880s.

## Traditions of Ancestry in Africa

Sheppard's relationship with Hampton had been ongoing throughout his career and established a unique frame of reference for his missionary enterprise. In December 1893, the *Southern Workman* published "Into the Heart of Africa," an exceptionally popular address Sheppard delivered at Hampton.[99] As elsewhere, Sheppard proclaimed his admiration of the Kuba, who "make one feel that he has again entered a land of civilization." In the capital city of

Mushenge, he saw the surest sign of "civilization": "The people all wore clothes, even the children," which he contrasts with the nakedness of the Luonga, Baluba, and Lulua.[100] This acknowledgment of Kuba "superiority" complemented Sheppard's pride in his royal welcome by such an auspicious nation.

The tale of Sheppard's reception by the Kuba was prominent in his Hampton speech, as in most of his autobiographical works, many of which appeared decades before the publication of *Presbyterian Pioneers in Congo*. In "Into the Heart of Africa," Sheppard related what Toenzaida, another son of the Kuba king, told him:

> My father called the wise men together and said to them, Who is this stranger? He knows our roads without a guide, yet he is a foreigner. He speaks our language, yet he is a foreigner. The wise men studied this mystery and they told my father, we know who this stranger is. He is no stranger, but Bo-pe Mekabe of your own family, who has returned to earth. Then my father was glad and said to me, Son go and tell all our people that "Bo-pe has returned to us." The people are rejoicing. You need not try to hide it from us longer. You are Bo-pe Makabe who reigned before my father and who died. His spirit went to a foreign land, your mother gave birth to it, and you are that spirit.[101]

Sheppard's *Southern Workman* article directly followed an announcement of the new Department of Folk-Lore and Ethnology, whose purpose was, according to a letter of endorsement from longtime Liberia missionary Alexander Crummell, to maintain connections to Africa.[102] Sheppard's oration appeared as the magazine was actively soliciting folktales that could be "traced back to Africa," "African words surviving in speech or song," "songs that go back to Africa," along with oral histories from "survivors of the later importations from Africa" in order to document "Traditions of ancestry in Africa, or of transportation to America."[103] At this same time, the *Southern Workman* was shifting direction under Armstrong's successor Hollis Burke Frissell and becoming a national vehicle "for useful information" relevant to "the development of the Negro race." Therefore, Sheppard's regular appearances in the increasingly cosmopolitan *Southern Workman* during the early 1900s—alongside essays by Anna Julia Cooper, W. E. B. Du Bois, and Kelly Miller; short fiction by Charles W. Chesnutt, Alice Dunbar, and Paul Laurence Dunbar; and poetry by Paul Dunbar, James Corrothers, and Daniel Webster Davis—should be understood as part of this broad-based interest in African American connections to Africa.[104] For *Southern Workman* readers, the Kuba explanation of the arrival of Sheppard was, by all means, a credible account of "transportation to America" that should not be casually dismissed.[105] The Kuba belief in reincarnation is consistent with Bo-pe Mekabe's return and Sheppard's account, which establishes his credibility as an informant. In addition, similar narratives of return circulated among indentured Africans throughout the diaspora in ways that suggest other possible sources for accounts of forced transatlantic migration during Sheppard's era.[106]

Sheppard's atypical relationship to the Kuba was long questioned by his white colleagues on the APCM. De Witt Snyder, who was elsewhere complimentary of Sheppard, privately disparaged his colleague's pursuit of the Kuba in January 1894: "From what I hear and see here I cannot endorse all Mr. S[heppard's] talk [since] he is given to draw on his imagination and in the end will, I am afraid, do more harm than good. . . . Personally, from what I know, I am sorry Mr. S[heppard] is saying what he did about the Bakuba and the king and the country, but say nothing of this."[107] In a letter to Arthur Rowbotham around the same time, Snyder affirmed his skepticism of Sheppard's report on the Kuba by comparing it to an account by the Adamsons: "Their report differs *very* much from Mr. S[heppard] and I am afraid Mr. S[heppard] is drawing much on his imagination."[108] Sheppard's unique approach does not imply the sort of fantastical imaginings that Snyder and others disparagingly attribute to him. Certainly Sheppard's studied fluency in the Kuba language, unprecedented for a foreigner, and his active pursuit of the city facilitated his success: "Every day we were secretly trying to get a clue to the right road."[109] Sheppard reached the capital by befriending people along the route and by arranging for an acquaintance to mark a trail for him to follow. Similarly, Sheppard gained access to the site of the 1899 Zappo Zap raid by manipulating a personal relationship. His innovations in missionary work enabled him to engage the Kuba people in ways different from those of many of his colleagues.

The relationship Sheppard envisioned with the Kuba was the basis for Presbyterian appointments of black missionaries to the APCM. In 1895, church authorities approved the appointment of Joseph Phipps, "whose grandfather was a native of the Congo region," and who grew up in St. Kitts, "where African dialects are still spoken among the Africans, who largely people that island, and he himself has a speaking knowledge of one or two of these dialects."[110] Phipps was directly informed by cultural heritage and memory. In this instance, the Presbyterian Board of Foreign Missions had use for Phipps's familial connections, which were similar to those ascribed to Sheppard. Phipps's denominational affiliation—he was a member of the Second Presbyterian Church of Scranton, Pennsylvania, a congregation of the PCUSA, which did not allow blacks to serve on their own missions—provides evidence of both the unique prominence of the APCM as a field placement for African American missionaries and the cordial relations between recently conflicting denominations, a reunion that was consistent with a broader reconciliation between the North and South, often executed by white men over such cases of racial accommodation.[111] This embrace of Phipps's background as "practically a trained native," despite inconsistent reports regarding which family members were born in Africa, contrasts with the rote disavowals that became pro forma for Sheppard.[112]

Phipps's appointment to the APCM, like Sheppard's writings about the Kuba, bring into focus the diasporic discourse that drove African American missionary work in Africa. Sheppard's reception must be situated within the critical history of the transatlantic slave trade that is evident in the *Southern Workman*'s calls for oral histories of the Middle Passage. As such, stories can be productively understood in terms of "a narrative continuity between past and present" defined by Stephanie Smallwood as "an epistemological means of connecting the dots between there and here, then and now, to craft a coherent story out of incoherent experience."[113] Hampton's interest in Middle Passage narratives was imbued by Sheppard with repatriation stories that resonate with memories of the transatlantic slave trade that lurk at the surface of this or any other conversation about America's relationship to Africa. In the case of Sheppard, this connection may be best appreciated outside the realm of the APCM and through the lens of his relationship to Hampton as a diasporic site. Sheppard's forced retirement from the APCM provided him with an opportunity to affirm his relationship with Hampton, which included a 1911 fundraising tour with his former teacher Booker T. Washington.[114] Through their association, local and transatlantic strategies of racial uplift came together, particularly in the work that Washington undertook on behalf of the CRA. In the process, Sheppard's career was being redefined for the domestic stage. Even the Presbyterian Church implicitly recognized the confluence of the foreign and domestic missions as evident in the November 1911 merger of the *Missionary*, which reported on their foreign missions, and the *Home Mission Herald*, its domestic counterpart, into the *Missionary Survey*, "a journal representing all the activities of the Southern Presbyterian Church at home and abroad."[115] This merger serves as a textual acknowledgment of the connectedness of their domestic and foreign work at a time when Sheppard was forging a new path at "home."

In 1912, Sheppard became pastor of Louisville's Grace Presbyterian Church, where the proselytizing skills he honed in Africa helped the congregation grow significantly under his leadership. His arrival in Louisville coincided with a period of civil rights organizing in the city, which between 1908 and 1915 saw the establishment of local chapters of the National Association of Colored Women, the NAACP, and the Urban League.[116] In 1916, at Robert Russa Moton's inauguration as Washington's successor at Tuskegee, before an audience of dignitaries that included Alabama Governor Charles

Henderson, philanthropist Julius Rosenwald, Wilberforce University president William Sanders Scarborough, and Morehouse College president John Hope, Frissell reflected on the privilege of teaching Hampton's students such as Moton and Washington, but told those assembled: "It is hard to conceive of a greater honor than that of having helped William H. Sheppard, a Hampton student who went to Africa and did splendid service because of the idea which he gained one Sunday from a missionary visit which we made together to 'Slabtown,' not far from the Hampton School."[117]

Sheppard's visibility continued to emphasize the connections between his work at home and his work abroad, which includes political activism. In naming Sheppard one of its "Men of the Month" for May 1915, the NAACP's *Crisis* acknowledged, "many of his friends felt sure that African labors and hardships had incapacitated him from further service. . . . That Dr. Sheppard has 'come back' physically is a genuine gain for the South. Today Dr. Sheppard is doing in Louisville, Kentucky, some notably constructive social uplift work for his people."[118] Sheppard was a member of the NAACP for a decade and served as chair of a petition committee in 1918.[119] While serving as a pastor and community activist in Kentucky, he continued his work with Hampton, which provided a forum for him to highlight his political accomplishments and, as discussed in chapter 6, share his art collection. While at Hampton to deliver the 1915 Founder's Day Address, Sheppard gave a lecture in the chapel, during which he "spoke of his arrest and trial on account of his exposure of the Belgian atrocities."[120] The publication of this oration was announced on the cover of the March 1915 issue of the *Southern Workman*. While his political work was effectively being erased from church accounts such as *Presbyterian Pioneers in Congo*, it was being recognized by the NAACP and Hampton.[121]

In retirement, Sheppard's activism took on a mythology of its own. A 1924 *Pittsburgh Courier* article recounts a speech Sheppard delivered at a Baptist conference: "He stated that he was in jail in Congo for 9 months because he betrayed the fact to the London Times that King Leopold was a murderer. King Leopold chopped off the hands and flesh of his subjects when rubber got scarce and for disclosing this fact, Dr. Sheppard was supposed to hang, but the British government sent word that Dr. Sheppard should have a trial and so he escaped hanging."[122] This sensational version of Sheppard's activist career appropriately uses Leopold to personify his colonial regime, and, intriguingly, the British play the role of hero. St. Clair Drake appreciates the role of missionaries in spreading news about Africa and colonialism as a marker of the church's ranging secular impact. From William Sheppard's visits to his home and church in Staunton, Virginia, he recalls, "he had attacked the colonial politics of the Belgians and was jailed for being outspoken."[123] The Sheppards' son Max, in a 1979 interview, recalls, only vaguely, learning of his father's case: "He was condemned to die but in some way the United States government, the French government, and the English government in some way or another ... —I wouldn't put this down, this isn't too accurate what I'm telling you—in some way came to his defense and saved his life."[124]

On the other side of the Atlantic, Sheppard continues to be remembered in a variety of ways. When his alma mater Stillman College was dedicating its new library to him in 1956, the Luebo Presbytery donated 30,000 francs ($600) toward the project.[125] Decades later, the independent Congolese Presbyterian church affirmed its strong affinity for Sheppard by naming its Université Presbyterienne Sheppard et Lapsley du Congo (UPRECO), located in Ndesha, a neighborhood on the outskirts of Kananga, for the cofounders of the APCM. (See Figure 2.7.) In addition, in 2002, the Imprimerie Protestante du Kasai (IMPROKA) published the first Tshiluba-language biography of William Sheppard, Etienne Bote-Tshiek and Ntambue Kazadi's translation of excerpts of William Phipps's biography. (IMPROKA has its origins in the APCM's J. Leighton Wilson Press, which shuttered its operations in Luebo in 1979 after a distinguished history as one of the country's premier Tshiluba-language publishers, which is considered in more detail in chapter 4. The new IMPROKA opened in Kananga in 1982.)[126] Meanwhile, there remain important forms of remembrance in the United States. In 1988, for example, the Presbyterian Church renamed its central Alabama region the Presbytery of Sheppards and Lapsley.[127] This renaming, somewhat subtly, pluralizes Sheppard, formally acknowledging the frequently overlooked contributions of Lucy Gantt Sheppard as a pioneer of its work.

This transatlantic history of recognition establishes connections between the foreign and domestic legacies of the Sheppards that demand more sustained forms of inquiry. Much writing about the Sheppards, like *Presbyterian Pioneers in Congo* itself, has tended to detach their work in the Congo from their more commonplace racial uplift work in the United States. With the exception of scholars like Wallace Short, the Sheppards' activism in Louisville, Kentucky, rarely receives more than a brief mention in biographical accounts. The ongoing underappreciation of Lucy Sheppard, a pioneer of social work in Louisville, is one particular outcome of this domestic neglect. Kennedy, who was able to construct a biography out of William Sheppard's incomplete archive, claims: "The circumstances of Lucy's own passing have become hazy; rarely do any of the brief accounts of her life include a death date. The *Biographical Dictionary of Christian Missions* does give the date 1940, but follows it with a question mark."[128] Lucy Sheppard did not die until May 26, 1955.[129] In her "last" interview, which appeared posthumously in the September 1955 *Presbyterian Survey*, she affirms the dearth of documentation: "No, I never kept a diary, and I regret it very much. . . . I regret it because

*Figure 2.7* Université Presbyterienne Sheppard et Lapsley du Congo (UPRECO), located in Ndesha, on the outskirts of Kananga (2006). (Photograph by author.)

I think a woman's point of view is quite different from a man's."[130] Her unique career demands further research into a written oeuvre that includes *Kassai Herald* columns and pamphlets such as "From Talladega College to Africa" and "Children of the Kassai."[131] Even more, while her historical legacy has faded more than that of her husband, her memory survives in important ways through the ongoing civic work of the Lucy Sheppard Art Club which was established on the occasion of her August 1911 visit to Tuscaloosa.[132]

The Sheppards' decades of work in Louisville provide their biographies with a crucial continuity between their commitments to African missionary work and domestic faith-based community service. Such continuity would have been commonplace. In the early part of the twentieth century, the field of international relations, for example, took race relations to be within its purview and did not assume the foreign-domestic split in the way that scholars often do today.[133] Based on this model, a transatlantic approach to the Sheppards could partly fill in the gaps that Kennedy identifies, by attending to the later social work career of Lucy Gantt Sheppard, which embodies a link between missionary work in the Congo and domestic strategies of social uplift. Combined with William Sheppard's involvement with the Louisville chapter of the NAACP, the domestic work undertaken by the Sheppards in the United States represents the crucial, yet still underappreciated way that local civic traditions have been shaped by transatlantic networks of writers and activists working on matters of colonialism and anticolonialism.

Country of My Forefathers 77

*Chapter 3*

# Booker T. Washington's African at Home

On January 17, 1890, Booker T. Washington addressed "a large audience of colored students and citizens" at Alabama State Normal School one month after George Washington Williams's address at his alma mater and his former student William Henry Sheppard's appointment to the American Presbyterian Congo Mission (APCM). Migration to the Congo was quite real and Washington took the opportunity to dismiss the entire prospect as misguided:

> You may talk of our disadvantages because of our color, because of race prejudice, because of friction in enjoying civil and political rights, may advise emigration to the West or the Congo, but I am free to say to you as young people preparing for life, that I had rather take my chances for an opportunity to lead a positive, helpful and independent life, right here in Alabama as a black man—and I would not change my color if I could—than in any other section of the Union or anywhere in the world.[1]

In doing so, Washington alludes to the contemporary prominence of Williams and Sheppard. Just two months after covering Williams's recruiting visit, the *Southern Workman* quoted Washington's speech opposing emigration.[2] Washington, Hampton's best-known graduate, and principal Samuel Chapman Armstrong, his mentor and editor of the *Southern Workman*, recognized the appeal the Congo held for many of their students, and may have been concerned that these two well-known travelers were foretelling a larger exodus.

In his speech, Washington refers simultaneously to the currency of African American interest in the Congo, tied as it was to Hampton and to Alabama Senator John Tyler Morgan. On January 7, 1890, a week and a half before Washington's speech, Morgan pleaded on the Senate floor for congressional funding to transport African Americans to the Congo. In this context, Washington's assertion that African Americans should remain in the South was not a conservative acceptance of racism, but rather a timely challenge to Morgan's racist proposal at a time when the "movement to deport negroes [*sic*]" was in the national spotlight.[3]

Washington's insistent claims to the South would come to define his career, which is synonymous with Tuskegee Institute, for which he served as principal from its establishment in 1881. However, Washington's regional devotion obscured, perhaps deliberately, Tuskegee's transnationalism and the vital role of Historically Black Colleges and Universities (HBCUs) in black Atlantic networks of exchange, which included both collaboration with and challenges to existing colonial regimes. From his 1890 speech at Alabama State Normal School up through his involvement with the Congo Reform Association (CRA) in the early twentieth century, Washington's attention to the Congo is exemplary of the vexed transnational networks that developed out of the work of folks like Sheppard and Williams and spread to people who had never traveled there. In this regard, Washington was in the dubious company of King Leopold II, who had a monstrous impact in the Congo, a place where he never set foot. These underappreciated aspects of Washington's career demonstrate how an interest in Africa existed at the elite levels of black leadership and across the ideological spectrum, even in instances of seeming contradiction.

Washington's African work fails, at first glance, to fit neatly with his self-fashioning as a southerner. His biographer Louis R. Harlan describes the perception and explains the congruity: "The Negroes' position in American society at the turn of the twentieth century was, after all, roughly analogous to that of Negroes in the African colonies."[4] Beyond the kind of affinity that Harlan describes, there is an institutional analogue, whereby Washington's involvement in Africa was deeply embedded in his better-recognized and quite successful efforts to build Tuskegee Institute. Despite excellent research not only by Harlan, but also by Milfred Fierce, Manning Marable, Basil Mathews, Elliott Skinner, Vernon Williams, Andrew Zimmerman, and others, many scholars continue to read Washington's interest in Africa as secondary to, if not incommensurate with, his Southern focus.[5]

Such assumptions are long-standing. Washington's Congo reform comrade Robert Park later recalled, "He wasn't really interested in the Congo natives, or in anything else for that matter, except for the American Negro and his school in Tuskegee." Park, who worked closely with Washington for many years and helped organize the International Conference on the Negro at Tuskegee in 1912, presumes a narrow opposition between Africa and America that overlooks Tuskegee's long-standing history of involvement in Africa. Indeed, "one could argue," as historian Frank Guridy does quite compellingly, that prior to the Harlem Renaissance, "Tuskegee was the prime epicenter of Afro-diasporic activity in the world."[6] While Fierce similarly asserts that Washington may be "the Black American individual with the most substantial record of active involvement, during the period, with Africa and Africans," Park's presumption is adopted by his biographer/former student Winifred Raushenbush, who sweepingly insists, "Historians agree that Washington cared little about the problems of Africans."[7] Even Park himself offers a seemingly contradictory account of Washington's myopia, describing him as "an inveterate reader of the newspapers [who] invariably kept abreast of events inside or outside his world."[8] St. Clair Drake disagrees with Raushenbush and August Meier's shared interpretation, insisting instead that both Washington and Park "had a deep interest in Africa."[9] "Tuskegee's policy toward Africa provides ample evidence of his breadth and vision," which, Wilson J. Moses argues, can provide the foundation for a much more inclusive assessment of Washington's legacy on American pragmatism, something that Park, who worked with William James and John Dewey, also asserts.[10] Indeed, an examination of Washington from the perspective of his involvement with the Congo does more than facilitate a reconsideration of his career; it enables a fuller appreciation of the contours of the African diaspora networks that circulated through HBCUs and other institutional sites in the late nineteenth and early twentieth centuries.

### Cast Down Your Bucket Where You Are

Five years after Washington's comments about emigration and the Congo were cited in the *Southern Workman*, he expressed strikingly similar ideas at the defining moment of his extraordinary career. In his September 18, 1895, address to the Atlanta Cotton States Exposition, which appears as the centerpiece of his 1901 autobiography *Up from Slavery*, Washington seemingly offers his listeners and readers, both black and white, a manifesto of localism:

> To those of my race who depend on bettering their condition in a foreign land or who underestimate the importance of cultivating friendly relations with the Southern white man, who is their next-door neighbour, I would say: "Cast down your bucket where you are"—cast it down in making friends in every manly way of the people of all races by whom we are surrounded.
>
> . . . .
>
> To those of the white race who look to the incoming of those of foreign birth and strange tongue and habits for the prosperity of the South, were I permitted I would repeat what I say to my own race, "Cast down your bucket where you are."[11]

In this, Washington's most famous moment, Africa lurks in the background of his allusions to emigration, which had been promoted by the American Colonization Society (ACS) since its founding in 1816. The ACS continued after the Civil War as part of a project to relocate African Americans primarily to Liberia, though the Congo was occasionally under consideration. John H. B. Latrobe, a longtime ACS leader, was the founding president of the American branch of Leopold's International African Association (AIA), and he worked with Sanford, and later Morgan, to secure Senate recognition of Leopold's Congo claim in April 1884.[12]

After Reconstruction, some African American leaders like Henry McNeal Turner were actively advancing an independent emancipatory colonizationist agenda, which greatly differed from the forcible deportation advocated by the ACS.[13] Despite its limited operational success, this movement was significant enough, as Vernon Williams points out, for Washington to open his 1895 "address by scolding black emigrationists"; however, the international aspects of the speech are typically little more than a footnote in discussions of it, which have largely been shaped by Du Bois's characterization of it as the "Atlanta Compromise."[14] In doing so, Du Bois, whose critique of the speech's conciliatory tone appears in his own signature work, *The Souls of Black Folk*, framed a debate between himself and Washington that has become not only definitive of both of their careers, but also paradigmatic of twentieth-century African American intellectual life. While Du Bois focuses on the domestic implications of Washington's address, he discusses the South's need for "discriminating and broad-minded criticism," which must include "exposing Senator Morgan," whose draconian proposal depended on a settler colony in the Congo.[15] On this point, among others, Du Bois and Washington shared common ground in opposition to white efforts to render African Americans a settler class in Africa.

Washington used his most prominent platform—his Atlanta Cotton States Exposition address—to recognize that the waters of the world were vast and that the abolition of slavery created new, albeit still profoundly limited, possibilities for African American movement. As in his 1890 advice to students, Washington raises the specter of black mobility before reaffirming his staunchly local rhetoric. After discouraging African Americans from looking abroad, he warns employers of "strikes and labour wars" to dissuade the hiring of European immigrants who he believes endanger African Americans' tenuous position in the U.S. labor market.[16] His message of conciliation between blacks and whites in the South was based on a defense of the region's integrity, without an exodus of African Americans or an influx of European immigrants. Washington relies on vaguely threatening "foreign lands" like the Congo to illustrate the depth of his commitment to the South. In taking a stand against mass migration, Washington directly addresses people who are negotiating their place on an expanding and increasingly complex global stage opened up by new forms of mobility in the aftermath of the Civil War. His career is full of examples that demonstrate that his localism was not a programmatic call for insularity (and certainly not one to which he himself was subject), but rather a broad philosophical dictum. Indeed, there were many disparities between Washington's rhetoric and actions; for instance, his advocacy of Southern autonomy did not preclude his ongoing collaborations with patrons and institutions in the North, where he himself spent up to half of each year.[17]

Washington's local rhetoric can best be interpreted as an attempt to reimagine Tuskegee's role in a global world on his own terms. The decision to cast down one's bucket at Tuskegee or Hampton is not an attempt to separate from the broader transnational sphere, but rather an effort to negotiate that sphere more effectively by cultivating extensive missionary networks, religious and secular, within HBCUs. So in an era when African American mobility was severely circumscribed, Washington's transnationalism was not coterminous with his physical travels. When Washington casts down his bucket in the rural South, he does so, at least in part, in order to construct Tuskegee (and other HBCUs) and his own oeuvre as locally grounded institutional and textual sites for his peculiar brand of transnationalism, which effectively assumed a colonial definition of the civilizing mission. While Washington's international record, much like his record in the United States, is subject to debate and criticism, its recovery can demonstrate the breadth and diversity of African American interests in the late nineteenth and early twentieth centuries. Colonialism proved formative even among the most conservative African American leaders.

One reason for misconceptions about Washington is that his archetypal autobiography *Up from Slavery* has become a synecdoche for a prolific, if uneven and sometimes redundant, literary career that includes multiple autobiographies, histories, travel narratives, and political essays. In *Up from Slavery*, Washington constructs his public profile as a unique leader, describing himself on the occasion of his Atlanta address as "a representative of the Negro race," making no mention of national or regional affiliation. In his 1911 autobiography *My Larger Education*, he makes a similar point even more sharply by positioning himself as the successor to the country's most famous black leader of the nineteenth century: "Frederick Douglass died in February, 1895. In September of the same year I delivered an address in Atlanta at the Cotton States Exposition."[18] *My Larger Education* acknowledges the influence of his international travels through chapters like "Meeting High and Low in Europe" and "What I Learned about Education in Denmark." Even the penultimate chapter of *Up from Slavery* is entitled "Europe." In that chapter, Washington recounts reading Douglass's account of his transatlantic voyage during his own return trip to the United States. In the ship library, Washington finds one of Douglass's autobiographies and notes that the mistreatment that Douglass experiences during his transatlantic trek is at odds with the welcome he feels aboard the ship. For Washington, this experience symbolizes a decline in racial hostility, marked by the invitation he received, while in Paris, from the mayor of Charleston, West Virginia, to visit the capital of his home state. Despite this international geography, readings of *Up from Slavery* presume its Southern focus as the basis for Washington's representative status. If Washington represents the "Negro," then *Up from Slavery*, aside from its often-ignored European excursion, represents Washington.[19] The wider world of Washington's literary oeuvre, however, includes underappreciated titles like *Some European Observations and Experiences* (1899), *The Story of the Negro* (1909), *My Larger Education* (1911), and *The Man Farthest Down: A Record of Observation and Study in Europe* (1912) plus a range of essays that document a much more central role for Africa in his political, intellectual, and ideological development.

Cruelty in the Congo Country

Washington's own inability to travel to Africa did not prohibit his involvement in the Congo, and in 1904 he became vice president of the CRA, lobbying both Congress and the White House to take action.[20] The starting point of Washington's relationship to the Congo differed substantially from that of predecessors like Williams and Sheppard in that he was made aware of the brutality taking place in the Congo without traveling there. While he acknowledged that he gained information and authority from Sheppard, who "I knew slightly as a fellow-student at Hampton Institute," Washington, the most prominent African American of his generation, was a crucial conduit for exposing those crimes to an international public.[21] On October 7, 1904, Washington cited Sheppard's investigation at the Universal Peace Congress in Boston, which Park, Jane Adams, Thomas Seymour Barbour, G. Stanley Hall, William James, E. D. Morel, and William Morrison attended or addressed.

The address was classic Washington. He began with a parable about spreading two tablespoons of molasses over an entire plate to "produce more," which garnered laughter while reminding his listeners of his slave past. Then Washington turned his attention to the Congo: "I have testimony direct from the lips of Dr. Shutworth [sic], a former school-fellow of mine at the Hampton Institute, and from the lips of Dr. Morrison, a Southern man—and incidentally I wish to add that the going of these two men into the Congo Free State furnishes almost a dramatic side of history. One of them was the son of a master in the South, the other the son of a slave in the South. Hand in hand they have gone to the Congo Free State in order to help free those people from mental and moral slavery. (Applause.)." Like many others, Washington views the experience of the APCM as a metaphor for interracial cooperation. Here Morrison is secondary to Sheppard. Washington skillfully shifts from the passive voice to an assertion of Sheppard's crucial ongoing witness and agency: "Villages to-day are burned; people are murdered or maimed. Dr. Shutworth tells me that with his own eyes in one village he saw eighty-one human hands which had been severed from the body and were hung up and dried, to be presented to the Belgian authorities as evidence that the soldiers had performed their duty."[22] Washington shares Sheppard's analysis by making it clear that the soldiers were following the orders of the Belgian authorities.

By contrast Morrison evokes his colleague Sheppard's report of "atrocities and cruelties in the cutting off of hands and mutilations and all those things" without naming him in the published Congress proceedings.[23] Washington makes strong statements about the transatlantic continuity of racist violence by making a seamless transition to lynching, "that debasing and demoralizing habit of burning and torturing human beings without a trial before the law," in the United States, "which concerns very largely my race, which should have the honest, the active sympathy and help of an organization such as is gathered here."[24] In the end, the Peace Congress issued an official resolution to pursue allegations "that the government of the Congo Free State has appropriated the land of the natives and the products of commercial value yielded by the land, thus leading to the committal of grave wrongs upon the native races, and to the infringement of the rights secured for international commerce by the Conference of Berlin."[25]

In the same month as the Congress, Washington published "Cruelty in the Congo Country" in *Outlook* magazine. The article excludes the comparison to lynching, his tale of molasses, and reference to Morrison. Most of his information comes directly from Sheppard's report of his interview with the chief of "a tribe of cannibals known as the Zapo-zaps" following a raid during which people's hands were cut off for failing to harvest their quota of rubber. In Washington's account, as in its source, Sheppard was told of the casualties and asked the chief to see the severed hands, which numbered 81. For Washington, Sheppard's matter-of-fact account was indispensable: "a report written on the spot by an eye-witness."[26] Significantly, Washington indicates that Sheppard's witness was not happenstance, but the result of him proactively seeking out the gory evidence. When his reliance on Sheppard was challenged by Robert Curtis Ogden, head of the Southern Education Board, Washington disingenuously revised his citation to appease his white patron: "While in my article I mentioned Mr. Sheppard's name, I would state that I got perhaps more information from Rev. Dr. Morrison, a

Southern white man who is engaged in missionary work in the Congo under the auspices of the Southern Presbyterian Church."[27] Of course, the most important information that Morrison shared was Sheppard's report.

Despite his personal connection to Sheppard, Washington anticipated that his entry into the public debate about the Congo State would be greeted with skepticism in part because the public image of Tuskegee downplayed its role as a site of international exchange. For this reason, he begins "Cruelty in the Congo Country" with a preemptive defense: "My interest in the race to which I belong, and in the advancement of the cause of humanity regardless of race, is my excuse for discussing a subject which I have not hitherto called attention to in public print." After broadly positioning himself in the service of "humanity," Washington quickly returns to the notion of transnational racial identification: "The oppression of the colored race in any one part of the world means, sooner or later, the oppression of the same race elsewhere."[28] His perspective was not especially radical. Rather, he thought that Leopold's brutal rule in the Congo undermined more benevolent colonial systems that, like Tuskegee's collaboration with Germany in Togo, should be replicated. Washington believed he could positively influence colonial rule, whether in Togo or Alabama. With regard to the Congo, Washington calls for reform of the excesses of the Belgian regime because of "the heritage of misunderstanding, mutual distrust, and race hatred that it inevitably leaves behind it. This alone, in my opinion, will render fruitless for many years to come every effort to bring the great mass of the natives under the better and higher influences of our Christian civilization"—a pragmatic goal shared by missionaries and colonialists.

Just as there are "Christian" colonial systems whose work is sullied by the Congo regime, there are also white colonists who find themselves victimized by the same system, thereby binding white and black people together in a web of mutuality that echoes one of Washington's most common refrains. In "Cruelty in the Congo Country," he concludes: "And what is the result of it all? Not the improvement and uplifting of the black men, since wherever the white man has put his foot in the Congo State the black man has been degraded into a mere tool in the great business of getting rubber. And what is the effect upon the white men who are condemned to perform this degrading work? All reports agree that these men almost invariably give themselves over to the worst vices. . . . It is clear that the native is not the only victim of this system."[29] For Washington, the Congo's brutality undermines the work of good imperialists, presumably those from Tuskegee and their German collaborators.

In the wake of Washington's Congo activism, Tuskegee expanded its African efforts to the Sudan to demonstrate the "liberal influence" he describes in "Industrial Education in Africa" (1906), which provided the "germ idea" for Tuskegee's International Conference on the Negro in 1912.[30] In a letter wishing the Tuskegee students well in the Sudan, he reminds them that "the reputation of the school [is] in your hands."[31] The warnings in the letter and in "Cruelty in the Congo Country" align with Conrad's gothic representation of Kurtz in *Heart of Darkness*, which, amid its indifference to the mistreatment of the African population, exposed the psychological toll of colonialism on settlers. Elsewhere, however, Washington's criticism of the degradation of Africans by rubber companies approaches a broad argument against imperialism that he had, despite his conservatism, come close to articulating at other points in his career. For example, Moses points to an 1896 dispatch from Tuskegee that inveighs against British violence and hypocrisy, while also mocking the principles underlying colonialism by asking, "Have not these Matabele warriors as much right to lay claim to the streets of London, as the English have to claim the native land of these Africans?" Here, Washington echoes Williams, who similarly speculates on his "legal claim . . . to be Commander-in-Chief of the Belgian army" in his *Open Letter* to King Leopold.[32] At a time when few reform-minded Americans or Europeans advocated independence, Washington asked questions that broadly challenged emigration and colonialism.

Throughout the colonial era, Leopold and Belgium sought, Zimmerman notes, "to improve their public image by associating themselves with Tuskegee and Hampton. Representatives of the Congo Free State approached Washington to secure African Americans to help develop the Congolese cotton industry in late 1903."[33] By 1905, as Washington gained prominence in the Congo reform movement, he was targeted by Leopold's top American lobbyist, the famously unscrupulous San Francisco attorney Henry I. Kowalsky. After notifying the king that "Dr. Washington is no small enemy to overcome," Kowalsky invited Washington to visit the Congo State: "You can select your own route, in every way be your own master, free from suggestion or dictation,—the fullest and widest latitude of your own choice alone shall map your footsteps, and every dollar of expense I will place in the bank for you to defray your wants."[34] Washington, however, never traveled anywhere as his "own master" and, in this case, to his credit, flatly refused Kowalsky's bribes. Other attempts to appeal to Washington and his circle were equally unsuccessful. In 1905, "a representative of King Leopold offered the Hampton library a collection of books on Africa, which sociologist Thomas Jesse Jones suspected was a ploy to oblige the institute to the Congo Free State."[35] In 1907, Robert Park exposed the Belgian propaganda campaign, including the king's Press Bureau, for distributing books like Wellington Wack's *The Story of the Congo State* to "most of the negro [sic] mission-schools of the South, and from which the negroes [sic] are being taught that Leopold is a benefactor of their race."[36] Rejection of such overtures did not stop Belgium from continuing to seek an association with Washington and Tuskegee, and even announcing unilaterally, in 1912, the establishment of its own "Tuskegee Institute."[37]

Washington's Congo reform activities not only drew the attention of Belgium's royal family, but also connected him to a diverse network of the era's most prominent intellectuals, including Sheppard, Park, Morel, Arthur Conan Doyle, and Mark Twain. Park, who was Secretary of the CRA when Washington was vice president, recalls that when they met in 1904, "I told him that I was thinking of going to Africa; that there was, I had heard, at Lovedale, South Africa an industrial school for natives, and that, if there was any solution of the Congo problem it would probably be some form of education." Hearing this, Washington recruited Park to Tuskegee, which he envisioned as an alternative to Lovedale, a Presbyterian mission school founded in 1841, which was, at the time, "the only institution equipped to prepare African students for the high school matriculation examination."[38] Washington steered Park away from Africa, as he had a generation of African American students; as a result, Park did not travel to Africa until the 1930s. Washington also convinced Park to decline a job offer from the University of Chicago, though he later spent several decades there making a name for himself as a pioneer of American sociology. Park, a Heidelberg PhD with two years of experience as an assistant to William James at Harvard, worked as a Tuskegee "publicist" for seven years.[39]

The Congo proved foundational to one of the most prolific associations of their distinguished careers. Washington's work with Park and Monroe Work, who became two of the era's most accomplished sociologists, connects him to the major social and intellectual movements of his time. Park himself describes Washington as a "man, whom I knew longer and from whom I learned more than from any of my other teachers," including James and Dewey, which suggests that the frequently used "pejorative term 'ghost writer' " flattens other dimensions of their collaboration.[40] Fred Matthews's assertion that "Park's career seems an anticipation of the anonymous corporate quality of work in the social sciences" indicates that alternatives to individual authorship are consistent with methodological developments in the field of sociology.[41] Indeed Harlan shows, for example, that Washington's previous secretary, Max B. Thrasher, who worked at Tuskegee from 1899 until his death in 1903, made limited editorial changes to his manuscripts and that even the most incidental of these were submitted to Washington for approval.[42] With regard to Park, Harlan explains, he "researched, drafted, or revised most of Washington's writings for publication between 1905 and 1912 ... while retaining the distinctive Washingtonian plainness of style."[43]

When requesting credit as a "joint author" for *The Man Farthest Down*, Park suggested that it would establish Washington as his equal: "I think the matter can be so presented that it will appear that whatever I have added to the book has really been yours as well as mine. In that way it can not be said that you hired an outsider to write the book as I fear they are likely to say otherwise."[44] Washington did not need Park to stoke anxieties around black authorship. He understood the presumptions and skepticism well enough to proactively discuss their collaborative process quite openly in the book's first chapter. By acknowledging Park as a collaborator (but not coauthor) on the title page and detailing their relationship so thoroughly in the text itself, Washington seems to acquiesce to Park's request while unequivocally claiming primary credit in a manner that affirms his narrative and editorial authority.[45] Robert Stepto sees a particular sophistication in the meticulous attribution of " 'outside' texts" in *Up from Slavery*, which Washington handles similarly in *The Man Farthest Down*: "Once assembled, these documents not only authenticate Washington's tale, but also, because they have been edited and contextualized within the tale, enhance Washington's authorial control."[46] Washington's sophisticated ability to maintain control of his texts, through a collaborative process that facilitated his prolific output, is evident throughout his oeuvre. In their personal correspondence, Park himself is clear on this point: "if the situation were not as I have stated I would never have been willing to do the work that I have done."[47] Such a conclusion is consistent with Drake's analysis that *The Man Farthest Down*, Washington's study of the conditions of the European working class, was "true collaboration."[48] (Indeed if there was an unacknowledged hand in *The Man Farthest Down*, it may belong to Washington's black stenographer, Nathan Hunt, who was in Europe with Park and Washington in 1910 and whose role has escaped notice in most accounts of Washington's writing process.[49])

Harlan credits Park with writing "Cruelty in the Congo Country," because Washington sent his payment from *Outlook* to him with a note that "this article was so largely prepared by you."[50] Despite such convincing evidence, it seems impossible that Park "prepared" the article independently of Washington. "Cruelty in the Congo Country" uses a personal reference to Sheppard, a black witness who establishes Washington's authority by noting their time together at Hampton. Moreover, Park utilizes very different sources when writing about the Congo under his own name. Although published in the same month as "Cruelty in the Congo Country," Park's "Recent Atrocities in the Congo State" makes no mention of Sheppard. In his own signed article, Park essentially reprints accounts of John Harris, A. E. Scrivener, and John Weeks, none of which were used in "Cruelty in the Congo Country." By 1906, however, Park appears to use, without attribution, the Sheppard report that was the basis for "Cruelty in the Congo Country" in his article "The Terrible Story of the Congo." For this reason, Park's writings might be just as fruitfully read to discern Washington's influence as Washington's are read for evidence of Park's hand.[51] While Park's seeming reliance on Sheppard and Washington may not compromise his narrative authority, it forces a reconsideration of the reliance of white authors on the groundbreaking reports of African American intellectuals and activists like Williams and Sheppard.

From the start of his association with Tuskegee, when Alabama replaced Lovedale (which was itself a substitute for the Congo) as his destination, Park was committed to the international aspects of the school's mission. In recommending that Washington accept an invitation to the 1905 Congress on Economic Expansion in Belgium, Park identified the compatibility of Tuskegee's mission with forms of colonialism: "I believe it will give you an opportunity to say something, at once for your school and our own colonial system, more fundamental than has yet been uttered. The difference between our colonial system and others consists in the fact that we are preparing the peoples we govern for citizenship, either in the United States or as independent states; other countries are interested only in the *economic development* (a vague term, which may be interpreted in many ways) of their possessions."[52] Park acknowledges Tuskegee as a "colonial system," albeit an alternative to European models, like Leopold's regime, which is the most monomaniacal in its pursuit of profit. Park's emphasis of "citizenship, either in the United States or as independent states" is indicative of how Tuskegee's global model of industrial education can be used to educate a student body that includes aspiring postcolonial subjects. The Belgian government's interest in Tuskegee and its principal was affirmed by the invitation to Leopold's congress.[53]

Park's international focus contrasts with the interest of Twain, whom Washington first met in England in 1899 and who served as vice president of the CRA for two years.[54] Despite holding similar posts, Twain and Washington saw their work differently. Twain's nationalist approach to reform serves to highlight the philosophical foundations of Washington's transnationalism. Whereas Washington recognizes that the "Congo State owes in large measure its existence" to the "timely intervention" of the United States "in what seemed to some people at that time a purely European affair," he spoke out on the basis of transnational identification and human rights.[55] Twain, on the other hand, saw the mission of the CRA in strictly national terms and resigned from the organization in 1906 upon learning that the Senate never approved the 1885 Berlin Act granting Leopold dominion over the Congo State. In a letter to Thomas Seymour Barbour of the Baptist Mission Society, who recruited Park to the CRA, Twain explained: "The American branch of the Congo Reform Association ought to go out of business, for the reason that the agitation of the butcheries can only wring the people's hearts unavailingly—unavailingly, because the American people unbacked by the American government cannot achieve reform in Congo."[56] Twain alludes to President Grover Cleveland's refusal to submit the Berlin Act to the Senate for ratification. Since the Senate never ratified the Berlin Act, Twain saw no legitimate target for U.S. activists.

Washington did not share Twain's nationalism, and his involvement was not contingent on official state policy. The U.S. government was not his target, as it rarely was for someone who disturbingly criticized African Americans for looking, during the era of Reconstruction, "to the Federal Government for everything, very much as a child looks to its mother."[57] His identity in his speeches, as in "Cruelty in Congo Country," was regional and racial rather than federal. The same ideology that limited his agitation toward the state created possibilities for transnational alliances, as evident, for example, in his collaborations with South Africans. The question of whether or not the federal government had been an official party to the Berlin Treaty was of minor importance for someone staunchly devoted to the South despite the power the government in Washington continued to exert over every aspect of his life and work.

Washington's analysis of Africa in general and the Congo in particular was shaped by his geographical understanding of race in the United States. For authors like Stanley and Conrad, the Congo symbolized an unknown frontier. Park revealed an analogous understanding of the South by titling an unpublished account of Alabama, "Land of Darkness."[58] Equally resonant for a writer like Washington was the dramatic corruption of something perceived as idyllic. The grotesqueness of Leopold's brutality sharply contrasted with a romantic vision of the interior regions. The very title of his *Outlook* article highlights not the city or the state, but rather the "Congo Country," the rural spaces of the "country districts."[59]

For all of its unique emphasis of Africa, "Cruelty in the Congo Country" nonetheless includes Washington's characteristic commentary on the United States. In order to accentuate the horrors of the contemporary Congo, Washington downplays the devastation of chattel slavery, indulging in the type of rhetoric for which he is often criticized: "there was never anything in American slavery that could be compared to the barbarous conditions existing to-day in the Congo Free State." Washington's abandonment of historical concerns can help explain, though not excuse, this reckless apologia for American slavery as a displaced attempt to address the present crisis in central Africa and to discourage African American emigration. Not only is the situation in the Congo worse than any in the United States, but it is also "harsher and more evil in its consequences than any form of slavery that has ever existed on African soil."⁶⁰ While such comparisons unnecessarily diminish the brutality of one slave system or another, the unique gravity of the Congo provides a rationale for Washington's uncommon involvement. His personal connection to Sheppard, the influence of his financial backers like Barbour and Huntington, and the role of the movement itself factored into Washington's activism. Cumulatively then, his participation was the product of a wide range of social networks. While this context may contradict the more individualistic persona that Washington tried to fashion, it hints at the significant ways that his personal involvement is in fact representative of broader interest in the Congo.

## My Ambition of Going to Africa

The subtitle of Washington's *The Story of the Negro: The Rise of the Race from Slavery* reveals it to be a collective variation on *Up from Slavery* that opens, appropriately enough, in Africa. The subtitle of the two-volume epic, which Washington collaborated on with Park and Work, casts its author's life as illustrative of the larger "story" indicated by the title.⁶¹ Such an approach fits what Houston A. Baker Jr. defines in *Turning South Again: Re-Thinking Modernism/Re-Reading Booker T.* as "mulatto modernism," a "chief tenet of [which] is 'uplift,' the translation of individual, bourgeois, class achievement into doctrinal and pedagogical imperatives for the black masses." Baker's "mulatto modernism" is inherent in Washington's embrace of the role of "representative," where his individual achievements provide a model for racial advancement. Washington's description of his relationship to Africa in "The African at Home," the third chapter of *The Story of the Negro*, exemplifies what Baker describes as "a project in ambivalence"⁶²:

> While I had been a student at Hampton Institute, Virginia, it was one of my ambitions, as it has been the ambition of a great many other Negro students before and since, to go out some day to Africa as a missionary. I believed that I had got hold at Hampton of a kind of knowledge that would be peculiarly helpful to the Native Africans and I felt that my interest in the people out there, vague and indefinite as it was, would in some way or other help and inspire me in the task of lifting them to a higher plane of civilisation.
>
> After I went to Tuskegee I gave up my ambition of going to Africa. I had not been long there, however, before I was convinced that I could, perhaps, be of larger usefulness through the work I was able to do in this country, by fitting, for the same service I wanted to perform, Africans who came as students to America, and by sending from Tuskegee men

and women trained in our methods, as teachers and workers among the native peoples.[63]

This quote reveals that Washington, like some of the young people he addressed in his 1890 speech, once wanted to be a missionary to Africa. He abandoned this goal, but was consoled by his conviction that he could better serve Africa by building Tuskegee into a black Atlantic nexus than by traveling to the continent himself. In recounting his own experiences at the intersections of Hampton, Tuskegee, and Africa, Washington imagines Tuskegee as a global space while remaining tied to the South. Despite their differences, Washington's innovative "cartography" resembles that of Du Bois, which, Amy Kaplan explains, "does not just reflect established boundaries between fixed geographical units, but discursively produces new aggregates of social space that can be policed, contested, and transformed."[64]

"The African at Home," which was simultaneously published in two of the era's most important periodicals, *Outlook* and the *Colored American Magazine*, delineates two specific roles that Tuskegee fulfilled—training Africans on its campus and sending its graduates abroad to work in Africa. This was a realistic vision. There were many African students at Tuskegee, as degree candidates and as visitors.[65] Among these, many ultimately set out on a more directly political path than that ostensibly promoted by the school curriculum. Neither Tuskegee nor its African students were unique in this regard; historian Robert Engs points out that many Hampton graduates were involved in political work in their home communities, and typically on a more progressive basis than Washington or Armstrong would encourage.[66] Washington himself came to realize that many of Tuskegee's international students were "sent here, not merely to get an education in the trades, such as they do not have an opportunity to do at home, but likewise to get acquainted with the plans and methods of this school, in order that they might be more helpful to their own people, either as teachers or in some other capacity, when they returned home."[67] Many students were more interested in the school as an institutional model than in any of the more parochial lessons that might be gleaned from their coursework.

For this reason, the Alabama campus became a frequent stop for Africans studying or traveling in the United States and, like other HBCUs, played a formative role in the education of several generations of African leaders, who, historian Manning Marable notes, were drawn to Washington's "racial pride and black nationalist tendencies."[68] Harlan explains the ease with which Washington's ideas were understood cross-culturally: "The separatist concept which was Tuskegee conservatism in the American context became radical nationalism in the African context."[69] The social segregation that

Washington advocated resembled anticolonialism, and Tuskegee's emphasis on land ownership at the individual and institutional levels resonated with people suffering under settler colonialism.[70] It may not be surprising, therefore, that Tuskegee had a particular allure for South Africans. As early as the 1890s, John Tengo Jababvu was promoting Washington's ideas among South Africans in the bilingual Xhosa-English newspaper he edited. Rev. John L. Dube, a South African Oberlin College graduate, spoke at the 1897 commencements at both Tuskegee and Hampton, and his Hampton address on the "Need of Industrial Education in Africa" was published in the *Southern Workman*.[71] In 1912, when Dube was named the founding president of the South African Native National Congress (which was renamed the African National Congress [ANC] in 1925), he wrote a letter to the other founders invoking Washington as his "patron saint."[72] Two subsequent presidents of the ANC also had direct connections to Washington. Pixley ka Isaka Seme, a Zulu graduate of Columbia University who headed the group from 1930 to 1936, visited Tuskegee in 1906.[73] Alfred Xuma, who served as ANC president from 1940 to 1949, arrived at Tuskegee as a student in 1913 and had the distinction of speaking about "Problems in Poultry Raising" at the 1916 commencement when Robert Russa Moton was inaugurated as Washington's successor.[74] On this auspicious occasion, Xuma and the other distinguished guests heard Hollis Burke Frissell speak about the "honor" of contributing to the development of Sheppard.[75]

John Jabavu's son, Davidson, graduated from the University of London and subsequently spent three months at Tuskegee, where he met Xuma in September 1913. Jabavu returned to South Africa, founded the South African Native College at Fort Hare in 1916, and published "Booker T. Washington: What He Would Do if He Were in South Africa" in 1920.[76] In 1936, Davidson Jabavu and Xuma collaborated to lead the All-African Convention, building on an acquaintance that began in Alabama more than two decades earlier. Xuma's biographer Steven Gish correctly points out that his subject's "contact with African-American individuals and institutions . . . symbolized the larger cross-fertilization of ideas that had occurred between the United States and South Africa since the nineteenth century."[77] However, the presence of African students at HBCUs did more than ensure an African American influence in Africa; African students transformed U.S. campuses by rendering modern Africa as something other than an abstraction for their American classmates. The relationships that developed lasted lifetimes, and managed to transcend seeming ideological rifts.

For example, in 1930, when Xuma was writing a book about fellow South African activist Charlotte Manye, he reached out to Du Bois, who taught at Wilberforce University in Ohio from 1894 to 1896, while Manye was a student there. Du Bois wrote a preface for Xuma's biography of Manye, who was friends with Nina Gomer, a Wilberforce student whom Du Bois married: "I have had the opportunity of following her work throughout the glimpses which I have had from far-off South Africa."[78] Du Bois's personal relationship to Manye, who came to the United States with the African Choir, a group in the style of the Fisk Jubilee Singers, complicates Gilroy's assertion that Du Bois's early writings, including *The Souls of Black Folk,* were "so deeply rooted in the post-slave history of the new world that it became difficult for Du Bois's understanding of modernity to incorporate contemporary Africa. Africa emerged instead as a mythic counterpart to modernity in the Americas."[79] Wilberforce, where Manye helped facilitate the enrollment of at least ten additional South African students (including John Dube's younger brother) in the next four years, is an exemplary transatlantic site that did not preclude contemporary Africa in favor of its "mythic counterpart." Du Bois knew Africans at Wilberforce, which, like his studies in Germany, warrants consideration as part of the intellectual and political development of his interest in Africa, even if, as Laura Chrisman observes, Du Bois seems to deliberately elide South Africa in his writings.[80] As Brent Hayes Edwards correctly points out, "'Diaspora' here ultimately functions more as one of the figures for Gilroy's obstinate anti-absolutism and anti-essentialism than as an elaboration of that 'new structure of cultural exchange,'" such as that which took place at Wilberforce in 1895 and 1896.[81]

Du Bois's contact with Manye defies the common presumption that the "concept of Negro liberation and the Pan-Africanism which he developed in the course of his life must be seen largely as an abstraction from his own experiences."[82] Far from an abstraction, Manye was a South African woman who toured the United States and Europe with an African singing group modeled on a black American choir based on the Jubilee tradition that Du Bois canonized in *The Souls of Black Folk.* She returned to South Africa, cofounded a school named Wilberforce Institute, and worked with the ANC. There she used her civil service post with the Johannesburg Juvenile Magistrate to issue passports for South Africans to study in the United States as she had. (With her assistance, Hastings Banda, the first president of Malawi, attended Wilberforce.) Via Manye, Gilroy's chronotope and its essential ingredients—Africa, Europe, and America; choirs, music, and politics—can suggest non-mythic, contemporary sources for Du Bois's understanding of Africa, despite his own seeming disinterest in acknowledging the contributions of personal relationships to his knowledge in this area. This alternative genealogy of Du Bois renders Africa something other than an abstraction for a wide spectrum of African Americans, including Washington who was influenced by his encounters with many South African activists at Tuskegee.

Washington was conscious of Tuskegee's role in this regard, as evident in his decision to host the International Conference on the Negro in April 1912. In his opening remarks, Washington describes the impetus for the meeting, which Sheppard attended and addressed: "For a number of years, we have received here at Tuskegee letters from various parts of the world, letters from missionaries in foreign fields, letters from Governmental officials, especially in Europe, asking for some information that would put them into touch with the methods of education employed here at Tuskegee."[83] Attendees were solicited through a very wide call; invitations were sent to missionaries and colonial governments with the assistance of the U.S. State Department. Representatives from dozens of countries, churches, and missionary organizations met to examine "the methods employed in helping the Negro people of the United States, with a view of deciding to what extent Tuskegee and Hampton methods may be applied to conditions, in these countries, as well as to conditions in Africa."[84] It brought together Sheppard, Work, Park, Turner, and Mark Hayford. Many invitees who could not attend, including Morel, Joseph Casley Hayford, Edward Wilmot Blyden, and Duse Mohamed Ali, sent papers or greetings. It was an extraordinary gathering, which, according to Washington, sought "a more systematic development of constructive educational work on the part of missionaries and governments" in order to more firmly and formally entrench Tuskegee in the colonial African world.[85]

The second role that Washington delineates in "The African at Home"—"sending from Tuskegee men and women trained in our methods, as teachers and workers among the native people"—was realized most comprehensively through a collaboration with German colonial authorities on industrial cotton production in Togo. This project, which "helped transform the political economy of race and agricultural labor characteristic of the New South into a colonial political economy of the global South," had its roots at the 1895 Atlanta Cotton States Exposition where the recently appointed German agricultural attaché Baron Beno von Herman first saw Booker T. Washington. Five years later, von Herman met Washington in Boston and convinced him to recruit African Americans to help the German government develop cotton production technology in Togo under the auspices of the private Colonial Economic Committee. Between 1900 and 1909, a total of nine agronomists from Tuskegee worked in Togo to introduce new methods and technology for cotton production. Several of them died there, including two in a dramatic boat accident that discouraged additional Tuskegee settlers. By 1909, the year *The Story of the Negro* appeared, the collaboration petered out with the tragic drowning death of the last remaining Tuskegee representative, John Winfrey Robinson.[86]

The project was an enormous success for German cotton production, with exports expanding at least sixty-fold during its tenure, reaching a peak of more than 500,000 kilograms per year by 1908–9. Along with increased exports, the project was recognized worldwide for its application of American educational and production methods, and for growing industrial-grade cotton. However, the initiative was disastrous for the Togolese as it was responsible for "bringing to many Africans what counted, by African, American, and European standards, as downward mobility." Its impact, Zimmerman argues, is still being felt in the twenty-first century, as "The work of Tuskegee personnel in German Togo began the colonial transformation of much of West Africa into the undercompensated exporter of raw cotton to international markets that it remains to this day." While Washington participated in at least one other colonial agricultural initiative when the British Cotton Growing Association hired students to work in the Sudan, his influence in colonial Africa extended beyond these commissioned alumni and faculty.[87] Over and above such formal arrangements, Tuskegee provided a model for many unaffiliated educational institutions and economic projects.

There is a literary corollary to the two roles that Washington delineated for Tuskegee in Africa, whereby his philosophies reached people who never visited Tuskegee or met any of its alumni. The North German Mission Society of Bremen distributed translations of *Up from Slavery* to its workers, which enabled Washington's writings to circulate not only in Togo, but throughout the world. *Up from Slavery* was translated into many languages including French, Spanish, German, Norwegian, Swedish, Danish, Dutch, Finnish, Russian, Hindi, Zulu, Marathi, Telugu, Urdu, Malayalam, Arabic, Chinese, and Japanese.[88] Givens its wide circulation, *Up from Slavery* functioned as a textual analogue to the HBCU campus as a "contact zone," which Mary Louise Pratt defines as "the space in which peoples geographically and historically separated come into contact with each other and establish ongoing relations, usually involving conditions of coercion, radical inequality, and intractable conflict."[89] Such entangled genealogies of HBCUs as diasporic contact zones complicate Washington's rhetoric of Southern autonomy. The wide circulation of texts and ideas, as much as the circulation of people, was central to Tuskegee's domestic mission. The extraordinary mobility of Washington's writings rendered his work important to South African activists, Presbyterian missionaries, German colonial administrators, and educators in Ghana, Kenya, Nigeria, Sierra Leone, and around the world.[90] Tuskegee's role in Africa was remarkably consistent with the missionary impulse that Washington uses to frame "The African at Home."

The connections between the Hampton–Tuskegee educational model and international missionary work are deeply rooted in a shared institutional history. Armstrong grew up in Hawai'i, where his missionary parents were stationed. Land reform policies in Hawai'i in the 1830s and 1840s created a demand for industrial education, a task that Armstrong's father embraced so wholeheartedly that he resigned from the pastorate in 1847 to join the government as Minister of Public Instruction.[91] Gary Okihiro reminds us that "The colonization of Hawai'i included prominently the educational work of missionaries . . . and its suppression of native culture and promotion of useful labor and subservience."[92] After the U.S. Civil War, Armstrong applied this colonial model to the rural South, developing Hampton Institute, whose mission was, in the words of historian James D. Anderson, "to train a corps of teachers with a particular social philosophy relevant to the political and economic reconstruction of the South."[93] Subsequently, both Hampton and Tuskegee trained educators to serve Southern rural communities, much as foreign missions like the APCM sought to establish an indigenous pastorate.

Christian missionaries frequently tried to apply Washington's educational model to colonies in Asia, South America, and Africa. In 1902, Robert Elliott Speer, who was Secretary of the Northern Presbyterian Board of Foreign Missions from 1891 to 1937, wrote to Washington about letters he had received with "frequent expressions of appreciation of the value of your example and methods to missionaries." Speer shared a letter from a white Presbyterian missionary who recognized the utility of the Southern example while reading Washington's "autobiography" aloud to a group in Kobe, Japan: "I am a Southerner of the Southerners yet I have a feeling of justifiable pride in recalling that I am a fellow-statesman of Booker T. Washington, also of William H. Sheppard that noble missionary on the lower Congo. His old mother used to be our bath-woman at the Warm Sulphur Springs back in old Virginia. When the negro [sic] race is capable of producing such high types as these truly there is great hope for it."[94] The nostalgia of the unnamed "Southerner of the Southerners" for Sheppard's "old mother" and for "old Virginia" indicates, from another perspective, a continuity between the plantation South and the foreign mission field. Washington's writings traveled seamlessly between missionaries and colonialists, extending far and wide the influence of his philosophy and "life story."[95] In this letter from Japan, the category "such high types" connects the representative Washington to Sarah Frances Martin Sheppard, a freeborn woman who worked at a bathhouse in Virginia.[96] African American missionaries saw the appeal of the Hampton-Tuskegee model; Hawkins published Washington's article "Industrial Schools as an Aid to Missions" in the July 1906 issue of the *Kassai Herald*. As Baker usefully reminds us, "Education becomes the *mission civilatrice* for colonialism everywhere," whether at home or abroad.[97]

Washington offers an extensive comparison of the "country districts" of the South to those regions of Africa, like the Kuba Kingdom, with relatively recent or otherwise limited direct experiences of colonization. Such is the particular appeal of the Congo with its limited ocean coastline and vast territory. In "The West Coast Background of the American Negro," the chapter that follows "The African at Home" in *The Story of the Negro*, Washington differentiates urban from rural, as coastal from "bush," in terms that privilege the latter: "The most self-reliant and substantial characters among my race that I know in the South are those who have been so surrounded as not to get hold of the vices and superficialities of towns and cities, but remained in the country where they lead an independent life."[98] Rather than being locations of modernist hybridity, these contact zones were morally bankrupt threats to the black autonomy Washington sought both in Africa and at Tuskegee, which he envisioned as "a Hampton run entirely by black people."[99] Indeed, Tuskegee's distinctive all-black faculty and staff represented a conservative approach to racial separation that was radical in many of its effects and implications, particularly from the perspective of the colonial world.

In his analysis of interracial contact in *The Story of the Negro*, Washington went even further in identifying a methodological quandary that Africa posed for white observers: "To judge the African by what one may see in these coast towns or by what one may see in South Africa, or in the Nile regions of the Soudan, or wherever the native African has come in close contact with white civilisation, is much the same as if one were to judge the civilisation of America by what one can see in the slums of great cities."[100] In these critical pronouncements, Washington decries white, not European, influence. While he never explicitly states whether or not black APCM missionaries are representatives of "white civilisation," his racial characterization leaves open the possibility that their presence is less destructive than that of their white peers. "Cruelty in the Congo Country" implies something similar when Washington, unlike Twain, notes Sheppard's race.

Washington finds a way to speak about race by comparing the relationship of coastal and interior regions in Africa to the rural-urban dialectic in the United States:

> The Negro people of the country districts in the Southern states are, I suspect, much more like the masses of the Africans, who live beyond the influences of the coast towns, than any other portion of any race in the United States. As often as I can find the time to do so, I get out into the country among this class of people. I like to sleep in their houses, eat their food, attend their churches, talk with them as they plant and

> harvest their crops. In this way I have gotten the inspiration and material for much that I have written and much that I have had to say from time to time about the Negro in America.
>
> In recent years I have noticed among the people, in what I have called "the country districts," a growing distrust for the city, not unlike that distrust of the Africans in the bush for the coast towns.[101]

Washington's comparison suggests that his analysis of the rural South is not only a product of firsthand participant observation but was also illuminated by his understanding of African geography. The appealing milieu of rural African Americans contrasts with city dwellers, positing a parallel relationship between residents of the African interior and the coast. Washington carefully notes intraracial distrust among residents of the American "country districts" and the African "bush." This attitude toward the "country districts" is consistent with Sheppard's experience as a student missionary in isolated areas of the South, which led him to establish African mission stations far away from historical European routes, relatively independent of colonial agents and infrastructure. Washington argues that the masses of continental Africans were more similar to African Americans in the rural South "than any other portion of any race in the United States," explicitly rejecting, as he did in *The Man Farthest Down*, a racially delimited field for comparison.

For Washington, race may be deployed as a point of political identification but not as a means of absolute sociological classification. Similarities between African Americans and Africans resulted as much from shared geographic experiences as from shared racial origins (in the pseudo-scientific sense that those origins were then understood). The absence of discernible parameters of racial categorization rendered race as much a red herring in Africa as in the United States: "it is as hard for one, not an expert, to find the 'true Negro' in Africa—that is without any mixture of foreign blood—as it is to find the colour line in the United States." His argument about Africa has clear implications for the United States. Washington argued, as did Homer Plessy in the Supreme Court case that resulted in the legal codification of the doctrine of separate but equal, that the color line was a fiction. Washington further complicates the notion of the "true Negro" by recognizing "the multitude of different peoples that inhabit Africa and the variety of civilisations represented among its inhabitants."[102] Washington presents an antiessentialist position, built on the premise that intraracial distinctions determined by geography, state, and class are more significant than generalized interracial demarcations. In his writings about Africa, Washington worked to demonstrate that the African continent was not monolithic. His appreciation of this diversity, predicated on an understanding of European colonialism, enables him to take different positions regarding different countries—from Togo to Liberia to the Congo.

## Mobility of the Black Flâneur

As a result of the widespread circulation of Washington's writings and ideas, the Tuskegee model traveled abroad in ways that his person could not. In "The African at Home," he rationalizes the transformation of his relationship to Africa by claiming, fairly enough, that he could be most useful to the continent by working in the United States. In this reappraisal, Washington presents himself as independently deciding not to travel to Africa. However, this obscures the broader colonial context of declining opportunities for African American travel; "The African at Home" was published in 1909, Sheppard's last full year in the Congo. At the time, historian Walter L. Williams explains, the appointments of African American missionaries were increasingly restricted by both white church officials and colonial administrators.[103] The exclusion of African Americans from overseas travel in the decades following George Washington Williams and William Sheppard's 1890 expeditions parallels disfranchisement in the United States. Despite occasional political advisory opportunities for Washington and a small cohort of race leaders, the restrictions on black mobility during the era that Rayford Logan famously labeled the "nadir" circumscribed the range of roles that Washington could imagine for himself. Washington's access to the transatlantic sphere was limited by structural impediments, whether or not he publicly drew attention to them.

"The African at Home" does not refer to Washington's stymied attempts to travel to the continent or how restrictions on black mobility by colonial governments may have helped define Tuskegee's relationship to Africa. Rather, it carefully presents Washington as an autonomous subject whose desire to travel to Africa was a matter of youthful naiveté that he abandoned upon his arrival at Tuskegee in 1881. Washington, however, apparently had not given up the notion entirely since he seriously considered several later invitations. His prospective travel always depended on invitations, which, like the "letters requesting Washington's participation in or presence at ceremonial functions" included in *Up from Slavery*, preserve "the essential illusion that Washington is a modest Negro whose mobility on the American landscape is, in effect, by invitation and not by acts of aggression."[104] Washington carefully prefaces the account of his first trip to Europe that appeared in *Up from Slavery* as such by noting his insistent refusal of the invitation until he "was compelled to surrender."[105]

Many colonial enterprises solicited the assistance of Washington and Tuskegee, the most fully realized being the German cotton industry in Togo, which Washington helped coordinate without traveling there. In 1903, Washington was recruited by British colonial authorities to serve as a consultant in Southern Rhodesia. A few years later, he was invited to serve as an educational advisor in South Africa, an offer he declined only after consulting with President Theodore Roosevelt, a gesture that not only affirmed his status in the United States, but also exposed the tension between his service to the U.S. government and his commitment to Africa.[106] Washington came even closer to traveling to Liberia. Liberian government advisor Harry Johnston, a British explorer who traveled to the Congo with Stanley, acquired a large loan to pay off the country's foreign debt in exchange for a personal rubber concession and British control of the military, which predictably "precipitated a Liberian political crisis."[107] In its aftermath, a Liberian delegation visited the United States, where they were chaperoned by Washington, who Liberia named a knight of the Order of African Redemption and tried to hire as its chargé d'affaires.[108] He attended a series of high-level meetings which gave Johnston the idea "of putting Booker Washington in charge of Liberia." Though Johnston was reportedly "opposed to the American type of Negroes," he and Lord James Bryce, British ambassador to the United States, spent a week at Tuskegee with Washington.[109] Secretary of State Elihu Root welcomed Washington's influence in Liberia. In early 1909, Root was organizing a delegation to Liberia and wanted Washington to join; however, President-Elect William Howard Taft demanded Washington stay in the United States to advise his transition team.[110] Washington "was very happy, however, when ... President Taft decided to relieve me from the necessity of making the trip."[111] In this instance, Washington's domestic service as a "representative of the Negro race" prevented a scheduled visit to Africa; his secretary Emmett J. Scott went in his stead. In the end, "Liberia became an American protectorate similar to that which had recently been imposed on the Dominican Republic," which Washington considered preferable to the seemingly imminent prospect of European colonization.[112]

On this occasion, as on many others, Washington rejected the "*mobility of the black flâneur*," as Baker describes it, and "settled instead for a personal triumphalism and an imperialist power over the back country that were, indeed, remarkable for a black man of his day, but far from the *black fantastic*, then or now."[113] While Washington's domestic imperial power thwarted his attempts to travel to Africa, he managed to visit Europe on three occasions (in 1899, 1903, and 1910) and was planning a fourth trip at the time of his death.[114] This "peculiar mobility," according to Baker, "is both determinately *personal* and *purchased*, at the price of a commitment to imperialism as

Tuskegee Institute's normative relationship to the black 'country districts.'"[115] Washington's European travels were "personal" in their emphasis on "rest" and "recreation," and "purchased" since he traveled with the financial support of Tuskegee's white patrons. He opens *Some European Observations and Experiences* (1899) with an apology that makes his disinclination clear: "It has been a severe and trying ordeal for me to leave the United States just at this time, when there is so much transpiring which concerns the interest of our people, but my friends insisted that I needed the rest and recreation which a trip through Europe would bring, and since they very kindly provided the means, there was nothing for me to do but to accede to their wishes."[116] Mobility is forced upon a reluctant Washington, who reassures his readers that neither his ambition nor his finances would normally permit such a vacation. The notion that Washington need to leave home to find rest contradicts his assertion in *Up from Slavery* that "the time when I get the most solid rest and recreation is when I can be at Tuskegee," which reinforces his deep ties to the South right before recounting his first trip to Europe.[117] More than a decade later, Washington, however, uses the same language to introduce his 1910 trip to Europe as an opportunity for more "rest and recreation."[118] Throughout such seeming contradictions, Washington configures his experiences abroad as "personal," which is distinct from his deep investments elsewhere in his status as "representative." In *Some European Observations and Experiences*, he goes so far as to recommend that others stay in the United States: "I should strongly advise our people against coming to Europe, and especially to Paris, with the hope of securing employment, unless fortified by strong friends and a good supply of money. Within the last week three Afro-American citizens have called to see me, and in each case I have found them in practically a starving condition, and my purse was the worse off by reason of their call."[119] Washington uses his own experiences abroad to oppose emigration and to endorse the Southern political economy that his patronage depended upon. His "personal and purchased" mobility is deployed to inhibit other African Americans.

Washington's observation about the poor living conditions of African Americans in Europe is not simply a happenstance anecdote, but is consistent with Washington's 1895 Atlanta address and integral to his travelogues throughout his career. In the early chapters of *The Man Farthest Down*, Washington tells a similar antiemigration parable with even greater flair. Amid the book's remarkably sober and serious account of social class in Europe, Washington depicts an African American man who, anxious to return to the United States, tells him: "It is a long time since I had watermelon, pig's feet and corn. . . . I can see the pork chops and the corn bread and the hot biscuits calling me to come over and get some and many a time I have tried but failed."[120] Here Washington uses dramatic dialogue to offer a literary variation on "cast down your buckets where you are" by personifying the culinary dangers of not casting down your bucket at home.

In a dispatch from his 1899 trip to Europe, Washington explicitly rejects emigration to Africa as "a solution for our Southern problem." African Americans should stay in the United States, not only because of what their Southern home offers, but also because European colonials have enveloped the entire continent: "All Europe—especially England, France and Germany—has been running a mad race for the last twenty years, to see which could gobble up the greater part of Africa; and there is practically nothing left," including the "Congo Free State [which] is an international African Association," which Washington denotes in pre-1885 nomenclature that marks its rapacious history more clearly than the deliberately misleading "Free State." Washington describes a litany of competing interests in the continent to make the case that, "If we are to go to Africa and be under the control of another government, I think we should prefer to take our chances in the 'sphere of influence' of the United States."[121] He understood the impossibility of an African American relationship to Africa outside of the grasp of European colonialism. The United States held the promise of autonomy in the form of land and home ownership. His suspicions of colonial Africa were reinforced by a meeting with Stanley, which made him "more convinced than ever that there was no hope of the American Negro's improving his condition by emigrating to Africa."[122] Stanley, who, a decade earlier, had advocated for African American involvement in the Congo State, was much less enamored of its prospects after his dealings with George Washington Williams.

In a July 1899 letter to the Washington, D.C., *Colored American* newspaper during his first journey abroad, Washington suggests that Europe is an adequate, if not superior, substitute for Africa: "Outside of Africa there is no better place to study Africa than London, and, in some respects, London is better for a careful investigation than Africa itself."[123] So Washington's immobility vis-à-vis Africa is not an intellectual impediment. More than a decade later, Europe remained a venue for studying Africa. His 1910 trip provided him an opportunity to reconnect with Congo reform comrades Doyle, Harris, and Morel in London. While these reunions are mentioned in *My Larger Education*, Washington curiously omits any reference to Morel or Doyle from *The Man Farthest Down*, his more detailed chronicle of the same voyage. And Washington limits his account of meeting Harris to a discussion of his work with the poor in London's East End, making no mention of Africa, his 1906 CRA tour of the United States, or their earlier association. Whereas Washington's *Colored American* letter and *My Larger Education* imply some connection between his understanding of Africa and his international experiences (even though his itinerary does not include Africa), *The Man Farthest Down*, his most extensive and most conceptually coherent treatment of his European expeditions, divorces his African work from his actual travels abroad, thereby rearticulating the vision that Washington proposes in "The African at Home." Washington's critique of European society can be read as an antiemigration homily that warns against seeing Europe as a utopia, offsetting any critiques of the treatment of African Americans in the United States with its emphasis on what Washington considers the far worse conditions of many white Europeans. *The Man Farthest Down* looks to Europe in order to debunk the more vicious racial explanations for inequality and discrimination in the United States.[124]

Washington consistently writes against the tradition of prominent African American travelers to Europe that Gilroy highlights in *The Black Atlantic*. The desire of Washington's informant to leave England for the South's cuisine, for instance, contrasts with Gilroy's reading of Ida B. Wells's account of "her productive times in England as like 'being born again in a new condition'" as "typical," which is an example of the kinds of "totalising claims" that Chrisman critiques in Gilroy.[125] Whereas Gilroy finds England to be a transformative site for African American intellectuals, Washington writes of an African American man who finds himself stuck in London, a site that is "historically, and structurally, oppressive for blacks from colonies."[126] While there is no evidence to suggest that Wells is necessarily less representative than Washington's informant, Washington's use of the anecdote reveals conflicting images of Europe among African American leaders. *The Black Atlantic*'s focus on Europe and its omission of Washington's travel writings is notable, albeit understandable. Washington's travels in Europe are a peculiar exposé of the limitations of cosmopolitan mobility that serves to claim a transatlantic mantle for Tuskegee Institute and other HBCUs as archetypes of emergent global black cultures.

However, in 1899, Washington anticipated that his first European tour would provide an opportunity for him to explore the African diaspora, an attitude very much in line with Gilroy's reading of Europe. Indeed, Washington writes, "One of the things I had in mind when I came to France, was to visit the tomb of Toussaint L'Ouverture," which is stymied when he realizes that there is no "proper memorial" to the leader of the Haitian Revolution.[127] In 1909, Washington privately noted that "during the past two or three years, I have been taking advantage of such leisures as I had to dig into the history of the African people."[128] By the time he wrote *The Man Farthest Down*, however, Washington publicly eschewed the significance of any sort of past as a matter of principle, going so far as to avoid museums during his European travels, claiming: "I have never been greatly interested in the past, for the past is something that you cannot change. I like the new, the unfinished and the problematic."[129] Washington's increasingly ahistorical pragmatism enables him to privilege contemporary concerns without acknowledging a continuity between the past experiences of African Americans and their current circumstances.

With regard to Africa, Washington's public disregard of the past contrasts with the romantic tradition that Gilroy identifies: "Blacks are urged, if not to forget the slave experience which appears as an aberration from the story of greatness told in African history, then to replace it at the centre of our thinking with a mystical and ruthlessly positive notion of Africa."[130] For Gilroy, the Afrocentric celebration of classical African civilization has obfuscated more pertinent, if less glamorous, aspects of black history. However, Washington does more than not romanticize the past; according to *The Man Farthest Down*, he does not even care about it. More importantly, Washington's oeuvre is part of a tradition of African American writers and intellectuals whose work on Africa is animated by modern political affairs. Washington's writings about the Congo suggest models of African American identification with Africa that are not "mystical," "ruthlessly positive," or obsessed with origins, but rather based on overlapping networks of influence that include African students, missionaries, political activists, and HBCUs.

The dramatic limitations on Washington's mobility and his modernity defined his relationship to diaspora. For all of his unrealized opportunities to travel to Africa, Washington represents one of the "precursor *modernisms*," which ultimately lacks the more inclusive transatlantic political vision of what Baker terms "Afro-modernity . . . the general effects of African, African diasporic, and Afro-American people's 'stride toward freedom,' their move toward cosmopolitan mobility of citizenship, work, cultural reclamation and production that enhance the lives of a black majority globally conceived." Baker concludes, "The preeminent dynamics of Afro-modernity are the 'search' for Africa, the query 'What is Africa to me?'" that opens Countee Cullen's poem "Heritage."[131] While Washington never achieved the level of cosmopolitan mobility needed to facilitate an Afro-modern realization of global black empowerment, his career manifests an implicit diasporic sensibility and a pragmatic, rather than meditative or poetic, "search" akin to Cullen's poetic query. Indeed pragmatism is built, in part, on a recognition that European colonialism saturated all connections to Africa.

Baker posits the South as a metonym for the United States, which had been defined by the racialized control of space and mobility—from the Middle Passage's ships to plantation slavery to convict labor to modern imprisonment. Baker adapts Washington's South for the critical sphere, a reconfiguration that can be expanded geographically to the international field. Such a maneuver should not be unexpected since, throughout this period, historian C. Vann Woodward acknowledges, "the North... was looking to Southern racial policy for national guidance in the new problems of imperialism resulting from the Spanish war."[132] Washington's South was an international exemplar for a nation defining new relationships with its colonies in the Caribbean and Pacific. Building on Zimmerman's research, we can move beyond the South, the Western Hemisphere, and the traditional U.S. sphere of influence to recognize the ways that Washington and Tuskegee promoted what Carla Willard calls "a model of global uplift based on southern example."[133]

Washington's ambivalence toward radical politics in Africa was offset by the international circulation of many of his best-known domestic writings, which made an anticolonial argument against Northern and federal government intervention in the South however problematic it might be in the context of the intensifying terrorism of the post-Reconstruction era. While Washington collaborated with European colonial administrators and was popular among conservative white missionaries, the mission of Tuskegee was appealing to black nationalist leaders throughout the diaspora. Marcus Garvey, for example, began a correspondence with Washington (and later with Scott and Moton) from his home in Jamaica after reading *Up from Slavery* and featured a Washington quote atop the Universal Negro Improvement Association's (UNIA) Jamaica letterhead.[134] More than Washington's colonial collaborations, Tuskegee provided a model for building independent institutions for people of African descent. The 1915 death of Washington, who came to international prominence in the year that Douglass died, was followed in 1916 by the arrival of Garvey in the United States. Despite Washington's popularity among radicals in the African diaspora, the wizard of Tuskegee remained committed to the South. As he was dying, he rejected his doctor's orders to remain in New York and insisted on returning to Tuskegee: "I was born in the South, I have lived and labored in the South, and I expect to die and be buried in the South."[135] Up until his death, he told the story of living and laboring in the South though he was, for two decades, a national leader and an international icon. As if scripted, Washington died the day after he disembarked the train at Chehaw Station, Alabama.

PART II

# The Twentieth-Century Cultures of the American Congo

*Chapter 4*

Missionary Cultures

*The American Presbyterian Congo Mission,*
*Althea Brown Edmiston, and the Languages of the Congo*

The American Presbyterian Congo Mission (APCM) was extraordinarily successful in recruiting African Americans to its ranks. For every William Sheppard who served in Africa, there were many more Booker T. Washingtons who dreamed of doing so but found themselves without the opportunity. Among the latter was a young Mary McLeod (Bethune) who, in 1894, submitted her application to the Northern Presbyterian Church (PCUSA), which, on the advice of white Lincoln University theology professor Robert Laird Stewart, decided against racially integrating its mission.[1] Her application is indicative of the popular appeal of Africa to accomplished young African Americans, and the unrealized possibilities for APCM recruitment: "They informed me that no openings were available where they could place Negro missionaries, so they sent me to Augusta, Georgia to work."[2] The Northern Mission Board did not refer McLeod to the APCM as they did Joseph Phipps, who, beginning in 1895, served in the Congo for fifteen years. Unlike Washington, Bethune eventually found her way to the continent. Nearly sixty years later in 1952, she traveled to Liberia "as a representative of the United States Government" for the second inauguration of President William V. S. Tubman.[3]

A few years after Bethune was rejected by the Northern Presbyterians, the APCM accepted the application of Althea Maria Brown, who became one of its most accomplished missionaries. She was born in Rolling Fork, Mississippi, on December 17, 1874, and grew up hearing family stories about Africa, including her grandfather James Madison Brown's tales of "his grandmother and the tales she told of how she was brought directly from Africa in chains."[4] James Madison Brown died in 1897, at the age of 100, while Althea was studying at Fisk University. She knew that Fisk had been sending missionaries to Africa since 1878 when Albert P. Miller and A.E. Jackson joined the American Missionary Association (AMA) Mendi mission in Sierra Leone.[5] Brown, who was a leader on campus, was focused on a similar goal.[6] She applied to the APCM even before she graduated. On May 14, 1901, she appeared before the Southern Presbyterian Church (PCUS) Executive Committee of Foreign Missions (ECFM), which conditionally supported her application

*Figure 4.1* William Henry Sheppard, "Maxamalinge" William Lapsley Sheppard, Lucy Sheppard, Althea Brown Edmiston, and Joseph E. Phipps, likely at Ibanche (c. 1903–4). (Box 4, WHSPA, Courtesy of Presbyterian Historical Society, Philadelphia, Pennsylvania.)

pending additional theological study.[7] A month later, as the only female graduation speaker, Brown delivered a valedictory address—"What Missionaries Have Done for the World"—that foretold her future plans.[8] A year later, on June 10, 1902, after a year at the Chicago Training School for City, Home, and Foreign Missions, Althea Brown returned to the committee, which, after conceding "we do not see our way clear to appoint a white missionary to Africa at present," approved her application.[9] In October, she arrived in Matadi, and after spending seven weeks at Luebo, she joined the Sheppards and Phipps at Ibanche: "Then and there I lost my American name, and have been known ever since by the Bakuba as Mbawota" (transcribed elsewhere as "Biwata" and "Mbawata").[10] (Among the Baluba, her name was Mamu Tshitolo.) (See Figure 4.1.)

Immediately after her appointment, she immersed herself in linguistic projects.[11] Her proclivity was consistent with several of the earliest African American pioneers like William Sheppard, whose addresses were often "intermingled with words and expressions in African dialect," and Maria Fearing, who earned her full appointment, in part, because "she had mastered the native language."¹² By 1905, Brown, writing as "Biwata," published *Nkana mu Ilonga. Bamamukalal a buola*, a Kuba catechism with a prefatory note: "Although the greek [sic] word Nyuma is used for the Holy Spirit, it will be interesting to foreign instructors to know that the Bakuba have the word Baxula, meaning the third in a trinity."¹³ This seemingly technical linguistic note anticipates questions from Kuba parishioners about the concept of the holy trinity, and demonstrates her interest in how a central tenet of Christianity can be incorporated into a Bantu language and worldview. After the catechism, Althea Brown Edmiston, as she was then known, turned to her more comprehensive linguistic project, completing the *Grammar and Dictionary of Bushonga or Bukuba Language* in 1913. The church, however, refused to authorize its publication for nearly twenty years.¹⁴

Brown took up the Bushong language of the Kuba at a time when the colonial government was promoting the Tshiluba language as a regional lingua franca. The APCM promptly followed the state's lead. In 1906, Henry Hawkins published some Tshiluba translations of scripture as *Mukanda wa Malu a Kukema* and, most crucially, William Morrison published his *Grammar and Dictionary of the Buluba-Lulua Language* to be "helpful to Government officials, traders or travelers."¹⁵ Ironically, Morrison, who had recently agitated against the colonial regime, provided, through his dictionary, an important cog in its wheel. By the time of his death in 1918, Morrison had translated much of the Bible and dozens of hymns into Tshiluba, further codifying the state's preferred regional language. As one of the largest colonial-era publishers of Tshiluba materials, the APCM's J. Leighton Wilson Press at Luebo provided crucial support for the colonial project.¹⁶

As a binational language spoken in variation by both Baluba and Lulua, Tshiluba was less identified with a unified indigenous political tradition than was Bushong whose speakers represented a single ethnic group. In the eyes of religious and governmental authorities, local languages like Bushong were deemed at best unnecessary and at worst a threat. Strong regional identities and, more importantly, indigenous political power could be undermined by language policy whereby "the Bakuba were being reached with the use of the Buluba tongue."¹⁷ Althea Brown Edmiston resisted this APCM policy, which helped transform citizens of linguistically identified cultural groups into colonial subjects. In Katanga at this time, for instance, centralized language policy was an increasingly important instrument of colonial management.¹⁸ Comparably, in the Kasai, the mission's devaluation of the Bushong language was a by-product of a shift toward Tshiluba. The participation of the APCM in the politically expedient regional promotion of Tshiluba, if not a deliberate effort to ingratiate themselves with the Belgian authorities, represents the increasingly intertwined relationship between missions and colonialism, both of which, V.Y. Mudimbe points out, "implied the same purpose: the conversion of African minds and space."[19]

Before the APCM fully shifted its focus to Tshiluba, they published several additional Bushong projects including, in 1902 and 1908, readers written by Lucy Sheppard. African Americans played an especially instrumental role in translating hymns, which are generally the mission's most popular religious texts. Fearing headed an early committee responsible for reviewing the musical integrity of all hymn translations.[20] In 1909, the APCM published a Bushong hymnal *Nkana mu Ncema*—entirely translated by African American missionaries including Althea Brown Edmiston, William Sheppard, Lucy Sheppard, Joseph Phipps, and Katie Taylor (Rochester)—in a volume bound with its Tshiluba hymnal, *Mukanda wa Misambu*, whose first edition Lucy Gantt Sheppard compiled in 1898.[21] In the first edition of *Mukanda wa Misambu*, nearly half of the translations were the work of African American missionaries (though later editions exclude many early translations by African Americans, including all of those from the Sheppards and Lillian Thomas DeYampert).[22] None of the Tshiluba translations in the 1909 volume, however, were the work of Althea Brown Edmiston, who was not, at this point, working in the language.

## The Edmiston Affair

Althea Brown became Althea Brown Edmiston after her July 8, 1905, marriage to Alonzo Edmiston. In early 1904, Alonzo arrived in the Congo with his Stillman Institute professor Samuel Phillips Verner, who was "on a business trip" to bring Congolese people for display at the St. Louis World's Fair.[23] They were joined by John Kondola, whom Edmiston knew as a Congolese fellow student at Stillman.[24] Within weeks of their arrival, Verner and Edmiston apparently had a falling out. Edmiston abandoned his former teacher and headed out alone to visit another Stillman classmate Lucius DeYampert at Luebo station. Was Edmiston's departure, as Pamela Newkirk speculates, a way of protesting his professor's troubling "assignment to hunt 'pygmies'?"[25] In early May 1904, Verner began his trek to St. Louis, via New Orleans, with nine Congolese young men, half the number commissioned, which indicates that Verner faced unanticipated resistance in his enterprise. Meanwhile, Edmiston walked from Luebo to Ibanche, where he met Althea Brown, who was appointed to the APCM at the same time as DeYampert.[26] Edmiston, a theology graduate of Stillman who, inspired by Sheppard, had begun medical studies with the intention of serving as a missionary in Africa, decided to remain in the Congo. He quickly fell in with the APCM, which welcomed him as "an unlooked for, but badly needed, assistant," and, on August 9, 1904, with the "hearty sympathy" and support of Verner, he was conditionally approved by the ECFM, which waited for the endorsement of his U.S. home presbytery before finalizing his appointment on November 8. Edmiston, who was "royally entertained" by Brown at her home in Ibanche, soon proposed marriage which was approved by the ECFM on October 11, 1904.[27]

Alonzo Edmiston's rapid affiliation with the APCM affirms his clear desire and intention, whether spoken or not, to remain in the Congo.[28] Although their marriage was a wedding of two missionaries, Alonzo's hiring was probably predicated on their relationship, which was the easiest avenue for appointment and a way to circumvent any racial restrictions. There was some drama when Chester wrote to a white missionary to "express the approbation of the Committee with reference to the action taken by the Mission in regard to the marriage," another instance of how the church policed the relationships of its black missionaries.[29] This cryptic "action," taken more than a year after the ECFM conditionally approved their marriage, suggests that the mission did something without executive approval. Whatever the details, Chester's correspondence reveals that the church had concerns about the role of the Edmistons on the APCM from the earliest days of their careers even though they were respected enough by their peers that Alonzo Edmistion was elected to chair the APCM in 1907.[30]

In early 1908, the couple went on leave under murky circumstances described in correspondence as "the Edmiston affair" for which Althea sent "a number of letters to different members of the Mission . . . expressing her deep regret at the turn matters have taken, and pleading to be returned."[31] After Althea left the Congo in January 1908 with their first child Sherman Lucius "Kuetu" Edmiston (born May 26, 1906), Alonzo submitted his resignation, but was forced to remain in the Congo another six months until Motte Martin returned.[32] (See Figure 4.2.) In a letter to Chester, Sheppard and Morrison described a "long provocation" and "deeply regret the whole affair and the pain which it has given both to us and to Mr. and Mrs. Edmiston."[33] The written record on their case is full of deliberate circumspection, but the transgression was not sexual since there was "no moral delinquency charged against the individuals involved."[34] After the Edmistons returned to the United States, the issues continued to be discussed, still obliquely, in the context of whether or not they should be allowed to go back in the field. An August 1910 letter from Chester to Morrison asserts the importance of dealing with "this matter so as to prevent its getting before the public in such a way as to give us trouble and possibly do harm to the Cause." The unspecified issues, including "Mr. Edmiston's business relations with the Mission at the time of his leaving and since," seem to have shifted to include the

*Figure 4.2* Althea Brown Edmiston, Alonzo Edmiston, and son Sherman Kuetu Edmiston (c. 1907). (Vass Family Papers, RG 476, Box 17. Courtesy of Vass Family and Presbyterian Historical Society, Philadelphia, Pennsylvania.)

now-retired William Sheppard, even though he was a signatory to the Edmistons' original censure. Chester sent Morrison a "word of caution suggesting that the brethren be very careful in writing both to the Edmistons and to Dr. Sheppard to avoid anything that would be likely to leave a wrong impression on their minds in regard to the Mission's attitude on any matter in which they are concerned."[35] Nearly a decade later, when Chester accused Lillian Thomas DeYampert of being "entirely occupied with your own domestic affairs," "extravagant in your manner of living," and "not always amaiable [sic] and pleasant in your dealings with other missionaries," he compared her case to that of the Edmistons.[36] Its legacy cast a long shadow.

It is likely that the broader cultural disconnect between African American and white APCM missionaries was at play. Chester suggested that the problem with Althea Edmiston was her Fisk education, writing to Morrison that "the origin of the trouble" lies with "certain influences exerted on the students of a certain institution in this country. I think we will be safe in the future in seeking all colored reinforcements for Africa among those who have not attended that institution."³⁷ Although Chester does not name the "certain institution," it seems likely that he had Fisk in mind. (The other possibilities would be Talladega College, an institution with American Missionary Association roots similar to those of Fisk, which sent three women to the APCM in the 1890s, or Stillman, where Alonzo studied with Verner.)

The Edmistons' case arose at a crucial moment in the annals of not only the APCM, with Sheppard's trial on the horizon, but also of the Congo, as Leopold was formally transferring control to Belgium. The PCUS recognized its stake in colonial politics by passing a resolution urging the United States to oppose Belgium's annexation of Congo on the grounds that it did not provide sufficient guarantees of reform. After Belgium took control of the Congo in 1908, tension between Belgian officials and American missionaries increased, as did pressure on African American missionaries, several of whom were dismissed at that time on the specious basis of sexual liaisons. In 1908, Chester unsuccessfully sought the resignation of William B. Scott, an unmarried white Scottish missionary, and Katie Ann Taylor, an unmarried African American woman, for a rumored romantic relationship that Taylor ultimately quashed by marrying Adolphus Rochester, a black colleague.³⁸ Morrison suggests some sort of collective guilt, if not punishment, of African Americans, noting that "our colored people especially regret the affair."³⁹

Whatever its motivation and rationale, the ECFM worked hard to block the return of the Edmistons to Africa, even after the APCM formally approved their return based on their "hope that the real cause of the previous trouble has been sincerely removed."⁴⁰ In an August 16, 1910, letter, Chester explained, "In view of all the experience of the past few years, I am confident that our Committee will deem it wise to send out white re-inforcements to Africa for the present," carefully noting that, "We do not think it necessary or wise to make any public proclamation of this policy."⁴¹ Indeed, there were no public proclamations; later church accounts explain the delay as due to "lack of funds."⁴² "All the experience of the past few years"—whether Sheppard's trial, the Edmiston affair, the Scott-Taylor affair, or the inability to control the sexual lives of its black missionaries—led the Presbyterian Church to reconsider the role of African Americans on its missions.

The ECFM continued to delay the Edmistons' reappointment, asking they be preceded by six white missionaries (euphemistically "first-class people"): "The Edmistons, of course, can fill a place, but we want men who can do theological teaching, superintend Schools and evangelistic work, and do translation."⁴³ The grammar of this sentence is difficult to parse, but it could be read to suggest that the ECFM wanted missionaries who do traditional religious tasks, as well as translation, rather than someone who prioritized translation as Edmiston did. On August 20, 1910, Chester sent Alonzo

Edmiston a differing account, attributing the decision to an APCM meeting at which "a motion was passed asking for your recall, but on the condition that your return would not interfere with the sending out of six other new missionaries."[44] The ECFM's stated preferences make it clear that "other" means "white." The public absence of racial rhetoric reflects the committee's conscious management of policy and information in racial terms. In any event, resistance to the reappointment of the Edmistons was consistent with a general prohibition against the appointment of new African American missionaries that Presbyterians shared with other denominations. Chester discourages the Edmistons, telling them that their return will be delayed at least one year, and that they should seek employment domestically. It was disingenuous of Chester to provide any hope since as late as February 14, 1911, "the Committee had difinitely [sic] decided not to send them back to Africa."[45] However, their supporters, including William Sheppard, who visited the Edmistons in Tuscaloosa during this period, ultimately held sway and the couple returned to the Congo on October 11, 1911. Their son Kuetu remained in the United States with relatives.[46]

## Do Bana Coba

After returning from furlough in 1911, Althea Edmiston remained steadfast in her commitment to her Bushong dictionary. As Tshiluba was becoming more deeply entrenched, she began to work in it by translating Presbyterian hymns. Soon thereafter, she added African American spirituals to the Tshiluba corpus. Through this project, she was able to mediate the hegemony of the colonial lingua franca by ensuring that the APCM promoted a version of Tshiluba that was not simply an instrument of the state, but rather a language that incorporated a musical tradition that James Weldon Johnson was "reaffirming . . . as the cultural centerpiece of African-America as a whole."[47] The transatlantic circulation of music was deeply embedded in the culture of the APCM. Music was also important to William Sheppard, who appears in archival photographs from the Congo variously with a phonograph, marching band, and banjo.[48] (See, for example, Figure 4.3.) Lucy Gantt Sheppard collaborated with her husband on public programs throughout the United States, where, to much acclaim, she used her experience as a Jubilee Singer to perform "with simple pathos and deep feeling hymns which, though in the dialect of an African tribe, were also in the language of the heart."[49] Edmiston conceptualized musical work as foundational to her missionary service: on her first trip, she "brought from America a portable organ, and though not a trained musician, she used what knowledge she had to teach the

*Figure 4.3* William Sheppard playing the banjo. (Box 4, WHSPA. Courtesy of Presbyterian Historical Society, Philadelphia, Pennsylvania.)

young people of the community the reading of musical scores, and to direct a chorus choir."[50]

The translations of spirituals such as "Swing Low, Sweet Chariot," "Nobody Knows da Trouble I Seen," "Steal Away," and "I Couldn't Hear Nobody Pray" into Tshiluba offer a narrative of colonial exchange whereby APCM missionaries like Edmiston introduced the cultural vehicles of postbellum African American religious, educational, and economic independence into a developing colonial language system.[51] These translations were contemporary to *The Souls of Black Folk*, which is a frequent starting point for discussions of spirituals. By the time Du Bois arrived at Fisk as a student in 1885, the pioneering Jubilee Singers, who "sang the slave songs so deeply into the world's heart that it can never wholly forget them again," were an international phenomenon.[52] Edmiston was likely familiar with *The Souls of Black Folk*, as it was published by the most celebrated alumnus of her alma mater a year after her graduation; she visited Fisk during her 1908–11 furlough, before she began translating spirituals. Du Bois uses the spirituals—African American religious music with roots both in Africa and the United States—as his book's

Missionary Cultures   117

central trope. Each of its fourteen chapters is headed by a poetic verse followed by several meters of musical notation. His sources for the musical transcriptions are *Hampton and Its Students* and *The Story of the Jubilee Singers*, publications that did not simply document performance, but also served to promote and raise funds for their institutions.[53] Furthermore, these books, like Du Bois's own, transformed the vernacular of performance into print form. The APCM accomplished something similar by publishing translations of several of these same songs in Tshiluba.

In the final chapter of *The Souls of Black Folk*, "The Sorrow Songs," Du Bois discusses the music directly and identifies the songs whose music he quoted earlier. "Of Our Spiritual Strivings," the first chapter, featured bars from "Nobody Knows da Trouble I Seen," which was translated in 1947 by Winifred Kellersberger Vass, a white missionary and one of the APCM's most accomplished linguists. "The Faith of the Fathers," chapter 10, begins with "Steal Away," which was translated by Lucius DeYampert, who served from 1902 to 1918.[54] Edmiston herself translated the iconic "Swing Low, Sweet Chariot," which Du Bois uses to head chapter 12, "On Alexander Crummell." For Du Bois, songs like "My Lord, What a Mourning! When the Stars Begin to Fall" (commonly titled elsewhere "My Lord, What a Morning"), which heads chapter 2 ("Of the Dawn of Freedom"), support an attempt "to refashion the notion of 'soul' into an idea capable of evoking race unity as well as resurrection from the bondage of race slavery." Eric Sundquist proposes an "African meaning" of the song because "in Kongo lore falling stars have been interpreted as spirits flashing across the sky." Sundquist's interpretation of "Kongo lore," based on Robert Farris Thompson's *Flash of the Spirit*, can be read as part of a broader diasporic formulation: "The failure of Reconstruction and the rise of more virulent, and often legally sanctioned, racism must now be answered by an awakening of the many 'nations' of Africa. The spirits of the ancestors, in the homeland as well as in the diaspora, need to be fused with those present generations who continue to lead an oppressed 'underground' existence."[55]

Du Bois's most notable and enigmatic gesture toward an African, possibly Kongo, musical lineage in "The Sorrow Songs" occurs when he introduces "Do bana coba," an African song sung by his great great grandmother:

> Do bana coba, gene me, gene me!
> Do bana coba, gene me, gene me!
> Ben d' nuli, nuli, nuli, nuli, ben d' le.[56]

This song is incorporated into the final chapter and the musical notation accompanies the undeciphered lyrics, which function, as Tsitsi Jaji describes South African music of the same era, as "an alternative to translation, conveying music as a sonic sign unbounded by linguistic specificity" which

*Figure 4.4* "Do bana coba" from chapter 14, "Of the Sorrow Songs," of W. E. B. Du Bois, *The Souls of Black Folk* (1903; Chicago: A. C. McClurg, 1915), p. 254.

enables it to "access common structures of feeling across diverse communities."[57] (See Figure 4.4.) Du Bois's use of musical notation places the song within the tradition that *The Souls of Black Folk* establishes even though none of the other spirituals (with the exception of "Let Us Cheer the Weary Traveller") feature titles or lyrics, making them easily identifiable only to those who can read music and recognize the melody—those who are, to use Du Bois's language, "within the Veil."[58] Musically, Farah Jasmine Griffin points out, "Do bana coba" "appear[s] as a modified blues form, with the repetition of the first two lines before the resolution of the third. Furthermore, he transcribes the song in the complex, dark key of D-flat, one of the keys favored by African American improvisers."[59] For Du Bois, the illegibility of the lyrics, here as in the musical headers, is effectively the point. In *The Souls of Black Folk*, he follows the music with the explanation: "The child sang it to his children and they to their children's children, and so two hundred years it has travelled down to us and we sing it to our children, knowing as little as our fathers what its words may mean, but knowing well the meaning of its music."[60] Following Du Bois's modus, Ivor Miller makes a similar point regarding "the importance of music in cultural transmission in the African Americas; through rhythm and repetition, language is remembered even if the meanings are lost to the present generation."[61] Miller foregrounds the music, despite providing Fu-Kiau Bunseki's compelling translation of the lyrics. Bunseki deems it a heavily creolized version of a Kikongo (Bantu)

Missionary Cultures 119

lullaby, which fits Du Bois's attribution of the song in *Darkwater* and *The Autobiography of W. E. B. Du Bois* to an eighteenth-century ancestor, "a little, black, Bantu woman, who never became reconciled to this strange land."[62]

The mystery of Du Bois's ancestry remained throughout his life, as he repeated the 1903 account in several autobiographical texts. Early in the first chapter of *Darkwater*, Du Bois quotes this Bantu song as a lyric couplet without repeating the first line or providing musical notation.[63] By doing so, he removes two of its structural qualities—repetition and key—that mark it as blues. The absence of musical notation heightens its illegibility and further dissociates it from the sorrow songs. Correspondingly, *Darkwater* does not include his explanation of "knowing well the meaning of its music," which even further highlights the incomprehensibility of the untranslated couplet. The lyrics are not accessible to readers of *Darkwater* in the same way they would be to the children who he describes hearing it in *Souls*. As a result, the song—and Africa—become much less legible. Another variation appears in *Dusk of Dawn: An Essay toward an Autobiography of a Race Concept* (1940), where Du Bois preserves the repetition but drops the musical notation. However he discursively privileges the absent music by directly quoting his own discussion of the song in *The Souls of Black Folk*, which emphasizes the generational transmission of musical knowledge. In addition, Du Bois here follows the account with the opening ten-line stanza from his former son-in-law Countee Cullen's 1925 poem "Heritage," whose repeated query "*What is Africa to me?*" is employed to foreground the ephemeral quality of his relationship to Africa.[64] In a final version in his posthumously published *Autobiography*, Du Bois recalls his Bantu ancestor from *Darkwater* without the musical accompaniment or lyrical repetition that appear in *Souls* and *Dusk of Dawn*.[65]

While Du Bois's attention to "Do bana coba" is evidence of his ongoing efforts, shared by black missionaries, to articulate a connection to Africa through music, he unconvincingly tries to minimize the affective possibilities of these earlier encounters: "My African racial feeling was then purely a matter of my own later learning and reaction."[66] This leads Sundquist to argue, "Du Bois's view of Africa, despite his command of recent historiography and his incisive theoretical understanding of the colonial problem (he was less precise when it came to local detail), was overwhelmingly romantic."[67] Kwame Anthony Appiah, who makes no mention of "Do bana coba," similarly sees a "romantic primitivism" in Du Bois's writings on Africa, but is compelled to clarify his remarks in a lengthy endnote: "I don't want to reduce Du Bois's scholarly engagement with Africa, let alone his Pan-African activism, to a mode of self-exploration: he was a committed foe of colonialism and imperialism."[68] While the readings by Sundquist and Appiah are exemplary,

Simon Gikandi sees greater intentionality in Du Bois's earlier essay "The Conservation of Races": "Africa, then, remained a realm of experience that was intangible and fragmentary, very much like the grandmother's song cited earlier; and yet it needed to be mobilized toward certain political ends, and in this sense, it needed to be made visible. In regard to the meaning of Africa to the African American, Du Bois needed to symbolize the imaginary, or to materialize the phenomenal."[69] Du Bois's own repetition of the lyric was a material gesture, rather than a romantic one, which transforms what Sundquist characterizes as his "transgeographical and Pan-African" appeal into the more direct forms of political engagement that are central to this study.[70]

By situating "Do bana coba" within a tradition of African American spirituals, Du Bois foregrounds an ongoing process of transatlantic exchange and invites a kind of inverted excavation that makes visible additional migrations from Afro-America to the Congo by way of Fisk University and figures such as Althea Brown Edmiston. While the precise source of "Do bana coba" remains subject to debate, the spirituals continued to circulate from the United States to Africa and back again across routes that were familiar to Du Bois. The international influence of the Fisk Jubilee Singers extended beyond their prestigious performances for Queen Victoria. After touring Europe and Australia with Frederick Loudin's Fisk Jubilee Singers (the group with which Lucy Gantt Sheppard also performed), Orpheus McAdoo, Washington's Hampton classmate, toured South Africa with his own ensemble, the Virginia Jubilee Singers (alternately known as the Virginia Concert Choir), throughout the 1890s. There they inspired South African singers to form the African Choir to raise funds for a black industrial school.[71] After successful tours of Europe and the United States, the African Choir's manager abandoned the singers in the United States where they managed to enroll at HBCUs. Through this network, Charlotte Manye became the first South African student to enroll at Wilberforce University, where her previously discussed friendship with Du Bois forcefully suggests that his appreciation of the transatlantic circulation of African American spirituals predates *The Souls of Black Folk* by nearly a decade.[72]

Later, in his *Autobiography*, written in the final years of his life, Du Bois implies that his arrival at Wilberforce exposed the limits of his European education: "I did not at all understand the implications of the Matabele War in 1893. I did not see how the gold and diamonds of South Africa and later the copper, ivory, cocoa, tin and vegetable oils of other parts of Africa and especially the black labor force were determining and conditioning the political action of Europe." In the same chapter, he recalls that his departure from Wilberforce for the University of Pennsylvania occurred in the same "year Abyssinia vanquished Italy; and England, suddenly seeing two black nations threatening her Cape-to-Cairo plans, threw her army back into the Sudan and recaptured Khartoum."[73] By the end of his life, Du Bois frames his experience at Wilberforce in terms of colonial history and politics, even if his failure to name Manye serves to mystify the process of exchange. Even before these anticolonial epiphanies, Du Bois's writings about culture, including the Fisk Singers, could not be confined within the parameters of "romantic primitivism." More than a half century before the *Autobiography*, Du Bois makes it clear that his interest in the sorrow songs is closely aligned with what Gikandi describes as an effort to "materialize the phenomenal." Writing in "The Sorrow Songs," Du Bois explains: "To me Jubilee Hall seemed ever made of the songs themselves, and its bricks were red with the blood and dust of toil. Out of them rose for me morning, noon, and night, bursts of wonderful melody, full of the voices of my brothers and sisters, full of the voices of the past."[74]

Althea Edmiston had a similar affinity for Jubilee Hall, which she tried to recreate as soon as she arrived in the Congo. She christened her home, "Jubilee Cottage," after the campus building raised by the Fisk Jubilee Singers.[75] Revenue from the Fisk Singers imbued the campus infrastructure with a strong material connection to its most well-known cultural product. Evidence was elsewhere in the physical plant—the entrance to Jubilee Hall was "wainscoted with beautiful wood, alternated in dark and light, brought from the Mendi Mission, West Africa."[76] Shortly after the 1876 dedication of Jubilee Hall, the American Missionary Association sent several Fisk graduates to the Sierra Leone mission.[77] At the building's dedication, Gustavus D. Pike, who first compiled the Jubilee Songs in 1872, spoke on "The Possibilities of African Civilization," covering topics from classical Egyptian civilization to the political economy of the transatlantic slave trade.[78] African missionary work was a central part of the university's broader transatlantic mission.

## Swing Low, Sweet Chariot

Like "Do bana coba," "Swing Low, Sweet Chariot" is another song with possible Congolese origins. Du Bois quotes its music to open "Of Alexander Crummell," a chapter's whose iconic Pan-African subject he met at Wilberforce (the same place he met Manye) in 1895.[79] As Sundquist persuasively argues, "'Swing Low, Sweet Chariot' was transparently available to being coded with the ideology of resistance to and escape from slavery.... A more radical interpretation would insist that the home was the motherland of Africa, the true destination of at least some slaves (or colonizationists) and the spiritual world to which some assumed they would return after death."[80] James Weldon Johnson makes a comparable musical association in *The Book of American Negro Spirituals* (1925), which presents "Swing Low, Sweet

Chariot" as an exemplary song "built upon the form so common to African songs, leading lines and response."[81]

The possible Congolese origins of "Swing Low, Sweet Chariot" come into clearer focus in Charles S. Johnson's 1927 New Negro anthology *Ebony and Topaz*. In a short essay, the white musicologist Dorothy Scarborough, a well-known figure among the Harlem cultural elite, recounts the story of a missionary who heard the melody to "Swing Low, Sweet Chariot" in the Congo.[82] Her informant, Catherine Wharton of Sherman, Texas, is the sister of white APCM missionary Conway T. Wharton, who served from 1915 to 1929 (and again from 1944 to 1950). Catherine Wharton's brother reported that "Swing Low, Sweet Chariot" was a "funeral dirge" that was, according to his unnamed sources, "as old as our tribe."[83]

Because of the publication of Scarborough's account in *Ebony and Topaz*, one of the era's major anthologies, edited by one of its most important scholars, this narrative, connected to the APCM, would have been widely known and of great interest, appearing as it did on the heels of the Johnson brothers' two volumes of spirituals. In *Ebony and Topaz*, Wharton's account of the Congolese routes of "Swing Low, Sweet Chariot" appears alongside writings by Jessie Fauset, Sterling Brown, Langston Hughes, Alice Dunbar Nelson, Countee Cullen, Arna Bontemps, Angelina Weld Grimké, Anne Spencer, Frank Horne, Gwendolyn Bennett, Helene Johnson, Georgia Douglas Johnson, Alain Locke, George Schuyler, E. Franklin Frazier, Allison Davis, and Zora Neale Hurston. Johnson's inclusion of Scarborough's account is part of a larger diasporic project that opens with Arthur Huff Fauset's Afro-Caribbean tale "Jumby" and features African proverbs throughout its pages. Scarborough's "New Lights on an Old Song" is followed by Edna Worthley Underwood's "La Perla Negra" set in Cuba.[84] In its entirety, the volume insists on the diversity and diasporic character of African American culture, celebrating the "return of the Negro writers to folk materials" while using images of Paul Laurence Dunbar's manuscripts and a Phillis Wheatley broadside to visually document the materiality of literary culture.[85]

The characterization of "Swing Low, Sweet Chariot" as a "funeral dirge" suits the song, which is often interpreted as a description of a journey to heaven. It also fits Scarborough's own stated desire elsewhere to have some of her "colored friends" sing it at her funeral.[86] In Wharton's account, there is no mention of the language of the song or the nationality of the singers. He reportedly heard the song being sung by porters "on the trail," which makes it impossible to determine its precise geographical origins.[87] However, by the time of Wharton's appointment, porterage, as a system of transport, was facing such massive Congolese resistance that even colonial authorities acknowledged it as "a plague to Central Africa."[88] By the early 1920s, a few years after Wharton was appointed, porterage was rarely used. By 1925, according to Alonzo Edmiston, it was outlawed.[89] A funeral dirge could, therefore, be heard as a form of protest against a brutal, and often deadly, labor practice that was nearing elimination.

If Wharton recognized the melody to "Swing Low, Sweet Chariot," then Althea Edmiston undoubtedly would have as well, since she translated it into Tshiluba. And if she had heard it, she either translated or transcribed the lyrics of a song that she knew to be African in origin. Alternately, Wharton may have heard "Swing Low, Sweet Chariot" unaware that he was listening to his colleague's translation. In any event, the language and origins of the song described by Wharton are impossible to confirm. The absence of African American spirituals from the 1909 Bushong hymnal does not mean that Edmiston and her colleagues did not translate, sing, or perform them. Who knows what other permutations happened to the song in the voices of its singers? Perhaps Wharton did not understand the language of the song well enough to identify it as a translation. And even if he did understand the individual words, he might not have recognized the lyrics as a translation since, like many of the APCM's published translations, Edmiston's rendering is not literal. Is it possible that Wharton was unfamiliar with his church's repertoire of spirituals? If so, this further suggests significant diversity among stations and missionaries within the APCM.

Edmiston's translation of the lyrics of "Swing Low, Sweet Chariot" reveals much about her interpretation of the song, which is less metaphorical in its Tshiluba incarnation. The chariot disappears and the title "Tanojilayi Banjelo" translates as "Look at the Angels." The refrain's second line "Coming for to carry me home" becomes "Badi balua kututuala" (literally, "They are coming to carry us").[90] In addition to a shift from the singular to the plural, the absence of *nsubu*, the Tshiluba word for "house" or "home," from Edmiston's translation is especially notable, suggesting an understanding that, from the perspective of the diaspora, the singers may already be home.[91] Alternatively "home" may lose some of its metaphorical significance outside the explicit context of diaspora. Her translation, then, implicitly shifts the setting of the song from Afro-America (and the diaspora) to Africa. Like the contemporary Francophone examples that Brent Edwards describes, her language "suggest[s] a link among discursive practices that aim (at a wide variety of points in a transnational print culture) to frame blackness as an object of knowledge beyond the nation-state."[92]

In Tshiluba, the brilliant fourth and final verse in the Jubilee Singers transcription—"I'm sometimes up, I'm sometimes down"—is replaced by the much more straightforward, "Pa buloba tudi ne dikengesha" ("On earth, we are suffering"). By locating the suffering on "earth" (or "land"), there is no possible site for earthly escape. The connotation also suggests that the lyric is about the land, rather than the sufferings at sea during the Middle Passage. Such an unequivocal statement reflects Edmiston's interpretation of the song as one of redemption in which "dikengesha"—defined by Morrison in his dictionary as "punishment, chastisement, suffering, retribution"—is paramount.[93] Edmiston's translation demonstrates a sophisticated contextual awareness of both the song's history and her Congolese audience. Suffering is referenced in the third verse of the Tshiluba translation, which appears to invert the final two verses from the Fisk version of the song.[94] Correspondingly, the song's one reference to Jesus—"When Jesus washed my sins away"—is moved from the third to the fourth verse with the more literal "Yesu wetu wakatupikula" (roughly "Our Jesus redeemed us"). The Edward Boatner transcription that Edmiston cites in a later hymnal has only three verses—it is missing the third ("Jesus") stanza of the Fisk version, so it is possible that Edmiston composed a new verse for the spiritual rather than reordering an extant version. Regardless, her version uniquely concludes with Jesus and redemption, rather than following the redemption with the ongoing and ambivalent struggle characteristic of the acknowledgement that "I'm sometimes up and sometimes down." The translation represents a deep reimagining of the song, and while the Tshiluba version addresses "dikengesha," its religious conclusion can be interpreted as more definitively evangelical than its source.

Tshiluba translations of African American spirituals are unique colonial religious texts that had value, albeit often contradictory, to both the Presbyterian Church and its Congolese congregations. This musical tradition, which was codified in the United States, served to support and challenge the missionary project of the church that used them. Edmiston's translation of "Swing Low, Sweet Chariot" is part of a larger cultural project undertaken by African American missionaries that should be understood in the context of colonial language policy and the church's relationship to it. These interventions occurred during an active time for J. Leighton Wilson Press, which seemed to expand its offerings once the complete Tshiluba Bible was published in 1928.[95] As Makim M. Mputubwele explains in his study of Kikongo, Bible translation opened up space for "more personal religious creations such as hymns, songs, prayers or somewhat secular works." White missionaries published abridged Tshiluba translations of Daniel Defoe's *Robinson Crusoe* (*Lusumuinu lua Robinson Crusoe*) in 1931 and John Bunyan's *Pilgrim's Progress* (*Luendu lua muena Kilisto*) in 1934. Edmiston's dictionary and grammar finally appeared in 1932, followed in 1933 by the Tshiluba hymnal *Misambu ya Kutumbisha n'ai Nzambi*, which included her translation of "Swing Low, Sweet Chariot." More broadly, religious print media, Mputubwele points out, "served as the points of departure of literatures in African languages."[96]

Within missionary print culture of the colonial era, these religious songs are evidence of a multilingual African American diasporic aesthetic that was embedded in the culture of colonialism while at the same time challenging fundamental aspects of the colonial project. The translations typically appeared in print without musical accompaniment though each song listed a source for its arrangement, typically a standard Presbyterian hymnal. "Swing Low, Sweet Chariot" cites Boatner and Willa Townsend's *Spirituals Triumphant*, an early work by two pioneering African American arrangers that was published by the Baptist Church in Nashville in 1927.[97] It appears likely that Edmiston, who was raised Baptist, acquired the songbook during her July 1928–August 1929 furlough and brought it with her when she returned to the Congo.[98] The absence of the musical arrangement from the hymnal requires outside knowledge or an intertextuality that runs counter to trends in musicology at a time when, as Jon Cruz notes, slave songs were being studied in academic ways that evacuated the tradition of its critical discursive relationship to American chattel slavery: "In place of historical testimonies of lived relationships triumphed a new and improved technical description that spoke in a proper new grammar of knowledge—a fledgling ethnomusicology."[99] Edmiston's emphasis on lyrics of suffering ("dikengesha") can be read as an effort to restore these "historical testimonies" of slavery and beyond. Amid a revival that included, for instance, the 1929 second edition of *Slave Songs of the United States* (1867), Edmiston provided translations that reemphasized, renewed, and re-created the subject matter of the spirituals rather than the formal musical dimensions.[100]

Edmiston's particular transcriptional practice has roots in Lucy Sheppard's 1898 hymnal, which also provides translated lyrics without music, and acknowledges a modern black musical tradition represented by Boatner and Townsend. Such practices were a part of global black culture during the late nineteenth and early twentieth century. Writing about South Africa, Jaji explains: "This generation placed a premium on fluid transitions between languages, ethnic identities, media, and art forms, a value they shared with other global movements of racial uplift. The aesthetic and political innovations in their modernism were couched in transcription, a set of writerly practices shuttling between sound and text. Transcription enabled an ambitious reimagining of the possibilities of citizenship and solidarity, both with other races within South Africa and with anti-racist and anticolonial movements in other regions."[101] For missionaries, transcription served to facilitate solidarity across linguistic difference. By the time Edmiston was in the Congo, spirituals were a widely recognized international phenomenon, emerging, according to Ronald Radano, as "aural signifiers of blackness for a world populace."[102] Edmiston had a unique understanding of the multidimensionality of the musical tradition and actively sought to use it as a form of cultural resistance in the colonial context.

In direct opposition to colonial policy, Edmiston was deeply invested in the lives of those people whom Cruz describes as being "on the receiving end of an imperial knowledge and an imperial power."[103] She publicly supported the development of "native leadership . . . both men and women" within the church, and, in 1930, endorsed "the formation of three or four self-supporting churches."[104] Edmiston had a particular audience in mind for her work, likely her "Congo sons and daughters [who] came to serenade" her and Alonzo before their 1925 furlough with "songs that their spiritual mother had taught them—lullabies and hammock melodies, African spirituals, and the great hymns of the Christian Church."[105] The Tshiluba spirituals were incorporated into the hymnal at a historical moment when Edmiston could envision their use by independent Congolese congregations. In the twenty-first century, the independent Communauté Presbytérienne au Congo continues to include African American spirituals in its hymnal.[106]

## Beautiful and Highly Inflected

While emphasizing Tshiluba, the APCM allowed some space for the Bushong language. In February 1918, Edmiston wrote a memo describing the status of her grammar and dictionary, as well as the needs for revisions of existing textbooks and hymnals, for new readers, for new math books, and for additional Bible translations, which she "would rather leave . . . to some one who knows more about the Bible and its interpretation than I do."[107] In response to her announced plans for Kuba materials, APCM officials noted its limited appeal: "It was not anticipated that the Bakuba work would ever require more than a half dozen missionary workers. Why spend three thousand dollars or more for the benefit of so few? Might not a brief, condensed outline of the Grammar serve every purpose required?"[108] Edmiston, however, stuck to her grander vision, and insisted on the documentary value of her work within print culture, which is something she recognized as early as 1908 when she describe her project as "a dictionary and grammar in the unwritten language of the Bakuba tribe."[109]

Meanwhile, a conflict emerged among missionaries regarding two competing Bushong language books, each in a different dialect. The debates followed lines similar to those with regard to Tshiluba, as both languages were used to consolidate forms of local governance that were beneficial to the Belgian colonial regime. Edmiston, who worked at Ibanche station in its local dialect, was at loggerheads with Wharton, who worked at Bulape in the Mushenge dialect (and whose account of hearing "Swing Low, Sweet Chariot" made its way to the Harlem Renaissance). The APCM's minutes from Bulape station include a letter from Wharton and Hezekiah M. Washburn that argues that the Mushenge dialect is superior to the Ibanche which is tainted by Baluba and Bakete influence. Coincidentally or not, the promotion of the Mushenge dialect was politically consistent with the Belgian policy of indirect rule among the Kuba, a system of governance predicated on a strong king and capital region. There were no state posts in the capital until 1910, which is indicative of the unique reliance of colonial authorities on local leadership.[110] This political conflict between dialects may also be reflective of APCM staffing patterns, which often placed white missionaries at stations closest to the seats of power so that they could be the most visible faces of the mission. Louis Franck, who served as Minister of Colonies from 1918 to 1924, takes Rwanda and Burundi as models, where Belgium was able "to maintain the existing political organisation and to rule through the two native sultans.... In both principalities we have rather strengthened the central power."[111] Franck was similarly committed to preserving the "great chiefdom" of the Kuba people, which "has some 150,000 to 200,000 subjects": "We wish not to let the indigenous organizations be broken up. When they disappear there remains usually only small chiefdoms; authority is scattered; the chiefs lose all genuine authority; this situation already exists in many other regions of the colony; one of the great problems for tomorrow will be to remedy this, for we don't want to be faced one day with a true indigenous anarchy."[112]

Language became one important mechanism for the strategic preservation of traditional forms of leadership. The conflict between Edmiston and Wharton quickly escalated in ways that reveal the stakes of linguistic practice within the mission.[113] This clash, among others, leads to the question as to what extent language policy, particularly when framed as a conflict between Bulape and Ibanche stations, became a proxy for racial tension on the mission, something that even Belgian authorities noticed.[114] In 1919, Ibanche, which was an all-black station for much of its history, was closed and the Edmistons were reassigned to Bulape, which like Ibanche was in the Kuba Kingdom. The Edmistons then were sent to establish a station in Mushenge, as Sheppard had attempted a few decades earlier. Although welcomed by the Kuba leadership, the Belgians blocked their request. Soon thereafter, the Edmistons were reassigned to Mutoto, which was outside the kingdom.[115]

At this point, even though Edmiston was no longer working among the Kuba, she remained resolute that her complete dictionary and grammar be published. Even Robert Dabney Bedinger, who took a rosy view of "cordial and harmonious relations . . . between the two races," acknowledged her frustration with the publication "delay which tested her. It tested her faith in her fellow-missionaries. It tested her loyalty" to the APCM and the ECFM.[116]

While she had the support of her APCM colleagues in earlier debates about her 1911 reappointment, this publication debacle exposed the fissure between how the church saw the work of its missionaries and how its black pioneers defined their own labors. The APCM adoption of the Belgian government's system of Bantu orthography in 1921 added to her labors as Edmiston was forced to spend two years revising her unapproved manuscript "to conform to the State method."[117] In this context, the conflict between Althea Edmiston and the Presbyterian Church over the publication of her *Grammar and Dictionary* must be understood as a fundamental disagreement about the APCM's mission and its relationship to the colonial state. Edmiston understood the obstacles and, as early as 1918, made clear her intentions "to secure the money for its publication from friends outside of our own Church."[118]

By the late 1920s, when the Presbyterian Church finally agreed to print her *Grammar and Dictionary*, they still refused to fund it. Edmiston was prepared; for nearly a decade, she had been soliciting external funds. For example, she used her 1921 Fisk commencement address to take up a collection for its publication. Edmiston's appeals and persistence were ultimately successful. Her ongoing loyalty to the church paid off when she received $2,000 from the Woman's Auxiliary to support the publication, which is acknowledged in the dedication. Final donations of $400 from Fisk alumni and $100 from her parents and other family members enabled J. Leighton Wilson Press to publish her 619-page *Grammar and Dictionary of the Bushonga or Bukuba Language as Spoken by the Bushonga or Bukuba Tribe Who Dwell in the Upper Kasai District, Belgian Congo, Central Africa* at Luebo in the Belgian Congo in 1932.[119] An inscribed copy of the book remains in the Fisk University library.

Even after thirty years of service as a Presbyterian missionary, Edmiston still relied on Fisk, which demonstrated a specific interest in the cultural work that African American missionaries undertook in Africa. During her first furlough, "she spoke in the chapel and before various and influential groups of students" at Fisk, and, by all accounts, "her visits to Fisk [were] delightful occasions to teachers and students alike."[120] The continuity of her connection to Fisk resembles Sheppard's ongoing relationship with Hampton. Like Hampton, Fisk had its own networks that extended to the Congo when Edmiston's classmate, George E. Haynes, a founder of the Urban League and Fisk's sociology department, took time from a 1930 Federal Council of the Churches of Christ in America trip to South Africa to visit her at Mutoto.[121] Her family's legacy continued. Her son Sherman Kuetu graduated from Fisk in 1928 as did her granddaughter (and namesake) in 1953.[122]

Althea Edmiston's achievement is so extraordinary because, over the course of the 1920s, it seemed increasingly unlikely that the Presbyterian

Church would publish a Bushong dictionary given its growing investment in Tshiluba. Although Edmiston uses her preface to insist that the mission was working "in two distinct languages" (Bushong and Tshiluba), her claim was more aspirational than accurate.[123] In 1927, the mission appointed a committee of three white men—Vernon Anderson, W. Frank McElroy, and George McKee—to revise Morrison's Tshiluba dictionary in accordance with government language policy. In 1933, the dictionary committee explained the church's position on language more bluntly than Morrison had: "This work is not being published for natives but is intended for the use of missionaries and other Europeans. . . . Possibly the material found between these covers may make some small contribution to that vast amount of data which is being accumulated by ethnographers and philologists concerning African languages and cultures, but our prime purpose in compiling this dictionary and our prayerful hope is that these pages, in a definite and far-reaching way, will be blessed and used of God to bring about a wider dissemination of the Gospel of Jesus Christ in Africa."[124] Any use of the church's Tshiluba dictionary for purposes other than religious conversion was incidental, which stands in contrast to Edmiston's more broadly humanistic and scholarly efforts.

Unlike the preface to Morrison's 1906 Tshiluba dictionary, which acknowledges several "native lads" along with the Sheppards and Hawkins, the APCM's 1939 volume thanks only other missionaries and previous editions.[125] Edmiston's preface points toward a broader constituency for her work by thanking her Congolese assistants by name—Mbohe Lumuana, Shamingi, Mishamikohi, Mukuna, Mingashanga, and Mabudi—and scholars from the University of London.[126] As early as 1908, she described the language of the Kuba as "beautiful, highly inflected, rhythmical, musical and full of stories, fairy tales and songs."[127] Her literary vision remained consistent over the course of several decades. A 1929 letter soliciting funds for the dictionary makes a similar academic case based on aesthetics and sophistication: the Kuba "are considered the most superior people of all Central Africa. Their language is beautiful and highly inflected. The verb has a full conjugation with many shades of tenses. There are ten classes of nouns as well as all the other various parts of speech."[128] She makes a secular appeal for support based on the complexity of the linguistic system rather than on its utility as an instrument of proselytizing. In an address to a group from the AMA—Fisk's founding body—Edmiston expressed her gratitude: "Never could I have accomplished what I have in systematizing one of the most difficult unwritten languages in Africa had it not been for the college training received at Fisk University," where the preparatory and college curricula required several years of Latin and Greek (as well as French and German).[129] The result was a complete grammar of the "Greek of the Kasai." Her ongoing debt—"I owe all I am and all I hope to be to you, through Fisk University"—extends beyond its financial support to include this intellectual foundation.[130]

The diminishing resistance to the publication of Edmiston's Bushong grammar and dictionary is likely indicative of the fact that by the 1930s language policy was not as contentious as it was in the 1910s. Tshiluba had won. By 1936, the APCM had completely phased out Bushong, and was using Tshiluba as the language of instruction among Bushong speakers in Kuba schools.[131] A 1939 edition of Morrison's dictionary excised his 139-page grammar and his thoughtful preface. In contrast, Edmiston's 1932 publication included more than 200 pages of grammar, further suggesting that she emphasized systematic linguistic analysis at a time when such an approach was devalued by the mission. Not only were her colleagues focusing exclusively on Tshiluba, but they were moving away from the scholarly linguistic method that Edmiston had learned at Fisk in favor of the kind of basic translation that could be accomplished with a dictionary alone.

Edmiston understood her linguistic work to be part of a larger scholarly project. Indeed its value was neither personal nor utilitarian; her commitment to the dictionary extended a decade beyond her own residence in the Kuba Kingdom and reveals a set of cultural priorities that differ from typical missionary aims and church policy. For her, Bushong was a literary language "full of many idioms, parables, fairy tales, lullabies and songs." Edmiston's preface gives careful attention to Kuba government traditions, as did Sheppard in his 1915 Hampton address, effectively using her *Grammar and Dictionary* to codify a political system that predated colonialism and continued to exist, in some form, outside of it. She explains that Kuba society features a "highly organized government with three judicial courts of appeal" and a democratic tradition that includes "many centuries" of woman suffrage and female parliamentarians.[132] She celebrated a robust matrilineal system that Catholic missionaries and others actively opposed as undermining family values. She chose to highlight a sophisticated, progressive, democratic, and feminist formation that stands in contrast to the Belgian colonial regime, and, in some respects, even outlasted it as "by the end of the colonial period, Kuba women still continue to enjoy a remarkably higher status than those in many other parts of rural Congo."[133]

Edmiston's achievements are affirmed by the generations of scholars who used her *Grammar and Dictionary*. When the Belgian anthropologist Jan Vansina was studying with the "famous Bantuist" Malcolm Guthrie at the School of Oriental and African Languages in England in the early 1950s, Edmiston's "missionary grammar" was the primary text for his language instruction and helped to impress upon him the critical importance of linguistics as an area of formal study rather than simply a tool for fieldwork.[134] As what

Vansina calls a "grammar," rather than a dictionary, Edmiston's contribution runs counter to the process of colonial pidginization, which, as in the case of Kiswahili in Katanga, effected an "extreme reduction" of the language "for limited purposes."[135] Although Guthrie "did not know a word of Bushong" and Vansina ultimately "learned no Bushong," Edmiston's book provided Vansina with a valuable appreciation for a system of linguistic study distinct from regnant colonial conventions.[136]

## The Garvey Danger

The reluctance of the Presbyterian Church to publish Edmiston's Bushong *Grammar and Dictionary* can be understood as part of a larger shift within the mission toward accommodating the colonial policies of the Belgian Congo. Correspondingly, Edmiston's insistence on her book's publication mediates the hegemony of colonial language policy. Her actions may not have been as dramatic or visible as those of Sheppard, but they are consistent with the broad-based vision that Sheppard and other early missionaries to the APCM had practiced. African American missionaries, who were increasingly marginalized in the APCM, developed a critical perspective on the power of the colonial state, which reached back to the United States through HBCUs and other channels. The efforts of figures like Sheppard and Edmiston, as political activists and linguists, demonstrate a willingness to defy the mission and the state in ways that critically expose their deeply racial dimensions. There is little evidence to suggest that Edmiston, or any of the other African American missionaries, was not deeply committed to the Christian evangelizing mission of the APCM. However, Althea Edmiston's scrapbook reveals some of her political interests at this stage in her career. Most of the newspaper clippings are taken from the *Chicago Defender*, and they include material related to the 1931 Scottsboro, Alabama, case of several African American teenagers sentenced to death within weeks of being falsely accused of assaulting two white women. She includes a 1930 article discussing anticolonial protests in both Leopoldville and Brazzaville, along with several installments of *Defender* editor Robert S. Abbott's European travelogue, "My Trip Abroad," including one on the Royal Museum for Central Africa (RMCA) in Tervuren, which criticizes Belgium's colonial regime.[137]

The mission history of the Edmistons, including the struggle for reappointment, is full of examples of ways in which their work was not universally welcomed by Presbyterian leadership. Not surprisingly, the increasing entanglement of the APCM and the colonial state coincided with the increasing marginalization of African American missionaries who contributed important racial narratives—such as Sheppard's account of ancestral return and Edmiston's translation of "Swing Low, Sweet Chariot"—into a dynamic missionary corpus. In the 1910s, the missionaries continued their efforts to maintain autonomy and neutrality by, for example, refusing an offer of military protection for an expedition to the Kuba Kingdom. In 1916, Alonzo found himself in the middle of a conflict with the state and was at loggerheads with a Belgian agent who sought to bring charges against the APCM for providing sanctuary to the Congolese.[138] James Campbell describes this as a source on ongoing tension: "Though leaders of the mission rarely admitted it, many of those who settled at Luebo and later at Ibaanche were less interested in Christianity than in finding some place where they could live in peace, free from the exactions of a violent colonial state. This fact was not lost on Belgian officials, who increasingly regarded the Presbyterian mission as an affront to constituted authority, a refuge for fugitives and loafers and others trying to avoid the state's legitimate demand for labor."[139] Alonzo is extremely direct in his criticism of a local state agent's failure to protect the Congolese people: "We must by all means try to give this young man Cambier a lesson or two. His head is mighty warm."[140] Within the mission, there was no consensus, but perhaps most notable is the report, later in the year, from a white missionary that "Edmiston is not reporting to [the] state the facts I gave him, though the state man inquired from him about it."[141]

While the increasingly white APCM was falling in line with the state, Alonzo Edmiston was unwilling to report to a regime that was becoming more and more fixated on the perceived threat posed by African Americans. In the early 1920s, the Belgian government feared the rising influence of Marcus Garvey and his Universal Negro Improvement Association (UNIA), and attributed Simon Kimbangu's messianic anticolonial activism to Garveyite agitation. When the Belgian ambassador to the United States subscribed to the Garvey's *Negro World*, U.S. authorities were notified because of their own surveillance of Garvey's mail and immediately saw an opportunity to collaborate on monitoring African Americans. The Belgian ambassador wanted to block outright African Americans from traveling to the Congo, but his proposal was rejected by Franck. As a compromise, Franck required his office's approval for any visas issued to African Americans and directed the colonial governor to monitor the activities of all African Americans in the Congo.[142] As Michael Meeuwis demonstrates, "Franck believed that bringing Belgium's colonial policy in line with the one adopted by the British and with segregationist educational theories developed in the United States . . . would allow Belgium to gain the diplomatic approval of these two important international players."[143] Not only was Franck deliberately appealing to the racial interests of the U.S. government, he was modeling the colony on the U.S. South. Most pronouncedly, he called on the Phelps-Stokes Fund, an organization that invested in segregationist industrial education for African Americans, to visit the Belgian Congo in 1921 on a tour that included visits to APCM mission stations.[144] The delegation, headed by former Hampton professor Thomas Jesse Jones, issued a report that predictably promotes "adapted education," as part of a racist colonial policy of indirect rule that included "selective management of . . . linguistic diversity."[145]

The Belgian system of indirect rule created more opportunities for Garveyism to circulate. As Adam Ewing explains, under such a system, local leaders' "direct appeals to the colonial state were rarely strident, and were always couched in a discourse of unflinching loyalty to the imperial project. But the very performance of those appeals" by an empowered indigenous leadership "posed a subversive challenge to the logic of colonial domination, one that authorities could not long ignore."[146] Belgian administrators called APCM members to a meeting to discuss Garvey's feared influence on black missionaries. Following the meeting, the APCM sought clarification as to whether the rejection of black missionaries was absolute and whether or not "such disqualifications (if they exist) extend to old and tried Missionaries, such as the Edmistons (1904), Mr. Rochester (1907), etc." The unsigned memo states that the rumored "disqualifications (if they exist) arise out of the Garvey danger." The APCM counters, "the Garvey propaganda [can] best be combatted from within,—that is, by the careful selection (for which we Americans are uniquely qualified) and importation of anti-Garvey men."[147] A second memo (possibly a draft of the first) discusses language policy as a point of contention with the mission's "desire to teach French, surrendered in deference to the demand of the Colonial Minister." The missionaries "agree with the Minister of the Colonies when he says, 'ces connaissances superficielles ne sont qu'un pretexte a vanite desplacee [sic]'" (this superficial knowledge is only a pretext for displaced vanity); in other words, French, not unlike the Latin and Greek that Edmiston studied at Fisk, is considered an uppity language associated with "les mulatres [sic]."[148] In her study of language policy, Barbara A. Yates convincingly argues, "French was an unnecessary intermediary, particularly as it made available non-religious ideas and the necessary skills for employment outside the mission orbit."[149] With regard to a "Native Lingua Franca" and debates about "Lingala, Swahili or Luba," the same memo expresses the APCM's commitment to "do all that we can to assist them and to further the interests of their Colony."[150]

In a private 1922 London meeting with the APCM's British agent, the governor general of the Belgian Congo, Maurice Lippens, laid out the racial policy of the colonial regime: "the point he made and repeated with most emphasis, was the vital importance of maintaining unimpaired the prestige and the supremacy of the White [sic] race." Lippens stressed that African converts must not be given any authority within the church, a position which Althea Edmiston publicly opposed by advocating for "native leadership." Nor should African American missionaries be appointed: "while he had no complaint to make of the coloured Missionaries from other lands, many of whom he had met and held in high respect, he yet regretted their being there, and hoped the Societies interested would send no more agents of colour for the present."[151] That same month, at a general meeting of British missionaries attended by an APCM representative, Lippens responded to a question about African Americans by stating "that there would be no interference with those who were already in the Congo, but that no more would be admitted under any condition."[152] The prohibition against black leadership, whether African American or Congolese, further exposes the racial bedrock of the Belgian colonial state.

As the colonial government issued such explicit directions (which were consistent with the racial beliefs of many within the church), the APCM bragged of their improved relationship. A 1923 church publication even recommends travelling missionaries bring some "small American and Belgian flags."[153] In the mid-1920s, APCM stations welcomed senior officials, most notably the Crown Prince of Belgium, who Luebo mission students regaled with the national anthem of Belgium.[154] By the end of the decade, the mission saw nothing wrong with directly serving the Belgian colonial regime: "Our own [education] program has been aligned as nearly as possible at this stage with that of the State, and it is hoped that in a few years it will be possible to have either a complete alignment or a program just as good as that of the Government."[155]

Subsequently, the APCM, including the few continuing African Americans, remained cozy with the Belgian colonial regime. In 1932, the year Althea Edmiston's *Grammar and Dictionary* was finally published, local government officials recommended that King Albert honor her and her husband with the *Médaille Commémorative du Congo* for their service, an award that was accompanied by the explicit "assurance 'That the Government is not prejudiced against colored missionaries and value[s] their services.'" The Edmistons responded with appreciation.[156] The alliance with Belgium reached even greater heights in 1936, when Hezekiah and Lillie Washburn were invited to visit the king and queen of Belgium. Initially, Hezekiah, who previously feuded with Althea Edmiston over the politics of language, "worried that someone had put up some charges against me," as they had Sheppard.[157] Instead the king hosted Hezekiah at his luxurious suite at the Cosmopolitan Hotel, and knighted him and his wife to the Royal Order for having "rendered a great service" including donations of corn produced on mission stations to government mining concessions.[158] The king's attempts to charm the Washburns had a lasting impact; nearly four decades later, Hezekiah titled his autobiography *A Knight in the Congo* and proudly included pictures of the awards the king gave him.

All the while, Belgium's fear of African Americans continued unabated in ways that continued to echo the "colonial anxieties" and "settler paranoia" that the Garvey movement inspired.[159] In 1924, the American explorer Herman Norden notes that wherever he travels in the Congo, colonial officials ask about Garvey, though, in his racist estimation, "They are too far away from the man and too close to the menace of their lands to see the absurdity of Garvey." Belgian officials throughout Africa feared the Garveyite and communist influence posed by African Americans. In 1925, the U.S. consul in Nairobi "found himself in a familiar position: reassuring" his Belgian counterpart "that he had nothing to fear from Black Americans." A Belgian journalist "found copies of Garvey's *Negro World* in Kinshasa and concluded that Bolshevik plans for colonial revolution lay behind the newspaper and movement."[160] Among the Congolese, "rumors circulated among adherents that the Belgians would be expelled from the colony by an arriving black American army," a long-standing image of African Americans returning as liberators.[161] During the late 1920s and early 1930s, there were rumors that the Trinidad-born U.S.-based Pan-Africanist George Padmore, then active in the Communist Party, headed "a gun-running expedition into the Belgian Congo to help a native revolt there."[162] In 1934, in her *Negro: Anthology*, Nancy Cunard included "Extracts from a Pamphlet Circulating in the Belgian Congo," advocating a unified uprising among black workers seeking "to be masters in their own country."[163] As late as 1947, Julia Lake Kellersberger attributed Althea Edmiston's mistreatment during a 1917 Cape Town layover not to South African racism, but rather to the Garvey movement, which is exceedingly unlikely since there is no evidence of the UNIA in the city until 1920.[164] Kellersberger's memory reveals the ongoing depths of anti-Garvey fear among APCM missionaries.

During World War II, the Ministry of Colonies asked the United States to redeploy its black soldiers who were stationed at Matadi as "a matter of the greatest importance not to raise any difficult problems of a social or an economic character among the native population."[165] The U.S. government, which in 1909 defended William Sheppard before a Belgian court, agreed to withdraw its black soldiers in 1942. Despite such accommodations, the Belgians considered African Americans, even in absentia, to be dangerous exemplars. A photo of African American officers that was found among Force Publique mutineers was blamed for an uprising in Kananga (then Luluabourg), the largest city in the Kasai province. Belgian authorities considered African American missionaries equally threatening. When Belgian censors, who were monitoring mission correspondence during World War II, discovered that American Protestant missions were considering appointing black missionaries, Governor General Pierre Ryckmans and Foreign Minister Paul-Henri Spaak both approached U.S. authorities on this subject.[166] Again, the U.S. government and the churches responded favorably to the colonial authorities' racist requests. As the APCM was aligning itself with Belgian racial policy, much of the fear that motivated racial segregation within its ranks was tragically misdirected. In 1945, white missionary William Pruitt began a decades-long career as a sexual predator responsible for the abuse of at least twenty children of other APCM missionaries.[167]

Shortly after the end of the war, in 1948, the Presbyterian Board of World Missions began to comply with a Belgian requirement that all appointed missionary families spend a minimum of a year in Brussels studying, among other things, "Belgian and colonial history and government" in colonial education programs.[168] The APCM complied without protest. At this same time, in 1948, the Presbyterian Church, for the first time, signed an agreement with the Ministry of Colonies for official recognition and financial subsidies in order to make its "training available to its people in a Christian atmosphere."[169] Fearing the loss of its religious foundation, the church debated the issue, but ultimately agreed to become an appendage to the state and effectively remained as such until independence.[170]

There is nothing especially unusual in the Presbyterian Church's complicity in Belgian colonialism; however, the shifting relationship between the mission and the state and its concordance with U.S. racial politics make visible forms of African American anticolonial activism. Its early years under black leadership offer a glimpse of the possibility of an alternative model of activist missionary work, albeit a deeply problematic sort of imperial anticolonialism, in which a mission need not be an uncritical arm of the state.[171] Beyond the unique activism of Sheppard, Edmiston's efforts to mediate the church's capitulation to the strictures of the colonial state represents an alternate trajectory of resistance. While language served Belgium as an instrument of political power, Edmiston's dictionary and translations recognize its potential as a space of resistance in the tradition of Du Bois's *The Souls of Black Folk*.

This history reveals colonialism's effective incorporation of nonstate actors and the foundational role that racist ideology played within that context. These relationships were forged, at least in part, by international opposition to black liberation—an alliance between the governments of Belgium and the United States, and supported by the Presbyterian Church. If nothing else, the Belgian government's ongoing campaign against African American missionaries indicates a perceived threat to colonial rule that U.S. churches and the government were all too willing to accommodate. By the 1940s, the APCM of the Sheppards and Edmistons no longer saw the state as its adversary. All the while, the colonial government had the continued support of the U.S. government. As late as 1957, the U.S. State Department had barred black Americans from traveling to the Congo, and following Alonzo's 1941 retirement, the mission was exclusively white for the first time in its fifty-year history.[172] Another African American was not appointed to the APCM until Bettye Jean Mitchell in 1958.

Alonzo, who died in Selma, Alabama, in 1954, was predeceased by his wife and colleague. When Althea Edmiston died at Mutoto on June 9, 1937, she was the senior member of the APCM, having served since 1902.[173] She was preceded in death by a few weeks by her retired senior colleague Maria Fearing in Alabama. Bedinger's obituary for Fearing concludes: "On May 23, 1937, to use the beautiful language of her colleague, Mrs. A. L. Edmiston, she heard 'the welcome voice of her Lord and the whir and hum of the 'Sweet Chariot,' accompanied by a band of angeles [sic], swinging low, coming for to carry her home."[174] Bedinger's association of Edmiston and "Swing Low, Sweet Chariot," the signal spiritual she included into the APCM's Tshiluba corpus, serves as an appropriate and timely memorial for Edmiston herself. At Althea Edmiston's own funeral a few weeks later and thousands of miles away in Mutoto, a choir sang her Tshiluba translations of two Presbyterian hymns, "Guide Me, O Thou Great Jehovah" and "'Tis Midnight, and on Olive's Brow."[175]

*Chapter 5*

Literary Cultures

*The Black Press, Pauline E. Hopkins, and the Rewriting of Africa*

In 1902–3, the *Colored American Magazine* published *Of One Blood; Or, the Hidden Self*, Pauline E. Hopkins's novel about Reuel Briggs, an African American doctor, who, like the African American missionaries of his day, travels to Africa, making it, according to John Cullen Gruesser, "one of the earliest known fictional accounts of the continent by a black American writer."[1] The novel, which was being serialized at the precise time when Althea Brown Edmiston was traveling to the Congo, features as its heroine Dianthe Lusk, a former Fisk University student and Jubilee Singer who uses African American spirituals as a medium to connect with Africa. Although Hopkins herself never traveled to Africa, the journeys of her contemporaries helped her to fashion an independent African American literary discourse that engaged the legacy and crisis of colonialism with a remarkable level of complexity that included, at times, profound ambivalence. The *Colored American Magazine*, which Hopkins edited, laid the groundwork for a twentieth-century black literary press that embedded a wide array of African engagements within its pages, including in fiction, and represents a means through which confrontations with the Congo shaped the wider political and cultural landscape. Hopkins, her novel, and her editorial career demonstrate the ways that such confrontations with colonialism were foundational to twentieth-century African American print culture.

In *Of One Blood*'s first scene, Reuel Briggs, an African American Harvard medical student passing for white, is invited by Aubrey Livingston, his fellow student and best friend, to attend a concert performance by the Fisk Jubilee Singers. At the concert, Reuel recognizes star vocalist Dianthe Lusk as an apparition who earlier interrupted his reading of Harvard psychologist William James's 1890 essay "The Hidden Self," which, although not properly attributed, provides the subtitle for the novel. Later, when Dianthe is injured in a train accident and ominously pronounced dead by Aubrey, Reuel miraculously revives her. Reuel falls in love with Dianthe, and they marry. Soon thereafter, Reuel, who is unable to find a job in the United States because of rumors about his racial identity, departs to work on a British-led scientific expedition to Africa. While traveling, Reuel loses consciousness and awakens in the Great Pyramid of the hidden biblical city of Telassar, where he uncovers both the African roots of Western civilization and his own family history. Ethiopian Prime Minister Ai, who was waiting for the "coming of our king who shall restore to the Ethiopian race its ancient glory," anoints Reuel "Ergamenes," the lost king of Ethiopia.[2] In so doing, Hopkins develops a classical protagonist who is granted a mantle similar to that bestowed on William Sheppard when he was received as a reincarnated member of the Kuba royal family in Mushenge and on Ernest Hogan when he sang the popular "My Little Jungle Queen: A Congo Love Song."

Dianthe Lusk's education, artistry, and mission in the novel recall the career of not only Althea Edmiston but also Lucy Gantt Sheppard, who toured with Fredrick Loudin's Fisk ensemble. According to Daphne Brooks, Dianthe's character is historic: *Of One Blood* is "the earliest novel by an African American woman to figure a black female performer . . . as its heroine." Even more importantly, Dianthe's "vocal talents ultimately open up transgeographical frontiers and negotiate chronotopical fields to reconnect her character with an individual past as a choir soloist and a collective history of black subjugation and cultural survival embedded in the lyrics of the spirituals."[3] The highlight of the Fisk Jubilee Singers concert occurs when she sings, "Go down, Moses, way down in Egypt's land, Tell ol' Pharaoh, let my people go," which more directly than any other spiritual advocates the freedom of African people from state oppression.[4] As Brooks explains, this performance "plants the seeds of Reuel's political and cultural evolution."[5] For her part, Hopkins was familiar with the activist use of "Go Down, Moses" on the eve of the passage of the Emancipation Proclamation, and she was one of the first novelists to invoke its spiritual power, something that both W. E. B. Du Bois and Ralph Ellison did for different purposes in later years.[6]

At a critical point later in the novel after Reuel has departed for Africa, Dianthe is inspired to sit at a piano to perform "Go Down, Moses," which causes her to faint. When she comes to, she regains the consciousness she had lost in the train accident: "Her thoughts were painful. Memory had returned in full save as to her name."[7] Her memories extend beyond her own life and family history to include her experience at Fisk University, the vernacular musical tradition represented by the song, and the African continent ("Egypt's land" and the site of Reuel's expedition). "Go Down, Moses," which was later distinguished as the opening piece in James Weldon Johnson's *Book of American Negro Spirituals*, has the power to raise her consciousness, and to connect her to the place for which her husband just departed.[8]

While Reuel is in Africa, Dianthe, who is still not fully conscious, remains in Massachusetts to continue her recovery under the watch of Aubrey, whose evil designs include kidnapping her to the South, where he will "renew the ancient splendor of his ancestral home."⁹ While roaming around Aubrey's Southern homeland, much as Reuel was roaming when he arrived at Telassar, Dianthe arrives not at a pyramid, but at a "typical Southern Negro cabin." There, she meets her grandmother, Aunt Hannah, whose regal stature is immediately apparent: "Somewhere she had read a description of an African princess which fitted the woman before her."¹⁰ This characterization, like the narrative structure of the novel, locates classical African civilization within African American folk culture. Aunt Hannah, who represents Africa so distinctively, reveals that Reuel, Dianthe, and Aubrey are the offspring of Hannah's enslaved daughter Mira and her late owner Aubrey Livingston (senior). All three are siblings, and all three are "black." However, due to a switched child scheme reminiscent of Twain's 1893 novel *Pudd'nhead Wilson* and other popular racial fiction of the era, Aubrey (junior) was raised white because Hannah replaced the Livingstons' dead child (the original Aubrey) with her own grandson (the current Aubrey). The recovery of their shared family history coincides with both Reuel's recovery of an African heritage and Dianthe's recovery of literal consciousness. Soon thereafter, Dianthe performs "Go Down, Moses" for the third time, on this occasion at the request of Aubrey, whom she married under the mistaken belief that Reuel was dead.¹¹ At the end of the novel, Aubrey poisons Dianthe, who manages to stay alive until moments after Reuel's temporary return from Africa, which serves as a reminder of the dynamic routes of transatlantic mobility. As she dies in Reuel's arms, the two transatlantic narrative threads converge. Although Aubrey is acquitted in court for Dianthe's murder, he commits suicide in accordance with royal tradition, which marks the way that African practices can help shape putatively American melodrama.

## Black Livingstone

In *Reconstructing Womanhood: The Emergence of the Afro-American Woman Novelist*, a major contribution to the resurgence of interest in Hopkins in the 1980s, Hazel V. Carby profitably reads *Of One Blood* as part of a wide range of early-twentieth-century intellectual discourses: "The network of these relations between *Of One Blood* and other, nonfictional, articles in the *Colored American Magazine* indicated the extent of an intertextual coherence, achieved under Hopkins's literary editorship, which aimed at the reconstruction of a sense of pride in an African heritage."¹² Carby's model of "intertextual coherence" can be usefully extended beyond the *Colored American Magazine* to encompass an array of sources on Africa that were available during this period. The connection of Dianthe Lusk to Althea Edmiston and Lucy Sheppard suggests that African American fictions of return to Africa function on a shared plane with contemporary nonfiction accounts of travel by missionaries and others. Hopkins's novel, like the various versions of the Sheppards' narrative, is part of a decidedly internationalist African American print culture that has shaped images of Africa, textual and otherwise.

Interpretations of the novel as emblematic of Afrocentrism's "dreamy, mystical quality" obscure the materiality of the diverse networks of ongoing transatlantic exchange that were available to Hopkins and her audience. These networks reveal that identity, as Stuart Hall explains, "is not a mere phantasm either. It is *something*—not a mere trick of the imagination. It has its histories."[13] The larger oeuvre of Hopkins, who worked as a novelist, essayist, editor, orator, and stenographer, suggests that substantive international political interests inform not only her creative writing, but also much of the era's cultural work for which she served as an important conduit. Following Carby's lead, scholars have taken productive intertextual approaches to *Of One Blood*, often highlighting its significant references to James's "The Hidden Self."[14] Scott Trafton argues that "the discourses of psychology that have featured so prominently in recent criticism can themselves be seen to be only half of a dual construction; underneath is something perhaps more materialist, certainly more historicist, and concerned not, as it were, with the archaeologies of identities but with the identities of the archaeological." Or, to use Hall's definition: "Not an identity grounded in the archeology, but in the *re-telling* of the past?"[15] This chapter attempts to excavate this materialist and historicist context by illuminating a fuller range of Hopkins's sources.

More recently, Geoffrey Sanborn has written provocatively of the novel's "plagiarism" which Hopkins uses to place "herself within various existing traditions of popular writing . . . by relocating bits and pieces of that writing into *Of One Blood*." His documentation is compelling, above all, for the portrait it provides of Hopkins's reading practices. Quoting Roland Barthes, Sanborn elaborates: "By allowing her writing voice to be haunted—overtaken, accompanied, possessed—by 'the voice of reading itself,' an ultimately nonsubjective vocalization, Hopkins amplifies the unowned, unownable flowing of language."[16] Sanborn's description of Hopkins's "vocalization" is quite similar to Hopkins's description of Dianthe's performance of "Go Down, Moses," where her own voice is followed by a disembodied echo that demonstrates her awareness of the possibility of literal polyvocality: "A weird contralto, veiled as it were, rising and falling upon every wave of the great soprano, and reaching the ear as from some strange distance. The singer sang on, her voice dropping sweet and low, the echo following it, and at the closing word, she fell back in a dead faint."[17] Hopkins locates her own authorial methods of polyvocality within African American musical traditions in ways that anticipate the poetry of the Black Arts movement. Her invocation of Egypt helps to render Africa visible through a kind of "transindividuality" that reveals layers and contexts for Hopkins's writing and Dianthe's path back to full consciousness.[18]

Although the Sheppards are not named in *Of One Blood*, William does appear in "Mrs. Jane E. Sharp's School," an essay Hopkins published in the *Colored American Magazine* a few months after the serialization of *Of One Blood* concluded. Sharp, who emigrated from Boston to Liberia in the early 1880s, was well known to Hopkins as an alumna of her alma mater, Boston Girls' High School.[19] Writing under the name "J. Shirley Shadrach," Hopkins quotes Senate Chaplain Edward Everett Hale's comparison of Sharp's work in Liberia to that of Sheppard in the Congo: "There is many a province, and barony, and kingdom, and empire in Africa, where a white man would be killed as soon as he was seen, while a black man is welcomed and made at home. The romantic and extraordinary experience recently of Mr. Shepherd [*sic*], in the very heart of Africa, is an interesting illustration of this."[20] In using this quote, Hopkins acknowledges a racial analysis of imperialism, a tradition of militant African resistance, and an African commitment to transnational racial solidarity. Sheppard's experience becomes representative of a contemporary African American relationship to Africa through the comparison to a familiar local figure in Sharp (who in 1916 was announced as a contributor to Hopkins's *New Era Magazine*).[21] As a result, neither Sheppard nor Briggs was outlandish in this regard. While such allusions may seem obscure to twenty-first-century scholars, the minimal explication that Hale and Hopkins provide indicates that Sheppard was identifiable to readers of the *Colored American Magazine* a century ago.

Hopkins's March 1904 profile of Sharp alludes to the gracious welcome that William Sheppard received from the Kuba who saw him as a royal heir. Yet prior to his initial departure, Samuel Lapsley's mother famously told Sheppard to "take care of Sam," while Aubrey told Jim Titus, an African American servant hired to spy on Reuel, "to 'take care of Dr. Briggs.'"[22] Both instances imply racialized dependency and caregiving, which is transformed by the agency of Sheppard and Jim, who makes a critical revelation of Reuel's family history. Although traveling under the auspices of the Presbyterian Church (U.S.), Sheppard immediately saw his mission as a "happy" return to "the country of my forefathers."[23] Published accounts of his African reception range from a "most kindly" one to a celebratory scene in which "the people are rejoicing."[24] Such accounts, which are alluded to in Hopkins's essay on Sharp, parallel the "great homage" offered to Reuel in Telassar.[25] Like Sheppard, Reuel is welcomed to the throne.

The Kuba saw Sheppard as the reincarnation of a past ruler, which finds an analog in the transatlantic spirits that populate *Of One Blood*. Dianthe's apparitional appearance in the novel's opening scene coincides with the Kuba concept of *nkala*, defined by Althea Brown Edmiston as "an apparition or being or ghost that can appear at will or at any time or place."[26] Sheppard's report on the Kuba belief "in the transmigration of souls" fits with Vansina's account that the Kuba believe, "Every alternating—i.e., second—generation saw the rebirth of a person who had lived some two generations before the baby was born."[27] In Hopkins's Telassar, the people, who "believe in reincarnation by natural laws regulating material on earth," are anticipating a royal successor from "lands beyond unknown seas."[28] In their parallel tales, Sheppard and Reuel both fit this bill. In West Africa, it also fits the Igbo, some of whom, Olaudah Equiano notes in his *Interesting Narrative of the Life of Olaudah Equiano, or Gustavus Vassa, the African*, "believe in the transmigration of souls."[29] Equiano's 1789 narrative, which Sheppard and Hopkins could have read, situates Hopkins's fiction within a long-standing discursive tradition that fashions a trope of transatlantic migration and return in the wake of the horrors of the Middle Passage. Indeed, Vincent Carretta's research into Equiano's birthplace, which ultimately questions the autobiographical veracity of his *Interesting Narrative*, could point to a form of transindividuality that further entrenches Hopkins within the narrative tradition represented by Equiano.[30]

In addition to the central trope of return and ascension, there are other notable parallels in the backgrounds of the Sheppards and the fictional characters in *Of One Blood*. Lucy Sheppard and Hopkins's Dianthe Lusk are both soprano soloists with the Fisk Jubilee Singers. Both women travel extensively with the ensemble, representing what Gilroy recognizes as the group's "distinctive patterns of cross-cultural circulation."[31] Lucy Sheppard was known for singing hymns in African languages to audiences in the United States and Africa. In addition, these two enormously accomplished women share a temporary separation from their Africa-bound husbands. William and Lucy were engaged before William's first trip to the Congo and married during his first furlough. Lucy returned to the Congo with William, though it was public knowledge that they took subsequent leaves at different times from one another.[32] To add another layer to this characterization, Dianthe Lusk is the namesake of abolitionist John Brown's first wife, who "loved singing hymns and praying alone in the woods."[33] The fictional Lusk, the historical Lusk, and Lucy Sheppard share a love of religious music, experiences of isolation, and husbands inspired by spiritual visions.

In *Of One Blood*, Reuel is given missionary credit for bringing Christianity to Africa (though historically Christianity existed in Ethiopia before it reached Europe). After invoking Jesus, Ai tells the returned ruler, "Your belief shall be ours."[34] With "missionary work ... one of the few means by which

African Americans gained firsthand experience in and knowledge about Africa," Gruesser explains that through Reuel's service as a de facto missionary, Hopkins chooses the ideal vocation for "asserting the necessity of maintaining this vital link between black Americans and Africa."[35] James Campbell points out the broad impact of "Missionaries such as William Sheppard [who] became celebrities, drawing packed houses during their periodic visits back to the United States. Their accounts became yet another source of information for African Americans anxious to know more about their ancestral continent."[36] Outside of the church, Sheppard was not primarily known for proselytizing; likewise, Reuel's evangelical success was incidental to a larger process of cultural reclamation. As St. Clair Drake, whose childhood home William Sheppard frequented, points out, African American leadership was only beginning to become secularized at the start of the twentieth century and the Ethiopianist "redemption of Africa" was, at the time of *Of One Blood*, the purview of missionaries and religious institutions.[37]

The missionary tradition is most prominent in Aubrey's family name, "Livingston," which approximates that of the iconic Scottish missionary David Livingstone and is consistent with Hopkins's use of historical names in the novel.[38] Livingstone, who was the subject of an 1869 expedition that brought Henry Stanley international renown, was a known figure in African American communities. His daughter was inspired by the Fisk Jubilee Singers to donate money for the construction of "Livingston Hall," which was completed in 1882 and shares its name with Aubrey's Southern manse. (Valeria G. Stone, who also contributed funds for the building, has her own namesake in the novel: Professor Stone, the leader of Reuel's African expedition.)[39]

In chapter 16, Hopkins literally inserts Reuel into Livingstone's narrative, using more than 300 words from John Hartley Coombs's popular *Dr. Livingstone's 17 Years' Exploration and Adventure in the Wilds of Africa* (1857) to describe her protagonist's travels.[40] In assuming David Livingstone's mantle, Reuel demonstrates his vision of what Coombs headlines as "HEROISM" and "MIRACULOUS ESCAPE" from a predatory lion.[41] Whereas in Coombs's account, the lion responds to the command "Begone!"—for Reuel it takes "the full force of his personal magnetism," a very individualized agency that is on display elsewhere in *Of One Blood*.[42] In her appropriation of Coombs, Hopkins transforms the landscape in meaningful ways. She deletes Coombs's "blackfaced" adjective used to describe "a goodly number of baboons," precluding its racial connotations (not long before Ota Benga would be displayed at the Bronx Zoo). While Livingstone and Reuel note that the "character of the country improved" in the interior region, Reuel appears demonstrably less surprised than Livingstone who uniquely finds it "Contrary to all his expectations."[43] In addition, the geographical nomenclature shifts as Hopkins writes of "the European idea respecting Central Africa, which brands these regions as howling wildernesses or an uninhabitable country," which is more precise than Coombs's explication of "the prevailing notions of Europeans respecting the central regions of Africa. It has been believed by many that the greater part of that ground which is marked on the maps as 'unexplored,' is a howling wilderness, or an arid, sterile and uninhabitable country."[44] Hopkins more decisively demarcates the place as "Central Africa" rather than Africa's "central regions," and corrects Coombs's passive voice ("It has been believed") by clearly ascribing such prejudices to a "European idea," something more deeply institutionalized than Coombs's "prevailing notions."

One of the passages that Hopkins added to her interpellation of Coombs remains troubling albeit characteristic: "Reuel remembered the loathsome desert that stood in grim determination guarding the entrance to this paradise against all intrusion, and with an American's practical common sense, bewailed this waste of material."[45] This moment is seemingly an example of what Jill Bergman has in mind when she describes how "Reuel adopts the imperialistic values associated with the United States," an understandably frightening prospect in the wake of a rapidly expanding U.S. empire in the Pacific and the Carribean.[46] While it remains disquieting and unclear what exactly constitutes "an American's practical common sense" in Africa, it seems plausible that Hopkins, like others before her, saw African American missionaries as bulwarks against the most sinister "intrusions" of European colonialism, much as Garveyites throughout Africa would claim throughout the 1920s.[47] Hopkins effectively articulated a variation of the moderate discourse of the emerging Congo reform movement which, though sadly unable to envision autonomous African statehood, aimed at ending King Leopold II's exploitative control. From the many available sources on Livingstone, Hopkins selected one that predates his entanglement with Stanley. In doing so, she circumvents the brutality that had come to be associated with Stanley in favor of a version of Livingstone whose abolitionist background made him, in the words of George Washington Williams, Stanley's "noble" and kind foil.[48]

As Reuel Briggs's family history is uncovered over the course of the novel, revealing him to be an actual Livingston, he adopts the identity of David Livingstone alongside his royal crown, which "enacts a dramatic inversion of nineteenth-century history, white agency, and African exploration."[49] This allows for a new Livingston to emerge within the text, which is a microcosm of what Hopkins achieves by supplementing Coombs's Livingstone with her own black missionary hero. Hopkins transforms Coombs's volume into a narrative of "self-knowledge" (represented in *Of One Blood* by the respective journeys of Reuel and Dianthe) that, as Elisabeth Engel writes of Charles

Smith's *Glimpses of Africa*, is unique to African American African travel narratives. Unlike white exploration narratives that express pride at being a pioneer in unexplored regions, Smith takes pride in finding Sheppard's name carved on a tree near Boma. By sticking to familiar coastal regions rather than claiming new knowledge, Smith "foregrounded his personal mission of producing knowledge by means of comparisons between colonial realties and books."[50] In her novel, Hopkins opens up space for a similar critique of colonial discourse by employing a system of allusion that includes what Sanborn calls plagiarism. *Of One Blood* revised Livingstone much as William Sheppard did during furlough speaking tours that proclaimed him the "Black Livingstone."[51] Hopkins's reinvention of a colonial archive can be read as a prototype of the postcolonial achievements of works like NoubeSe Philip's 1991 prose poem *Looking for Livingstone: An Odyssey of Silence*, which invents an elaborate archival history for its purported source.[52]

## The Colored American Magazine

*Of One Blood* shares the central conceit of missionary William Sheppard's narrative. Sheppard is, like *Of One Blood* protagonist Reuel Briggs, an educated reformer who is surprised to find himself embraced as the heir to an African throne. The return enacted by Reuel, like that of the Sheppards, represents what Brent Hayes Edwards characterizes as a central urge in the African diaspora: "If black New World populations have their origin in the fragmentation, racialized oppression, and systematic dispossession of the slave trade, then the Pan-African impulse stems from the necessity to confront or heal that legacy through racial organization itself: through ideologies of a real or symbolic return to Africa."[53] Whereas the Sheppards' return to Africa represents the "real," their experiences, documented and circulated through speeches and writings, provide a source for American constructions of a "symbolic return," such as that undertaken in Hopkins's fictional narrative. This connection between the real and the symbolic, which has a parallel in Gilroy's model of routes and roots, is a crucial element of fiction about Africa.

Hopkins's familiarity with the Congo and the Sheppards was not happenstance, but rather was facilitated through a dynamic African American print culture of which she was both a consumer and a producer. One of Sheppard's most prominent forums, and one of the places where Hopkins may have encountered him, was the *Southern Workman*, the monthly organ of Hampton Institute, which was "published regularly longer than any other black journal with the exception of the *Crisis*."[54] At that time, the Hampton Folklore Society's Department of Folk-Lore and Ethnology column may have been one attraction for Hopkins as it was for Alexander Crummell, Anna Julia Cooper, Robert Moton, Daniel Webster Davis, and William Scarborough.[55] As the *Southern Workman* blossomed into a forum for the best-known women and men of Afro-America, the periodical was distributed in thirty-five (of forty-five) states and internationally to supporters, alumni, and other publishers.[56] Subscription records indicate that it circulated extensively in Boston, where 30 percent of the city's rapidly increasing black population was born in Hampton's home state of Virginia, including all four officers of its publisher, the Colored Co-operative Publishing Company.[57] Both of the parents of Walter W. Wallace—the company's president, the magazine's managing editor, and one of Hopkins's firmest allies—attended Hampton; his mother Nannie J. Ellerson was one of its first graduates, proudly marking him as "the oldest grand-child of that institution."[58] Under these circumstances, the *Southern Workman*, to say nothing of other periodicals featuring Sheppard, was readily available to Hopkins as she wrote *Of One Blood*.

The *Southern Workman* may have shaped Hopkins and Wallace's vision for the *Colored American Magazine*, which, with a circulation of close to 20,000, became "the first significant Afro-American journal to emerge in the twentieth century."[59] The Colored Co-operative Publishing Company simultaneously envisioned itself as a book publisher whose first and most prominent title was Hopkins's novel *Contending Forces: A Romance Illustrative of Negro Life North and South*. The magazine describes Hopkins's fiction as a means of "reaching those who never read history or biography,"[60] so it fits that she would share the Sheppards' story in *Of One Blood*, as she did the tale of the *Creole* slave ship rebellion in "A Dash for Liberty" in which, as Ivy Wilson writes of Frederick Douglass's *The Heroic Slave*, "the protagonist can find refuge only in another country," the British colony in the Bahamas.[61]

The Colored Co-operative Publishing Company provided an institutional model of nationalist enterprise across all of its platforms.[62] In addition to hiring a mostly black staff, the *Colored American Magazine* developed a cooperative model in which subscribers were members who owned a portion of the magazine and writers were compensated in part with certificates of deposit in the cooperative.[63] The magazine had branch offices and agents throughout the United States, mainly in Northern cities, as well as in the West Indies and in Liberia. Its organizational apparatus affirmed the political autonomy and transnational affiliations that were articulated in its pages. As Colleen O'Brien points out, throughout Hopkins's career, "there is a consistent underlying theme of transnational racial cooperation among those whom she referred to as 'The Dark Races of the Twentieth Century.' Her periodical work thus looks less like bourgeois uplift literature and more like the oppositional Paris literary world of the 1920s analyzed by Walter Benjamin."[64]

Venues such as the *Southern Workman* and the *Colored American Magazine* were more than outlets for the circulation of fully formed narratives. They were also, critically, the space in which such narratives were nurtured, through a body of literature that included fiction. In *The Golden Age of Black Nationalism, 1850–1925*, Wilson J. Moses reflects on *Of One Blood*: "Certainly, no one was converted to black nationalism as a result of this, but Pan-Africanism was insinuating its way even into sentimental magazine serials. This symbolizes the pervasiveness of Pan-African ideals, whose contact was unavoidable if one happened to be a literate urban black during the early 1900s."[65] Moses is correct to point out the underappreciated pervasiveness of Pan-African thought, which he has done as much as any scholar to recover. Yet Pan-Africanism was not a ubiquitous force that inevitably insinuated its way into fiction, but was constructed and reinvigorated by literary producers, including the *Colored American Magazine*. Lois Brown believes that Hopkins's "primary contribution to the growing pan-Africanist movement was her solicitation of potential *Colored American Magazine* articles from Africans active in the international conference movements and African expatriate press," which "introduced them to American readers, and . . . provided a dynamic forum in which they could build new ventures to achieve African autonomy. Indeed, the magazine, under Hopkins's supervision, had the potential to create a mobilized and progressive international coalition of people of African descent."[66] Brown situates the *Colored American Magazine*, whose readers included many important intellectuals, among the vibrant diasporic cultural traditions, including Pan-African meetings, that animated the first half of the twentieth century.[67]

Furthermore, sentimentalism was an important instrument for Hopkins, as it was for Garvey, whose "conception of African liberation," Moses argues elsewhere, "seems melodramatic, romantic, sentimental and ironically 'Eurocentric.'"[68] The rhetoric shared by Hopkins and Garvey need not be understood as a matter of direct influence, but may be seen as similar to certain recurrent tropes in the Works Progress Administration (WPA) interviews with formerly enslaved people. According to historian Michael A. Gomez, these interviews "reveal . . . the collective consciousness of the African-based community," which is not some preternatural phenomenon or a direct reflection of lived experience as much as it is "an intergenerational crafting by those who were actually captured and by those who were born on American soil. The story was not told as it actually happened but recast." Narratives of return are codified, therefore, through a practice of storytelling that circulates in communities that include people with firsthand knowledge of Africa as well as those without, which illuminates the relationship of Hopkins's novel to Sheppard's tale. The oral traditions documented by the WPA and the

Hampton Folklore Society are similarly shared through print culture, where, for example, Sheppard's speeches about the Congo were read alongside the work of the Department of Folk-Lore and Ethnology. The confluence of *Of One Blood* and the story of the Sheppards suggests a discursive process whereby collectively these tales attempt "to convey what the African-based community perceived as the essential truth of the experience."[69] An insistence on a firm distinction between "reports by others" and "firsthand experiences" neglects the cultural significance of the travelers whose work made Africa familiar in ways that demystified "firsthand" exposure, allowing a more inclusive definition of Engel's "self-knowledge" at a historical moment when, as Houston A. Baker Jr. points out, African American experience was shaped by limited mobility.[70]

In *Of One Blood* and elsewhere, experiences of the African diaspora are narrated and comprehended through the collective "vocalization" of musical performance. Individual consciousness alone fails to provide Dianthe with redemption. Even after her private performance of "Go Down, Moses" enables her to recuperate her memory, Aubrey tells her, "Yes, Felice, there *is* a story in your life! I can save you." Memory is incomplete or dysfunctional without a story, which is highlighted by the misrecognition within the terms of address: Aubrey addresses her as Felice, her fabricated name. Hopkins does not include their dialogue in the novel, but self-referentially states, "he recounted . . . the story of Dianthe Lusk as we have told it here."[71] In this sentence, the novel adopts a collective narrative persona. At this point, Aubrey is as reliable—or unreliable—as Hopkins herself. However Aubrey's deeply troubling narrative hegemony is predicated on his manipulation and exploitation of an African American woman. In the end, the revelation that Aubrey is not white and that Dianthe's story is effectively his, even if neither of them realized as much at its original telling, complicates his supposed authority. There may be some discomfort in suggesting that Aubrey gives Dianthe's story its narrative shape, yet in scenes like this the novel is conscious, if not critical, of its own devices as readers are forcefully reminded that the author and her plural narrator have the final authoritative word.

## The Broad Field of International Union and Uplift for the Blacks in All Quarters of the Globe

The contributions of Hopkins and the *Colored American Magazine* should be situated within Boston's vibrant political and literary culture. Hopkins worked closely with Geraldine Pindell Trotter in the Colored National League—the city's "most daring, outspoken, and unapologetic African American political collective." Not only was the Colored National League forthright in its criticism of the hypocrisy of U.S. imperialism, but it also met at Hopkins's church.[72] In 1899 she read to the group from the *Contending Forces* manuscript, as she did to the Woman's Era Club, a Boston affiliate of the National Association of Colored Women. She later was a charter member of the Boston Literary and Historical Association, of which William Monroe Trotter, Geraldine's activist husband and a Hopkins ally, was a founder. In 1903, she spoke to that group's membership two months after Du Bois had done so.[73] An essential element of the Boston Literary and Historical Association's political commitments was its internationalism, which included discussions about Cuba and China in order to explore what Elizabeth McHenry describes as "the possibility of creating a unified front with other 'darker races' throughout the world."[74] These conversations coincided with issues that were addressed by the *Colored American Magazine*'s acknowledgment in its coverage of the 1900 Pan-African Conference that isolation was not viable in the modern world: "People did make their way all over the world's surface, and it was no longer a tenable proposition for the inhabitants of any part of the world's surface to say: 'We do not want to see anybody else, we prefer to isolate ourselves; we won't have visitors. . . .' The question they had to settle now was: How was the universal intercourse of man, which they had to recognize as an established fact, to be carried on in the best possible way?"[75] The challenge facing the Pan-African Conference was the same as that facing the Boston Literary and Historical Association and characters in *Of One Blood*— how to conduct transnational interactions in the least exploitative or otherwise "best possible" manner. According to Hopkins and many of the conference delegates, which included missionaries, diasporic blacks were the agents best suited to the task. This attitude was neither unusual nor unproblematic. As Kevin Gaines points out, "Because it shared many of the assumptions of an evangelical worldview, the rhetoric of racial uplift often resembled the imperialist notion of the 'civilizing mission.'"[76] Such attitudes would have been quite familiar within these Boston circles.

Gaines explicates the connections between missionary politics and racial uplift, which connects the international and the domestic in a way that is useful for situating the *Colored American Magazine* within the broader sphere of African American political culture. As Lois Brown points out, the magazine began publication in May 1900 as "a resource for the increasingly mobilized African American organizations that were rallying to end lynching and institutionalized racism and inequality."[77] Although the magazine was committed to a progressive agenda, it was not overtly antagonistic. Its very first issue, for instance, acknowledged its largely Northern readership's disagreement with many of Booker T. Washington's positions, but pacifically suggested that he be supported: "we of New England can, with credit to ourselves, forbear the spirit of criticism and lend him our encouragement in every method of work he may undertake believing him to be as loyal to the welfare of the race as we are." The magazine's explication of its editorial position toward Washington in its inaugural issue marked their entry into a discussion of African American affairs at a time when Washington was a touchstone. This was not shallow or sarcastic rhetoric about "his manly and courageous efforts"; the *Colored American Magazine* published a substantial excerpt of a Washington speech alongside its coverage of the Pan-African Conference in September 1900.[78]

In November 1900, Hopkins opened her *Famous Men of the Negro Race* series with a profile of Toussaint L'Ouverture, the leader of the Haitian Revolution, which, like Williams's historical epics, indicated a fundamental commitment to charting a tradition of diasporic black leadership that was not bound by the borders of the United States. In October 1901, Hopkins concluded the series with a markedly ambivalent profile of Washington that more harshly, though still politely, exposed the disparity between the rhetoric and reality of his professed localism by contrasting the European postmark of his letter opposing federal intervention against lynching with a speech by Rev. Quincy Ewing of Mississippi advocating federal legislation. In her conclusion, Hopkins tentatively asserted Washington's "stupendous" influence while insisting that the jury was still out: "Dr. Washington's motives will be open to as many constructions and discussions as are those of Napoleon today, or of other men of extraordinary ability, whether for good or evil, who have had like phenomenal careers."[79] Her clever ambivalence escaped the notice of historian August Meier, whose 1953 essay "Booker T. Washington and the Negro Press: With Special Reference to the *Colored American Magazine*" makes no mention of Hopkins. Meier instead reads an article advocating liberal arts education as a "vigorous attack" on Washington based on the reputation of its author, George Washington Forbes, who was William Monroe Trotter's coeditor at the Boston *Guardian* which began publishing in November 1901.[80]

Still Washington saw newspapers and magazines as means to counter his opponents; he quietly financed several Boston newspaper ventures and even secretly tried to purchase the *Guardian*. Following a series of failures, Washington set his sights on the *Colored American Magazine*.[81] His interest was partly opportunistic; the magazine's financial difficulties led it to rely on the subsidy of John C. Freund, a white New York publisher and an eventual correspondent of Washington's. These struggles created an opening Washington could exploit as part of his broader efforts to amplify his voice in the African American press and to undermine the Boston-based progressive community centered around Trotter and the *Guardian*. In this way, the

*Colored American Magazine* became an important proxy in one of the defining conflicts in twentieth-century African American political culture, although the centrality of Trotter has been overshadowed by a simplified portrait of Washington's conflict with Du Bois.[82]

In a lengthy letter to Trotter, solicited at the behest of Du Bois, Hopkins was clear about her ouster, which was, Du Bois later explained in the *Crisis*, because "her attitude was not conciliatory enough."[83] Hopkins believed that her commitment to international affairs cost her career, as Freund "was curtailing my work from the broad field of *international* union and *uplift* for the Blacks in all quarters of the globe, to the narrow confines of the question as affecting solely the Afro-American." Hopkins cites a letter from Freund in which he insists: "If you people, therefore, want to get out a literary magazine, with article [*sic*] ON THE FILIPINO, I refuse to work one minute longer with you. That is my ultimatum and I shall say no more on the subject."[84] Hopkins's consistent attention to the "dark races" and autonomous black states seems to mark the political differences between her and Washington. Her celebration of Toussaint in *Famous Men of the Negro Race* contrasts with the failed attempt by Washington, despite his international mobility, to pay homage at Toussaint's "tomb."[85] Her glorification of Ethiopia in *Of One Blood* and her allusions to the Congo indicate a different position from the apologetic reformist platform on which Washington stood. Their dissimilar political ideologies, which can be read through the institutional history of the *Colored American Magazine*, suggested the wide range of the Congo's appeal, which, for Hopkins, was consistent with her commitment to black self-governance in political and civic institutions of all scales. Hopkins's belief in autonomy applied no less to the black press than to international politics. In her self-published 1905 pamphlet, *A Primer of Facts Pertaining to the Early Greatness of the African Race and the Possibility of Restoration by Its Descendants*, Hopkins uses her experiences at the *Colored American Magazine* to reflect on the plight of the black press: "The Propaganda of Silence is in full force. Newspapers and magazines have been subsidized or destroyed if the editors fearlessly advocated the cause of humanity."[86] The pamphlet established a parallel between Washington's financial shenanigans and the destructive violence aimed at black journalists by white supremacist groups.[87]

By January 1904, the financially struggling *Colored American Magazine* declared itself "Under New Management" and began offering copies of Washington's books as premiums to entice new subscribers. By the middle of the year, Washington arranged for Fred R. Moore to purchase the magazine, move its offices from Boston to New York, and fire Hopkins. As late as May 1904, the magazine announced that Hopkins would undertake a summer tour to distribute the magazine to agents around the country. One month later, Moore replaced her in the masthead, thereby effectively ending the heyday of one of the premier independent black publications of the twentieth century's first decade. In November 1904 and again in June 1905, the *Colored American Magazine* accounted for Hopkins's departure by claiming her "ill-health," indicating that she remained on the minds of readers a full year after abruptly disappearing from the pages of the magazine.[88] These explanations seem unlikely because Hopkins covered the October 1904 opening of the New York City subway for the *Voice of the Negro* and continued to write for them through 1905. She maintained her popularity at the *Voice of the Negro*, where she was advertised alongside Du Bois's series *The Beginnings and Endings of Slavery*: "Many people have written us and spoken to us about Miss Hopkins' articles. Evidently they have awakened great interest in the history of the colored people of the world."[89] Indeed, Lois Brown notes a shift in tone with her 1905 *Voice of the Negro* nonfiction series, *The Dark Races of the Twentieth Century*, which is "noticeably forthright and unsentimental. The absence of emotional language in Hopkins's work also reaffirmed her studious effort to participate fully in pan-African discourse and also to cultivate the impression that she could be a promising leader in those same global circles."[90] The sentimentalism that she used so expertly in *Of One Blood* gave way to new discursive forms that enabled her to continue to address international affairs not only in a different venue but also in a different genre with a different voice.

In October 1909, long after its Hopkins-edited heyday, the penultimate issue of the *Colored American Magazine* published Washington's "The African at Home" along with a story about the acquittal of William Sheppard. Washington's rosy explanation of Tuskegee as the voluntary site for his African work contrasted with the legal campaign that Sheppard faced because of his outspokenness in the Congo. In the magazine's final issue in November 1909, another brief notice on Sheppard's court victory appeared.[91] These materials evoke an ongoing community that bridges the local and international worlds that Hopkins also incorporated into her fiction. In her writings and her relationships with her readers, she developed a literary discourse that synthesized the careers of Sheppard, Washington, Williams, Sharp, and others. Amid a contentious state of affairs in Boston, Hopkins argued in her fiction and nonfiction for a unity based on Africa as both a site of origins and a site of future political interests. The institutional history of the *Colored American Magazine* provides one location for reading Hopkins's career for its commentary on the conflicted political scene. Meanwhile the world of black periodical publishing was shifting. While the *Colored American Magazine* was languishing, the *Voice of the Negro*, which was published from 1904 to 1907, was instrumental in promoting the work of the Niagara movement and "laid a basis for" the NAACP's definitive *Cri-*

*sis* magazine, whose first issue appeared in November 1910 exactly one year after the *Colored American Magazine* was shuttered.⁹²

## Black Classics Series . . . Number One

After her editorial career at the *Colored American Magazine* ended, Hopkins continued to cultivate her audience and to focus on Africa. Beyond the evidence of Hopkins's familiarity with the Sheppards, their connection exemplifies a shared African American discourse about Africa that is grounded in the predicament of the modern African state. The visibility of the Sheppards reveals that African American interest in Africa is not, as Gilroy contends, "frozen at the point where blacks boarded the ships that would carry them into the woes and horrors of the middle passage." Hopkins's representation of classical African civilization in the novel is much more than an uncomplicated appeal to mystical roots; indeed, her narrative's "movement and meditation" highlight the centrality of routes to the formation of an African diasporic identity.⁹³ Cedric R. Tolliver makes a compelling case that "the back-to-Africa section of the novel . . . makes legible the limits of the project of seeking to discover the ancient racial past. This project, while it resists the white denial of civilization in the black racial past, also embraces that discourse's construction of history as a hereditary science." Given early-twentieth-century conceptions of "heritable traits," Hopkins's adherence to some notion of continuity, a corollary to Gilroy's "roots," seems unavoidable.⁹⁴ In doing so, however, Hopkins rejects an artificial juxtaposition of "routes" and "roots," offering instead a critique of "roots" that opens up space for African American engagement with imperialism even if the space for critique contains its own limitations.

Hopkins's involvement with discourses of colonialism eschews the confines of a racial discourse that is narrowly delimited by heritable traits. *Of One Blood* acknowledges as much in its final paragraphs when, even as Reuel returns to Africa following the deaths of his siblings, a romantic future for the restored ruler is not a foregone conclusion. Rather, it is "with serious apprehension" that Reuel reflects on "the advance of mighty nations penetrating the dark mysterious forests of his native land."⁹⁵ This dynamic view of Africa demonstrates an understanding of "cultural identity," which in Hall's definition, "is not a fixed origin to which we can make some final and absolute Return."⁹⁶ Hopkins's concluding note of caution concerning imperialism seems a fitting end to the novel, since it demonstrates that her interest in Africa, finally, is not exclusively classical; like the Sheppards, she understands the threat that European interlopers pose to modern Africa. Such political awareness reflects the impact of the Sheppards' routes on Hopkins's construction of diaspora identity. In the end, Hopkins's image of Africa, despite its strong "mystical" qualities, is not "ruthlessly positive," but is actually quite cautious.[97]

*Of One Blood* manifests its author's understanding of the multivalent political dynamics of modern Africa. Susan Gillman recognizes this complex amalgam as "a transculturated Africa, a fictional representation derived largely from factual sources and black history, not all of it glorious, and inclusive of both the contemporary United States and the colonial world as well as of a diasporic, Pan-African future, itself contingent on colonial incursions in present-day Africa."[98] Through this lens of sources, including Williams, Rufus Perry, Martin Delany, and William Wells Brown, Hopkins's references to Ethiopia must be viewed as deliberatively inclusive engagements with all of Africa that skillfully appropriate the regional glories of ancient and contemporary Ethiopia for what she effectively sees as a Greater Ethiopia. If Gay Wilentz is correct in her observation that "very few, if any, Africans were actually transported from this part of the continent to be slaves in the Americas," Hopkins's Ethiopianism is only "geographically confused" if it is assumed to be a narrow articulation of hereditary origins, rather than part of a larger political project that, while infused with the idea of roots, is not limited by them.[99] Hopkins's "Ethiopia" represents a strategic response to the political realities of modern Africa, and *Of One Blood* articulates an African American connection to the continent that is not principally genealogical.

Of course, Hopkins's references to Ethiopia also drew on Psalm 68's oft-cited biblical prophecy of rejuvenation: "Ethiopia shall soon stretch forth her hand unto God." This propitious divination was widely used by nineteenth-century religious leaders such as Henry Highland Garnet as proof of the coming salvation of African peoples.[100] In its broadest sense as a long-standing synecdoche for the entire continent, "Ethiopia" was already inclusively Pan-African, encompassing blacks in Africa and throughout its diaspora.[101] Hopkins also drew on a tradition in African American letters that consistently links Ethiopia to Egypt. She ascribed to the popular belief that, in the words of Professor Stone, the British leader of *Of One Blood*'s African expedition, "It is a *fact* that Egypt drew from Ethiopia all the arts, sciences and knowledge of which she was mistress."[102] Hopkins was in the tradition of Frances Ellen Watkins Harper, who published a long poem, *Moses: A Story of the Nile*, that described ancient Egypt as a product of Ethiopian civilization, in 1869; Harper spoke to the Boston Literary and Historical Association in the same month that *Of One Blood* opened.[103] Similarly Williams's *History of the Negro Race in America* detailed evidence of a Negro presence in ancient and modern Egyptian militaries.[104] Professor Stone's explanation includes a reference to the "Shepherd kings," who, according to Williams, were the last in a long line of the "Ethiopian Kings of Egypt" and, according to Perry, the source of racial amalgamation in the Nile valley.[105] Whether or not Hopkins alludes to William "Shepherd," as he appears in her Sharp article, she recognizes that the Shepherd Kings were not innocent but that they "subjugated the whole of Upper Egypt."[106] In his account, Williams is clear that they were, ultimately, overthrown by the last in a lineage of Nubian rulers.

*A Primer of Facts* is significant because it is primarily about Africa and explicitly addresses readers familiar with Hopkins as the "Author of 'Contending Forces,' 'Hagar's Daughter,' "Winona,' 'Talma Gordon,' 'Famous Men of the Negro Race,' 'Famous Women of the Negro Race,' Etc." Moreover, *A Primer of Facts* echoed many of the arguments that appear in her fiction. She described places (Meroe, the "queen city of Ethiopia") and people (Ergamenes and Candace) whose namesakes were familiar to readers of *Of One Blood*.[107] *A Primer of Facts* was identified on its cover as "Black Classics Series . . . Number One," suggesting that Hopkins's Cambridge, Massachusetts–based enterprise projected an ongoing commitment to writing about Africa in a climate where black magazines and newspapers were under attack. When she and Walter Wallace established the short-lived *New Era Magazine* more than a decade later, they planned to run a series of articles under the same title.[108]

Continuing what she had begun at the magazine, Hopkins opened *A Primer of Facts* with a version of the "one blood" argument that gave the novel its title: "Man began his existence in the creation of Adam, therefore all races of mankind were once united and descended from one parentage." In Hopkins's lexicon, the flow of "blood" represents the unstoppable motion of historical progress: "Blood will flow, but not by the seeking of the Black, and he will only participate in the fight when the government places in his hands arms for its protection. . . . When labor and capital become contending forces, the Black will float into the full enjoyment of citizenship. Blood will flow, for humanity sweeps onward, and God's purposes never fail."[109] In this passage, Hopkins referenced her first novel, *Contending Forces*, to assert that blood is not only a marker of racial unity, but is also a product of struggle, which she presents within a very distinctive political apparatus that suggests both militancy and loyalty to the state. As O'Brien explains, "Hopkins clothes her Marxian ideology in biblical prophesy," which may be an attempt to gain an audience around matters of political economy, where she knew her ideas were taken less seriously than they would be were she a man: "I have argued the union of the Negro with labor for a number of years, but being only a woman have received very small notice; however, it matters not who moves the sun as long as we are convinced that 'she do move.' "[110] Her awareness of this perception provides valuable context for her shifting relationship with the sentimental form during the first years of the twentieth century.

This more literal vision of blood as the product of struggle, whether in a war against slavery or in the struggle of labor and capital, was part of the larger historical lens through which Hopkins viewed the Congo State. She explicitly outlined the possibilities for the modern fulfillment of the biblical prophecy of the restoration of Ethiopia, taking as evidence,

> The establishment of the Liberian Republic, the Anglo-Boer war in South Africa and the rapid opening up of the Continent of Africa by civilized powers during the nineteenth century and the rapid intellectual improvement of Africans and their descendants in all parts of the world.
>
> What is the obligation of the descendant of Africans in America?—To help forward the time of restoration.
>
> HOW MAY THIS BE DONE?—By becoming thoroughly familiar with meagre details of Ethiopian history, by fostering race pride and an international friendship with the Blacks of Africa.
>
> Are we obliged to emigrate to Africa to do this successfully?—No. Friendly intercourse and mutual aid and comfort are all that are necessary at the present time.[111]

In the absence of emigration, print culture becomes a critical medium for "Friendly intercourse and mutual aid and comfort."

Hopkins's vision of a Greater Ethiopia in *A Primer of Facts* is "Compiled and Arranged from the Works of the best known Ethnologists and Historians."[112] Composed as a series of questions and answers that borrows language directly from Delany's *Principia of Ethnology: The Origin of Races and Color, with an Archeological Compendium of Ethiopian and Egyptian Civilization, from Years of Careful Examination and Enquiry* (1879), Hopkins asks, "WERE ETHIOPIA AND EGYPT EVER UNITED KINGDOMS?" and, citing Pliny, Diodorus Siculus, and Herodotus, affirms, "That the rule of Cush extended from the Nilotic borders of Egypt in toward the interior of darkest Africa, and known as Ethiopia, is not to be disputed, all historians of ancient history agreeing on this point."[113] *Of One Blood*'s "Ethiopia," therefore, includes the *Primer*'s "interior of darkest Africa." With such language, Hopkins recalls the title of Stanley's 1890 bestseller *In Darkest Africa*; foreshadows Sheppard's 1905 address in the *Southern Workman*, "Light in Darkest Africa"; and carefully appropriates what Patrick Brantlinger terms "the myth of the Dark Continent," a "widely shared . . . view of Africa which demanded imperialization on moral, religious, and scientific grounds."[114]

*A Primer of Facts* was part of a larger African American revision of Eurocentric genealogies of African civilization. Meroe, the capital of ancient Nubia (in present-day Sudan), was commonly referred to as "Ethiopia" in classical texts, as it is in *Of One Blood*, which strategically melds classical and modern geographies. In conjunction with Hopkins's definition of Ethiopia, her novel's geography associates the glories of the ancient Nile valley with central Africa: "In the heart of Africa was a knowledge of science that all the wealth and learning of modern times could not emulate."[115] Her Ethiopianist genealogy is similar to that of Sheppard, who audaciously suggests, "Perhaps they [the Kuba] got their civilization from the Egyptians—or the Egyptians theirs from the Bakuba (!)."[116] Like Hopkins, he expands the idea that Ethiopia was the source of Egyptian civilization in order to make specific claims for central Africa. Even the language Hopkins uses to make her assertions—"In the heart of Africa"—recalls Hale's description of "Mr. Shepherd [*sic*], in the very heart of Africa" and the titles of two *Southern Workman* articles, one about William Sheppard ("In the Heart of Africa") and one by him ("Into the Heart of Africa"). The convergence of language suggests a form of collective consciousness similar to what Gomez locates within WPA interviews. In the end, these texts use contemporary geographical rhetoric to describe Ethiopianist and Kuba-ist genealogies that associate African Americans with the renowned magnificence of ancient Egypt.

Such formulations developed in communities where, at the time, modern Ethiopia was as familiar as the Ethiopia of Psalm 68. On March 1, 1896, Ethiopian forces under the command of Menelik II resoundingly defeated the Italian military at Aduwa. The Italians suffered 7,500 casualties (43 percent of their forces) and 1,800 captives. The military victory of the Ethiopian state, which was covered extensively in the black press, fortified "Ethiopianism" as a proud contemporary Pan-African formulation.[117] Menelik II was a hero who, the *Colored American Magazine* reported, the Pan-African Conference named an "honorable" member, a position shared only with the presidents of the independent black republics of Liberia and Haiti. For both Williams and Hopkins, independent African states were instructive models for the United States. While Ethiopia provided cause for optimism at the close of *Of One Blood*, the novel avoided naive euphoria. In late 1903, Ethiopia signed a commercial treaty with the U.S. Department of State that affirmed the cautionary tenor of her novel's concluding observation.

Cognizant of these maneuvers, Hopkins pointed out the government's hypocrisy in the final installment of *The Dark Races of the Twentieth Century*, stating "A treaty has just been signed between the United States' government and 'Menelik II, by the Grace of God King of Kings of Ethiopia.' It is a curious fact that the United States authorities maintain friendly relations with all independent black governments, although dealing severely with its own Negro population."[118] At the moment when Hopkins was writing *Of One Blood*, concerns about imperial threats were allied less with modern Ethiopia, the professed setting of the novel, than with the Congo State, which was then, thanks in part to the Sheppards, emerging as a rallying point for activists internationally. This divergence was a relatively recent phenomenon, however, because "Ethiopia and Congo shared comparable and mutually intelligible political cultures during the sixteenth and seventeenth centuries."[119] While modern Ethiopia provided a cause for cautious optimism for Hopkins, the Congo was the clearest cause for alarm: "With the rapid advance which exploration has made in Africa in recent years, there has followed a great rivalry among European nations for colonies and protectorates; but while great wealth and boundless avenues for commerce have been opened up, civilization has been a mixed blessing to the natives, and today the eyes of Christendom are fastened upon the Congo Free State and its attendant acts of atrocity in the enforcement of slavery within its borders. The regeneration of Africa is upon us, but blood and tears flow in its train."[120] Despite her ambivalence about imperialism, Hopkins's explicit commentary on the Congo exhibits a discernment of the foreign threat to modern Africa, reminiscent of Reuel Briggs's reflections at the end of *Of One Blood*. Gaines notes that here, "a denunciation of the atrocities of Belgian authorities in the Congo contended, in the same breath, with a generally benign missionary view of colonialization."[121] In essays such as this, Hopkins is clearly struggling to offer a critique of colonialism by building an alternative literary discourse on the problematic dream that she shared with so many of her contemporaries.[122] *Of One Blood* envisions racial uplift as an alternative to European imperialism even if today readers are struck by their uncomfortable similarities.

## Virginia Dreams

Hopkins's storied career is only one form of literary engagement with Africa. Her "transculturated" incorporation of the Sheppards is distinct from the poetry of Maggie Pogue Johnson, an African American writer from Virginia, whose 1910 collection *Virginia Dreams: Lyrics for the Idle Hours. Tales of the Time Told in Rhyme* features "Dedicated to Dr. W. H. Sheppard (The returned missionary, who spent twenty years in Africa)." Much like *Of One Blood*, Johnson's poem offers a detailed narrative of its protagonist's religious achievements in "Ethiopia" without naming the Congo. From its opening line—"On, on to the darkest continent"—Johnson relies on conventional imperialist discourse. Colonial images of darkness and light are repeated throughout the poem, affecting an uncritical take on the missionary project without referring to Sheppard's activism or trial. The sole footnote explicates the "Forbidden Land" as a "reference to a tribe of savages in the interior, known as Bakubas," a description that runs counter to Sheppard's more nuanced accounts of Kuba culture. Johnson's characterization—here and throughout the poem—demonstrates the facility with which Sheppard's painstaking ethnographic project can be shoehorned into existing paradigms of the continent.[123] Her poem translates the historical specificity of his accomplishments into a more generic narrative of Christian conversion:

> For twenty years he struggled,
>   In Africa's darkened land,
> Giving them the light
>   As they heeded his command.[124]

This 108-line poem elevates William Sheppard to the status of a mythologized hero, and demonstrates how ostensibly political stories about colonialism in Congo can be transformed into romantic Ethiopianist literature about Africa. Both political and romantic discourses exist within the same sphere.

Sheppard's place in Johnson's larger poetic project is equally intriguing in that *Virginia Dreams* follows books like Paul Laurence Dunbar's *Lyrics of Lowly Life* in its combination of standard English verse and dialect poetry. Her tribute to Dunbar, "Poet of Our Race," is, like "Dedicated to Dr. W. H. Sheppard," composed in standard English verse. "Dedicated to Dr. W. H. Sheppard," however, is directly preceded by a dialect tribute to Washington.[125] The language of "To See Ol' Booker T." affirms Washington's status as a Southern subject and provides both a counterpoint and context for Sheppard, who exists beside his Hampton teacher yet within a distinct discursive realm that gives his two decades of work in "Ethiopia" a gravity that is marked by its geography, labor, language, and imagery. Her tribute to Washington's "Cullered Skool" lacks the religious imagery and pastoral landscape of the other two poems' subjects, both of who won the "victor's crown" in strikingly similar language—Dunbar (who died in 1906 at the age of thirty-three) in memoriam and Sheppard for:

> After toiling daily,
>   With Ethiopia's sons,
> Many were brought to Christ,
>   A victor[']s crown was won.[126]

Johnson's poem does the work of the Presbyterian Church on the occasion of Sheppard's retirement by situating his achievements squarely within the religious realm as part of a romantic evacuation of their political significance.

Hopkins's Ethiopia is as much a product of the Congo as is Johnson's *Virginia Dreams*. As a discourse about modern Africa circulated through networks of HBCUs such as Hampton and through the press, a wide cross section of African American writers fashioned a complex relationship to the entire continent, born of both their backgrounds in the United States and their knowledge of Africa. As the author of four novels and numerous stories, Hopkins evoked the Congo in more traditional literary forms, albeit less directly than writers like Williams and Washington. The identification of direct sources for Hopkins's *Of One Blood* makes a larger argument about the utility of a full accounting of the routes within roots. The methodological and interpretive challenge remains for scholars to map the black Atlantic routes between African Americans and Africa to appreciate the full range of sources that informed Hopkins's writing and her audience's reading, which reveal the contours of their profound engagement with colonialism.

*Chapter 6*

Visual Cultures

*Hampton Institute, William Sheppard's Kuba Collection, and African American Art*

In 1916, more than a decade removed from her tenure at the *Colored American Magazine* and *Voice of the Negro*, Pauline Hopkins made one final foray into publishing with her *New Era Magazine*, whose two issues featured decidedly international coverage of Ethiopia, Liberia, Haiti, and Puerto Rico. One feature that appeared in both issues was Meta Vaux Warrick Fuller's column, "Helpful Suggestions for Young Artists," as part of its art department.[1] As early as 1915, Fuller, who married Liberian doctor Solomon Fuller in 1909, had begun corresponding with the pioneering art historian Freeman Murray about "her interest in the theme 'The Rise of Ethiopia,' which she hoped 'someday to attempt.'" At the time, she was also, Renée Ater explains, learning about Egyptian art from reading the *Crisis*'s "exclusive coverage of archaeological excavations in the Sudan and Ethiopia, which stressed the reign of the Kushite kings and the ancient city of Meroe."[2] Her interest in Meroe could also have been piqued by her colleague Hopkins, whose novel *Of One Blood* had made many similar observations earlier in the century. Hopkins had mentioned Fuller in her 1905 pamphlet *A Primer of Facts Pertaining to the Early Greatness of the African Race and the Possibility of Restoration by Its Descendants*, and both of their oeuvres recognized Ethiopia "as a lone symbol of African autonomy at the height of the age of imperialism, serving as a beacon of hope to Africans and African Americans in the early twentieth century, as they began to imagine a postcolonial future."[3] Fuller's interest culminated in her best-known sculpture, *Ethiopia* (or *The Awakening of Ethiopia*), which was commissioned by James Weldon Johnson, acting on the recommendation of W. E. B. Du Bois, for the 1921 America's Making Exposition in New York.[4]

These networks—connecting figures like Fuller, Hopkins, Du Bois, and Johnson, through the black press, the NAACP, and other intellectual communities—have played a critical role in nurturing African American engagement with Africa across various media. Art historian Judith Wilson points out how in the sculpture of Fuller, along with earlier work by Edmonia Lewis, "we can trace the origins of African American modernism in the visual arts to an upsurge of politically-motivated identification with Africa's ancient Nile valley civilizations and a conflation of this romantic attachment to ancient Egypt and Nubia with concern for modern Ethiopia's fate."[5] Wilson makes the compelling argument that African American images of Ethiopia, like Hopkins's contributions in the literary realm, allude not only to Psalm 68, but also to the 1896 Ethiopian victory over Italian invaders at Aduwa. This practice extends beyond the historic Nile valley; visual artists appreciated the Congo as a state, like Ethiopia, with its own unique and familiar history of "politically-motivated identification."

These black Atlantic routes build on the cultural retentions that have been brilliantly documented by Melville Herskovits and Robert Farris Thompson to provide material links to ongoing political movements that continue to inform African American literature and art.[6] Thompson has devoted decades to examining Kongo cultural retentions within African American culture, usefully distinguishing it from the Congo state. Yet, as Jemima Pierre warns, too narrow a focus on African cultural survivals can obscure modern Africa: "the 'Africa' part of this cultural continuum exists in the (traditional) *past*, rendering continental phenomena static and bounded."[7] As a result it is easy to lose sight of how African American visual culture is shaped by experiences of and engagements with the state, over the course of multiple incarnations of colonialism and neocolonialism. Rather than understanding African material culture as simply "loci of memory, testifying about and illustrating the space of their origin," this chapter is interested in tracing the dynamic ways that African American visual artists have transformed African aesthetics in order "to revive the historical activity and the reactiveness of a culture with its motions and exemplary beauty."[8]

William Sheppard's storied activism provides a political framework, echoed in contemporary accounts, for his collection of what V. Y. Mudimbe terms "worked objects."[9] By consensus, art historians and anthropologists consider Sheppard's collection to be the first of the "three great early collections" of Kuba art, the others being those of Emil Torday of Hungary and Leo Frobenius of Germany.[10] The intersection of Sheppard's two identities, as an art collector and a political activist, provides a node for understanding how African American visual aesthetics, like art and culture more generally, are shaped by the wider culture of anticolonialism. Art historian Patricia Leighten similarly argues that the anarchists and socialists in Pablo Picasso's circle at the time he painted *Les Demoiselles d'Avignon* (1907) would have appreciated its contemporary allusions: "In this period, to evoke scarified African masks was to evoke a larger Africa, and all its associations with colonial exploitation, legalized slavery, and resistance to French rule."[11] Visual art must be understood alongside the lives and knowledge of the artists that created the work and the contemporary communities that experienced it. What Leighten describes for Picasso in France applies equally to African Americans at HBCUs: at the same time that Congolese art was gaining prominence in European museum collections, it was also being collected by figures like Sheppard and displayed at Hampton. African American encounters with African art materially entwine diasporic consciousness with contemporary political engagement.

Gilroy argues that in Du Bois's early writings, including *The Souls of Black Folk*, Africa serves "as a mythic counterpart to modernity in the Americas—a moral symbol transmitted by exquisite objects seen fleetingly in the African collection at Fisk University but largely disappearing from Du Bois's account, leaving an empty, aching space between his local and global manifestations of racial injustice."[12] Gilroy acknowledges the art collection in the basement of Bennett Hall at Fisk University as a potential source of Du Bois's interest in Africa; however, he may be understating its significance, including its influence on Du Bois, who attended Fisk from 1885 to 1888, and its contemporary connections to Africa via the American Missionary Association (AMA) missionaries whose donations established it.[13] Fisk began to exhibit its African art holdings in 1876 in a gallery whose installation was worthy of notice by *Harper's Weekly*.[14] Even Du Bois's beloved Jubilee Singers were committed to the project and over the years "by solicitation, obtained books, apparatus, works of art and collections for the museum."[15]

By all accounts, exposure to Fisk's collection nurtured an appreciation for African art. Through this Fisk missionary network, Althea Brown Edmiston was exposed to African culture as Du Bois had been. During her 1908 to 1911 furlough, Edmiston, and her husband "brought back with them many beautiful African curios and finely wrought Congo palm-fiber cloth," which they used to decorate their Tuscaloosa home where they frequently entertained. Not only did the Edmistons appreciate the aesthetic value of these pieces, but they also recognized their economic value as they organized "curio exhibits" to raise money for the return passage to the Congo that the Executive Committee of Foreign Missions of the Presbyterian Church was trying to block.[16] An inventory of Alonzo Edmiston's possessions at the time of his retirement in 1941 includes a list of art objects and "curios."[17] On his first post–American Presbyterian Congo Mission (APCM) lecture tour, Alonzo Edmiston featured them as visual aids, much as Sheppard did nearly fifty years earlier.[18]

Even earlier, George Washington Williams amassed a substantial collection of Congolese art, whose market and value he appreciated. In February 1891, he wrote to Collis Huntington from Cairo, offering him "six boxes of African curios—a veritable museum containing 'at least $1,000 worth of ivory'" as reimbursement for a debt.[19] In July 1891, Williams contacted Francis W. Fox about selling "60 or 70 African curios comprising ivory tusks, spears, shields, arrows, &c." for $1,000 to cover his medical expenses. Fox wrote to Huntington, proposing they lowball the terminally ill Williams with installments of $250 because, "I fancy, the money would be more than acceptable to Col. Williams, as he seems in a very low spot in body and spirits and in outward means." Despite his desperation, Williams had the forethought to suggest "these might form an interesting exhibit for the great Exhibition at Chicago next year."[20] While seeing a reasonable opportunity to solicit needed funds, Williams remained focused on the ethnological value of the collection, and held out hope of cultivating a wider audience for it. Williams died less than a month after meeting Fox. In the end, U.S. Consul Thomas H. Sherman auctioned Williams's African art collection to settle some of his debts. Although Sherman estimated the collection of "copper knives, quaint daggers and swords, carved spears, ornamental paddles, shields, bows and arrows, ivory tusks, trumpets, brass rings for neck, ankles and wrists, fishing spears, and other interesting objects" would bring between $500 and $1,000, the sale raised less than $250.[21]

Apparently, the collection was neither purchased by Huntington nor exhibited at the Columbian Exposition. Still, Williams foresaw a future of African installations at World's Fairs, which proved to be contested sites of racial representation. The case of the Columbian Exposition may be the best known, with its resultant pamphlet *The Reason Why the Colored American Is Not in the World's Columbian Exposition*, written by Frederick Douglass, Ida B. Wells, and other prominent figures. These expositions—with their associated expeditions—were part of a colonial project in which lives were, literally and directly, at stake. Following the controversy at the Columbian Exposition, subsequent events of that ilk, beginning with the 1895 Atlanta Cotton States Exposition (best known as the occasion of Washington's famed address), often featured dedicated African American exhibits. In Paris in 1900, Du Bois curated photographs for the *American Negro* exhibit, which functioned, in the words of Shawn Michelle Smith, as a visual "counterarchive" that "was forced implicitly to negotiate such constructions of 'Negro savagery'" as was displayed in popular African village exhibitions such as those in St. Louis in 1904.[22] African American pavilions became venues for independent curation, providing opportunities for intellectuals and artists to tell their own stories. Meta Fuller, for instance, received high-profile commissions for the Jamestown Exposition in 1907 and the Emancipation Proclamation celebration in Boston in 1913, leading up to her *Ethiopia* in New York in 1921.[23] For Congolese people, these occasions were often tragic—during the 1897 fair at Tervuren, Belgium, on the site that became the Royal Museum for Central Africa (RMCA), at least seven Congolese people who were brought for human display died from exposure. These results did not cease the penchant for human display, and the horrific case of the St. Louis Exposition remains well known. Less well known is that Verner parlayed his St. Louis commission into a 1905–6 art removal expedition to the Congo with Frederick Starr that acquired 4,000 objects for the American Museum of Natural History in New York.[24]

Simultaneous with these exhibitions, the African art collections at HBCUs were contributing to the larger diasporic visual project described by Smith. Williams's 1891 requests demonstrate a commitment to the broader cultural function of African art in the United States that was, by that time, already institutionalized at places like Hampton and Fisk. If Williams's goals were unrealized in the instance of the Columbian Exposition, Sheppard successfully shepherded his collection to Hampton, where for more than a century it has functioned as an important counterarchive. His collection, like Du Bois's 1900 Paris exhibition and contemporary work by the Hampton Camera Club, served a visual culture of uplift.[25] From its home at Hampton, Sheppard's African art collection does similar work toward what Smith describes as "the reconstruction of racial knowledge" by cultivating a diaspora consciousness among students and the community.[26]

Curiosity Room

As groundbreaking as Sheppard's collection was, it was built upon a strong foundation. Hampton's "Curiosity room" was established soon after the school itself as a way of facilitating cross-cultural understanding. (See Figure 6.1.) Many of the curios that students like Sheppard encountered as part of the curriculum had missionary origins from sources including Principal Armstrong's missionary parents in Hawai'i and Hampton alumni in Sierra Leone. Hampton had an African studies program as early as 1873 and, like Fisk, started to acquire African objects in the 1870s. African pieces were listed (without provenance) among the losses from an 1879 fire at Academic Hall. Soon thereafter, while Sheppard was a student, the newly constructed Marshall Hall became the museum's home. In the 1880s, Ackrel E. White, class of 1876, donated objects that he acquired during his service on the AMA's Mendi mission in Sierra Leone from 1876 to 1883 (where he served with former students of Atlanta, Howard, and Fisk universities).[27] According to Mary Lou Hultgren, who spent several decades as curator and later director of the museum, White is responsible for the earliest extant African objects in Hampton's collection—"a 'country cloth' acquired in 1880 and neck ornament and headdress" from Sherbro Island.[28]

Unlike a traditional art museum, Hampton's "Curiosity room" was modeled on "the ethnographical museum," which "articulated" the colonial

*Figure 6.1* Curiosity room, Hampton Institute (c. 1904–5). (Courtesy of Hampton University Archives, Hampton, Virginia.)

enterprise "of converting overseas territories to the self and imagination of the West."[29] However, Hampton demonstrated prescient early interest in collecting fine art in addition to curios. In 1894, trustee Robert Ogden donated paintings by Henry Ossawa Tanner, which were displayed in the library and at special events like graduation, initiating one of the world's most distinguished collections of African American art. In 1903, when Cora Mae Folsom became curator of the Hampton Museum, she wrote up a plan for a new space for its ethnographic collections and took as her model the Boston Museum of Art, rather than a natural history museum.[30] So even before the 1911 acquistion of Sheppard's collection, the Hampton Museum envisioned moving beyond the traditional pedagogical uses of a curiosity room.

Sheppard acquired his collection during an era when African art, particularly from the Congo, was newly being codified as such. It was not until 1891 that African art—specifically a pillaged collection of bronze sculptures from Benin—began to be appreciated in Europe in a fine arts context.[31] "The transformation from curio to object of art began," Johannes Fabian speculates, "when the products of certain groups only (people near the court, or certain ethnic groups of 'nobility') were praised as pure and refined. Aesthetics and politics meshed."[32] The criteria of African art was overdetermined by colonial politics. The removal of cultural artifacts was instrumental to Leopold II's reign. By 1891, he explicitly instructed state agents to "keep all confiscated 'arts and crafts.'" By 1894–95, the state was sponsoring small exhibitions dedicated to Congolese art, which led directly to the collecting expedition for the 1897 exposition at Tervuren, whose "purpose," according to Enid Schildkrout and Curtis A. Keim, "was to justify and publicize Leopold's activities in the Congo."[33] Kuba textiles and sculpture were popular attractions at the Tervuren fair: "By then it had become commonplace among well-informed colonials to believe that the Kuba were somehow heirs to the old civilization of pharaonic Egypt."[34] In this way, the prestige of the Nile valley tradition described by Wilson, Ater, and others is extended to the Congo.

In 1890, when Sheppard first arrived in the Congo, he wrote to Armstrong: "I have many spears, knives, idols, etc., [and am] saving them for the curiosity room at Hampton."[35] Though not part of Sheppard's religiously defined mission, his commitment to Hampton and its cultural tradition is representative of the institution's foundational role in his Congo work, and the extent to which his mission within the APCM was self-defined.[36] Sheppard took notice of Kuba textiles, which his fellow pioneer, Samuel Lapsley, also collected. He began to collect Kuba art even before reaching Mushenge and developing a personal relationship with the royal family.[37] After reaching the royal court at Mushenge, Sheppard noticed four *ndop* statues. He was the first outsider to describe these unique carved wooden seated king figures in terms of material (ebony), subject ("King Xamba Bulngunga" [Shyaam aMbul aNgoong]), value ("highly prized" and "sacred"), and accoutrements (checkerboard) or *ibol* that, as art historian Elisabeth L. Cameron explains, was included as "the king's individualized and identifying symbol attached to the pedestal at his feet." (See Figure 6.2.) Sheppard clearly recognized the significance of the *ndop*, which symbolically served as the king's "surrogate when he was absent from the capital," yet he declined to collect them.[38]

However, these exact same statues did show up in the British Museum as the most "outstanding" of more than 3,000 objects acquired by Torday, according to him, through negotiations that promised prestige and preservation.[39] Although Torday himself describes the transactions in terms of "lavish bribery," John Mack of the British Museum defends the legitimate provenance of the collection—"there is little sense that he set out to hoodwink naïve hosts"—and even suggests that Torday overpaid.[40] David A. Binkley and Patricia J. Darish, however, note that "the dramatic effects of the colonial enterprise on the Kuba go unnoted in most discussions of *ndop* figures," making the prospect of a fair negotiation unlikely if not impossible. The failure to account for the overarching colonial context of these transactions gives the mistaken impression that "the *nyim* and other high-ranking titled officials readily gave the *ndop* of the culture hero Shyaam aMbul aNgoong and other objects to Emil Torday so that they could be safeguarded in the British

*Figure 6.2* Unidentified artist (Bushong), *ndop* of King Shyaam aMbul aNgoong, late eighteenth century, wood carving, 21⅔×8⅔×8⅔ in. (55×22×22 cm). Collected by Emil Torday, acquisition Af1909,1210.1, Mushenge, 1909. Sheppard described this statue of "King Xamba Bulngunga" on his first visit to Mushenge. Emil Torday removed it for the British Museum in 1909. For more on King Shyaam aMbul aNgoong, see Vansina, *Children of Woot*, pp. 59–65. (Collection of the British Museum, London, United Kingdom.)

Museum."[41] Art-removal practices were dependent upon colonial and missionary infrastructures. Torday, for example, prepared a box of objects for the British Museum in early 1905, while he was still working for the Compagnie du Kasai (C.K.).[42] For its part, the APCM hosted imperial collectors like Verner, Starr, and Frobenius at its stations.[43]

Sheppard's decision to allow the *ndop* statues to remain in Mushenge sheds light on the integrity of his collection, whose provenance is embedded in his most iconic story—his reception as "a dead son of King Lukenga." In a 1921 article for the *Southern Workman*, Sheppard describes his reception at Mushenge as replete with royal gifts of cups, a scepter, and a knife.[44] The contextualized transaction—that he received these items as gifts rather than through theft, pillage, or purchase—corroborates his frequent accounts of his reception as an esteemed member of the Kuba royal family. The objects from the royal court in his collection are material evidence of his relationship with Kuba King Kot aMbweeky II. Sheppard, for example, describes being given a seventeenth-century knife that "had been handed down through the reigns of seven Lukengas," and there is evidence that his hosts may have given him works of art that were several centuries old at the time, rather than disingenuously flattering him for political gain.[45] Interestingly enough, his collection does not include much sculpture, even though it was the most popular medium for European collectors during this era. (Despite its renown, the *ndop* is actually a somewhat rare representational carving within the Kuba tradition.[46]) The sculptural lacuna in Sheppard's collection might reasonably be connected to his criticism of idolatry. Following his admiring description of the *ndop* statues in *Presbyterian Pioneers in Congo*, Sheppard wants to be clear: "I have seen in no Bakuba village an idol. I mean a large piece of wood carved into an image to be dreaded or adored."[47] Some of the differences between Sheppard's collections and those of his European contemporaries could be attributed to the fact that textiles, such as ceremonial skirts that are well represented in his collection, are not traditionally commercial products, but rather transferred as inheritance.[48]

Sheppard accumulated his collection while working against both of Torday's employers—the C.K. and the Belgian state. He developed his collection over the course of two decades from people among whom he lived and worked, whereas Torday used networks of C.K. employees to collect Kuba items before he ever traveled to the Kasai region.[49] Demonstrating some of the ways that "collecting [practices] were always mediated by, among other things, political and economic relations," Torday promised his C.K. employers that in exchange for "a subsidy of 5,000 francs outright, free passage onboard the company steamers, and local credit for another 5,000 francs," "he would not make any unfavorable 'political' comments."[50] Torday and other European collectors further exploited "the massive instability and change that occurred during the late nineteenth and early twentieth centuries" by "quickly amassing large collections of objects that removed in short order the majority of precontact examples of Kuba objects from the region."[51] Fabian explains, "The ruler must have interpreted this as a way to establish a real presence of Kuba political power in one of the centers of imperialism."[52] Given the unique colonial history of indirect rule and the relative autonomy of the Kuba, the sale of its cultural heritage presented a sensible strategy to utilize their artistic prestige to facilitate political power and preserve limited forms of self-governance at a moment when they were increasingly in danger.

They Decorate Everything

The dominance of the *ndop* statues in art historical studies of the Congo region has shaped the international market for Kuba art (and subsequently the artistic practices of the Kuba themselves). "Although there are more than seventeen distinct ethnic groups under the designation Kuba, with varying degrees of cultural and artistic diversity, only Bushoong culture as manifested at the royal capital of *Nsheng* [Mushenge] has held sustained interest for Kuba scholars during most of the twentieth century." While Sheppard and Torday both favored art associated with the royal court, Torday believed that "any artistic tradition that did not support the authority of chiefs was not significant in the corpus of Kuba arts," and in 1908 he insinuated that Morrison was spreading false rumors of instability in an attempt to weaken the Kuba king.[53] Torday, who considered the king "more of a gentleman in one toe than the whole American mission," also accused "un missionnaire américain minègre" (likely Sheppard) of attempting to influence the royal line of succession for his own benefit.[54] Of course, Torday's own commercial interests as a collector depended on preserving the royal lineage. Sheppard's unique relationship with the royal family was a concern for Torday only because Sheppard manifested real political power.

Sheppard's collection is as notable for what it excludes—*ndop* and other sculpture—as for what it includes. The emergent influence of African art on European painters like Picasso is largely based on sculpture. In this regard, his collecting interests differ from most twentieth-century Western collectors of African art, who have demonstrated a preference for figurative work. Kuba textiles are representative of a design tradition whose influence can best be appreciated in broadly aesthetic rather than representational terms. Despite frequent claims of Kuba exceptionalism, the Kuba textiles have likely origins in the Kongo Kingdom, dating back to at least the early sixteenth century. Although raffia textiles from Kongo were seen in Europe as early as the seventeenth century, by the late nineteenth century, they were produced exclusively by the Kuba.[55] Among those that Sheppard collected at Mushenge, there is a great deal of diversity. There may be textiles that date back to the middle of the eighteenth century while others may have been regifted raffia that the royal family received "as tribute from affiliated groups."[56] Given patterns of migration and intermarriage among different ethnic groups in the Kuba Kingdom, precise ethnic categorization of textiles is difficult.[57] Nonetheless, this varied genealogy indicates that the presumptively Kuba aesthetic was actually part of a regional artistic practice in central Africa.

Among nonfigurative Kuba media, textiles—particularly pile-cut raffia cloths, sometimes called "Kasai velvets," associated with the Shoowa people (one of the ethnic groups in the Kuba Kingdom)—were in the late nineteenth century a source of national pride for the Kuba and today remain among their most influential products. In the Kuba tradition, men use looms to weave the original raffia fibers and women then pound the fabric for softness, dye the fibers, design the patterns, and embroider it. The velvets range in color from white to light brown and the traditional dye palette is an array of beiges, reds, blacks, and browns, all described in exquisite detail by Sheppard.[58] Their most distinguishing feature is their patterning, which uses a broadly geometric grid that demonstrates a "command of orderly structures" within which

*Plate 1* Unidentified artists (Shoowa), no date, raffia cut-pile cloth, l. 27 in. (l. 68.6 cm). Collected by William Sheppard, acquisition 11.152. (Collection of the Hampton University Museum, Hampton, Virginia.)

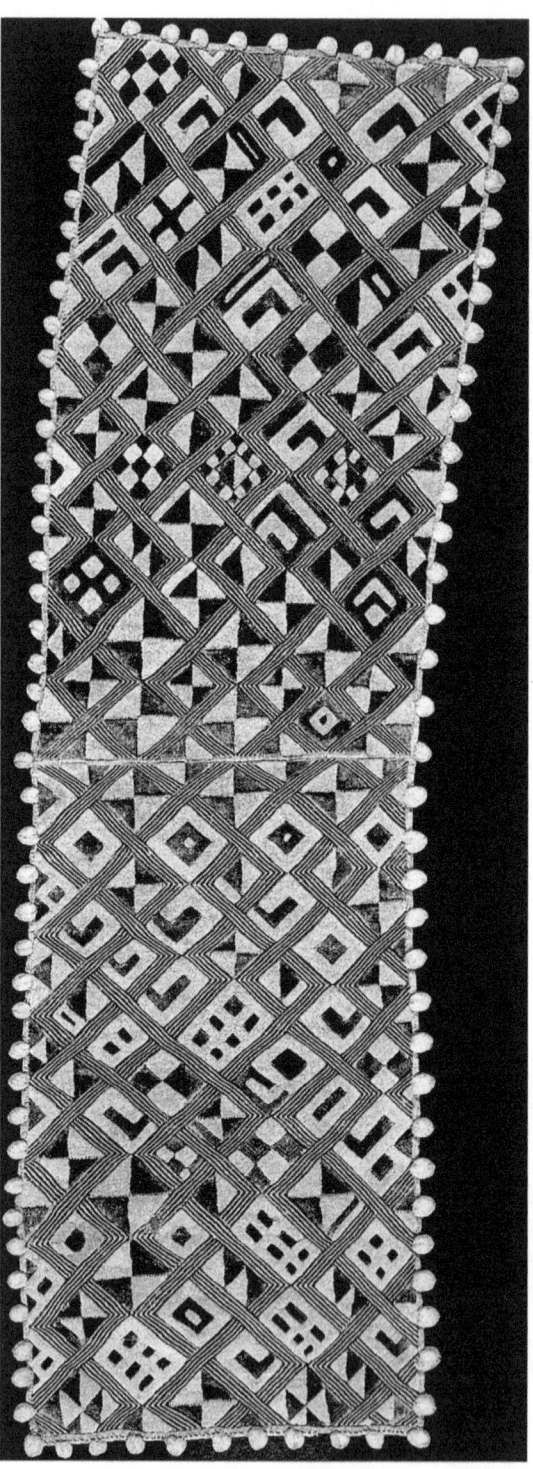

*Plate 2* Unidentified artists (Shoowa), no date, raffia cut-pile cloth, l. 55 in. (l. 139.7 cm). Collected by William Sheppard, acquisition 11.174. (Collection of the Hampton University Museum, Hampton, Virginia.)

*Plate 3* (*above*)
Palmer Hayden, *Fétiche et Fleurs*, c. 1926–33, oil on canvas, 23 ½ × 29 in. (59.7 × 73.7 cm). (Artwork of Palmer Hayden, used with the permission of the Museum of African American Art, Los Angeles, California.)

*Plate 4* (*left*)
Malvin Gray Johnson, *Negro Masks*, 1932, oil on canvas, 20 × 18 in. (50.8 × 45.7 cm). (Collection of the Hampton University Museum, Hampton, Virginia.)

*Plate 5* John Biggers, *Quilting Party*, 1980–81, oil and acrylic, 83 × 252 in. (210.8 × 640.1 cm). (Art © John T. Biggers Estate/Licensed by VAGA, New York. Photograph © David A. Brown, dabfoto creative. Courtesy of City of Houston Art Collection, Houston, Texas.)

*Plate 6* John Biggers, *Starry Crown*, 1987, acrylic and mixed media on masonite, 61 × 49 in. (154.9 × 124.5 cm). (Art © John T. Biggers Estate/Licensed by VAGA, New York. Courtesy of Dallas Museum of Art, Museum League Purchase Fund, Dallas, Texas.)

*Plate 7* (*left*)
John Biggers, *House of the Turtle*, 1991, acrylic on canvas, 20 × 10 ft. (609.6 × 304.8 cm). (Art © John T. Biggers Estate/Licensed by VAGA, New York. Collection of the Hampton University Museum, Hampton, Virginia.)

*Plate 8* (*right*)
John Biggers, *Tree House*, 1991, acrylic on canvas, 20 × 10 ft. (609.6 × 304.8 cm). (Art © John T. Biggers Estate/Licensed by VAGA, New York. Collection of the Hampton University Museum, Hampton, Virginia.)

*Plate 9* James Phillips, *The Soul and Spirit of John Biggers*, 1995, acrylic on canvas, 4 × 7 ft. (121.9 × 213.4 cm). (Collection of the Hampton University Museum, Hampton, Virginia.)

*Plate 10* Faith Ringgold, *Breakfast in Bed, Windows of the Wedding Series #2*, 1974, acrylic on canvas, 65 ½ × 27 in. (166.4 × 68.6 cm). (© 1974 Faith Ringgold and courtesy ACA [American Contemporary Art Gallery], New York, New York.)

*Figure 6.3* Kuba textiles from William Sheppard's collection from William Sheppard, *Presbyterian Pioneers in Congo* (1917), p. 119. (Courtesy of Princeton Theological Seminary Library, Princeton, New Jersey.)

there is an individuated vocabulary that often defies expectations of symmetry. (See Figure 6.3; see Plates 1 and 2.) Eli Leon characterizes this style as "improvisational patterning."[59] The patterning that originates "within the sphere of women's textile production and decoration" appears frequently as a design feature of other Kuba objects such as cups, bowls, boxes, mats, knife handles, and combs.[60] Kuba art is noted "for decorating almost all of an available surface with an intricate network of patterns" that is visible on everything from a royal knife in the Sheppard collection to the "intricate geometric patterning" on the walls of the homes of Kuba royalty and others.[61] These decorative uses of textiles suggest how Kuba patterning can envelop a domestic space, making it part of the aesthetics of daily life since, as Sheppard simply put it, "They decorate everything."[62] The design elements of African art were incorporated into the built environments of HBCU campuses, APCM mission stations, and personal homes. On the Fisk campus, Jubilee Hall, the namesake and inspiration for Althea's home at Ibanche, was adorned with wood from Sierra Leone. Soon after their arrivals on the mission, the Sheppards and the DeYamperts decorated their station homes with Kuba art, including mats that are similar to other textiles in their patterning if not

Visual Cultures   173

texture. The Edmistons' Tuscaloosa home was adorned with African art, which served a similar function by materializing an African diaspora aesthetic as part of the daily lives of its occupants.[63]

African American communities encountered Kuba textiles through such institutional links of missionary networks, HBCUs, and the black press. These engagements are entangled with significant cultural ties often framed primarily in terms of cultural retention traced through a strong African lineage within diasporic communities. However, the institutionalization and circulation of Sheppard's art collection at Hampton—in the museum, classroom, and beyond—made Kuba visual culture available to generations of African American artists and designers beyond campus. In 1967, for instance, Richard Long brought national attention to Hampton's collection when he organized the *Primitive Art of Africa, North America and Oceania from the College Museum* at the Union Carbide Building in New York. The following year, Sheppard's collection was featured as part of the *Exhibition of Bakuba Art*, which accompanied the "Symposium on Traditional African Art" that Long organized on campus on the occasion of Hampton's centennial. The conference featured distinguished speakers and attendees including Leon Damas, Jacqueline Delange, William Fagg, Eugene Grigsby, James Herring, James Porter, Roy Sieber, Stanley Shaloff, Robert Farris Thompson, and Jan Vansina, who delivered a keynote address at the "William H. Sheppard Memorial Banquet."[64] As Long explained, "The Conference was the occasion of introducing a large group of major scholars to this collection and to the pioneering role of Black Americans in bringing Africa to the consciousness of the West."[65] Its proceedings were published as a special double issue of *African Forum*.

Sieber first saw Sheppard's collection at Hampton during the symposium, and in 1972 he curated *African Textiles and Decorative Arts* for the Museum of Modern Art (MoMA) in New York, marking "the first time works from the collection were included in a major national traveling exhibition."[66] Sieber was assisted by one of his graduate students, Roslyn Walker (Randall), Hampton class of 1966, who later became the director of the Smithsonian's National Museum of African Art.[67] The MoMA exhibit introduced four pieces from Sheppard's collection to a national audience: an ornate ceremonial knife from King Kot aMbweeky II (distinct from the heirloom knife Sheppard received), a copper comb also from the Kuba king, a beaded hat, and a "woman's raffia wraparound."[68] Beyond its inclusion of objects from Sheppard's collection, *African Textiles and Decorative Arts* was groundbreaking in that it challenged the strong predilection toward sculpture that had dominated African art exhibitions and scholarship for most of the century. Subsequent exhibits further showcased Sheppard's collection—in 1988 the traveling

*Art/Artifact* show organized by the Center for African Art displayed more than sixty objects from Hampton, the plurality from Sheppard, and recreated a curiosity room. Significantly, among other African objects from Hampton in *Art/Artifact* were Kikuyu and Zulu objects donated by Hampton students who, inspired by Sheppard's collection, wanted to see their cultures represented as they saw the Kuba.[69] The Kikuyu collection was sent directly by a Kikuyu chief whose son, Mbiyu Koinange, attended Hampton's secondary school from 1927 to 1931, where he "helped to sensitize a few potentially influential Afro-Americans to Kenya's problems," including St. Clair Drake. Koinange maintained close relationships with African Americans throughout a career that, according Gerald Horne, "could well be regarded as on [Jomo] Kenyatta's level as a Founding Father," and which further establishes an anticolonial political context for Hampton's African art collection.[70]

## Many Curios

From its inception, Sheppard's collection of Congolese art circulated widely, fulfilling its intended educational function. In his lectures on and off campus, Sheppard regularly used the pieces as visual aids. During a speech at Hampton in 1893, he exhibited the royal knife. During his popular 1904 furlough tour, he "showed many curios" and "interesting relics, illustrative of the manner and customs of the natives," which local newspapers often highlighted (along with Lucy's songs) in their coverage of his addresses.[71] He used the same media—music and material culture—to illustrate his 1905 Hampton lecture "Light in Darkest Africa." When printed in the *Southern Workman*, this talk was accompanied by musical notation from Lucy Gantt Sheppard and an image of textiles captioned "Dresses and Rugs made by Negroes of Central Africa who have never seen White People."[72]

Sheppard donated several small items to Hampton in 1900, sent some curios as gifts to Principal Hollis Burke Frissell in October 1910, and arranged for Hampton to purchase most of his collection in 1911.[73] In a letter to Frissell, he wrote, "I must thank you, more than I can express in this letter, for your great kindness in buying my African Collection. You cannot imagine, perhaps, the great good which you have done for my family. I hope some day to tell you of this signal act of kindness."[74] The language and timing of his letter suggest that his sale of his collection may have been, in part, the result of financial necessity after his forced retirement from the APCM and suspension from the church. Whatever his personal needs, he sold the collection for a rather modest sum of $500.[75] Although there were already African objects in the museum, the Sheppard acquisition was immediately recognized as Hampton's "largest and most valuable."[76] There were additional smaller accessions during Sheppard's lifetime and from his estate after his death.[77] Principal James Edward Gregg, Frissell's successor, personally thanked Sheppard for a 1923 acquisition, noting his hope that "we may often have you here to lecture upon it." He appreciated the dynamic uses of Sheppard's collection, tied as strongly as it is to the collector, to educate folks about Africa. Gregg published more than sixty articles on Africa in the *Southern Workman* during his decade overseeing the journal.[78]

By that point, Sheppard had been lecturing at Hampton for thirty years, almost always with visual aids from his collection, making them important elements of his political commentaries. In 1911, after recounting "the story of his trial by the Belgian Government for telling the truth about some of the cruelties and atrocities practiced against the natives by the Kassai Rubber Company, whose stock is controlled by the Belgian Government—how, as a result of a force labor system, the natives were oppressed, mutilated, and even killed for failing to bring to the company the amount of rubber demanded of them," the *Hampton Student* immediately noted that he "showed many curiosities from Africa. . . . The cloth he showed, woven by them on their looms, was most extraordinary."[79] Sheppard's intertwined commentary on both the political economy of colonialism and African culture was appealing to students. With the benefit of some distance and detachment following the 1908 accession of the state to Belgium and his own 1910 retirement, Sheppard used both rubber and raffia to humanize the African victims of European colonialism in a way that was unique in the Congo reform movement.

Similarly, during a 1915 visit to Hampton, Sheppard used these objects in multiple venues, as noted by the *Hampton Student*: "One day the Seniors were invited to the museum to hear him tell about the African curios in the cases, many of which he gave to the school."[80] In another speech, "He shows and gives a description of curios—palm fiber, cloth made from it, cloth after it has been sewed together, wet, and pounded to make it soft, a piece of embroidery," as well a comb, spoon, hat, ring, and knife. Then Sheppard showed a piece of rubber as a visual aid to a personal discussion of Belgian annexation and colonialism: "This is a piece of Congo rubber. You have heard of the rubber and the Belgian regime. I have been acquainted with the Belgians for 20 years. I speak their language. I have been in Brussels and Antwerp. You have heard of the murder of people in the Congo for rubber. I would like to let you into the secret of that. The Congo was private domain. It is not now. It is a colony and belongs to the Belgians. When we went there it belonged to King Leopold alone—his own private property the Congo was."[81] During this speech, rubber was displayed along with Congolese art, as evidence of his authority and firsthand knowledge of Belgian colonialism. This implicit juxtaposition highlights the violence of colonialism by reminding the audience of precontact forms of labor that produced these artistic objects. By seeing Congolese art in European galleries in the early 1920s, Claude McKay similarly came to appreciate that, "The Congo, it turns out, has an interest independent of rubber and savages."[82] In 1929, after visiting the RMCA in Belgium, *Chicago Defender* publisher Robert Abbott echoes Sheppard by highlighting the fact that "this wonderful display of art . . . was made before the coming of the white man."[83] Abbott fuses criticism of European colonialism with expressions of appreciation for Congolese art.

Hampton's earliest curio collections were intended to be part of a "practical method" of instruction, which was consistent with the overarching philosophy of industrial education.[84] After the initial Sheppard acquisition, hundreds of academic classes were held at the museum every year.[85] By this point, the Hampton Museum was overcrowded and kept so much of its popular collection in storage that the director appealed for additional space: "The students are particularly interested in these African things and I wish they might be able to see more of them."[86] The importance of the museum extended far beyond the immediate school community. Up through at least the 1920s, it was the only Southern museum regularly open to blacks.[87] By 1920, Folsom acknowledged the collection's value for ethnology and for "artists in search of the new designs and suggestions."[88] In 1925, Folsom's successor Sara Lane noted that the collection was particularly valuable for "those studying textiles and art" and was used in home economics classes in ways consistent with the early mission of the curiosity room.[89] (See Figure 6.4.) Today, all Hampton students are required, as part of the curriculum, to visit Sheppard's collection at the museum and study its history.[90]

Beyond its classroom use, Sheppard's collection was the subject of illustrated articles in the *Southern Workman*, making it familiar to the journal's national audience. The first acquisition was announced in 1911: "The many varieties of fibre cloth, beautiful in design and texture, with mats and baskets of artistic form and pattern, give one a new idea of the ancestors of the American Negro and are of especial interest to their descendants."[91] After Sheppard's death in 1927, Lane wrote a series of articles about African art, which use his collection in such a way that Kuba art, the centerpiece of the museum, becomes representative of African art as a whole: "In no department of African craftsmanship is greater skill shown than in the metal work of the Bushongo smiths." At a time of increasing international interest in African art, Sheppard's objects remained unique because "Many of them, he said, were old and choice, made long before European influence had been felt."[92] Similar to Abbott's preference for precolonial art, Lane finds evidence in Sheppard's textile collection that "those made long before the Congo tribes

*Figure 6.4* Domestic science students at Hampton Institute use Kuba textiles from Sheppard's collection in the classroom (c. 1920s). (Courtesy of Hampton University Archives, Hampton, Virginia.)

had felt European influence are much finer and softer than the newer pieces."[93] Her qualitative assessment provides material corroboration of his narrative account of the "gift" provenance of several knives, which illustrate that "he had been received into the king's family and would be granted the protection accorded any other member of the royal family."[94] The *Southern Workman* took many cues from Sheppard, with Lane virtually repeating the opening sentence of a 1921 article ("The natives of Africa have a decided taste for the beautiful") in 1927: "The primitive African has a real devotion to beauty."[95] Their shared sentiments are distinguished by Lane's repeated use of the pejorative word "primitive," which contrasts with Sheppard's preferred nomenclature, here and elsewhere, of "native." This terminology is indicative of the ways in which Sheppard worked to shape interpretations of his collection, and the ways in which he was not always successful.

During this time, the *Southern Workman* itself was taking its cover designs from Kuba textiles, noting that their "beauty in texture is the result of tedious and painstaking work."[96] (See Figure 6.5.) Similarly, Natalie Curtis used Sheppard's Kuba textiles to decorate the cover and title page of her *Songs and Tales from the Dark Continent* (1920), even though the text itself is about southern Africa, providing another example of the synecdochal use of Kuba art.[97] Hampton's African aesthetic was distinct from both the Egyptian and

178   Chapter Six

*Figure 6.5 Southern Workman 57, no. 6 (June 1928) cover featuring Kuba textile from William Sheppard collection. (Courtesy of Hampton University Archives, Hampton, Virginia.)*

Ethiopian influences represented by Fuller and the figurative tradition that privileges sculpture and masks. Subsequent generations, at Hampton and beyond, sought to use Sheppard's collection not only as an instrument of cross-cultural education, but also as a building block of an emergent African American aesthetic practice.

Art Lessons from the Congo

Beyond the Hampton campus, Congolese art was circulating widely throughout Europe and the United States during the twentieth century. In a 1934 list of fourteen U.S. museums featuring African art, Nancy Cunard included Hampton, Fisk, and the 135th Street Branch of the New York Public Library. Overall, Schildkrout and Keim estimate that between 70,000 and 100,000 art objects were removed from the Congo prior to World War I with most of it ending up in European collections.[98] As a Rhodes scholar in the century's first decade, Howard University philosophy professor Alain Locke had visited African collections in European museums.[99] Delegates to the 1921 Pan African Congress visited the RMCA, which is an exemplary encounter of politics and visual art that would have been familiar to thousands of readers of Jessie Fauset's report in the *Crisis*.[100] As African American interest in

African art grew during the period, Kuba art was frequently in the spotlight in ways that brought attention to Sheppard's collection.

In 1923, a major Brooklyn Museum exhibit *Primitive Negro Art, Chiefly from the Belgian Congo,* highlighted "the work of the Bushongo . . . [who] have a high artistic sense and are the most advanced in the arts, especially those of wood carving and weaving."[101] The show, whose catalog echoed Sheppard's *Presbyterian Pioneers in Congo* in its assertion that the Kuba "knowledge of weaving, embroidering, wood carving and smelting was the highest in equatorial Africa," caught Locke's attention as it did Tuskegee's Robert Moton, the Urban League's Charles S. Johnson, and the NAACP's Walter White.[102] The curator, Stewart Culin, sought to mark a clear distinction between this show and more typical ethnological formats in that it "is shown under the classification of art; as representing a creative impulse, and not for the purpose of illustrating the customs of the African peoples."[103] The appreciation for the Kuba textiles in the design community was substantial; Culin developed relationships with Bonwit Teller and Blanck and Company to produce blankets and other products using Kuba patterns (without any attempt to compensate their Kuba designers).[104] Locke borrowed items, including textiles, from the Brooklyn collection for a June 1924 lecture at the 135th Street Branch library.[105]

By 1925, Locke, who met African students and toured historical sites in Egypt and Sudan while a Rhodes scholar, began trying to acquire a permanent collection of artwork for a proposed Harlem Museum of African Art. He was already in touch with collectors, having met Albert Barnes and Paul Guillaume in early 1924.[106] After seeing Belgian diplomat Raoul Blondiau's collection in Europe, Locke arranged for *Theatre Arts Monthly*, a magazine edited by arts patron Edith Isaacs, to purchase it for $10,000 in 1927.[107] During this time, Locke was traveling to Europe to do research for the Foreign Policy Association on the Brazzaville railway construction and on the mandate system of colonial governance under the League of Nations.[108] "His mandates report," Robert Vitalis explains, "frames the issue in terms of the centrality of imperialism in leading to the recent world conflict and the threat that 'the imperialistic world powers, America included' continue to pose to world peace." Locke's research shaped his vision for Howard's African studies program, which further embeds his art collection, like Sheppard's, within the political culture of colonialism and anticolonialism.[109]

Although the plans to sell or donate the Blondiau–*Theatre Arts* purchase to the Harlem Museum of African Art were unrealized and Locke's museum never found a permanent home, the collection was at the center of the New Negro Renaissance. Locke first met "Godmother" Charlotte Osgood Mason when she introduced herself to him at the West 57th Street opening of the

Blondiau–*Theatre Arts* exhibit on February 6, 1927. Within the week, Locke introduced Mason to Langston Hughes and within the year to Zora Neale Hurston, initiating relationships that would prove as contentious as they were significant.[110] The Blondiau collection soon made its way to Harlem and was shown in 1927 at the 135th Street Branch, the precursor to the Schomburg Center for Research in Black Culture, which became the permanent home to much of it.[111] Another portion became a permanent part of the Hampton collection when trustee George Foster Peabody spent $500 for "some 50 pieces that would complement the Sheppard collection."[112] Indeed Blondiau "found many of his rarest articles among the tribes with whom Dr. Sheppard worked."[113] In "Art Lessons from the Congo," a 1927 article for *Survey*, Locke notes that the Blondiau collection, like the Brooklyn Museum exhibit, is "especially strong in those of the most artistic of the Bushongo peoples, the Bakuba, Baluba tribes and the Kasai," essentially the field covered by Sheppard.[114]

Locke may have inspired one the most direct representations of Kuba textiles in African American art from that era: Palmer Hayden's still life oil painting *Fétiche et Fleurs* was a product of his "call for artists to look to African art for inspiration and design ideas."[115] (See Plate 3.) In early 1927, after winning a prestigious Harmon Foundation award, Hayden moved to France for five years, where he got to know Locke and see his personal collection of African art. *Fétiche et Fleurs*, whose title echoes Lane's report, won an award at a 1933 Harmon exhibition. The painting features a vase of lilies, a cigarette in an ashtray, and a stand-mounted Fang mask; on the table underneath the base of the mask is a distinctive Kuba textile used as a table covering. There is much debate among scholars about the date of the painting: some place it in 1926 and others in 1932–33. The latter date accounts for his likely exposure to African art during his years in Paris. However, the Blondiau exhibit opened in New York in February 1927, so he could have seen Kuba textiles on West 57th Street before he left for Paris in March.[116]

At the time, the artist Edward J. Brandford suggested another U.S. source for its "African background—gained not through his studies abroad—but rather through close contact and inspirations of that well known pioneer of primitive Negro art, Cloyd Boykin."[117] Boykin, Hayden's friend since the early 1920s, was born in Hampton, Virginia, in 1877 and attended Hampton Institute.[118] Boykin founded the Primitive African Art Center and hosted exhibits of African art in New York in 1931 and 1932. In addition, he established an art school that offered courses in "the African method of weaving and coloring cloth."[119] While Hayden once claimed that African art held "no meaning to we Americans," he was nonetheless interested in its formal dimensions and design aesthetics.[120] Hayden's later artwork codifies the formal influence of African objects with identifiable similarities between the composition of the Fang mask in *Fétiche et Fleurs* and a human figure in *The Janitor Who Paints*. Hayden stated that the figure in *The Janitor Who Paints* was Boykin, further marking the Hampton alumnus as an African art conduit if not an actual African sculptural subject.[121]

Around the same time that Hayden painted *Fétiche et Fleurs*, Malvin Gray Johnson, a close associate of Hayden and Boykin, painted *Negro Masks*.[122] (See Plate 4.) Johnson depicts masks that, according to Jacqueline Francis, are based in part on Congolese headdresses. These masks appear propped against a backdrop that has the distinct lines and coloration of Kuba textiles, similar to, but not as well defined as, what appears in *Fétiche et Fleurs*. Furthermore, in a well-known self-portrait, Johnson distinctively includes *Negro Masks* behind him, which implies something quite different from Hayden's oft-cited quote that African art had "no meaning to we Americans." Francis notes that contemporary critics rarely looked carefully at the African objects when they were used in African American paintings and that, in Hayden's painting, the Kuba cloth, when noted at all, was secondary to the masks.[123] This reflects the broader bias in the field of African art where we can appreciate Sheppard's aesthetic intervention into a predominantly figurative field.

Connections between African art and contemporary African American art were on prominent display during the *Negro in Art Week* program sponsored by the Chicago Woman's Club in November 1927.[124] This exhibition, which featured Congolese art from the Blondiau collection, served as a model for an HBCU tour that was organized by Locke, who was a visiting professor at Fisk in 1926–27. For the tour, he made specific recommendations that "an exhibit of works by contemporary Negro artists such as was held in Chicago in conjunction with our exhibit is the most effective way of emphasizing the artistic possibilities of the Negro."[125] In addition, for Hampton, Locke specifically suggested that the Blondiau exhibit be mounted with items from its Sheppard collection.[126] Locke, who regularly traveled with the exhibit, lectured at Hampton on May 11, 1928. (On that visit, he apparently was accompanied by Langston Hughes.[127]) Shortly thereafter, Locke visited Lucy Sheppard, perhaps with an interest in purchasing art objects from her.[128]

Throughout this period, the visual arts continued to have a role on the Hampton campus. In the late 1920s, students and faculty established the Art Group. In the mid-1930s, Hampton was the opening venue for *Photographs of African Negro Art*, an exhibit of 75 photos (mostly masks and statues from MoMA) by Walker Evans that were displayed at fifteen HBCUs in 1935 and 1936.[129] By the time that Viktor Lowenfeld, a Jewish refugee from Austria, arrived on Hampton's campus in 1939, there was general appreciation for African art nationally and an established tradition of classroom use of

Sheppard's collection locally. Though Lowenfeld was trained in psychology and hired in the field of "industrial arts," he was previously the director of an African art museum in Vienna and his immediate aims for Hampton included "a voluntary class in art."[130] After hesitation on the part of the administration and a year of informal evening offerings, Lowenfeld began teaching his art classes for credit in 1940. They were exceedingly popular with students. As Hampton was moving toward a more traditional liberal arts curriculum with the establishment of the School of General Studies in 1941, the art program grew at a rapid pace at a time when programs in music, dance, and architecture suffered wartime cuts.[131]

Lowenfeld envisioned a central role for Sheppard's collection in this new department. Ironically, as the artistic importance of the collection was increasingly recognized, Sheppard's name was fading from public view: the 1939–40 Hampton catalog is the first in three decades not to name Sheppard, opting instead for a broader notice that "The Negro is represented by collections made by friends in East, West, and South Africa."[132] By 1942–43, Hampton's course catalog made wider assertions about the aesthetic role of African art, with less attention to the history of its own collection: "More and more it is being realized that African art is one of the fundamental influences on all modern art expression. Recognizing the value of the rich heritage to American Negroes, as well as the obligation to discover and develop the creative powers of its students, Hampton Institute offers an education in various related fields of art."[133] Drawing on intimate knowledge of European fine arts and museums, Lowenfeld more firmly situated the African collection in a modern artistic realm distinct from the curiosity room.

In the early 1940s, Hampton was a dynamic environment for visual artists, who brought with them a diverse array of knowledge and experience. By the time Lowenfeld arrived on campus, Joseph Gilliard, an innovative sculptor who would teach at Hampton for more than forty years, was already an undergraduate student, as was Reuben V. Burrell, who worked as university photographer for 65 years.[134] Joseph Mack entered in 1939 as an interior design major, but in 1941 won a new art department scholarship. In 1941, George Spencer arrived from Gastonia, North Carolina, along with another future art student from Gastonia, John Biggers. Persis Jennings, who later taught at Hampton, arrived in 1941 as a student.[135] In terms of faculty, in spring 1943, muralist Charles White and sculptor Elizabeth Catlett were both in residence. White arrived on campus with a prestigious Julius Rosenwald Fellowship, after his plans to study in Mexico with the great muralists were blocked by the draft board because of his association with the Communist Party.[136] Hampton became a surrogate location that, as Stacy I. Morgan explains, like other HBCUs gave "African American artists relatively autonomous institutional support for the continued exploration of politically engaged themes and aesthetics in the mural medium following the curtailment of government sponsorship for such cultural work."[137] Biggers assisted White on his campus mural *The Contribution of the Negro to Democracy*, leaving a lasting impression visible in the naturalism of Biggers's own early murals. Already an accomplished artist, Catlett felt she learned about both craft and pedagogy from Lowenfeld. Indeed she was so impressed with Lowenfeld that she encouraged Samella Sanders (Lewis), her star pupil from Dillard University, to decline a scholarship from the University of Iowa in favor of attending Hampton.[138] Through such networks, Hampton quickly developed a reputation that enabled it to attract art students from across the country.

The artwork of this distinguished cohort received local and national attention. In 1943, Lowenfeld included Biggers, Sanders, and at least fifteen other Hampton students in a 1943 MoMA exhibition that he curated on *Young Negro Artists*. Jennings appeared in the *Crisis* in 1944.[139] Also in 1944, *New Names in American Art*, whose catalog included an essay by Locke, undertook a national tour that included Hampton and featured a painting by Biggers, alongside work by Catlett, Hayden, White, Lois Mailou Jones, Jacob Lawrence, and Hale Woodruff.[140] A few years earlier, in 1942, Woodruff began a series of highly influential annual exhibitions at Atlanta University that created important opportunities for African American artists, including many from Hampton.[141] White and Catlett had works in the first iteration in 1942; Catlett had a watercolor in the April 1943 exhibit and did not win an award despite White serving as a member of that year's jury.[142] Catlett and White encouraged their Hampton protégés to submit work. The following year, five Hampton undergraduates—Biggers, Jennings, Burrell, Samella Sanders (Lewis), and Annabelle Baker—were included in the annual show, where their work was displayed alongside that of Romare Bearden, Aaron Douglas, and many of the best-known artists of the day.[143]

One visitor to campus in the late 1940s was the Trinidad-born, New York–based dancer Pearl Primus, perhaps best known at that time for her inspired performance of Langston Hughes's poem "The Negro Speaks of Rivers," which invokes the Congo in ways that are considered in chapter 7. As part of a spring 1948 tour, she performed at Hampton and at Fisk, where President Charles S. Johnson was so impressed that he arranged for her to receive a Rosenwald Fellowship. One year later, she used that award to study among the Kuba in the Kasai region of the Congo. There, her "interpreter explained in halting French, 'The chief . . . he plenty surprised that there be such a wonderful one outside Mushenge. He heart tell him you come from his Mushenge heaven.'"[144] When Primus visited Mushenge, the capital of the Kuba Kingdom and the site of Sheppard's famous excursion more than a half-century earlier, she was likewise graciously welcomed into the royal court, where she met King Mbop Mabinc maMbeky ("Bope Mabintshi"), who ruled from 1939 to 1969.[145] Whether intentionally or not, from May to August 1949, Primus found herself tracing Sheppard's routes from Hampton to Mushenge.

Hampton's contributions are part of a broader network of arts programs at HBCUs. The academic program at Atlanta University, which Woodruff took over in 1931, was groundbreaking, as was its affiliation with Morehouse College and Spelman College, where Nancy Elizabeth Prophet joined the faculty in 1934.[146] At Fisk in the late 1940s, Charles S. Johnson, who enthusiastically responded to Culin's Brooklyn Museum show decades earlier, began to emphasize modern acquisitions to complement the university's African collection.[147] Howard University had perhaps the most established program, dating back to drawing and painting classes offered as part of its "Manual Training" program as early as 1871 and incorporated into the academic "Normal department" by 1891.[148] In 1921, James Vincent Herring founded Howard's art department, and in 1930 opened a campus gallery in Rankin Chapel; in 1943, Herring and Alonzo J. Aden, who studied at Hampton in the mid-1920s when Sheppard's collection was celebrated, opened the private Barnett Aden Gallery. With these resources at hand, Locke personally encouraged his Howard colleague Loïs Mailou Jones to use African images in her painting, which she did quite successfully during this era in works such as *The Ascent of Ethiopia* (1932), influenced by her mentor Meta Fuller, and *Les Fétiches* (1938), whose title echoes Hayden's. In the 1970s and 1980s, Jones, who taught at Howard for fifty years, produced stylistically distinct work influenced by African and Haitian art; she had rooms in her home that were each dedicated to one of her collections. Jones used masks from the Congo in several of her paintings over the years, and her career is one more example of the institutional connections between African art collections and African American aesthetics deserving of further study.[149]

## My Early Interest in Africa

One of the students who was deeply influenced by Sheppard's collection was the painter Biggers, who originally intended to study plumbing at Hampton:

> We, the students, had no idea of our rich heritage in art until Lowenfeld came. I must give him the credit for making us conscious of this. Previously, this art was looked upon as inferior art. Blacks wanted to

become more American at that time and not become, in the common vernacular, ostracized in terms of their own African heritage.

Lowenfeld broke through that kind of stereotype. He told us how highly regarded African art was in Europe.[150]

According to Alvia Wardlaw, Lowenfeld believed that "the bridge to African heritage that former Hampton student William Sheppard had hoped to build by donating Kuba and Central Kongo art to Hampton" would enable students to "discover a direct and palpable link with their African heritage."[151]

Biggers's exposure to central African culture and missionary traditions predated his 1941 arrival at Hampton. He credited his high school principal Henry Curtis McDowell, a Talladega graduate just back from nearly twenty years as a missionary in Angola, "for part of my early interest in Africa."[152] At Lincoln Academy, the Kings Mountain, North Carolina, school, which he, like both of his parents, attended, Biggers's classmates included several students from Africa.[153] There, McDowell "gave us a daily diet of the very wonderful concepts of Africa which was different from what you got in the movies and daily through the popular mediums. We got a very dignified and wonderful concept of what Africa was all about . . . in his sermons he used African proverbs and African philosophy . . . so we had an understanding about Africa very early that was different from the average kind of information that was being moved around through popular media."[154] McDowell imparted on Biggers the value of firsthand knowledge of Africa. He also recommended Biggers attend Hampton.[155] McDowell had a career path similar to Sheppard's, and came to appreciate that in Angola, "The people are precisely like people I have been with all my life. I have never felt more at home anywhere. They are thoroughly justified in referring to us as 'our brethren.'"[156] With this background, Biggers must have well understood Sheppard, who he came to appreciate as "a forerunner of Alain Locke," by the time he arrived at Hampton.[157]

Lowenfeld made sure students had access to Sheppard's African art collection. After the museum closed in 1943 because of a wartime demand for space, he organized a trip to see it at the Virginia Museum of Fine Arts in Richmond, where it was on loan (and would remain until 1960).[158] In a 1982 interview, Samella Lewis highlighted the importance of its provenance: "I know about the collection; who left it, who gave it, and understood under what circumstances Hampton got it. I got more . . . understanding about that collection while Lowenfeld was there, than I have gotten since or even in writing, trying to get information."[159] Biggers had similar recollections: "In Hampton Institute, it had and still has a very wonderful collection of African Art. From the Zaire—we used to call it 'Congo.' It was marvelous! One of the best collections in this country of textiles, sculptures, carvings, and so forth. And he [Lowenfeld] made it his business to give us a very close relationship with this. And, so, in my early training, really the first year that I took drawing and painting, I was introduced to African Art from this source, and the interest started at that time."[160]

Well before Biggers first traveled to Africa in 1957, his interest in the continent drew directly on academic sources—McDowell, Sheppard, and Lowenfeld. It continued for the rest of his life: "the more I study African Art, the greater my vocabulary will grow because I am finding new things almost every day."[161] His work evokes multiple layers of influence that do not lend themselves to a facile genealogy. He is not unique in this regard. All of the students who saw Sheppard speak or studied his collection and then became educators themselves helped to shape aesthetic sensibilities throughout the United States in ways that are impossible to fully trace. Consider, for example, Harvey Johnson, whose high school art teacher was a student of Biggers; Johnson himself later became Biggers's student, colleague, and collaborator, and spent several months studying in Sierra Leone.[162] No doubt there are countless other students of students (of students) touched in some way by Biggers's education. African Americans encountered African material culture through schools and churches and newspapers, such that many people, who may not have traveled to the continent or otherwise directly encountered it, did so at once, twice, or thrice remove. Beyond family and ancestral memories, these ongoing institutional networks of cultural exchange provide some of the "documentary evidence for direct transmission of African textile design to the New World" that art historians have found missing.[163]

In the second mural Biggers ever painted, *Country Preacher* (1943), the subject is "talking about Africa" while surrounded by African musicians, dancers, shepherds, carvers, sculptures, straw homes, pyramids, and a sphinx.[164] While Biggers uses White's methods to represent "a much more personalized past, recalling the rural ministries of his childhood," his pencil sketches demonstrate the particular detail and care that Biggers took with African subject matter as a young art student at Hampton.[165] (See Figures 6.6 and 6.7.) The mural is built on the interplay between its American foreground and the distinctive and carefully rendered African background that includes a woman weaving a geometrically patterned cloth that looks similar to textiles in Sheppard's collection.[166]

The early image of a weaver in *Country Preacher* anticipates one of Biggers's iconic visual motifs, the quilt, which he uses to establish diasporic connections. Quilting scholars frequently cite Kuba textiles as an antecedent tradition.[167] For Biggers, the quilt emerged as a touchstone from familial

*Figure 6.6* John Biggers, *Country Preacher*, 1943, mural sketch, pencil on paper, 12×9 1/16 in. (30.5×23 cm). (Art © John T. Biggers Estate/Licensed by VAGA, New York. Collection of the Hampton University Museum, Hampton, Virginia.)

*Figure 6.7* John Biggers, *Africa*, 1942–43, detail sketch for *Country Preacher*, pencil on paper. (Art © John T. Biggers Estate/Licensed by VAGA, New York. Collection of the Hampton University Museum, Hampton, Virginia.)

experiences that were later amplified and elaborated by educational experiences in North Carolina, at Hampton, and in his own subsequent travels to Africa. As children, Biggers and his siblings "were taught early to do the preparatory work for quilting."[168] John later came to realize that "Experiences that I participated in back home—quiltmaking, building, carving, whittling—we didn't call art. So what I had done as a child—for instance, putting geometric parts together into a whole creatively new concept in quiltmaking—I later realized was really my basic art training."[169] Olive Jensen Theisen notes, Biggers's "mother once made him a quilt that he kept by his side as he worked."[170] Quilting is everywhere in Biggers's work, including a 1964 drawing of his mother.[171] He acknowledges, "It has really been there from the beginning. In the very first mural in the Eliza Johnson Home of the Aged [1950], the quilt is there. . . . I don't think I've done a mural without that. I think that the pattern or structure of the quilt has been very basic. For a long time it was almost unconscious." From his early education in the geometry of quilting, his work over time developed beyond incorporating images of quilts to becoming "the structure of the mural."[172]

While African American quiltmaking had a generalized influence on much of Biggers's work, it appears directly as the subject of *Three Quilters* (1952). (See Figure 6.8.) The drawing features three women, two seated and a third in the middle standing between them. Together they are working on a large quilt that sits on the laps of the two seated subjects, while the standing figure is holding a corner and a needle while seemingly stretching it by clenching an end between her teeth. The quilting party represents a rare venue for African American control of the means and process of production. The collaborative nature of their labor represents art as communal and functional, which further connects it to African textile production.[173] The result of such a process may reflect multiple individual aesthetics, even creating some seeming irregularities in the final product. Similar internal variation distinguishes Kuba textiles, which "are a composite of the work of several different hands."[174] In this way, the collaborative process manifests itself in the aesthetic structure of the work. In the Kuba textile tradition, Kasai velvets, those common among the Shoowa, are governed by a geometric grid of straight "diagonal 'streets' or 'paths' (Mboka), or black linear zones."[175] However the designs within their borders vary. Within this structure, "improvisation occurs in a context of traditional limitations," incorporating elements that Leon sees as central to what he terms "Afro-traditional" quilts.[176] The lines are preserved but there is significant improvisation contained within the squares, which allows for individual expression. Within Kuba textiles, such "irregularity," Adams explains, serves "as a means of particularizing the thing, of exemplifying individuality."[177]

*Figure 6.8* John Biggers, *Three Quilters (Quilting Party)*, 1952, conté crayon, 58×48 in. (147.3×121.9 cm). (Art © John T. Biggers Estate/Licensed by VAGA, New York. Courtesy of Museum of Fine Arts Houston, from *The Art of John Biggers: View from the Upper Room* by Alvia Wardlaw, New York: Harry N. Abrams and the Museum of Fine Arts, Houston, 1995, Figure 21, cat. no. 31, p. 59.)

Stylistically, the realism of *Three Quilters* is similar to Biggers's other work of the period and the women resemble many of the figures in Catlett's prints. Their powerful oversized hands are consistent with the social realist aesthetic he learned from White and Catlett. The setting lacks any obvious American cultural markers, and the three women are wearing head wraps that could be African or American. Biggers uses conté crayon to give the work a two-tone sensibility that brings attention to the irregular geometric patterning of the quilt rather than the juxtapositions of a wider color palette. Other than the checkered skirt of the seated woman on the left side of the drawing, all of the other visible clothing items—including the headscarves—appear to be unpatterned solids. The quilt rests on her lap on top of the patterned skirt, yet remains distinct: the patterning on the skirt appears to be symmetrical and is composed of smaller squares than those of the quilt. The open hand of one of the quilters draws the viewer's attention to the point where the quilt and the skirt are layered, bringing the contrast into focus. Biggers's visual interest in textiles—and the fabric culture of the African diaspora—here demonstrates an aesthetic understanding of the quilt as not only a symbol, but also a visual aesthetic effect.

Biggers's interest in African art came into sharper focus during his first trip to the continent in 1957, on a United Nations Educational, Scientific, and Cultural Organization (UNESCO) grant to the newly independent republic of Ghana with his wife Hazel, whom he had met at Hampton. Upon their arrival, Biggers recalled Hampton as the place where "our art master, Viktor Lowenfeld, taught us something about the noble meaning of African sculpture." Biggers's experiences in Ede, Nigeria, recall those of Sheppard in Mushenge; King Timi welcomes Biggers as a returned ancestor: "The drums announced that two foreigners had arrived through the palace gates. I have just told my people that you are not foreigners, but brothers who have returned home after an absence of three hundred years."[178] Biggers reflected, "sometimes I felt that I had been there before."[179] Like Sheppard, McDowell, Reuel Briggs, and countless other historical and literary figures, Biggers found Africa, particularly its visual art, to be familiar. During a visit to a weaving center in Abomey, Benin, he saw "a colorful checkered cloth about the size of a bedspread. We examined it, and I saw the piece had been made in much the same way that my mother made patchwork quilts back home in Gastonia."[180] Biggers here affirms what is otherwise visible in his art: the impossible-to-overstate influence of his mother, which represents the broader generational transmission of knowledge. His interest in textile patterns is shaped by his memories of his North Carolina upbringing, his travels in Africa, and his Hampton education.

Biggers's first African trip, which is beautifully documented in his book *Ananse: The Web of Life in Africa* (1962), is generally seen as marking a shift toward African subject matter. However in pre-1957 works such as *Country Preacher* and *Three Quilters*, African iconography was embedded within works otherwise set in the United States. As Theisen points out, "Many of the rural Southern images in Biggers's works have African antecedents, including the peaked roof shotgun house, the wash pot, and the vibrant textiles."[181] The African origins of shotgun house architecture are well known.[182] On Biggers's two-dimensional plane, the roof patterns are strikingly similar to quilt patterns, which he had used as a visual icon "since his Hampton days."[183] African American connections to Africa are not limited to manifestations in subject matter, but include the formal aesthetic qualities that Biggers continued to develop in his later work from *Shotgun, 3rd Ward, #1* (1966) to *Christia Adair* (1983) and *Shotguns, 4th Ward* (1987). Thompson beautifully links Bigger's shotgun house aesthetic to African American yard art, terming it "American Kongo," a signifying revision of Grant Wood's *American*

*Gothic.*[184] The home designs of African American missionaries seemingly fit within a tradition that includes the elaborate Kongo-influenced decorated Kentucky home of Henry Dorsey, who, like Sheppard, worked in Louisville in the 1920s.[185]

During his travels to West Africa, Biggers drew incredibly detailed scenes from Ghana (including and especially from its northern regions) and Nigeria—mostly rural and "traditional" images, often featuring boats, fishing, agriculture, animals, and drummers. Given his earlier encounters with African culture at places like Hampton Institute and Lincoln Academy, however, his African travels might be best understood as part of a continuum rather than as signaling an immediate change in focus. In this regard, Biggers had an established relationship to Africa prior to his actual travels, similar to what Farah Jasmine Griffin argues for Primus before her trip to the Congo (and the same argument can apply to many other figures including the early career of Langston Hughes, which is discussed in chapter 7).[186] Travel is only one part of a much more complex cultural matrix that produces traveling subjects such as Primus and Biggers in the first place. Therefore, while *Ananse* reflects a growing interest in Africa in terms of subject matter, his style much more gradually moved away from the expressionistic distortion of his earlier social realist influences. Over subsequent decades, the technical figures from his Ghana drawings slowly deconstruct, leading to his development of an aesthetic built less on discernibly African subject matter than on the influence of African design, which in the case of the Kuba has roots in women's embroidery.[187]

In a revealing exchange in Abomey, Biggers's own bias toward sculpture is challenged. His hosts ask, "Why should a person ask for sculpture when weaving was displayed for sale?" This question signals their preference for the abstract design of textiles rather than figurative sculpture. The detail in Biggers's drawings from the trip reveals a profound appreciation for the patterns of textiles, dresses, and clothing, and a concern that "imported, printed cotton goods have almost eliminated the African craft of weaving." Biggers also expresses concern about threats to indigenous cultural forms and has a visceral reaction to a weaving class at the university in Kumasi where he is based: "I loved to hear the singing treadles of the looms as brilliant threads of many colors were woven into the luxuriant designs of *kente* cloth."[188] As head of the art department at Texas Southern University (TSU), Biggers introduced weaving to the curriculum and oversaw a weaving studio in the campus Arts Center.[189]

Biggers understood his travel as part of a larger diasporic project to fulfill his "lifelong desire . . . to bridge the gap between African and American culture."[190] An exploration of a full range of influences does not diminish the "positive shock" of his first trip to Africa: "Ghosts of my ancestors writhed before me, laughing insanely and rattling their chains, and a stench from that open gutter seemed to become unbearable."[191] Biggers was haunted, and found it challenging to return to his craft: "Settling down to interpreting African life was the most difficult task I had encountered during my eighteen years of painting and drawing. The impact of Africa almost paralyzed my creative efforts; the drama and the poetic beauty were devastating. Until I was able to reorient myself I was literally broken; I felt unequal to the task."[192] Biggers makes it clear that such totalizing challenges manifest themselves in aesthetic ways as he later reflects, "I'd never seen color like the color there."[193]

The cumulative impact of Biggers's several trips to Africa is probably best measured by the range of distinctive and influential aesthetic practices he developed over the course of three decades, rather than exclusively by the work produced immediately on his first return from Ghana.[194] Over that time, other influences included his mother Cora, who lived with John and Hazel in Houston from the early 1960s until her death in 1975, serving as a reminder of the early interest in quilting that she inspired.[195] Art historian Edmund Barry Gaither describes the development of Biggers's aesthetic as "the artist's work became more abstract, more preoccupied with architecture and architectonic complications, and more symbolic. Especially after a serious illness in the mid-1970s, he began to synthesize, merge, and combine southern and African symbols into a new language of visual poetry and mystery. His paintings became like quilts, unified by their geometric patterns." In effect, Biggers increasingly moved away from realism, and by the 1980s, he had "virtually abandoned scientifically constructed pictorial space, replacing it with a highly patterned ground where flattened figures inhabit very shallow spatial windows."[196] Where his earlier work demonstrates an interest in textiles, in his work in the 1980s, the entire wall or canvas becomes a textile. Biggers acknowledges quilts as the "basic structure" of his murals: "These are architecturally sound things. The same mathematical formula that you erect buildings with, these women had put these things, consciously or unconsciously in these quilts."[197]

This developing style, predicated on the geometric sophistication of the quilt form, reflects the ongoing influence of the Kuba aesthetic forms that Biggers encountered in Sheppard's collection at Hampton. It emerges quite distinctively in the ways that his Houston mural *Quilting Party* (1980–81), which Wardlaw sees as contiguous with his earlier work, "represent[s] the continuity of an ancient and majestic culture."[198] (See Plate 5.) In *Quilting Party*, the identifiable figures are predominantly women, many of whom are dancing and playing music. Toward the center-left of the image, there are three women holding looms, who, according to Biggers, are "making a quilt pattern." The presence of the weavers suggests the mural's title, which is less a description of what the mural's figures are doing than an indication of the way *Quilting Party* uses their patterns as its "grid, with images woven in that serve to unify the complex mural." Those images are heavily African-influenced and include stools, sculptures, calabashes, tortoises, balaphons and xylophones, and shotgun houses with wings and heads. At the center is what Biggers calls a "morning star" figure that is modeled on an African sculpture from his personal collection, which he started in Ghana with gold weights and wood sculpture.[199] Also from his collection, at the bottom left is a comb or Afro hair pick, iconic images common in both African and African American society, and ubiquitous in his paintings as "our transcended symbol and that's why it[']s in the head, in the hair."[200] The geometry of Kuba design envelops much of the mural, as it is visible on the ground surface, in the clothing of the figures, on the shells of the tortoises, and in the background. The muted color palette, which is heavily tan, brown, and gray, is further characteristic of the earth tones of Kuba textiles. However, Biggers subtly foregrounds the browns and lighter hues to add depth to a work whose overarching geometry otherwise flattens its surface. The Africanness of Biggers's work is embedded as deeply in its formal and aesthetic dimensions as in its topical counterparts. Ultimately, its title *Quilting Party* is not a descriptor of the image Biggers paints, but rather the spirit, form, and structure of the work, which mark the development of the role of Africa in his work over the course of four decades and provides an interpretive roadmap for considering later work by him and other artists influenced by him.

Sacred Geometry

In the late 1940s, when Lowenfeld left Hampton for Penn State University, Biggers followed and eventually earned a PhD there.[201] In 1949, the new president of TSU in Houston, Raphael O'Hare Lanier, formerly U.S. minister to Liberia, hired Biggers, whom he knew from Hampton, as founding chair of the art department.[202] The strong Hampton connection to TSU, especially the art department, is the direct result of an academic migration from other HBCUs.[203] In addition to Biggers, Lanier hired Joseph Mack, another of his Hampton peers, in 1949 as the only other full-time art instructor. Sculptor Carroll Harris Simms, who attended Hampton from 1944 to 1948, joined the TSU faculty in 1950. The cohort immediately brought local and national recognition to the program. In 1950, both Biggers and Mack had work exhibited in shows at the Houston Museum of Fine Arts and at Atlanta University's annual exhibition; Simms appeared in the Atlanta University show in 1949 (as had Mack), and again in 1952. Under Lanier and his successor Samuel Nabrit, TSU was a remarkable intellectual environment; Toni Morrison taught there for two years in the mid-1950s and a series of prominent cultural figures visited campus. By 1960, the art department was offering 23 undergraduate and 8 graduate courses. Biggers required that all art majors paint public murals, which is indicative of his efforts to shape the built environment of the campus, which remains home to several of his major pieces.[204]

Simms, like Lanier and Biggers, had a great interest in Africa. He studied African art with William Fagg at the British Museum in the 1950s and traveled to West Africa in the late 1960s; in a variation of accounts by Sheppard, Biggers, and others, he was recognized as Beninois during his travels. Over the years, the school nurtured those connections by enrolling African students and providing opportunities for its students to study in Côte d'Ivoire.[205] Furthermore, though it did not come to fruition until the 1970s, "a TEACHING COLLECTION" of African art, modeled on Hampton's, was part of Biggers's founding vision for the department.[206] A 1980 catalog of 171 items from the TSU collection includes several on loan from the collection of Hazel Biggers. Of ten catalog objects from Zaire, the Kuba Kingdom is represented in the library's permanent collection by a Mwaash aMbooy mask that features some characteristic patterning in its beadwork on the rear of the mask.[207] A 1974 exhibition of Dogon art in Houston "awakened Biggers once again to the richness of West African culture," and Biggers likely felt a strong connection to a 1979 exhibition of Kuba art in Austin (even though the published catalog fails to mention Sheppard). Meanwhile, after Biggers retired from full-time teaching in 1983, he read African history with great intensity.[208] In Biggers's consciousness and in his art, Africa remained a dynamic subject accessible through a diverse range of sources for more than a half-century.

These renewed African influences shape later work like *Starry Crown* (1987), which not only reimagines the *Three Quilters* as identifiably African figures, but creates a two-dimensional plane in which Kuba-inspired geometric floor patterns are contiguous with the backdrop. (See Plate 6.) The overarching patterns encompass the entire painting in such a way that background and foreground come together. The backdrop is shaded by the shadows of the seated figures. Above their heads, this Kuba textile pattern dissolves into stars giving the painting its title. Furthermore, there is variation within the geometry, and the browns, beiges, blacks, and reds emphasize the colors common in Kuba textiles. According to Gaither, "its pictorial space ... is more completely dominated by what Biggers called 'sacred geometry.'"[209]

Amid the energy of his ever-expanding interests, Biggers accepted a commission to paint a mural for Hampton's new William R. and Norma B.

*Figure 6.9* John Biggers, Mary Alice Ford Armstrong (Samuel Chapman Armstrong's widow), and Margaret Armstrong Howe (daughter of Mary Alice and Samuel Chapman Armstrong, and wife of former Hampton president Arthur Howe) at the January 30, 1949, Founder's Day presentation of the bronze casting of a bust of Samuel Chapman Armstrong that Biggers sculpted in 1943. (Courtesy of Hampton University Archives, Hampton, Virginia.)

Harvey Library, which brought him back to the campus from 1990 to 1992 for a residency that included weekly community lectures.[210] (The new construction also enabled the stately former library to serve as the home of what is now called the Hampton University Museum.) The commission further embeds Biggers within the history and built environment of Hampton; a bust he sculpted of Samuel Armstrong while an undergraduate remains on display.[211] (See Figure 6.9.) As Biggers reflected at the time, Hampton "really had been a place of initiation for me," and that "I have used Hampton as a means of motivation" and "an invisible background for the things I have been doing all through the years." When he received the invitation to paint the murals, he felt he'd "been waiting for this."[212] Biggers was aware of the tradition as he recalled that "Du Bois's book, *The Souls of Black Folk*, was the first book I bought at Hampton as a student. It has taken me fifty years to give visual expression to his words. They are a part of these murals."[213] He also recalled that the African connection was evident as early as *Country Preacher*.[214] To draw on this personal and institutional history, he "surrounded himself with pieces of African art, photographs of campus buildings, Native American designs, and examples of vegetation native to the Tidewater area" in his makeshift Hampton studio.[215] The resulting work, which he painted with his nephew James Biggers, includes two panels, each of which is twenty feet high and ten feet wide: *House of the Turtle*, on the left, representing the past and *Tree House*, on the right, representing the future.[216] (See Plates 7 and 8.)

The bottom half of *House of the Turtle* features three women: "a kneeling 'African Mother,' a kneeling 'Native American Mother,' and a 'Church Mother' sitting on a turtle in Hampton's Memorial Chapel holding a smaller version of the Chapel in her hands." The top half includes two young people who, according to Jeanne Zeidler, director of the Hampton University Museum for more than two decades, represent Hampton students.[217] The clothing of the figures merges with the background and the icons are embedded in the background pattern. Here, the built environment takes over the landscape, and human figures predominate. Biggers took great care to represent many of the historic buildings on the Hampton campus, most of which were built by students as part of the industrial curriculum.[218] Biggers also recalled the role of music in the physical campus, where buildings like Virginia Hall "were sung up by the Hampton choirs." Biggers and his students were also attached to the Johnsons' *The Book of American Negro Spirituals*, and, through his world travels, he "found places in Africa and other places that the music of Hampton was home."[219]

This dynamic is reflected in the distinctive titles Biggers gave to the two halves of the mural. The title of the *Tree House* foregrounds the campus's historic Emancipation Oak, which envelops the canvas. A face is visible behind a rounded geometric pattern in the bottom third of the painting. Absent the human figures featured in *House of the Turtle*, Biggers merges the background and foreground so completely in *Tree House* that his distinctive geometric patterning comes to the foreground. In these paintings, Biggers creates an aesthetic that is similar to the Kuba, who have developed "an internally consistent design system which is found on costumes, pressed *tool*, wood carvings, and raffia cloth."[220] Throughout his paintings of the 1980s and 1990s, the design patterns increasingly swathe the work in ways that make the icons inseparable from the overarching aesthetic project.

In *House of the Turtle*, Biggers uses color to project a particular vision. Brown is the dominant color in the bottom half of the painting, which is where Biggers represents historical and contemporary buildings from the Hampton campus. Much of the iconography in the library murals is familiar. A series of six combs adorn the cemetery, growing like trees behind a series of headstones, while to their right, in the bottom center foreground, is a larger, more ornate comb. His scaling of the combs employs a type of fractal geometry that is characteristic of Kuba textiles, particularly in their development over the first half of the twentieth century, when increased demand by an international market resulted in older patterns being reproduced on a larger scale so that less intricate, yet still identifiable, designs could be produced more rapidly.[221] If the small combs are found in the campus cemetery, the enlarged combs are prominent structural elements in both halves of the mural, and their fine teeth serve as windows through which the viewer must gaze. In *Tree House*, two larger combs appear on the left and right sides of the canvas, effectively framing the tree at the center of the work.

Relative to Biggers's other work, the mural colors appear to be bright, as *House of the Turtle*, according to Biggers, "wanted a checkerboard structure of orange, burnt sienna and blue-green, suggesting fire and water."[222] *House of the Turtle* has a pronounced sense of illumination emanating from its center. The brightness of the green colors with some pink highlights on the clothes of the two standing figures is similar in his two final murals, *Salt Marsh* (1998) and *Nubia: The Origins of Business and Commerce* (1999), both painted in Houston in collaboration with Harvey Johnson in the years prior to Biggers's 2001 death.[223] Even there, such relatively bright coloration does not approach that of the artists of the Chicago-based AFRICOBRA group, or African Commune of Bad Relevant Artists, who were influenced by Biggers.[224] As Biggers found his color palette developing along the lines of AFRICOBRA artists, it becomes impossible to chart a linear genealogy of influence. In paintings like *Water Spirits* (1982) and *Mojo* (1987), AFRICOBRA artist James Phillips, who taught at Hampton in 1993, exhibits the geometric influence of Kuba textiles, while eschewing its color palette in favor of "coolade colors," the bright hues characteristic of AFRICOBRA artists like Wadsworth Jarrell.[225] Today, Phillips's unstretched canvas *The Soul and Spirit of John Biggers* is displayed on the second floor of the Hampton University Museum, directly above Sheppard's Kuba collection. (See Plate 9.) In its galleries, we can trace a visual tradition of direct and indirect influence, rooted in and routed through Sheppard's collection, on later generations of artists.[226]

Faith Ringgold has described the influence of Kuba textiles on her work, which is especially notable given her storied career in fabric art. In the late 1960s and early 1970s, Ringgold, like Biggers, represented Kuba patterns on her canvases, as well as her political posters.[227] Well before Ringgold's first trip to Africa in 1976, the geometry and structure of Kuba patterning informed her approach to decidedly American political images, including invocations of Rosa Parks in *For the Women's House* at the New York Women's House of Detention and designs on behalf of Angela Davis and the Black Panthers.[228] Lisa Farrington explains how "Ringgold's Bakuba triangles frame each vignette within the painting, strengthening the narrative by allowing the viewer to read each 'episode' like a succession of comic strip panels. Although the scenes may change and the configuration of space, shapes, and proportions may vary from one panel to the next, the Bakuba grid holds these various elements together."[229] Ringgold's incorporation of the African textile media into her craft predates yet expanded with her turn to fabric art. In 1974, Ringgold painted *The Windows of the Wedding Series*, a foundational series of fabric paintings based on Tibetan thangkas, which, she explains, "represent a visual language I was trying to invent based on Kuba designs."[230] (See Plate 10.) Ringgold discussed the topic of African influences with Biggers and Lowery Sims at length. While European modernism was Ringgold's portal to African art, Biggers appreciated the influence of his Hampton education, where Charles White "explained the meanings and qualities in African art, showing me the meaning of form."[231]

Among other artists influenced by Biggers is his cousin Sanford Biggers, a Morehouse College graduate, who explained to the late artist Terry Adkins, a Fisk University graduate, that he grew "up looking at his [John's] art and was very inspired, not only by the physical work, but also by his field of research, his use of history, his weaving of vernacular—U.S. Southern vernacular, African vernacular and culture, mythology, revisionist history, pro-positive black imagery, African diaspora imagery, sacred geometry."[232] African combs, which are among the most prized objects in Sheppard's collection and a frequent conceit in John Biggers's paintings, are the basis for one of Sanford's best-known works, *Afropick*, a six-foot-tall woodcut print in the shape of a Black power fist with its teeth extending like long tree roots. Sanford, who cites the influence of John Biggers's use of quilts on his own textile pieces, included a reproduction of *Quilting Party* in a 2012 Massachusetts Museum of Contemporary Art show he dedicated to his cousin.[233]

Samella Lewis's distinguished students have been equally influenced by Sheppard's collection. At Scripps College in the 1970s and early 1980s, she taught the Congo art historian Mary Nooter Roberts and multimedia artist Alison Saar, who later collaborated on *Body Politics: The Female Image in Luba Art and the Sculpture of Alison Saar*.[234] In her dialogue with Roberts, Saar appreciates the influence of her studies with Lewis, but notes that the aesthetic connections that Roberts makes between Saar's work and the female body in Luba art "are not necessarily conscious crossovers," and that "a lot of my work is informed by African ideas but not necessarily directly."[235] Sheppard's collection is one of the indirect channels through which African art shapes the aesthetic practices of contemporary art. Nick Cave, a multimedia artist whose work includes fabric, has described the influence of Kuba textiles, which he first saw at the Metropolitan Museum of Art when he was 18 years old.[236] The textile artist Karen Hampton, who works in raffia fiber, includes repurposed Kuba textiles in some of her work.[237] Susan Cooksey,

Robin Poynor, and Hein Vanhee's recent exhibition and catalog *Kongo across the Waters* brilliantly expands the conversation among artists, audiences, and scholars even wider by considering the Kongo tradition in the works of Renée Stout, Radcliffe Bailey, and other African-descended artists in the United States and the Caribbean.[238]

Amid the extended discussion of Sheppard's artistic heirs, it is worth considering his own son, Maxamalinge, who attended the Art Institute of Chicago to study design, with a focus on jewelry making.[239] (The offspring of Sheppard's colleagues the Edmistons also pursued a distinguished career in the arts: their grandson Sherman has owned and operated the Essie Green Gallery in Harlem for several decades.) Though Max did not graduate, his interests recall the Kuba tradition of adornment. It also places him at the Art Institute during a period when there were many great African American artists enrolled before, during, and after his time there. In the 1910s and 1920s alone, Richmond Barthe, Hale Woodruff, Archibald Motley, Charles Sebree, Dox Thrash, Ellis Wilson, and Walter Ellison all studied there.[240] When he returned to Louisville, he taught African art and design. One of his students was Gloucester Caliman Coxe (1907–99), the son of one of his father's ministerial colleagues, who went on to become "the dean of Louisville's African American artists," as part of a vibrant scene that produced such luminaries as Sam Gilliam and Bob Thompson.[241]

This rich array of connections is foundational to the development of African American visual practices that remain entangled within ongoing histories of colonialism and resistance. These African American engagements with the Congo enable us to see black Atlantic routes in their historical complexity and to understand the material connections that are foundational to diasporic aesthetics. Sheppard's art collection remains a dynamic site of transatlantic exchange. While studying at Hampton, Ngoloshang Mbeky, who earned an MBA in 1993, provided the museum with additional documentation on Sheppard's collection and, in 2000, arranged for his uncle, the Kuba King Kwete Mbuek III, to visit the museum.[242] Hampton's connection to the Kuba is one of many stories that suggest the importance of the transatlantic movements of people, art, texts, and ideas. As a permanent collection and centerpiece of the Hampton University Museum, Sheppard's art collection has contributed to an ongoing aesthetic practice whose genealogy suggests that modern African American interest in African art is not only a matter of heritage, but rather the product of ongoing contact and exchange, much of it through networks of politically engaged figures whose commitment to African art was forged as an integral part of a colonial and, at its best, anticolonial project.

PART III

# The Congo in Modern African American Poetics and Politics

*Chapter 7*

Near the Congo

*Langston Hughes and the Geopolitics
of Internationalist Poetry*

Langston Hughes's "The Negro Speaks of Rivers," which has become a signature meditation on African American heritage and ancestry, includes one of the most famous invocations of the Congo in American letters: "I built my hut near the Congo and it lulled me to sleep."[1] The poem, which was originally published in the June 1921 issue of the NAACP's *Crisis*, has become an iconic representative of Hughes and the Harlem Renaissance. With an opening couplet whose long, reflective second line begins by repeating the first line—"I've known rivers: / I've known rivers ancient as the world and older than the flow of human blood in human veins," the poem traverses major waterways on three continents.[2] Along the way, the poem's innovative geopolitics inaugurate Hughes's relationship with the Congo, which makes it representative of an ongoing internationalist sensibility both in his verse and in the larger cultural movement of which it is an exemplary part.

The poem's image of the Congo captures an African landscape seemingly so calm and peaceful as to obscure its sources in black political discourse. For Rachel Blau DuPlessis, "The Negro Speaks of Rivers" reinterprets Vachel Lindsay's "The Congo" in presenting the Congo River "as a pastoral, nourishing, maternal setting."[3] Lindsay certainly influenced Hughes, and the poem's pastoral resonance is no doubt partly responsible for its enduring popularity. Yet as this line about the Congo subtly illustrates, such seductive serenity can dull people's full awareness of their surroundings. In 1920, at the time of the poem's writing, African American intellectuals recognized the Congo as the subject of the most brutal extremes of European colonialism. Rather than a synecdoche for the African continent, as much commentary on the poem implies, the Congo was a discrete political site that had recently been the target of a massive, international human rights campaign in which the writings of African American travelers like George Washington Williams and William Henry Sheppard were instrumental. Within this political context, Hughes's Congo reference, along with other images in the poem, contains allusions that would likely have been apparent to thousands of *Crisis* readers, even as they remain obscure in the writings of later critics.

By 1930, "The Negro Speaks of Rivers," which "promptly became," "along with the Du Bois editorials and Jean Toomer's 'Song of the Son,' the voice of the Association [NAACP] itself," had been reprinted at least eleven times, appearing in such major Harlem Renaissance anthologies as *The New Negro* (1925) and *Caroling Dusk* (1927).[4] The frequent republications have transformed, if not obscured, the context in which it was written and read. Much like the *Colored American Magazine* before it, journals like the *Crisis* complemented their creative offerings with broad political coverage, so it is especially important "to see the poetry as part of a whole critical and transformative social project."[5] For a writer like Hughes, who "learned to read with *The Crisis* on my grandmother's lap,"[6] the monthly periodical, edited by W. E. B. Du Bois, was peerless and the "only magazine that came by mail to my grandmother's house in Kansas."[7] The poem's early history in the *Crisis* illuminates a political geography that, through the figure of the Congo, extends from the Harlem Renaissance to the Black Arts movement.

An analysis that locates a political sensibility in Hughes's earliest poetry can prompt a rethinking of the work, its author, and his community, thereby illuminating the centrality of the internationalist imperative to twentieth-century African American literature. While references to modern Africa abound in African American poetry of the 1960s and are understood to be products of the confluence of African national independence movements and the Black Arts movement, Hughes's earliest poetry extends that continuity back at least to the 1920s and the Harlem Renaissance. Throughout his career, Hughes maintained an active association with a range of political and literary institutions in which the Congo was as much a contemporary political figure as a romantic image. While Hughes's late poems from the 1960s include indisputably political references to the Congo, they are not anthologized or read as frequently as his earlier work. And while "The Negro Speaks of Rivers" remains an integral part of his canon, it is rarely read as a political work that includes Africa and the wider colonial world. Yet this poem, Hughes's first major publication, reveals some of the ways in which an internationalist political sensibility around the figure of the Congo was vital to literary culture at the dawn of the Harlem Renaissance and throughout the twentieth century.

Rivers in Our Past

For more than half a century, the most common point of departure for interpreting "The Negro Speaks of Rivers" has been Hughes's autobiographical account in *The Big Sea* (1940), in which he acknowledges, "The one of my poems that has perhaps been most often reprinted in anthologies . . . was written just outside St. Louis, as the train rolled toward Texas." En route to see his father in Mexico, Hughes recounts how the sight of the Mississippi River inspired him "to think about other rivers in our past—the Congo, and the Niger, and the Nile in Africa—and the thought came to me: 'I've known rivers,' and I put it down on the back of an envelope I had in my pocket, and within the space of ten or fifteen minutes, as the train gathered speed in the dusk, I had written this poem."[8] For decades, scholars accepted his straightforward account and focused on the poem as a transcendent and romantic meditation on racial heritage.[9] Yet the geography of *The Big Sea* has at least as much in common with Benjamin Brawley's assertion in *Africa and the War* (1918) that "four great rivers—the Nile, the Niger, the Congo, and the Zambezi—rival the Mississippi," and with the later distribution routes of Garvey's *Negro World* along "the uncharted reaches of the Nile, the Congo, the Zambesi and the Niger" as it does with the published version of the poem.[10] Although *The Big Sea* presents a compelling genealogy for the poem, the published version suggests an image of Africa that differs significantly from what Hughes describes writing.

The opening two stanzas—three lines in all—are followed by the poem's longest, most geographically specific verse:

> I bathed in the Euphrates when dawns were young.
> I built my hut near the Congo and it lulled me to sleep.
> I looked upon the Nile and raised the pyramids above it.
> I heard the singing of the Mississippi when Abe Lincoln went down to New Orleans, and I've seen its muddy bosom turn all golden in the sunset.[11]

The four rivers named in "The Negro Speaks of Rivers" differ from those referenced in *The Big Sea*, with the poem excluding the Niger River in West Africa and beginning in Iraq (Mesopotamia) with the Euphrates, a river that is not in Africa. While many commentators have looked to *The Big Sea* to explicate the poem, they have not accounted for this geographic change (or Hughes-the-autobiographer's decision to make this rupture visible), despite the acknowledged importance of Hughes's poetic geography as part of an African American "discourse of spatial signing [that] has evolved into a literary strategy of allusion to a diversity of symbolic and spiritual spaces." By focusing on three distinct sites—"the unremembered place of origin in Africa, the unrealized yet perfectible social space of America, and the unprecedented enclave of black Harlem," James de Jongh points toward a multivalent interpretation of Hughes's spatial allusions, which serve a diversity of purposes.[12]

As a result of Hughes's assertion that "The Negro Speaks of Rivers" is about "rivers in our past," the poem is typically read as what Brent Hayes Edwards defines as an "abstraction" of diaspora that "ground[s] identity claims and transnational initiatives in a history of 'scattering of Africans' that supposedly offers a principle of unity—as Paul Gilroy phrases it, 'purity and invariant sameness'—to those dispersed populations."[13] Indeed, the structure of the poem seems to support such an abstract reading by neatly rendering its four rivers in parallel. This approach seems endemic to readings of the Congo. As Bill Ashcroft writes, "The Congo, a metonymy put for the mysterious chthonic regions of the human imagination called Africa, is a peculiarly appropriate sign of the post-colonial. It emerges out of the distinction between the town and the spiritual jungle, the centre of power and the colonised margin; it acknowledges the identifying importance of place, because above all, the post-colonial is a discourse of place; it acknowledges the terror of the unknown which will always keep the margin distanced and powerless." Ashcroft, however, has little to say about the Congo even though he follows Homi Bhabha's criticism of "the metaphorising tendency . . . 'to introduce the principle of equivalence,' a totalising act which is a device for importing universalism into the post-colonial text."[14] Hughes's poem, which is not postcolonial, sets up such an equivalence, but then offers a critique of its own use of place. The murky image of the Mississippi's fleeting transparency—its daily flow from muddy to golden—defies any configurations of uniformity. For his part, Edwards prefers to highlight "the anti-abstractionist uses of *diaspora*," which emphasize such a difference.[15] When "The Negro Speaks of Rivers" is read in this African American internationalist context, particularly via the *Crisis*, the poem appears more concerned with the kind of "multilocational history" that Houston A. Baker Jr. calls for than with some unified, abstract ideal.[16] The poem thus exemplifies how articulations of Africa or the global can be read as part of a perspicuous political discourse.

As *The Big Sea* nods toward an abstract interpretation of "The Negro Speaks of Rivers," it obscures the Euphrates, which, as the poem's first river, can guide readers toward a concrete interpretation of its geography. The Euphrates was not only the cradle of ancient civilization (with African origins, according to Du Bois) but also a politically charged location that was on the vanguard of antiimperialism at the time when Hughes was writing.[17] Iraq had, until recently, been under Ottoman rule. In return for Arab and Kurdish support in the Allies' Ottoman campaign of World War I, England and France promised independence to both groups. When the European powers reneged, their occupation met fierce resistance across the region. In the summer of 1919, the Kurds rebelled and were crushed by the British. One year later, the League of Nations provided international sanction to the occupation by giving England a mandate over Iraq on April 28, 1920. Iraq responded with military action on June 30, 1920, beginning what is known today as the 1920

Revolution.[18] Hughes's own account indicates that he wrote the poem three weeks after the start of the revolution, which spread quickly throughout the Euphrates valley.[19] Amid this massive uprising, which claimed the lives of 10,000 Iraqis and more than 1,000 British and Indian colonial troops, Hughes's narrator recalls literally immersing himself in the Euphrates, which was the frontline of the struggle against British colonialism.[20]

A passing reference in an unpublished diary Hughes kept between July 20 and July 23, 1920, provides one viable source for his reference to the Euphrates. During the train ride to Mexico when he wrote the poem, Hughes mentions sitting next to an Assyrian man who was reading an Arabic-language paper.[21] This encounter connects the poem to the vibrant, if now largely forgotten, early-twentieth-century Arabic-language press in the United States.[22] Regardless of who Hughes's train companions were, he, like his *Crisis* readers, was well-enough informed to recognize that the Euphrates River, the location of his narrator's bath, was a pivotal site of anticolonial resistance. Today, such recognition stands out because Hughes understood Iraq's anticolonial history, which so many U.S. leaders in the twenty-first century catastrophically misunderstand. Regarding the 2003 U.S. invasion of Iraq, Rashid Khalidi explains: "Nothing so ambitious, or so fraught with peril, has been tried there since just after World War I, when Britain and France engaged in their last burst of colonial expansion under the guise of League of Nations mandates. Their effort was strongly resisted by Middle Easterners, but it also resulted in the creation of many of the states, and produced many of the problems, in that region today. This historical context was largely ignored in the lead-up to war. Even less attention was paid to how Middle Easterners perceived American actions in terms of that recent history."[23] The historical ignorance that Khalidi describes is a far more consequential corollary to the decontextualization that has made it difficult for many readers to appreciate the range of allusions at work in Hughes's poem.

## Upon the Nile

In a September 1920 review essay in *The Nation* (a magazine to which Hughes subscribed and in which he published "The Negro Artist and the Racial Mountain" in 1926), Du Bois rhetorically links the Euphrates with the Nile. Du Bois insists that Africa's centrality to world history transcends both racial identification and animus: "No age of the world, ancient or modern, has been able to escape Africa. We may, according to our birthplace or color or lineage, bewail this or feel a secret uplift because of it; but it is, in either case, true that from the beginning of human civilization, on the Nile and Euphrates, around the shores of the Mediterranean, in central and in northern

Europe and in America, continually, each century, at one time or another, centers world interest in this old and mighty continent." Here Du Bois uses the rhetoric of "human civilization" to advance a political argument that becomes more clearly contemporary as he reviews *The Belgian Congo and the Berlin Act* (1919) by "the orthodox British imperialist" Arthur Berriedale Keith and *The Black Man's Burden* (1920) by CRA-founder E. D. Morel, who is likewise "no particular lover of Africans."[24]

Hughes's poem similarly links the Nile, Euphrates, and Congo to construct a broad commentary about Africa that connects the classical and modern worlds. By associating Egypt and Iraq, Hughes challenges the conventional wisdom of the British authorities, who claimed that this era of Arab uprisings (which included Palestine and Jordan) was a series of unrelated local matters.[25] Hughes recognizes the connection between struggles in the region at a time when colonial authorities publicly denied such linkages, even as telegrams and private communications from British officers revealed their fear, by the summer of 1919, that rising nationalism would create "another Egypt" in Iraq.[26]

Hughes utilizes the Nile valley as he does the Euphrates, by using the location of an active anticolonial struggle for poetic purposes. While the political resonances of the Nile were multifaceted and reached into the Sudan and Ethiopia, the most immediate reference for readers of the *Crisis* was the Egyptian revolution.[27] The March 1919 exile of Saad Zaghloul, the Egyptian nationalist leader of the Wafd Party, resulted in mass resistance throughout much of Egypt. British fear increased following "widespread attacks on British military personnel."[28] "The Negro Speaks of Rivers" uses the singular pronoun to describe a construction project that would be impossible for any individual—"I looked upon the Nile and raised the pyramids above it." Therefore, the poet's voice is necessarily collective, reflecting the anticolonial mobilization underway in the same Nile valley at the time he was writing.

In a June 1919 editorial "Egypt and India," the *Crisis* declared its solidarity with Egypt (along with India). Even as they acknowledge that militancy is not suited for the United States, the editors ask, "Who sitting in America can say that Revolution is never right on the Ganges or the Nile?" The editorial concludes, "Only our hearts pray that Right may triumph and Justice and Pity over brute Force and Organized Theft and Race Prejudice, from San Francisco to Calcutta and from Cairo to New York."[29] *Crisis* editorials such as this, Hughes acknowledged, were crucial to his literary development, just as articles like Jessie Fauset's "Nationalism in Egypt" in the April 1920 *Crisis* helped him better understand modern Africa.[30] Fauset's article, published three months before Hughes wrote "The Negro Speaks of Rivers," recounts in detail the Egyptian campaign for independence from Britain, who "prevented the Egyptians from sending a popular delegation to the Paris Peace Conference, thereby providing the spark that ignited the 1919 Egyptian revolution."[31] Fauset focuses on U.S. complicity, sharply noting that President Woodrow Wilson irresponsibly recognized Britain's unjust claim without even responding to letters he received from the Egyptian delegation.

Fauset unequivocally frames the conflict as Egypt rightly asserting its independence from a belligerent colonial power. The struggle, she insists, must not be justified by ideological sophistry: "The East and the West are clashing not only over separate and distinct ideas, but also over ideas which are practically similar. Each is determined to gain and maintain its own supremacy. England, having seized Egypt in her grip, is holding on with all her bulldog tenacity. Egypt's request for autonomy means practically nothing to England." Fauset cites Zaghloul in her penultimate paragraph to argue that the clash is simply England's attempt to maintain imperial control: "The struggle becomes fiercer. The struggle is unequal, if one judges from the viewpoint of brutal force against unarmed right; but it is a struggle from which Egypt, sooner or later, will come forth victorious, because she defends an ideal, and there is no force on earth that can indefinitely conquer an idea." Fauset follows Zaghloul in her own diasporic voice, concluding: "Who doubts that Egypt is really speaking for the whole dark world? Thus is the scene being staged for the greatest and most lasting conflict of peoples."[32] Fauset has a savvy appreciation for the politics of the Nile valley and in her conclusion can see the struggle in Egypt as paradigmatic of a global movement of people of color, which would make it consistent with "The Negro Speaks of Rivers." Indeed, Hughes began his correspondence with Fauset a few months after she published "Nationalism in Egypt," and in January 1921, Fauset accepted the then-unknown teenager's poem for publication in the *Crisis*.[33]

Any early reader of Hughes's poem in the June 1921 issue of the *Crisis*, where it debuted, could not escape recognizing Egypt as a beacon of modern anticolonial nationalism: "The Negro Speaks of Rivers" is immediately followed by an article honoring Egypt's Zaghloul as one of the magazine's "Men of the Month." The unsigned profile, likely the work of Fauset or Du Bois, notes Zaghloul's "triumphant" return from exile when he was "received by the natives with unprecedented enthusiasm." The article concludes that Zaghloul, whose picture accompanies the text, "embodies the new spirit of Egyptian nationalism."[34] This celebration of Zaghloul at the precise moment when his Wafd Party was becoming increasingly militant in its demands for "the termination of the British protectorate, the abolition of martial law, and complete independence" belies any interpretation of Hughes's geography as simply pastoral or romantic.[35] While reprints of "The Negro Speaks of Rivers" conceal its proximity to Zaghloul, *Crisis* readers needed only to turn the page to find an exegesis of what could be seen, beyond the Pyramids, if they collectively "looked upon the Nile."

Near the Congo

In 1921, amid rising Arab militancy and European fear of the influence of Garvey and his apparent allies in the Belgian Congo, Fauset attended the Second Pan-African Congress in Brussels, Paris, and London as a delegate of Delta Sigma Theta sorority. While the Belgian press was spreading rumors that Congolese delegate Paul Panda Farnana, a Du Bois correspondent, was in league with Garvey, Fauset affirmed the importance of the Congo by making Farnana's photo the sole illustration to accompany her report in the *Crisis*.[36] In her article, she also describes a visit to the Royal Museum for Central Africa, which helped the delegation "to understand the unspoken determination of the Belgians to let nothing interfere with their dominion in the Congo. Such treasures! Such illimitable riches! What a store-house it must plainly be for them. For the first time in my life I was able to envisage what Africa means to Europe.... All the wealth of the world—skins and furs, gold and copper—would seem to center in the Congo."[37] The Pan-African Congress, which drew on earlier missionary traditions, is also situated on the cusp of expanding U.S. interest in Congolese art. Fauset's report from Brussels makes the Pan-African importance of the Congo clear to anyone reading the *Crisis*.

Similarly, Hughes recognized the Congo as a touchstone for activists in "The Negro," his third poem for the *Crisis*, which was published in January 1922, six months after "The Negro Speaks of Rivers" and soon after Fauset returned from the Pan-African Congress. Its fifth stanza reads:

> I've been a victim:
> The Belgians cut off my hands in the Congo.
> They lynch me now in Texas.[38]

By July 1924, the transatlantic poem made its way to Paris as it was reprinted in its original English in *Les Continents*.[39] Hughes considered this poem, and its political specificity, to be representative enough to use it as the opening "Proem" in his first book, *The Weary Blues* (1926), where it heralds "The Negro Speaks of Rivers," which appears later in the same volume.[40]

"The Negro" bluntly refers to one of the colonial administration's most infamous instruments of terror—the cutting off of hands, a gruesome accounting system for the bullets allocated to the colonial military. This hand-severing practice, which was used against many living people, was first exposed in Europe and the United States in an 1899 eyewitness report by Sheppard, who had been, like Zaghloul, recognized as one of the *Crisis*'s "Men of the Month."[41] Sheppard's January 1919 address to a national NAACP meeting on "The Future of Africa" was covered in the *Crisis*, which reports that he saw "eighty-one right hands which had been cut off and were in the process of being cured!" while, "Above them waved the flag of Belgium and the king [M'lumba N'kusa] on being questioned produced papers from Belgian Leopold, of evil fame, asking for ivory, rubber or *hands of men*!"[42] The Belgium references attributed to Sheppard are striking since his initial communiqué on the subject, written nine years before Belgian rule officially supplanted Leopold's unchecked private reign, makes no mention of the flag or of any papers from Leopold.[43] Still, Sheppard's 1919 assertions about Leopold and the flag, whether observation or embellishment, by him or the *Crisis*, suggest the importance of Belgium to the NAACP version of this narrative. This is not a matter of individual rapaciousness but rather state colonialism. The "Future of Africa" conference, where Sheppard delivered his remarks, was significant enough for Hughes to refer to it in his 1962 history of the organization, *Fight for Freedom: The Story of the NAACP*.[44]

Where the NAACP and Sheppard did not see eye to eye, Hughes and "The Negro" follow the NAACP's Du Boisian line. For instance, Sheppard insisted that the shift of control from Leopold to Belgium, which he helped spark more than a decade earlier, was consequential and "that the horrors of the Congo were the immediate result of Leopold's personal interest and not connected with the interests of the Belgian Government." The *Crisis* remained unwilling to absolve Belgium of any responsibility, opining, "The distinction is fine."[45] While the *Crisis* was correct in that the "central part of what Morel had called the 'System,' forced labor, remained in place" after Leopold was forced to cede control of Congo to the Belgian government in 1908, the nuanced disagreement highlights the level of African American discourse on the Congo.[46] Across such differences, the Congo is consistently rendered a political site, even when its precise ideological position is difficult to classify. Hughes's poem "The Negro," then, is consistent with the NAACP's vilification of the colonial state: "The Belgians cut off my hands in the Congo." Hughes's "Negro" is not, in this instance, the subject of the clause; the "Belgians" are. The brutal cutting exists in both the past and present tenses, indicating its ongoing prevalence.

Nor was Hughes the only poet to use this graphic image to address Belgian colonialism. A young Lester B. Granger published "Belgium" in *The Dunbar Speaker and Entertainer* (1920). Though Granger employs a Congolese persona whose chief, after being held hostage for rubber, returns with "arms but useless stumps," his poem's imagery and its assignment of responsibility to "Belgium" make it comparable to "The Negro."[47] Such violent

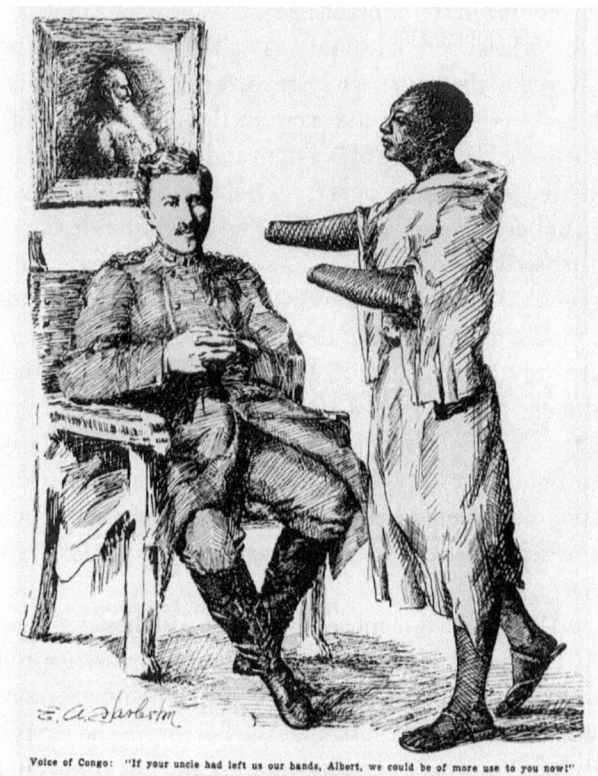

Figure 7.1
E. A. Harleston, "Voice of Congo: 'If your uncle had left us our hands, Albert, we could be of more use to you now.'" From *Crisis* 13, no. 5 (March 1917): 247. (Courtesy of Library of Congress, Washington, D.C.)

images establish "Belgium" as shorthand for the eternal colonial state. In his 2014 song "Evil Knievel," Mississippi hip-hop artist David Banner, for example, can draw a straight line, similar to "The Negro," from racist state violence in Tulsa, Rosewood, and Philadelphia up through the present: "This for Harlem when the pigs stop and frisk / All my folks from the Congo tell Belgium suck a, suck a."[48] By literally dropping the understood near-rhyme at the end of this couplet, Banner adeptly abbreviates the implied vulgar colloquialism in a way that demonstrates that "Belgium" continues to function as a recognizable allusion to colonialism more than fifty years after the formal end of its central African regime.

The earlier narrative that spotlights Belgian culpability is visible elsewhere in the *Crisis*. A 1917 editorial cartoon by E. A. Harleston presents a uniformed white figure seated in a chair in front of a portrait profile of a bearded man. A black man dressed in white cloth and sandals stands before the seated figure with his handless arms outstretched. The caption reads: "Voice of Congo: 'If your uncle had left us our hands, Albert, we could be of more use to you now.'" (See Figure 7.1.) The appearance of the cartoon without explanatory details indicates the editors' belief that *Crisis* readers knew the Congo crisis well enough to identify the pictured uncle as Leopold II and the seated figure as the current King Albert I of Belgium.[49] Readers encountering "The Negro Speaks of Rivers" in the same magazine a few years later would be similarly prepared to recognize the political connotations of a reference to the Congo.

While Harleston's powerful image may be the most graphic trace of the Congo in the pages of the *Crisis*, it is hardly alone. As St. Clair Drake, who as a child met Sheppard, recalls, "Black newspapers and opinion magazines like Du Bois' *Crisis* were the major sources of information in black communities about African affairs and prominent personalities. They kept Africa very much before us."[50] The attention aimed at Belgium can be traced through Du Bois, whose "poetic and stirring, passionate and indignant editorials" Hughes had idolized since he "was old enough to read."[51] During Hughes's teenage years, Du Bois was developing an internationalist analysis in works like "The African Roots of the War," which use the Congo as a touchstone for "the tale of all Africa in this rape of a continent already furiously mangled by the slave trade."[52] After the essay's first appearance in the *Atlantic Monthly*, the NAACP reprinted it as a pamphlet. For *Darkwater*, Du Bois incorporated material from the essay in two separate chapters, one of which, "The Hands of Ethiopia," insists that "for the development of Central Africa, Egypt should be free and independent, there along the highway to a free and independent India; while Morocco, Algeria, Tunis, and Tripoli must become a part of Europe, with modern development and home rule." His deeply disconcerting prescription for northern Africa west of Egypt highlights his exceptionalist belief in the existence of a particular link between Congo and Egypt. Furthermore, Du Bois made sure that wartime sympathy for Belgium did not obscure its history of colonial violence in the Congo: "Behold little Belgium and her pitiable plight, but has the world forgotten Congo? What Belgium now suffers is not half, not even a tenth, of what she has done to black Congo since Stanley's great dream of 1880."[53]

In *Darkwater*, Du Bois bridges contemporary and classical discourse by invoking Queen Nefertari as an inspiring symbol for the liberation of modern Africa.[54] The connections that Du Bois elicited were consistent with the work of Pauline Hopkins and Meta Fuller with regard to Ethiopia. For Du Bois, Egypt exists simultaneously in both eras; for Hughes, whom he influenced so profoundly, it did the same. When "The Negro Speaks of Rivers" appeared in *The Weary Blues*, Hughes dedicated it to Du Bois, increasing its likelihood of being read through a political lens. While the influence of Du Bois's anticolonialism may be more easily legible in "The Negro," the consistency of reference between the two poems published in the same magazine six months apart and later in the same collection provides a contextual continuity that informed readings of "The Negro Speaks of Rivers" in its early years.

## The Big Sea

While "rivers in the poem, such as the Congo and the Nile, also have connotations of slavery and exploitation by colonial powers," the fourth and final river reference is the most obviously recent:[55] "I heard the singing of the Mississippi when Abe Lincoln went down to New Orleans, and I've seen its muddy bosom turn all golden in the sunset." This line alludes to a popular story that Hughes recalls "reading [about] how Abraham Lincoln had made a trip down the Mississippi on a raft to New Orleans, and how he had seen slavery at its worst, and had decided within himself that it should be removed from American life."[56] Although Hughes supposedly wrote the poem while looking at the river (the only one from the poem he had seen at that time), his reference point is not firsthand observation, but rather something he read.[57] The author's view of the river is further mediated, through a characteristic musical interface ("singing") that evokes New Orleans's musical heritage. The name of the historic park at the center of the city's rich jazz culture—Congo Square, so named because it served as a place where Africans gathered to dance during the antebellum era—further acknowledges its cultural ties to central Africa.[58]

The confluence of the Mississippi and Congo rivers finds political expression in the December 17, 1919, edition of Hughes's hometown *Cleveland Advocate*: "'American Congo' to be Subject at this Gathering."[59] The headline refers to a Du Bois speech at a January 1920 NAACP meeting in New York, which was being widely publicized in the African American press.[60] The frequent use of "American Congo" in NAACP vernacular at the time is noteworthy, especially when Du Bois, in his speech, describes "the Mississippi Valley, from Memphis to New Orleans . . . [as] a region whose history is as foul a blot on American civilization as Congo is a blot on Belgium and Europe."[61] Such "startling parallels between the evils of Belgian administration in the Congo and the authoritarian rule of Jim Crow in the New South" have an extensive history.[62] "American Congo" was the title of a chapter in *The Negro Faces America* (1920), a book written by the NAACP's white publicity director Herbert J. Seligmann. In the March 1921 edition of *The Nation*, NAACP Field Secretary William Pickens used "American Congo" as the title of an article on the lynching of Henry Lowry, an African American tenant farmer in Mississippi County, Arkansas, that was reprinted in the *Chicago Defender*, in a pamphlet by the American Civil Liberties Union, and later in *Negro:*

*Anthology Made by Nancy Cunard, 1931–1933*.⁶³ Frank Marshall Davis opens his 1935 volume *Black Man's Verse* with "Chicago's Congo (Sonata for an Orchestra)," which provides a musical framework for a poem that engages similar comparisons in a refrain that directly reflects on the Middle Passage and other forms of transatlantic migration:

> *From the Congo*
> *to Chicago*
> *is a long trek*
> *—as the crow flies*⁶⁴

Such examples reveal that the Congo, like the Mississippi, was a long-standing political figure in African American discourse and that its connotations were not exclusively pastoral.

While the geopolitical discourse circulating in the 1920s made the allusions in "The Negro Speaks of Rivers" legible to its readers, scholars have tended to accept Hughes's explanation that the poem presents an apparently apolitical racial heritage in which Africa is seen as "dim and distant" or a "romantic motherland."⁶⁵ Yet the statement by his authoritative biographer Arnold Rampersad that Hughes's "leftist involvements have vanished without a trace"⁶⁶ from *The Big Sea* usefully reminds us of his political discretion, a point that Kate Baldwin affirms in her gloss of Arna Bontemps's 1939 letter suggesting that Hughes was dissuaded from publishing anything about the Soviet Union around the time he published the autobiography.⁶⁷ While the autobiography may downplay Hughes's affinity for the NAACP and Eugene Debs's antiwar socialism, it nevertheless leaves more than a trace of the political origins and context of "The Negro Speaks of Rivers."⁶⁸

In *The Big Sea*, Hughes opens the short five-page chapter "I've Known Rivers" by noting "That November the First World War ended," and that his high school classmates in Cleveland celebrated Lenin's ascension in Russia. The structure of the chapter frames "The Negro Speaks of Rivers" as a product of World War I, which, according to the Du Bois–NAACP thesis, was a result of European imperialism in Africa and set the stage for the dissolution of the Ottoman Empire and for the uprisings in the Euphrates and Nile valleys. Although *The Big Sea* does not mention it in detail, as a high school student during this period, Hughes was active in the NAACP and attended its annual convention in Cleveland in 1919, which Du Bois addressed.⁶⁹ Yet *The Big Sea* reconfigures Hughes's leftist sympathies as youthful naïveté: "The daily papers pictured the Bolsheviki as the greatest devils on earth, but I didn't see how they could be that bad if they had done away with race hatred and landlords—two evils that I knew well at first hand."⁷⁰ However, the Russian revolution provides a useful context for understanding his invocation of Egypt at a time when British officials feared the "Bolshevik tendency" of the Egyptian nationalists who had "the sympathy of all classes and creeds."[71]

Rampersad's insight that *The Big Sea* deliberately deemphasizes Hughes's leftist history should lead readers to take with a grain of salt the book's explanation for "The Negro Speaks of Rivers" twenty years later. The autobiography itself even concedes a more complicated composition: "No doubt I changed a few words the next day, or maybe crossed out a line or two."[72] His basic acknowledgment that he did not publish the precise poem that he composed on the train in fifteen minutes in July 1920 leaves a trace of an undocumented process. Hughes consciously used *The Big Sea* to fashion himself as a "folk poet, who 'finds' poems nearly complete and has to write them down quickly before they disappear," a deliberate "antithesis of the high Modernist poetic craftsman." David Roessel convincingly argues that the way the autobiography plays down Hughes's major revisions to "When Sue Wears Red" "should give pause to anyone who thinks that 'The Negro Speaks of Rivers' was composed when Hughes crossed the Mississippi on a train at sunset."[73]

Interestingly enough, Hughes never changed the geography of "The Negro Speaks of Rivers" after he published it, as he did "The Negro," for example, following the lynching of Emmett Till.[74] Such inaction is striking, since Hughes frequently altered his own work even after it was initially published; 59 of the 186 pieces in his *Selected Poems* (1959) differ from their original publication.[75] Yet the only significant revision to "The Negro Speaks of Rivers" was his addition of the aforementioned dedication to Du Bois in *The Weary Blues* (a gesture omitted from *The Big Sea* and *Selected Poems*). Still, Hughes's narrative in *The Big Sea* destabilizes the poem's riverscape by erasing the Euphrates and inserting the Niger and then compromising this revision by following it with the full published version of the poem.[76] With its two coexisting geographies, the poem is something more than an impulsive reflection on "rivers in our past."

The poetry Hughes wrote around the time he published this account in *The Big Sea* suggests he was interested in exploring the boundaries of racial identification. In the 1937 Spanish Civil War poem "Letter from Spain: Addressed to Alabama," an African American soldier named Johnny tells of an encounter with a North African colonial subject fighting on behalf of Franco. The epistolary poem recognizes the expectation of racial identification in which "The initial rhetoric of recognition in the encounter is tempered by incommensurability—first of all, due to linguistic difference: 'He answered something in a language / I couldn't understand,'" while ultimately belying a naive understanding of diaspora.[77] The inability of Johnny to communicate with a "wounded Moor" who is "just as dark as me" suggests that the author of *The Big Sea* was aware that not all encounters conformed to the "mystic union of Negroes in every country and every age" that Jean Wagner claims to find in "The Negro Speaks of Rivers."[78] Where Wagner sees a "mystic union," a radically different "potential internationalist solidarity," similar to what Edwards finds in Hughes's work in the 1930s, is visible in the national liberation struggles that populate "The Negro Speaks of Rivers."[79]

Despite its politicized geography, scholars often use "The Negro Speaks of Rivers" as a counterpoint to Hughes's more overtly political verse of the 1930s: "Although many of his radical poems are powerful and valuable, it is almost certain that under the radical aesthetic, a poem such as 'The Negro Speaks of Rivers' would have been impossible."[80] Although Rampersad correctly identifies a shift in Hughes's poetics, his juxtaposition of "The Negro Speaks of Rivers" and radicalism mischaracterizes Hughes's early work, which participates in a larger transatlantic project that recognized Africa as a site of anticolonial internationalist activism.

### We, Too

While numerous scholars have written valuably on Hughes's radical poetry of the 1930s, Daniel Won-gu Kim makes a compelling case for expanding the parameters of Hughes's radicalism to include the late 1950s and 1960s.[81] In doing so, Kim follows established periodizations and juxtaposes "The Negro Speaks of Rivers" with Hughes's later work: "The source of this sharp change in Hughes's semiotics of Africa is the anti-colonial, pan-Africanist and radical nationalist politics of Hughes's African (re)turn."[82] One exemplary poem from that period that employs similar geographical range is "Memo to Non-White Peoples" (1957):

> It's the same from Cairo to Chicago,
> Cape Town to the Caribbean,
> Do you travel the Stork Club circuit
> To dear old Shepherd's Hotel?
> (Somebody burnt Shepherd's up.)[83]

By the time Hughes published this poem, the Stork Club, a one-time leading light of New York cafe society infamous for its discriminatory treatment of African Americans (including Josephine Baker in a 1951 case in which the NAACP got involved), was in decline, in part because of its antiunion policies.[84] The club's worn-out image is linked to "Shepherd's Hotel," a misspelling of "Shepheard's Hotel," a former colonial outpost in Cairo that was destroyed during the January 1952 Egyptian nationalist revolution that brought Pan-Africanist Gamal Abdel Nasser to power.[85] With echoes of

William Sheppard in the background, Hughes engages with history in a way that disrupts colonial society, which is what he did far more idyllically in "The Negro Speaks of Rivers." Contextualized readings of his early poetry reveal a "semiotics of Africa" that shares many political elements, including those that Kim lists, with Hughes's late work. The black activist and intellectual discourse that influenced Hughes in the late 1910s and early 1920s came to seem newly prescient with the overthrow of European colonial regimes in the 1950s and 1960s. As the Congo, whose colonial plight he mourned in the 1920s, struggled for independence, Hughes continued his written engagement with the region in ways that prompt readers to rethink the geopolitics of African American culture throughout the twentieth century.

In September 1959 in the *Chicago Defender*, Hughes wrote "Bread Not Enough in Congo," which begins, somewhat surprisingly, by describing a relatively benign Belgian colonial state. However, Hughes warns that an efficient social welfare apparatus is not, per the title, a substitute for independence. Judging from an editorial mark on an unpublished typescript of the essay, Hughes appreciated the dynamic African political landscape enough to change "Africans" to "The Congolese" in the penultimate sentence: "The Congolese feel that it is unfortunate that their first requests for negotiations were met with arrests, armoured police cars, and the banning of public meetings."[86] What's more, Hughes published his essay several months before the Roundtable Conference determined the date for full independence, at a time when many observers considered Belgium to be one of the most entrenched colonial regimes on the continent.[87]

On August 2, 1960, little more than a month after Congolese independence and on the heels of Prime Minister Patrice Lumumba's only visit to the United States, Hughes wrote "Simple and the Congo," a dialogue between Jesse B. Simple, his popular comedic folk hero, and an interlocutor.[88] Hughes creatively uses the "Simple" story, which appeared in the August 13 *Chicago Defender* alongside an editorial and a cartoon on Katangan secession, to argue that the new Congolese state be allowed to control the valuable uranium resources at the heart of the imperial conflict. When Simple questions Ralph Bunche's role as head of the U.N. Congo mission, claiming that the light-skinned diplomat is "not black," his target is the cynical exploitation of Bunche's race to justify neocolonial intervention: "If they knew what they was doing, they would send some colored folks the color of African colored folks." Simple's anticolonial folk analysis sees Bunche's involvement as a distraction from the goal of independence: "How come they have to have Ralph Bunche or anybody else help them eat? Me, I believe them Congo people could straighten out their own affairs, if they was just let alone." The article concludes with a comparison that reaches back to "The Negro Speaks of Rivers" and "American Congo" rhetoric by comparing the Congo to Mississippi in their shared need of "help in becoming a democracy." Simple proposes, "Why don't the UN send Ralph Bunche to Mississippi?" When his interlocutor proposes that the U.N. send Simple, he responds, "Then I would need a whole lot of uranium to take with me . . . Boom!"[89] In a later column, Simple repeats these ideas in a speech he envisions himself delivering to the United Nations: "let us consider the backward countries like Mississippi and give them aid. In fact, let's send in a few Congolese troops with Dr. Bunche as trouble shooter."[90] These stories exemplify how Hughes situates a sophisticated commentary on global affairs within African American vernacular culture.

Beyond these prose pieces, Hughes addresses the Congo in his late poetry in ways that connect directly to his work in the 1920s. "We, Too," which he first drafted on October 12, 1960, revises one of his best-known poems, "I, Too" (published first in Alain Locke's March 1925 issue of *Survey Graphic* and soon thereafter as the "Epilogue" to *The Weary Blues*).[91] Whereas "I, Too" concludes "I, too, am America," a dozen drafts of "We, Too" from 1960 to 1963 document Hughes's struggles over precisely how to end the poem.[92] This example reveals how his engagement with the Congo is embedded within his poetic process, including the transformation of the Whitmanesque aesthetics of his early verse into an economical affirmation of postcolonial political solidarity.

The first two drafts of "We, Too," which conclude "We, too, excite / the sky," were written when the house arrest of Lumumba was not yet widely known as the death sentence it proved to be. Hughes did not return to the poem until February 1962. In the interim, Hughes took two trips to Nigeria in November 1960 and December 1961, which were his first visits to the continent since 1923 and undoubtedly informed his ideas about Africa.[93] By the time he continued writing "We, Too," Lumumba had been dead for a year, and any initial optimism had given way to a clear view of a developing neocolonial state, represented well in his 1961 column in which Simple reflects, "Were I making a Christmas gift to Old Satan, I would give him the Uncle Tom of the Congo, Moise Tshombe, so Tshombe could turn his machine guns on the Devil. Then they would both have fun seeing who could be the most treacherous."[94] Following Lumumba's assassination, Hughes changed the word "scared" to "scarred" in the poem's second quatrain:

We, too, emit
A frightening cry
From body scarred,
Soul that won't die.[95]

His addition of a single letter transforms these lines from foreboding about the future to suffering in the past, where "tribal marks" are replaced by "great welts." Such markings may look the same at first glance; however, their similar appearance obscures dramatic differences in their sources and significations. This revision further represents a shift from collective longing ("We who have no tribal marks to bear," which survives in lines 2 and 11 of the final version), to a clear affirmation of Congolese identity ("Oh, Congo brother / With your tribal marks").⁹⁶ In 1963, Hughes finally published the poem with a direct gesture of affinity in its concluding lines:

> We, too,
> Congo brother,
> Rise with you.⁹⁷

The revisions of "We, Too" reflect the shifting mood that followed the assassination of Lumumba. The diaspora poet's "We," which still begins five of the published poem's twenty-one lines, remains a significant contrast to the singular pronoun that defined "I, Too" nearly forty years earlier. As a revision of "I, Too," "We, Too" is an accumulation of nearly four decades of internationalist writings through which Hughes articulates multivalent visions of the Congo. There, the political coexists beside the cultural, a process whose most mature example is his underappreciated masterpiece *Ask Your Mama: 12 Moods for Jazz* (1961), which he began composing within days of Lumumba's inauguration.⁹⁸

In *Ask Your Mama*, Lumumba, the Congo, and Belgium are prominent figures, appearing in six of the twelve moods (all of which are accompanied by running musical instructions). The first reference to the Congo, in "Ride, Red, Ride," asks of the poet's grandmother: "WAS SHE FLEEING WITH LUMUMBA?"⁹⁹ Within the book's rhetorical framework of the dozens, "SHE" raises unanswered questions about the poetics of political inheritance and the mysterious depth of the poet's involvement with the Congo. The next section, "Shades of Pigmeat," opens "IN THE QUARTER OF THE NEGROES / BELGIUM SHADOW LEOPOLD" which, four decades after "The Negro," reveals the continued presence of Belgium in the newly postcolonial era.¹⁰⁰ "Blues in Stereo" features a historical reference to "A TOWN NAMED AFTER STANLEY," Lumumba's stronghold of Stanleyville (Kisangani).¹⁰¹

To add another layer to *Ask Your Mama*, "Ode to Dinah" includes the line "BONGO-BONGO! CONGO!" alluding to the primitivism of Lindsay's poem and to "Bongo Bongo Bongo / I don't want to leave the Congo," the refrain of the 1947 song "Civilization (Bongo Bongo Bongo)" popularized by the Andrews Sisters and Danny Kaye.¹⁰² The section entitled "Ask Your Mama" invokes "LUMUMBA LOUIS ARMSTRONG / PATRICE AND PATTI PAGE," and uses a line break to split the political leader's name, locating him in equal measure beside musical performers of two different traditions (jazz and country), each an icon of a distinct place (New Orleans and Tennessee, respectively).[103] Lumumba surrounds Armstrong, to whom Hughes dedicated the book and who is arguably its most important icon.[104] Part of Armstrong's iconicity at that moment was his return from an African tour that was widely covered in the press. Over the course of a couple of months, Armstrong was barred from South Africa, "touched off a clash between police and African nationalists" in Kenya, and was "welcome[d] to the land of your ancestors" in Congo, where he performed in October and November 1964.[105] These allusions brilliantly encapsulate the multiplicity of registers on which the Congo functions for Hughes. The final reference to Lumumba in *Ask Your Mama* affirms his place beside his political peers:

> STARS AT STARS STARS. . . .
>    TOURÉ DOWN IN GUINEA
>    LUMUMBA IN THE CONGO
>    JOMO IN KENYATTA. . . . STARS. . . .[106]

Here, in "Bird in Orbit," Hughes reinscribes Lumumba and the Congo as political actors rather than simply sounds or icons. The positioning of Lumumba beside both Patti Page and Sekou Touré allows the political to coexist with the popular, synthesizing Hughes's musical sensibility and the social ideals of the 1960s.

As he was finishing *Ask Your Mama*, Hughes began writing "Lumumba's Grave." He composed the first draft on March 31, 1961, less than two months after learning of Lumumba's murder, at a time when news coverage of the Congo became so frequent that articles on the latest crisis often shared the page with his columns in the *Chicago Defender*.[107] Unlike "We, Too" which he spent several years, if not decades, revising, "Lumumba's Grave" was published within six months of its initial composition. The finality of Lumumba's death seems to have resulted in a less vexed writing process.[108] Not only are Hughes's revisions to "Lumumba's Grave" much less substantial than those he made to "We, Too," but the language of the poem is much more direct:

> Lumumba was black
> And he didn't trust
> The whores all powdered
> With uranium dust.[109]

The concluding stanza includes one revision to the verb tense referring to the poet's commemoration of Lumumba's grave:

> I've marked it there
> As tomorrow
> Has marked it
> Everywhere.

became:

> And it's marked there.
> *Tomorrow will mark*
> *It everywhere.*¹¹⁰

The shifts from the active to the passive voice and from the past to the future create an uncertainty that leaves alive the potential of Lumumba's ongoing legacy, serving as "a sort of gesture of literary solidarity with the black radicals and/or nationalists" who, as discussed in chapter 8, protested the assassination at the U.N.¹¹¹ Indeed, when Simple posits himself as a missionary to whites in Mississippi, he imagines traveling South with "Them cats that created the riot at the UN on Lumumba . . . so as to have protection."¹¹²

Within Hughes's capacious oeuvre, Patrice Lumumba was much more than an icon; he was a speaking subject, whose poem "Dawn in the Heart of Africa" Hughes included in his edited volume, *Poems from Black Africa* (1963), which Amiri Baraka reviewed for *Poetry* magazine in March 1964.¹¹³ When excerpts from the collection appeared in *Time* magazine in September 1963, an unsigned headnote singled out for scorn "a part-time poet named Patrice Lumumba, the late, rabblerousing Congolese leader."¹¹⁴ While there may be temptation to see Hughes's work on Lumumba as commonplace amid the Black Arts movement, *Time* magazine's cruel caricature is a reminder that it placed Hughes well outside the mainstream of white America. Still, as in his 1964 poem "Final Call," which proclaims, "SEND (GOD FORBID—HE'S NOT DEAD LONG ENOUGH!) / FOR LUMUMBA TO CRY, 'FREEDOM NOW!,'" Hughes insistently recognizes Lumumba's words and voice.¹¹⁵

By consistently engaging with Lumumba in the 1960s, Hughes situated himself squarely at the center of a new generation of writers and activists who saw the Congo as central to what John Henrik Clarke termed, "the new Afro-American Nationalism." Yet, Clarke understood that this interest was "really not new," and had long-standing roots in the African American tradition.¹¹⁶ According to "The Negro Speaks of Rivers," one of the most iconic works in the history of African American letters, the Congo, poetically positioned in between Iraq and Egypt, was always already a political site engaged with nationalist discourse. When read in this context, this poem revises familiar genealogies of Hughes's career and the literary movements to which he was central. Archival sources help situate the literary text within a larger internationalist network that includes the NAACP, the *Crisis* magazine, the Pan-African Congresses, and African American missionaries among others, providing resources for reading texts whose romantic flourishes have sometimes overshadowed their political gestures. Such an understanding of the internationalist engagement that undergirds commonplace references to Africa can illuminate individual works of literature as well as the communities in which they circulated. As a result, "The Negro Speaks of Rivers" can be read as part of a literary, cultural, and intellectual tradition that saw the Congo much like Hughes and his contemporaries did, not as a euphemism for the "dark continent" but as, in fact, the Congo, a familiar place whose nearness is both invoked and evoked by Hughes's verse.

*Chapter 8*

# Another Black Magazine with a Lumumba Poem
*Patrice Lumumba and African American Poetry*

In John Oliver Killens's novel, *The Cotillion, or, One Good Bull Is Half the Herd* (1971), a young woman named Yoruba is forced to negotiate her mother's bourgeois aspirations with her own rising nationalist sensibilities. Yoruba's burgeoning racial pride is entangled with her romantic relationship with a young poet, Ben Ali Lumumba: "It seemed like every day Yoruba came into the house with another Black magazine with a Lumumba poem and face somewhere inside."[1] In this scene, Yoruba is carrying a magazine with a "Lumumba poem," a verse written by her prolific and increasingly successful boyfriend, who represents the new generation of militant writers. In the world outside the novel, another sort of Lumumba poem that memorialized the first prime minister of the independent Democratic Republic of Congo, Patrice Lumumba, became ubiquitous over the course of the 1960s. Elegiac verse like Langston Hughes's "Lumumba's Grave" became as commonplace within the exciting new print culture of journals like *Black Dialogue*, *Black World*, *Freedomways*, *Journal of Black Poetry*, *Soulbook*, and *Umbra* as pieces by his fictional namesake are in Killens's novel.

Within weeks of Lumumba's June 30, 1960, inauguration, Belgian forces joined with his other political opponents, including secessionists from the wealthy mining region of Katanga, to remove him from office. By early September, Lumumba was under house arrest and spent most of the remaining months of his life under various forms of detention. By the middle of September, U.S. government advisors were convinced that he "would cause trouble in power, in jail, or upon release." And despite Lumumba's incarceration, throughout December and into January, his political party—Mouvement National Congolais (MNC)—was getting stronger. By January 1961, soldiers at Camp Hardy in Mbanza-Ngungu (known then as Thysville, named for the Belgian businessman who commissioned George Washington Williams), where Lumumba was being held, were in rebellion and the government feared its ability to continue to hold him prisoner, especially since he had support among the troops. With his opponents sensing that imprisonment could not contain Lumumba and everything he represented, he was transferred to Katanga and was secretly executed along with two aides Maurice Mpolo and Joseph Okito on January 17, 1961, in a plot for which Belgium, the United States, the United Nations, and his Congolese opposition all bear responsibility.[2] When news of his death emerged on February 13, people took to the streets of Accra, Amsterdam, Brussels, Caracas, Dakar, Dublin, Havana, Jakarta, Johannesburg, Khartoum, Lagos, Melbourne, Montreal, Rome, Tehran, and other cities around the world. A demonstration in Shanghai reportedly drew 500,000 people. The international outcry targeted Belgian embassies and consulates in Belgrade, Chicago, London, Moscow, New Delhi, and Warsaw. In Cairo, huge protests gripped the city, as the Belgian Embassy was burned and the U.S. Embassy, the British Embassy, and U.N. offices were attacked. In Washington, a group of Howard University students protested by throwing eggs and snowballs at the Belgian Embassy.[3]

And famously, on Wednesday, February 15, 1961, the United Nations was the target of a dramatic demonstration organized by young African American activists. At the New York demonstration, "Them cats that created the riot at the UN on Lumumba," to quote Simple, entered the U.N. and sat in the gallery.[4] While U.S. Ambassador Adlai Stevenson was delivering an address, a group that included many artists and cultural activists rose in protest as Aishah Rahman describes: "We raised the brutalized images of the Congo's Premier Patrice Lumumba, betrayed by Britain, France, Belgium and the U.S. and delivered to his enemies. . . . We raised photos of his widow, Pauline, walking ahead of the mourners her head shaved, her breasts bared before the world."[5] An attack on the protestors by the U.N. police provoked a melee that resulted in several injuries. Though participants have over the course of several decades provided differing accounts about how the protest was coordinated, what kind of disruption was intended, and what exactly occurred, there is a consensus that, unlike the sort of "riot" that the *New York Times* suggested on its front page, the coordinated political action was, like the "Boston Riot" that interrupted Booker T. Washington's 1903 speech to the National Negro Business League, a transformative moment in African American cultural politics.[6] After "bursting into the Security Council gallery," Rahman recalls, "we remembered our mission in that darkened chamber where our presence was a fissure, a fault line in the gathering of august men dividing the plunder of the Congo."[7]

The U.N. action was "a turning point" that, according to Daniel Watts of the Liberation Committee for Africa (LCA), which was founded in June 1960, "marked the beginning of the departure of Negro militants from passive, peaceful, largely legalistic protests."[8] The protest, wrote John Henrik Clarke in the fall 1961 *Freedomways*, "introduced the new Afro-American Nationalism," which "is only a new manifestation of old grievances with deep roots. Nationalism, and a profound interest in Africa, actually started among Afro-Americans during the latter part of the nineteenth century," in the wake of the 1884–85 Berlin Conference. Clarke analyzes the links between the United States and the Congo, by presenting Lumumba's assassination within a comparative American context:

> The demonstrators in the United Nations gallery interpreted the murder of Lumumba as the international lynching of a black man on the altar of colonialism and white supremacy. Suddenly, to them at least, Lumumba became Emmett Till and all of the other black victims of lynch law and the mob. The plight of the Africans still fighting to throw off the joke [*sic?*] of colonialism and the plight of the Afro-Americans, still waiting for a rich, strong and boastful nation to redeem the promise of freedom and citizenship became one and the same. Through their action the U.N. demonstrators announced their awareness of the fact that they were far from being free and a long fight still lay ahead of them. The short and unhappy life of Patrice Lumumba announced the same thing about Africa.[9]

While the year 1960 was a watershed for African nationalism, as seventeen countries gained their independence, it also saw in the Congo the continent's first postcolonial coup.[10] Dramatically punctuated by Lumumba's assassination, the Congo coup tempered any newfound hubris and served as a call for renewed vigilance. Lumumba, "whose struggle was made noble by his unswerving demand for centralism against all forms of Balkanization," represented youthful leadership, nationalist unity, and principled commitment at a crucial moment for the black freedom movement.[11] When many established activists expressed "wariness" about Lumumba, an "increasingly militant segment of black America" embraced him in a manner "that reflected the rising tide of domestic militancy and interest in broader pan-African ties."[12]

Cynthia Young argues, "The fact that the Lumumba protest occasioned the articulation of a new black identity demonstrates how 1960s anticolonialism and black cultural politics were mutually constitutive."[13] The protest at the U.N. "marked a personal crossroads and was seen as a larger cultural turning point by a number of the young militants who would be pivotal in the Black Arts movement."[14] The demonstration placed its participants at odds with many figures in the civil rights establishment. Ralph Bunche apologized to the General Assembly two days after the protest. Although leaders like the NAACP's Roy Wilkins and the Urban League's Lester Granger (who forty years earlier had criticized colonialism in his poem "Belgium") sided with Bunche, the leadership of such organizations did not always reflect the attitudes of its local affiliates or its rank-and-file membership.[15] Still the *Crisis* stuck to the Bunche/Wilkins narrative by describing a "violent black nationalist demonstration" and implying that activist groups were simplistic for having "enshrined as patron saint the late Patrice Lumumba, who is depicted as a black hero singlehandedly opposing the imperialist machinations of the Western countries and murdered conspiratorially at the behest of those nations."[16] Of course, subsequent research has conclusively established that Lumumba was killed on precisely those terms.

Such predictable efforts to disparage the protestors were, in some instances, part of an organized campaign to undermine emerging alliances between African Americans and Africans.[17] Perhaps more surprisingly, the African American communist leader Benjamin J. Davis Jr. was, according to some reports, excluded from the U.N. protest, which signaled the younger progressive artistic community's movement toward a new brand of nationalism that fused the cultural and political realms.[18] Poet, playwright, and political activist Amiri Baraka explains, "as the whole society heated up with struggle and rebellion and revolution, I suppose the most politically sensitive of us began to pull away from the bourgeois rubric that art and politics were separate and exclusive entities." Baraka recognized that a new set of political icons had replaced those of the established civil rights movement: "That's why the Cuban revolution was so heavy in our sensibility. That's why Robert Williams was our hero. That's why we demonstrated for Lumumba and wrestled in those streets with the police despite Ralph Bunche telling us he was embarrassed that we were in public acting like niggaz."[19] Baraka's explanation reveals how the U.N. protest exposed the chasm that separated him and his comrades from figures like Bunche in terms of both ideology and tactics.

According to Maya Angelou, she, Rosa Guy, and Abbey Lincoln announced news of Lumumba's assassination and plans for the demonstration in front of Lewis Michaux's National Memorial African Bookstore in Harlem.[20] The U.N. protest introduced many of the period's most important collaborators to one another for the first time. Writing in 1994, Baraka recalls, "In 1961, I 1st met Askia Toure, along with other life long comrades, in front of the U.S. Mission to the U.N. where we were gathered with hundreds of other people, including Aishah Rahman and Mae Mallory and Calvin Hicks to protest the murder of Patrice Lumumba by the U.S., Belgium and the traitorous scum who still sits in the seat of power of Zaire, Joe Mobutu."[21] Baraka was arrested for the first time ever while demonstrating outside the U.N., marking it as a radicalizing moment for one of the era's foremost artists and intellectuals.[22] A partial list of those who were involved is useful for appreciating the extraordinary talents who converged on that February day. In addition to Baraka and those he names above, various sources list Angelou, Guy, Lincoln, Nab Eddie Bobo, Carlos A. Cooks, James Rupert Lawson (United African Nationalist Movement), Louise Meriwether, Carlos Moore, Larry

Neal, Max Roach, Paul Robeson Jr., Dan Watts, and Sarah Wright, among other participants.[23] In subsequent weeks, with participants facing ongoing criticism, Lorraine Hansberry and James Baldwin, two of the country's best-known writers, expressed their solidarity with the "riot" by publicly announcing in the *New York Times* that they "intended" to be there.[24]

## The Spirit of Patrice Lumumba Lives

The demonstration at the U.N. was the culmination of months of celebrations of Lumumba by African Americans since his election the previous year. Less than a month after his inauguration, he visited the United States to appeal to the U.N. and the international community for the withdrawal of Belgian troops from his country. Once he arrived, "The black Americans in Harlem carried him in triumph, with the result that they provoked what amounted to a pitched battle with the police who were supposed to be protecting Lumumba." Thomas Kanza, Lumumba's ally and the Congo's U.N. representative, describes the scene, "In their mass meeting at the corner of 7th Avenue and 125th St, speakers acclaimed Lumumba as 'one of the few blacks who has been brave enough to drive the white men out of Africa without a cent.'"[25] In New York, Guy, an active member of the Harlem Writers Guild, and Marie McBroom joined Lumumba's "entourage, going from place to place, standing as guards outside of doors, deciding who should or should not enter."[26] By unfortunate coincidence, however, at the time of Lumumba's visit several of the activists who were involved in the February 1961 demonstration as planners (Richard Gibson and Robert Williams), participants (Baraka and Wright), or chroniclers (Clarke) were in Cuba in July as part of the Fair Play for Cuba delegation and therefore missed an opportunity to meet him.[27]

Cooks, the Dominican Republic–born leader of the Harlem-based African Nationalist Pioneer Movement, immediately celebrated Lumumba's election for its "orthodox African Nationalism, along the Garveyan pattern."[28] In the same issue of the organization's *Black Challenge* journal, R. Waldo Williams published "The Awakening Call," a rare poetic tribute to Lumumba written before his assassination.

> Hail Lumumba! man of Africa
> Who stands like a mighty dam
> Against the floods of oppression-[29]

Cooks met Lumumba at the airport when he arrived in New York in July 1960 and had conversations with the leader that led the African Nationalist Pioneer Movement to initiate a recruitment drive, advertising in the *Black Challenge*: "The Congo Wants Young Black Men—Talented and Intelligent

Young Black Men of Trades—Interested in Opportunity For Advancement."[30] While the direct results of Cooks's efforts are unclear, they nonetheless represent an explicit organizational effort to find places for African Americans in the newly independent Congo. And, through a range of mechanisms, several African Americans did make the journey in the coming years.

During the same trip, his only visit to the United States, Lumumba used a lecture at Howard University to express his hope that "in the future ... this university [will] send to Africa, to help their ancestors, dentists and doctors and engineers with all possible skills." Like George Washington Williams, who solicited Hampton students in 1889, Lumumba recognized the unique role of HBCUs like Howard in "the liberation of the Black Race." Lumumba similarly recruited people from elsewhere in the African diaspora "to come to the land of your ancestors."[31] During the trip, Lumumba "signed an agreement with Phelps Stokes Fund ... ensuring the recruitment of skilled African Americans to work in the Congo." Although the agreement was never executed, historian Seth Markle considers the Pan-African Skills Project, which developed in Tanzania later in the decade, to be "an institutional legacy" of Lumumba's recruitment efforts.[32] Indeed, though his recruits never rivaled the numbers attracted to Kwame Nkrumah's Ghana, he did attract Yvonne Reed (Seon) (the mother of visionary actor and comedian Dave Chappelle), who met Lumumba in Washington. Although he invited her to travel to the Congo immediately, Seon did not make the trip until after Lumumba's assassination, when, in March 1961, she began more than two years of work on the Inga Dam hydroelectric project. While in the Congo, she was joined by an impressive cohort of African Americans including Albert Berrian, James "Ted" Harris Jr., James L. Hope, Shirley Barnes Kalunda, David McAdams, Douglas E. Moore, Charles Robinson, Robert L. West, and others.[33]

Lumumba's admiration for African Americans was not limited to the context of recruiting. In September 1960, he spoke to a large crowd of Congolese supporters in Kinshasa about how "Africans built America. They are the reason America has become a great world power. If Africans could achieve that in the new world, they can achieve it in their own continent. That is what we must do here."[34] A November 1961 incident provides further insight into how African Americans were perceived in the newly independent country, where attitudes may have been shaped by a longer history of direct and indirect contact. An Associated Press (AP) newspaper story mentioned an attack on APCM missionaries in the Kasai by Congolese soldiers. According to the report, however, "A third American, Miss Betty [*sic*] Jean Mitchell, believed to be from Albany, Ga., was not touched by the patrol. She was ordered into her residence. She remained at the post to continue teaching at the mission school." The wire story, as printed in the *Baltimore Sun*, did not mention that Mitchell was black, let alone Congolese perceptions of African Americans; the *New York Times*, which ran the first half of the same story, did not mention Mitchell at all.[35] One year later, Mitchell resigned and married M. Paul Fabo, Dahomey's ambassador to the Congo.

Lumumba made an impression well beyond those folks who traveled to the Congo. Some older activists and writers, like Hughes, rapidly took to him. By September 1960, Du Bois, who in 1958 thought Lumumba was "an unthinking fanatic," realized he had been wrong in his earlier assessment. At the age of 92, Du Bois reflected, "I pride myself on ability to learn."[36] Around the same time, Malcolm X, who is the subject of chapter 9, used his personal audience with Fidel Castro to discuss the fate of Lumumba.[37] In November 1960 in Paris, novelist Richard Wright spoke enthusiastically, shortly before his own untimely death, about how Pan-Africanism "lives ... in the Congo ... in the person of Lumumba."[38] The same can be said of the LCA, which organized a campaign to support Lumumba in November 1960 as a way to counter the State Department's "anti-democratic" support of Mobutu.[39] While Lumumba was alive (or at least thought to be alive), groups, including the LCA and the Harlem Writers Guild (led for many years by Killens), expressed solidarity and advocated for his release from prison.[40] In the days before news of his death broke, the Cultural Association for Women of African Heritage, headed by Abbey Lincoln, collected 1,500 signatures on a petition protesting Lumumba's imprisonment, which it presented to Guinea (Conakry) Ambassador Diallo Telli, the future head of the Organization of African Unity (OAU), who was part of a group of African diplomats who met Lumumba in Washington.[41]

Following such foundational interest, Lumumba emerges in death as a major figure in work by global intellectuals such as Frantz Fanon and Jean-Paul Sartre.[42] In particular, Clarke recognizes that Lumumba's "spirit was a natural choice to rekindle the flame of Afro-American nationalism."[43] As James Smethurst, Christopher Tinson, Komozi Woodard, and others have written, Lumumba's assassination galvanized a new kind of black nationalist activism in the United States that shaped publishing houses, literary journals, and community theaters.[44] Historian Peniel Joseph explains, "Lumumba's martyrdom carried more than symbolic notions for many of these demonstrators. This assassination, along with the Cuban Revolution and African decolonization efforts, provided the practical and ideological building blocks for a black radical solidarity that was fueled by a resurgence in black nationalism, street corner speaking, study groups, and community organizing."[45] Several organizations that were central to the Black Arts movement, including the Harlem Writers Guild, the Cultural Association for Women of African Heritage, On Guard for Freedom, Provisional Committee for a Free

Africa, and the United African Nationalist Movement, were involved in organizing the protest or were otherwise animated by it.[46] Cheryl Higashida feels that much of this work has been lost to posterity as later accounts like Angelou's autobiographies present a "diasporic identity [that] ultimately appears to be routed less (if at all) through the internationalist challenge to the racist and imperialist U.S. state than through romantic visions of 'Africa's maternal welcome.'" This romantic definition of "diasporic identity" has, at times, obscured the internationalist politics that defined the movement and which this book aims to recover.[47]

Many organizations and publications marked their ideological positions with statements on the assassination of Lumumba. For example, the multiracial LCA was not only represented at the February 15 action, but it also participated in a second U.N. demonstration on February 18 and organized a "Lumumba Memorial" the following week. The LCA presented its ideas to the public in its organ, *Liberator*, which was launched to capitalize on the publicity surrounding the February 15 action. Indeed, its first mimeographed issue in March 1961 (then titled *Liberation*) consisted of a single article: "The Death of Lumumba." Subsequent content on Lumumba used the U.N. protest as its point of reference. The article "Lumumba's Murderers Exposed: UN Demonstrations Justified" indicates that the U.N. report on the assassination was noteworthy not simply because it uncovered details about the murder, but because, in doing so, it vindicated the protesters. In August 1961, the LCA moved its offices closer to the U.N. even though Watts, one of the group's leaders, had been barred from entering the building.[48]

Correspondingly, when *Freedomways: A Quarterly Review of the Negro Freedom Movement* published its inaugural issue in Spring 1961, edited by Shirley Graham Du Bois, W. Alphaeus Hunton, Margaret Burroughs, and Esther Jackson (Burroughs and Jackson, the youngest of the quartet, were born in 1917), its longest article, by far, was the March 7, 1961, speech that Ghana president Kwame Nkrumah delivered at the U.N. following Lumumba's assassination. The first issue also includes a quote from Lorraine Hansberry rebuking Bunche's criticism of the protest and an article on the January 1961 Afro-Asian Women's Conference expressing the "respect, sympathy, and admiration" of "the whole world" for Patrice Lumumba's widow Pauline.[49] At the magazine's first public event in 1961, Kanza shared keynote duties with W. E. B. Du Bois.[50] In print, *Freedomways*'s coverage of the Congo continued. The second issue contains a statement by Lumumba's MNC comrade Antoine Gizenga; the third features Clarke's brilliant "The New Afro-American Nationalism"; the fourth contains Walter Lowenfels's poem "Patrice Lumumba Speaks"; the fifth includes journalist Charles P. Howard Sr.'s article on Katanga and Harry Schachter's "Barebreasted in

Leopoldville—A Poem"; the sixth includes Clarke's critical review of Philippa Schuyler's "shameful piece of anti-African propaganda" *Who Killed the Congo?*; the seventh includes Howard's critique of American media coverage of Africa (with a focus on Lumumba), Desmond Victor's poem "Star of the Congo," and a speech by Nkrumah which includes additional comments on Lumumba; the eighth includes Clarke's review of Lumumba's *Congo, My Country* plus references to the Congo in a short story by Loyle Hairston and in an article by historian William Leo Hansberry (Lorraine's uncle); the ninth includes another article by Howard that comments on the Congo and Shirley Graham Du Bois's review of Conor Cruise O'Brien's *To Katanga and Back: A UN Case History*.[51] The Congo was at the heart of the magazine's work.

*Liberator* and *Freedomways* were two of the many periodicals that "radicalized a generation" and, through the figure of Lumumba, "raised the international awareness of young African Americans" at a time when the major black newspapers were becoming much more ambivalent toward Lumumba following his appeals to the Soviet Union for support.[52] In New York, *On Guard*, the eponymous journal of a Greenwich Village organization, included a tribute to Lumumba in its inaugural issue in 1961. In California, Anthony James Ratcliff points out, *Soulbook: The Quarterly Journal of Revolutionary Afro-America*, began publication in 1964 with an issue dedicated to several martyred freedom fighters, including "the great Black martyr Patrice Lumumba." Its opening editorial cites a widely circulated letter Lumumba wrote to his wife: "without dignity there is no liberty, without justice there is no dignity, and with[out] independence there are no free men."[53] The second issue of *Soulbook*, "a semi-organ of RAM" (Revolutionary Action Movement), includes an article by editor Kenn M. Freeman that asks "Did the United Nations Benefit Congo?" Freeman, who changed his name to Mamadou Lumumba, and whose brother Don became Baba Lumumba, concludes, "I am convinced that my Brothers and Sisters in the Congo will not in the final analysis be decieved [sic] by the likes of Tshombe, [U.N. official Andrew] Cordier, Carl Rowan or Ralph Bunche. They will be strengthened by the memory of Lumumba, Malcolm X and the support of all Black Peoples of the world."[54]

Lumumba's writings and speeches continued to circulate throughout the decade. In 1970, the *Black Panther* quoted Lumumba's June 30, 1960, independence day speech and concluded, "By liberating North America and in the reality of intercommunalism we therefore liberate the Congo and Lumumba's death will at last be avenged. His dream will be a reality. He was one of the greatest leaders the African community ever had and with deep reverence the Black Panther Party pays tribute to his memory on this the

Figure 8.1 The Black Panther 4, no. 29 (January 16, 1971). John Huggins is represented by five repeated background images. Alprentice Bunchy Carter appears in the foreground with sunglasses and a leather jacket. (Courtesy of Dr. Huey P. Newton Foundation.)

anniversary of his assassination. He lived and died for what he believed in—the liberation of all peoples."[55] For the Panthers, the death of Lumumba hit especially close to home when on January 17, 1969, the eighth anniversary of his assassination, party members Alprentice "Bunchy" Carter and John Huggins were killed in Los Angeles. The *Black Panther* added to the intrigue of that coincidence with a cover image of Carter and Huggins superimposed over Lumumba, highlighted in bright pink, and an article noting that a few weeks earlier Carter had had an argument about Lumumba with Larry "Watani" Stiner, a member of Maulana Karenga's US Organization; Stiner was later convicted in association with the Panther murders.[56] (See Figure 8.1.)

By 1970, the connections articulated by the *Black Panther* can be seen in more traditionally mainstream African American periodicals, such as the former *Negro Digest*, which editor Hoyt W. Fuller brilliantly revived and, in

1970, renamed *Black World* because "the empowerment of the Black people of Harlem is not possible until Black men in the Congo are in full control of the vast mineral wealth of that country."[57] As editor, Fuller's commitment to poetry was epic and *Negro Digest/Black World*, like many other publications, featured Lumumba references in poetry ranging from Keorapetse Kgositsile's "Lumumba Section" (1968) to work by Baraka and Haki Madhubuti in the 1970s.[58] The development of *Black World* is an example of how the figures of Lumumba and the Congo served as catalysts for transformations within African American print culture of the period.

After Lumumba's death, a rich poetic practice developed through the memorial efforts of African American artists. The seemingly ubiquitous Lumumba poem emerged as an elegiac genre resembling the memorials to composer and saxophonist John Coltrane, which, during the same era, served as a rejoinder to the silencing of his musical voice. As Kimberly Benston explains in *Performing Blackness: Enactments of African-American Modernism*, "the Coltrane Poem—like the music of the figure whom it eulogizes, and like the modern African-American poetics of which it is a complex microcosm—traverses the regenerative itinerary of loss, outrage, and restitution through a theoretically infinite series of beginnings and forestallings of final resolution."[59] Indeed the Coltrane poem remains a frequent topic of scholarly analysis.[60]

Given Benston's insistence that Coltrane's voice is part of a musical tradition that has long been a form of political speech, it is not surprising that the poetry written in tribute after his 1967 death resembles that invoking Lumumba, who quickly became an icon of the Black Arts movement for "his unyielding resistance to the forces of neocolonialism which finally killed his body, but not his spirit."[61] This genre of elegiac meditation covers the developmental range of responses to Lumumba's death, reaching beyond simple mourning and toward a textual resurrection, as in the title of Ted Joans's "LUMUMBA LIVES!" which resists the absoluteness of his death as a "final resolution." Such rhetoric appears in the earliest poetic reactions to the assassination, including "The Spirit of Patrice Lumumba Lives," which the Nigerian poet Dennis Osadebay published in the February 15, 1961, *West African Pilot*.[62] Two days later, Olatunde Lawrence published "Lumumba's Death" in the same newspaper:

> Nationalists of Africa! Fresh courage take
> The Blood and spirit of Lumumba this provide
> Thus On the march! . . .

Lawrence's poem concludes: "And thou dear Lumumba shalt not have died in vain."[63]

These early Lumumba poems are indicative not only of the immediate adoption of Lumumba as an icon, but also of the appeal of verse as a vehicle for tribute. When poets attempt to erase or revise Lumumba's death, they effectively preserve the fleeting moment of independence that is under immediate neocolonial threat. In this context, these poems represent the urgent beginnings of an elegiac tradition that is grounded in what Jennifer Wenzel calls "anti-imperialist nostalgia [which] is a desire not for a past moment in and for itself but rather for the past's promise of an alternative present: the past's future." Accordingly, such poems do not attempt to reclaim particular accomplishments of Lumumba's brief reign, but rather to recuperate "the past's visions of the future."[64]

The discourse of survival that such works initiate is not strictly African or Anglophone. It includes the Indonesian poet Sabarsantoso Anantaguna and an extensive archive of Francophone poems from Africa and the Caribbean cataloged by Charles Djungu-Simba and Marie-José Hoyet.[65] And Aimé Césaire's play *Une Saison au Congo* (1967) illustrates that the discourse is not exclusive to poetry. Lumumba frequently appeared in popular dramatic works published in Onitsha, Nigeria.[66] The best-selling playwright Ogali A. Ogali published two pamphlet dramas on Lumumba, the second of which, *The Ghost of Patrice Lumumba: A Drama*, appeared after the September 1961 death of U.N. Secretary General Dag Hammarskjold in a plane crash near Katanga. Ogali produces this afterlife at a moment when the nationalist future that Lumumba imagined was rapidly disappearing as a result of the Katanga debacle and the intervention of the U.N. Lumumba similarly appears as a ghost in the African American dramatic canon via Adrienne Kennedy's surrealist masterpiece, *Funnyhouse of the Negro* (1962). At the time of Lumumba's assassination, Kennedy was in Ghana, where she could have seen or read Onitsha plays.[67] Around this time, Lorraine Hansberry, who spoke in defense of the U.N. demonstration, began writing *Les Blancs*, a play based at least in part on the Congo, which she had studied, years earlier, under the supervision of W. E. B. Du Bois.[68]

This transnational literary discourse involved not only African Americans abroad, but also diasporic black folks in the United States. The black nationalist artistic community that created the Lumumba poem included many important international and multilingual contributors. New York–based Puerto Rican poet Victor Hernandez Cruz offers the Spanish version—"Viva Lumumba"—in his poem "third world."[69] In *Negro Digest* and *Black World*, and in books published by Third World Press, Kgositsile, an exiled South African poet, wrote about Lumumba as a diaspora subject by associating him with African American music in "The Nitty-Gritty" and "Point of Departure," and with Malcolm X in "For Afroamerica."[70] Congolese writer Florian

Alphonse Ngoma was on the American scene long enough to publish his Lumumba poem "Tom-Tom" in *City Lights Journal* in 1963 and in *Black Dialogue* in 1965.[71] Pioneering literary scholar Stephen Henderson observes that writers like Kgositsile and the Jamaican Lebert "Sandy" Bethune "absorbed the Afro-American Soul into their own African and West Indian consciousness respectively," serving as a valuable reminder of the geographic scope of the Black Arts movement.[72] Indeed, the remarkable diversity of Lumumba poets enabled the genre to reach stylistically, ideologically, geographically, and chronologically beyond the bounds of what is typically defined as the Black Arts movement.[73]

The ubiquity of Lumumba poems marks their namesake's influence on African American expressive culture. Kiarri T-H. Cheatwood, Jayne Cortez, Michael S. Harper, Langston Hughes, Hurley X, Rashidah Ismaili, Ted Joans, Keorapetse Kgositsile, Raymond Patterson, Ishmael Reed, and Lorenzo Thomas all published Lumumba poems. Even more widespread are passing reference to Lumumba in poems by Ahmed Alhamisi, Ernie Allen, Charles Anderson, Amiri Baraka (LeRoi Jones), Melba Joyce Boyd, Victor Hernandez Cruz, Nikki Giovanni, David Henderson, Percy Johnston, June Jordan, Haki Madhubuti (Don L. Lee), Larry Neal, Sterling Plumpp, Yvonne Seon, and Edward S. Spriggs, among others.[74] Such literary works are too extensive to comprehensively catalog given the number of journals, anthologies, and small-press chapbooks that were in circulation during the 1960s and 1970s, but they suggest avenues for future research. Taken cumulatively, the frequency of reference provides a context for appreciating the ways that three particular poems—"LUMUMBA LIVES!" by Ted Joans, "Festivals & Funerals" by Jayne Cortez, and "Lumumba Blues" by Raymond Patterson—are part of a discrete genus of literary discourse on the Congo. The three exemplars, all by poets who are deeply engaged with black musical traditions, provide insight into the contribution of this political discourse to the development of an "innovative" elegiac poetics.[75] Not coincidentally, all three poems initially appeared in either self-published or small-press volumes, which makes them representative of movements driven by independent press initiatives. Like Benston's Coltrane genre, these disparate versions of modernist poetics are rooted in forms of African American expressive culture that provided the foundation for a distinctive transnational voice for the diasporic hero.

Lumumba Lives!

In response to an early version of Benston's work, Stephen Henderson notes similarities between the Coltrane genre and poems mourning other jazz musicians, including Charlie "Bird" Parker.[76] Perhaps Parker's most distinctive elegist was Joans, his former New York roommate and "an important transitional figure between the New American Poetry and the Black Arts movement."[77] Following Parker's death in 1955, Joans and several friends traveled around New York chalking "Bird Lives!" on the streets and walls.[78] In the eyes of the law, Joans was committing vandalism; however, his daring performance was a prototype of the innovative response to the death of Lumumba. In its transgressive public performance of mourning, the immediacy of Joans's graffiti, like the poems by Osadebay and Anantaguna, helped to defer the death of a man at the peak of his powers. This work is "part of a critique," as Fred Moten writes of Baraka's poetry, "immanent to the black radical tradition that constitutes its radicalism as a cutting and abundant refusal of closure."[79] By initiating an utterance that through anarchic repetition ensured its own circulation and survival, Joans articulated a kind of public outrage that, drawing on musical traditions of improvisation, leaves open "a theoretically infinite series" of possibilities.

Joans's repetition of his "Bird Lives" tagline figures in "Him the Bird," which marks the death of Parker as a collective loss. The poem concludes with a consideration of Parker's cultural and economic legacy:

> He blew his horn in the Village and wailed for the world
> He died a pauper although now his every
> Effort on wax will sell    So the BIRD is gone and
> in the outer-world he cooks   therefore women and
> Men like me will always have the BIRD influence in
> Their   music   paintings   and poetry books
>
> Bird Lives   Bird Lives   Bird Lives   Bird Lives!![80]

After locating Parker's legacy in an expansive cultural and commercial sphere, which includes "music paintings and poetry," Joans emphatically concludes that such cultural productions ensure Parker's survival. In the revised version of the 1958 poem that appears in the collection *Teducation* (1999), Joans begins by dedicating the poem to the memory of jazz vocalist and impresario Babs Gonzales, who passed away in 1980.[81] Gonzales, who helped to codify the language and style of bebop, and Joans seem like kindred trickster spirits. Musically, Gonzales (who also performed standup comedy and, according to Joans, deserved a PhD in "Hipsterism") was known for his 1953 recording of a vocal version of Parker's "Ornithology." His music, like Joans's graffiti, was a heartfelt, creative tribute to their mutual friend.[82] "Him the Bird" acknowledges Gonzales as someone who made his meager living (his autobiography is subtitled "Good Times . . . No Bread"), in part, off of the culture that Parker helped to build. By invoking Gonzales, Joans extends the parameters of the elegy by rendering "Him the Bird" a dynamic and inclusive text whose ongoing improvisations facilitate the memorialization of figures who were alive at the time of its original composition.

Joans's writings on Parker address Benston's interrogation of the Coltrane poem: "How, each asks, can the paralyzing pain of loss be transformed into collective progress and productive speech? For the elegist, the task is to find celebratory praise where only lamentation seems possible; for the poet, the quest is for song that dispels the suspensions of silence, for an incandescence of language that reclaims banished creativity and restores the eclipsed world."[83] "Him the Bird" inverts the standards of lamentation, refuses silence through repetition, and uses the poetic form to ensure that terrible loss is transmogrified into the continuing artistic voices of Joans, Gonzales, and others in a broad-based community of musicians, painters, and writers, accomplishing "a restorative *poiesis* that reestablishes culture as possibility."[84]

Joans's innovative use of poetry to resurrect the banished voice takes on new significance when the figure is an assassinated political leader. "LUMUMBA LIVES!" first appeared as an illustrated poem in Joans's 1961 chapbook *All of Ted Joans and No More*. (See Figure 8.2.) The text is accompanied at the top by an image of a knife delicately slicing a rubber tree and at the bottom by a nearly naked black woman on her knees, leaning back, with her arms and face reaching upward. The rubber tree image appears immediately to the right of the poem's title. The knife bisects the vertical tree limb and is parallel to, and thus a part of the title, providing historical continuity with earlier regimes of colonial terror in the Congo. His collages, like his visual work in *The Hipsters*, draw on ethnographic images of colonial Africa and Du Bois's lectures at the Jefferson School, which Joans attended soon after moving to New York in 1951 and where Lorraine Hansberry and others were studying the Congo.[85]

In this version of the poem, "Lumumba" makes his first five appearances parenthetically, as in the opening couplet:

For he (Lumumba)
Perhaps (Lumumba)[86]

The use of parentheses, even in the first instance where the pronoun seems unambiguous, is a mechanism that Joans uses to reaffirm a specific individual in the face of a generic referent. In an analysis of Amos Tutuola's novel *The Palm-Wine Drinkard*, which Joans read and in which he found inspiration, Joseph Slaughter observes, "Things and people change form constantly; the definite parenthetic clarification of the indefinite pronoun may be a necessity in a world where 'he' could be an old man, or god, or Death,

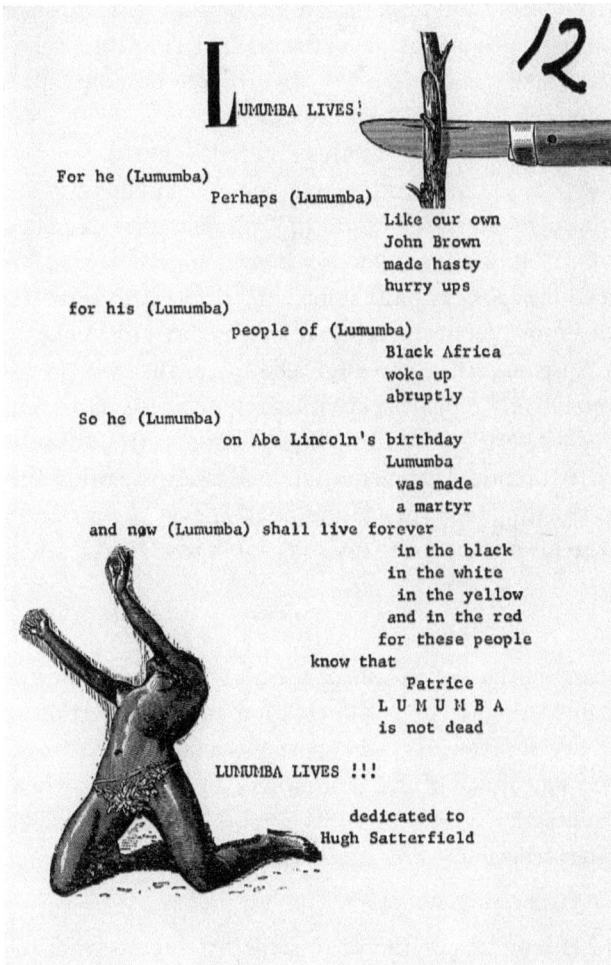

*Figure 8.2* Ted Joans, "LUMUMBA LIVES!," From *All of Ted Joans and No More* (1961). (© Estate of Ted Joans, courtesy of Laura Corsiglia.)

or something yet to be determined."[87] While the range of possible referents is different for Joans than for Tutuola, Joans acknowledges a similar world in which Lumumba functions both as an individual and as a figure who is transcendent in death. For Joans, the parentheses also separate Lumumba from the instability of "perhaps." This version of the poem otherwise repeats and affirms Lumumba's presence. Lumumba's final two appearances are, like the title, in capital letters:

> Patrice
> L U M U M B A
> is not dead
>
> LUMUMBA LIVES ! ! ![88]

The result, in part, is to offset "Lumumba" as an incantation that, through Joans's syntax, exists both inside and outside of the poem. In these lines, Lumumba is both a person and a symbol in a way that is more broadly representative of African American discourse on the Congo.

In other versions of the poem, Joans explores different syntactic ways to mark that distinction, which, to him, must be retained. A revised version of the poem appears without illustrations under the title "LUMUMBA LIVES L U M U M B A   L I V E S!!" in Joans's collection *Black Pow-Wow: Jazz Poems* (1969). The later version uses nearly all capital letters and compresses the language of twenty-seven mostly short lines into thirteen mostly longer lines, which leaves less room for the words to breathe. The spaces that remain are highly charged. Joans effectively replaces parentheses with caesuras around "LUMUMBA," visually offsetting Lumumba's name while surrounding it with an implied silence that renders it a memorial site despite the title's emphatic claim. Whereas wording like "he (Lumumba)" makes the pronoun directly referential in the 1961 version, the revised syntax renders the poem polyvocal:

FOR HE    LUMUMBA      PERHAPS    LUMUMBA    LIKE THEIR

Lumumba's name appears on the same plane as the rest of the line, but disrupts its grammar through the absence of punctuation and the insertion of capacious blank space. In each of the first three stanzas, the word "LUMUMBA" first appears immediately and abruptly after a pronoun ("he" or "his"), where it grammatically and syntactically interrupts its English language fluidity. Among the few lowercase terms in the *Black Pow-Wow* version is "patrice":

PEOPLE    KNOW that patrice L U M U M B A    IS    NOT    DEAD![89]

This line emphasizes his iconicity by detaching his first name from his symbolic surname. In the literary realm, "LUMUMBA"—whether rendered in capital or lowercase letters, with additional spaces between letters, in repetition, or parenthetically—is not the same as "patrice." As such, "LUMUMBA" serves as a poetic figure rather than a word consistently subject to conventional grammar or syntax.

Whereas the *All of Ted Joans and No More* version concludes with the declaration "LUMUMBA LIVES   ! ! !," the *Black Pow-Wow* version ends with the statement's repetition five times over the course of two lines, with the full series punctuated with two, rather than three, exclamation points. The repetition extends the urgent declaration through a form of echolalia. A parallel revision is visible in the shift of the title from "LUMUMBA LIVES!" to the elongated "LUMUMBA LIVES    L U M U M B A   L I V E S!!" The version that appears in *Teducation* shares the title and most of its text with the *Black Pow-Wow* version; however, it appears, with the exception of the title, entirely in capital letters. Over time, these changes to the poem increase its volume and minimize the kinds of modulations that seemed possible in its earliest incarnation. While these changes suggest the work's evolution, the sensibility of the first publication is maintained over the course of four decades during which Mobutu dominated Congolese politics. Later versions of the poem continue to mark this increasing historical uncertainty with the use of "PERHAPS" as a modifier:

> SO HE LUMUMBA   ON PERHAPS ABE LINCOLN'S BIRTHDAY
> LUMUMBA WAS MADE   A   MARTYR[90]

The poem notes that the martyring (distinct from the killing) occurred "on Abe Lincoln's birthday," (February 12, the day before the news was officially announced), which recalls the identification of Lumumba as the "Lincoln of the Congo."[91] Furthermore, it is an example of how Joans uses his elegies to "layer events from different historical epochs over current sites and events."[92] Joans constructs a historical landscape that is grounded in uncertainty. The repetition of "PERHAPS" over the course of the later version of the poem, and the unknown date of Lumumba's death, acknowledge that the uncertainty surrounding it has increased over time. As a result, "LUMUMBA" seems to appear at random in the first three stanzas, which heightens its indeterminacy while his presence is inescapable. The poem, like its subject, remains alive.

The anarchic possibilities of "LUMUMBA" resemble those of Bird's appearance on walls throughout New York City. Diane di Prima, a Greenwich Village–era collaborator of Baraka, describes a similar phenomenon: "green posters LUMUMBA LIVES flooded Harlem in those days."[93] Such attention was international and multilingual as in Joans's poem "Afrique Accidentale" (1963), which appeared with Ngoma's "Tom-Tom" in *City Lights Journal* and which notes that along the route from Senegal to Mali, "there's a sign to remember Vive Notre Frere [sic] Lumumba."[94] A bilingual poetic invocation of a physical marker of Lumumba's afterlife suits a visual poet like Joans, for whom illustrations, space, varieties of indentation, and layout are central to his work. His use of capitalization and creative spacing between lines and words defy definitive oral performance. What does capitalization accented by exclamation points sound like? Or as Meta DuEwa Jones asks, "How do you make audible a font size and style?"[95] As a result, any transcription is imprecise, present text included.

Given the difficulties in precisely reproducing the varieties of syntax and spacing that Joans uses, each publication of one of his poems varies from the supposed original in some way, thereby becoming a new work. In this fashion, his written works emulate the improvisational nature of the musical traditions that have influenced him. This is consistent with Stephen Henderson's affirmation of Larry Neal's notion that the poem is simply one "score," not a definitive version, but rather "a single possible form of a poem."[96] For Joans, any publication of the poem—given the irreproducible qualities of his graphics, style, and syntax—could be considered a rendition. The result is deliberately open-ended, consistent with what Benston finds in his reading of Sonia Sanchez's "a/coltrane/poem": "In effect, the poem has ceded elements of its narrative authority to readerly performance, maintaining ideological perspective while granting to another voice the responsibility and satisfaction of rhythmic embodiment. Sanchez has gradually destabilized poetic space in order to render it susceptible to pluralized redefinition."[97] Benston's description of "readerly performance" is similar to the kind of "pluralized redefinition" that shaped the signification of Hughes's geography in "The Negro Speaks of Rivers." While Joans's poem may not have the same rhythmic properties as Sanchez's, his remains a deliberately unstable text that, like the "Bird Lives" graffiti, takes on a life of its own. The "rhythmic embodiment" of the poem's repetition of "LUMUMBA" plays with the aural properties of his name, whose first two syllables are a near rhyme, which makes it an especially suitable candidate for poetic invocation. These strategies of repetition facilitate the kind of "pluralized redefinition" that Sanchez creates in her Coltrane poem.

"LUMUMBA LIVES!" is an integral part of Joans's oeuvre, as it carefully revises "Bird Lives!" and shifts an ostensibly cultural discourse into a political realm, breaking down the commonly perceived split between "musical sensation and political thought," or what Baraka terms "art and politics."[98] Indeed Joans's ability to make this seamless transition is indicative of the ways in which political and musical discourse overlap within African American poetry. Lumumba and the Congo are prominent throughout Joans's oeuvre, as they are throughout poetry of the period, and Joans's discourse functions as a sort of prototype of the Lumumba poem. This tradition can be seen by unique pairings of political and popular icons in poems like Hughes's *Ask Your Mama*, as discussed in chapter 7, and Baraka's "Black Dada Nihilismus," which places "patrice" beside "mantan" Moreland, a film actor well known for his performances that emerge out of the minstrel tradition.[99] Baraka's poem, as Aldon Lynn Nielsen observes, was a successful musical collaboration with the New York Art Quartet and was also effective as a visual text. Nielsen explains that the limited roles available to Moreland and other African American actors of his era parallel the silencing of Lumumba, whom Baraka elsewhere characterized as an "artist."[100] This juxtaposition encapsulates the essence of the poem, described by Moten as "the absence, the irrecoverability of an originary and constitutive event; the impossibility of a return to an African, the impossibility of an arrival at an American, home."[101]

Similarly, Joans pairs Lumumba with cultural figures in his poem "Who Shook" (1985), which links many of the characters who appear in this study—Langston Hughes, John Coltrane, Jayne Cortez, LeRoi Jones, Don L. Lee, Hoyt Fuller, James Baldwin, Jean-Paul Sartre, and Frantz Fanon—through a series of poetic handshakes. The poem undertakes a process of association that starts with André Breton; travels through African American musical, literary, and political culture; and ends with Breton's surrealist colleague Man Ray. Unlike most of the sixty-five named figures in the poem, Lumumba's first name is excluded, giving him a rare status (shared only with [Pablo] Picasso, [Guillaume] Apollinaire, [Heriberto] Cogollo, and [Roberto] Matta), which further establishes his iconicity:

> the hand of Kwame Nkrumah
> who had shook
> the hand of Lumumba
> who had shook
> the hand of Louis Armstrong[102]

Within this poem, Lumumba is aptly positioned between the Pan-African canon represented by Nkrumah and the diasporic cultural tradition represented by Armstrong, whose hometown of New Orleans is known for its historic Congo Square. Unfortunately, despite such literary associations, Lumumba never had the chance to shake Armstrong's hand because he was under house arrest when Armstrong played in Kinshasa in October 1960. Fatefully, when Armstrong played in Lubumbashi, the capital of secessionist Katanga, in November 1960, he performed for and stayed with Moise Tshombe, the antinationalist leader who would soon be implicated in Lumumba's death.[103]

Such a meeting of Lumumba and Armstrong could only be realized in creative work where cultural and political icons share common ground, a poetic innovation that, like the memorials that Benston analyzes, provides an outlet for poets and activists struggling with Lumumba's legacy. For Joans, Lumumba's death is an occasion not just for an elegiac statement like "LUMUMBA LIVES!" but an opportunity to critically explore the larger process of memorialization. In "Black February Blood Letting," Joans writes:

> L U M U M B A   WAS MURDERED   AND MADE A MARTYR
>                                          IN THE MONTH
> OF FEBRUARY . . .

After recounting other February tragedies—including the assassination of Malcolm X and the overthrow of Nkrumah, Joans concludes:

> .... STILL YET I CAN NOT FORGET
> that not one:
> CHINESE RED  RUSSIAN RED  OR ANY OTHER
> KINDA RED
> DID ANYTHING MILITANTLY TO HONOR THESE BLACK
> FEBRUARY DEAD[104]

Although Russia symbolically, if not "MILITANTLY," named a university devoted to international education in Lumumba's memory, government efforts "to sponsor an official 'Lumumba cult'" or to rename institutions in his memory are distinct from more popular literary forms of memorialization.[105] Joans is less interested in establishing a state-sponsored, prescriptive, or otherwise definitive tribute than in allowing the kind of ambiguity that is inherent in his earlier work writing "Bird Lives" to flourish. His writings about Lumumba, like his writings about Parker, do more than memorialize an individual musical or political figure; they facilitate a meta-exploration of the possibilities and limitations of the process of commemoration itself.

Much in the way that Benston considers the Coltrane poem "a complex microcosm" of a broader tradition, the frequent reappearance of Lumumba and the Congo throughout Joans's oeuvre is reflective of Lumumba's rich functionality in African American poetry.[106] Furthermore, Joans's poems, like those of Baraka and Hughes, locate Lumumba in an American context by placing him beside American figures (Moreland, Armstrong, Lincoln, John Brown) and framing his death as a lynching. While Lumumba is obviously front and center in works such as "LUMUMBA LIVES!" his more common appearances as a passing reference (as in "Afrique Accidentale") or as an allusion are indicative of his integral role within a broader discourse.

One allusion to Lumumba appears in "The Sax Bit" (1971), which links lynching, Congo, and African American music in a paean to jazz saxophonist Coleman Hawkins:

> This curved shiney tune gut / hanging lynched like / J
> shaped initial of jazz / wordless without a reed  when
> Coleman Hawkins first fondled it/kissed it with Black
> sound  did Congo blood sucking Belges frown  ?[107]

The use of slashes fuses the musical and political spheres, facilitating the continuity that Joans establishes between Hawkins and an image of vampire Belgian colonialism, where the possibility of the silent or "wordless" saxophone lurks. Joans characteristically combines slashes, irregular spacing, caesuras, and line breaks to provide the reader with multiple levels of enjambment. These conjunctions match the poem's assemblages of associations, which, within this one stanza, move from the saxophone to lynching to Belgian colonialism. Half a century earlier, Joans's mentor Hughes compared Belgian colonialism to lynching in "The Negro." Joans's poem combines musical language and poetic discourse, which intersect in ways that lead to an implicit commentary on the colonial regime that took the life of Lumumba, who is unnamed in this poem. In his adoption of the "blood sucking" vampire figure to describe colonialism, Joans shares a discourse with Ogali, who writes, "Lumumba was killed by the Congo Vampires—Tshombe, Kasavubu and Mobutu," and George Washington Williams, who describes white colonial officers in similar terms.[108] This invocation of Belgian colonial history in the neocolonial era looks to its past, present, and future in Africa and the United States, even though we are well served to remember Luise White's warning that such discourse should not be universalized across time or place at the expense of "regional histories and regional economies": "stories may travel, but they do not travel through or to passive storytellers."[109]

From its opening epigraph, "The Sax Bit" reflects on the possibilities and limitations of poetry as an instrument of commemoration:

This poem is
just a poem of
thanks

Joans's awareness of what a poem "is" led him to other forms of memorialization—from "Bird Lives" to his decision, like Malcolm X, Michael S. Harper, and others, to name his son in memory of Lumumba. Patrice Lumumba (Joans) stands in for Hughes, in whose honor the child was nearly named. Joans told Hughes about the decision and Hughes responded graciously.[110] The interchangeability of Hughes and Lumumba is indicative of how closely the Congolese leader came to be associated with a particularly vibrant musical place within the poetic world. For poets, Lumumba becomes "American" not only because his unaccountable murder resembles the unsuccessfully prosecuted assassinations of African American leaders like Medgar Evers, but also because he is memorialized in poems that are deeply rooted in African American musical practice.[111]

## Who Killed Lumumba

Ted Joans's surrealist approach to lynching, blood, and colonialism is shared by Jayne Cortez, whose volume *Festivals and Funerals* (1971) addresses the criminality of the Belgian regime and the legacy of Lumumba. *Festivals and Funerals* opens with "Initiation," a meditation on the Middle Passage and colonialism. The surrealist poem, which includes many of Cortez's characteristic tropes like the body and blood, suggests a continuity and collectivity in which memories of emancipation merge with the profoundly tragic colonial history of the Congo:

> During the season of cut organs we
> shot forward like teeth spokes from runaways
> a lost cargo of part flesh part ash part
> copper and zinc
> sucking in names like katanga
> like congo
> we dissolved our chains
> celebrated the slit nose reality of
> our severed hands and
> at the base of a fifty million skull pyramid
> we rehearse life
> second headed face circles of
> one handed life calling:[112]

Cortez's reference to the "severed hands" of the colonial era evokes Sheppard's widely distributed report. Such history does not foreclose the possibility of "one handed life," as a possible answer to Benston's question about how "the paralyzing pain of loss [can] be transformed into collective progress and productive speech?"[113] The "blood blood blood / and once again blood" that dominates the final third of the poem ("blood" appears in five of its final eight lines) is reclaimed in its concluding couplet: "No / take us to the place for the new birth blood."[114] Cortez's image of "new birth blood," which recalls Pauline Hopkins's language, represents the reclamation of something powerful "during" what the poem's opening line calls "the season of cut organs."

That poem initiates a volume whose title, *Festivals and Funerals*, announces a simultaneous engagement with and, in its coupling with the celebratory "festival," challenge to the conventions of the elegy, a genre that Cortez explores throughout her oeuvre in works in memory of musicians ("How Long Has Trane Been Gone"), writers ("For the Poets"), and victims of police violence ("Give Me the Red on the Black of the Bullet").[115] Poet-scholar Eugene B. Redmond finds Cortez's provocative coexistence of festivals and funerals to be "Musical, daring, ambivalent, complex and technically dexterous, [and] it summarizes the uncertain world of blacklife" such that he uses it as the title to his chapter on the 1960s and 1970s in *Drumvoices: The Mission of Afro-American Poetry: A Critical History* (1976).[116]

The opening triplet of the poem "Festivals & Funerals" foregrounds spiritual and verbal injuries that, for their tragedy and brutality, do not expedite the prospect of death:

> They winged his spirit &
> wounded his tongue
> but death was slow coming

The second stanza repeats the first one, with two subtle changes that serve as textual equivalents to oral inflection: the ampersand is moved from the end of the first line to the start of the second line, and the third line is punctuated with a question mark. One of the poem's refrains, which appears three times, asks or, given the absence of question marks, states: "Who killed Lumumba / What killed Malcolm." After repeating this couplet, Cortez repeats another triplet:

> There are no tears
> we have no friends
> this is the word[117]

From the opening reference to the injured tongue to the insistent presence of the "word," Lumumba and Malcolm are eulogized as speakers who are remembered here for their words much as they were in the black journals of the period.

Cortez is conscious of her unique poetic use of historical figures in her verse. In response to a question from poet-scholar D. H. Melhem about the mythologization of people in her work, Cortez replies, "Most of the names in my work are there as examples."[118] While it is easy to appreciate the ways in which Cortez's references function as representative figures, her explanation belies the terms on which she undertakes this process of mythmaking. By basing her work so forcefully in flesh and blood, her "examples" are embodied in an inescapably confrontational manner. As a result, what Cortez calls her "supersurrealism" maintains an uncommon concreteness that is grounded, as Jennifer D. Ryan points out, in "her poems' graphic imagery, for which she is indebted to both blues lyrics and the early-century surrealist movement."[119] Cortez's approach resembles that of Joans, which, Kathryn V. Lindberg explains, offers "an embodied history of race and racial violence, [as either] a critique of Surrealism or a neglected aspect of the Surrealist project."[120] In either case, a uniquely African American genus foregrounds a historically specific form of embodiment that brilliantly redresses the legacies of physical dismemberment that began during Leopold's regime and culminated in the bodily dissolution that punctuated Lumumba's assassination.

This embodiment holds particular significance in light of the physical disappearance of Lumumba; after being shot and buried, the bodies of Lumumba and two comrades were exhumed twice, and ultimately dissolved with sulfuric acid and the remains ground up. All told, it took nearly two weeks to "obliterate all traces of the corpses."[121] The absence of a body made the funeral service and wake with an effigy of "Lumumba Lying in State" that Michaux held at his Harlem bookstore especially poignant.[122] (See Figure 8.3.) "The void left by a period of mourning that could have no end—because there was no body to bury—was gradually filled with images," explains Bogumil Jewsiewicki, writing about Congolese visual representations of the martyred leader: "The destruction of Lumumba's biological body was meant to tear him from the world and make him a nonbeing; instead . . . it has strengthened the aesthetic and political power of his image as Christ."[123] Clarke's characterization of Lumumba as a "Black Messiah" resembles Lorenzo Thomas's "A Tale of Two Cities," which appeared in the first issue of the New York journal *Umbra* and recounts protestors "running amok at the UN shouting, / 'You've crucified our saintly Lumumba. . . .'"[124] Thomas uses Christian imagery to imply Lumumba's resurrection, which represents one way of escaping his death. Cortez resurrects his image in a tradition of African American martyrs like Malcolm X and Evers. Her rendering of Lumumba evades a disembodied iconic martyrdom, and is wholly consistent with Benston's understanding of the poetic subgenre as emerging to regenerate a silenced voice. The innovative artistic forms that predominate in the Black Arts movement are means of creative expression that are ideologically, institutionally, and aesthetically well suited to engage the assassination of Lumumba.

In this context, Cortez attends to Lumumba's voice and body with alliterative animation and vitality, as near the end of "Festivals & Funerals":

> backing the beat of our brains was the
> speech of his thoughts & the death of
> our fear through the dark of his meat
> sits the flesh of Patrice
> our flesh of a flesh is Lumumba our flesh Lumumba
> flesh[125]

Cortez, like Joans, repeats "Lumumba" as an incantation that varies its part of speech to emphasize her declaration that Lumumba lives. Also like Joans and Hughes, she separates "Patrice" from "Lumumba," which marks a distinction between the person and the icon as she moves between the "flesh" and the "word." In a single line, "Lumumba" appears to be a noun modified by the first person plural possessive, an adjective modifying "flesh," and a noun modified by "flesh" as an adjective. Lumumba lives through the "speech of his thoughts," which continues to reverberate in "our brains." The stanza instantly returns to the "flesh" of Lumumba (repeated five times in three lines). Cortez sought to restore, if not resurrect, Lumumba's body, a critical

*Figure 8.3* Lewis Michaux's National Memorial African Bookstore in Harlem announcing "Lumumba Lying in State" (1961). A photograph of Lumumba is also visible in the center of the display window. (© Henri Cartier-Bresson/Magnum Photos.)

resurrection of a figure whose death was marked by the literal absence of a body.

This stanza, which forces the reader to confront Lumumba's flesh, is followed by a repetition of the triplet that, like Joans's epigraph to "The Sax Bit," serves as a reminder that language seemingly supersedes all else:

> There are no tears
> we have no friends
> this is the word

After a stanza break, Cortez follows "the word" with a quatrain that concludes the poem by presenting the new and innovative alongside the sensual and musical:

> the vanguard of precision
> the virgin of communications
> the erotic improvisation of uprooted
> perfection the Blues[126]

By ending "Festivals & Funerals" with a reference to the "Blues" (with a capital B), Cortez situates this mourning praise song within a specific African American musical tradition whose vernacular differs markedly from the language of the poem itself, even while the poem's refrain announces a lonely commitment to the "word."

"Festivals & Funerals" is also one of the highlights of *Celebrations and Solitudes* (1974), the album that Cortez recorded with bassist Richard Davis. Davis uses his bow to punctuate Cortez's questions in a way that contrasts with the pizzicato bass line that he uses elsewhere in the song and throughout the album. The unusual combination of the two bass styles in a single song destabilizes its relationship to a blues musical tradition while emphasizing the unanswerability of Cortez's questions, "Who killed Lumumba / What killed Malcolm." In a review in *Black World*, poet June Jordan posits that the album, which she considers the finest collaboration between a poet and musician since Hughes worked with Charles Mingus on *The Weary Blues* in 1957, affirms Stephen Henderson's belief in the important connections between speech and music.[127] For Jordan, Cortez's incorporation of the "Blues" into her surrealist verse represents an aesthetic innovation that accords with Henderson's conceptualization of the era. As Robin D. G. Kelley, citing Paul Garon, explains in his analysis of black surrealists like Joans and Cortez, this sensibility is in fact part of the blues; "through its fidelity to fantasy and desire, the blues generates an irreducible and, so to speak, habit-forming demand for freedom and what Rimbaud called 'true life.' "[128] Cortez's formal innovations articulate this "demand for freedom" in a way that grounds her within blues aesthetics that, according to Tony Bolden, "reflect a radical internationalist politics shaped by the specific historicity of the African American experience and committed to the liberation of colonized subjects globally."[129]

## Lumumba Blues

In Raymond R. Patterson's "Lumumba Blues," that same "demand for freedom" is articulated explicitly within a poetic structure that is directly based on the rhythmic form of the blues. The title of the poem—"Lumumba Blues"—defines "Lumumba" as a type of blues; these are not "Lumumba's Blues" because the blues that are being described do not belong to him. They are the blues of the people, who are suffering from the loss of Lumumba's voice. Here, "Lumumba" functions as a poetic figure, similar to the "LUMUMBA" of Joans's "LUMUMBA LIVES!" which describes "people of (Lumumba)," making it clear that Lumumba belongs to the people. Like the blues singer described by Neal in "Any Day Now: Black Art and Black Liberation," Patterson's blues poet "is not an alienated artist moaning songs of self-pity and defeat to an infidel mob. He is the voice of the community, its historian, and one of the shapers of its morality."[130] The blues, therefore, provide a community-based form of memorialization, similar to Onitsha writings, well suited to represent Lumumba.[131]

Patterson elegizes Lumumba within a characteristically American genre, which is itself a poetic rearticulation of a musical mode that has established poetic roots in works by Hughes and Sterling Brown, among others. The form of the poem is highlighted by its publication in the collection *Elemental Blues*. In contrast to the fluid and unstable architectonics of Joans's and Cortez's verses, Patterson's poem uses a traditional blues structure to mourn the Congolese leader. Patterson explains, "As a poetic form, a blues stanza consists of three lines of verse in which the first line presents a statement that is repeated in the second line, with or without variation. The third line of a blues provides a rhymed response or resolution to the repeated statement."[132] Patterson's poem undertakes this process as it opens with a question: "Did you hear about Lumumba?," which gives the poem a dialogic tenor that is maintained throughout its five stanzas.[133]

The opening stanza of "Lumumba Blues" follows that formula (in five, rather than three, lines), concluding: "Take folks more than a little to forget that crime."[134] The verb tense of "take," adroitly rendered indeterminate (either present or future) by the vernacular, excludes the past to suggest that the "crime" continues to reverberate. "Little" can be read as a noun or as an adjective that modifies an omitted noun. The absence of the noun (perhaps "time") leaves open a range of potential interpretations, all of which are predetermined to be substantial ("more than a little"). The stanza also resonates with Benston's reading of Cortez's "How Long Has Trane Been Gone," in which "the hero appears as arch signifier or Image of communal meanings rendered insecure only by a hypothetical forgetfulness that the poet dispels with preacherly admonishment."[135] The blues provide the ideal structure for the process described by Benston. The opening questions posit a "hypothetical forgetfulness" that the poet, inhabiting the voice of a blues persona rather than a preacher, dismisses as a short-term impossibility. The danger of forgetting, which these poetic memorials intend to avert, is introduced and overcome. Within "Lumumba Blues," memory serves two distinct purposes. First, the inability to forget the criminal manner in which Lumumba died is transformed into a defiant insistence that he will be remembered for "language that reclaims banished creativity and restores the eclipsed world."[136] Second, the refusal of the blues poet to forget is a variation on "LUMUMBA LIVES!" which, much in the way Neal explains, establishes the speaker—the African American blues musician or folk poet—as the bearer of cultural memory for the postcolonial black Atlantic world. Such work, according to Bolden, is central to the Black Arts movement goal to develop, often through musical forms and devices, "an affective poetics similar to affective preaching, which allows the listener to experience the poem sensually and thereby gain understanding through memory."[137]

The second stanza of Patterson's poem reminds readers of the community that includes the poet and the poet's audience: "Well, he didn't want much, / Just like you and me." This communalism is followed by the transition of Lumumba to a speaking subject:

> He was speaking for his people.
> He said, Set my people free.
> (Don't you think we ought to be free?)[138]

The remembrance of Lumumba's words—by the black radical press that frequently cited him, in the poetry that Langston Hughes included in *Poems from Black Africa*, and beyond—ensures that such wide visibility does not reduce him to silent symbolism. In Patterson's poem, his words are not "quoted" per se, but rather are incorporated and articulated by the persona as collective speech. Such poetic recovery of Lumumba's actual voice represents a very specific response to the silencing of Lumumba, something that predates his physical death. Lumumba's *Congo, My Country*, which was written in 1956 and submitted to Belgian publishers in 1957, was not published until after his death.[139] Journalist Howard describes a Kinshasa press conference where impatient American reporters left before Lumumba arrived, highlighting the need for activists to create new discursive spaces for Lumumba's voice.[140]

In Patterson's poem, the voice of Lumumba emerges along with a comparable dialogic aside between the blues poet and the blues audience, reinforcing a transatlantic communal sensibility. The language and structure of "Lumumba Blues" are marked as American, which make the "we" a reference to African Americans who are included under the umbrella of "his people." This sensibility is reinforced in the third stanza, which describes his assassination as a lynching, thereby contextualizing it within a particular U.S. regime of domestic racial terror, which is similar to the earlier rhetoric of Clarke, Joans, and others. That sense of transatlantic racial identification is stated outright in the fourth stanza:

> Lord, Lumumba! See what they did to you!
> Poor black boy, I see what they did to you.
> I can't help feeling they done that to me, too.[141]

This stanza shifts from an imperative, direct address of Lumumba to a first-person form of vernacular identification between the subject, the poet, and the audience, which, in its final appearance, is revealed to be more empathetic than individualistic.

Patterson's poem implicitly makes the case that Lumumba's legacy remains as important in the 1980s as it did in the 1960s. Echoing Hughes's invocation of "freedom" in "Final Call," "Lumumba Blues" concludes:

> Freedom! Lumumba,
> I hear you calling still,
> Freedom! Oh, Freedom!
> I hear you calling still.
> I won't forget,
> Don't think I ever will.[142]

The final line can be read as a colloquial affirmation with an implied first person subject ([I] "Don't think I ever will" [forget]) that allows for future uncertainty, even while the poem's repetition itself directly challenges that prospect. Secondarily, the line serves as a command directed to the reader or listener ("Don't [you] think I ever will" [forget]), which acknowledges the skepticism against which it cautions. Regardless of how this concluding line is interpreted, the blues poet ("I") is positioned on the front line of protecting and preserving Lumumba's words as what Neal would describe as the group's "historian." In the end, the poem is less about Lumumba than about the act of remembrance and the perils of amnesia.

Although Patterson was himself a central figure in African American literary circles in New York as early as the late 1950s, his poem about the danger of forgetting was written several decades hence.[143] This final stanza specifically recognizes the ongoing presence of Lumumba by repeating the word "still" to insist that, even in the 1980s with Mobutu in power, Lumumba's call for freedom will not soon be forgotten. The unromantic recovery of Lumumba's anticolonialism becomes particularly germane at a time when, Wenzel points out, "Critiques of neocolonialism, as urgent as they certainly are, still risk another kind of amnesia, forgetting independence (even if it was not liberation) rather than forgetting colonialism."[144] "Lumumba Blues" avoids direct mention of Leopold or Belgium, which makes it effective in its poetic recovery of Lumumba. Patterson's innovative blues focuses on Lumumba's vision, which is consistent with both Kelley's appreciation of the genre (musically and poetically) and Wenzel's "anti-imperialist nostalgia."

Patterson's poem asserts that Lumumba's voice was not silenced by the assassination, but was symbolically transferred to the African American masses through its survival in the blues lyric. As in Joans's "LUMUMBA

LIVES!," Lumumba is placed within a discursive context that builds and brings together musical, literary, performative, and political traditions. Whereas Cortez's contribution is marked by her surrealist blues aesthetic, for Patterson, it is the blues form and vernacular language that make "Lumumba Blues" a unique accomplishment. These qualities make these examples of the Lumumba poem archetypes as explained by Stephen Henderson: "Structurally speaking, however, whenever Black poetry is most distinctly and effectively *Black*, it derives its form from two basic sources, Black speech and Black music." Such engagements provide readers with the Lumumba poem as exemplary of African American poetics which is, Henderson explains, a tradition constituted "in the movement toward the forms of Black music."[145]

## Who Cut Off Peoples' Hands in the Congo

In addition to the poems by Joans, Cortez, and Patterson, there are dozens of others worthy of examination ranging from Hurley X's pastoral broadside "Poem for Patrice Lumumba: Murdered for Seeking Justice for His People" (1974) to Kiarri T-H. Cheatwood's chapbook *Elegies for Patrice* (1984). More recently, hip-hop group X-Clan shouts out Lumumba on "Raise the Flag" from its classic album *To the East, Blackwards* (1990) as does Nas in the song "My Country" (whose title echoes that of Lumumba's posthumously published *Congo, My Country*) on *Stillmatic* (2001). Michael S. Harper's poem "Patrice Lumumba" (1997) self-consciously acknowledges that the power of colonialism lies, at least in part, in its ability to control the stories that are told. Harper's concluding stanza begins with the coded date of Congolese independence, but insists that:

> 30 6 60
> Belgian
> Congo
> still
> Conrad's
> Intended[146]

European domination continues its reign in the Congo in part through the resilience of scripts written by figures like Conrad. The power of Conrad's literary representation remains intact more than a century after he, Williams, and Sheppard all traveled to the Congo. While the genre of the Lumumba poem may not supplant Conrad's dominant image, it does open up space for more critical literary engagements with the tradition it represents.

By using the Lumumba poem to address the Leopoldian/Conradian era, Harper extends the chronology of the genre into the late colonial era, suggesting that its parameters are much less narrow than might be presumed. Indeed, given Harper's own vexed relationship to the Black Arts movement, his "Patrice Lumumba" is a particularly significant mark of the breadth of Lumumba's influence. This is an important point—for all their ideological differences, Harper shared certain cultural, aesthetic, and poetic principles (as well as spaces of publication) with Baraka and other architects of the Black Arts movement.[147] Lumumba was one point of intersection.

As a poet who remained prolific until his death in 2014, Baraka elongates this trajectory in "Somebody Blew Up America," his epic post–September 11, 2001, interrogation of the international functioning of U.S. imperial power. Baraka, like Cortez, uses rhetorical questions to construct a historical continuity that extends the Lumumba canon into the post-Mobutu twenty-first century with his pointed framing of the January 2001 assassination of Congolese leader Laurent Kabila:

> Who killed Kabila, the ones who wasted Lumumba, Mondlane,
>     Betty Shabazz, Princess Margaret,
> Ralph Featherstone, Little Bobby.

Baraka answers Cortez's query ("Who killed Lumumba") and punctuates its continued relevance while posing his own questions. Its anticolonial and nationalist rhetoric is a direct product of the Black Arts era and emerges from meaningful political engagements of artists who converged at the United Nations in February 1961. As one of the twenty-first century's best-known poems—due to a line about the World Trade Center that caused controversy after Baraka's appointment as poet laureate of New Jersey—"Somebody Blew Up America" establishes a continuity of death and violence that, like Cortez's "Initiation," extends to the Leopoldian era by asking: "Who cut off peoples' hands in the Congo."[148] For more than a century, images of hand severing have circulated through the writings of Sheppard, Hughes, and others. Baraka's invocation, as part of a wider internationalist milieu, emerges as the product of a sustained literary history of which the work itself is conscious.

Baraka and Harper use characteristically different points of reference to extend the chronology of the Lumumba poem. Between them, the genre covers the Leopoldian and postindependence eras. Such a long-range interest is visible in the works of other writers from the 1960s. In 1964, college student Alice Walker wrote a research paper on Belgian colonialism.[149] Forty years later, Walker traveled to the Congo and published a book based, in part, on that experience, recalling Leopold's "policy of cutting off the hands of enslaved Africans who didn't or couldn't fulfill their rubber quota."[150] In 2009, Lynn Nottage won the Pulitzer Prize for drama for *Ruined*, which sets Bertolt Brecht's *Mother Courage* in eastern Congo. She traveled to East Africa with her director, who, on visiting refugees in Uganda, recalled the hand-cutting violence of the Leopoldian era, asserting "Stanley cut off the hands of anyone refusing to work," while drawing a line from "Such butchery, practiced by colonizers one hundred years earlier" to "current acts of violence in a post-colonial Congo."[151] The literary trajectories of Walker and Nottage, like those of Hughes and Baraka, are indicative of the ways in which interest in the Congo during the early years of independence was both the product of and the foundation for sustained intellectual, artistic, and political attention. Through such works, the figure of "Lumumba" is situated within a broader discursive tradition that spans more than a century, and becomes representative of what is best understood as this long history of African American engagement with the Congo.

*Chapter 9*

# The Chickens Coming Home to Roost

*Malcolm X, the Congo, and Modern Black Nationalism*

While the Black Arts movement was engaging the postcolonial politics of the Congo, Malcolm X took Patrice Lumumba as the patron saint for the Organization of Afro-American Unity (OAAU). Overall, Malcolm X took a longer historical view on the Congo. On November 28, 1964, a few days after returning to the United States from several months abroad, he appeared as a guest on the Barry Gray Show on WMCA radio in New York to discuss the Congo, a timely subject following the disastrous attempt by U.S. and Belgian forces four days earlier to rescue white hostages from Stanleyville (Kisangani), a city in northeastern Congo that was under Lumumbist control.[1] During an exchange with fellow panelist Sanford Griffith, who defended Belgium's "fine administration" of the Congo, Malcolm X mentioned that he was reading Mark Twain's book about the Congo, *King Leopold's Soliloquy*. When Griffith questioned Malcolm X's assertion that the population of the Congo was reduced from 30 million to 15 million people under Leopold II's reign, Malcolm X challenged Griffith to offer specific data. All Griffith could muster was, "there were undoubtedly many thousand casualties, but certainly not a hundred thousand and certainly not fifty thousand," an absurd underestimation of what remains a highly contentious figure.[2]

Mindful of Theodor Adorno's assertion that to "haggle over numbers is already inhumane," Malcolm X turned his attention to the cutting off of the hands of Congolese people by the colonial administration.[3] As the host tried to steer the conversation away from colonial history and toward the present crisis, Malcolm X insisted on their inseparability: "when you start talking about what the Congolese are doing in retaliation today, they have pictures that are historic fact, that Leopold made it mandatory that when a black man didn't produce a certain quota of rubber, his hand was cut off."[4] Drawing, albeit indirectly, on the research of William Sheppard, Malcolm X foregrounds the bodies of the Congolese victims of Belgian colonialism. Malcolm X insisted that the 1960s crisis was shaped by the ongoing circulation of historical images, visual evidence of colonial violence, part of what he later described as the "science of imagery."[5]

Malcolm X's Congo readings were guided by Lewis Michaux, whose legendary National Memorial African Bookstore was literally his second home and sometimes office. A few years earlier, Michaux gave a copy of Twain's book to Carlos Moore when he came to the bookshop to learn more about the Congo. Malcolm X, like others whom Michaux directed to *King Leopold's Soliloquy*, was building on Sheppard's seminal eyewitness report of hand severing, which adds an important layer to Saladin Ambar's observation that this reference was exemplary of "Malcolm's effective employ of white literary and intellectual icons."[6] When Malcolm X discussed the history of the Congo during the final months of his life, he advanced a lineage of African American involvement in central Africa that reaches back to the nineteenth century. The distribution of *King Leopold's Soliloquy* by Michaux, a towering figure of Harlem intellectual and political life, ensured the continued circulation of Sheppard's words. While Malcolm X, to my knowledge, never mentioned Sheppard by name, it seems reasonable that he could have been a topic of conversation with Michaux.

In February 1961, the New York Police Department and other authorities rushed to hold the Nation of Islam (NoI) and its New York leader Malcolm X responsible for the U.N. demonstration that Angelou, Guy, and Lincoln announced in front of Michaux's bookstore.[7] While Malcolm X occasionally continues to be misplaced at the scene of the demonstration and Peter Goldman vaguely claims that he "actually turned down an invitation to join the demonstrators," he did meet with two of the principal organizers—Angelou and Guy—a couple of days afterward.[8] According to Angelou, Malcolm X was bluntly critical on the grounds that "going to the United Nations, shouting and carrying placards will not win freedom for anyone, nor will it keep the white devils from killing another African leader. Or a black American leader." Yet, he appreciated that the demonstration was "symbolic of the anger in this country," and refused to repudiate the protestors publicly, as he correctly predicted other leaders would.[9] According to FBI documents, Malcolm X threatened "some retaliatory action" unless the New York City Police Commissioner publicly apologized for its "false statement," which "has ruined the good name of the NOI."[10] Malcolm X's own public statements were much more measured: "I refuse to condemn the demonstrations . . . because I am not Moise Tshombe, and will permit no one to use me against the nationalists."[11] By naming Tshombe, the secessionist leader of Katanga who was widely understood to be involved in Lumumba's death, Malcolm X's response implicitly announces a deep commitment to the fate of postcolonial states in Africa, while demonstrating that neocolonial factionalism in the Congo was instructive for the dissension that threatened black nationalist movements in the United States.

Like Du Bois, whose anticolonial radicalization a half-century earlier coalesced around a strong World War I–era critique of Belgium's empire,

Malcolm X's expanding internationalism took the Congo as its geopolitical touchstone. In an October 20, 1962, address at Yale University, Minister Malcolm X described the Congo as a "racial volcano" that "could easily touch off the dreaded 3rd World War."[12] Malcolm X remained contemptuous of Tshombe, whom he considered an agent of white economic interests, "a cold-blooded murderer," and "the worst African that was ever born"—a widely shared assessment, explains Thomas Borstelmann, because of Tshombe's "leadership of the unsuccessful Katanga secession of 1960–63, his ready use of white mercenary troops against fellow Congolese, his intimate ties with colonialist Belgian enterprises, and, above all, his responsibility for the murder of the Congolese independence leader and first prime minister Patrice Lumumba."[13]

Malcolm X was not alone in his invocation of Tshombe's name as the archetypal neocolonial villain. As soon as news of Lumumba's assassination became public in February 1961, the *Chicago Defender* reported "Chicagoans Blast Tshombe as 'Uncle Tom,'" employing an appellation that Malcolm X frequently used to caricature African Americans suspected of racial betrayal.[14] When it came to the Congo, Tshombe had company in Ralph Bunche, whom Malcolm X unmistakably lambasted in Philadelphia in September 1963 as "a twentieth century Uncle Tom": "He runs to the Congo and tries to settle differences there, but he can't go to Mississippi and settle differences that his own people are confronted with in the face of these Mississippi southerners."[15] His criticism of Bunche resembles that of Hughes's Jess B. Simple in substance, if not in style. Like many contemporary poets, Malcolm X uses his own American vernacular to bring his audience's critical attention to the racial dimensions of the relationship between the Congo and the United States and to evoke caution regarding a facile understanding of racial identification.

The U.N. demonstration exposed fissures among African American activists; Malcolm X believed that this kind of ideological fracturing had parallels in neocolonial Africa, where new fault lines within and between nations and blocs were emerging. While such lines were relatively easy to identify in the colonial era, they became less clearly demarcated in postcolonial Africa, and the Congo exemplified the dangers of disunity. Malcolm X himself recognized the Congo as an object lesson for intra-Muslim conflict, pointing out in a September 1962 letter to a Sudanese student in the United States: "The Belgians are still in the Congo because they are able to keep the Congolese fighting against each other."[16] Malcolm X believed that internecine conflicts, like those he witnessed within the NoI and the wider African American community, made independent political movements more vulnerable to their enemies. His insistence during his appearance on the Barry Gray Show that the Congo crisis had inextricable roots in Belgian colonialism represented a radical reconfiguration of the current postcolonial/neocolonial moment—one that implicitly invoked Sheppard, reperiodized colonial history, and materialized transnational connections to the political crisis. Malcolm X's consistent political specificity with regard to the Congo enables us to understand his transnationalism as a formation with precise historical investments in the contours of modern nation-states so that "Africa" is recognizable as a diverse network of political struggles.

## The Chickens Coming Home

Nearly three years after the assassination of Lumumba, the conflicts between Malcolm X and the Honorable Elijah Muhammad of the NoI famously came to a head on the occasion of another killing of a head of state. After his December 1, 1963, speech to an audience of 700 at the Manhattan Center, Minister Malcolm X responded to a question about the November 22 assassination of John F. Kennedy. As he recounts in his *Autobiography*, "Without a second thought, I said what I honestly felt—that it was, as I saw it, a case of 'the chickens coming home to roost.' I said that the hate in white men had not stopped with the killing of defenseless black people, but that hate, allowed to spread unchecked, finally had struck down this country's Chief of State. I said it was the same thing as had happened with Medgar Evers, with Patrice Lumumba, with Madame Nhu's husband."[17] Malcolm X's comparison of the Kennedy murder to other violent attacks for which the U.S. government bears responsibility—including the Lumumba assassination—has achieved a sort of mythic status; no audio recording of it is known to exist (though the speech itself was published). As a result, the full context remains unavailable, though the existing reports, from the autobiography to the *New York Times*, are consistent in noting that he referred to Lumumba in his remarks.[18] When his famous description of the "chickens coming home to roost" is "taken out of context," as Malcolm X asserted it was, his larger analysis, one in which the Congo plays a central role, is obscured.[19] He may have adopted the expression from Michaux, who did so much to educate him about the Congo.[20]

Although Malcolm X's commentary on the Kennedy assassination violated instructions from Elijah Muhammad and resulted in his suspension from the NoI, he did not steer away from his "chickens coming home to roost" analysis. In a December 1963 interview with Louis Lomax during the suspension, he clarified: "I did not say that Kennedy's death was a reason for rejoicing. That is not what I meant at all. Rather, I meant that the death of Kennedy was the result of a long line of violent acts, the culmination of hate and suspicion and doubt in this country."[21] In April 1964, after his final split with the NoI, at a Militant Labor Forum event in New York, Malcolm X elaborated on his analysis that the chickens were coming home because of the actions of the United States in the Congo: "One of the greatest black leaders was Lumumba. Lumumba was the rightful ruler of the Congo. He was deposed with American aid. It was America, the State Department of this country, that brought Kasavubu to this country, interceded for him at the UN, used its power to make certain that Kasavubu would be seated as the rightful or recognized ruler of the Congo. And as soon as Kasavubu, with American support, became the ruler of the Congo, he went back to the Congo, and his first act upon returning home was to turn Lumumba over to Tshombe. So you can easily see whose hand it was behind the murder of Lumumba. And chickens come home to roost."[22] Instead of backtracking, he doubled down on his controversial comments in a manner that refocused attention on the Congo.

Less than a week after this speech, Malcolm X left the United States for his pilgrimage to Mecca and his second trip to Africa. (He first traveled to the continent in 1959 as a representative of the NoI.) Even without traveling to the Congo as the *New York Amsterdam News* initially reported he would, Malcolm X had a full itinerary that included Saudi Arabia, Lebanon, Egypt, Nigeria, Ghana, Morocco, and Algeria, with additional layovers in Liberia and Senegal.[23] At the outset, he saw this trip as an opportunity to connect with leaders of "Independent nations [that] could pressure 'justice' for 22 million Amer (Africans)."[24] Throughout his travels, he remained deeply invested in the Congo, and reminders of its importance were unavoidable. At the insistence of the Nigerian ambassador, he addressed a crowd at an Accra Press Club party: "Now, dance! Sing! But as you do—remember Mandela, remember Sobokwe [sic]! Remember Lumumba in his grave! Remember South Africans now in jail!"[25] In Algiers, the Ghanaian ambassador "related many of his experiences in the Congo at the time of Lumumba's death."[26] The week Malcolm X spent in Ghana is the best-known segment of this trip thanks to accounts of members of the country's large African American expatriate community and the groundbreaking scholarship of Kevin Gaines. During that week, Malcolm X established a branch of his secular OAAU, modeled on the Organization of African Unity (OAU), which he considered "the best thing that has ever happened on the African continent."[27]

Malcolm X returned to the United States on May 21, 1964, and soon thereafter "announced the formation of 'his new political group,' the Afro-American Freedom Fighters . . . [and] emphasized the right of Afro-Americans to defend themselves and to engage in guerilla warfare." Malcolm X sent letters offering military support to civil rights activists in Philadelphia, Mississippi, and St. Augustine, Florida. However, Malcolm X's nationalist allies "feared giving public exposure to organizing efforts for self-defense and guerilla warfare," so he formed the OAAU instead of a visibly paramilitary group. According to William W. Sales Jr., "These discussions, in fact, reflected the impact of Malcolm's interaction with the representatives of national liberation movements and guerilla armies during his trip to Africa."[28] In turn, a similar discourse was prominent in Malcolm X's extensive conversations about strategies for solidarity with the Congo.

From the start, the Congo and its struggles were central to the organization, which took Lumumba as a sort of patron saint. At its June 28, 1964, founding rally at the Audubon Ballroom, Malcolm X instructed members to read Lumumba's independence day "speech ['The greatest speech'] and tack it up over your door." (See Figure 9.1.) Malcolm X took this admiration a step farther, announcing at the rally that he and his wife Betty planned to name their fourth child in memory of "the greatest black man who ever walked the African continent."[29] Three days later, their daughter was born: Gamilah Lumumba, named for Gamal Abdel Nasser and Patrice Lumumba.[30] Malcolm X and Betty's gesture resonates with NoI members and others for whom the act of naming was a sacred assertion of freedom.

A few days after Gamilah Lumumba was born, the OAAU held its second rally. On that occasion, Malcolm X declared that "one of the worst slaps in the face that the black man in this country has received was when the State Department had the audacity last week to admit that American pilots were bombing defenseless Africans in the Congo." To make matters worse, he continued, African American leaders were "too busy talking about rowdyism on the subways" to address this international calamity.[31] Within a week of these remarks to the OAAU, Malcolm X went back to Africa on a four and a half month trip that would prove to be his final visit to the continent.

As the Congo crisis escalated, Malcolm X attended the July 17–21 OAU conference in Cairo and afterward reached out to Diallo Telli, the secretary general of the OAU: "Before Western Imperialists and Neocolonialists succeed by using racism to turn American completely into a Fascist State that can seriously threaten the peace and security of the entire world, The Organization of Afro-American Unity calls upon our elder brothers of the Organization of African Unity to demand that the United Nations Commission on Human Rights launch an immediate investigation into the inhuman destruction of Afro-American life and property which the present United States Government seems either unable or unwilling to protect."[32] This letter suggests Malcolm X's "considerable trust" in Telli, who served as Guinea's U.N. representative since independence in 1958. Telli may have met Malcolm X earlier in New York, where he had strong connections with African American activists including the Cultural Association for Women of African Heritage, who appealed to him on behalf of Lumumba in early 1961.[33]

*Figure 9.1* Malcolm X with Patrice Lumumba picture in background. Carlos Moore and Lebert Bethune, "L'heritage de Malcolm X," *La Vie Africaine* 57 (1965). (Courtesy of Melville J. Herskovits Library of African Studies, Northwestern University, Evanston, Illinois.)

Malcolm X remained in Egypt until September 1964, after which time he traveled to Palestine, Saudi Arabia, Kuwait, Lebanon, Ethiopia, Kenya, Tanzania, Nigeria, Ghana, Liberia, Guinea, and Algeria. These visits included meetings with heads of state ranging from PLO president Ahmed al-Shukairy to Guinea president Sekou Touré.[34] Although Malcolm X did not travel to the Congo, it remained a central topic for him and his African allies. In another letter to Telli, Malcolm X asserted: "We want the OAU to know that there are thousands of Afro-Americans who are ready to place ourselves at your service to help drive those South African murderers from the Congo. Many Afro-Americans are unemployed ex-servicemen who are experienced in every form of modern warfare and guerilla fighting. . . . We of this generation are fed up with colonialism, imperialism . . . and all other forms of racism . . . and we are ready to strike whatever blow is necessary to sweep the racists from this earth, at once and forever." Subsequently, the Information Bureau of the OAAU in Accra issued a statement endorsing Malcolm X's "scathing attack on the use of white mercenaries in the Congo" and his call for "Afro-American Troops" to take up the cause.[35]

Malcolm X's advocacy coincided with the height of the period that historian Georges Nzongola-Ntalaja terms, using Amilcar Cabral's analysis of the struggle against neocolonialism, the "second independence movement."[36] In the years following Lumumba's assassination, Tshombe, long the target of Malcolm X's ire, went into exile in Spain after his secessionist efforts in Katanga failed. Meanwhile Lumumbist rebels gained control of significant parts of the country and established their own government, which the United States actively sought to undermine. The extent of U.S. involvement became common knowledge in June 1964 after *Time* magazine reported on the use of American aircraft and pilots against the rebels. CIA documents from that month indicate the presence in country of seventy U.S. military advisors, along with ninety Belgians and ten Israelis.[37] As a result of their exposure, two pilots named by *Time* were pulled off the job but "headed back to Leopoldville to help train replacements—a dozen anti-Castro Cuban volunteers, most of them survivors of the Bay of Pigs fiasco."[38] And Tshombe, who the United States considered a "realist who wanted to restore civil order and . . . to unite the Congo and make it a viable, independent nation," returned to Congo as prime minister following the June 30, 1964, departure of U.N. troops.[39]

Between July and September 1964, the United States sent aircraft and other military devices along with personnel to aid a neocolonial counterinsurgency by white mercenaries from the apartheid states of South Africa and Southern Rhodesia in support of Tshombe's government. When the *New York Times* reported on U.S. military assistance in August, government officials discouraged the newspaper from editorializing critically on the subject, and the white press remained sympathetic toward the mercenaries. As it became more widely known that the United States was actively assisting the Congolese National Army in every way imaginable (with the possible exception of providing ground troops), the rebels, who took control of Stanleyville in early August, began restricting the movements of all foreigners living in and around the city. The initial provocation against the U.S. consulate occurred on August 5, the same day the United States began bombing Vietnam in response to the supposed Gulf of Tonkin attack.[40] Since Congolese "rebels blame[d] the air attacks on the United States, as opposed to Belgium," the entire U.S. consular corps (consisting of five members, at least four of whom were CIA officers under cover) was variously imprisoned or under house arrest until November.[41]

On August 14, 1964, Carl Rowan, the first African American director of the United States Information Agency (USIA), urged President Lyndon Johnson to make U.S. involvement "more palatable internationally."[42] Despite "substantial evidence . . . that the hostages may have been released in exchange for assurances that the air force would be grounded," the United States continued its air operations under the auspices of the CIA, whose supposedly secretive practices enabled the government to plausibly deny the entire campaign.[43] The false claim that the operation's Cuban exile pilots were hired and supervised by Congolese authorities was another U.S. strategy for claiming innocence. Malcolm X's speeches on the Congo consistently reference the critical alliance of anti-Castro Cubans and the United States, which was an important corrective to the government's misleading official account. Despite appeals from the OAU, the United States stood by its lie and continued its air campaign, which, according to more recent analysis based on declassified documents, was essential to its counterinsurgency efforts.[44]

The Congo remained prominent in the news during Malcolm X's months in Africa, where he was meeting with political figures like N. A. Welbeck, a cabinet minister in Nkrumah's government who recounted his time in "the Congo as Ghana's emissary to Patrice Lumumba."[45] Many of the figures Malcolm X met were actively supporting the struggles of Congolese rebels against Tshombe's illegitimate rule. By September 1964, the OAU, whose leaders Malcolm X had worked with in Cairo during the summer, was trying to negotiate a settlement between the rebels and the Tshombe regime. In early October, Malcolm X observed with admiration as President Nasser, with the support of other delegates, blocked Tshombe from attending the Conference of Non-Aligned States.[46]

On October 9, 1964, Malcolm X traveled from Kenya to recently unified Tanganyika and Zanzibar (which was renamed Tanzania at the end of the month). There, he was hosted by Mohamed Abdul Rahman Babu, a revolutionary Zanzibari government minister whom he had met at the July OAU meetings in Cairo. Babu, who quickly became one of Malcolm X's closest African allies, met Lumumba in Congo in 1958 and facilitated meetings for Malcolm X with Congolese rebels, African American expatriates, and Tanzanian dignitaries, including an initially reluctant President Julius Nyerere. After a scheduled three-minute October 13 meeting with Nyerere lasted three hours, Malcolm X decided to remain in Tanzania a few additional days.[47] Whether by fluke or not, his extended stay coincided with both a meeting of the Liberation Committee of the OAU and an October 15–16 summit between the presidents of Tanzania, Zambia, Uganda, and Kenya to discuss the Congo.[48] In any event, on an October 17 flight from Dar es Salaam to Nairobi, Malcolm X was seated between Uganda prime minister Milton Obote and Kenya president Jomo Kenyatta, who was chairing a series of OAU meetings about the Congo crisis.[49] Malcolm X noted the irony of Kenyatta, who was once considered a "monster" by the West, becoming "so highly respected" that he was selected "to moderate the conference that took place between [U.S.] Ambassador [to Kenya William] At[t]wood and Tom Kanza in Nairobi."[50] From his time in New York, Kanza, who represented the Congolese rebels, was as beloved by African American activists as he was reviled by U.S. diplomats.[51]

Malcolm X and Telli spent a great deal of time together in Nairobi, meeting on a daily basis from October 19 to 21. Telli "was very enthusiastic in praise of" Malcolm X's work and invited him to Guinea.[52] On one occasion, after finding that the restaurant "'crowded us' too much," the two men reconvened in Telli's room, where they ate and had a private conversation.[53] It seems probable that they would have followed up on Malcolm X's recent offer to recruit African Americans to fight on behalf of the Congo rebels. Malcolm X and Telli met again in Addis Ababa from October 27 to 29. The precise purpose of Malcolm X's visit to Ethiopia, where the OAU was headquartered, is unclear, and Marika Sherwood speculates that he may have made this trip specifically to meet with Telli, who had just completed a 17-country tour of the continent.[54] In November, Malcolm X made his first trip to Guinea. After meeting Telli in the airport on his arrival on November 9, Malcolm X stayed in the Conakry home of President Touré, who had two months earlier hosted Student Nonviolent Coordinating Committee (SNCC) activists including Fannie Lou Hamer.[55] Moving in these circles among activists and politicians, it would have been impossible for Malcolm X to avoid conversations about the Congo and the kinds of support African Americans could offer. As the Congo crisis intensified, he left Africa for Geneva on November 16, traveling soon thereafter to London and Paris. On his final night in Paris, November 23, 1964, at a meeting of the *Présence Africaine* group, Malcolm X strongly criticized progressive voters for supporting Lyndon Johnson for president at a time when "he had troops invading the Congo and South Vietnam!"[56] For Malcolm X, the Congo continued to serve as the representative example of criminal foreign policy at a time when Vietnam was beginning to dominate—with seeming permanence—popular consciousness of U.S. imperialism. Malcolm X, like Du Bois, worked to make sure that imperialism was understood as part of a U.S. regime of antiblack racism and domination.

A Violent Harvest

Malcolm X's assertion was prescient. The following day, November 24, 1964, the United States undertook its largest direct Congo operation when it airlifted Belgian paratroopers into Stanleyville to attack Congolese nationalists, supposedly in order to rescue approximately 2,000 hostages, including 58 U.S. citizens.[57] The day of the operation was the same day that Malcolm X, its most forceful critic, returned to the United States. He lost no time in offering his analysis. After greeting family, friends, and supporters, he told reporters at the newly renamed John F. Kennedy Airport: "Congolese have been killed year after year after year, and what ever the United States gets in the Congo, she is getting what she asked for; the Congo killings is [sic] like the chickens coming home to roost."[58] The *New York Times* reported Malcolm X's comments "that the killing of white hostages in Stanleyville by Congolese rebels was the responsibility of President Johnson because of his financial support of 'Moise Tshombe's hired killers.'"[59] Although the deaths of white Americans like missionary Paul Carlson captured public attention, as evident by his appearance on the cover of the December 4 issue of *Time* magazine, Malcolm X considered the violence visited upon white Americans—whether in Stanleyville or Dallas—to be the direct result of government policies, not an abstract form of retribution. Malcolm X was relentless in attacking "the most criminal operation that has ever been carried on by a so-called civilized government since history was recorded!"[60]

Malcolm X's view was widely shared by African Americans, even those who did not share his admiration of Lumumba or disapproved of his vehemence. Twelve hours before the Belgian invasion, six leaders of established civil rights organizations—Martin Luther King Jr., James Farmer, Dorothy Height, A. Philip Randolph, Roy Wilkins, and Whitney Young—wrote to President Johnson and Secretary of State Dean Rusk asking them to discontinue U.S. support for the Tshombe regime.[61] King spoke from Europe in early December about the "need at this time for a withdrawal of all foreign troops and all mercenaries" from the Congo. At a press conference on the eve of the

Nobel Peace Prize award ceremony, King acknowledged, as Malcolm X had on the Barry Gray Show, that "the Congo situation has a great deal of history, as we know, and what we see now in the Congo is the harvest, a violent harvest, that came into being as a result of seeds of injustice, seeds of neglect and seeds of man's inhumanity to man planted across the years." While King was clear that he did not "see a military solution to the problem in the Congo," he supported the involvement of the OAU and the U.N.[62] Even Eartha Kitt, a performer, who, though active in the civil rights movement, did not ally herself with Malcolm X, surprised Michael Hoyt, the U.S. consul and a former hostage in Stanleyville, during a talk show appearance during which she "broke into a litany of how it was another example of whites killing blacks." Malcolm X effectively framed African American discourse on the Congo as a transnational racial narrative.[63]

Following the events of November 24, Malcolm X stepped up his staunch criticism of U.S. intervention. Having returned from Africa for the final time, Malcolm X—like Williams, Sheppard, Washington, and others—increasingly focused on determining a role for African Americans in the Congo, albeit a much more militant one than his predecessors had envisioned. On December 3, 1964, David Du Bois sent Malcolm X a copy of a cable that Nasir El-Din Mahmoud, the president of the Executive Committee of the American Muslim Student Association in Cairo, sent to President Nasser.[64] The cable, dated November 28 (the same day as Malcolm X's appearance on the Barry Gray Show), opens with an expression of "deepest appreciation of and full accord in the condemnation of the U.S.-Belgian imperialist intervention in the landing of Belgian paratroopers in the Congo." On behalf of the group, Nasir El-Din, who spent a great deal of time with Malcolm X in Egypt, offered to assist "our brother, El Hajj Shabazz (Malcolm X) who was recently granted the authority of spiritual leadership of the American Muslim community by Alazhar, in assuring you that there are many U.S. military trained young Afro-American[s] that if equipped and supplied, are ready to volunteer today to take up arms beside our Congolese brothers in their just struggle against U.S.-Belgian, Armed, British Assisted Aggression."[65] The cable, which was covered in the Egyptian press, further expresses solidarity with demonstrators who protested the November 24 invasion in front of the U.S. Embassy in Cairo. In response to the cable, Malcolm X wrote David Du Bois that he would like to bring Nasir El-Din's group, whose plans include having African Americans fight in the Congo, under the umbrella of the Muslim Mosque Inc. (MMI).[66]

On November 29, one day after the radio debate and the cable, Malcolm X spoke at his homecoming OAAU rally in New York and expressed his support for direct action, not only by inviting a Ghanaian student to announce an anti-Tshombe protest planned for the U.N., but also by publicly proposing that African Americans volunteer to serve as counter-counterinsurgency forces in the Congo:

> Many of us are vets, we've had all kind of experience.... We might put on a drive right here in Harlem to raise up some black mercenaries to take over there to show them what to do.... Okay, we've got black people who can fly planes—we've been flying them for the man. Instead of you sitting around here driving a bus, remember how you used to fly a plane for him, get on over there and get with it on the right side. If they can send white ones against black ones, we can recruit and send black ones against white ones. I frankly believe that it would be most exciting. I know a whole lot of Afro-Americans would go for free—would go for fun. We don't need any money, we just want to get even.

Malcolm X anticipated that the media would use his proposal for sensational fearmongering: "As long as there are white people going over there shooting black people, nothing is said—they glorify them. But when you and I start talking like we want to do the same thing to some of them, then we're *fanatics*, we're *bloodthirsty*."[67] An FBI report asserting that Malcolm X "said black men should send black mercenaries to help the African people in their fight for freedom and that this rally 'was all for this'" indicates that he correctly anticipated the concern his remarks would elicit.[68] Seeking to maintain the momentum, Malcolm X announced that the next OAAU rally, on December 13, would be dedicated to the Congo, with historian Earl Raymond Sweeting scheduled to speak.

In the interim, Malcolm X traveled to England to participate in the December 3 Oxford Union Debate. The first half of his speech—per the debate topic, a defense of extremism—features extensive commentary on the Congo: "I am for the kind of extremism that the freedom fighters in the Stanleyville regime are able to display against these hired killers, who are actually using some of my tax dollars which I have to pay up in the United States, to finance that operation over there."[69] His address uses the *Daily Express* newspaper's morning coverage of the Congo as a point of departure, and Stephen Tuck contends that "The reason he devoted more than a third of his speech to the Congo, though, was that it reinforced his argument about the media's creation of extremist images."[70] Malcolm X had expressed concern about misrepresentations of Africa since his time with the NoI. And Tuck correctly notes a pivot whereby the media became an important lens onto the Congo crisis for Malcolm X. However, his interest in the Congo was not purely a rhetorical ploy or a media critique, but rather a product of an unfolding crisis that piqued his staunch antiracist and anticolonial indignation. Malcolm X admired Lumumba, who was his same age (Lumumba was a mere six weeks his junior), and wished to support his followers in Stanleyville whose political commitments he shared. As for so many other diaspora activists and intellectuals across generations, his interest was a part of his education, his politics, and his travels, and the *Daily Express* gave him a way to talk about the breadth of international complicity in the Congo crisis in a prominent forum.[71]

*Time* magazine, which defamed Lumumba as a "wild leftist demagogue" in the same issue that venerated Carlson, is another example of the media Malcolm X had in mind. Indeed much of the rhetoric seems to be responding directly to the December 4 issue of the magazine, which defends the South African "mercenaries" as "no more mercenary—and far less brutal—than the African soldiers on either side of the Congolese civil war," and insultingly and inaccurately describes the deaths of twenty Belgians as "deliberate savagery reminiscent of the Nazi death camps." *Time* concludes with an obstinate dismissal of history, "In the 'nonaligned' and Communist worlds, though, a well-organized propaganda effort made it sound as if the Americans and Belgians, not the savage Simbas, had committed the atrocities of Stanleyville. Whatever Belgium's guilt in the past, whatever the U.S.'s mistakes, it was a dizzying and infuriating perversion of the reality."[72] Such a powerful media campaign was the backdrop to Malcolm X's unyielding criticism of the press in the coming weeks for making "the murderers look like saints and the victims like criminals . . . and indeed the devil look like an angel and angels like the devil."[73]

Malcolm X continued to denounce media distortions at a December 12 speech to the Domestic Peace Corps: "The world press projected the scene in the Congo as one wherein the people who were the victims of the crime were made to appear as if they were the actual criminals and the ones who were the actual criminals were made to appear as if they were the actual victims. The press did this, and by the press doing this, it made it almost impossible for the public to analyze the Congo situation with clarity and keep it in its proper perspective."[74] At the December 13 OAAU rally, he planned to show a film about the Congo, but technical difficulties prevented the screening. Activist and comedian Dick Gregory filled the time followed by Malcolm X who emphasized: "Right now, in the Congo, defenseless villages are being bombed, black women and children and babies are being blown to bits by airplanes. Where do these airplanes come from? The United States, the U-n-i-t-e-d S-t-a-t-e-s." After carefully highlighting the role of the United States and the hypocrisy that privileges white lives over those of the Congolese, he again turned to the press: "If you'll notice, as long as the blacks in the Congo were being slaughtered on a mass scale, there was no outcry. But as soon as the lives of a few whites were involved, the whole world became in an uproar. What caused the world to become involved in an uproar? The press. The press made it appear that 2,000 white people are being held hostage. And they started crying in big headlines if any of them were killed. Now the Africans didn't kill any of them, the brothers there in Stanleyville didn't kill any of them until the paratroopers landed."[75] Subsequent scholarship corroborates Malcolm X's analysis that the landing of the paratroopers, not the actions of the rebels or even the white mercenary ground troops, sparked the killings.[76] Over the course of the New York rally, he called out the *Daily Express* by name and ended by making it clear that this conversation was ongoing. He promised to go even "deeper into the Congo question" next week.[77]

In the intervening week, Malcolm X reiterated his criticism of the media at a Harvard Law School Forum on "The African Revolution and Its Impact on the American Negro": "The headlines were used to mislead the public, [to create] wrong images. In the Congo, planes were bombing Congolese villages, yet Americans read that (How do they say it?) American-trained anti-Castro Cuban pilots were bombing rebel strongholds. These pilots were actually dropping bombs on villages with women and children. But because the tags 'American-trained' and 'anti-Castro Cubans' were applied, the bombing was legal. Anyone against Castro is all right."[78] The involvement of anti-Castro Cubans in the CIA operation serves as an acknowledgment that the Congo was a Cold War battleground shaped, in part, by a fear of "a communist dominated black Africa."[79] Malcolm X's emphasis on Cuban participation enabled a foundational critique of U.S. imperialism and its investment in the geopolitical importance of the Congo, understanding that a nationalist victory was critical to the liberation of the entire African continent. He strategically insisted that Africa not be lost in the Cold War conversation by repeatedly drawing connections to the more prominent Cuban theater and, increasingly, to Vietnam.

Malcolm X acknowledged the importance of independent autonomous African states to African Americans, not exclusively as a matter of racial pride, but also as a provider of political support in international bodies like the U.N.[80] Malcolm X knowingly addressed criticism that considered African liberation irrelevant to the United States:

> What effect does all this have on Afro-Americans? What effect will it have on race relations in this country? In the U.N. at this moment, Africans are using more uncompromising language and are heaping hot fire upon America as the racist and neo-colonial power par excellence. African statesmen have never used this language before. These statesmen are beginning to connect the criminal, racist acts practiced in the

Congo with similar acts in Mississippi and Alabama. The Africans are pointing out that the white American government—not all white people—has shown just as much disregard for lives wrapped in black skin in the Congo as it shows for lives wrapped in black skin in Mississippi and in Alabama.[81]

Malcolm X would, during the coming months, speak in detail about the direct bearing that African national liberation struggles had on African Americans. As Malcolm X became more deeply involved in the Congo, he logically returned to his explanation of the chickens coming home to roost. His remarks remained volatile enough that the respondent to his Harvard speech, an African American university administrator, felt compelled to express his disappointment at hearing Malcolm X repeat his characterization of the Kennedy assassination "without real qualification and rather gleefully."[82] For Malcolm X, however, events in Stanleyville only affirmed the centrality of the Congo to his analysis.

Malcolm X provocatively seemed to repeat his "chickens" comments most frequently for white or racially integrated audiences (rather than in OAAU speeches), to those who might be most surprised by the return of the chickens: a December 1963 interview with African American journalist Louis Lomax whose work appeared frequently in white publications; an April 1964 Militant Labor Forum; a November 1964 press conference at JFK airport; a December 1964 Harvard University event; and a January 1965 interview with Jack Barnes and Barry Sheppard for the *Young Socialist* in response to a question about "the role of the U.S. in the Congo":

> Probably there is no better example of criminal activity against an oppressed people than the role the U.S. has been playing in the Congo, through her ties with Tshombe and the mercenaries. You can't overlook the fact that Tshombe gets his money from the U.S. The money he uses to hire these mercenaries—these paid killers imported from South Africa—comes from the United States. The pilots that fly these planes have been trained by the U.S. The bombs themselves that are blowing apart the bodies of women and children come from the U.S. So I can only view the role of the United States in the Congo as a criminal role. And I think the seeds she is sowing in the Congo she will have to harvest. The chickens that she has turned loose over there have got to come home to roost.[83]

Just as Tshombe remained an integral figure in Malcolm X's understanding of neocolonialism and a yardstick of international attitudes, the "chickens" allegory remained central to his analysis of U.S. foreign policy. By continuing to use the language that got him expelled from the NoI, while sharing King's invocation of a "harvest," Malcolm X implies that the deaths of Americans in Stanleyville were only the continuation of a much larger ongoing blowback. For white audiences, his analysis served as a particular kind of cautionary tale. While his original statement on the Kennedy assassination is a famous marker of Malcolm X's break with the NoI, its core analysis, framed through an ongoing critique of U.S. actions in the Congo, remains, as Gaines notes, "largely ignored."[84] Shortly after Malcolm X's assassination, *Muhammad Speaks* reprinted an editorial by Julian Mayfield, one of his strongest allies among the African American community in Ghana, from the November 25, 1964, *Ghanaian Times*, demonstrating that his analysis of the Congo crisis in the wake of Stanleyville extended from his radical comrades in Ghana to his former colleagues in the NoI.[85]

## Mississippi in Disguise

During the final months of his life, Malcolm X not only expanded his commitment to the Congo, but also became more directly involved with the Black Freedom movement in the South. On December 20, 1964, he spoke at two events with Hamer, who was visiting New York on behalf of the Mississippi Freedom Democratic Party's efforts to block the seating in Congress of the white representatives of Mississippi's segregated Democratic Party. First, at a Harlem church event with Malcolm X and the SNCC Freedom Singers, Hamer compared the U.S. government's policies in Mississippi and Congo: "We have made an appeal for the president of the United States and the attorney general to please protect us in Mississippi. And I can't understand how it's out of their power to protect people in Mississippi. They can't do that, but when a white man is killed in the Congo, they send people there." Hamer, who had recently returned from Guinea, challenges the geography of American racism, describing Northern cities as "Mississippi in disguise," arguing, like Malcolm X, that their struggle is not local or regional, but rather national and international.[86]

Hamer's speech was followed by the Freedom Singers, who performed "Oginga Odinga," a song written on the occasion of the Kenyan leader's visit to Atlanta, Georgia.[87] In his remarks, Malcolm X acknowledged the song and pointed out the importance of Odinga (whom he met in Kenya in October), Kenyatta, and their Mau Mau rebellion: "if you analyze closely those words, I think you'll have the key to how to straighten the situation out in Mississippi.... In Mississippi we need a Mau Mau. In Alabama we need a Mau Mau. In Georgia we need a Mau Mau. Right here in Harlem, in New York City, we need a Mau Mau." Malcolm X was inspired by the song and by

Hamer's analysis: "some people wonder, well, what has Mississippi got to do with Harlem? It isn't actually Mississippi; it's America. America is Mississippi." He invited Hamer and the SNCC Freedom Singers to the Audubon Ballroom that same evening to "let some people hear you singing about Oginga Odinga and Kenyatta and Lumumba."[88]

While Hamer and Malcolm X represent distinct geographic and political positions, both made efforts to internationalize the Black Freedom movement. While both deploy the full rhetorical weight of "Mississippi," their strategic engagements suggest that neither of them saw Mississippi, or the South more generally, as a simple symbol. Similarly, both understood from their recent travels to Africa that the Congo was not a one-dimensional synecdoche for the African continent or European colonialism. For Malcolm X, the Congo was a specific site in his increasingly detailed critical geography of imperialism. During the Audubon forum with Hamer, he analyzed the geopolitical importance of the Congo as,

> the gateway to Southwest Africa [Namibia], Southern Rhodesia [Zimbabwe], Basutoland [Lesotho], Swaziland, and South Africa . . . which is so strategically located geographically that if it were to fall into the hands of a real dyed-in-the-wool African nationalist, he could then make it possible for African soldiers to train in the Congo for the purpose of invading Angola. When they invade Angola, that means Angola must fall, because there are more Africans than there are Portuguese, and they just couldn't control Angola any longer. And if the Congo fell into good hands, other than Tshombe, then it would mean that Angola would fall, Southern Rhodesia would fall, Southwest Africa would fall and South Africa would fall. And that's the only way they would fall.

With "one of the best freedom fighters in America today" beside him, Malcolm X saw an opportunity to expand on the global dimensions of the struggle for racial justice by staking the liberation of the Portuguese colonies and the apartheid states of southern Africa on the Congo. Here, he recognizes the centrality of the Congo to the entire African diaspora: "You can't understand what is going on in Mississippi if you don't understand what is going on in the Congo. And you can't really be interested in what's going on in Mississippi if you're not also interested in what's going on in the Congo. They're both the same. The same interests are at stake. The same sides are drawn up, the same schemes are at work in the Congo that are at work in Mississippi."[89] The Mississippi connection was not an occasional reference for the benefit of Hamer, but was an integral part of Malcolm X's discourse to audiences throughout the world. Malcolm X frames the connections between the Congo and Mississippi as part of a broader interlocking network of colonial, neocolonial, and apartheid regimes. While his rhetoric is part of a tradition that includes Wells, Pickens, and Hughes, all of whom compared the United States to the Congo, his interrogation of the relationship between domestic and imperial regimes derives directly from modern African politics. Such comparisons are part of a strategy for developing political alliances whose lineage includes the 1955 Bandung Conference—which Malcolm X increasingly referenced in his speeches—and continues through the Non-Aligned Movement, the U.N., and the OAU, which were dependent on the power of newly independent African states.[90]

On January 1, 1965, Malcolm X found himself discussing the Congo with another group of visiting Mississippi activists to whom he explained the folly of international support for Tshombe's return to power: "It's like saying Jesse James is the only one can run the bank. Therefore you should let Jesse James run the bank; and the only reason the bank is in trouble is because Jesse James already was in the bank."[91] For Malcolm X, Tshombe was an outlaw servant of powerful economic interests who sought to preserve a colonial regime in many of the same ways that James was invested in the restoration of former Confederates to political power in the postbellum United States. Malcolm X uses American cultural references to explain the Congo, while offering a critique of an iconic American "outlaw" whose character was well known in Africa because of his frequent appearances in Hollywood films.[92]

The transnational connections that Malcolm X expressed to representatives of the Southern movement were consistent with ideas being articulated by African U.N. delegates, who strongly identified with Mississippi.[93] Malcolm X himself noted approvingly during a December 27 interview that African envoys were beginning "to link what's happening in the Congo with what's happening in Mississippi."[94] Within a couple of days, the *New York Times* picked up on Malcolm X's assertion "that he had prepared the political groundwork in the capitals of Africa for the recent concerted attack on American 'racism' in the debate on the Congo in the United Nations. . . . The spokesmen of some African states acted precisely within the framework of these recommendations last month in the Congo debate at the United Nations. They accused the United States with being indifferent to the fate of the blacks and cited as evidence the attitude of the United States Government toward the civil rights struggle in Mississippi."[95] Articles like this fueled the public association of African U.N. representatives with Malcolm X, who was frequently asked about his role "in the recent debate on the Congo in the United Nations." *Muhammad Speaks* provided even more extensive coverage of the African delegates' leadership in debates at the U.N. about the Congo, a striking confluence of opinion around a critical issue.[96] In a January 28, 1965, radio interview, Malcolm X insisted on the autonomy of the African delegates: "I have never taken responsibility or credit, you might say, for the stance taken by the African nations. The African nations today are represented by intelligent statesmen." Still, he uses the occasion to describe racism as a global system: "Now the African nations are speaking out and linking the problem of racism in Mississippi with the problem of racism in the Congo, and also the problem of racism in South Vietnam. It's all racism. It's all part of the vicious racist system that the Western powers have used to continue to degrade and exploit and oppress the people in Africa and Asia and Latin America during recent centuries."[97] Ultimately, Malcolm X argued, the relationship between the Congo and Mississippi must be understood as not simply similar or parallel, but rather structurally contingent.

The connective tissue across this global landscape is the American racial empire, and Malcolm X focuses his attention on the role of the United States in counterinsurgency operations in the Congo. At a January 7, 1965, Militant Labor Forum event, he explains: "In the Congo, the People's Republic of the Congo, headquartered at Stanleyville, fought a war for freedom against Tshombe, who is an agent for Western imperialism—and by Western imperialism I mean that which is headquartered in the United States, in the State Department." Here, Malcolm X deftly acknowledges the illegitimacy of neocolonial state formation as he distinguishes between the "Congo" and the "People's Republic" in order to posit a legitimate alternative to the political apparatus recognized by the United States: "The struggle is still going on, and America's man, Tshombe, is still losing."[98] During the question-and-answer period, Malcolm X conveys a conversation he had with a "very highly placed African official" about the aggressive lobbying tactics of the U.S. government on behalf of the Tshombe regime. This unnamed official, Malcolm X recounts, "told me that one of the most powerful men in the State Department jumped on an airplane and followed an African leader all the way home over a year ago, begging him to use his influence to get other African heads of state to accept Tshombe as the prime minister of the Congo."[99] As with the refusal of Nasser and others to permit Tshombe to attend the Conference of Non-Aligned States, newly independent African nations were unwilling to bow to U.S. pressure.

Intense American interest in the Congo was premised on the government intelligence community's belief that it represented "the key 'domino' in Africa."[100] Throughout 1964, there was increasing fear that the Congo could become "another Vietnam," where the United States was on the brink of a full-scale ground war.[101] U.S. actions in Vietnam deeply concerned Malcolm X; however, he refused to allow it to displace the Congo, emphasizing instead shared experiences of both U.S. imperialism and resistance to it, providing U.S. activists with "a powerful example in the young *Simbas* in the Congo and the young fighters in South Vietnam."[102] Malcolm X continued to insist on the relevance of the Congo on this global landscape: "when you find a person who has a knowledge of things of the world today, he realizes that what happens in South Vietnam can affect him if he's living on St. Nicholas Avenue, or what's happening in the Congo affects his situation on Eighth Avenue or Seventh Avenue or Lenox Avenue." In order to become educated in the way that Malcolm X suggests, the internationalist imperative is clear for groups like the OAAU "to try and broaden the scope and even the reading habits of most of our people."[103]

As Malcolm X continued to compare the Congo to Harlem, he was getting more directly involved with the Southern movement. In February 1965, he traveled to Alabama. African American Congo activism may have come full circle when Malcolm X criticized the Johnson administration's support for Tshombe in front of 3,000 students at Tuskegee Institute, recalling the importance of HBCUs as sites of Congo education for figures like Williams and Sheppard. His Tuskegee audience was especially interested in the Congo, as evident by the inclusion of his Congo commentary as part of a short excerpt of his remarks that were printed in the student newspaper. In Selma, during the same trip, he spoke to activists and met with Coretta Scott King about possible collaborations a few weeks before the "Bloody Sunday" assault by Governor George Wallace's state troopers on unarmed protestors on the Edmund Pettus Bridge. Malcolm X planned to attend a Mississippi Freedom Democratic Party rally in Jackson, Mississippi, on February 19, 1965, but postponed the visit after the bombing of his home.[104]

As Malcolm X ventured into the heart of the Southern movement, he continued to travel abroad to share his reports from Selma with an international audience in Europe.[105] The Congo was never far from his mind. In London, the *West Indian Gazette* (founded by Claudia Jones, who had died a month earlier) reported that during a February 8 address to the Committee of African Organisations (CAO), Malcolm X said, "He was happy that Africans were realising that 'the monster' operating in the Congo was the same as that oppressing US Negroes." His speech inspired the CAO to adopt a resolution in support of the Congolese people and in opposition to Tshombe.[106] During that week in England, an interviewer asked Malcolm X "if he was involved in recruitment for revolution in Afrika. He declined comment."[107]

On February 11, 1965, Malcolm X spoke to a meeting organized by the African Society at the London School of Economics about press accounts describing "the pilots that are dropping the bombs on these babies as 'American-trained, anti-Castro Cuban pilots.' As long as they are American-trained, this is supposed to put the stamp of approval on it, because America is your ally. As long as they are anti-Castro Cubans, since Castro is supposed to be a monster and these pilots are against Castro, anybody else they are against is also all right." After forcefully using Cold War politics to frame public discourse around the Congo, Malcolm X highlighted the involvement of the United States and criticized the media for maintaining white support for military intervention: "after the press had gotten the whites all whipped up, then anything that the Western powers wanted to do against these defenseless, innocent freedom fighters from the eastern provinces of the Congo, the white public went along with it." With his audience responding to his speech with calls of "It's true," Malcolm X extended his criticism of racial discourse to an economic and political analysis of the Congo as the linchpin to the liberation of the entire continent: "the Congo is so situated strategically, geographically, that if it falls into the hands of a genuine African government that has the hopes and aspirations of the African people at heart, then it will be possible for the Africans to put their own soldiers right on the border of Angola and wipe the Portuguese out of there overnight."[108] The fate of Portugal's African empire will be determined by the struggle in the Congo.

At a critical moment during the London School of Economics speech, Malcolm X sharply describes how "American planes with American bombs being piloted by American-trained pilots, dropping American bombs on Black people, Black babies, Black children, destroying them completely—which is nothing but mass murder—goes absolutely unnoticed. . . ."[109] Then, at this exact moment, the transcript published in both *February 1965: The Final Speeches* and *Malcolm X Talks to Young People* is interrupted by a "gap" in the source tape.[110] When the transcript resumes, he continues speaking about the Congo, though the length of the gap, which would reveal the extent of his comments if not their substance, is unknown. The remaining traces ensure that his analysis of the Congo is not entirely "unnoticed," but the historical record is sadly diminished. Such inconsistencies are frequent within the corpus of transcribed Malcolm X speeches. A similar lacuna is reported in the transcript of his remarks to the Oxford Union that Steve Clark includes in *Malcolm X Talks to Young People*. "The first part of Malcolm X's remarks is not available," but Clark notes that press reports indicate he spoke about the Congo.[111] Clark's edition is missing more than half of Malcolm's address; of the missing 3,000 words, two-thirds regard the Congo. Ambar's *Malcolm X at Oxford Union* (2014) valuably appends the full speech, thereby restoring a critical chapter in the history of his subject's engagement with the Congo.[112]

A similar gap appears in a transcript of a speech Malcolm X delivered a few days later on February 14, 1965. Less than seven hours after the early-morning firebombing of his home in Queens, Malcolm X flew to Detroit, where he delivered an especially extraordinary address, as he often seemed to do on visits to the city.[113] At Ford Auditorium, he spoke about the bombing campaign in the Congo in deeply personal terms on the same day that his home had been bombed: "they're able to take these hired killers, put them in American planes with American bombs, and drop them on African villages, blowing to bits black men, black women, black children, black babies, and you black people sitting over here cool like it doesn't even involve you. You're a fool. [applause] They'll do it to them today, and do it to you tomorrow. Because you and I and they are all the same." Malcolm understood the violence visited on black families in the Congo did involve him. However, the version of that speech that appears in George Breitman's *Malcolm X Speaks* excludes this passage and effectively erases the Congo. Of the thirty-six references in the original speech, thirty-three are excised. Breitman's only explanation for such editorial liberties is his general acknowledgment that he "omitted sections that were repeated or paraphrased in other speeches."[114] Some of the cuts are attributed to a gap in the source tape, but Breitman eliminates, without explanation, additional passages on colonialism and Bandung, as well as several hundred words about Malcolm meeting Nasser, Nyerere, Kenyatta, Azikiwe, Nkrumah, and Touré, and praising the Mau Mau in Kenya.[115] From this lengthy cut, Breitman bizarrely preserves two sentences alluding to the treatment of Jews in Nazi Germany, but completely changes its meaning by delinking it from the Congo. Two-thirds of the material that Breitman excised appear in Clark's *The Final Speeches: February 1965*, which restores more than 2,800 of the 4,200 total words that Breitman cut from throughout the speech. However, Clark's edition has its own extended eight-minute "gap" (nearly 1,400 words) of commentary about the Congo which is included, with published variants noted, as an appendix to the present volume.[116] These publications substantially diminish the significance of the Congo in this speech, which is one of Malcolm X's most comprehensive commentaries on the subject delivered hours after his home was bombed and a week before his assassination. A restored version of this speech can facilitate an appreciation of his unique analysis and more broadly of the importance of the Congo to Malcolm X at a critical juncture in his life.

Malcolm X began this speech by acknowledging its unusualness—he wasn't wearing a tie and had taken some medicine to treat the effects of having spent the winter night outside in his pajamas. Malcolm X was clearly shaken by the violent attack on his family. Emotion, fatigue, informality, and infirmity could have shaped his Detroit remarks, which are exceptionally candid with regard to his organizing activities. During the speech, he sharply criticizes African American expatriates in Africa for their "tendency . . . to, what I call lollygag" and for "partying." Such behavior, Malcolm X believed, stood in sharp contrast to other exiled diaspora groups who remained focused on their homelands. In response, "during the summer, when I went back to Africa, I was able in each country that I visited, to get the Afro-American community together and organize them and make them aware of their responsibility to those of us who are still here in the lion's den." These summer meetings provided an impetus for the formation of OAAU chapters throughout the world. Malcolm X "organized a group in Paris and just within a very short time they had grown into a well-organized unit," which was significant enough that French authorities had prevented him from entering the country less than a week earlier.[117]

One day after the Detroit speech, Malcolm X was back in New York City to deliver an address to an OAAU rally at the Audubon Ballroom about the "worldwide revolution going on." The revolution did not single out the United States, Belgium, or another European regime as its target, but aimed at the entire "international Western power structure." Malcolm X criticized the failure of President Johnson to protect Alabama civil rights activists whom he had met earlier in the month, explaining, "Old Lyndon is all tied up in South Vietnam and the Congo and other places, but he's not minding his business in Mississippi, in Alabama."[118]

On February 16, Malcolm X presented another detailed account of the role of the United States in the Congo—its bombing campaign, its support of Tshombe, and its media misrepresentations—at Corn Hill Methodist Church in Rochester, New York.[119] Through the last week of his life, at a moment of profound concern for the safety of his family, the Congo remained a defining, strategic issue. As he insisted that African Americans reframe their demands as "human" rather than "civil" rights and that they address them through the U.N. and other international bodies like the OAU, Malcolm X understood the necessity of strong independent, progressive African states.[120] The ascension of Tshombe and his ilk to leadership positions throughout the African continent directly threatened to undermine, if not eliminate, what Malcolm X considered the vanguard of the Black Freedom movement in the United States, namely its internationalization.

## Malcolm's African Project

Unfortunately, Malcolm X is often misrepresented as a figure whose career is characterized by "symbolic action" and "polemic." Goldman contends that Malcolm X "was a revolutionary without an army, or an ideology, or any clear sense of how the revolution was to be waged and what it would do if it won."[121] Contrary to Goldman's assessment, Malcolm X established the OAAU with Lumumba as its guiding light because he identified the need for a militant practice. His involvement with the Congo was a practical commitment to a revolutionary agenda, not a polemic. Malcolm X understood the militant history of African American involvement in Africa. At the OAAU's second rally, in July 1964, he insisted that the bombings in the Congo were "worse than what the Italians did to our brothers in Ethiopia."[122] This comparison is striking because the father of Malcolm X's friend Adam Clayton Powell Jr. invited Emperor Haile Selassie to "Abyssinian Baptist Church in 1936 to plead for help in obtaining African American fighter pilots" after Italy's invasion of Ethiopia.[123] Malcolm X was aware of the historic Harlem church's connection to Africa through the younger Powell, who attended the Bandung Conference and introduced him to Algeria president Ahmed Ben Bella in 1962. He knew about Abyssinian Baptist's connections to Ethiopia, since during a June 1963 address to the congregation, an audience member pointed out a cross that Selassie had given to the church.[124]

In 1964, Malcolm X spent time in Ethiopia, which was the headquarters of the OAU. He may have recalled Ethiopia's modern history when he wrote a letter to the MMI about plans to recruit African Americans to fight on behalf of the nationalists against Tshombe's mercenaries.[125] Given the necessarily secretive nature of such an enterprise, it is impossible to determine the extent of the plan. However, Malcolm X definitely had personal contact with Congolese "liberation fighters" who fought against Tshombe's white mercenaries, and there is otherwise quite a bit of evidence that the plan he mentioned publicly at the November 29, 1964, homecoming rally of the OAAU was already under way.[126]

A week before that rally, while in France, Malcolm X met with Carlos Moore about organizing an OAAU chapter in Paris. Moore, whose outspoken criticism of the Cuban revolution places him at odds with many African American radicals, remains a controversial figure and an unreliable, albeit intriguing, source. However, he did help coordinate the U.N. demonstration in February 1961, worked with Kanza in New York in 1960 and 1961, and collaborated with Malcolm X during the final months of his life.[127] The two men shared a desire to support the Stanleyville rebels, and what we know of their conversations suggests that Malcolm X solicited Moore as part of a plan to provide African American military aid to the Simbas. In late 1964, Malcolm X corresponded with Kojo Amoo-Gottfried, president of the CAO in London, noting somewhat obliquely that Moore, Sylvia Boone, and Sandy Bethune, all "can be depended on in this work that we are trying to do for the benefit of our people who have been scattered all over the earth and those who are still in our African homeland."[128] Bethune attended the Oxford debate and, Ambar points out, there was some unaccounted-for time during that trip that could have been spent politicking.[129] Writing more than forty years after the events, Moore provides few details about "Malcolm's daring project":

We saw eye to eye. So when he requested my help in a wide-ranging plan to assist the Congolese rebels, I agreed.

I had been in France only a month and a half when I decided to involve myself with Malcolm's daring project. Despite my own fragile position there, I began recruiting volunteers with military and medical expertise to assist the Lumumbist insurrection, fully aware that I was opening myself to extreme danger.[130]

Moore describes his organizing efforts in the French Caribbean community: "the French secret police . . . had been monitoring my recruitment activities for Malcolm's movement among French nationals from Guadeloupe and Martinique. Moreover, they suspected me of collusion with the Groupement des Organisations Nationalistes Guadeloupéennes (GONG), a pro-independence movement, some of whose sympathizers I had approached for Malcolm's African project."[131] Such attention from the authorities provides a possible explanation for the decision to bar Malcolm X's admission to France in February 1965.

Despite serious questions about Moore's credibility, other European collaborators offer similar accounts. The esteemed Guyanese writer and scholar Jan Carew recounts Malcolm X, in England, telling him that, "the OAAU . . . from the very start was collecting the names of all the people of African descent who have professional skills, no matter where they are. Then we could have a central register that we could share with independent countries in Africa and elsewhere. Do you know, I started collecting names, and then I gave the list to someone who I thought was a trusted friend . . . and the list disappeared."[132] Betrayal like this discouraged activists from keeping written records of their activities. At a December OAAU rally Malcolm X was deliberately circumspect about the organization's work: "I purposely, to this day, have not in any way mentioned what our program is, because there will come a time when we will unveil it so that everybody will understand it."[133] Moore reasonably, albeit conveniently, claims that there is little trace because, "For security reasons, presumably, Malcolm had centralized the project to the extent that none involved had but a sketchy idea of how it would materialize."[134] Nonetheless there seems to be enough circumstantial corroboration to support the likelihood that Malcolm X and his comrades were involved in conversations about diaspora Africans providing material support to the Congo. While it remains unclear to what extent Malcolm X followed through, there is overwhelming evidence that his plan was a profoundly serious one.

A few weeks after Belgian paratroopers invaded Stanleyville, one of Malcolm X's international allies, Ernesto "Che" Guevara, the Argentinean guerilla and hero of the Cuban revolution, came to New York to address the

U.N. General Assembly on behalf of Cuba. On December 11, 1964, he presented the delegates with a racial analysis of the Congo crisis that echoed Malcolm X's speeches: "those who used the name of the United Nations to commit the murder of Lumumba are today, in the name of the defense of the white race, murdering thousands of Congolese." Guevara, much like Malcolm X, frequently drew on Lumumba in his speeches. In his 1964 U.N. address, Guevara reminded his audience that in 1960, "dramatic mobilizations were carried out to avoid the secession of Katanga, but today Tshombe is in power, the wealth of the Congo is in imperialist hands—and the expenses have to be paid by the honorable nations.... Who are the perpetrators? Belgian paratroopers, carried by U.S. planes, who took off from British bases." Malcolm X and Guevara shared an analysis of the Congo with a clear understanding of the multinational dynamics of neocolonialism. Guevara also echoed Malcolm X's criticism of the hypocrisy of U.S. racism, using language similar to that of African delegates: "Those who kill their own children and discriminate daily against them because of the color of their skin; those who let the murderers of blacks remain free, protecting them, and furthermore punishing the black population because they demand their legitimate rights as free men—how can those who do this consider themselves guardians of freedom?... It must be clearly established, however, that the government of the United States is not the champion of freedom, but rather the perpetrator of exploitation and oppression against the peoples of the world and against a large part of its own population."[135] Here, Guevara makes a crucial connection between U.S. imperialism abroad and domestic racial oppression.

Two days later, at an OAAU rally that was dedicated to the Congo, Malcolm X told the audience that Guevara had been invited to speak, but was unable to attend. Guevara did, however, send a "statement of solidarity," which included greetings from Fidel Castro, "who remembers enthusiastically his visit to Harlem" in September 1960 when he was welcomed by supporters including many holding pro-Lumumba signs.[136] When Castro met Malcolm X late one night at Harlem's storied Hotel Theresa in 1960, he inquired: " 'Is there any news on Lumumba?' Malcolm X smiled broadly at the mention of the Congolese leader's name. Castro then raised his hand. 'We will try to defend him (Lumumba) strongly. I hope Lumumba stays here at the Theresa.' "[137] Indeed, Lumumba figured prominently in Castro's address to the U.N. General Assembly that week. Castro argued that the Congo, like Cuba, was a victim of colonialism, presciently comparing Mobutu to Batista in their support by the United States. Cuba, he insisted, was "on the side of the only leader who remained there to defend the interests of his country, and that leader is Lumumba."[138] Malcolm X spent time with Castro at a watershed moment when he "unveiled Cuba's policy toward Africa" and most fully articulated its solidarity with the decolonization struggle in Africa.[139] At a Harlem rally the following week, Malcolm X shared a platform with Nkrumah and other distinguished speakers who addressed a crowd of supporters holding signs of Lumumba and in support of "Congo for the Congolese."[140]

Four years after Castro's historic visit, Guevara, as his representative, continued Cuba's connections with African American activists.[141] Even though Guevara did not attend the December 11 OAAU meeting, Malcolm X biographer Manning Marable believes, "Circumstantial evidence provided by James 67X suggests that Malcolm and Guevara briefly met that week in December."[142] Baba Zak A. Kondo goes farther in suggesting that they met as part of Malcolm's efforts "to organize a continental Afrikan army for service in the Congo."[143] Even if a personal encounter is difficult to fully document due to legitimate reasons of secrecy, Guevara's letter to the OAAU confirms they were in correspondence. More importantly, Guevara was evidently aware of and influenced by Malcolm X at a time when they shared a deep concern for the Congo.

On December 17, 1964, Guevara left New York and headed directly to Algeria, one of Cuba's closest political allies since its July 1962 independence from France.[144] Malcolm X had met several Algerian ambassadors during his travels. In May 1964, one week after meeting Algeria's representative in Accra, he traveled to Algiers, where he discussed the Congo with the Ghanaian ambassador, who had been in Kinshasa at the time of Lumumba's assassination. Ambassador Nutako, in turn, tried to arrange other high-level meetings in Algeria though the details remain vague.[145] Malcolm X later wrote to Angelou, whom he worked with in Ghana, that he "failed to see *the man* in Algeria," adding "I was successful in making some friends on my own initiative, but whatever was set up in advance evidently failed to materialize."[146] When he returned to Algeria in November, he recorded in his diary his decision to depart immediately "after trying hard to make my contacts." This entry seems circumspect with regard to "contacts," such that he would try so "hard" yet then leave the next day from what was a planned excursion.[147] By this time, Malcolm X had already established important connections with Cuban government representatives throughout the continent. In May 1964, he met Armando Entralgo Gonzalez, Cuba's ambassador to Ghana, and "reportedly discussed . . . the idea of recruiting black Americans to help fight in Africa's wars," which Malcolm X told him Nkrumah had approved.[148] When he visited Dar es Salaam in October 1964, he met the Cuban ambassador as well as President Nyerere and Congolese activists.[149] According to Kondo, Malcolm X used this time to engage with the logistics of his plan, and "even discussed passports for recruits and other vital essentials with diplomats."[150]

By December 1964, Marable explains, Guevara was "carrying out Malcolm's revolutionary agenda for the continent." Guevara "literally traced Malcolm's steps," visiting Mali, Congo (Brazzaville), Guinea, Ghana, Algeria, Benin, Tanzania, and Egypt, while meeting African leaders like Ben Bella, Touré, and Nkrumah, all of whom welcomed Malcolm X less than two months earlier.[151] During these months, Guevara's travel companion was Jorge Serguera, Cuba's first ambassador to Algeria, who held that office in May 1964 when Malcolm X visited.[152] When Guevara went to Ghana in January 1965, Gonzalez introduced him to African American expatriates.[153] According to Moore, Guevara asked African American novelist and journalist William Gardner Smith, "How do you think Africans would react to an internationalist brigade made up of black Cubans and black Americans fighting alongside liberation movements in Africa to defeat colonialism, imperialism and apartheid?"[154] On February 19, Guevara met Gaston Soumialot, Defense Minister of the rebel government of the People's Republic of Congo, in Cairo and later spent time with Congolese rebel leaders including Laurent Kabila in Tanzania, where he also met with Malcolm X's close ally Mohamed Babu. Meanwhile, Malcolm X was planning a March trip to Cuba.[155]

In March 1965, Castro appointed Pablo Rivalta ambassador to Tanzania with instructions "to establish very close relations with the government of that country and to contact the representatives of African liberation movements who lived in Dar es Salaam."[156] Guevara's military mission, begun two months after Malcolm X's assassination, would soon be based out of Rivalta's office, which Malcolm X had also visited. There, Rivalta worked with Babu, who was secretary general of the Zanzibar Nationalist Party (ZNP), which, a few years later, sent some of its members for military training in Cuba.[157] Babu's ties to Lumumba and the Congo were even longer standing. In 1958, while en route to the All African People's Conference in Accra, Babu and his comrades stopped in the Belgian Congo, where he met Lumumba and arranged for him to accompany their delegation to Ghana. Babu was present when Lumumba met Nkrumah, an experience that initiated Nkrumah's sustained commitment to the liberation of the Congo.[158] Babu immodestly, though not inaccurately, explains that their invitation to Lumumba "was a historic decision which was to change the entire political atmosphere in sub-Saharan Africa."[159]

In December 1964, Babu, as the head of Tanzania's U.N. delegation, arrived in New York directly from Cuba.[160] In New York, he delivered Guevara's December 13 message to the OAAU.[161] That week, he also gave speeches to several Harlem groups, including the OAAU, the May 2 Movement, and the Harlem Progressive Labor Club.[162] Not surprisingly the Congo figured prominently in Babu's lectures, including an Audubon Ballroom speech that was covered in the OAAU's *Blacklash* and reprinted in RAM's *Black America*: "That's why they are trying to shoot the Congolese people. They are testing. They are testing our position on this question of the Congo. It is a serious test because if today they can prop up a Tshombe—that renegade who can sell his own brother and sisters (the Tshombes are the same type who sold their brothers and sisters two centuries ago), and if they can keep that renegade then we are weak. To what extent will the people of Africa resist him? If today they succeed in the Congo, tomorrow it will be Mozambique, it will be Kenya, it will be the United Arab Republic, it will be all of Africa."[163] After this speech, which connects Tshombe to the transatlantic slave trade, Babu and Malcolm X had a long meeting with Amiri Baraka and a couple of other leaders in New York, suggestive of an intense ongoing collaboration.[164]

Beyond the Babu connection, there are indications that Guevara intended to include African Americans in his mission into Congo, even after Malcolm X's assassination. In the days before Guevara departed Cuba for Tanzania, he visited Robert F. Williams, the former head of the Monroe, North Carolina, branch of the NAACP, who was well known for his advocacy of armed self-defense and who had lived in Cuba since 1961. Prior to his exile in Havana, Williams was a member of the Fair Play for Cuba Committee and traveled to the island twice in 1960, where he met Castro and Guevara. In the United States, Williams had a strong national platform, speaking frequently in New York at NoI Mosque Number 7 while Malcolm X was minister. Williams, who also frequented Michaux's bookstore, "agreed" with Malcolm X's assessment of the Kennedy assassination as a case of the chickens coming home to roost.[165] When Castro stayed at the Hotel Theresa, Williams, like Malcolm X, had a private audience with the Cuban leader. Like Guevara and Malcolm X, Williams also had a long-standing interest in the Congo. He helped organize the February 1961 U.N. action that followed the news of Lumumba's assassination.[166] At the end of July 1964, Muhammad Ahmad (Maxwell Stanford Jr.) went to Cuba to meet with Williams on behalf of RAM as part of a coordinated effort with Malcolm X, who was then in Africa "to try to find places for eventual political asylum and political/military training for cadres."[167]

In late March 1965, Guevara visited Williams during a two-week trip to Cuba when he was making arrangements to leave his entire life, including his family, for his Congo mission. Guevara must have had good reason to reach out to Williams at such a time, and he may have had some idea of recruiting him for the Congo mission. Robert Carl Cohen's biography of Williams, which is based on extensive 1968 interviews with its subject, contends that the impetus for the meeting was that Guevara heard from Africans and African Americans that Williams felt mistreated by Cuban authorities. According to Moore, however, it was a recruiting meeting that was derailed by Williams's critical comments on Cuban racism.[168] It seems unlikely that Guevara would have been surprised to hear such criticisms from Williams, although it certainly remains plausible that the conversation somehow discouraged Guevara from confiding in Williams as planned. The timing of the meeting remains a powerful suggestion of a possible collaboration, and, at the least, suggests Guevara's profound awareness of the global challenges of racism as he headed off to lead an all-black unit on his Congo mission.

Malcolm X's efforts to recruit African Americans to the Congo recall George Washington Williams's plans seventy-five years earlier. Although Williams never traveled with any of his recruits, his project was manifest in the work of William Sheppard and the APCM. Although Malcolm X never visited the Congo despite plans to do so, he too "has sown seed which will be fruitful of greater interest in Africa."[169] Malcolm X's insistent emphasis of the ongoing import of the history of the Leopoldian era established a historical continuum with contemporary African American engagement with the Congo, which includes the February 1961 U.N. demonstrations and Guevara's African mission, which, though widely considered a failure, laid the groundwork for much more successful Cuban military support in Angola and elsewhere in southern Africa.[170]

The issue of the Congo was not a freestanding one, but rather was integral to Malcolm X's larger philosophy, mission, and activism. His understanding of black nationalism and internationalism remain inextricably tied to the politics of state formation in the postcolonial era as he sought to negotiate the challenges of using international bodies for forms of redress. Nonaligned countries maintained the U.N. was a valuable tool, even if their confidence was profoundly tested by its failure to effectively support Lumumba.[171] All of these forms of political engagement are predicated on an understanding of and investment in these systems in ways that redefine African American transnationalism. In these materials, there is enough to unequivocally assert that within Malcolm X's capacious commitment to antiracism and Pan-Africanism, there was a staunch commitment to the Congo. Though excised from *Malcolm X Speaks* and other publications, his invocations of the Congo transcend the oratory for which he is so justly remembered. Like the literary forms in which Malcolm X's idol Lumumba was memorialized, these cultural instantiations are indelible commitments that exist within a cultural and material field that enables us to see anew the African American commitment to Africa and the contours of diaspora identity.

# Conclusion

Malcolm X was deeply disturbed by media coverage of the Congo. In an address at the London School of Economics less than two weeks before his assassination, he explained the utter dehumanization he experienced: "If you recall reading in the paper, they never talked about the Congolese who were being slaughtered. But as soon as a few whites, the lives of a few whites were at stake, they began to speak of 'white hostages,' 'white missionaries,' 'white priests,' 'white nuns'—as if a white life, one white life, was of such greater value than a Black life, than a thousand Black lives. They showed you their open contempt for the lives of the Blacks, and their deep concern for the lives of the whites." He made similar remarks a few days later in Detroit on February 14, 1965: "You know what the paper said right here in Detroit—'white missionaries,' not just a missionary; a 'white nun'—as if there's a difference between a white nun and a black nun, or a white priest and a black priest, or if the life that's in a white skin is more valuable than a life within a black skin."[1] Malcolm X understood that the brutality of the Belgian colonists was facilitated by powerful U.S. interests who drew on domestic forms of racism to misrepresent the Congo. In this encounter between the United States and the Congo, Malcolm X saw the need to affirm the value of black life, much as a more recent generation of African American activists continue to do under the banner of "Black Lives Matter."

This history is far less remote—geographically or temporally—than it might initially appear. The murder of Trayvon Martin by George Zimmerman, which inspired a group of activists to organize around "Black Lives Matter," occurred in Sanford, Florida, a town founded by Henry Shelton Sanford, who, as King Leopold II's U.S. agent, was responsible for incalculable amounts of colonial violence. Soon after the Civil War, in 1870, Sanford purchased thousands of acres of cheap Florida land and helped pioneer the state's citrus industry. Sanford's ambition continued amid a series of violent attacks on African American laborers employed on his plantation. He developed his domestic businesses while simultaneously pursuing his imperial mission in central Africa. These efforts were intertwined. Sanford was responsible for Henry Stanley's relationship with Leopold and for U.S. recognition of the AIA. At the end of Reconstruction, Sanford was devising new ways to systemically exclude African Americans from exercising full citizenship, selling Secretary of State William

Evarts on the possibilities of the Congo: "I think we more than any other country, will profit of it and an outlet will be found for the enterprise and ambition of our colored people in more congenial fields than politics."[2] In 1880, he established the Florida Land and Colonization Company, one of whose main investors was William Mackinnon, who he met through their work for Leopold's AIA. As Sanford continued his work for Leopold, he even named a son, born in 1880, for the Belgian king. At the 1884–85 Berlin conference, he, Stanley, and John Kasson represented the United States. In 1886, Leopold thanked Sanford for his help in Berlin by granting him a concession to establish the Sanford Exploring Expedition in the Congo. In 1888, the failing Sanford Exploring Expedition was taken over by Société Anonyme Belge pour l'Industrie et Commerce du Haut Congo, which was headed by Albert Thys, who soon commissioned George Washington Williams to recruit Hampton students for the Congo. Though Thys was never able to hire the Hampton cohort Williams recruited, his commercial enterprises became some of the great profiteers of the brutal rubber collection practices that took off in the 1890s.[3]

Before he even set foot in the Congo, Williams realized that the interests of Sanford—whom President Chester Arthur introduced him to in 1884—had nothing in common with his own. Still, their paths intersected, as inevitably as Sanford's had with Sheppard and the APCM, whose own vexed origins include Sanford's assistance via Senator Morgan and Judge Lapsley. In a February 1890 letter from Sierra Leone, Williams confronted Sanford directly:

> Before leaving Bruxelles it was intimated to me by a gentleman of position, character, ability that you was [sic] the instigation of all the opposition with which my mission to the Congo was beset.
>
> I carefully investigated the facts before my departure from Europe, and reached the conclusion that it was necessary to inform my friends in America, the President and Senator Sherman, that my mission had been secretly and publicly beset and that I expected protection as an American citizen in visiting a country that had been opened to a great international commerce and free-trade.
>
> I have also the assurances of several eminent English Statesmen that if I am in any way obstructed that the provisions of the Berlin Conference will be urged to an honest fulfillment, respecting the right of travellers to pass through the Congo State freely.
>
> If the Congo Country is what you have claimed it to be, there need be no uneasiness about travellers visiting it on their own account. I am now, as ever before, a true friend of the State of Congo; but I shall discharge my mission without fear or favor; and if any thing should happen to me

you will be held responsible. I represent four hundred (400) daily newspapers in the United States, and the "London Times."[4]

Williams insists that he, not Sanford, is a "true friend of the State of Congo" and recognizes himself as a figure whose own mistreatment represents the failures of the colonial state. Sanford poses a threat to Williams's life and livelihood, as well as to the Congo. His recognition that his own predicament is entangled with U.S. involvement in the Congo was as profoundly transformative for Williams as it was for Malcolm X.

Williams's career is defined by his willingness to directly confront powerful men—government officials, financiers, and their agents. He sought support where he could find it—increasingly outside of the government, as evident by his turn to the press and business leaders during the final year of his life. Malcolm X's Congo activism marks a break with the path pursued by Williams. During the last year of his life, Malcolm X recognized that the criminality of U.S. human rights violations necessitated forms of intervention outside the apparatus of the nation-state—hence his own nascent OAAU and MMI, and the ongoing appeal of the OAU, the Non-Aligned Movement, and the U.N. Malcolm X's involvement with those groups depended on the independent political power of postcolonial African states, a possibility that Williams sought but was unable to fully realize.

The political violence that Williams feared from Sanford has been foundational and ongoing in the United States. The Congo framed Malcolm X's understanding of his vulnerability to state violence when he told Jan Carew a few weeks before his assassination that "the chances are that they will get me the way they got Lumumba before he reached the running stage."[5] Malcolm was not alone in imagining himself as a Lumumba-style martyr struck down before realizing his full political potential. Immediately after his assassination, the CAO in England issued a statement asserting, "the butchers of Patrice Lumumba are the very same monsters who have murdered Malcolm X in cold blood."[6] The Pan Africanist Congress of South Africa called Malcolm, "another Lumumba."[7] In the United States, RAM published a statement in the *Liberator*, asserting that Malcolm "was to black America what Lumumba was to the Congo. In this way, his spirit should be to black revolutionary nationalists what Lumumba's spirit is to the Congolese National Liberation Front. In the Congo the word is: 'Lumumba lives.' In black America the word must be: 'Malcolm lives! Keep on pushin'! Change is gonna come!'"[8] RAM's statement combines Joans's poetic mantra and the modern soul music of the Impressions and Sam Cooke, embedding Malcolm X's relationship to Lumumba within the highest echelons of black song.[9] These cultural associations ensure Malcolm X's survival as they did Lumumba's.

As in Jayne Cortez's "Festivals and Funerals," Malcolm X and Patrice Lumumba were frequent companions in their literary afterlives. In his novel *Comes the Voyager at Last: A Tale of Return to Africa* (1992), the late Kofi Awoonor, then Ghana's ambassador to the U.N., traces the development of the fictional "Sheik Lumumba Mandela," an African American who is imprisoned for a crime he did not commit.[10] After his release, he joins the NoI but follows Malcolm X after his split with Elijah Muhammad. Wenzel insightfully reads the novel as reaching toward "a transhistorical African poetic voice" that is achieved by the Lumumba character's guardianship of the historical Malcolm on the night of his assassination.[11] The novel provides a real encounter between a fictionalized historical Malcolm and an activist fictional Lumumba that makes real the "transhistorical" and transnational association of two figures who probably never met.[12] Awonoor's Lumumba, who travels to Africa and is recognized as a returning member of the family, ultimately undertakes a familiar journey that represents a literary crossroads of global African American political culture.[13]

Novels like *Comes the Voyager at Last* acknowledge the delayed inevitability of African American movement toward Africa, representing a long history of U.S.-African relationships that is fundamentally different from the ongoing use of *Heart of Darkness* as a defining trope for the entire continent. In July 1960, in an editorial headlined "Heart of Darkness," the *Washington Post* bemoaned the threat to "Belgian lives and property" during the three weeks since independence rather than the impact of a century of colonialism on the Congolese people.[14] More recently, the second installment of an ABC News *Nightline* series about the Democratic Republic of Congo was scheduled to be broadcast Tuesday, September 11, 2001, leading anchor Ted Koppel to reflect later on its delayed airing due to the "3,000 people [who] died in the World Trade Center alone. In the Congo, almost that many people have died each and every day for more than three years now." While acknowledging this devaluation of black life and, as Malcolm X had, the contributing role of the media, Koppel comforts his viewers by describing this lack of attention as a historical inevitability: "Hardly anyone noticed the loss of a few million Congolese back then, either."[15] Despite citing Hochschild's *King Leopold's Ghost*, which documents extensive resistance to Leopold's reign, Koppel asserts that twenty-first-century ignorance of the Congo existed from time immemorial. Vansina has made it clear that European observers and the Congolese themselves were aware of what social scientists politely call the "demographic decline."[16] Also, among the people who did notice the deaths of "a few million Congolese" were African Americans like Williams, Sheppard, and their compatriots based in the United States. These traditions belie the history of the Congo that is told in ABC's "Heart of Darkness."

William Henry Sheppard witnessed the skeletons left by Stanley and the hands left by Leopold's henchmen; for this he was put on trial and fired. Booker T. Washington wrote about Sheppard's reports and used his platform to encourage others to do the same. Althea Brown Edmiston understood the cultural stakes of colonialism and used her Fisk education to challenge the hegemony of colonial language policy. Pauline Hopkins created a body of literature that saw blood everywhere. Malcolm X was assassinated at a time when his domestic and international work was coalescing around the Congo. African American stories about the Congo are often ignored and result in the evacuation of diaspora's political entanglements with colonialism in Africa. More importantly, all of these figures, and so many others, were mainstays of religious, educational, literary, and political institutions where their work grounded African American communities and identities in the colonial politics of the Congo. Nonetheless, all of these voices, sometimes at odds with one another, found ways to tell the story. Those stories insist on the relevance of the Congo to the United States. As Philippe Wamba describes in his beautiful memoir *Kinship: A Family's Journey in Africa and America*, his personal history as the son of a Congolese father and African American mother, both politically active, is embedded within the longer and wider history of African American connections to the Congo, which itself "has in many ways been representative of processes taking place in the continent at large."[17] Likewise, his family's experience, including his own untimely death in an automobile accident in Kenya in 2002, is itself part of a much larger transatlantic story.

If Sanford serves as a reminder that the savagery associated with the Congo is located domestically in the United States—in the violence of George Zimmerman, the police, and the legal system—Williams's writings serve as a reminder of the importance of witnessing and confronting the apparatus of state power that continues to disregard black lives. As Alicia Garza recognizes, the love that Malcolm X expressed for black people throughout his life is profoundly political: "One thing I really admire is that Malcolm talked about self-actualization, self-love and being really rooted in who we are unapologetically. When (Opal Tometi, Patrisse Cullors and I) created Black Lives Matter, it absolutely was about: how do we live in a world that dehumanizes us and still be human? The fight is not just being able to keep breathing. The fight is actually to be able to walk down the street with your head held high— and feel like I belong here, or I deserve to be here, or I just have [the] right to have a level of dignity."[18] As a nation seeks justice for its countless Sanford, Floridas, where the laws, police, courts, and legislature consistently refuse to recognize the police murders of black people as a crime, Williams's bold challenge to state power at home and abroad remains relevant. Williams was as adamant in his appeal to Sanford as he was to King Leopold and President

Harrison, but never had a chance to return to the country whose president he addressed. He died in England at the age of 41 shortly after visiting the Congo. He did outlive Sanford, who died in May 1891, by three months, though Sanford's ghost continues to haunt his town and country as part of the domestic landscape of U.S. imperialism, the "American Congo" that has been the target of activists for more than a century.

## Appendix
Malcolm X on the Congo, February 14, 1965, Detroit

A few hours after Malcolm X's home in Queens was firebombed in the early morning hours of February 14, 1965, he flew to Detroit to deliver an address at Ford Auditorium. For reasons explored in chapter 9, the most prominent published versions of that speech exclude Malcolm's extraordinary insight and analysis of the bombing of the Congo at a moment when he understood better than ever the experience of being victimized by a bomb attack. The thirteen-minute segment of the speech about the Congo is reproduced here. The *italicized text* indicates the portions of the speech included in George Breitman's *Malcolm X Speaks*. The point when the excerpt in Steve Clark's *The Final Speeches* is interrupted is indicated below; *The Final Speeches* picks back up at the same place that *Malcolm X Speaks* does. The transcription below is my own, taken from an audio recording.

*When you begin to start thinking for yourself, you frighten them, and they try and block your getting to the public for fear that if the public listens to you, then the public won't listen to them anymore. And they've got certain Negroes whom they have to keep blowing up in the paper to make them look like leaders so that the people will keep on following them, no matter how many knots they get on their heads following him. This is how the man does it. And if you don't wake up and find out how he does it, I tell you, they'll be building gas chambers and gas ovens pretty soon—I don't mean those kind you've got at home in your kitchen.*

Another example at the international level of how skillfully they use this trickery was in the Congo. In the Congo, airplanes were dropping bombs on African villages. African villages don't have a defense against bombs. And the pilot can't tell who the bomb is being dropped upon. When a bomb hits a village, everything goes. And these pilots flying planes filled with bombs, dropping these bombs on African villages, were destroying women, were destroying children, were destroying babies. You never heard any outcry over here about that. And it had started way back in June. They would drop bombs on African villages that would blow that village apart and everything in it—man, woman, child, and baby. No outcry, no sympathy, no support, no concern because the press didn't project it in such a way that it would be designed to get your sympathy. They know how to put something so that you'll sympathize with it, and they know how to put it so you'll be against it. I'm telling you: they are masters at it. And if you don't develop the analytical ability to read between the lines in what they're saying, I'm telling you again: they'll be building that gas oven, and before you wake up *you'll be in one of them just like the Jews ended up in gas ovens over there in Germany. You're in a society that's just as capable of building gas ovens for black people as Hitler's society was.* [*applause*]

This was mass murder in the Congo—of women and children and babies. But there was no outcry even from the white liberals, even from your friends. Why? Because they made it appear that it was a humanitarian project. They said that the planes were being flown by American-trained anti-Castro Cuban pilots. This is propaganda too. Soon as you hear that it's American-trained, you say, "Oh that's all right. That's us"; and the anti-Castro Cubans, "Oh that's all right too because if they're against Castro whoever else they're against, that's good because Castro is a monster." But you see how step by step they grab your mind? And these pilots are hired; their salaries are paid by the United States government. They're called mercenaries, these pilots are. And a mercenary is not someone who kills you because he's patriotic. He kills you for blood money; he's a hired killer. This is what a mercenary means. And they're able to take these hired killers, put them in American planes with American bombs and drop them on African villages, blowing to bits black men, black women, black children, black babies, and you black people sitting over here cool like it doesn't even involve you. You're a fool. [*applause*] They'll do it to them today, and do it to you tomorrow. Because you and I and they are all the same.

They call it a humanitarian project and that they're doing it in the name of freedom. And all of this, these glorious terms, are used to pave the way in your mind for what they're going to do. Then they take Tshombe. You've heard of Tshombe. He's the worst African that was ever born. The lowest type that was ever born. [*applause*] He's a murderer himself. He's the murderer of Lumumba, the former prime minister of—the first and only rightful prime minister of—the Congo. He's an international—he's a murderer with an international stature as a murderer. [Here, Clark's edition stops due to a "gap in tape."]

Yet the United States government went and got Tshombe in Spain and put him as the head of the Congolese government. Imagine that. This is criminal. Here's a man who's a murderer. So the United States takes him, puts him in over the Congo, and supports his government with your tax dollars. Now, in other words, they hire him to occupy the position as head of state over the Congo. A killer! He is a hired killer himself! His salary paid by the United States government. And he turns his first move is to bring in South Africans, who hate everything in sight. He hires those South Africans to come and kill his own Congolese people. And the United States again pays their salary.

You know it's something to think about. How do you think you would feel right now if some Congolese brothers walked up to you—and they look just like you, don't think you don't look Congolese. You look as much Congolese as a Congolese does. [*applause*] They got all kinds of Congolese over there. How would you feel if one of them walked up to you and asked you about what your government is doing in the Congo? I was asked that when I was over there. But they didn't have to come to me like that because they know where I stand automatically anyway. And for once I'm thankful to the press for letting everybody know where I stand. [*applause*] See. But you have no explanation. Your tongue stays in your mouth. And you have to then become, go to the extreme to convince them that you don't go along with what the United States government is doing in the Congo. But again, your image-making comes into importance here. And they justify the usage of Tshombe as the present head of state by saying that he's the only African who can unite or bring unity to the Congo. Has he brought unity to the Congo?

But, see, this is their game. And their real reason for wanting Tshombe there was so that Tshombe could invite them to come in. No other African head of state would have dared to invite outside powers. So they put Tshombe there, and as soon as Tshombe got there then he invited them to bring paratroopers from Belgium in the United States transport planes to try and recapture the Congo. This is all a cold-blooded act on the part of your Western powers, namely the Western powers here in the United States—interests in the United States, in England, in France, and in Belgium and so forth. They want the wealth of the Congo, plus its strategic geographic position.

The step-by-step process that was used was used by the press: first they fanned the flame in such a manner to create hysteria in the mind of the public. And then they shift gears and fan the flame in a manner designed to get the sympathy of the public. And once they go from hysteria to sympathy, their next step is to get the public to support them in whatever act they're getting ready to go down with. You're dealing with a cold calculating international machine that's so criminal in its objectives and motives that it has the seeds of its own destruction right within it.

They use the press to emphasize that white hostages are being held by cannibals—imagine that—or white priests, white missionaries, white nuns. They don't say "nuns"—"white nuns." You know what the paper said right here in Detroit—"white missionaries," not just a missionary; a "white nun"—as if there's a difference between a white nun and a black nun, or a white priest and a black priest, or if the life that's in a white skin is more valuable than a life within a black skin. This is what they're implying. And the press—look at the press when this thing was going on—and you will see what I'm talking about. They're vicious in their whiteness!

But still I wouldn't judge them just cause they're white, cause they'd call me a racist. [*laughter*] Judging by their deeds, by their conscious behavior—and you know how they've been consciously behaving in the Congo, and how they consciously behave in Vietnam, and how they consciously behave right now in Alabama and Mississippi. So you and I got to get conscious, and start behaving in a way that we can offset this thing before it's too late—and this is what they don't want to hear.

One more thing concerning Tshombe—if you notice—and I must go all over there on the African continent in order to give you a better understanding of what is going on right here—the next thing that is good to know about Tshombe: no Congolese troops have ever won any victories, whatsoever, for the present Congolese government. Congolese soldiers won't even fight unless they're forced to.

But the fighters in the Congo were the freedom fighters, these brothers from the Orientale eastern province. And they fought with stones and sticks and rocks, spears and arrows. And the only time they had a gun was when they got some soldier who had it, and they'd kill him and take his gun. But they were winning; they took over two-thirds of the Congo, showing you they were fighting from their hearts, whereas these other people their heart wasn't in it. And because of the fighting spirit of these people, it will be impossible for Tshombe to remain as head of state over the Congo without additional troops—white troops—constantly being brought in from South Africa or elsewhere. But sooner or later, these troops are going to give out, and then America's going to have to increase her troops like she did in South Vietnam, you know. She's not at war over there, you know. They're only there advising. They've got about 20,000 advisors, you know, on the front lines. But it's not a war. It's just—they're in an advisory capacity while they insult the intelligence of their own public. And they're going to have to end up doing the same thing in the Congo. They'll be trapped. They'll have to eventually send American troops to occupy the Congo. Because the African freedom fighters are going to fight. They're not going to give up one inch without fighting back. And this is something that you should know: that they realize now on the African continent what's at stake, and how much all of these Western powers have in common and what they're doing in cahoots with each other behind the closed doors.

So on the African continent, they are training Africans to be soldiers so that they can invade each one of these countries and take it over and give it to their rightful people. One of the last things I must say concerning the Congo: not only do they not intend for the Congo to fall into African hands because of its mineral wealth—and it has the greatest deposits of some of the richest elements or minerals of any other area on this earth. They don't intend to give it up because of its wealth. Another reason they don't intend to give it up if you look at the map you'll see that it is so strategically located geographically wherein if a real genuine African government were to come in power over the Congo, then it would be possible for African troops from all countries to invade Angola, which is a Portuguese possession, and if Angola fell—and it would fall—then it would only be a matter of time before South-West Africa [Namibia], Southern Rhodesia [Zimbabwe], and Betuanaland [Botswana] also would fall, and it would put African troops right on the border of South Africa. And that's where they really want to get at that man down there in South Africa.

And the United States interests are involved in blocking this, yes. Some of these liberals who grin in your face like they're your best friend, they got money tied up in the Congo. Some of the most powerful political figures in this country, some of them governors over states got interests in the Congo and got interests in South Africa and got interests all over the African continent and go there! And as the Africans awaken and realize this, they—it makes them filled with the incentive to never rest until that exploiter is driven out.

So *now, what effect does this have on us? Why should the black man in America concern himself since he's been away from the African continent for 400 years—three or 400 years—why should we concern ourselves? What impact does what happens to them have upon us?*

# Notes

## Introduction

1. Levy, *James Weldon Johnson*, 89.
2. Hogan, Northrup, and O'Dea, *My Little Jungle Queen*, [3].
3. Kaplan, *Anarchy of Empire*, 180; James Weldon Johnson, "Africa at the Peace Table," 17.
4. Oliver, "'Jim Crowed' in Their Own Countries," 218.
5. For the purpose of consistency, I refer to the area that was known as the Belgian Congo (1908–60) as the Congo state. Since 1997, the country has been known as the Democratic Republic of the Congo, which replaced Zaire (1971–97), which was the name of the country for most of the three decades under the rule of Mobutu Sese Seko (1965–97). It is not my intention to flatten the distinctions between historical periods.
6. James, *Holding Aloft the Banner of Ethiopia*, 292; Fleming, *James Weldon Johnson*, 2; Adelman, "Study of James Weldon Johnson," 131–32; Seniors, *Beyond Lift Every Voice and Sing*, 23.
7. James Weldon Johnson, *Along This Way*, 295. For more on *Tolosa*, see Gruesser, *Empire Abroad*, 99–112.
8. Adelman, "Study of James Weldon Johnson," 137; Oliver, "'Jim Crowed' in Their Own Countries," 211.
9. Jerome Dowd, quoted in James Weldon Johnson, *Native African Races and Culture*, 11.
10. Jacobs, *African Nexus*, 87.
11. Eisenberg, "Only for the Bourgeois?," 111; Simmons, "Europe's Reception to Negro Talent," 638–42; Fleming, *James Weldon Johnson*, 14; James Weldon Johnson, *Along This Way*, 362; Jacobs, *African Nexus*, 87–98.
12. Wells, *Red Record*, 112.
13. James Weldon Johnson, "Lynching—America's National Disgrace," 73.
14. James Weldon Johnson, *Along This Way*, 299.
15. Morrissette, *James Weldon Johnson's Modern Soundscapes*, 38.
16. Sundquist, *To Wake the Nations*, 21.
17. Chinitz, *T.S. Eliot and the Cultural Divide*, 115–17; Jacques, *Change in the Weather*, 5; North, *Dialect of Modernism*, 77–99; Leighten, "White Peril," 609.
18. Sanders, "Brief Reflections on the Discourse of Transnationalism," 812.
19. McHenry, *Forgotten Readers*, 10–12.
20. Gilroy, *Black Atlantic*, 19.
21. Hochschild, *King Leopold's Ghost*, 87.
22. Sanford, "Report of Hon. Henry Shelton Sanford," 93. See Fry, *Henry S. Sanford*, 137–38.

23. Hochschild, *King Leopold's Ghost*, 59–60; Jeal, *Stanley*, 292; Bontinck, *Aux origines de l'État Indépendant du Congo*, 51–52.

24. Bontinck, *Aux origines de l'État Indépendant du Congo*, 162. See Hochschild, *King Leopold's Ghost*, 79–80; Baylen, "Senator John Tyler Morgan," 118–20. See John Tyler Morgan, "Future of the American Negro," 81–84.

25. Shepperson, "Centennial of the West African Conference," 40; Boya, *DR Congo*, 80.

26. George Washington Williams, *Report [ . . . ] to the President*, 279.

27. Ndaywel è Nziem, *Nouvelle histoire du Congo*, 319. See Hochschild, *King Leopold's Ghost*, 233. The causes of and data on colonial-era depopulation continue to be debated by historians.

28. Stengers and Vansina, "King Leopold's Congo," 358.

29. Ibid., 319, 331.

30. Stearns, *Dancing in the Glory of Monsters*, 113.

31. Hochschild, *King Leopold's Ghost*, 164–66.

32. Mahaniah, "Presence of Black Americans in the Lower Congo," 407, 417–19.

33. Bowser, "Studies of the African Diaspora," 4–5.

34. "Men of the Month: A Missionary" (May 1915), 15. Phipps attributes authorship to Du Bois. Phipps, *William Sheppard*, 180.

35. Du Bois, "Poem on the Negro," 18.

36. Du Bois, "Looking Glass," 182.

37. Du Bois, "African Roots of the War," 643. A version of the argument appeared in 1920 as "The Hands of Ethiopia," chapter 3 of Du Bois, *Darkwater*, 32–42.

38. David Levering Lewis, *W. E. B. Du Bois*, 1:503–4. Vitalis identifies an earlier version of Du Bois's argument in a Howard University lecture by Alain Locke. Vitalis, *White World Order*, 58.

39. Du Bois, "On Migration to Africa," 48.

40. Johnson, "Africa at the Peace Table," 13; James Weldon Johnson, *Along This Way*, 591–92.

41. Adam Hochschild, "A Congo Lesson for Bush," *Los Angeles Times*, December 22, 2006.

42. Campbell, *Songs of Zion*, xii–xiii.

43. Hall, "Cultural Identity and Diaspora," 226.

44. Nwankwo, *Black Cosmopolitanism*, 18, 11.

45. Kabamba, "Heart of Darkness," 268.

46. Nwankwo, *Black Cosmopolitanism*, 13.

47. Murphy, *Shadowing the White Man's Burden*, 125.

48. Kaplan, "'Left Alone with America,'" 8, 4.

49. Houston A. Baker Jr., *Turning South Again*, 85; Horne, "Toward a Transnational Research Agenda," 300.

50. Kaplan, "'Left Alone with America,'" 3.

51. Pierre, *Predicament of Blackness*, 210. Emphasis in source.

52. Kaplan, "'Left Alone with America,'" 19.

Chapter 1

1. Bontinck indicates that Williams returned to the United States on December 1, 1889, and spoke at Hampton on December 12, 1889. See Bontinck, *Aux origines de l'État Indépendant du Congo*, 444.

2. Collis P. Huntington, Letter to Samuel Chapman Armstrong, December 6, 1889, box 88, SCA.

3. George Washington Williams, Letter to Samuel Chapman Armstrong, December 16, 1889, box 92, SCA. For information on the students, see Hampton Normal and Agricultural Institute, *Catalogue of the Hampton Normal and Agricultural Institute* (1889–90).

4. Samuel Chapman Armstrong, Letter to Collis P. Huntington, December 16, 1889, box 108, folder "Correspondence Dec. 1st-16th 1889," CPH. See "Items of Intelligence," 62; Cleveland, "Reversing Current," 23.

5. George Washington Williams, Letter to Samuel Chapman Armstrong, December 17, 1889, box 92, SCA.

6. Thornton, "African Experience of the '20. And Odd Negroes,'" 421–34. Thanks to Juliette Harris for informing me of the location of Old Point Comfort. For demographic details on the Kongo population in the transatlantic slave trade, see Jason Young, *Rituals of Resistance*, 24–35.

7. Jason Young, *Rituals of Resistance*, 3. Emphasis in source.

8. George Washington Williams, Letter to Collis P. Huntington, December 18, 1889, box 108, folder "Correspondence Dec. 18th-31st 1889," CPH.

9. Samuel Chapman Armstrong, Letter to George Washington Williams, December 19, 1889, box "Letter Books 6 and 7," pp. 511–13, SCA.

10. George Washington Williams, Letter to Samuel Chapman Armstrong, December 21, 1889, box 92, SCA.

11. Franklin, *George Washington Williams*, 186–87.

12. "Negroes from This Country," *New York Times*, January 14, 1890, 2; Blyden, *African Problem*, 16. As Liberian ambassador to England, Blyden met Leopold in Belgium in 1892. Lynch, *Edward Wilmot Blyden*, 208–9.

13. George Washington Williams, Letter to Samuel Chapman Armstrong, January 21, 1890, box 97, SCA.

14. "Americans in Africa," *New York Tribune*, March 2, 1890, 19.

15. [Armstrong], "Invitation to Congo," 2. Although "Invitation to Congo" is unsigned, Armstrong authored most of the *Southern Workman* until he suffered a paralyzing stroke in November 1891. In addition, the article refers to the "seed" of Williams's visit, which is the same language that Armstrong used in an unpublished letter to Huntington about the visit. See Franklin, *George Washington Williams*, 186.

16. [Armstrong], "Invitation to Congo," 2.

17. "'Appeal to Pharaoh,'" 121. See also, Campbell, *Middle Passages*, 124–25.

18. "African Slave Trade," 122.

19. Quoted in Franklin, *George Washington Williams*, 20.

20. Horne, "Toward a Transnational Research Agenda," 293.

21. George Washington Williams, *Centennial*, 25.

22. George Washington Williams, *History of the Negro Race*, 1:x.

23. George Washington Williams, *Report [ . . . ] to the President*, 279.

24. Franklin, *George Washington Williams*, 123.

25. George Washington Williams, *History of the Negro Race*, 1:34, 61.

26. Moses, *Afrotopia*, 65.

27. George Washington Williams, *History of the Negro Race*, 1:110.

28. Franklin, *George Washington Williams*, 8.

29. Jacobs, *African Nexus*, 210. African Americans held consular positions in Liberia without interruption from the early 1870s to the early twentieth century.

30. Leonard, *Who's Who in New York City and State*, 1219; "Negroes Run Steamship Line," *New York Times*, June 9, 1904, 1; Spurgeon, "New York and Liberia Steamship Company," 734–42. The December 1904 issue of the *Colored American Magazine* also featured an advertisement for the New York and Liberia Steamship Company, listing Spurgeon as "Chief Promoter."

31. George Washington Williams, *History of the Negro Race*, 1:107.

32. George Washington Williams, "Liberia," *Commoner*, December 4, 1875, 2; typescript in box W1, folder "Books: George Washington Williams—Editor (2 of 2)," JHF. The John Hope Franklin Papers at Duke University include Franklin's research notes for his biography on Williams. Franklin began his research at a time when Williams's papers were in the possession of Henry Slaughter. Slaughter's collection of Williams's papers, which consisted of his Congo diaries and several letters, has been lost, so Franklin's papers are the only surviving proxy. Franklin, *George Washington Williams*, xvii–xix. For a description of Franklin's notes, see McStallworth, "United States and the Congo Question," 196–203.

33. George Washington Williams, *History of the Negro Race*, 1:98, 101.

34. Stanley, *Congo*, 2:382; Jacobs, *African Nexus*, 218, 230n36.

35. "Americans in Africa," *New York Tribune*, March 2, 1890, 19.

36. George Washington Williams, Letter to Henry Shelton Sanford, October 31, 1889, box 22, folder 5, HSS; Fry, *Henry S. Sanford*, 133–55; Baylen, "Senator John Tyler Morgan," 118–20; John Tyler Morgan, "Future of the American Negro," 81–84; Bontinck, *Aux origines de l'État Indépendant du Congo*, 162–63.

37. McStallworth, "United States and the Congo Question," 196.

38. Franklin, *George Washington Williams*, 308n28. In 1862, Lincoln issued an emancipation order for the District of Columbia, which offered remuneration to slaveholders who affirmed their loyalty to the Union. On Emancipation Day 1883, Frederick Douglass criticized Williams for telling "his readers that it was the dissolution of the Union that abolished slavery," and emphasizing war rather than reunion. Douglass, *Address by Hon. Frederick Douglass*, 13.

39. George Washington Williams, *Negro as a Political Problem*, 38–39.

40. Ibid., 39.

41. Hochschild, *King Leopold's Ghost*, 65, 81, 87; Stanley, *Congo*, 1:38. Leopold and Stanley deliberately fostered confusion around several similarly named organizations.

42. Bontinck, *Aux origines de l'État Indépendant du Congo*, 196.

43. Nzongola-Ntalaja, *Congo from Leopold to Kabila*, 16.

44. R. S. Smith, "The National Capital," *New York Globe*, April 26, 1884, 1. The *New York Globe*, which was edited by T. Thomas Fortune, later changed its name and became better known as the *New York Age*.

45. "England on the Congo River," *New York Globe*, April 26, 1884, 2.

46. George Washington Williams, "The New South: The Measures Which Will Result in the Solution of the Negro Problem and the Regeneration of Africa," *New York Globe*, May 24, 1884, 2.

47. George Washington Williams, *Negro as a Political Problem*, 39.

48. George Washington Williams, *History of the Negro Race*, 1:x. Emphasis in source.

49. Bontinck, *Aux origines de l'État Indépendant du Congo*, 213n179.

50. Charles de Lalaing, Letter to Henry Morton Stanley, August 19, 1884, item no. 775, HMS.

51. Paul de Borchgrave, Letter to Henry Morton Stanley, September 2, 1884, item no. 710, HMS.

52. Bontinck, *Aux origines de l'État Indépendant du Congo*, 221n22.

53. Ibid., 442.

54. Stanley, *Congo*, 2:383.

55. Bontinck, *Aux origines de l'État Indépendant du Congo*, 292–97. The Monroe Doctrine was central to the public debate as the 1891 deadline for formal ratification of the Berlin Act approached. See, for example, "Can the Congo Treaties Be Saved?," *New York Tribune*, April 18, 1891, 6.

56. Stanley, *Congo*, 2:383.

57. Franklin, *George Washington Williams*, 148–49; *New York Freeman*, February 7, 1885, box W3, folder "Books: George Washington Williams [Research Notes (1 of 7)]," JHF. Williams was sworn in two hours before the noon inauguration of President Grover Cleveland, whose secretary of state subsequently denied Williams clearance to assume his post in Haiti.

58. *Washington Bee*, March 7, 1885, p. 3, box W4, folder "Books: George Washington Williams [Research Notes (7 of 7)]," JHF. See reports from the *Boston Advocate* and *Washington Bee* from November 13, 1886, box W1, folder "Books: George Washington Williams—Columnist and Orator," JHF; *Washington Bee*, February 12, 1887, p. 3, box W3, folder "Books: George Washington Williams—His Brother's Keeper II (2 of 2)," JHF. For related correspondence, see box W2, folder "George Washington Williams—His Brother's Keeper I (2 of 2)," JHF.

59. James Johnston, *Report of the Centenary Conference*, 1:135.

60. Franklin, *George Washington Williams*, 145. For additional information on this address, see box W1, folder "George Washington Williams—Civic Leadership and Activities II," JHF.

61. Although Williams's articles in the *New York Tribune* were published without bylines, Franklin confirms his authorship. Franklin, *George Washington Williams*, 319n32, 321n1; [George Washington Williams], "On the Congo. First Impressions of the Great African State," *New York Tribune*, June 8, 1890, 19.

62. [George Washington Williams], "The Opening of Africa," *New York Tribune*, November 24, 1889, 15.

63. Franklin, *George Washington Williams*, 181–82.

64. [George Washington Williams], "The Opening of Africa," *New York Tribune*, November 24, 1889, 15.

65. George Washington Williams, *Report [ . . . ] to the President*, 265. Emphasis in source.

66. Franklin, *George Washington Williams*, 187, 189, 208–9.

67. George Washington Williams, Letter to Collis P. Huntington, February 6, 1890, box 108, folder "Correspondence Feb. 1st-28th 1890," CPH.

68. George Washington Williams, Letter to Collis P. Huntington, April 14, 1890, box 108, folder "Correspondence Apr. 13th-31st 1890," CPH.

69. Franklin, *George Washington Williams*, 190–91.

70. George Washington Williams, Letter to Collis P. Huntington, April 14, 1890, box 108, folder "Correspondence Apr. 13th-31st 1890," CPH. Emphasis in source.

71. Stengers and Vansina, "King Leopold's Congo," 357–58, 318.

72. Ibid., 319.

73. Hochschild, *King Leopold's Ghost*, 112.

74. George Washington Williams, *Open Letter*, 244.

75. Ibid., 246, 252, 253. Emphasis in source.

76. Stanley, *Congo*, 2:379.

77. George Washington Williams, *Open Letter*, 244–45.

78. Ibid., 252.

79. Hochschild, *King Leopold's Ghost*, 110.

80. Franklin, *George Washington Williams*, 104.

81. Ibid., 206–7, 238.

82. George Washington Williams, *Report on the Proposed Congo Railway*, 260, 255, 260.

83. Ibid., 262.

84. George Washington Williams, *History of the Negro Race*, 1:x. Emphasis in source.

85. George Washington Williams, *Memorial Day*, 4.

86. George Washington Williams, *History of the Negro Race*, 1:110. On Livingstone's position toward slavery, see Kilbride, "Old South Confronts the Dilemma of David Livingstone," 806–7.

87. Bierman, *Dark Safari*, 74–78.

88. George Washington Williams, *History of the Negro Race*, 1:73.

89. George Washington Williams, *Report on the Proposed Congo Railway*, 260.

90. Driver, *Geography Militant*, 128, 129.

91. Stanley, *Autobiography of Sir Henry Morton Stanley*, 407. Emphasis in source.

92. Hochschild, *King Leopold's Ghost*, 81.

93. Ibid., 67.

94. George Washington Williams, Letter to Collis P. Huntington, February 6, 1890, box 108, folder "Correspondence Feb. 1st-28th 1890," CPH.

95. He takes his lack of national identity a step farther: "Whether the complicated colours, red, blue, white, were arranged properly, or the crosses according to the standard, I am ignorant." Stanley, *Through the Dark Continent*, 1:49.

96. Jeal, *Stanley*, 156. Stanley was born in Wales, moved to the United States as a young man, volunteered for the Confederate Army during the Civil War, and, after being captured at the Battle of Shiloh, volunteered for the Union Army as a condition of his release. Jeal, *Stanley*, 48.

97. Mudimbe, *Invention of Africa*, 12.

98. Driver, *Geography Militant*, 144.

99. Jeremy Bernstein, "Dark Continent of Henry Stanley," 105.

100. Youngs, *Travellers in Africa*, 133. See also, Bontinck, *Aux origines de l'État Indépendant du Congo*, 322. In 1892, Stanley was renaturalized as a British citizen, which paved the way for his 1895 election to Parliament and his 1899 knighting. Jeal, *Stanley*, 424–25, 436, 457.

101. Stanley, *Autobiography of Sir Henry Morton Stanley*, 400.

102. For more on Bumbire Island, see Coupland, *Exploitation of East Africa, 1856–1890*, 324–26; Stanley, *Stanley's Despatches to the "New York Herald,"* 241–62, 257n8; Stanley, *Through the Dark Continent*, 1:178–86; and Stanley, *Exploration Diaries of H. M. Stanley*, 92–97.

103. Franklin, *George Washington Williams*, 215.

104. Leonard K. Wilson, Letter to Henry Morton Stanley, January 2, 1891, item no. 2229, HMS. It is not clear what Stanley did with the pamphlets, which Wilson told him that he did not need to return; those copies do not survive to accompany the associated correspondence in the Henry Morton Stanley Papers, and it seems likely that they were destroyed either by Stanley or members of his family. On the history of the Stanley papers, which have been available to researchers at the Royal Museum for Central Africa since 2003, see Bierman, *Dark Safari*, 363; Daerden and Wynants, "About the Stanley Archives."

105. "Stanley the Bugbear of Congo Land," *New York Herald*, April 14, 1891, 8.

106. Collis P. Huntington, Letter to Henry Morton Stanley, January 28, 1891, item no. 3752, HMS.

107. Franklin, *George Washington Williams*, 222–24.

108. Henry Morton Stanley, Letter to William Mackinnon, June 6, 1891, item no. 1418, HMS.

109. William Mackinnon, Letter to Henry Morton Stanley, June 8, 1891, item no. 1419, HMS. When Mackinnon responded to Stanley two days later, he made no mention of Williams, but apologized for a pamphlet that one of his clerks had published.

110. Franklin, *George Washington Williams*, 210.

111. Ibid., 211–12.

112. Ibid., 213–15; George Washington Williams, *Open Letter*, 248–53.

113. Franklin, *George Washington Williams*, 223. See also, George Washington Williams, Letter to Collis P. Huntington, April 25, 1891, box 112, folder "Correspondence Apr. 23rd-31st 1891," CPH.

114. George Washington Williams, Letter to Collis P. Huntington, February 11, 1891, box 112, folder "Correspondence Feb. 11th-19th 1891," CPH.

115. William Mackinnon, Letter to Collis P. Huntington, June 11, 1891, box 113, folder "Correspondence Jun. 10th-19th 1891," CPH.

116. Francis W. Fox, Letter to Collis P. Huntington, July 6, 1891, box 113, folder "Correspondence July 1st-6th 1891," CPH. After Williams's death, Fox and a collector from the Arts Club in Manchester both expressed interest in purchasing the journals; however, they were returned to Williams's widow, who entrusted them to Slaughter from whose possession they disappeared. Deputy Consul Sherman, Letter to Francis W. Fox, August 7, 1891, box W5, folder "Books: George Washington Williams—General Correspondence (1 of 2)," JHF; Deputy Consul Sherman, Letter to R. C. Phillips [of Arts Club, Manchester], August 27, 1891, box W5, folder "Books:

George Washington Williams—General Correspondence (1 of 2)," JHF; Franklin, *George Washington Williams*, xix–xxi.

117. Franklin, *George Washington Williams*, 224.

118. Cookey, *Britain and the Congo Question*, 36.

119. George Washington Williams, Letter to Collis P. Huntington, December 1, 1890, box 111, folder "Correspondence Dec. 1st-10th 1890," CPH. Emphasis in source.

120. The *New York Tribune* obituary prominently notes his engagement to a British woman, Alice Fryer, who "applied to Consul General [John C.] New for information regarding Williams, according to this authority, and upon learning in what light marriages between whites and negroes [sic] in the United States are regarded she broke the engagement." "George W. Williams," *New York Tribune*, August 5, 1891, 7. See also, Franklin, *George Washington Williams*, 96, 102.

121. *Cleveland Gazette*, April 25, 1891, p. 2, box W4, folder "Books: George Washington Williams—CH. XIII-Observer and Critic (12 of 12)," JHF.

122. See transcription of an article on a meeting of the Christian Endeavor Society from *Worcester Telegram*, April 9, 1889, p. 3, box W1, folder "Books: George Washington Williams—Republican Politician," JHF.

123. George Washington Williams, *Report [ . . . ] to the President*, 269.

124. Ibid., 278–79. Emphasis in source.

125. Ibid., 276.

126. Ibid., 272.

127. George Washington Williams, *Report on the Proposed Congo Railway*, 262–63. Emphasis in source.

128. [George Washington Williams], "The Opening of Africa," *New York Tribune*, November 24, 1889, 15.

129. Franklin, *George Washington Williams*, 186; James Anderson, *Education of Blacks in the South*, 35. Although the Congregationalist American Missionary Association helped Armstrong found Hampton Institute, the group later moved away from industrial education. Meier, *Negro Thought in America*, 88.

130. George Washington Williams, *Report [ . . . ] to the President*, 276. Emphasis in source.

131. Du Bois, "Talented Tenth," 842–61.

132. Gates, *Figures in Black*, 25.

133. Ibid., 26.

134. Said, *Culture and Imperialism*, 51.

135. Banning, *Mémoires politiques et diplomatiques*, 295–96. See also, Banning, *Mémoires politiques et diplomatiques*, 279.

136. Conrad, *Heart of Darkness* (Norton Critical Edition, 3rd ed., edited by Robert Kimbrough), 82–125. Williams's reports to Leopold and Harrison are reprinted in their entirety; his report on the Congo railway is represented by substantial excerpts.

137. Hawkins, "Mark Twain's Involvement with the Congo Reform Movement," 166.

138. George Washington Williams, *Open Letter*, 248.

139. Lyman, *Militarism, Imperialism, and Racial Accommodation*, 47.

140. White, *Speaking with Vampires*, 9.

141. Hochschild, *King Leopold's Ghost*, 144–46.

142. Dunn, *Imagining the Congo*, 4.

143. Firchow, *Envisioning Africa*, 116. Firchow does mention Williams to corroborate accusations of cannibalism. Firchow, *Envisioning Africa*, 121.

144. Armstrong supplants an excerpt from Franklin with one from Hochschild's *King Leopold's Ghost*, which has familiarized a large audience with the roles of Williams and Sheppard in the international movement for Congo reform. Conrad, *Heart of Darkness* (Norton Critical Edition, 4th ed., edited by Paul B. Armstrong), 120–31, 171–81. In September 2016, Norton published a 5th edition, edited by Paul B. Armstrong, whose contents with regard to Williams appear to be identical to those of the 4th edition.

145. Campbell, *Middle Passages*, 130; Charles Smith, *Glimpses of Africa*, 153.

146. Charles Smith, *Glimpses of Africa*, 154.

147. Blyden's political and commercial connections rendered him unwilling to confront Leopold even when the reform movement was gaining momentum. Lynch, *Edward Wilmot Blyden*, 208–9.

148. duCille, *Skin Trade*, 124.

Chapter 2

1. "Minutes of Committee—Foreign Missions," December 9, 1889, 3:176, ECFM; Owen and Owen, *History of Alabama*, 1012.

2. Charles Smith, *Glimpses of Africa*, 218. See Campbell, *Middle Passages*, 136–37.

3. "Minutes of Committee—Foreign Missions," August 12, 1889, 3:160, ECFM; "Minutes of Committee—Foreign Missions," October 13, 1889, 3:167–68, ECFM. During the Civil War, the Presbyterian Church split into Northern and Southern factions, which did not reunite until 1983. Although the Southern Presbyterian Church (U.S.) had very few African American members, it provided opportunities for black missionaries to serve in Africa in the nineteenth and early twentieth centuries. All references to the Presbyterian Church will be to the Southern Presbyterians unless otherwise specified. The Northern Presbyterian Church was known officially as the Presbyterian Church (U.S.A.). Alvis, *Religion and Race*, 2–7, 132–45; Barber, *Climbing Jacob's Ladder*, 31–45; Andrew Murray, *Presbyterians and the Negro*, 139–49.

4. "Minutes of Committee—Foreign Missions," November 1889, 3:171, ECFM; Phipps, *William Sheppard*, 11–13; Fry, *John Tyler Morgan*, 5; Lapsley, *Life and Letters*, 30–31.

5. William Sheppard, "Letter" (September 1, 1890), 168.

6. Abbott and Seroff, *Out of Sight*, 85. Loudin, the former director of the Fisk Jubilee Singers, formed his own group that used the Fisk name though they were not affiliated with the university. Ward, *Dark Midnight When I Rise*, 388–89. For more on Loudin, see Cook, "Finding Otira," 84–111.

7. Of the first five black women appointed to the APCM, only Lucy Gantt Sheppard was married. Of the four unmarried women, three later married black APCM colleagues. During the first twenty years of the APCM, no unmarried white women were appointed as missionaries. For biographical data on APCM missionaries and their terms of service, see Ethel Wharton, *Led in Triumph*, 58, 84.

8. "Remarkable Missionary," 273.

9. Edmiston, *Maria Fearing*, 18.

10. [Armstrong], "Invitation to Congo," 22.

11. Lapsley, "Letters from the Missions" (October 2, 1890), 33–34.
12. Lapsley, "Letters from the Missions" (October 5, 1892 [sic]), 151. Emphasis in source.
13. Lapsley, *Life and Letters*, 94.
14. "Congo Boat Company," 114.
15. Rowbotham, "Letters from the Missions," 232.
16. De Witt Snyder, "Letters from the Field" (April 20, 1895), 410.
17. Morrison, Letter (June 5, 1897), 109.
18. Morrison, Letter (December 7, 1897), 113. Throughout the book, I have opted to use the "Kuba" root to describe the people often referred to in primary and secondary sources as the Bakuba, which is the correct Bantu plural prefix, meaning the "Bakuba people." A complete and correct use of Bantu prefixes throughout the manuscript, however, could cause confusion, so for the sake of consistency I have elected to use the root alone.
19. Morrison, "Late War as Reported on the Congo," 30.
20. William Sheppard, "Interview with Chief M'lumba N'kusa," 121.
21. Hochschild, *King Leopold's Ghost*, 165.
22. William Sheppard, "Interview with Chief M'lumba N'kusa," 122–23. On the spelling of the chief's name, see Benedetto, *Presbyterian Reformers in Central Africa*, 125n2.
23. Benedetto, *Presbyterian Reformers in Central Africa*, 126n6.
24. Chester, Letter to APCM (January 9, 1900), 127.
25. "Atrocities in the Congo Free State," 61.
26. Morrison, "Africa Between the Upper and Nether Millstones," 66.
27. "In the Heart of Africa," 220.
28. Ludovic Moncheur, Letter to Adolphe de Cuvelier, January 18, 1904, AAB; Phipps, *William Sheppard*, 155; Sprunt, "Augusta County's Pioneer Missionary," 27.
29. Washington, "Address of Dr. Booker T. Washington," 258; Morrison, "Treatment of the Native People," 189. The version of Morrison's speech included in the congress proceedings does not name Sheppard. Morrison, "Address of Rev. W. H. [sic] Morrison," 235–39.
30. Morrison, Letter to Samuel Clemens, 219; Twain, *King Leopold's Soliloquy*, 52–54.
31. The *Kassai Herald* was published from March 1901 until November 1916 albeit "somewhat irregularly" because of "shortages of paper and type, and lack of editorial and production staff." Benedetto, *Presbyterian Reformers in Central Africa*, 68n22.
32. William Sheppard, "From the Bakuba Country," 282.
33. Dreypondt [sic], Letter to the *Kassai Herald*, 284.
34. Morrison, Letter to Gustave Dreypondt [sic], 287.
35. Compagnie du Kasai, *Question congolaise*; Vandervelde, *La Belgique et le Congo*, 89.
36. Ludovic Moncheur, Letter to Adolphe de Cuvelier, January 18, 1904, AAB; Benedetto, *Presbyterian Reformers in Central Africa*, 196–97n5. Benedetto provides an English translation of part of the letter.
37. Ferdinand de Hemricourt de Grunne, No. 175 Confidentielle, April 6, 1908, (attached to Vice-Gouverneur Général, Letter to Secrétaire d'État, May 11, 1908), AAB.

38. Morrison, Letter to Lachlan Cumming Vass II, 357–58.
39. Hochschild, *King Leopold's Ghost*, 110.
40. Vandervelde, "Speech for the Defense," 388.
41. Vandervelde, *Souvenirs d'un militant socialiste*, 90.
42. Phipps, *William Sheppard*, 169; Pagan Kennedy, *Black Livingstone*, 182.
43. Doyle, *Crime of the Congo*, 93, iv.
44. Émile Vandervelde, "Interview de Vandervelde; Retour du Congo," *Le Peuple*, October 19, 1909, 3; Gianpetri, "Verdict of the Tribunal of the First Instance at Léopoldville," 413.
45. Morrison, Letter to E. D. Morel, 417.
46. Phipps, *William Sheppard*, 215; Pakenham, *Scramble for Africa*, 593. Matthews, *Quest for an American Sociology*, 58; Cookey, *Britain and the Congo Question*, 171. A 1908 "note" in the Belgian colonial archives claims that Sheppard told someone that Morrison "n'est pas un missionnaire que c'est, au contraire, un agent politique" (is not a missionary but, on the contrary, a political agent). I don't find the charge consistent with anything else Sheppard ever said about Morrison or consider the source to be wholly credible; however, it does seem to reflect Belgian efforts to exploit known rifts among APCM missionaries. Gustave Gustin, "Note," (attached to Vice-Gouverneur Général, Letter to Secrétaire d'État, May 11, 1908), AAB.
47. Benedetto, *Presbyterian Reformers in Central Africa*, 423–25n5; Pagan Kennedy, *Black Livingstone*, 189–91, 178; Phipps, *William Sheppard*, 177–78; James O. Reavis, Letter to William Morrison, September 10, 1910, box 78, folder 1, CMP. Phipps and Hawkins, the only two black male missionaries who spent their entire tenures without wives in the Congo, were forced to resign in 1908 and 1910 respectively, based on Morrison's charges of sexual misconduct. When the PCUS appointed Hawkins, they refused to allow his wife to go to the Congo, effectively ending his marriage, and he may have been in a long-term monogamous relationship with an African woman. Luebo Station minutes from 1899 indicate that it was common knowledge that Hawkins was caring for a child who bore his name, which makes the timing of his dismissal especially curious. See Luebo Station Minutes, August 17, 1899, box 17, folder 2, CMP. During travels in the Kasai in 2006, I met an individual who claimed to be Sheppard's great grandson. Other people disputed his claim, and I was unable to confirm or refute his account.
48. Samuel Chester, Letter to James McClung Sieg, August 16, 1910, box 78, folder 5, CMP.
49. After marrying active missionary Adolphus A. Rochester of Jamaica, Edna Atkinson Rochester, also of Jamaica, served from 1923 to 1939. Adolphus's previous wife, Annie Katherine Taylor Rochester of Alabama, died in 1914 after eight years with the APCM. For more on Annie Rochester, see Jacobs, "Their 'Special Mission,'" 169–71.
50. Kaplan, "'Left Alone with America,'" 16.
51. Phipps, *William Sheppard*, 103.
52. Chester, "Help Needed for Africa," 398. Emphasis in source.
53. See, for example, Robert Gordon, "Black Man's Burden," 58.
54. Chester, "Man Needed at Once," 446–47.
55. May Snyder, "Letter from Luebo" (October 18, 1895), 78.
56. John Crawford, "Pioneer African Missionary," 45.

57. Chester, "Foreign Mission Committee Notes" (November 1895), 491; Newkirk, *Spectacle*, 80.

58. Sotiropoulos, "'Town of God,'" 61.

59. John Crawford, "Pioneer African Missionary," 53; Bradford and Blume, *Ota Benga*, 92. Following the unceremonious end of Verner's tour, appeals for white missionaries continued. See "Needs of the Congo Mission," 339; "Congo Mission," 5; and "Wanted—Another White Missionary for Africa," 461.

60. Parezo and Fowler, *Anthropology Goes to the Fair*, 409; Bradford and Blume, *Ota Benga*, 110.

61. Sotiropoulos, "'Town of God,'" 72–73.

62. J. Lee Greene, *Time's Unfading Garden*, 69–81; Spencer, *Who Is Chauncey Spencer?*, 15; Kalumvueziko, *Le Pygmée congolais exposé dans un zoo américain*, 105–8; McCray, *Ota Benga under My Mother's Roof*, xii. Carrie Allen McCray insists that Ota Benga lived with her family in Lynchburg, not with the Spencers as Chauncey Spencer claimed.

63. Bradford and Blume, *Ota Benga*, 93.

64. *Eleventh Annual Report of the Executive Committee of Colored Evangelization to the General Assembly, Sitting at Jackson, MS, May 15, 1902 and the Catalogue of the Stillman Institute, 1901–1902*, p. 19, box "Stillman College History," WHSML; Sikes, "Historical Development of Stillman," 48; Pagan Kennedy, *Black Livingstone*, 124; Newkirk, *Spectacle*, 80; Bradford and Blume, *Ota Benga*, 93, 99.

65. Ludovic Moncheur, Letter to Adolphe de Cuvelier, January 18, 1904, AAB; Newkirk, *Spectacle*, 137, 161–62.

66. Newkirk, *Spectacle*, 90; Schildkrout, "Personal Styles and Disciplinary Paradigms," 172–73. The APCM's *Kassai Herald* notes that Verner went out in search of Kuba curios for Starr. American Presbyterian Congo Mission, "Secular News" (April 1906), 24.

67. Verner, *Pioneering in Central Africa*, 4.

68. Phipps, *William Sheppard*, 149. For a more extreme defense of Verner, see Bradford and Blume, *Ota Benga*, 75–76. Even more remarkably, Crawford's *Journal of Presbyterian History* article on Verner makes no mention of Ota Benga or the Bronx Zoo, mistakenly claiming that the Congolese people brought to St. Louis all returned "home safely." John Crawford, "Pioneer African Missionary," 55.

69. Samuel Chester, Letter to Motte Martin, February 28, 1907, box 78, folder 2, CMP; Morrison, Letter to "Whom it May Concern," 244–48; Hill, "Antislavery Work by the American Women," 216–17.

70. John Crawford, "Pioneer African Missionary," 51; Phipps, *William Sheppard*, 215.

71. Pagan Kennedy, *Black Livingstone*, 4; Fields, "Ideology and Race in American History," 159.

72. Pagan Kennedy, *Black Livingstone*, xiii–xiv.

73. Phipps, *William Sheppard*, xi.

74. William Sheppard, *Presbyterian Pioneers in Congo*, 15, 150.

75. Chester, "Introduction," 11.

76. Ibid.

77. William Sheppard, *Presbyterian Pioneers in Congo*, 83.

78. Ibid., 101, 107–8. *Lukenga* is the Tshiluba title for the king; *Nyimi* is the Bushong or Kuba royal title.

79. William Sheppard, Letter (May 17, 1890), 355.
80. Charles Smith, *Glimpses of Africa*, 148; Hogan Northrup, and O'Dea, *My Little Jungle Queen*. Smith makes a similar statement about his "long-cherished desire to see Africa" on the first page of his preface to *Glimpses of Africa*, a point which is cited by Henry McNeal Turner in his introduction to the volume. Charles Smith, *Glimpses of Africa*, 5, 12. As cited, Maria Fearing also was noted for her "long cherished desire to be a missionary to Africa." "Remarkable Missionary," 273. The rhetoric that Smith shares with the APCM marks the broad influence of the mission.
81. Campbell, *Middle Passages*, 159.
82. "Congo Boat Company," 113–14.
83. "Bakuba," 170.
84. William Sheppard, *Presbyterian Pioneers in Congo*, [5].
85. Ibid., 79, 21, 49, 81.
86. Jacobson, *Barbarian Virtues*, 111.
87. Newkirk, *Spectacle*, 69.
88. Edmiston, *Maria Fearing*, 24.
89. Lapsley, *Life and Letters*, 174.
90. Rebecca Harding Davis, "In Proof of To-Morrow," 787. Her son Richard Harding Davis traveled to the Congo in 1907 to investigate the atrocities. For his criticism of Leopold and his U.S. commercial collaborators, see Richard Harding Davis, *Congo and Coasts of Africa*, 93–104.
91. Jacobson, *Barbarian Virtues*, 121.
92. William Sheppard, "Into the Heart of Africa," 186.
93. William Sheppard, "Semi-civilization in Africa," 82.
94. William Sheppard, *Presbyterian Pioneers in Congo*, 81, 137.
95. Ibid., 113.
96. Ibid., 117–18.
97. Lapsley, *Life and Letters*, 55.
98. William Sheppard, *Presbyterian Pioneers in Congo*, 28, 34.
99. The full text of the oration was reprinted in two installments in April and May 1895 "to satisfy frequent requests." William Sheppard, "Semi-civilization in Africa," 82.
100. William Sheppard, "Into the Heart of Africa," 185.
101. William Sheppard, "Into the Heart of Africa," 185. Spellings of names vary from one source to another and sometimes even within a single source (e.g., "Bo-pe Makabe"). I have been faithful to my sources, despite irregularities.
102. Crummell, Letter, 5; Moody-Turner, *Black Folklore*, 87–89. Hampton had ties to the developing field of anthropology: in 1893, Alice Bacon, who worked at Hampton while Sheppard was a student, established the Hampton Folklore Society which soon placed the school near the center of emergent academic anthropology thanks to its close connections with the new American Folklore Society. Lee Baker, "Research, Reform, and Racial Uplift," 44n3, 63–65. See also, Moody-Turner, *Black Folklore*, 64–72.
103. "Folk-Lore and Ethnology," 181.
104. "*Southern Workman* Prospectus 1898" (January 1898), 2. See also, Frissell, "Twenty-Seventh Annual Report of the Principal," 88; Hollis Burke Frissell, "Letters to *Southern Workman* Contributors," January 18, 1899, SWP.
105. See, for example, Pagan Kennedy, *Black Livingstone*, 89.

106. William Sheppard, "Into the Heart of Africa," 185; Phipps, *William Sheppard*, 73–74; Vansina, *Children of Woot*, 7; Heywood, *Central Africans and Cultural Transformations*, 17. Vansina cites Sheppard as a credible source on a range of topics. See Vansina, *Children of Woot*, 79, 344n73, 145, 111, 197, 208.

107. De Witt Snyder, Letter to Brother Phillips, 97.

108. Benedetto, *Presbyterian Reformers in Central Africa*, 98n4. Emphasis in source.

109. William Sheppard, "Into the Heart of Africa," 184.

110. Chester, "Foreign Committee Mission Notes" (November 1895), 491.

111. Joseph Phipps was not listed as a member of Second Presbyterian and did not appear in the minutes of the Lackawanna County (Pennsylvania) Presbytery until 1896, after his appointment to the APCM. The lack of prior Presbyterian affiliation makes it possible that church membership was intended as an entree to African service. Following his return to the United States in 1908, Phipps lived in New York, Florida, and South Carolina though he remained affiliated with the Lackawanna Presbytery until at least 1915.

112. Chester, "Foreign Mission Committee Notes" (October 1895), 446.

113. Smallwood, *Saltwater Slavery*, 191.

114. Phipps, *William Sheppard*, 179.

115. See the cover of the *Missionary Survey* 1, no. 1 (November 1911). The *Missionary Survey* changed its title to the *Presbyterian Survey* in April 1924, and to *Presbyterians Today* in 1995.

116. George Wright, *Life behind a Veil*, 148; Short, "William Henry Sheppard," 445.

117. "Dr. Frissell/H.N.I. Grad Class 5/23/16/Tuskegee 5/25/16," box "William H. Sheppard (Edmiston to Great Britain)," folder "Frissell," "Supplementary William Henry Sheppard Materials," WHSVA (2003). See also, "Principal Washington's Successor Installed," *Tuskegee Student*, June 3, 1916, 1–2.

118. See "Men of the Month: A Missionary" (May 1915), 15. William Phipps attributes authorship of the article to Du Bois. See Phipps, *William Sheppard*, 180.

119. Short, "William Henry Sheppard," 452, 447–49.

120. "At Home and Afield: Hampton Incidents," 183.

121. In 1915, Hampton Institute Press published "Four Little 'True African Stories' written by Rev. W. H. Sheppard," a series of children's morality tales set in Africa. See William Sheppard, *African Daniel*; William Sheppard, *Little Robber*; William Sheppard, *Story of a Girl*; William Sheppard, *Young Hunter*; "Graduates and Ex-Students," 125.

122. "Local Baptist Conference in Uproar as Dr. Batchelor 'Classifies' Preachers," *Pittsburgh Courier*, May 31, 1924, 8.

123. Bowser, "Studies of the African Diaspora," 4.

124. Max W. Sheppard, Interview, August 12, 1979, three unlabeled audio cassettes, box "William H. Sheppard—Negatives, Photographs, Slides and Tapes," WHSVA (2003).

125. Samuel Burney Hay, Letter to Luebo Presbytery, April 18, 1956, WHSML.

126. Bote-Tsheik and Ntambue, *Shapeta, Tshilobo Tshia Mu Kasayi*, 3–4. I am grateful to Simon Ntumba Tshitenga, director of IMPROKA, for sharing the history of the press, where he began working in 1986 and which he has directed since 1993, during a June 12, 2006, conversation.

127. See "History: The Presbytery of Sheppards and Lapsley," http://pslpcusa.org/history. June 20, 2016.

128. Pagan Kennedy, *Black Livingstone*, 204.

129. Kennedy's fifteen-year error is peculiar given her citation of a 1941 interview. Pagan Kennedy, *Black Livingstone*, 105, 218n107[a].

130. Horner, "Last Chat with a Congo Pioneer," 28.

131. See also, Lucy Sheppard, "Progress at Ibanj," 16–17; Lucy Sheppard, "Sunshine in Congo-Land," 41–42.

132. Mary Jacq Rainey, "Art Club Gives Historic Records to Stillman," *Tuscaloosa News*, October 6, 1978, 8. Special thanks to Martha J. Hall-Cammon for sharing the history of the Lucy Sheppard Arts Club, which she joined in 1963, in a March 15, 2004, telephone conversation.

133. Vitalis, *White World Order*, 26.

Chapter 3

1. Washington, "Helpful Life," 3:24–25.

2. "Mr. B. T. Washington on the Emigration Question," 25.

3. Jeanette Jones, *In Search of Brightest Africa*, 36; Hochschild, *King Leopold's Ghost*, 314n80; Baylen, "Senator John Tyler Morgan," 121–22.

4. Harlan, "Booker T. Washington and the White Man's Burden," 441.

5. See, for example, Norrell, *Up from History*, 201–3, 372–75; Pagan Kennedy, *Black Livingstone*, 158.

6. Guridy, *Forging Diaspora*, 22–23.

7. Fierce, *Pan-African Idea in the United States*, 176; Raushenbush, *Robert E. Park*, 39. Raushenbush mentions only one historian by name—August Meier.

8. Park, "Methods of Teaching," 316.

9. Drake, Introduction, xi. See also, Drake, "Tuskegee Connection," 83; Drake, Review of *Negro Thought in America*, 330.

10. Moses, *Creative Conflict in African American Thought*, 163. See also, Park, "Methods of Teaching," 311–12.

11. Washington, *Up from Slavery*, 1:331–32.

12. Fry, *Henry S. Sanford*, 138, 144.

13. Power-Greene, *Against Wind and Tide*, 196–97. Washington attributes his "careful and unbiased study of the question" of emigration to Africa to his "respect" for its partisans, namely Turner. Washington, *Some European Observations*, 10.

14. Vernon Williams, *Rethinking Race*, 57; Du Bois, *Souls of Black Folk*, 393.

15. Du Bois, *Souls of Black Folk*, 402–3.

16. Washington, *Up from Slavery*, 1:332.

17. Harlan, *Booker T. Washington*, 1:298, 223–35.

18. Washington, *Up from Slavery*, 1:330; Washington, *My Larger Education*, 106.

19. Washington, *Up from Slavery*, 1:368–69. Although Washington does not specify which of Douglass's autobiographies he read, the encounter appears in both Douglass, *My Bondage and My Freedom*, 370–72 and Douglass, *Life and Times of Frederick Douglass*, 677–99. When writing about Douglass's status as "representative," Henry Louis Gates Jr. misattributes Washington's juxtaposition of Douglass's death and Washington's

own ascension to *Up from Slavery* rather than *My Larger Education*. Gates, *Figures in Black*, 109.

20. Harlan, "Booker T. Washington and the White Man's Burden," 450.
21. Washington, "Cruelty in the Congo Country," 8:88.
22. Washington, "Address of Dr. Booker T. Washington," 258–59.
23. Morrison, "Address of Rev. W. H. [sic] Morrison," 237. A lengthier version of Morrison's address that appears as an appendix to the missionary's biography does mention Sheppard by name. Morrison, "Treatment of the Native People," 189.
24. Washington, "Address of Dr. Booker T. Washington," 260, 259.
25. Rose, *Official Report of the Thirteenth Universal Peace Congress*, 303.
26. Washington, "Cruelty in the Congo Country," 8:88.
27. Washington, Letter to Robert Curtis Ogden, 8:94.
28. Washington, "Cruelty in the Congo Country," 8:85–86.
29. Ibid., 8:88, 90.
30. Emmett Scott, quoted in "International Conference on the Negro," *Tuskegee Student*, April 20, 1912, 1. See Washington, "Industrial Education in Africa," 8:549. Washington's article also appeared in the *Independent* on March 15, 1906, and the *New York Age* on March 22, 1906. Jeanette Jones, *In Search of Brightest Africa*, 237n45.
31. Washington, Letter to Cain Washington Triplett and Others, 8:153.
32. Moses, *Creative Conflict in African American Thought*, 164; Washington, "Christianizing Africa," 4:252; George Washington Williams, *Open Letter*, 252.
33. Zimmerman, *Alabama in Africa*, 179.
34. Harlan, "Booker T. Washington and the White Man's Burden," 450–51.
35. Zimmerman, *Alabama in Africa*, 179.
36. Park, "Blood-Money of the Congo," 237.
37. Zimmerman, *Alabama in Africa*, 179.
38. Park, "Methods of Teaching," 312; Gish, *Alfred B. Xuma*, 16. See also, Jeanette Jones, *In Search of Brightest Africa*, 102.
39. Raushenbush, *Robert E. Park*, 43. See Matthews, *Quest for an American Sociology*, 62; Raushenbush, *Robert E. Park*, 40–41.
40. Park, "Methods of Teaching," 311; Drake, "Tuskegee Connection," 84. For characterizations of Washington's oeuvre as largely ghostwritten, see Harlan, *Booker T. Washington*, 2:290; Norrell, *Up from History*, 372.
41. Matthews, *Quest for an American Sociology*, 64.
42. Harlan, *Booker T. Washington*, 1:246–47.
43. Ibid., 2:291.
44. Park, Letter to Booker T. Washington, 11:116–17.
45. Washington, *Man Farthest Down*, 14–17. For an alternate perspective that "Park's white authorial presence permeates the text, compromising Washington's narrative authority," see Totten, "Southernizing Travel in the Black Atlantic," 123.
46. Stepto, *From behind the Veil*, 41. See, for example, Washington, *Man Farthest Down*, 269–70.
47. Park, Letter to Booker T. Washington, 11:117.
48. Drake, Introduction, xxiii.
49. Mathews, *Booker T. Washington*, 225.
50. Harlan and Smock, *Booker T. Washington Papers*, 8:90n1.

51. Park, "Recent Atrocities in the Congo State," 205–9; Park, "Terrible Story of the Congo," 230.

52. Robert Park, quoted in Harlan, "Booker T. Washington and the White Man's Burden," 451. Emphasis in source.

53. "Belgian Legation," April 28, 1905, box 16, folder "Correspondence Jan.-Oct. 1905," BTW.

54. Washington, *Up from Slavery*, 1:366.

55. Washington, "Cruelty in the Congo Country," 8:86. Williams and Stanley made the same point. See John Hope Franklin's transcription of an article about a meeting of the Christian Endeavor Society from the *Worcester Telegram*, April 9, 1889, p. 3, box W1, folder "Books: George Washington Williams—Republican Politician," JHF; Stanley, *Congo*, 2:383.

56. Hawkins, "Mark Twain's Involvement," 169. See Raushenbush, *Robert E. Park*, 36; Matthews, *Quest for an American Sociology*, 57–59.

57. Washington, *Up from Slavery*, 1:258.

58. Raushenbush, *Robert E. Park*, 44.

59. Washington, *Story of the Negro*, 1:62.

60. Washington, "Cruelty in the Congo Country," 8:86, 87.

61. Vernon Williams, *Rethinking Race*, 67.

62. Houston A. Baker Jr., *Turning South Again*, 34, 33.

63. Washington, *Story of the Negro*, 1:36–37.

64. Kaplan, *Anarchy of Empire*, 180.

65. In 1912, Washington reported, "From year to year we have from 100 to 150 students representing foreign countries and we are anxious that these students be fitted to go back to their homes and render the highest and best service." Washington, "Opening Address of the International Conference on the Negro," 11:521. See also, Zimmerman, *Alabama in Africa*, 182; Washington, Letter to James Jenkins Dossen, 9:617–18.

66. Engs, *Educating the Disfranchised and Disinherited*, 130–43.

67. "International Conference on the Negro," *Tuskegee Student*, April 20, 1912, 1. For another version of the address, see Washington, "Opening Address of the International Conference on the Negro," 11:520–22.

68. Marable, "Booker T. Washington and African Nationalism," 403–4.

69. Harlan, "Booker T. Washington and the White Man's Burden," 461.

70. On the importance of land ownership, see Norrell, *Up from History*, 95; Matthews, *Quest for an American Sociology*, 69.

71. R. Hunt Davis, "John L. Dube," 499; Marable, "Booker T. Washington and African Nationalism," 401. See Dube, "Need of Industrial Education in Africa," 141–42.

72. R. Hunt Davis, "John L. Dube," 497. On Dube's admiration for and connections to Washington, see Heather Hughes, *First President*, 70–72, 155.

73. Harlan, "Booker T. Washington and the White Man's Burden," 463–64; R. Hunt Davis, "John L. Dube," 528.

74. "Principal Washington's Successor Installed," *Tuskegee Student*, June 3, 1916, 1–2; Gish, *Alfred B. Xuma*, 61.

75. "Dr. Frissell/H.N.I. Grad Class 5/23/16/Tuskegee 5/25/16," box "William H. Sheppard (Edmiston to Great Britain)," folder "Frissell," "Supplementary William Henry Sheppard Materials," WHSVA (2003).

76. Marable, "Booker T. Washington and African Nationalism," 402; Gish, *Alfred B. Xuma*, 16; Jabavu, *Black Problem*, 27–70.

77. Gish, *Alfred B. Xuma*, 205.

78. Du Bois, "Foreword," 8.

79. Gilroy, *Black Atlantic*, 113. Sundquist recognizes Manye as a source for Du Bois's Africa in *The Souls of Black Folk*. Sundquist, *To Wake the Nations*, 561. For more on Manye and her circle, see Campbell, *Songs of Zion*, 249–94.

80. Chrisman, "Du Bois in Transnational Perspective," 22; Heather Hughes, *First President*, 81. For a list of African students at Wilberforce, see Walter Williams, *Black Americans and the Evangelization of Africa*, 193.

81. Edwards, "Uses of Diaspora," 61.

82. Berghahn, *Image of Africa*, 68.

83. Washington, "Opening Address of the International Conference on the Negro," 11:521. See "International Conference," *Tuskegee Student*, February 3, 1912, 1; "International Conference on the Negro," *Tuskegee Student*, April 20, 1912, 1.

84. Booker T. Washington, "Internation[al] Conference on the Negro," *Tuskegee Student*, February 10, 1912, 3.

85. Quoted in Harlan, "Booker T. Washington and the White Man's Burden," 465. See also, Zimmerman, *Alabama in Africa*, 183–87.

86. Zimmerman, *Alabama in Africa*, 1, 4–5. See Herman, Letter to Booker T. Washington, 5:633–36; Harlan, "Booker T. Washington and the White Man's Burden," 446.

87. Zimmerman, *Alabama in Africa*, 113, 174. See Zimmerman, *Alabama in Africa*, 170–71; Harlan, "Booker T. Washington and the White Man's Burden," 447–48; Washington, Letter to Cain Washington Triplett and Others, 8:153.

88. Zimmerman, *Alabama in Africa*, 164; Drake, "Introduction," xv; Norrell, *Up from History*, 221; Harlan, "Booker T. Washington and the White Man's Burden," 459; Harlan, *Booker T. Washington*, 2:278; Mathews, *Booker T. Washington*, 224.

89. Pratt, *Imperial Eyes*, 6.

90. Harlan, "Booker T. Washington and the White Man's Burden," 459n73.

91. Engs, *Educating the Disfranchised and Disinherited*, 10. See also, Moody-Turner, *Black Folklore*, 46–52.

92. Okihiro, "Toward a Black Pacific," 324.

93. James Anderson, *Education of Blacks in the South*, 77.

94. Speer, Letter to Booker T. Washington, 6:524–25.

95. Mathews, *Booker T. Washington*, 310.

96. For more on Sarah Frances Martin Sheppard, see Phipps, *William Sheppard*, 1; Pagan Kennedy, *Black Livingstone*, 7–8; Langhorne, "Mother of a Famous Missionary," 218–19.

97. Houston A. Baker Jr., *Turning South Again*, 63. See Washington, "Industrial Schools as an Aid to Missions," 30–31.

98. Washington, *Story of the Negro*, 1:63.

99. Harlan, *Booker T. Washington*, 1:140.

100. Washington, *Story of the Negro*, 1:64.

101. Ibid., 1:62.

102. Ibid., 1:20–21, 28.

103. Walter Williams, *Black Americans and the Evangelization of Africa*, 42; Seraile, "Black American Missionaries in Africa," 200–201.

104. Stepto, *From behind the Veil*, 42–43.

105. Washington, *Up from Slavery*, 1:360.

106. Harlan, "Booker T. Washington and the White Man's Burden," 448.

107. Ibid., 453.

108. Ibid., 454n48.

109. Mathews, *Booker T. Washington*, 248; Lyon, Letter to Booker T. Washington, 9:626.

110. Harlan, "Booker T. Washington and the White Man's Burden," 455.

111. Mathews, *Booker T. Washington*, 249.

112. Washington, *Up from Slavery*, 1:330; Harlan, "Booker T. Washington and the White Man's Burden," 452. For more on Washington's relationship to Liberia, see Skinner, *African Americans and U.S. Policy toward Africa*, 291–347; Mathews, *Booker T. Washington*, 241–54.

113. Houston A. Baker Jr., *Turning South Again*, 63. Emphasis in source.

114. In addition to Washington's accounts of his first and third trips in *Some European Observations* and *The Man Farthest Down*, respectively, on his short fall 1903 trip and the unrealized trip planned for 1915, see Harlan, *Booker T. Washington*, 2:282–83, 293–94.

115. Houston A. Baker Jr., *Turning South Again*, 59. Emphasis in source.

116. Washington, *Some European Observations*, 1.

117. Washington, *Up from Slavery*, 1:355.

118. Washington, "Man Farthest Down," 11:131. In the opening paragraph of the first chapter of the book version, Washington writes of "recreation and rest." Washington, *Man Farthest Down*, 3.

119. Washington, *Some European Observations*, 5.

120. Washington, *Man Farthest Down*, 35.

121. Washington, *Some European Observations*, 10, 11. See also, Washington, *Future of the American Negro*, 159.

122. Washington, *Up from Slavery*, 1:366. See also, Washington, *Some European Observations*, 10.

123. Washington, Letter to *Colored American* (Washington, D.C.), 5:164.

124. Washington, *My Larger Education*, 259; Washington, *Man Farthest Down*, 343; Harlan and Smock, *Booker T. Washington Papers*, 8:484n1; Bruce, "Booker T. Washington's *The Man Farthest Down* and the Transformation of Race," 239–53.

125. Gilroy, *Black Atlantic*, 17–18; Chrisman, *Postcolonial Contraventions*, 80.

126. Chrisman, *Postcolonial Contraventions*, 79.

127. Washington, *Some European Observations*, 3. See Dubois, "Free Man."

128. Harlan, "Booker T. Washington and the White Man's Burden," 442.

129. Washington, *Man Farthest Down*, 13.

130. Gilroy, *Black Atlantic*, 189.

131. Houston A. Baker Jr., *Turning South Again*, 34.

132. Woodward, *Origins of the New South*, 324.

133. Willard, "Timing Impossible Subjects," 640.

134. Washington, Letter to Marcus Garvey, 13:133–34; Marcus Garvey, Letter to Emmett Scott, February 4, 1916, box 8, folder 56, RRM; Marcus Garvey, Letter to Robert Russa Moton, Febuary 29, 1916, box 8, folder 56, RRM.

135. Holloway, *Passed On*, 116.

Chapter 4

1. Minutes of Foreign Missions of the Presbyterian Church (U.S.A.), December 17, 1894, 12:146, box 2, BFM; Minutes of Foreign Missions of the Presbyterian Church (U.S.A.), February 18, 1895, 12:191–92, box 2, BFM.

2. Bethune, Interview by Charles S. Johnson, 42. See also, Holt, *Mary McLeod Bethune*, 45.

3. Bethune, "Yes, I Went to Liberia," 275.

4. Kellersberger, *Life for the Congo*, 18.

5. Ibid., 20; Richardson, *History of Fisk University*, 46.

6. At Fisk, Althea Brown served as president of the Young People's Society of Christian Endeavor, organized the Duodecem Literae Virgines Club, memorialized the university's founding president, Erastus Milo Cravath, in the *Fisk Herald*, and accompanied his successor James Merrill on a tour of Andrew Jackson's Hermitage. "Literary Notes," *Fisk Herald* 18, no. 5 (February 1901): 13; "Club Directory," *Fisk Herald* 17, no. 8 (May 1900): 10; "Extracts from Letters from Students," *Fisk Herald* 18, no. 2 (November 1900): 19; "A Drive to the Hermitage," *Fisk Herald* 18, no. 9 (June 1901): 8–9.

7. PCUS *Minutes of Committee—Foreign Missions*, May 14, 1901, 7:156–58, ECFM. Anna Thankful Ballantine, principal of the women's section of Fisk, accompanied Althea Brown to her ECFM interview.

8. "Commencement Day," *Fisk Herald* 18, no. 10 (July 1901): 4–6.

9. PCUS *Minutes of Committee—Foreign Missions*, April 8, 1902, 7:196, ECFM.

10. Bedinger, "Althea Brown Edmiston," 268. For her date and port of arrival, see Alonzo Edmiston, Letter to Joseph Savels, August 21, 1930, box 71, folder 15, CMP; Kellersberger, *Life for the Congo*, 56–58.

11. Bedinger, "Althea Brown Edmiston," 277.

12. "Africa and the World Democracy," 173; Edmiston, *Maria Fearing*, 18.

13. Edmiston, *Nkana mu Ilonga*, [iv].

14. Bedinger, "Althea Brown Edmiston," 277.

15. Morrison, *Grammar and Dictionary*, ix; Starr, *Bibliography of Congo Languages*, 44, 55. On Samuel Verner's early language contributions, see John Crawford, "Pioneer African Missionary," 54–55.

16. Bedinger, *Triumphs of the Gospel*, 52; Benedetto, "Presbyterian Mission Press," 65–68. For the predominance of APCM publications among Tshiluba holdings at Northwestern University and the School of Oriental and African Studies, see Bade, *Books in African Languages*, 2:660–69; Mann and Sanders, *Bibliography of African Language Texts*, 132–43.

17. Bedinger, "Althea Brown Edmiston," 278.

18. Fabian explains, "colonial authorities considered Swahili (rather than Luba or Bemba) to be *the* language of Katanga around 1910." Fabian, *Language and Colonial Power*, 133. Emphasis in source.

19. Mudimbe, *Invention of Africa*, 47. The APCM was in competition with Catholic stations, whose collaborations included at least one case where missionaries worked for the Compagnie du Kasai. Vansina, *Being Colonized*, 91.

20. Mputubwele, "Zairian Language Policy," 285; Luebo Station Minutes, March 25, 1901, box 17, folder 2, CMP.

21. Benedetto, "Presbyterian Mission Press," 60, 65–67. Starr presumptuously credits "white [sic] authors" (Hawkins, Lillian Thomas, William Sheppard, Lucy Sheppard, and Fearing) for their Tshiluba translations in the 1902 hymnal, which is a peculiar error, since Starr had visited APCM stations a couple of years before publishing his bibliography. Starr, *Bibliography of Congo Languages*, 82.

22. In the 1909 Tshiluba hymnal, African American missionaries translated forty-four of ninety-five songs. In the expanded edition I acquired in 2006, produced by the independent Congolese church but based on earlier APCM works, only thirty-three songs, less than 10 percent of the total, are translated by African Americans. After the Sheppards, Hawkins, and Phipps were sent home, Morrison replaced their translations with his own. Communauté Presbytérienne au Congo (31$^e$), *Misambu Ya Kutumbisha Nayi Nzambi*, 23, 87, 92.

23. Kellersberger, *Life for the Congo*, 74.

24. *Catalogue of Stillman Institute, Located at Tuscaloosa, Alabama. 1900–1901, Tenth Annual Report to the General Assembly*, Stillman College History Box, WHSML.

25. Newkirk, *Spectacle*, 115. Verner maintained a relationship with the Edmistons, who he visited on a return trip to the Congo in 1906 and defended against rumors that they "return[ed] to savagery." See Samuel P. Verner, "Edmiston Did Not Return to Savagery," Letter to the Editor of *Times-Gazette*, [n.d.], box 1, folder 3, ALENC.

26. PCUS *Minutes of Committee—Foreign Missions*, June 10, 1902, 7:204–5, ECFM.

27. Kellersberger, *Life for the Congo*, 73–75. See PCUS *Minutes of Committee—Foreign Missions*, August 9, 1904, 8:[n.p.], ECFM; PCUS *Minutes of Committee—Foreign Missions*, November 8, 1904, 8:[n.p.], ECFM; PCUS *Minutes of Committee—Foreign Missions*, October 11, 1904, 8:[n.p.], ECFM.

28. Edmiston later reported his APCM start date as early as January 1904 (and at least one other time as February 1904), effectively dating his missionary term from his arrival with Verner. The early date may be an accurate representation of his involvement with the mission even if it predates his formal appointment. See, for example, "Etats [sic] de Service du Reverend A Edmiston," box 17, folder 15, CMP; Alonzo L. Edmiston, Letter to Joseph Savels, August 21, 1930, box 17, folder 15, CMP.

29. Samuel Chester, Letter to Motte Martin, October 4, 1905, box 78, folder 2, CMP.

30. Phipps, *William Sheppard*, 215.

31. William Sheppard and William Morrison, Letter to Samuel Chester, January 24, 1909, box 78, folder 1, CMP.

32. PCUS *Minutes of Committee—Foreign Missions*, c. June 1903–March 1914, 8:[n.p.], ECFM; Kellersberger, *Life for the Congo*, 77.

33. William Sheppard and William Morrison, Letter to Samuel Chester, January 24, 1909, box 78, folder 1, CMP.

34. Samuel Chester, Letter to William Morrison, October 23, 1908, p. 2, box 78, folder 3, CMP.

35. Samuel Chester, Letter to William Morrison, August 23, 1910, box 78, folder 5, CMP.

36. Samuel Chester, Letter to Lillian DeYampert, March 18, 1916, box 78, folder 9, CMP. See Samuel Chester, Letter to William Morrison, December 15, 1915, p. 1, box 78, folder 8, CMP.

37. Samuel Chester, Letter to William Morrison, October 23, 1908, p. 1, box 78, folder 3, CMP.

38. PCUS *Minutes of Committee—Foreign Missions*, September 8, 1908, 8:[n.p.], ECFM; Émile Vandervelde, "Procès de presse au Congo," *Le Peuple*, October 19, 1909, 1; Samuel H. Chester, Letter to William Morrison, August 31, 1908, box 78, folder 3, CMP; Samuel H. Chester, Letter to William Morrison, September 11, 1908, box 78, folder 3, CMP.

39. William Morrison, Letter to Samuel Chester, December 9, 1908, p. 1, box 78, folder 3, CMP.

40. APCM, Letter to the Executive Committee, July 1, 1910, box 78, folder 5, CMP.

41. Samuel H. Chester, Letter to James McClung Sieg, August 16, 1910, box 78, folder 5, CMP.

42. Kellersberger, *Life for the Congo*, 85. Bedinger and Kellersberger attribute Althea's 1908 departure to homesickness and her son's health. Bedinger, "Althea Brown Edmiston," 271; Kellersberger, *Life for the Congo*, 80-81.

43. APCM, Letter to the Executive Committee, July 1, 1910, box 78, folder 5, CMP.

44. Samuel H. Chester, Letter to Alonzo Edmiston, August 20, 1910, box 1, folder 7, ALEPA.

45. PCUS *Minutes of Committee—Foreign Missions*, February 14, 1911, 8:[n.p.], ECFM.

46. William Sheppard, Letter to Alonzo Edmiston, March 31, 1911, box 1, folder 8, ALEPA; "Edmiston, Alonzo Elmore," box 71, folder 15, CMP; Bedinger, "Althea Brown Edmiston," 271.

47. Radano, *Lying up a Nation*, 166.

48. "First Phonograph," box 6, WHSPA; "WHS Entertaining the Natives," Photograph no. 835.02.11c, box 3, WHSPA; "Off for a Picnic—Ibanj (Ibanche)," Photograph no. 835.02.18a, box 3, WHSPA; "Sheppard and 'the Luther Maxwell Brass Band—Ibanche,'" Photograph no. 835.03.09, box 4, WHSPA.

49. "W.H. Sheppard, F.R.G.S.: Missionary Spoke to Large Audiences Yesterday," *Daily Evening Advance* (Lynchburg, Va.), January 30, 1905, box 1, WHSNC. After her retirement from the APCM, Lucy Sheppard served as musical director of the John Little Mission in Louisville and went to a Marian Anderson concert, which illustrates something of her musical interests. See Lucien V. Rule, "A Daughter of the Morning," Historical Synod of Indiana, typescript, [p. 4], box 1, WHSNC.

50. Kellersberger, *Life for the Congo*, 161.

51. Communauté Presbytérienne au Congo (31$^e$), *Misambu Ya Kutumbisha Nayi Nzambi*, 227, 228, 224, 229.

52. Du Bois, *Souls of Black Folk*, 537.

53. Sundquist, *To Wake the Nations*, 491.

54. On early versions of the essays that became *The Souls of Black Folk*, see Stepto, *From behind the Veil*, 53-57.

55. Du Bois, *Souls of Black Folk*, 540; Sundquist, *To Wake the Nations*, 499, 676n53.

56. Du Bois, *Souls of Black Folk*, 539. In the source, these lyrics appear with the musical notation.

57. Jaji, *Africa in Stereo*, 24.

58. Du Bois, *Souls of Black Folk*, 359.

59. Griffin, "When Malindy Sings," 114.

60. Du Bois, *Souls of Black Folk*, 539.

61. Miller, "Introduction," 146. Scholars have tried to find the meaning of the song for years. Lewis speculated that it may have been "originally a Wolof song from Senegambia." Although Wolof is part of the Niger-Congo language group, it is not a Bantu language. David Levering Lewis, *W. E. B. Du Bois*, 1:585n7; Nurse and Philippson, *Bantu Languages*, 1–3.

62. Miller, "Introduction," 145–46; Du Bois, *Darkwater*, 3. Nancy Cunard included the musical notation for several "Congo Songs" of the "Bacongo Tribe" in Cunard, *Negro: Anthology*, 419–20.

63. Du Bois, *Darkwater*, 3.

64. Du Bois, *Dusk of Dawn*, 638–39.

65. Du Bois, *Autobiography*, 62.

66. Du Bois, *Dusk of Dawn*, 638.

67. Sundquist, *To Wake the Nations*, 588–89.

68. Appiah, *Lines of Descent*, 138, 213n29.

69. Gikandi, "W. E. B. Du Bois and the Identity of Africa."

70. Sundquist, *To Wake the Nations*, 530.

71. On the Virginia Jubilee Singers, see Campbell, *Songs of Zion*, 128; Erlmann, "'Feeling of Prejudice,'" 334–38, 345–47; Thelwell, "Toward a 'Modernizing' Hybridity," 3–28; Erlmann, "'Spectatorial Lust,'" 107–34.

72. For more on Manye and her circle, see Campbell, *Songs of Zion*, 252–94. For a list of African students in the United States prior to 1900, see Walter Williams, *Black Americans and the Evangelization of Africa*, 191–94.

73. Du Bois, *Autobiography*, 184, 192.

74. Du Bois, *Souls of Black Folk*, 536.

75. Kellersberger, *Life for the Congo*, 58. See Fisk University, *Fisk University. History, Building and Site*, 5–6.

76. Fisk University, *Fisk University. History, Building and Site*, 10.

77. Richardson, *History of Fisk University*, 46.

78. See Pike, "Possibilities of African Civilization," 48–63. See also, Fisk University, *Fisk University. History, Building and Site*, 26, 35. See Jon Cruz, *Culture on the Margins*, 168.

79. Du Bois, *Souls of Black Folk*, 512; David Levering Lewis, *W. E. B. Du Bois*, 1:164–66.

80. Sundquist, *To Wake the Nations*, 519.

81. James Weldon Johnson, "Preface," 25.

82. Scarborough attended Charles S. Johnson's famous 1924 Harlem banquet in honor of Fauset's novel *There is Confusion*, and served as a juror for that year's *Opportunity* literary awards. Scarborough later served as a judge for the Harmon Awards in

1928 and 1929, which was coordinated by Edmiston's Fisk classmate George Haynes. North, *Dialect of Modernism*, 205n134; Scarborough, *On the Trail of Negro Folk-Songs*, 283. Thanks to Sylvia Grider for sharing her findings of correspondence from Haynes to Scarborough in the Dorothy Scarborough Papers at Baylor University, Waco, Texas.

83. Scarborough, "New Lights on an Old Song," 59.

84. Scarborough's essay appears in the table of contents of *Ebony and Topaz* as "New Light on an Old Song." See Charles S. Johnson, *Ebony and Topaz*.

85. Charles S. Johnson, "Introduction," 12.

86. Scarborough, *On the Trail of Negro Folk-Songs*, 28.

87. Scarborough, "New Lights on an Old Song," 59. Scarborough uses the language—"on the trail"—that she attributes to Wharton as the title for her own study of African American music.

88. Franck, "Recent Developments in the Belgian Congo," 713.

89. Kellersberger, *Life for the Congo*, 150. The APCM introduced motorcycles in 1919 and cars a few years later. The railroad was built between 1923 and 1928. The roads and railroads that replaced porterage became new symbols of colonial brutality; not only was the construction work often deadly, but the technology also serviced colonial tax collection. Alonzo Edmiston reports the use of airplanes at Luebo as early as 1925. Vansina, *Being Colonized*, 155–56; Likaka, *Naming Colonialism*, 37, 40; Kellersberger, *Life for the Congo*, 150.

90. The English translations from Tshiluba were prepared with assistance from Felly Kalonda of the University of Kinshasa and based on Morrison's dictionary.

91. Morrison's dictionary defines *nsubu* as "house, home, residence, mansion, edifice, building, room, chamber." Morrison, *Grammar and Dictionary*, 386.

92. Edwards, *Practice of Diaspora*, 67.

93. Morrison, *Grammar and Dictionary*, 327.

94. Marsh, *Story of the Jubilee Singers*, 160. The transcription is based on Pike, *Jubilee Singers*, 166.

95. Kellersberger, *Life for the Congo*, 152.

96. Mputubwele, "Zairian Language Policy," 284–85.

97. Boatner and Townsend, *Spirituals Triumphant*, hymn no. 28. As a young man in Boston, Boatner studied with Hampton's Nathaniel Dett. Glover, "Life and Career of Edward Boatner," 92. The Boatner and Townsend citation is not included in Communauté Presbytérienne au Congo (31[e]), *Misambu Ya Kutumbisha Nayi Nzambi*.

98. Kellersberger, *Life for the Congo*, 38; Alonzo Edmiston, Letter to Joseph Savels, December 9, 1932, box 71, folder 15, CMP.

99. Jon Cruz, *Culture on the Margins*, 183.

100. Ibid., 165.

101. Jaji, *Africa in Stereo*, 24.

102. Radano, *Lying up a Nation*, 177.

103. Jon Cruz, *Culture on the Margins*, 185.

104. Althea Brown Edmiston, *The Development of the Native Church of Our Congo Mission*, Nashville: Educational Department, Executive Committee of Foreign Missions, Presbyterian Church (U.S.), 1930, p. 9, box 88, folder 35, CMP.

105. Kellersberger, *Life for the Congo*, 148.

106. The current edition of Communauté Presbytérienne au Congo (31ᵉ), *Misambu Ya Kutumbisha Nayi Nzambi*, includes eleven African American spirituals, most of which were translated by white missionaries.

107. Althea Brown Edmiston, Memo to the APCM, February 1918, box 37, folder 20, CMP.

108. Bedinger, "Althea Brown Edmiston," 278.

109. Edmiston, "Missions in Congo Free State," 308.

110. Vansina, *Being Colonized*, 178, 208, 53–54.

111. Franck, "Recent Developments in the Belgian Congo," 717.

112. Vansina, *Being Colonized*, 181.

113. Wharton and Washburn contended that the Bushong project was assigned to Wharton in 1915. On April 10, 1918, Wharton and Washburn asked Edmiston to accept Wharton's elementary first reader as a substitute for her work. In response, she sent a letter of protest to which Washburn and Wharton replied: "We cannot believe that there is anything in this correspondence to justify Mrs. Edmiston in thinking that she has been unfairly dealt with by us, or to furnish grounds for an appeal.... We feel that our dealings with Mrs. Edmiston in all matters pertaining to this language work have been unfailingly courteous and just, hence our surprise at her appeal to the Com[mittee]." Edmiston was able to continue her work, and the result was something more substantial than a first reader, even though Wharton and Washburn made the "radical claim" that earlier readers written by Edmiston were not even good enough to warrant revision. They insisted that entirely new work of the sort undertaken by Wharton was required. Hezekiah M. Washburn and Conway T. Wharton, "Letter to the Committee Sent Out by the Ad-Interim Committee to Investigate a Supposed State of Friction Existing between Ibance and Bulape Stations Concerning the Bakuba Language Work," April 27, 1918, p. 3, box 10, folder 6, CMP. See Hezekiah M. Washburn and Conway T. Wharton, "Copy of Letter Sent to the Ad-Interim Committee Concerning Bukuba Translation Work," March 20, 1918, box 10, folder 6, CMP; "Minutes, 1917–1927," pp. 1–2, box 10, folder 6, CMP.

114. In 1908, a Belgian government report states that "les missionaires *noirs* et *mulâtres* d'Ibanche n'entretiennent pas des bons rapports avec les missionnaires *blancs* de Luebo." See Gustave Gustin, "Note," (attached to Vice-Gouverneur Général, Letter to Secrétaire d'État, May 11, 1908), AAB. Emphasis in source.

115. Kellersberger, *Life for the Congo*, 107–8, 122–28; Bedinger, "Althea Brown Edmiston," 280.

116. Bedinger, "Althea Brown Edmiston," 263, 277.

117. Ibid., 278. Among the orthographic changes, $x$ became $sh$, and $c$ became $tsh$.

118. Althea Brown Edmiston, Memo to the APCM, February 1918, box 37, folder 20, CMP.

119. See *Fisk University News* 11, no. 9 (June 1921): 17, 25; Fisk University, *General Anniversary Program of Fisk University in the City of Nashville Tennessee* (April 8, 1921–June 1, 1921); Bedinger, "Althea Brown Edmiston," 280. See also, "Life Membership and Printing of Bukuba Grammar," an incomplete memorandum that I found folded in the pages of a duplicate copy of Edmiston's *Grammar and Dictionary* that I purchased at the Presbyterian Historical Society in Montreat, North Carolina, in 2002.

120. Kellersberger, *Life for the Congo*, 83, 84.

121. Ibid., 153; Richardson, *History of Fisk University*, 64.

122. Just as the elder Althea spoke at her graduation, the younger Althea was part of a group that performed Margaret Walker's poem "For My People" at hers. *Mission to Africa*, [2].

123. Edmiston, *Grammar and Dictionary*, v.

124. Anderson, McElroy, and McKee, "Preface," ii–iii.

125. Morrison, *Grammar and Dictionary*, ix. To its credit, Pruitt and Vass's 1965 dictionary restores Morrison's acknowledgment of his Congolese assistants: Kazadi, Kabata, Kamuidika, Kachunga, and Malendola. Pruitt and Vass, *Textbook of the Tshiluba Language*, 11–13.

126. Anderson, McElroy, and McKee, "Preface," ii; Edmiston, *Grammar and Dictionary*, vii–viii.

127. Edmiston, "Missions in Congo Free State," 309.

128. Bedinger, "Althea Brown Edmiston," 279.

129. Kellersberger, *Life for the Congo*, 84. See Fisk University, *Catalogue of the Officers and Students of Fisk University* (1898), 44–49. Although the AMA no longer directly managed Fisk, it maintained an advisory role. See Richardson, *History of Fisk University*, 42.

130. Kellersberger, *Life for the Congo*, 129; Edmiston, "Missions in Congo Free State," 310.

131. Vernon Anderson, Annual Letter, October 14, 1936, box 40, folder 21, CMP.

132. Edmiston, *Grammar and Dictionary*, vi, v. For earlier speeches emphasizing the efficacy of Kuba governance, see Edmiston, "Missions in Congo Free State," 309; "At Home and Afield: Hampton Incidents," 183.

133. Vansina, *Being Colonized*, 239.

134. Vansina, *Living with Africa*, 11, 259n13.

135. Fabian, *Language and Colonial Power*, 133, 135.

136. Vansina, *Living with Africa*, 11.

137. "Facsimile of Letter Repudiating Testimony," box 1, folder 15, ABE; "Congo Natives Rise Up against Belgium," *Chicago Defender*, May 10, 1930, box 1, folder 12, ABE; Robert S. Abbott, "My Trip Abroad V: The Congo Museum," *Chicago Defender*, December 7, 1929, box 1, folder 15, ABE.

138. Hezekiah Washburn, *Knight in the Congo*, 71; Alonzo Edmiston, "Report to the Ad-Interim Committee," February 28, 1916, box 27, folder 3, CMP; Alonzo Edmiston, "Report to the Ad-Interim Committee," March 6, 1916, folder 1, CCR.

139. Campbell, *Middle Passages*, 167. In archival materials, Ibanche is alternately spelled as Ibaanche, Ibanj, and Ibance. In all instances, I have preserved the spelling as it appears in the source.

140. Alonzo Edmiston, "Report to the Ad-Interim Committee," March 6, 1916, folder 1, CCR.

141. Roy Fields Cleveland, Letter to William Morrison, August 7, 1916, box 9, folder 16, CMP.

142. Ewing, *Age of Garvey*, 94–95; Kodi, "1921 Pan-African Congress at Brussels," 267–75.

143. Meeuwis, "Origins of Belgian Colonial Language Policies," 196.

144. Hakiza, "Les États-Unis d'Amérique et l'enseignement en Afrique noire," 223n13, 247.

145. Seghers, "Phelps-Stokes in Congo," 462; Meeuwis, "Origins of Belgian Colonial Language Policies," 198. See Thomas Jesse Jones, "L'éducation des nègres," 162–75. For an important critique of Jones and the Phelps-Stokes Fund, see Woodson, "Thomas Jesse Jones," 107–9.

146. Ewing, *Age of Garvey*, 201.

147. "Memoranda" ("Colored Missionaries on the Staff of the A.P.C.M."), [n.d.], p. 1, box 39, folder 7, CMP.

148. "Memoranda" ("Concessions"), [n.d.], p. 2, box 39, folder 7, CMP.

149. Yates, "Origins of Language Policy in Zaire," 262.

150. "Memoranda" ("Concessions"), [n.d.], p. 2, box 39, folder 7, CMP.

151. Robert Whyte, Letter to Samuel Chester, July 1922, p. 3, box 80, folder 17, CMP.

152. A.L.W., "Memorandum of Interview with the Governor-General of the Belgian Congo," July 6, 1922, p. 2, box 80, folder 17, CMP.

153. *Hand-book for New Missionaries Going to the Belgian Congo*, 33.

154. Roy Fields Cleveland, "Annual Letter for Year Ending Mar. 31st, 1925," box 40, folder 11, CMP.

155. Charles L. Crane, "Annual Letter" (Mutoto), October 1, 1929, p. 8, box 40, folder 14, CMP.

156. Alonzo and Althea Edmiston, Letter to Joseph Savels, September 10, 1932, box 71, folder 15, CMP.

157. Hezekiah Washburn, *Knight in the Congo*, 196. Elsewhere in the book, Washburn mentions Sheppard's work with the Kuba. See Hezekiah Washburn, *Knight in the Congo*, 159.

158. Hezekiah Washburn, *Knight in the Congo*, 200.

159. Ewing, *Age of Garvey*, 162, 215.

160. Norden, *Fresh Tracks*, 64; Horne, *Mau Mau in Harlem?*, 39; Hunt, *A Nervous State*, 96.

161. Ewing, *Age of Garvey*, 95. See also, Hunt, *Nervous State*, 105.

162. Edwards, *Practice of Diaspora*, 248.

163. Cunard, *Negro: Anthology*, 795.

164. Kellersberger, *Life for the Congo*, 89; Vinson, "'Sea Kaffirs,'" 292, 292n49.

165. Helmreich, *United States Relations with Belgium and the Congo*, 38.

166. Ibid., 38, 41, 150.

167. In conversations with several Congolese and Americans who grew up on or near APCM mission stations in the late Belgian colonial era, I heard extensive reports of restrictions placed on social interactions between Congolese and American children. These restrictions intensified as white American girls and Congolese boys entered their teen years. William Pruitt began his career as an APCM missionary in 1945, shortly after Alonzo Edmiston's retirement. His decades of misdeeds were not acknowledged publicly for more than fifty years. The Presbyterian Church has recently committed itself to addressing this case and others of abuse among its missionary ranks. See Beardslee, Edmund, Evinger, Poling, Stearns, and Whitfield, *Final Report of the Independent Committee of Inquiry* (2002), 133; Evinger, Whitfield, and Wiley, *Final Report of the Independent Abuse Review Panel* (2010), 393.

168. Vernon Anderson, *Still Led in Triumph*, 31.

169. Ethel Wharton, *Led in Triumph*, 175. See also, Vernon Anderson, *Still Led in Triumph*, 37.

170. As late as 1959, the Presbyterian Church continued to accept the colonial government as the arbiter of missionary accomplishments as when C. Darby Fulton, the Executive Secretary of the Board of World Missions, wrote exultantly that Vernon Anderson "has been decorated by the Government for services rendered the Colony." Vernon Anderson, *Still Led in Triumph*, [iii].

171. For a consideration of recent scholarship on the relationship of missionaries to colonialism, see McAlister, "Guess Who's Coming to Dinner," 36.

172. Helmreich, *United States Relations with Belgium and the Congo*, 167.

173. Charles L. Crane, Annual Letter, October 1937, box 40, folder 22, CMP.

174. Robert D. Bedinger, "Maria Fearing, 1838–1937," typescript, July 19, 1937, pp. 2–3, box 1, folder A-F, BWM.

175. Kellersberger, *Life for the Congo*, 168–69.

## Chapter 5

1. Gruesser, *Black on Black*, 40.
2. Hopkins, *Of One Blood*, 547.
3. Brooks, *Bodies in Dissent*, 286, 319.
4. Hopkins, *Of One Blood*, 453.
5. Brooks, *Bodies in Dissent*, 303.
6. Trafton, *Egypt Land*, 2, 264n4; Du Bois, *Dark Princess*, 19, 26, 221; Ellison, *Invisible Man*, 312. In *The Negro in the American Rebellion*, a work Hopkins frequently referenced, William Wells Brown recounts the use of the song on the occasion of the Emancipation Proclamation. Hopkins, "*Famous Men of the Negro Race* III," 34–39; Hopkins, "*Famous Men of the Negro Race* VIII," 71n75; Hopkins, "*Heroes and Heroines in Black* 1," 288n33, 289n35.
7. Hopkins, *Of One Blood*, 502.
8. Johnson, Johnson, and Brown, *Book of American Negro Spirituals*, 51–53.
9. Hopkins, *Of One Blood*, 493. The location of Livingston's "ancestral home" is given once each as Virginia and Maryland. See Hopkins, *Of One Blood*, 493, 597.
10. Hopkins, *Of One Blood*, 603.
11. Ibid., 609.
12. Carby, *Reconstructing Womanhood*, 159–60.
13. Moses, *Afrotopia*, 39; Hall, "Cultural Identity and Diaspora," 226. Emphasis in source.
14. Gillman, *Blood Talk*, 58–65; Otten, "Pauline Hopkins and the Hidden Self of Race"; Posnock, *Color and Culture*, 64–69; Schrager, "Pauline Hopkins and William James."
15. Trafton, *Egypt Land*, 242; Hall, "Cultural Identity and Diaspora," 224. Emphasis in source.
16. Sanborn, "Wind of Words," 73, 74.
17. Hopkins, *Of One Blood*, 502.
18. Sanborn, "Wind of Words," 80.

19. Lois Brown, *Pauline Elizabeth Hopkins*, 387.
20. Hopkins, "Mrs. Jane E. Sharp's School," 184. In my edition of Hopkins's nonfiction, I silently correct this misspelling and consider Hopkins's use of the J. Shirley Shadrach pseudonym. See Dworkin, *Daughter of the Revolution*, 300–303, xli–xlii.
21. "Announcement and Prospectus of the *New Era Magazine*," 5.
22. Lapsley, *Life and Letters*, 240; Hopkins, *Of One Blood*, 511.
23. William Sheppard, Letter (May 17, 1890), 355.
24. "Congo Boat Company," 113; William Sheppard, "Into the Heart of Africa," 185.
25. Hopkins, *Of One Blood*, 553.
26. Edmiston, *Grammar and Dictionary*, 572.
27. William Sheppard, "Into the Heart of Africa," 185; Vansina, *Children of Woot*, 198.
28. Hopkins, *Of One Blood*, 562, 534.
29. Equiano, *Interesting Narrative*, 26.
30. Moore, Carretta, Nwokeji, Erkkila, and Rust, "Colloquy with the Author," 1–14.
31. Gilroy, *Black Atlantic*, 88.
32. "In the Heart of Africa," 221.
33. Reynolds, *John Brown*, 37. On Hopkins's choice of Dianthe's name, see Martha Patterson, "'Kin o' Rough Jestice fer a Parson,'" 447.
34. Hopkins, *Of One Blood*, 563.
35. Gruesser, *Black on Black*, 39.
36. Campbell, *Middle Passages*, 143.
37. Drake, *Redemption of Africa*, 73. See also, Rosa, "Roots and Routes of 'Imperium in Imperio,'" 58.
38. In *Life and Letters*, Lapsley spells "Livingston" without the concluding "e" multiple times. Lapsley, *Life and Letters*, 17, 26, 238.
39. Hopkins, *Of One Blood*, 601; Marsh, *Story of the Jubilee Singers*, 85–86; Richardson, *History of Fisk University*, 53; "Benefactions: Mrs. Valeria G. Stone," 69–70.
40. Sanborn, "Wind of Words," 71; Louise Henderson, "David Livingstone's *Missionary Travels*," 128.
41. Coombs, *Dr. Livingstone's 17 Years' Explorations*, 126. Emphasis in source.
42. Coombs, *Dr. Livingstone's 17 Years' Explorations*, 133; Hopkins, *Of One Blood*, 566.
43. Coombs, *Dr. Livingstone's 17 Years' Explorations*, 131; Hopkins, *Of One Blood*, 565.
44. Hopkins, *Of One Blood*, 565; Coombs, *Dr. Livingstone's 17 Years' Explorations*, 131.
45. Hopkins, *Of One Blood*, 565.
46. Bergman, *Motherless Child*, 133.
47. Ewing, *Age of Garvey*, 164–65.
48. George Washington Williams, *History of the Negro Race*, 1:110; Kilbride, "Old South Confronts the Dilemma of David Livingstone," 806–7. See also, Brawley, *Africa and the War*, 13–18.
49. Lois Brown, *Pauline Elizabeth Hopkins*, 391.
50. Engel, *Encountering Empire*, 83, 91.
51. Pagan Kennedy, *Black Livingstone*, 159–60. William visited the grave of Livingstone prior to going to Africa (which was reported in Lapsley's published letters) and Lucy, despite being ill, made the pilgrimage four years later. Lapsley, *Life and Letters*,

39; William Sheppard, *Presbyterian Pioneers in Congo*, 20; Kellersberger, *Lucy Gantt Sheppard*, 11.

52. Philip, *Looking for Livingstone*, 77–78.

53. Edwards, "Uses of Diaspora," 46.

54. Benson, "*Southern Workman*," 350.

55. Lee Baker, "Research, Reform, and Racial Uplift," 57, 65. The American Folklore Society and Hampton are further linked though several trustees, including Mary Hemenway (who helped finance the start-up of the *Southern Workman*) and faculty member Alice Bacon. Lee Baker. "Research, Reform, and Racial Uplift," 62–65.

56. Frissell, "Thirty-Second Annual Report of the Principal of Hampton Institute," 300; "*Southern Workman*" (December 1898), 234; and "Editorial: The *Southern Workman*" (January 1892), 3; "*Southern Workman* Prospectus 1898" (January 1898), 2.

57. Pleck, *Black Migration and Poverty*, 46. In 1901, Frissell sent a free subscription to the Boston Public Library and elsewhere described a "Boston Committee." James L. Whitney, Letter to Hollis Burke Frissell, January 22, 1901, SWP; Draft Rules for Free *Southern Workman* List to Hollis Burke Frissell, May 29, 1901, SWP.

58. Elliott, "Story of Our Magazine," 45; Lois Brown, *Pauline Elizabeth Hopkins*, 256–57.

59. Johnson and Johnson, *Propaganda and Aesthetics*, 4. On circulation, see Carby, *Reconstructing Womanhood*, 193n12.

60. "Pauline E. Hopkins," 219; Elliott, "Story of Our Magazine," 47.

61. Ivy Wilson, "On Native Ground," 463. See also, Hopkins, "Dash for Liberty," 98.

62. The Colored Co-operative published only four books, which included Hopkins's *Contending Forces*. Lois Brown, *Pauline Elizabeth Hopkins*, 276; Joyce, *Black Book Publishers*, 80–83; Joyce, *Gatekeepers of Black Culture*, 60–62, 187.

63. Carby, *Reconstructing Womanhood*, 124.

64. O'Brien, "'Blacks in All Quarters of the Globe,'" 249.

65. Moses, *Golden Age of Black Nationalism*, 200. Elsewhere Moses has taken Appiah to task for overlooking Hopkins's attempts to link African Americans to classical Ethiopia. See Moses, *Afrotopia*, 84.

66. Lois Brown, *Pauline Elizabeth Hopkins*, 387, 433.

67. James Weldon Johnson, for example, was a *Colored American Magazine* subscriber. Oliver, "'Jim Crowed' in Their Own Countries," 211.

68. Moses, *Afrotopia*, 196.

69. Gomez, *Exchanging Our Country Marks*, 199. Gomez makes a similar example of the stories of flying Africans, which are foundational to late-twentieth-century works like Toni Morrison's *Song of Solomon* and Julie Dash's *Daughters of the Dust*. Gomez, *Exchanging Our Country Marks*, 117.

70. Wallinger, *Pauline E. Hopkins*, 329–30n2.

71. Hopkins, *Of One Blood*, 503.

72. Lois Brown, *Pauline Elizabeth Hopkins*, 168. See also, Lois Brown, *Pauline Elizabeth Hopkins*, 180, 165.

73. Knight, *Pauline Hopkins and the American Dream*, 73; Lois Brown, *Pauline Elizabeth Hopkins*, 193–94, 309, 314, 408–9; McHenry, *Forgotten Readers*, 184.

74. McHenry, *Forgotten Readers*, 171. See also, McHenry, *Forgotten Readers*, 179–83.

75. Hamedoe, "First Pan-African Conference of the World," 225.
76. Gaines, "Black Americans' Racial Uplift Ideology," 437.
77. Lois Brown, *Pauline Elizabeth Hopkins*, 267.
78. "Editorial and Publishers' Announcements" (*Colored American Magazine*), 62; Washington, "Storm before the Calm," 203–4.
79. Hopkins, "*Famous Men of the Negro Race* XII: Booker T. Washington," 110.
80. Meier, "Booker T. Washington and the Negro Press," 69. Forbes was rumored to have said that "it would be a blessing to the race if the Tuskegee school should burn down." See Harlan, *Booker T. Washington*, 2:36.
81. For example, the *Colored American Magazine* advertised in the August 8, 1903, issue of the *Guardian*.
82. Harlan, *Booker T. Washington*, 2:52–54; Fox, *Guardian of Boston*, 68–71; Hopkins, "How a New York Newspaper Man Entertained," 226–37; Lois Brown, *Pauline Elizabeth Hopkins*, 414–41; David Levering Lewis, *W. E. B. Du Bois*, 1:298, 302.
83. [Du Bois], "Colored Magazine in America," 33; Knight, *Pauline Hopkins and the American Dream*, 46–47.
84. Hopkins, Letter to William Monroe Trotter, 242–43. Emphasis in source.
85. Washington, *Some European Observations*, 3.
86. Hopkins, *Primer of Facts*, 345.
87. Within the same pamphlet, Washington is also subtly impugned by his notable absence from a roll call of more than forty "phenomenally intellectual men [and women] produced in Africa and America," whose success is evidence of their descent "from the once powerful and mighty Ethiopians." Hopkins, *Primer of Facts*, 342–43.
88. "Publishers' Announcements" (*Colored American Magazine*), 700; Fred Moore, "Retrospection of a Year," 342.
89. "*Voice of the Negro* for July 1905," 364.
90. Lois Brown, *Pauline Elizabeth Hopkins*, 481.
91. "Congo Missionaries Acquitted," 248; "Acquittal of Sheppard," 381.
92. Johnson and Johnson, *Propaganda and Aesthetics*, 24.
93. Gilroy, *Black Atlantic*, 189, 19.
94. Tolliver, "Racial Ends of History," 36, 37.
95. Hopkins, *Of One Blood*, 621.
96. Hall, "Cultural Identity and Diaspora," 226.
97. Gilroy, *Black Atlantic*, 189.
98. Gillman, *Blood Talk*, 53.
99. Wilentz, "'What Is Africa to Me?,'" 641.
100. Garnet, *Past and the Present Condition*, 11. See also, Geiss, *Pan-African Movement*, 132–34.
101. Drake, *Redemption of Africa*, 9–11. See also, Moses, *Afrotopia*, 51.
102. Hopkins, *Of One Blood*, 521. Emphasis in source.
103. McHenry, *Forgotten Readers*, 184, 361n89.
104. George Washington Williams, *History of the Negro Race*, 1:15.
105. George Washington Williams, *History of the Negro Race*, 1:459, 454. See Rufus Perry, *Cushite*, 18; Lois Brown, *Pauline Elizabeth Hopkins*, 389, 402–3.
106. Hopkins, *Of One Blood*, 532.
107. Hopkins, *Primer of Facts*, 334, 340.

108. "Announcement and Prospectus of the *New Era Magazine*," 4.
109. Hopkins, *Primer of Facts*, 335, 351.
110. O'Brien, "'Blacks in All Quarters of the Globe,'" 264; Lois Brown, *Pauline Elizabeth Hopkins*, 557.
111. Hopkins, *Primer of Facts*, 344–45. Emphasis in source.
112. Ibid., 334.
113. Ibid., 339. Emphasis in source. See Delany, *Principia of Ethnology*, 41–42.
114. Brantlinger, *Rule of Darkness*, 174.
115. Hopkins, *Of One Blood*, 576.
116. William Sheppard, "Into the Heart of Africa," 187.
117. Jacobs, *African Nexus*, 194–96.
118. Hopkins, "*Dark Races of the Twentieth Century*, Part IV," 323.
119. Gebrekidan, "Ethiopia and Congo," 235.
120. Hopkins, "*Dark Races of the Twentieth Century*, Part IV," 322.
121. Gaines, "Black Americans' Racial Uplift Ideology," 447.
122. Her investment in colonial discourses of "civilization" is similar to that of contemporary Congolese intellectuals such as Stephano Kaoze. See Mudimbe, *Invention of Africa*, 75.
123. Maggie Johnson, *Virginia Dreams*, 36, 39n.
124. Ibid., 40.
125. Ibid., 50–51, 34–36.
126. Ibid., 34, 51, 38.

## Chapter 6

1. Meta Fuller, "Helpful Suggestions to Young Artists" (February 1916), 44–45; Meta Fuller, "Helpful Suggestions to Young Artists" (March 1916), 109–11.
2. Ater, "Making History," 20, 17. See Ater, *Remaking Race and History*, 25–26.
3. Judith Wilson, "Hagar's Daughters," 105. See also, Hopkins, *Primer of Facts*, 343.
4. Ater, "Making History," 13.
5. Judith Wilson, "Hagar's Daughters," 106.
6. Thompson, *Flash of the Spirit*, 103.
7. Pierre, *Predicament of Blackness*, 210. Emphasis in source.
8. Mudimbe, *Idea of Africa*, 61, 69.
9. Ibid., 62, 69.
10. Vansina, *Children of Woot*, 211. See also, Binkley and Darish, *Kuba*, 7; Austin, "Extraordinary Generation," 78.
11. Leighten, "White Peril," 610.
12. Gilroy, *Black Atlantic*, 113.
13. Kirschke, *Art in Crisis*, 133; Wardlaw, "Spiritual Libation," 63.
14. Grogan, "Fisk University Galleries," 41.
15. Fisk University, *Catalogue of the Officers and Students* (1884), 31. See also, Fisk University, *Catalogue of the Officers and Students* (1893), 71.
16. Kellersberger, *Life for the Congo*, 83, 85.
17. "Inventory of Household and Personal Effects, April 1941," box 1, folder 28, ALEPA.

18. Binkley and Darish, "'Enlightened but in Darkness,'" 61n26.

19. Franklin, *George Washington Williams*, 200.

20. Francis W. Fox, Letter to Collis P. Huntington, July 6, 1891, box 113, folder "Correspondence July 1st-6th 1891," CPH.

21. Franklin, *George Washington Williams*, 230; Thomas H. Sherman, Letter to Sarah Williams, February 24, 1892, box W5, folder "Books: George Washington Williams—General Correspondence (2 of 2)," JHF; Thomas H. Sherman, Letter to William F. Wharton, August 27, 1891, box W3, folder "Books: George Washington Williams [Research Notes (3 of 7)]," JHF. It is possible that some objects were traded separately to pay off other debts.

22. Shawn Smith, *Photography on the Color Line*, 2, 16.

23. Ater, "Making History," 14–15. A couple of decades later, in a fascinating reversal of sorts, the entire Belgian building from the 1939 New York Fair was donated to Virginia Union University, an HBCU in Richmond, where today the edifice with its huge stone relief of the Belgian Congo remains the centerpiece of the historic campus. The family of longtime *Pittsburgh Courier* publisher Robert Vann, a former Virginia Union student, funded its transport in his memory. Watson, "Case of the Missing Bells," 1, 4–5; "Bells Appealing," 14–16; *Bells for Peace*, http://www.bellsforpeace.org. September 18, 2015. Thanks to Dianne Watkins for sharing information about her work with *Bells for Peace*.

24. Rahier, "Ghost of Leopold II," 63; Stanard, *Selling the Congo*, 38; Schildkrout, "Personal Styles and Disciplinary Paradigms," 172–73; American Presbyterian Congo Mission, "Secular News" (April 1906), 24.

25. Austin, "Extraordinary Generation," 81.

26. Shawn Smith, *Photography on the Color Line*, 3.

27. Cureau, "William H. Sheppard," 344; Phipps, *William Sheppard*, 93; Zeidler and Hultgren, "'Things African Prove,'" 97–98, 106; Zeidler, "Hampton University Museum Collections," 46; "Items of Intelligence," 62.

28. Hultgren, "Roots and Limbs," 45.

29. Long, "Major Art Collections," 9; Mudimbe, *Idea of Africa*, 60–61.

30. "Hampton's Collections and Connections," 5; Zeidler and Hultgren, "'Things African Prove,'" 106.

31. Vogel, "Introduction," 14; Dunbar, "Influence of Negro Art," 13. A larger collection of Benin bronzes stolen by British forces in a famous 1897 raid remains the subject of legal debates about repatriation and restitution. See Coombes, *Reinventing Africa*, 7–27; Kiwara-Wilson, "Restituting Colonial Plunder," 375–425.

32. Fabian, *Anthropology with an Attitude*, 139.

33. Schildkrout and Keim, "Objects and Agendas," 23, 24.

34. Vansina, *Being Colonized*, 182.

35. William Sheppard, Letter, September 1, 1890, 168. See also, Lapsley, *Life and Letters*, 159, 161.

36. Benedetto, who mistakenly claims that Sheppard sold the 1911 collection to Hampton for $5,000 instead of $500, "wonders what prompted the venerable Sheppard to spend his time and energy collecting boxes and trunks full of Kuba curios ... art collecting activities which seem to run counter to his primary purpose for being in the Congo"; however, Phipps finds that his "appreciation of Congolese art illustrates

one way by which he established an extraordinary rapport with the people he was sent to serve." Benedetto, *Presbyterian Reformers in Central Africa*, 29–30; Phipps, *William Sheppard*, 216. For the accurate purchase price, see Zeidler and Hultgren, "'Things African Prove,'" 102. On later Kasai missionaries, including Presbyterians, who got into the Kuba art export business, see Vansina, *Being Colonized*, 274–75; Elisabeth Cameron, "Coming to Terms with Heritage," 34.

37. Lapsley, *Life and Letters*, 157–59, 161.

38. William Sheppard, *Presbyterian Pioneers in Congo*, 112; Elisabeth Cameron, "Coming to Terms with Heritage," 28. Cameron explains, the checkerboard was the *lyeel* game introduced by King Shyaam aMbul aNgoong who is "credited for bringing a time of peace that gave people leisure time to play games." An image of the *ndop* of King Shyaam aMbul aNgoong is included in Cunard, *Negro: Anthology*, 725. Sheppard also notes seeing the *ndop* of Mbop Pelyeeng aNce, identifiable by his "blacksmith's anvil." See also, Vansina, *Children of Woot*, 213. For more on the *ibol*, see Mabintch, "La statuaire royale kuba," 82–88.

39. Mack, *Emil Torday*, 17. See also, Vansina, *Children of Woot*, 213, 358–59n8.

40. Mack, *Emil Torday*, 72, 76. See Torday, *On the Trail of the Bushongo*, 150.

41. Binkley and Darish, *Kuba*, 51. Vansina provides political context, describing Torday as "pestering the king," and having "eventually obtained four statues, helped no doubt by the troubled political climate at that moment." Vansina, *Being Colonized*, 111.

42. Mack, *Emil Torday*, 33.

43. The *Kassai Herald* notes only that Frobenius was in Luebo "studying the origin of the various tribes, their manners, customs, folk-lore, and their possibilities," without mentioning his art gathering. American Presbyterian Congo Mission, "[untitled note]," 39. See also, American Presbyterian Congo Mission, "Secular News" (October 1905), 48.

44. William Sheppard, "African Handicrafts and Superstitions," 403.

45. "Bakuba," 171. The 14½-inch knife, composed of iron, copper, wood, and brass, can be seen in Hultgren and Zeidler, *Taste for the Beautiful*, 60. See also, Vansina, *Children of Woot*, 211–12.

46. Binkley and Darish, *Kuba*, 34.

47. William Sheppard, *Presbyterian Pioneers in Congo*, 113.

48. Van Beurden, "Authentically African," 316; Cureau, "William H. Sheppard," 346; Adams, "Kuba Embroidered Cloth," 31. The preference for sculpture is exemplified by Sweeney, *African Negro Art* (aside from two Kuba textiles from the collection of Henri Matisse).

49. Mack, *Emil Torday*, 52. Despite working for the C.K., Torday did not visit the Kasai until his third and final trip to the Congo in 1907, when he was effectively commissioned by the British Museum.

50. Fabian, *Anthropology with an Attitude*, 126; Vansina, *Being Colonized*, 113n13.

51. Binkley and Darish, *Kuba*, 51.

52. Fabian, *Anthropology with an Attitude*, 133.

53. Binkley and Darish, "'Enlightened but in Darkness,'" 55, 51.

54. Mack, *Emil Torday*, 68; Torday, *Causeries congolaises*, 143. See also, Shaloff, "William Henry Sheppard," 58–59.

55. Vansina, *Children of Woot*, 84, 220; Sieber, *African Textiles*, 28.

56. Dorothy Washburn, "Style, Classification and Ethnicity," 95n2. See also, Austin, "Extraordinary Generation," 89.

57. Adams, "Kuba Embroidered Cloth," 39.

58. Lucy Gantt Sheppard, Letter to Mrs. Godden, October 19, 1895, box 1, WHSNC; Adams, "Kuba Embroidered Cloth," 34; William Sheppard, "African Handicrafts and Superstitions," 408.

59. Adams, "Beyond Symmetry," 36; Leon, *Who'd A Thought It*, 26.

60. Binkley and Darish, *Kuba*, 22.

61. Mack, "Bakuba Embroidery Patterns," 163; Binkley and Darish, *Kuba*, 19. See also, Cureau, "William H. Sheppard," 343.

62. William Sheppard, "African Handicrafts and Superstitions," 401.

63. Fisk University, *Fisk University. History, Building and Site*, 10; Binkley and Darish, "'Enlightened but in Darkness,'" 48.

64. Van Beurden, "Authentically African," 335; Long, "*Exhibition of Bakuba Art*," April–May 1968, box "Annual Reports/Historical Information," folder "Museum—Collection Descriptions," HMC; List of registrants, box "Annual Reports/Historical Information," folder "Museum Reports 1966–1971," HMC. For an image of the 1967 Union Carbide exhibition gallery, see Hultgren, "African Art Collections," 39. On Grigsby, a Morehouse graduate who wrote a dissertation on Kuba art with Woodruff, see Grigsby, "Ba Kuba Art at the Brussels International Exposition," 143–61; Grigsby, "African and Indian Masks"; Bernard Young, *Eye of Shamba*, 54–56.

65. Long, "Perspectives on African Art," 10.

66. Hultgren, "Roots and Limbs," 52.

67. Randall, "Selected Bibliography," 228–38. See also, Hultgren, "African Art Collections," 39; Hultgren, "Roots and Limbs," 60n44.

68. Sieber, *African Textiles*, 88, 116, 64, 166.

69. Schildkrout and Keim, "Objects and Agendas," 33; Vogel, *Art/Artifact*, 112–52; Hultgren, "Roots and Limbs," 53, 49–50. More than sixty objects from Sheppard's collection were displayed in Richmond in 1979. See Regenia Perry, *Art of the Kuba*.

70. Drake, "Mbiyu Koinange," 167; Horne, *Mau Mau in Harlem?*, 97. See also, Sara Lane, Letter to George P. Phenix, January 28, 1930, box "Annual Reports/Historical Information," folder "Museum Reports, 1924–1941 and Undated," HMC. Other African collections from this period were donated to Hampton by Doyle L. Sumner, a student from Sierra Leone, and Reuben Tholakele Caluza, a student from South Africa. Sara Lane, Letter to James E. Gregg, February 12, 1929, box "Annual Reports/Historical Information," folder "Museum Reports, 1924–1941 and Undated," HMC; Hultgren, "African Art Collections," 38.

71. "Many Experiences. Of Missionaries to Africa and Related. The Rev. W. H. Sheppard, a Negro, Addresses Big Congregation at Second Presbyterian Church," *Louisville Courier Journal*, October 10, 1904, box "William H. Sheppard (Sheppard—*Blazing the African Trail* to Sheppard, William Henry)," folder "Sheppard Clipping File," WHSVA (2003); "Rev. H. [sic] H. Sheppard, Missionary for the Past Twelve Years in the Heart of Africa, Will Speak at Madison Avenue Presbyterian Church," *Cincinnati Times-Standard*, October 29, 1904, box "William H. Sheppard (*Twenty-Two Years Work* to Wharton-*The Leopard Hunts Alone*)," folder "Photocopies of Materials in W. H. Sheppard Clippings Scrapbook," WHSVA (2003). See also, "Rev. Wm. H. Sheppard.

The Missionary Addressed Second Church Congregation," *Staunton News*, December 27, 1904, box "William H. Sheppard (*Twenty-Two Years Work* to Wharton-*The Leopard Hunts Alone*)," folder "Photocopies of Materials in W. H. Sheppard Clippings Scrapbook," WHSVA (2003).

72. William Sheppard, "Light in Darkest Africa," 227, 224.

73. Singletary, "William H. Sheppard African Art Collection," 64–65; Hollis Burke Frissell, Letter to William Sheppard, October 10, 1910, letter books (carbon), HBF. Singletary lists a 1910 accession of a "palm fiber in its first state as it comes out of the hand loom," which does not fit the decorative description in Frissell's letter so perhaps Frissell sent it to the museum instead of keeping it for his home office.

74. William Sheppard, Letter to Hollis Burke Frissell, June 5, 1911, box 3, folder "1911," WHSVA (2015).

75. Zeidler and Hultgren, "'Things African Prove,'" 102.

76. Hampton Normal and Agricultural Institute, *Forty-Sixth Annual Catalogue* (1914), 31. This language is repeated nearly verbatim through the 1930s.

77. Singletary, "William H. Sheppard African Art Collection," 64–115.

78. William Sheppard, Letter to James E. Gregg, January 26, 1923, box 3, folder "1923," WHSVA (2015); Rosa, "New Negroes on Campus," 216.

79. "Dr. Sheppard on Africa," *Hampton Student* 2, no. 23 (February 15, 1911), 4.

80. "Founder's Day Exercises," *Hampton Student* 6, no. 6 (February 15, 1915), 5. See also, "At Home and Afield: Hampton Incidents," 183.

81. "Dr. Wm. H. Sheppard on Africa, Cleveland Hall Chapel, January 31, 1915," pp. 9–11, box 7, WHSVA (2015).

82. McKay, *Negroes in America*, 63.

83. Robert S. Abbott, "My Trip Abroad V: The Congo Museum," *Chicago Defender*, December 7, 1929, 1. Abbott points directly to the responsibility borne by the United States for the brutal Belgian regime owing to its endorsement of King Leopold II's rule at the Berlin Conference in 1884.

84. Samuel Chapman Armstrong, quoted in Zeidler, "Hampton University Museum Collections," 46.

85. Annual reports indicate that in 1913, a total of 155 academic classes were held at the museum; in 1914, a total of 148 classes; and in 1915, a total of 104 classes plus 7 outside lectures and 15 receptions and parties. Cora Mae Folsom, "Museum Report, 1915," January 29, 1916, box "Annual Reports/Historical Information," folder "Museum Reports, 1913–1915," HMC; Cora Mae Folsom, Letter to Hollis Burke Frissell, January 1, 1914, box "Annual Reports/Historical Information," folder "Museum Reports, 1913–1915," HMC.

86. Cora Mae Folsom, Letter to Hollis Burke Frissell (draft), December 23, 1915, box "Annual Reports/Historical Information," folder "Museum Reports, 1913–1915," HMC. As of 1918, the museum was operating in Marshall Hall, with 5,400 square feet of dedicated exhibition space. See Hultgren, "Roots and Limbs," 49.

87. Zeidler and Hultgren, "'Things African Prove,'" 106.

88. Zeidler, "Hampton University Museum Collections," 54. See Cora Mae Folsom, "The Museum" (c. 1918–1922), box "Annual Reports/Historical Information," folder "Museum Reports 1924–1941 and Undated," HMC.

89. Sara Lane, Letter to James E. Gregg, March 1, 1924, box "Annual Reports/Historical Information," folder "Museum Reports 1924–1941 and Undated," HMC.
90. Hultgren, "Roots and Limbs," 55.
91. "Museum Additions," 448.
92. Lane, "African Weapons and Tools," 353, 360.
93. Lane, "African Textile Craftsmanship," 263.
94. Lane, "African Weapons and Tools," 355.
95. William Sheppard, "African Handicrafts and Superstitions," 401; Lane, "Some Musical Instruments," 552.
96. Lane, "African Textile Craftsmanship," 262.
97. Ibid., 264; Folsom, Review of *Songs and Tales from the Dark Continent*, 133.
98. Cunard, *Negro: Anthology*, 732; Schildkrout and Keim, "Objects and Agendas," 23.
99. Wardlaw, "Spiritual Libation," 60.
100. Fauset, "Impressions of the Second Pan-African Congress," 13–15.
101. Culin, *Primitive Negro Art*, [4].
102. William Sheppard, *Presbyterian Pioneers in Congo*, 137. See also, Shannon, "From 'African Savages' to 'Ancestral Legacy,'" 181–183, 121–122.
103. Culin, *Primitive Negro Art*, [4].
104. Siegmann, "Collection Grows in Brooklyn," 67.
105. Shannon, "From 'African Savages' to 'Ancestral Legacy,'" 182.
106. Wardlaw, "Spiritual Libation," 60; Harris and Molesworth, *Alain Locke*, 220–21.
107. Shannon, "From 'African Savages' to 'Ancestral Legacy,'" 249–51; Harris and Molesworth, *Alain Locke*, 223–24; Alain L. Locke, Letter to James E. Gregg, April 11, 1928, box "General Correspondence Agard H. L.-Yabunchi K.," folder "Alain Locke," JEG.
108. Harris and Molesworth, *Alain Locke*, 226–28.
109. Vitalis, *White World Order*, 81.
110. Harris and Molesworth, *Alain Locke*, 239–41, 247; Locke, "Blondiau-Theatre Arts Collection," 127–28; Rampersad, *Life of Langston Hughes*, 1:146–47.
111. Deacon, "Arts and Artifacts Collection of the Schomburg Center," 152; Locke, "American Negro as Artist," 134.
112. Hultgren, "African Art Collections," 37. See "Museum Articles from the Belgian Congo Purchased from the Blondiau Theatre Arts Collection," box "Annual Reports/Historical Information," folder "Museum—Collection Descriptions," HMC.
113. Lane, "Some Musical Instruments," 552. See Sara Lane, Letter to James E. Gregg, February 17, 1928, box "Annual Reports/Historical Information," folder "Museum Reports 1924–1941 and Undated," HMC.
114. Locke, "Art Lessons from the Congo," 587.
115. Hanks, "Journey from the Crossroads," 34.
116. Regenia Perry, *Free within Ourselves*, 88; Allan Gordon, *Echoes of Our Past*, 19–21; Wolfskill, "Caricature and the New Negro," 357, 364n103; Bearden and Henderson, *History of African-American Artists*, 161.
117. Edward J. Brandford, quoted in Francis, "Modern Art, 'Racial Art,'" 123.

118. Bearden and Henderson, *History of African-American Artists*, 159.

119. Calo, "Community Art Center for Harlem," 160. See also, Carlyle Burrows, "Harlem Artists Make Bid for Recognition," *New York Herald Tribune*, July 17, 1932, 8; and the Boykin school advertisement in *"Crisis* School Directory," 328.

120. Bearden and Henderson, *History of African-American Artists*, 162.

121. Ott, "Labored Stereotypes," 111; Wolfskill, "Caricature and the New Negro," 358; Bearden and Henderson, *History of African-American Artists*, 159.

122. Boykin's relationship with Palmer Hayden, Malvin Gray Johnson, and Meta Fuller (who joined Boykin's board of directors after he moved the center to Boston in 1934) suggests another possible avenue of influence around an understudied Hampton figure. Calo, "Community Art Center for Harlem," 166.

123. Francis, "Modern Art, 'Racial Art,'" 121–24.

124. Meyerowitz, *"Negro in Art Week,"* 76, 82.

125. Alain L. Locke, Letter to James E. Gregg, January 18, 1928, box "General Correspondence Agard H. L.-Yabunchi K.," folder "Alain Locke," JEG. On the Howard exhibition, see Harris and Molesworth, *Alain Locke*, 224. See also, Shannon, "From 'African Savages' to 'Ancestral Legacy,'" 272.

126. Alain L. Locke, Letter to James E. Gregg, May 2, 1928, box "General Correspondence Agard H. L.-Yabunchi K.," folder "Alain Locke," JEG.

127. Alain L. Locke, Letter to Mary Livingston Hinsdale Gregg, May 21, 1928, box "General Correspondence Agard H. L.-Yabunchi K.," folder "Alain Locke," JEG.

128. Wallace Short speculates that Locke may have incorporated any purchased objects into either his personal collection or the Blondiau Collection. Lucy Sheppard gave Locke an inscribed copy of *Presbyterian Pioneers in Congo*, dated December 28, 1928, that he held onto until his death. Short, "William Henry Sheppard," 460–61, 461n37.

129. Ritter, *Five Decades*, 7; Webb, *Perfect Documents*, 40–42, 102–4. The images included several objects from the Congo, including a Kuba mask. Webb, *Perfect Documents*, 89. The traveling art exhibit itself featured Kuba textiles. Petridis, "'World of Great Art for Everyone,'" 113.

130. Viktor Lowenfeld, quoted in Peter Smith, "Hampton Years," 38; Hultgren, "African Art Collections," 38.

131. Samella Lewis, Interview by Peter Smith, May 29, 1982, p. 5, PSP; Ritter, *Five Decades*, 8–9. Thanks to Professor Ralph Raunft for providing transcripts of Smith's interviews with John Biggers and Samella Lewis.

132. Hampton Normal and Agricultural Institute, *Seventy-Second Annual Catalogue* (1940), 19.

133. Hampton Normal and Agricultural Institute, *Hampton Bulletin* 39, no. 6 (1943–44), 84. The same description appeared in the 1942–43 *Bulletin*.

134. "Hampton's Collections and Connections," 14; "Reuben V. Burrell, 95, Hampton University Photographer," *Richmond Free Press*, February 12, 2015, http://richmond freepress.com/news/2015/feb/12/reuben-v-burrell-95-hampton-university -photographe. August 24, 2015. See also, Burrell, *One Shot*.

135. Ritter, *Five Decades*, 30, 13, 28; Museum of Modern Art, "Biographical Notes of Exhibiting Artists."

136. LeFalle-Collins, *"Contribution of the American Negro to Democracy,"* 39.

137. Stacy Morgan, *Rethinking Social Realism*, 63.

138. Herzog, *Elizabeth Catlett*, 35; Samella Lewis, Interview by Peter Smith, May 29, 1982, pp. 4, 9, PSP.

139. Ritter, *Five Decades*, 18–20.

140. "Press Release: *New Names in American Art*" (1944), box "Art Conference 1945–1946/Department of Art 1944–1948," folder "Art Conferences (1945)," HART; "*New Names in American Art*" (Renaissance Society); Abbott, "Barnett Aden Gallery," 100–101. The Hampton press release notes that Samella Sanders (Lewis) had work in the show; however, her name is not listed by the Chicago Renaissance Society, which may indicate that her work was not included in the touring exhibition. Locke inscribed a copy of one of his books for Biggers, and later purchased two Biggers drawings for the Barnett Aden Gallery. In 1945, when Viktor Lowenfeld proposed that Hampton use the Navy Boat House as a center for the arts, he cited Alain Locke, who, after visiting campus, noted that the new space was needed, in part, to preserve Biggers's murals. Wardlaw, *Art of John Biggers*, 29; Viktor Lowenfeld, "Memorandum on the Improvement of Building Facilities of the Art Center," June 12, 1945, box "Annual Reports/Historical Information," folder "Museum—Collection Descriptions," HMC.

141. Cureau, "Visual Arts in Black Colleges," 31.

142. Dunkley and Cullum, *In the Eye of the Muses*, 52.

143. See Dunkley, "Compendium of Atlanta University Art Annual Participants."

144. Primus, "People and Ideas," 98–99.

145. Perpener, *African-American Concert Dance*, 164–65; Schwartz and Schwartz, *Dance Claimed Me*, 44, 58, 69; Primus, "People and Ideas," 145; Vansina, *Children of Woot*, 247.

146. Wardlaw, "Spiritual Libation," 65; Amaki, "Hale Woodruff in Atlanta," 23; Amaki, "Nancy Elizabeth Prophet," 43.

147. Shannon, "From 'African Savages' to 'Ancestral Legacy,'" 182–83; Cureau, "Art Gallery in the Negro College," 174; Driskell, *African Art*, [3]; Charles S. Johnson, "Creative Art of Negroes," 240–45.

148. Cureau, "Art Gallery, Museum," 456.

149. Wardlaw, "Spiritual Libation," 60–61; Long, "Major Art Collections," 9; Abbott, "Barnett Aden Gallery," 44; Harris and Molesworth, *Alain Locke*, 224; Chapman, "'Full Circle,'" 96; Bernard, "Patterns of Change."

150. John Biggers, Interview by Peter Smith, October 26, 1982, p. 14, PSP.

151. Wardlaw, *Art of John Biggers*, 28.

152. Theisen, *Life on Paper*, 12. Theisen mistakenly records his name as "McDonald."

153. Biggers, Simms, and Weems, *Black Art in Houston*, 7; Lawrence Henderson, *Galangue*, 28.

154. John Biggers, Interview by David Courtwright.

155. In an application letter describing his dream of attending Hampton, Biggers listed McDowell as a reference. John Biggers, Letter to Dean Walter R. Brown, April 22, 1941, JBA. Many years later at a Lincoln Academy reunion, Biggers got reacquainted with McDowell, who returned to Angola from 1947 to 1959. See Theisen, *Walls That Speak*, 9.

156. Henry McDowell, quoted in Lawrence Henderson, *Galangue*, 14.

157. John Biggers, "Interview: John Biggers," by Christian Walker, 8.

158. Samella Lewis, Interview by Peter Smith, May 29, 1982, p. 16, PSP. See also, Samella Lewis, Interview by Peter Smith, May 29, 1982, p. 12, PSP; Zeidler and Hultgren, "'Things African Prove,'" 109.

159. Samella Lewis, Interview by Peter Smith, May 29, 1982, pp. 16–17, PSP.

160. John Biggers, Interview by David Courtwright.

161. John Biggers, Interview [by Jeanne Zeidler], November 18, 1991, p. 38, JBA.

162. Harvey Johnson, Interview by Danielle Burns; Reaves, *Walk Together Children*, 4.

163. Leon, *Accidentally on Purpose*, 11.

164. John Biggers, quoted in Theisen, *Life on Paper*, 16. See also, Zeidler, "John Biggers' Hampton Murals," 51.

165. Alison de Lima Greene, "John Biggers," 98.

166. In 1946, *Country Preacher* (alternately known as *Community Preacher* or *Rural Preacher*) and *The Dying Soldier* were given as gifts to the Chicago chapter of the United Transport Service Employees, a Congress of Industrial Organizations (CIO) union, by a Hampton trustee. In a remarkable instance of transatlantic circulation, these two paintings were later sent to Liberia. Their current whereabouts are unknown. See Viktor Lowenfeld, Brochure for Hampton Gift of *The Dying Soldier* and *The Rural Preacher* to United Transport Service Employees, CIO, Chicago, JBA; Biggers, Simms, and Weems, *Black Art in Houston*, 78.

167. See, for example, Leon, *Accidentally on Purpose*, 19, 23, 53, 90–91, 115–17, 131, 153; Wahlman, *Signs and Symbols*, 36; Livingston, *Quilts of Gee's Bend*, 53.

168. Wardlaw, *Art of John Biggers*, 22.

169. John Biggers, "Interview: John Biggers," by Christian Walker, 8.

170. Theisen, *Life on Paper*, 6.

171. Wardlaw, *Art of John Biggers*, 17.

172. John Biggers, "Artists Series," by Rebecca N. Felts and Marvin Moon, 9.

173. Leon, *Accidentally on Purpose*, 25–28.

174. Adams, "Beyond Symmetry," 42.

175. Dorothy Washburn, "Style, Classification and Ethnicity," 33. See also, Dorothy Washburn, "Style, Classification and Ethnicity," 144.

176. Leon, *Accidentally on Purpose*, 67, 37.

177. Adams, "Beyond Symmetry," 40.

178. John Biggers, *Ananse*, 4, 26.

179. John Biggers, Interview by David Courtwright. Wardlaw suggests his trip may have been "inspired" by Sheppard. Wardlaw, *Art of John Biggers*, 47.

180. John Biggers, *Ananse*, 15.

181. Theisen, *Walls That Speak*, 6.

182. Vlach, *By the Work of Their Hands*, 185–213.

183. Theisen, *Life on Paper*, 87.

184. Thompson, "John Biggers's *Shotguns* of 1987," 111.

185. Thompson, *Flash of the Spirit*, 147–51.

186. Griffin, "Pearl Primus and the Idea of a Black Radical Tradition," 43n9.

187. Adams, "Kuba Embroidered Cloth," 34.

188. John Biggers, *Ananse*, 15, 76, 29. See also, John Biggers, *Ananse*, 9.

189. Biggers, Simms, and Weems, *Black Art in Houston*, 91–92.

190. John Biggers, *Ananse*, 4.

191. John Biggers, quoted in Eglash, "Geometric Bridge across the Middle Passage," 29; John Biggers, *Ananse*, 21.

192. John Biggers, *Ananse*, 27.

193. John Biggers, "Artists Series," by Rebecca N. Felts and Marvin Moon, 20.

194. Although most biographical accounts only cite the 1957 UNESCO trip, Biggers made at least four trips to Africa, including an especially profound 1969 trip to Sudan, Egypt, and Ethiopia. See Theisen, *Life on Paper*, 18, 57, 71–72; John Biggers, Interview by David Courtwright.

195. Theisen, *Life on Paper*, 101.

196. Gaither, "John Biggers," 88, 93–94.

197. John Biggers, Interview [by Jeanne Zeidler], November 18, 1991, pp. 29, 30, JBA.

198. Wardlaw, *Art of John Biggers*, 55.

199. Theisen, *Walls That Speak*, 80–81, 79. On Biggers as an art collector, see Theisen, *Walls That Speak*, 62–66.

200. John Biggers, Interview [by Jeanne Zeidler], November 18, 1991, p. 22, JBA. The interview typescript contains some transcriptional and typographical errors.

201. Lewis followed Lowenfeld to Penn State as well but left after a semester. See Samella Lewis, Interview by Peter Smith, May 29, 1982, p. 7, PSP.

202. Lanier served as acting president of Hampton in 1943–44, which made him its first African American head. He left Hampton to serve as U.S. minister to Liberia, and in 1948 he became president of the Texas State University for Negroes (which was soon thereafter renamed Texas Southern University). Biggers, Simms, and Weems, *Black Art in Houston*, 14; Theisen, *Life on Paper*, 18; John Biggers, Interview by David Courtwright; Malval, *Guide to the Archives of Hampton Institute*, 80.

203. Wardlaw, "Interview," 263.

204. Biggers, Simms, and Weems, *Black Art in Houston*, 58, 92–93; Dunkley, "Compendium of Atlanta University Art Annual Participants"; Wardlaw, *Art of John Biggers*, 44–47; Terry, *Origin and Development of Texas Southern University*, 82–83.

205. Biggers, Simms, and Weems, *Black Art in Houston*, 83–84; John Biggers, Interview by David Courtwright; Wardlaw, "Spiritual Libation," 70; Sawyer, "Preface," 6.

206. John Biggers, "Introduction," 11.

207. Biggers, Mothershed, and Hudnall, *Traditional African Art Collection*, 57–59.

208. Wardlaw, *Art of John Biggers*, 54–55. See also, Bilotta, "Royal Art of the Kuba," 77; Rogers, *Royal Art of the Kuba*.

209. Gaither, "John Biggers," 94.

210. William R. Harvey, Letter to John Biggers, April 17, 1989, JBA. The commission was arranged by Hampton's longtime president, William Harvey, a major art collector greatly responsible for the school's continued commitment to the visual arts. "Hampton's Collections and Connections," 16. On "the pervasive influence of the presidency" as a signal institutional force impacting arts programs at HBCUs, see Cureau, "Art Gallery in the Negro College," 172.

211. "News Release: Presentation of Bust/Highlights Hampton's Founder's Day," 92-1/2-2-49, JBA.

212. John Biggers, Interview [by Jeanne Zeidler], November 18, 1991, p. 1, JBA.

213. Theisen, *Walls That Speak*, 99.

214. John Biggers, Interview [by Jeanne Zeidler], November 18, 1991, p. 27, JBA.

215. Zeidler, "John Biggers' Hampton Murals," 54.

216. John Biggers, Interview [by Jeanne Zeidler], November 18, 1991, p. 7, JBA.

217. Zeidler, "John Biggers' Hampton Murals," 55.

218. Theisen, *Walls That Speak*, 101.

219. John Biggers, Interview [by Jeanne Zeidler], November 18, 1991, pp. 8, 1, JBA. See also, Theisen, *Walls That Speak*, 131; Harvey Johnson, Interview by Danielle Burns.

220. Dorothy Washburn, "Style, Classification and Ethnicity," 11. Emphasis in source.

221. Ibid., 129.

222. John Biggers, quoted in Theisen, *Walls That Speak*, 100.

223. Harvey Johnson, Interview by Danielle Burns.

224. Wardlaw, *Art of John Biggers*, 53.

225. Lock, "Wadsworth Jarrell and AFRICOBRA," 153; Spellman, "James Phillips," 6–7; Wardlaw, *Black Art, Ancestral Legacy*, 213. See also, Gerdes, "Interweaving Art and Mathematics," 48–49; Thompson, "Song That Named the Land," 110–13.

226. In an AFRICOBRA manifesto, Jeff Donaldson, a cofounder of the group and later Dean of the Howard University College of Fine Arts, recalls a July 1962 conversation with Jarrell "before the Washington picnic, its eloquent dream and its dynamite reality at the church in Birmingham. This was before the very real physical end of Malcolm. And the end of the 'negro' in many of us. And it was before James Chaney. Afro-American. Before Lumumba. Before Jimmie Lee Jackson. Before Selma. Black. Before the Meredith March. Black Power." All of the events signaled in this passage occurred after 1963, except the election and assassination of Patrice Lumumba. Donaldson's recollection indicates that the Congo increased its prominence over time and that the assassination of Lumumba took on increased meaning in African American political consciousness in the wake of these other critical moments in the Civil Rights movement. Donaldson, "Africobra 1," 80.

227. Ringgold, *We Flew over the Bridge*, 189–90.

228. Farrington, *Faith Ringgold*, 107; Wallace, "Faith Ringgold's Political Posters." See Collins and Fitzpatrick, *American People, Black Light*, 101, 102, 108, 117–19, 125.

229. Farrington, *Faith Ringgold*, 36. For additional commentary, see Lee Bernstein, *America Is the Prison*, 84; Martha Schwendener, "Art of Upheaval, and Cross-Pollination," *New York Times*, October 15, 2010, http://www.nytimes.com/2010/10/17/nyregion/17artwe.html. October 15, 2010.

230. Ringgold, *We Flew over the Bridge*, 203. For more, see Farrington, *Faith Ringgold*, 63; Dan Cameron, *Dancing at the Louvre*, 150. In a 1993 show at the Textile Museum in Washington, curator Nashormeh Lindo exhibited work by Ringgold alongside Kuba textiles and Tibetan thangkas. Elaine Louie, "Using Textiles to Tell Many Stories." *New York Times*, April 1, 1993, http://www.nytimes.com/1993/04/01/garden/using-textiles-to-tell-many-stories.html. November 1, 2015.

231. John Biggers, "Interview: John Biggers," by Christian Walker, 8–9. Lowery Sims has written of the similarity between Ringgold's portraits and "the serial portraits of the Kuba kings." See Sims, "Race Riots, Cocktail Parties," 20.

232. Sanford Biggers, Interview by Terry Adkins.

233. Theisen, *Life on Paper*, 115; Cash, "In the Studio: Sanford Biggers," 98.

234. While teaching at Scripps, Lewis was active in the preservation of the Sheppard family papers held by their daughter Wilhelmina in California. Before depositing them at Hampton, she made them available to her Scripps students for research. Kebede, "Visit with Collector Extraordinaire Samella Lewis," 17–21.

235. Roberts and Saar, *Body Politics*, 14, 28.

236. Cave, "On Kuba Cloths."

237. Coker, "Textile Artist's Historical and Anthropological Mission."

238. Cooksey, Poynor, and Vanhee, *Kongo across the Waters*, 355–405. See, especially, essays by Michael Harris on Renée Stout and Carol Thompson on Radcliffe Bailey.

239. Max W. Sheppard, Interview by Julia Vodicka and Larryetta Schall, May 13, 1980, Washington, D.C., audio cassette no. 2, box "William H. Sheppard—Negatives, Photographs, Slides and Tapes," WHSVA (2003).

240. Rossen, *African Americans in Art*, 4.

241. Martin, "Gloucester Caliman Coxe," 228; Morrin, "Cutting a Swath," 14; Phipps, *William Sheppard*, 187.

242. Hultgren, "African Art Collections," 43; Ivy Paglia, "Kuba's Art and History Display at HU," *Daily Press* (Newport News), December 13, 2000, http://articles.dailypress.com/2000-12-13/news/0012130003_1_kuba-art-collection-africa. December 5, 2016.

## Chapter 7

1. Langston Hughes, "Negro Speaks of Rivers," lines 5.
2. Ibid., lines 1–2.
3. DuPlessis, *Genders, Races, and Religious Cultures*, 95.
4. Bontemps, "Marching Song," 122. See Dickinson, *Bio-bibliography of Langston Hughes*, 220–21.
5. Nelson, *Repression and Recovery*, 200.
6. Langston Hughes, *Fight for Freedom*, 10:197.
7. Langston Hughes, "Golden Anniversary," 10:253.
8. Langston Hughes, *Big Sea*, 54, 55.
9. See, for example, Isaacs, *New World of Negro Americans*, 240; Barksdale, *Langston Hughes*, 17; Wagner, *Black Poets of the United States*, 394; and Emanuel, *Langston Hughes*, 150–51.
10. Brawley, *Africa and the War*, 4; Ewing, *Age of Garvey*, 165–66.
11. Langston Hughes, "Negro Speaks of Rivers," lines 4–7.
12. de Jongh, "Poet Speaks of Places," 65, 66.
13. Edwards, *Practice of Diaspora*, 12.
14. Ashcroft, "Is That the Congo?," 3.
15. Edwards, *Practice of Diaspora*, 12. Emphasis in source.
16. Houston A. Baker Jr., *Turning South Again*, 85.
17. Du Bois, *Negro*, chapter 8.
18. Zangana, *City of Widows*, 27.
19. Fromkin, *Peace to End All Peace*, 452.
20. Khalidi, "Fallujah 101."

21. See Langston Hughes, "A Diary of Mexican Adventures (If There Be Any)," July 20 to July 23, 1920, pp. 15–16, box 492, folder 12432, LHPCT. For a reference to the diary, see Rampersad, *Life of Langston Hughes*, 1:41, 401.

22. While Hughes does not specify what newspaper his interlocutor was reading, among the most prominent New York–based Syrian newspapers, the daily *Meraat al-Gharb*, which was established in 1899 by "Arab nationalist" Najeeb M. Diab "to speak for the Syrian Orthodox in America and for Arabism," and the thrice-weekly *Al-Bayan* are reasonable candidates, as both advocated for national independence following the fall of the Ottoman Empire. There were four Arabic-language dailies published in New York in the 1920s. Naff, "Arabic-Language Press," 7–8; Hitti, *Syrians in America*, 135.

23. Khalidi, *Resurrecting Empire*, v.

24. Du Bois, "Eternal Africa," 350, 351. See Rampersad, *Life of Langston Hughes*, 1:55.

25. Fromkin, *Peace to End All Peace*, 416.

26. Busch, *Britain, India, and the Arabs*, 343.

27. Egyptian nationalists used the "Nile" nomenclature to be inclusive of the Sudan, as in the name of the General Federation of Labor Unions in the Nile Valley, a Wafd Party umbrella group. See Beinin and Lockman, *Workers on the Nile*, 158. On the black press's coverage of the Sudan and Ethiopia, see Jacobs, *African Nexus*, 181, 193–200.

28. Fromkin, *Peace to End All Peace*, 419.

29. "Egypt and India," 62.

30. Langston Hughes, "Golden Anniversary," 10:253.

31. Khalidi, *Resurrecting Empire*, 56–57.

32. Fauset, "Nationalism and Egypt," 316.

33. Rampserad, *Life of Langston Hughes*, 1:45.

34. "Men of the Month" (June 1921), 72.

35. Beinin and Lockman, *Workers on the Nile*, 122.

36. Kodi, "1921 Pan-African Congress at Brussels," 266–71, 280–83; Fauset, "Impressions of the Second Pan-African Congress," 15. Du Bois and Farnana corresponded from 1919 until 1929, the year before Farnana's death. See, for example, Paul Panda Farnana, Letter to W. E. B. Du Bois, September 14, 1919, no. mums312-b015-i094, WEBD; W. E. B. Du Bois, Letter to Paul Panda Farnana, February 13, 1929, no. mums312-b050-i339, WEBD.

37. Fauset, "Impressions of the Second Pan-African Congress," 13–14.

38. Langston Hughes, "Negro," lines 14–16.

39. Langston Hughes, "Negro," was reprinted in *Les Continents*, July 15, 1924, 2. See Edwards, *Practice of Diaspora*, 99.

40. Langston Hughes, *Weary Blues*, 19, 51.

41. "Men of the Month: A Missionary" (May 1915), 15.

42. "Africa and the World Democracy," 174. Emphasis in source.

43. William Sheppard, "Interview with Chief M'lumba N'kusa," 121–26.

44. Langston Hughes, *Fight for Freedom*, 10:65.

45. "Africa and the World Democracy," 174. A similar report on Sheppard's address, along with other speeches from this NAACP meeting, were published in pamphlet form as *Africa in the World Democracy* (1919). While much of the pamphlet and *Crisis* text are identical, the pamphlet omits this last sentence.

46. Hochschild, *King Leopold's Ghost*, 278.

47. Granger, "Belgium," 184.

48. For the lyrics to David Banner, "Evil Knievel" (2014), see http://genius.com/4888867. May 31, 2016.

49. In her valuable *Art in Crisis*, art historian Amy Helene Kirschke mistakes the "seated white man [for] Prince Albert of England," when it is actually King Albert I of Belgium, who was the nephew of King Leopold II and reigned from 1909 to 1934. Kirschke, *Art in Crisis*, 163.

50. Bowser, "Studies of the African Diaspora," 5.

51. Langston Hughes, "Golden Anniversary," 10:253.

52. Du Bois, "African Roots of the War," 643.

53. Du Bois, *Darkwater*, 41, 22.

54. Ibid., 42.

55. Leach, *Langston Hughes*, 12.

56. Langston Hughes, *Big Sea*, 55.

57. Hughes stopped in the Belgian Congo during his first trip to Africa in 1923. He traveled to Egypt for the first time in 1962. Langston Hughes, "Ships, Sea and Africa," 69–71; Rampersad, *Life of Langston Hughes*, 2:354.

58. Hughes commonly invokes "Congo Square" in his writings in the *Chicago Defender* in the 1950s and in his late poem "Drums." See, for example, Langston Hughes, *Langston Hughes and the* Chicago Defender, 207, 213, 216; Langston Hughes, *Collected Poems*, 543–44. Other examples include Langston Hughes, "Negro History Week: The Unsung but Not Unswung," *Chicago Defender* (national edition), February 13, 1954, 11; Langston Hughes, "Jazz from Africa via America Now Goes Back to Africa," *Chicago Defender* (national edition), May 7, 1955, 9. On the origins of "Congo Square," see Sublette, *World That Made New Orleans*, 119–21.

59. "'American Congo' to Be Subject at This Gathering," *Cleveland Advocate*, December 27, 1919. In *The African-American Experience in Ohio, 1850–1920*, Ohio Historical Society, http://dbs.ohiohistory.org/africanam/det.cfm?ID=8958. May 14, 2011.

60. See also, "'The American Congo' to Be Described," *Baltimore Afro-American*, December 26, 1919, 1; "To Contrast Conditions in South with Congo," *Chicago Defender*, December 27, 1919, 1.

61. See W. E. B. Du Bois, "The American Congo," box I, C420, folder "Speech and Article File—W. E. B. Du Bois," NAACP.

62. Guterl, *Color of Race in America*, 138.

63. Seligmann, *Negro Faces America*, 218–52; Pickens, "American Congo"; Pickens, *Lynching and Debt-Slavery*; Cunard, *Negro: Anthology*, 29–31. In 1921, the NAACP reprinted the coverage of the Lowry case from national newspapers, including the *Chicago Defender*, as "An American Lynching" (1921). See Todd Lewis, "Mob Justice in the 'American Congo,'" 156–84. For an earlier use in a different context, see Bourke, "American Congo," 590–610.

64. Frank Marshall Davis, "Chicago's Congo," lines 6–9. The comparison of Chicago and the Congo is also used by the Art Ensemble of Chicago on its 1970 album *Chi-Congo*.

65. Isaacs, *New World of Negro Americans*, 240; Barksdale, *Langston Hughes*, 17.

66. Rampersad, "Introduction," xxiii.

67. Kate Baldwin, *Beyond the Color Line*, 86.

68. Langston Hughes, *Big Sea*, 31; Senate Permanent Subcommittee on Investigations of the Committee on Government Operations, *State Department Information Program*, 988.

69. Langston Hughes, *Fight for Freedom*, 10:197; David Levering Lewis, *W. E. B. Du Bois*, 2:6.

70. Langston Hughes, *Big Sea*, 51, 52.

71. Fromkin, *Peace to End All Peace*, 419.

72. Langston Hughes, *Big Sea*, 56.

73. Roessel, "Process of Revision and Hughes," 328, 329.

74. Langston Hughes, *Collected Poems*, 620n24.

75. Schatt, "Langston Hughes," 115.

76. Langston Hughes, *Big Sea*, 55–56.

77. Edwards, "Langston Hughes," 694.

78. Langston Hughes, "Letter from Spain," lines 5–6; Wagner, *Black Poets of the United States*, 394.

79. Edwards, "Langston Hughes," 704.

80. Rampersad, *Life of Langston Hughes*, 1:339.

81. See, for example, Edwards, "Langston Hughes"; Nelson, *Revolutionary Memory*, 66–75, 200–207; Smethurst, *New Red Negro*, 93–115; and Thurston, *Making Something Happen*, 86–134.

82. Kim, "'We, Too, Rise with You,'" 433.

83. Langston Hughes, "Memo to Non-White Peoples," lines 15–19.

84. Blumenthal, *Stork Club*, 162–79, 215–20.

85. Annabel Wharton, *Building the Cold War*, 43–45, 212n11.

86. Langston Hughes, "Bread Not Enough in Congo"; Langston Hughes, "Bread Not Enough in Congo," 1959, box 415, folder 9011, LHPCT.

87. Nzongola-Ntalaja, *Congo from Leopold to Kabila*, 88.

88. The title "Simple and the Congo" appears on two typescript versions of the story, though the *Chicago Defender* published it under the generic headline of Hughes's regular column, "Week by Week," with no subtitle. See Langston Hughes, "Simple and the Congo," 1960, box 416, folder 9056, LHPCT.

89. Langston Hughes, "Week by Week" ("Simple and the Congo"), 10.

90. Langston Hughes, "Simple at the U.N.," 10.

91. Langston Hughes, *Collected Poems*, 625n46.

92. Langston Hughes, "I, Too," line 18; Langston Hughes, "We, Too," 1960–62, box 386, folder 7109, LHPCT. All manuscript citations refer to material in this folder.

93. Rampersad, *Life of Langston Hughes*, 2:324–25, 347.

94. Langston Hughes, "Christmas Gifts for Satan," *Chicago Defender* (national edition), December 16, 1961, 8.

95. Langston Hughes, "We, Too," lines 5–8.

96. Ibid., lines 1–2.

97. Ibid., lines 19–21.

98. Rampersad, *Life of Langston Hughes*, 2:316.

99. Langston Hughes, "Ride, Red, Ride," line 16.

100. Langston Hughes, "Shades of Pigmeat," lines 1–2.

101. Langston Hughes, "Blues in Stereo," line 21.

102. Langston Hughes, "Ode to Dinah," line 44.

103. Langston Hughes, "Ask Your Mama," lines 39–40. A few years after the poem was published, both Sam Cooke and Otis Redding recorded "Tennessee Waltz," which was originally popularized by Patti Page.

104. Rampersad, *Life of Langston Hughes*, 2:319.

105. United Press International, "South Africa Bars Satchmo," *Chicago Defender* (national edition), October 8, 1960, 12; United Press International, "Louis Sets Off Clash in Kenya," *Chicago Defender* (national edition), November 12, 1960, 1; George Weeks, "U.S. Wants More Jazz on Tour," *Chicago Defender* (national edition), December 24, 1960, 12.

106. Langston Hughes, "Bird in Orbit," lines 57–60.

107. See, for example, Editorial, "Tragedy in the Congo," *Chicago Defender* (national edition), February 25, 1961, 10; Editorial, "Testimonials to a Patriot," *Chicago Defender* (national edition), March 4, 1961, 10; John V. Fox, "UN Riot Symbol of Black Unrest," *Chicago Defender* (national edition), March 4, 1961, 10.

108. Langston Hughes, *Collected Poems*, 686n533.

109. Langston Hughes, "Lumumba's Grave," lines 1–4.

110. Ibid., lines 21–23.

111. Smethurst, "'Don't Say Goodbye to the Porkpie Hat,'" 1232.

112. Langston Hughes, "Simple as a Missionary," *Chicago Defender* (national edition), April 22, 1961, 10.

113. Lumumba, "Dawn in the Heart of Africa," 135–36.

114. "Where God Is Black," 22–23.

115. Langston Hughes, "Final Call," lines 11–12. "Final Call" originally appeared under the title "Harlem Call: After the 1964 Riots."

116. Clarke, "New Afro-American Nationalism," 285.

## Chapter 8

1. Killens, *Cotillion*, 145.

2. Gerard and Kuklick, *Death in the Congo*, 190, 195; De Witte, *Assassination of Lumumba*, 75–77, 109, xiii.

3. Rubango, "Patrice Lumumba at the Crossroads of History and Myth," 56; Meriwether, *Proudly We Can Be Africans*, 233; Hébert, "'Stronger in Death Than Alive'"; Zeilig, *Patrice Lumumba*, 131–32; De Witte, *Assassination of Lumumba*, 148; Plummer, *Rising Wind*, 303–4; "1961: Lumumba Rally Clashes with UK Police"; "Rioters Protest Lumumba Death," *New York Times*, February 15, 1961, 16; "Crowd Sets Fire to Belgian Embassy," *Egyptian Gazette*, February 16, 1961, 1; "Embassies Attacked in Cairo," *New York Times*, February 16, 1961, 11; "Negroes Hurl Eggs at Belgian Embassy," *New York Times*, February 16, 1961, 11.

4. Langston Hughes, "Simple as a Missionary," *Chicago Defender* (national edition), April 22, 1961, 10.

5. Rahman, "Living in the Black Arts Movement."

6. "Riot in Gallery Halts U.N. Debate," *New York Times*, February 16, 1961, 1; Tinson, "'Voice of the Black Protest Movement,'" 5–6; Baraka, *Autobiography of LeRoi Jones*, 267; Angelou, *Heart of a Woman*, 182–88; Carlos Moore, *Pichón*, 153–58; Monson,

*Freedom Sounds*, 246; Smethurst, *Black Arts Movement*, 129; Plummer, *Rising Wind*, 302–3; Guy, "Castro in New York," 18.

7. Rahman, "Living in the Black Arts Movement."
8. Plummer, *Rising Wind*, 303.
9. Clarke, "New Afro-American Nationalism," 285.
10. Dudziak, *Cold War Civil Rights*, 153.
11. Clarke, "New Afro-American Nationalism," 286.
12. Meriwether, *Proudly We Can Be Africans*, 238.
13. Cynthia Young, *Soul Power*, 50.
14. Smethurst, *Black Arts Movement*, 129.
15. Meriwether, *Proudly We Can Be Africans*, 228–29, 236, 302–3n47; Gaines, *American Africans in Ghana*, 126; Hoyt Fuller, Review of *The Negro*, 86; Schuyler, *Who Killed the Congo?*, ix; Tillery, *Between Homeland and Motherland*, 99, 101; Cincinnati Branch NAACP, "Negroes Protest Lumumba Death," *Pittsburgh Courier*, March 18, 1961, A26.
16. Morsell, "Meaning of Black Nationalism," 69, 73. The article by Morsell, an NAACP official, was reprinted in *Negro Digest* in April 1963.
17. Polsgrove, *Divided Minds*, 133–46; Gaines, *American Africans in Ghana*, 110–35; Drake, "Negro's Stake in Africa," 42–43.
18. The exact basis for Davis's exclusion, like many details surrounding the event, remains unclear. "Riot in Gallery Halts U.N. Debate," *New York Times*, February 16, 1961, 2, 10; Smethurst, *Black Arts Movement*, 129, 397n56; "U.N. Rioting Laid to Pro-Africans," *New York Times*, February 16, 1961, 11.
19. Baraka, "Black Arts Movement," 495, 496.
20. According to Angelou, Guy received news of Lumumba's death from contacts in the Congolese diplomatic corps before the news was public. Angelou recounts the speech in front of Michaux's bookstore, but indicates the demonstration was planned for a Friday, when it took place on a Wednesday. Angelou, *Heart of a Woman*, 170, 177; Guy, "Castro in New York," 18.
21. Baraka, "Black Arts Movement," 495.
22. Baraka, *Autobiography*, 267; Baraka, *Conversations with Amiri Baraka*, 133; Watts, *Amiri Baraka*, 376.
23. Smethurst, *Black Arts Movement*, 118, 129; Bobo, "Carlos Cooks," 22; Tinson, "'Voice of the Black Protest Movement,'" 5–6; Carlos Moore, *Pichón*, 153; "Riot in Gallery Halts U.N. Debate," *New York Times*, February 16, 1961, 10; Baraka, "Post-Racial Anthology?"
24. James Baldwin, "Negro Assays the Negro Mood," 25; Lorraine Hansberry, "Congolese Patriot" (Letter to the Editor), 4.
25. Kanza, *Conflict in the Congo*, 242.
26. Guy, "Castro in New York," 15.
27. Baraka, "Cuba Libre," 11–62; Tinson, "'Voice of the Black Protest Movement,'" 5–6.
28. Cooks, "There Is Going to Be a New Day," 17.
29. R. Waldo Williams, "Awakening Call," lines 1–3.
30. African Nationalist Pioneer Movement, "Wanted," [21]. See Rivera, "Carlos Cooks and Garveyism," 130n48.

31. Dana Adams Schmidt, "Lumumba Urges U.S. to Aid Congo," *New York Times*, July 28, 1960, 3; Hunt, "Lumumba Views Howard as 'Pride of World,'" *Baltimore Afro-American*, August 6, 1960, 2. After visiting the United States, Lumumba traveled to Canada, where his repeated appeal for "technicians, doctors, nurses, construction engineers, professors and lawyers" was reported by the *Chicago Defender*. United Press International, "Denies White Women Raped by Congolese," *Chicago Defender* (national edition), August 6, 1960, 1. Many Haitians traveled to the Congo—including the parents of filmmaker Raoul Peck, who documents the experience in his 1992 film *Lumumba: Death of Prophet*. Mwissa, *Les Haitiens au Congo*, 37–38; Peck, *Stolen Images*, 111–62, 207–371.

32. Markle, "'We Are Not Tourists,'" 211n520, 199.

33. Brooke Bryan, "A Lifetime of Making a Difference," *Yellow Springs News*, July 16, 2009, http://www.ysnews.com/stories/2009/07/071609_seon.html. December 4, 2011; Bostick, "Tribute to Albert H. Berrian," 241; Cedric Johnson, *Revolutionaries to Race Leaders*, 115. I am exceptionally grateful to Yvonne Seon for sharing her experiences in the Congo with me in a June 22, 2016, telephone conversation.

34. Cecil Gregory, "Crowd Shouts, 'Gallows for Tshombe': 'Africans Built America,' Says the Congo's Lumumba," *Pittsburgh Courier*, September 10, 1960, 21.

35. Associated Press, "Congolese Beat 2 Missionaries," *Baltimore Sun*, November 11, 1961, 2. See also, Associated Press, "2 U.S. Missionaries Assaulted in Kasai," *New York Times*, November 11, 1961, 7.

36. Du Bois, "World Must Soon Awake," 318, 319. See also, Du Bois, "Logical Program for a Free Congo," 323–24.

37. Mealy, *Fidel and Malcolm X*, 43.

38. Gaines, *American Africans in Ghana*, 68. For more on Wright's speech, see Lawrence Jackson, *Indignant Generation*, 506.

39. "Campaign Started to Aid Lumumba," *Chicago Defender* (national edition), November 19, 1960, 2. See also, "Group Denounces U.S. 'Race' Stand in Africa," *Chicago Defender* (national edition), December 31, 1960, 10.

40. Tinson, "'Voice of the Black Protest Movement,'" 6; Sarah Wright, "Lower East Side," 594. See also, Meriwether, *Proudly We Can Be Africans*, 231.

41. "Petition Backing Patrice Lumumba Signed by 1,500," *Pittsburgh Courier*, February 18, 1961, A7; Marie McNair, "They Had 48 Hours Notice," *Washington Post*, July 29, 1960, C1.

42. Sartre, "Introduction," 1–52; Fanon, "Lumumba's Death," 191–97.

43. Clarke, "New Afro-American Nationalism," 286.

44. Smethurst, *Black Arts Movement*, 118; Tinson, "'Voice of the Black Protest Movement,'" 6; Woodard, *Nation within a Nation*, 56.

45. Joseph, "Dashikis and Democracy," 185–86.

46. See also, "Lumumba Tribute Held," *New York Times*, February 27, 1961, 9.

47. Higashida, *Black Internationalist Feminism*, 170. In other popular accounts, the movement itself is obscured by a failure to acknowledge Angelou's collaborators. Smiley, *My Journey with Maya*, 56.

48. Philip Benjamin, "400 Picket U.N. in Salute to Castro and Lumumba," *New York Times*, February 19, 1961, 18; Beveridge, *Domestic Diversity*, 269; "Death of Lumumba,"

1–5; "Lumumba's Murderers Exposed," 1; "Six Months Later," 1; "Secretary General and the Congo," 1; Tinson, "'Voice of the Black Protest Movement,'" 7, 12.

49. Nabaroui, "African Women Seek Independence and Peace," 106. See also, Nkrumah, "Address to the United Nations," 45–72; Lorraine Hansberry, "Congolese Patriot," quoted in *Freedomways* 1.1 (Spring 1961): 94.

50. Esther Cooper Jackson, *Freedomways Reader*, xxvii.

51. Gizenga, "Declaration of the Government of the Congo," 173–84; Clarke, "New Afro-American Nationalism," 285–95; Lowenfels, "Patrice Lumumba Speaks," 32; Howard, "Katanga and the Congo Betrayal," 136–48; Schachter, "Barebreasted in Leopoldville," 149; Clarke, "Cry Rape!," 335; Howard, "How the Press Defames Africa," 361–70; Victor, "Star of the Congo," 407; Nkrumah, "Africa's Liberation and Unity," 431–32; Clarke, "Martyr's Legacy," 119–20; Hairston, "Winds of Change," 55; William Leo Hansberry, "Africa: The World's Richest Continent," 76–77; Howard, "Last Phase of the African Revolution," 181–83; Graham [Du Bois], "History as It Is Made," 221–27. Charles P. Howard Sr., who reported from Africa for *Freedomways*, *Muhammad Speaks*, and other African American publications, was the grandson of Henry McNeal Turner. "Charles P. Howard, AFRO UN Reporter, Dies," *Baltimore Afro-American*, February 1, 1969, 21.

52. Joseph, "Dashikis and Democracy," 186. Alvin Tillery's "content analysis of 439 items that appeared in the" *Atlanta Daily World, Chicago Defender, New York Amsterdam News,* and *Pittsburgh Courier* "between 1958 and 1962 shows that the percentage of items that framed Lumumba negatively increased markedly after he invited the Soviets to intervene in the crisis. Whereas only 3 percent of the items that appeared in the black press before Lumumba courted Soviet intervention framed him negatively, 46 percent of the items that ran after he sought help from the Soviets presented negative frames of his actions." Tillery, *Between Homeland and Motherland*, 118. For excellent surveys of coverage of Lumumba and the Congo in periodicals as different as *Jet* and *Muhammad Speaks*, focusing on 1960–62, see Hickner, "'History Will One Day Have Its Say,'" 215–24, 240–46.

53. *Soulbook* editors, "To the Peoples of Afroamerica, Africa, and to All the Peoples of the World," 2. See Joseph, "Dashikis and Democracy," 185; Ratcliff, "Liberation at the End of a Pen," 71n107. The *Liberator* printed the same letter from Lumumba to his wife in February 1963. Lumumba, "Lest We Forget," 15. For the full letter, see Lumumba, "Letter to Pauline Lumumba," 422.

54. Smethurst, *Black Arts Movement*, 170; Freeman, "Did the United Nations Benefit Congo?," 99. In the first issue of *Soulbook*, articles appear under both "Mamadou Lumumba" and "Kenn M. Freeman." See also, Ahmad, *We Will Return in the Whirlwind*, 137.

55. Tabor, "In Memoriam—Patrice Lumumba," 15. On the circulation of the *Black Panther*, see Streitmatter, "*Black Panther* Newspaper," 229.

56. Black Panther Party, Southern California Chapter, "You Can Kill a Revolutionary but You Can't Kill a Revolution," 12; Scot Brown, *Fighting for US*, 91–99; Tammerlin Drummond, "Legendary Black Revolutionary Freed 46 Years after UCLA Murders," *Santa Cruz Sentinel*, February 3, 2015, http://www.santacruzsentinel.com/article/NE/20150203/NEWS/150209909. December 8, 2016.

57. Hoyt Fuller, "Editor's Notes," 4. See Semmes, *Roots of Afrocentric Thought*, xi.

58. Rambsy, *Black Arts Enterprise*, 28, 21; Kgositsile, "Lumumba Section," 46; Baraka, "[Conakry, Guinea, February 4, 1973 after Amilcar Cabral's funeral]," 45; Brimah, "Nkrumah Never Dies," 11; Don Lee, "Rise Vision Comin," 28. For Nicholas Guillén's poem "Angela Davis," which mentions Lumumba, see De Costa, "Poetry for Afro-Americans," 15.

59. Benston, *Performing Blackness*, 148.

60. See, for example, Meta Jones, *Muse Is Music*, 85–126, and Rambsy, *Black Arts Enterprise*, 116–24.

61. Clarke, "New Afro-American Nationalism," 286.

62. Dennis Osadebay, "Spirit of Patrice Lumumba Lives," *West African Pilot*, February 15, 1961, 5.

63. Olatunde Lawrence, "Lumumba's Death," *West African Pilot*, February 17, 1961, 5, lines 19–21, 24. The *West African Pilot* was founded by Hughes's Lincoln University classmate Nnamdi Azikiwe who "fancied himself a bit of a poet in the Afro-American tradition." Awoonor, Interview by Jane Wilkinson, 23.

64. Wenzel, "Remembering the Past's Future," 17, 15.

65. Sabarsantoso Anantaguna, quoted in Legum, "Foreword," xxvi. Hoyet, "Quelques images de Patrice Lumumba dans la littérature du monde noir d'expression française," 49–80; Djungu-Simba, "La figure de Patrice Lumumba," 81–91.

66. As the focus of at least ten publications, Lumumba "has been the subject of more Nigerian chapbooks than any other non-Nigerian political leader." Lindfors, "Heroes and Hero-Worship in Nigerian Chapbooks," 6; Obiechina, *African Popular Literature*, 237–44.

67. Adrienne Kennedy, *People Who Led to My Plays*, 119–20; Lindfors, "Heroes and Hero-Worship in Nigerian Chapbooks," 17n25. Guy writes that after the death of Hammarskjold, "Africans liked to joke grimly, 'That was Lumumba calling him, you know. "Come, come, Hammarskjold, don't go to Rhodesia, don't trouble those people too."'" Guy, "Castro in New York," 16.

68. Nemiroff, *Les Blancs*, 37–38, 41–44. Lorraine Hansberry, "The Belgian Congo: A Preliminary Report on Its Land, Its History and Its Peoples" ("For Dr. Du Bois—African History Seminar, Jefferson School—New York City, 1953"), box 1, folder 5, LHPNY; Jefferson School of Social Science (New York), background of "African Liberation Struggles" seminar preliminary reports and discussion, February 9, 1953, mums312-b140-i156, WEBD.

69. Cruz, "third world," 144.

70. Kgositsile, *My Name is Afrika*, 45, 55–56, 82.

71. Ngoma, "Tom-Tom," 104–9; Ratcliff, "Liberation at the End of a Pen," 73.

72. Stephen Henderson, "'Survival Motion,'" 117. See also, de Jongh, *Vicious Modernism*, 193–96.

73. Several white poets who were engaged with and influenced by African American culture published poems referencing Lumumba. See, for example, Lowenfels, "Patrice Lumumba Speaks," 32; di Prima, "Goodbye Nkrumah," line 32.

74. See, for example, Cheatwood, *Elegies for Patrice*; Cortez, "Festivals & Funerals," 9–11; Harper, "Patrice Lumumba," 290–91; Langston Hughes, "Lumumba's Grave," 533; Hurley X (Smith), *Poem for Patrice Lumumba*; Ismaili, "Bajji," 33–34; Joans, "LUMUMBA LIVES!," 12; Kgositsile, "Lumumba Section," 46; Raymond Patterson,

"Lumumba Blues," 36; Reed, "Patrice," 36; Thomas, "Tale of Two Cities," 36–37; Alhamisi, "Black Narrator," 40; Allen, "For Malcolm," 85–86; Charles Anderson, "Finger Pop'in," 190; Baraka, "Black Dada Nihilismus," 73; Boyd, "Sierra Maestra," 12; Victor Cruz, "third world," 144; Giovanni, "Adulthood," 18; David Henderson, "They Are Killing All the Young Men," 417; Percy Johnston, "Variation on a Theme by Johnston," 46; Jordan, "Poem about My Rights," 87; Don Lee, "Rise Vision Comin," 28; Neal, "Black Boogaloo," 44; Plumpp, "Half Black Half Blacker," 386; Seon, "Uhuru Hop Scotch," 29–30, "Alphabet Name Game," 26–28; Spriggs, "Every Harlem Face Is AFROMANISM Surviving," 341.

75. My use of the term *innovative* to describe experimental and avant-garde poetics borrows from the extensive scholarship of Aldon Lynn Nielsen. See, for example, Nielsen, *Integral Music*, xv–xvi. Nielsen and Ramey's *Every Goodbye Ain't Gone: An Anthology of Innovative Poetry by African Americans* features works by Cortez, Joans, and many other authors who invoked Lumumba, including Baraka, David Henderson, Percy Johnston, June Jordan, Ishmael Reed, and Lorenzo Thomas.

76. Stephen Henderson, "Response," 192. Henderson responds to Benston, "Performing Blackness: Re/Placing Afro-American Poetry," 164–85, an earlier version of chapter 4 of Benston, *Performing Blackness*, 145–86. Coltrane and Parker are each named in more than 200 poems listed in Feinstein, *Bibliographic Guide to Jazz Poetry*, 115–20, 168–72.

77. Smethurst, *Black Arts Movement*, 39.

78. Joans, "Bird Lives!," 45.

79. Moten, *In the Break*, 85.

80. Joans, "Him the Bird," lines 16–22.

81. Joans, *Teducation*, 167. For an early version of "Him the Bird" from 1962, see Reisner, *Bird*, 120.

82. Joans, "Bird and the Beats," 14; Gonzales, *I Paid My Dues*, 52–53.

83. Benston, *Performing Blackness*, 145.

84. Benston, "Performing Blackness: Re/Placing Afro-American Poetry," 177. Emphasis in source.

85. Joans, "Bird and the Beats," 14.

86. Joans, *All of Ted Joans* ("LUMUMBA LIVES!," lines 1–2), 12.

87. Slaughter, "Pathetic Fallacies," 9. Joans, *In Thursday Sane*. Sandra McPherson found Joans's personal copy of *The Palm-Wine Drinkard* for sale in a bookshop, with the previously unpublished 1976 poem "In Thursday Sane," dedicated to painter Beauford Delaney, written in its back cover.

88. Joans, *All of Ted Joans* ("LUMUMBA LIVES!," lines 24–27), 12.

89. Joans, *Black Pow-Wow* ("LUMUMBA LIVES    L U M U M B A   L I V E S!!," lines 1, 11), 16.

90. Joans, *Black Pow-Wow* ("LUMUMBA LIVES    L U M U M B A   L I V E S!!," lines 5–6), 16.

91. Clarke, "New Afro-American Nationalism," 286; Hébert, "'Stronger in Death Than Alive.'"

92. Lindberg, "Mister Joans, to You," 214.

93. di Prima, "Goodbye Nkrumah," line 32.

94. Joans, "Afrique Accidentale," line 5. A version of this poem was reprinted in Joans, *Afrodisia*, 4–8.

95. Meta Jones, *Muse Is Music*, 229.
96. Stephen Henderson, *Understanding the New Black Poetry*, 30.
97. Benston, *Performing Blackness*, 158.
98. Ibid., 147.
99. Baraka, "Black Dada Nihilismus," line 67.
100. Nielsen, *Black Chant*, 190–94; Baraka, *Conversations with Amiri Baraka*, 48; Baraka [as LeRoi Jones], quoted in Black Panther Party (Northern California) and House of Umoja (Unity), "Editorial" (*Black Power!*), 20.
101. Moten, *In the Break*, 94.
102. Joans, "Who Shook," lines 68–72.
103. Von Eschen, *Satchmo Blows Up the World*, 66–68. See also, Reuters, "Armstrong in Katanga: Trumpeter and U.S. Aide Go to Area on Goodwill Tour," *New York Times*, November 21, 1960, 5; Paul Hofmann, "Satchmo Plays for Congo's Cats: Trumpeter Arrives on Red Throne and Crew of Bearers," *New York Times*, October 29, 1960, 8.
104. Joans, "Black February Blood Letting," lines 1–3, lines 15–20.
105. Post, "Nigerian Pamphleteers and the Congo," 411. The Patrice Lumumba Friendship University was renamed the Peoples' Friendship University of Russia in 1992. See Peoples' Friendship University of Russia, http://www.rudn.ru/en. July 11, 2011. Robert Williams visited the university in September 1963. See Cohen, *Black Crusader*, 311.
106. In addition to the poems discussed in this chapter, Joans refers to Lumumba alongside musicians in "I Am the Lover," and references either Congo, Zaire, or Kinshasa in works such as "For the Viet Congo," "Africa," "Mahalia Jackson," "A Powerful Black Starmichael," "Happy Headgear to They," "I Told On It," "No Mad Talk," "Laughter You've Gone and . . . ," "Okapi Passion," and "The Statue of 1713." See Joans, *Black Pow-Wow*, 13–14, 46; Joans, *Black Manifesto*, 78; Joans, *Teducation*, 168, 8, 29, 44, 63, 178, 189, 220.
107. Joans, "Sax Bit," lines 4–7.
108. Ogali, *Ghost of Patrice Lumumba*, 246; George Washington Williams, *Open Letter*, 248.
109. White, *Speaking with Vampires*, 16.
110. Joans, "Langston Hughes I Knew," 16. Joans's tributes to Hughes include Joans, "Passed On Blues," 26–27; and "Ego-sippi" (1968); "Happy 78 Hughes Blues" (1978); "Another Dream Deferred" (1988). Joans, *Teducation*, 24, 28, 7. *Black Pow-Wow* is dedicated

> To
> Langston Hughes
> and allyall

111. After two previously deadlocked juries, Byron De La Beckwith was convicted in 1994 for the 1963 murder of Evers.
112. Cortez, "Initiation," lines 1–13.
113. Benston, *Performing Blackness*, 145.
114. Cortez, "Initiation," lines 14–15, 20–21.
115. Benston, *Performing Blackness*, 149–52; Melhem, *Heroism in the New Black Poetry*, 188.

116. Redmond, *Drumvoices*, 415.
117. Cortez, "Festivals & Funerals," lines 1–3, 24–25, 28–30. The title of the book—*Festivals and Funerals*—spells out the word "and," while the title of the poem—"Festivals & Funerals"—uses an ampersand ("&").
118. Melhem, *Heroism in the New Black Poetry*, 208.
119. Ibid., 206; Ryan, *Post-Jazz Poetics*, 92.
120. Lindberg, "Mister Joans, to You," 212.
121. Gerard and Kuklick, *Death in the Congo*, 208; De Witte, *Assassination of Lumumba*, 141.
122. "'Funeral' for Lumumba," *New York Times*, February 26, 1961, 21; Emblidge, "Rallying Point," 272; Willis, "Harlem Education."
123. Jewsiewicki, "Congolese Memories of Lumumba," 75.
124. Thomas, "Tale of Two Cities," lines 2–3.
125. Cortez, "Festivals & Funerals," lines 92–97.
126. Ibid., lines 98–104.
127. Jordan, "On Record," 63.
128. Kelley, *Freedom Dreams*, 164.
129. Bolden, "All the Birds Sing Bass," 62.
130. Neal, "Any Day Now," 55.
131. Lindfors, "Heroes and Hero-Worship in Nigerian Chapbooks," 1.
132. Raymond Patterson, *Elemental Blues*, 46.
133. Raymond Patterson, "Lumumba Blues," line 1.
134. Ibid., line 5.
135. Benston, *Performing Blackness*, 149.
136. Ibid., 145.
137. Bolden, "All the Birds Sing Bass," 63.
138. Raymond Patterson, "Lumumba Blues," lines 6–7, 10–12.
139. Legum, "Foreword," vii–xi; Lumumba, *Congo, My Country*, xxxi–xxxii, 1–5; Clarke, "Martyr's Legacy," 119.
140. Howard, "How the Press Defames Africa," 364.
141. Raymond Patterson, "Lumumba Blues," lines 19–21.
142. Ibid., lines 22–27.
143. Smethurst, *Black Arts Movement*, 112.
144. Wenzel, "Remembering the Past's Future," 22.
145. Stephen Henderson, *Understanding the New Black Poetry*, 30–31, 68.
146. Harper, "Patrice Lumumba," lines 41–46.
147. Rambsy, *Black Arts Enterprise*, 151.
148. Baraka, "Somebody Blew Up America," 201–2. On the controversy, see Jeremy Pearce, "When Poetry Seems to Matter," *New York Times*, February 9, 2003, http://www.nytimes.com/2003/02/09/nyregion/when-poetry-seems-to-matter.html. October 8, 2013.
149. Alice Walker, "Belgian Rule in the Congo: Saga of Irresponsibility," Sarah Lawrence College, May 29, 1964, box 88, folder 6, AWP (subseries 2.4e, college papers, 1961–66).
150. Alice Walker, *Overcoming Speechlessness*, 8–9.
151. Whoriskey, "Introduction," x.

Chapter 9

1. Although "Stanleyville" is now known as "Kisangani," I use the former name in order to maintain consistency with period sources.

2. Malcolm X, "Exchange on Casualties in the Congo," 159–60. For a summary of more recent demographic debates, see the exchange following Hochschild's review of Vellut's *Memory of Congo: The Colonial Era* exhibition at the RMCA. See Hochschild, "In the Heart of Darkness"; Vellut, "Letter"; Hochschild, "Reply to Jean-Luc Vellut." Among earlier African American discourse on the population decline, see Ford, *Communists and the Struggle for Negro Liberation*, 36.

3. Sliwinski, "Childhood of Human Rights," 358n4.

4. Malcolm X, "Exchange on Casualties in the Congo," 161.

5. Abernethy, *Iconography of Malcolm X*, 38.

6. Ambar, *Malcolm X at Oxford Union*, 47; Collins and Bailey, *Seventh Child*, 94; Twain, *King Leopold's Soliloquy*, 52–54; Moore, *Pichón*, 100–101. Moore recalls buying a copy of *King Leopold's Soliloquy* in 1960, although the International Publishers reprint that Michaux likely sold and Malcolm likely read has a 1961 publication date.

7. The U.N. demonstration spurred the *New York Times* to investigate nationalist groups. See Peter Kihss, "Negro Extremist Groups Step up Nationalist Drive," *New York Times*, March 1, 1961, 1, 25; Robert L. Teague, "Negroes Say Conditions in U.S. Explain Nationalists' Militancy," *New York Times*, March 2, 1961, 1, 17.

8. Goldman, *Death and Life of Malcolm X*, 156. See also, Temkin, "From Black Revolution to 'Radical Humanism,'" 278; Ambar, *Malcolm X at Oxford Union*, ix.

9. Angelou, *Heart of a Woman*, 198–99.

10. Malcolm X Little, Department of Justice, New York, New York, February 21, 1961, FBI file no. 100-399321, 1.

11. Marable, *Malcolm X*, 190.

12. Malcolm X, "Malcolm X at Yale," 157.

13. Malcolm X, "Not Just an American Problem, but a World Problem," 163; Malcolm X, "At the Audubon" (December 13, 1964), 94; Borstelmann, *Cold War and the Color Line*, 182.

14. Alvin C. Adams, "Chicagoans Blast Tshombe as an Uncle Tom," *Chicago Daily Defender* (daily edition), February 14, 1961, 1. See also, Malcolm X, "Not Just an American Problem, but a World Problem," 163. On the use of "Uncle Tom" as an epithet to attack black leaders, see Reynolds, *Mightier Than the Sword*, 260; Krosney, "America's Black Supremacists," 390.

15. Malcolm X, "Old Negro and the New Negro," 89.

16. Malcolm X, Letter to Yahya Hayari, September 1, 1962, box 3, folder 4, MXP. For a similar letter from October 1962, see Marable, *Malcolm X*, 223.

17. Malcolm X, *Autobiography of Malcolm X*, 307.

18. "Malcolm X Scores U.S. and Kennedy: Likens Slaying to 'Chickens Coming Home to Roost,'" *New York Times*, December 2, 1963, 21; Paul Lee, "When the Chickens Came Home to Roost: What Malcolm X Actually Said," *Michigan Citizen* (Highland Park), September 23–29, 2001; Malcolm X, "God's Judgment of White America (The Chickens Are Coming Home to Roost)," 121–48; Marable, *Malcolm X*, 269–73.

19. Malcolm X, "Whatever Is Necessary: The Last Television Interview, with Pierre Berton," 180. For a domestic framing of his remarks with no reference to Lumumba, see Collins and Bailey, *Seventh Child*, 141–42.

20. Goldman, *Death and Life of Malcolm X*, 53.

21. Malcolm X, "Louis Lomax Interviews Malcolm X," 177. See Marable, *Malcolm X*, 285.

22. Malcolm X, "Answers to Questions at the Militant Labor Forum," 41–42.

23. James Booker, "Seek to Evict Malcolm X from Home in Queens," *New York Amsterdam News*, April 18, 1964, 1.

24. Malcolm X, *Diary of Malcolm X*, 46.

25. Malcolm X, *Autobiography of Malcolm X*, 364–65. See also, Malcolm X, *Diary of Malcolm X*, 52. For another account of this occasion, see Smiley, *My Journey with Maya*, 62.

26. Sherwood, *Malcolm X Visits Abroad*, 63.

27. Malcolm X, "At the Audubon" (December 20, 1964), 129.

28. Sales, *From Civil Rights to Black Liberation*, 106. See Malcolm X (OAAU), Letter to Martin Luther King Jr., [June 1964], box 14, folder 2, MXP; Malcolm X (OAAU), Letter to James Farmer, [June 1964], box 14, folder 2, MXP; Sales, *From Civil Rights to Black Liberation*, 153; Ahmad, *We Will Return in the Whirlwind*, 126.

29. Malcolm X, "Founding Rally of the OAAU," 92.

30. Rickford, *Betty Shabazz*, 197.

31. Malcolm X, "Second Rally of the OAAU," 136.

32. Malcolm X, Message to Diallo Telli, July 28, 1964, box 24, folder 25, JHC. See also, Malcolm X, *Diary of Malcolm X*, 92.

33. Sherwood, *Malcolm X Visits Abroad*, 89, 12; "Petition Backing Patrice Lumumba Signed by 1,500," *Pittsburgh Courier*, February 18, 1961, A7.

34. Marable, *Malcolm X*, 367, 384–85.

35. Information Bureau of the OAAU (Accra), "Press Release: Afro-American Troops for Congo—Malcolm X," [n.d.], box 24, folder 25, JHC. See also, Sherwood, *Malcolm X Visits Abroad*, 89; Gaines, *American Africans in Ghana*, 200. Kondo notes a similar correspondence from an FBI report: "Malcolm sent a letter to an unknown Afrikan delegate to the OAU Conference in Addis Ababa, Ethiopia, stating that if the OAU needed recruits to aid Afrikan revolutionaries fighting to liberate the Congo, he could guarantee 10,000 recruits in Harlem." Kondo, *Conspiracys*, 51.

36. Nzongola-Ntalaja, *Congo from Leopold to Kabila*, 122–24.

37. Hoyt, *Captive in the Congo*, 27; Minter, "Limits of Liberal Africa Policy," 42.

38. "Congo: Is Anyone in Control?," 32.

39. Attwood, *Reds and the Blacks*, 192.

40. Weissman, *American Foreign Policy in the Congo*, 239–40; Gleijeses, *Conflicting Missions*, 129–31; Hoyt, *Captive in the Congo*, 27, 110–11, 46–58. Congress authorized the Gulf of Tonkin Resolution on August 7, 1964. Tom Wickers, "Johnson Calls Air Strike a Warning to Aggressors," *New York Times*, August 9, 1964, 1; Lyndon Johnson, "Transcript of President's News Conference on Foreign and Domestic Affairs," *New York Times*, August 9, 1964, 48.

41. Michaels, "Breaking the Rules," 142. See Hoyt, *Captive in the Congo*, 10, 259n1.

42. Gleijeses, *Conflicting Missions*, 125–26, 430n4.

43. Michaels, "Breaking the Rules," 142.

44. Ibid., 139–40; Attwood, *Reds and the Blacks*, 195–202.

45. Sherwood, *Malcolm X Visits Abroad*, 126.

46. Malcolm X, "Homecoming Rally of the OAAU," 179; Weissman, *American Foreign Policy in the Congo*, 245. The Egyptian and Algerian embassies in Kinshasa were occupied in retaliation. See Ismael, *U.A.R. in Africa*, 221. Nasser's rejection of Tshombe was noted as a signal moment by *Muhammad Speaks* as part of its extensive coverage of the Congo. See "Egypt's New Army May Back Africa's Freedom Struggle," *Muhammad Speaks*, January 1, 1965, 11.

47. Marable, *Malcolm X*, 371–74; Malcolm X, "Homecoming Rally of the OAAU," 178–79; Babu, *Future That Works*, 101; Markle, "'We Are Not Tourists,'" 58.

48. Sherwood, *Malcolm X Visits Abroad*, 106–7. Sherwood raises the intriguing possibility that Malcolm may have extended his stay in Tanzania in order to attend some of these meetings.

49. Marable, *Malcolm X*, 372. Hoyt and Attwood acknowledged Kenyatta's efforts. Hoyt, *Captive in the Congo*, 196; Attwood, *Reds and the Blacks*, 215–16. When the OAU sent a delegation to the United States to negotiate the release of hostages in Stanleyville, Secretary of State Dean Rusk initially refused to meet with the group because of its exclusion of Tshombe and ultimately rejected an offer of a ceasefire in exchange for U.S. withdrawal of its airplanes. Weissman, *American Foreign Policy in the Congo*, 244–45, 247.

50. Malcolm X, "See for Yourself," 75.

51. Hoyt, *Captive in the Congo*, 199. Kanza appeared at Lumumba's side when he visited the United States in July 1960. See Patrice Lumumba, "Excerpts from Transcript of News Conference by Premier Lumumba of the Congo," *New York Times*, July 26, 1960, 2. While living in New York, Kanza became close to activists such as Guy and Moore and was a keynote speaker at a *Freedomways* event. See Angelou, *Heart of a Woman*, 134; Carlos Moore, *Pichón*, 135–37; Esther Cooper Jackson, *Freedomways Reader*, xxvii. By contrast, Attwood describes Kanza as "an itinerant and usually unemployed Congolese politician" and "a confidence man." Attwood, *Reds and the Blacks*, 195.

52. Malcolm X, *Diary of Malcolm X*, 154.

53. Malcolm X, Travel Diary, microfilm (October 21, 1964, box 6), MXP. See also, Malcolm X, *Diary of Malcolm X*, 155. During this time, Malcolm was almost certainly being trailed by a U.S. spy, Leo Milas.

54. Sherwood, *Malcolm X Visits Abroad*, 118–19; Malcolm X, *Diary of Malcolm X*, 159–60.

55. Sherwood, *Malcolm X Visits Abroad*, 111–12, 132; Chana Kai Lee, *For Freedom's Sake*, 103–8.

56. Malcolm X, "On Politics," 202. See Malcolm X, "La communauté noire américaine et la révolution africaine," 44.

57. Weissman, *American Foreign Policy in the Congo*, 248.

58. Malcolm X Little, Department of Justice, New York, New York, November 25, 1964, FBI file no. 100-399321, section 13, serials 183, 3.

59. "Malcolm X, Back in the U.S., Accuses Johnson on Congo," *New York Times*, November 25, 1964, 17.

60. Malcolm X, "See for Yourself," 80. *Time* magazine's attention to Carlson is especially ironic, since Henry Luce agreed to pull Lumumba's picture from the cover a few years earlier at the personal request of Ambassador Clare Timberlake. Devlin, *Chief of Station, Congo*, 46.

61. John W. Finney, "Africans' Charge Rejected by U.S.," *New York Times*, November 29, 1964, 5.

62. King, "Press Release and Interview from Radio Norway," 3–4. King calls the OAU the "Organization of African States," apparently combining the name of the one-year-old OAU with the name of its predecessor organization, the Union of African States.

63. Hoyt, *Captive in the Congo*, 236. Hoyt encountered Kitt on the Irv Kupcinet show, which frequently had Malcolm as a guest. See Goldman, *Death and Life of Malcolm X*, 129, 155, 251; Kitt, *Confessions of a Sex Kitten*, 124; Malcolm X, "Twenty Million Black People in a Political, Economic, and Mental Prison," 34. Malcolm and Kitt's political circles did occasionally overlap. See Emblidge, "Rallying Point," 273.

64. David Graham Du Bois, Letter to Malcolm X, December 3, 1964, box 3, folder 14, MXP.

65. Nasir El-Din Mahmoud, Cable to Gamal Abdel Nasser, November 28, 1964, box 14, folder 2, MXP. See also, Sherwood, *Malcolm X Visits Abroad*, 91n62; Malcolm X, *Diary of Malcolm X*, 109, 117–22.

66. Malcolm X, Letter to David Graham Du Bois, December 15, 1964, box 3, folder 4, MXP; Malcolm X, Letter to David Graham Du Bois, December 17, 1964, box 3, folder 14, MXP. Malcolm's December 15 and December 17, 1964, letters to David Graham Du Bois are nearly identical; presumably one is a draft of the other.

67. Malcolm X, "Homecoming Rally of the OAAU," 182–83. Emphasis in source.

68. Malcolm X Little, Department of Justice, New York, New York, January 20, 1965, FBI file no. 100-399321, section 14, serials [214–227], 41–42.

69. Malcolm X, "Oxford Address at the Oxford Union Debate," 173.

70. Tuck, *Night Malcolm X Spoke*, 157.

71. Malcolm X, "Old Negro and the New Negro," 112–13; Malcolm X, "Elijah Is Willing to Sit and Wait—I'm Not," 21; Malcolm X, "Oppressed Masses of the World," 50–51; Malcolm X, "Educate Our People in the Science of Politics," 92.

72. "Congo Massacre," 28, 30, 32. *Time* publisher Bernhard M. Auer credits several writers including Leopoldville-based reporter Robin Mannock, West Africa bureau chief Jonathan C. Randal, and New York–based contributing editor Robert F. Jones for the unsigned cover story. Auer reports that Mannock works in Africa because of his interest "in abnormal psychology." Auer, "Letter from the Publisher," 19. For earlier examples of *Time*'s defamation of Lumumba, see "Where God Is Black," 22–23.

73. Malcolm X, "Harvard Law School Forum of December 16, 1964," 166.

74. Malcolm X, "Communication and Reality," 309.

75. Malcolm X, "At the Audubon" (December 13, 1964), 93, 96.

76. Weissman, *American Foreign Policy in the Congo*, 253.

77. Malcolm X, "At the Audubon" (December 13, 1964), 97, 104.

78. Malcolm X, "Harvard Law School Forum of December 16, 1964," 165.

79. Michaels, "Breaking the Rules," 134.

80. Malcolm X, "Harvard Law School Forum of December 16, 1964," 173–74.

81. Ibid., 167. For example, Albert Murray clumsily makes strange bedfellows in claiming that it has not "been shown that the fall of Lumumba, Tschombe [sic], or Nkrumah added to the problems of black Americans." Albert Murray, *Omni-Americans*, 182.

82. Epps, *Malcolm X: Speeches at Harvard*, 179. See Malcolm X, "Harvard Law School Forum of December 16, 1964," 165.

83. Malcolm X, "'Young Socialist' Interview," 194.

84. Gaines, "Malcolm X in Global Perspective," 164.

85. Julian Mayfield, "Congo—A Lesson for the Apologists," *Ghanaian Times*, November 25, 1964, 5, reprinted as Julian Mayfield, "Black American in Africa; 'Congo Is a Lesson for the Apologists,'" *Muhammad Speaks*, March 19, 1965, 11.

86. Hamer, "I'm Sick and Tired of Being Sick and Tired," 62, 64. In Guinea, the group visited a printing shop named for Lumumba. After Guinea, two members of the delegation—John Lewis and Donald Harris—traveled throughout the continent and ran into Malcolm in Nairobi. John Lewis, *Walking with the Wind*, 293–96; Chana Kai Lee, *For Freedom's Sake*, 105; Wilkins, "Making of Black Internationalists," 479–82.

87. Matthew Jones, "Oginga Odinga," 124–27.

88. Malcolm X, "With Mrs. Fannie Lou Hamer," 106, 108, 114. See Marable, *Malcolm X*, 371.

89. Malcolm X, "At the Audubon" (December 20, 1964), 124–25, 133, 125.

90. Malcolm X, "Malcolm X on 'Unity,'" 130; Malcolm X, "Oppressed Masses of the World," 56; Malcolm X, "Educate Our People in the Science of Politics," 94–95; Malcolm X, "Not Just an American Problem, but a World Problem," 167–68.

91. Malcolm X, "See for Yourself," 79. Excerpts of this talk published elsewhere provide a different transcription and indicate the date as December 31, 1964. See Malcolm X, "Moise Tshombe and Jesse James," 218. On the correct date, see Malcolm X, *Malcolm X Talks to Young People*, 103n17.

92. Stiles, *Jesse James*, 5–6; Awoonor, *African Predicament*, 19.

93. Attwood, *Reds and the Blacks*, 227.

94. Malcolm X, "Our People Identify with Africa," 93.

95. M. S. Handler, "Malcolm X Cites Role in U.N. Fight: Says He Swayed Africans to Attack U.S. 'Racism,'" *New York Times*, January 2, 1965, 6.

96. "Africans Fight Back to Free the Congo," *Muhammad Speaks*, January 1, 1965, 1–2.

97. Malcolm X, "Linking the Problem," 217–18.

98. Malcolm X, "Prospects for Freedom in 1965," 148–49.

99. Malcolm X, "Congo, Cuba and Law," 220.

100. Michaels, "Breaking the Rules," 134.

101. Schraeder, *United States Foreign Policy toward Africa*, 72.

102. Malcolm X, "'Young Socialist' Interview," 198. Emphasis in source.

103. Malcolm X, "Malcolm X on Afro-American History," 14.

104. Marable, *Malcolm X*, 411–12, 420; Malcolm X, "Elijah Is Willing to Sit and Wait—I'm Not," 20; Malcolm X, *February 1965*, 272n5.

105. Malcolm X, "Telephone Conversation," 206, 208–9.

106. Sherwood, *Malcolm X Visits Abroad*, 186.

107. Kondo, *Conspiracys*, 244n297.

108. Malcolm X, "Oppressed Masses of the World," 49–52.

109. Ibid., 49.

110. The same gap appears in two published transcriptions of the speech. Malcolm X, "Oppressed Masses of the World," 49; Malcolm X, *Malcolm X Talks to Young People*, 30.

111. Malcolm X, *Malcolm X Talks to Young People*, 20.

112. Malcolm X, "Oxford Address at the Oxford Union Debate," 169–80. The full text of the speech is available online. See Malcolm X, "Oxford University Debate (December 3, 1964)."

113. Carson, *Malcolm X: The FBI File*, 82.

114. Breitman, "Foreword," viii. There are many minor differences in the transcriptions of the speech in *Malcolm X Speaks* and *February 1965*.

115. Compare Malcolm X, "After the Bombing" (*Malcolm X Speaks*), 161; and Malcolm X, "Educate Our People in the Science of Politics," 81–82.

116. Malcolm X, "After the Bombing" (*Malcolm X Speaks*), 168; Malcolm X, "Educate Our People in the Science of Politics," 91–93. The most complete version is available online at Malcolm X, "After the Bombing/Speech at Ford Auditorium"; Malcolm X, "After the Firebombing (February 14, 1965)." An audio recording of the speech without the "gap" is also available as Malcolm X, *The Last Message* (Discos Hablando LP1300). These conflicting transcriptions highlight the need for a complete scholarly edition of Malcolm X's speeches.

117. Malcolm X, "Educate Our People in the Science of Politics," 77–79. See also, Malcolm X, "Telephone Conversation," 205–11.

118. Malcolm X, "There's a Worldwide Revolution Going On," 127, 146.

119. Malcolm X, "Not Just an American Problem, but a World Problem," 162–65.

120. See, for example, ibid., 180–81.

121. Goldman, *Death and Life of Malcolm X*, 398–99. See also, Goldman, *Death and Life of Malcolm X*, 158.

122. Malcolm X, "Second Rally of the OAAU," 135.

123. Evanzz, *Judas Factor*, 19. See Powell, *Adam by Adam*, 54; Hamilton, *Adam Clayton Powell, Jr.*, 208.

124. Daulatzai, *Black Star, Crescent Moon*, 27; Evanzz, *Judas Factor*, 127; Malcolm X, "Black Revolution," 76–77; Gebrekidan, *Bond without Blood*, 176.

125. Malachi D. Crawford explains, "The FBI learned of a letter that Malcolm had allegedly written to an unnamed African delegate at the OAU Conference in Egypt, which stated that, if requested to do so, he would rally 10,000 U.S. African soldiers from Harlem in support of the Congolese nationalists against the regime of Moise Tshombe, which was backed by neocolonial powers. However, the agency could not verify whether Malcolm X had suggested plans of a recruitment drive to deploy U.S. Africans in Harlem to the Congo. . . . A memorandum concerning Malcolm's speculation was sent by the FBI to the Central Intelligence Agency (CIA) and the intelligence-gathering communities in the U.S. Army, Navy, and Air Force." Malachi Crawford, "Malcolm X and Human Rights," 231. Malcolm X Little, Department of Justice, New York, New York, January 20, 1965, FBI file no. 100-399321, section 14, serials [214–227], 8, 130. FBI documents refer to an OAU meeting in Addis Ababa, Ethiopia, but Egypt hosted the

second annual OAU conference in July 1964. The founding meeting of the OAU was held in Addis Ababa in May 1963.

126. Malcolm X Little, Department of Justice, New York, New York, January 20, 1965, FBI file no. 100-399321, section 14, serials [214–227], 41.

127. For the ongoing rift between Moore and other African American activists, see Azikiwe et al., "North American African Activists, Intellectuals and Artists Speak," 463–66. Moore was suspected of being a CIA spy and, for some time, was implicated in an attempt to assassinate Malcolm X. See Carlos Moore, *Pichón*, 283. On Moore, see Gosse, *Where the Boys Are*, 169n55; Carlos Moore, *Castro, the Blacks, and Africa*, 204, 404n57. For further evidence of his relationship with Malcolm X, see Malcolm X, "Telephone Conversation," 205–11; Himes, *My Life of Absurdity*, 291–92.

128. Malcolm X, Letter to Kojo Amoo-Gottfried, December 30, 1964, box 3, folder 4, MXP.

129. Tuck, *Night Malcolm X Spoke at the Oxford Union*, 3; Ambar, *Malcolm X at Oxford Union*, 146–48.

130. Carlos Moore, *Pichón*, 279. In earlier writings, Moore made the same assertion that he "was one of those to whom Malcolm X turned to request help in the recruitment of qualified Blacks living in Europe." See Carlos Moore, *Castro, the Blacks, and Africa*, 402n8.

131. Carlos Moore, *Pichón*, 283.

132. Carew, *Ghosts in Our Blood*, 61.

133. Malcolm X, "At the Audubon" (December 20, 1964), 116.

134. Carlos Moore, *Castro, the Blacks, and Africa*, 404n58.

135. Guevara, "At the United Nations," 329, 337–38. See also, Porra, "L'Afrique du Che," 279–85; Gálvez, *Che in Africa*, 27–28.

136. Marable, *Malcolm X*, 396; Malcolm X, "At the Audubon" (December 13, 1964), 102. See Marable, *Malcolm X*, 172.

137. Mealy, *Fidel and Malcolm X*, 43.

138. Castro, *Speech at the United Nations*, 24.

139. Cynthia Young, *Soul Power*, 22.

140. Strickland and Greene, *Malcolm X*, 108–9.

141. Cohen, *Black Crusader*, 359, 335–38; Mitchell, "Monumental Plot." In New York, Guevara saw Robert Steele Collier, a member of the Black Liberation Front and later the Panther 21, whom he met in Cuba during the summer. Collier and three colleagues, including Khaleel Sultran Sayyed, "a member of RAM who had been sent into Malcolm's organization to develop a security wing," were convicted of a February 1965 plot to blow up the Statue of Liberty and other monuments, which is sometimes linked (without substantiation) to Guevara. Ahmad, *We Will Return in the Whirlwind*, 129. The comrades were arrested on February 16, less than a week before Malcolm X's assassination.

142. Marable, *Malcolm X*, 396. Moore states that Che Guevara "held long discussions with Malcolm X," which Sherwood repeats. Jon Lee Anderson makes no mention of a personal meeting, but notes, "the reason Che didn't show up [at the Audubon] was to avoid an appearance that the U.S. government could claim was an 'intromission' in its internal affairs." Carlos Moore, *Castro, the Blacks, and Africa*, 189; Sherwood, *Malcolm X Visits Abroad*, 176; John Lee Anderson, *Che Guevara*, 618.

143. Kondo, *Conspiracys*, 51.

144. Soon after independence, Cuba provided Algeria with military assistance in a conflict with Morocco, effectively marking Castro's entrance into African military affairs. In 1963, Guevara visited Algeria to celebrate the first anniversary of independence. Gleijeses, *Conflicting Missions*, 30–56.

145. Malcolm X, *Diary of Malcolm X*, 50, 57.

146. Malcolm X, Letter to Maya Maki [Maya Make (Angelou)], June 1, 1964, box 3, folder 4, MXP. Emphasis in source.

147. Malcolm X, *Diary of Malcolm X*, 172. A letter from Betty was waiting for Malcolm in Algeria, which indicates that it was a planned destination.

148. John Lee Anderson, *Che Guevara*, 618.

149. Marable, *Malcolm X*, 371. On his meetings with Congolese activists, see Malcolm X, "Homecoming Rally of the OAAU," 178–79.

150. Kondo, *Conspiracys*, 244n297.

151. Marable, *Malcolm X*, 396. See also, Rojo, *My Friend Che*, 168–70; John Lee Anderson, *Che Guevara*, 619; Marable, *Malcolm X*, 384–85; Gálvez, *Che in Africa*, 32; Carlos Moore, *Castro, the Blacks, and Africa*, 193–95.

152. Gleijeses, *Conflicting Missions*, 78, 406n6.

153. Gaines, *American Africans in Ghana*, 227.

154. Carlos Moore, *Castro, the Blacks, and Africa*, 197. As his source, Moore cites his October 1970 Paris interview with William Gardner Smith.

155. Rojo, *My Friend Che*, 170; Gálvez, *Che in Africa*, 35–37; Reitan, *Rise and Decline of an Alliance*, 58.

156. Pablo Rivalta, quoted in Gálvez, *Che in Africa*, 35. See also, Villafana, *Cold War in the Congo*, 127; Gott, "Introduction," xxvi.

157. Babu, "Memoirs," 13; Issa, *Walk on Two Legs*, 72. Although Babu left the ZNP in 1963, some of the members who were trained in Cuba joined him in the newly formed Umma Party. See Hunter, *Zanzibar*, 34, 50; Amrit Wilson, "Abdul Rahman Mohamed Babu," 11. See also, Burgess, "Imagined Generation," 216–49.

158. Babu, *Future That Works*, 63–64.

159. Ibid., 101.

160. Sherwood, *Malcolm X Visits Abroad*, 177.

161. Babu, "Memoirs: An Outline," 20.

162. Markle, "'We Are Not Tourists,'" 60–63.

163. Babu, "Dedication, Discipline, Decisiveness," 17. See Bailey, "Sheikh Babu Speaks at Rally," 4.

164. Babu, "Memoirs: An Outline," 20; Baraka, *Autobiography of LeRoi Jones*, 441.

165. Cohen, *Black Crusader*, 328. See also, Tyson, *Radio Free Dixie*, 204.

166. Tyson, *Radio Free Dixie*, 224–31, 205, 234. Williams was unable to attend the U.N. demonstration because of an engagement in Michigan, but spoke at a Harlem rally the day before. Tinson, "'Voice of the Black Protest Movement,'" 5–6.

167. Ahmad, *We Will Return in the Whirlwind*, 126.

168. John Lee Anderson, *Che Guevara*, 628–29; Cohen, *Black Crusader*, 358–61; Carlos Moore, *Castro, the Blacks, and Africa*, 213.

169. [Armstrong], "Invitation to Congo," 2.

170. Gott, "Introduction," xli.

171. Heikal, *Cairo Documents*, 162, 175.

## Conclusion

1. Malcolm X, "Oppressed Masses of the World," 50–51; see appendix "Malcolm X on the Congo, February 14, 1965, Detroit."

2. Bontinck, *Aux origines de l'État Indépendant du Congo*, 29. See also, Fry, *Henry S. Sanford*, 94–96, 100–101, 134.

3. Fry, *Henry S. Sanford*, 112, 77, 157, 163.

4. George Washington Williams, Letter to Henry Shelton Sanford, February 12, 1890, box 28, folder 19, HSS.

5. Carew, *Ghosts in Our Blood*, 36.

6. "World Pays Little Attention to Malcolm Slaying," *New York Times*, February 28, 1965, 74. The *New York Times* article compiles the extremely limited observations of the newspaper's international correspondents, who themselves present evidence to contradict the inaccurate accompanying headline.

7. Markle, "'We Are Not Tourists,'" 65.

8. Revolutionary Action Movement, "Why Malcolm X Died," 10.

9. The single "Keep on Pushing" by the Impressions (on an eponymously titled album) was on the Billboard Top 40 R&B charts for fifteen weeks beginning June 13, 1964 (spending two weeks at number one), and "A Change is Gonna Come" by Sam Cooke was on the same chart for eleven weeks beginning January 30, 1965. Whitburn, *Billboard Book of Top 40 R&B and Hip-Hop Hits*, 262, 121.

10. Smith McKoy, "'This Unity of Split Blood,'" 208n9.

11. Wenzel, "Intertextual Africa," 243.

12. I am unaware of any documentary evidence that Malcolm X and Patrice Lumumba ever met. Their one possible opportunity would have been in New York in July 1960, during Lumumba's only visit to the United States.

13. Awoonor, *Comes the Voyager at Last*, 109–13.

14. Editorial, "Heart of Darkness," *Washington Post*, July 21, 1960, A16.

15. ABC News, "Heart of Darkness: Part One-War in the Congo"; ABC News, "Heart of Darkness: Part Three-Kisangani."

16. Vansina, *Being Colonized*, 133.

17. Wamba, *Kinship*, 185.

18. Garza, "Q&A with Alicia Garza."

# Bibliography

Archival Source Abbreviations

| | |
|---|---|
| AAB | African Archives (Portefeuille M580, Liasse 88), Brussels, Belgium |
| ABE | Althea Brown Edmiston Papers (MS no. 883), Emory University Manuscript, Archives, and Rare Book Library, Atlanta, Ga. (U.S.) |
| ALENC | Alonzo Lmore Edmiston Papers (Montreat no. 129485), Presbyterian Historical Society, Montreat, N.C. (U.S.) |
| ALEPA | Alonzo Lmore Edmiston Papers (PCUS no. 129485), Presbyterian Historical Society, Philadelphia, Pa. (U.S.) |
| AWP | Alice Walker Papers (MS no. 1061), Emory University Manuscript, Archives, and Rare Book Library, Atlanta, Ga. (U.S.) |
| BFM | Board of Foreign Missions of the Presbyterian Church (U.S.A.) (Accession no. 02 0812a), Presbyterian Historical Society, Philadelphia, Pa. (U.S.) |
| BTW | Booker T. Washington Papers, Tuskegee University Archives and Museums, Tuskegee, Ala. (U.S.) |
| BWM | Board of World Missions of the Presbyterian Church (U.S.) (RG no. 839), Presbyterian Historical Society, Philadelphia, Pa. (U.S.) |
| CCR | Charles Cameron Ross Papers (Accession no. 06 0814c), Presbyterian Historical Society, Philadelphia, Pa. (U.S.) |
| CMP | Congo Mission, Records, 1891–1980, Division of International Mission (RG no. 432), Presbyterian Historical Society, Philadelphia, Pa. (U.S.) |
| CPH | Collis Potter Huntington Papers, Syracuse University, Syracuse, N.Y. (U.S.) |
| ECFM | Executive Committee of Foreign Missions, Office of Executive Secretary (Accession no. 05 0610a), Presbyterian Historical Society, Philadelphia, Pa. (U.S.) |
| HART | Collection 19.1 Education: Art, Hampton University Archives, Hampton, Va. (U.S.) |
| HBF | Hollis Burke Frissell Papers, Hampton University Archives, Hampton, Va. (U.S.) |
| HMC | Hampton Museum Collection, Hampton University Archives, Hampton, Va. (U.S.) |
| HMS | Henry Morton Stanley Papers, Royal Museum for Central Africa, Tervuren, Belgium |
| HSS | Henry Shelton Sanford Papers, Sanford Museum, Department of Recreation, Sanford, Fla. (U.S.) |

| | |
|---|---|
| JBA | John Biggers: Artist File, Hampton University Archives, Hampton, Va. (U.S.) |
| JEG | James E. Gregg Papers, Hampton University Archives, Hampton, Va. (U.S.) |
| JHC | John Henrik Clarke Papers (SCM no. 94), Schomburg Center for Research in Black Culture, New York, N.Y. (U.S.) |
| JHF | John Hope Franklin Papers, Duke University, Rare Book, Manuscript, and Special Collections Library, Durham, N.C. (U.S.) |
| LHPCT | Langston Hughes Papers (MSS no. 26), James Weldon Johnson Collection in the Yale Collection of American Literature, Yale University, Beinecke Rare Book and Manuscript Library, New Haven, Connecticut (U.S.) |
| LHPNY | Lorraine Hansberry Papers (MG no. 680), Schomburg Center for Research in Black Culture, New York, N.Y. (U.S.) |
| MXP | Malcolm X Papers (Sc MG no. 721), Schomburg Center for Research in Black Culture, New York, N.Y. (U.S.) |
| NAACP | NAACP Papers, Library of Congress, Washington, D.C. (U.S.) |
| PSP | Peter Smith Papers, John and Betty Michael Autobiographical Lecture Series of Prominent Art Educators, Miami University, Center for the Study of the History of Art Education (1972–), Oxford, Ohio (U.S.) |
| RRM | Robert Russa Moton Papers, Tuskegee University Archives and Museums, Tuskegee, Ala. (U.S.) |
| SCA | Samuel Chapman Armstrong Papers, Hampton University Archives, Hampton, Va. (U.S.) |
| SWP | *Southern Workman* Papers, Hampton University Archives, Hampton, Va. (U.S.) |
| WEBD | W. E. B. Du Bois Papers (MS no. 312), University of Massachusetts, Amherst, Special Collections and University Archives, Amherst, Mass. (U.S.) |
| WHSML | Stillman College, William H. Sheppard Memorial Library, Tuscaloosa, Ala. (U.S.) |
| WHSNC | William Henry Sheppard Papers, Presbyterian Historical Society, Montreat, N.C. (U.S.) |
| WHSPA | William Henry Sheppard Papers (RG no. 457), Presbyterian Historical Society, Philadelphia, Pa. (U.S.) |
| WHSVA (2003) | William Henry Sheppard Papers (accessed 2003), Hampton University Archives, Hampton, Va. (U.S.) |
| WHSVA (2015) | William Henry Sheppard Papers (accessed 2015), Hampton University Archives, Hampton, Va. (U.S.) |

Archival Sources

My gratitude for the archives and archivists who have made possible my research is boundless. There are a few notes that bear explanation. I have made multiple visits over several years to the Hampton University Archives and to the Presbyterian Historical Society. In the case of Hampton, the William Henry Sheppard Papers, which I use here, have been recataloged in the time since my first research visit to the collection. This is because additional materials that Samella Lewis acquired from William Sheppard's daughter in California had previously been listed as "Supplementary" before being incorporated into the main collection. In the case of the Presbyterian Historical Society, the Montreat, North Carolina, affiliate merged with its northern partner in Philadelphia in the mid-2000s. Though the cataloging information appears to be consistent, to ensure accuracy, I have specified the location where I reviewed the items.

Amherst, Massachusetts (U.S.)
 University of Massachusetts, Amherst, Special Collections and University Archives
  W. E. B. Du Bois Papers (MS no. 312)
Atlanta, Georgia (U.S.)
 Emory University Manuscript, Archives, and Rare Book Library
  Althea Brown Edmiston Papers (MS no. 883)
  Alice Walker Papers (MS no. 1061)
Brussels, Belgium
 African Archives (Portefeuille M580, Liasse 88)
Durham, North Carolina (U.S.)
 Duke University, Rare Book, Manuscript, and Special Collections Library
  John Hope Franklin Papers
Hampton, Virginia (U.S.)
 Hampton University Archives
  Samuel Chapman Armstrong Papers
  John Biggers: Artist File (five boxes; unnumbered and unprocessed)
  Collection 19.1 Education: Art
  Hollis Burke Frissell Papers
  James E. Gregg Papers
  Hampton Museum Collection
  William Henry Sheppard Papers
  *Southern Workman* Papers
Montreat, North Carolina (U.S.)
 Presbyterian Historical Society
  Alonzo Lmore Edmiston Papers (Montreat no. 129485)
  William Henry Sheppard Papers
New Haven, Connecticut (U.S.)
 Yale University, Beinecke Rare Book and Manuscript Library
  Langston Hughes Papers (MSS no. 26), James Weldon Johnson Collection in the Yale Collection of American Literature
New York, New York (U.S.)
 Schomburg Center for Research in Black Culture
  John Henrik Clarke Papers (SCM no. 94)
  Lorraine Hansberry Papers (MG no. 680)
  Malcolm X Papers (Sc MG no. 721)

Oxford, Ohio (U.S.)
: Miami University, Center for the Study of the History of Art Education (1972–)
: : Peter Smith Papers, John and Betty Michael Autobiographical Lecture Series of Prominent Art Educators

Philadelphia, Pennsylvania (U.S.)
: Presbyterian Historical Society
: : Board of Foreign Missions of the Presbyterian Church (U.S.A.) (Accession no. 02 0812a)
: : Board of World Missions of the Presbyterian Church (U.S.) (RG no. 839)
: : Congo Mission, Records, 1891–1980, Division of International Mission (RG no. 432)
: : Alonzo Lmore Edmiston Papers (PCUS no. 129485)
: : Executive Committee of Foreign Missions, Office of Executive Secretary (Accession no. 05 0610a)
: : Charles Cameron Ross Papers (Accession no. 06 0814c)
: : William Henry Sheppard Papers (RG no. 457)

Sanford, Florida (U.S.)
: Sanford Museum, Department of Recreation
: : Henry Shelton Sanford Papers

Syracuse, New York (U.S.)
: Syracuse University
: : Collis Potter Huntington Papers

Tervuren, Belgium
: Royal Museum for Central Africa
: : Henry Morton Stanley Papers

Tuscaloosa, Alabama (U.S.)
: Stillman College, William H. Sheppard Memorial Library

Tuskegee, Alabama (U.S.)
: Tuskegee University Archives and Museums
: : Robert Russa Moton Papers
: : Booker T. Washington Papers

Washington, D.C. (U.S.)
: Library of Congress
: : NAACP Papers

List of Newspapers

Additional newspaper sources found among archival materials are listed with archive location information in the endnotes.

*Baltimore Afro-American*
*Baltimore Sun*
*Chicago Daily Defender*
*Chicago Defender*
*Cleveland Advocate*
*Daily Press* (Newport News)

*Egyptian Gazette*
*Fisk Herald*
*Ghanaian Times*
*Hampton Student*
*Le Peuple* (Belgium)
*Los Angeles Times*
*Michigan Citizen* (Highland Park)
*Muhammad Speaks*
*New York Amsterdam News*
*New York Globe* (*New York Age*)
*New York Herald*
*New York Herald Tribune*
*New York Times*
*New York Tribune*
*Pittsburgh Courier*
*Richmond Free Press*
*Santa Cruz Sentinel* (California)
*Tuscaloosa News* (Alabama)
*Tuskegee Student*
*Washington Post*
*West African Pilot* (Nigeria)
*Yellow Springs News* (Ohio)

Published Sources

Abbott, Janet Gail. "The Barnett Aden Gallery: A Home for Diversity in a Segregated City." PhD dissertation, Pennsylvania State University, State College, 2008.
Abbott, Lynn, and Doug Seroff. *Out of Sight: The Rise of African American Popular Music, 1889–1895.* Jackson: University Press of Mississippi, 2003.
ABC News. "Heart of Darkness: Part One—War in the Congo." Narrated by Ted Koppel. *Nightline.* ABC. January 21, 2002. Transcript, http://more.abcnews.go.com/sections/nightline/dailynews/congo1-transcript.html. January 4, 2003.
———. "Heart of Darkness: Part Three-Kisangani." Narrated by Ted Koppel. *Nightline.* ABC. January 23, 2002. Transcript, http://more.abcnews.go.com/sections/nightline/dailynews/congo3-transcript.html. January 4, 2003.
Abernethy, Graeme. *The Iconography of Malcolm X.* Lawrence: University Press of Kansas, 2013.
"The Acquittal of Sheppard." *Colored American Magazine* 17, no. 5 (November 1909): 381.
Adams, Monni. "Beyond Symmetry in Middle African Design." *African Arts* 23, no. 1 (November 1989): 34–43+.
———. "Kuba Embroidered Cloth." *African Arts* 12, no. 1 (November 1978): 24–39+.
Adelman, Lynn. "A Study of James Weldon Johnson." *Journal of Negro History* 52, no. 2 (April 1967): 128–45.
Adoff, Arnold, ed. *The Poetry of Black America: Anthology of the 20th Century.* New York: HarperCollins, 1973.

"Africa and the World Democracy." *Crisis* 17, no. 4 (February 1919): 173–76.
African Nationalist Pioneer Movement. "Wanted." *Black Challenge* 1960, [21].
"The African Slave Trade." *Southern Workman* 18, no. 12 (December 1889): 122.
Ahmad, Muhammad (Maxwell Stanford Jr.). *We Will Return in the Whirlwind: Black Radical Organizations, 1960–1975*. Chicago: Charles H. Kerr, 2007.
Alhamisi, Ahmed [Le Graham]. "The Black Narrator." 1966. In *Black Poetry: A Supplement to Anthologies Which Exclude Black Poets*, edited by Dudley Randall, 39–40. Detroit: Broadside Press, 1969.
Allen, Ernie. "For Malcolm." *Soulbook* 1, no. 2 (Spring 1965): 85–86.
Alvis, Joel L., Jr. *Religion and Race: Southern Presbyterians, 1946–1983*. Tuscaloosa: University of Alabama Press, 1994.
Amaki, Amalia K. "Hale Woodruff in Atlanta: Art, Academics, Activism and Africa." In Amaki and Brownlee, *Hale Woodruff, Nancy Elizabeth Prophet, and the Academy*, 23–41.
———. "Nancy Elizabeth Prophet: Carving a Niche at Spelman College and Beyond." In Amaki and Brownlee, *Hale Woodruff, Nancy Elizabeth Prophet, and the Academy*, 43–61.
Amaki, Amalia K., and Andrea Barnwell Brownlee, eds. *Hale Woodruff, Nancy Elizabeth Prophet, and the Academy*. Atlanta: Spelman College Museum of Fine Art, 2007.
Ambar, Saladin. *Malcolm X at Oxford Union: Racial Politics in a Global Era*. New York: Oxford University Press, 2014.
American Presbyterian Congo Mission. [untitled note]. *Kassai Herald* 5, no. 4 (October 1905): 39.
———. *Misambu ya Kutumbisha n'ai Nzambi*. Luebo, Belgian Congo: Imprimerie A.P.C.M., 1949.
———. "Secular News." *Kassai Herald* 5, no. 4 (October 1905): 48.
———. "Secular News." *Kassai Herald* 6, no. 2 (April 1906): 24.
Anderson, Charles. "Finger Pop'in." In Baraka (Jones) and Neal, *Black Fire*, 189–90.
Anderson, James D. *The Education of Blacks in the South, 1860–1935*. Chapel Hill: University of North Carolina Press, 1988.
Anderson, John Lee. *Che Guevara: A Revolutionary Life*. New York: Grove, 1997.
Anderson, Vernon A. *Still Led in Triumph*. [Nashville, Tenn.]: Board of World Missions, Presbyterian Church (U. S.), [1959].
Anderson, Vernon A., W. Frank McElroy, and George T. McKee. "Preface." In *Dictionary of the Tshiluba Language* by William M. Morrison, ii–iii. Rev. ed. Luebo, Belgian Congo: J. Leighton Wilson Press, 1939.
Angelou, Maya. *The Heart of a Woman*. 1981. New York: Bantam, 1997.
"Announcement and Prospectus of the *New Era Magazine*: An Illustrated Monthly Devoted to the World-Wide Interests of the Colored Race." *New Era Magazine* 1, no. 1 (February 1916): 1–7 [i–vii].
"The 'Appeal to Pharaoh.'" *Southern Workman* 18, no. 12 (December 1889): 121.
Appiah, Kwame Anthony. *Lines of Descent: W. E. B. Du Bois and the Emergence of Identity*. Cambridge, Mass.: Harvard University Press, 2014.
[Armstrong, Samuel Chapman.] "Invitation to Congo." *Southern Workman* 19, no. 1 (January 1890): 2.

Ashcroft, W. D. [Bill]. "Is That the Congo? Language as Metonymy in the Post-Colonial Text." *World Literature Written in English* 29, no. 2 (1989): 3–10.

Ater, Renée. "Making History: Meta Warrick Fuller's 'Ethiopia.'" *American Art* 17, no. 3 (Autumn 2003): 12–31.

———. *Remaking Race and History: The Sculpture of Meta Warrick Fuller*. Berkeley: University of California Press, 2011.

"At Home and Afield: Hampton Incidents." *Southern Workman* 44, no. 3 (March 1915): 182–88.

"Atrocities in the Congo Free State." *Missionary* 33, no. 2 (February 1900): 61–63.

Attwood, William. *The Reds and the Blacks*. New York: Harper and Row, 1967.

Auer, Bernhard M. "A Letter from the Publisher." *Time*, December 4, 1964, 19.

Austin, Ramona. "An Extraordinary Generation: The Legacy of William Henry Sheppard, the 'Black Livingstone' of Africa." *Afrique et Histoire* 4 (February 2005): 73–101.

Awoonor, Kofi Nyidevu. *The African Predicament: Collected Essays*. 2006. Accra, Ghana: Sub-Saharan Publishers, 2012.

———. *Comes the Voyager at Last: A Tale of Return to Africa*. Trenton, N.J.: Africa World, 1992.

———. Interview by Jane Wilkinson. 1987. In *Talking with African Writers: Interviews with African Poets, Playwrights and Novelists*, edited by Jane Wilkinson, 19–31. London: James Currey, 1992.

Azikiwe, Abayomi, et al. "North American African Activists, Intellectuals and Artists Speak." *Journal of Pan-African Studies* 4, no. 2 (December 2010): 463–66.

Babu, Abdul Rahman Mohamed. "Dedication, Discipline, Decisiveness: Babu's Harlem Speech." *Black America* (Summer–Fall 1965): 5–6, 17.

———. *The Future That Works: Selected Writings of A.M. Babu*, edited by Salma Babu and Amrit Wilson. Trenton, N.J.: Africa World, 2002.

———. "Memoirs: An Outline." In *Babu: I Saw the Future and It Works; Essays Celebrating the Life of Comrade Abdulrahman Mohamed Babu, 1924–1996*, edited by Haroub Othman, 9–23. Dar es Salaam, Tanzania: E and D, 2001.

Bade, David W. *Books in African Languages in the Melville J. Herskovits Library of African Studies, Northwestern University: A Catalog*. Program in African Studies Working Papers, no. 8. 3 vols. Evanston, Ill.: Northwestern University, 2000.

Bailey, Peter. "Sheikh Babu Speaks at Rally." *OAAU Blacklash* 1, no. 9 (December 22, 1964): 4.

Baker, Houston A., Jr. *Turning South Again: Re-Thinking Modernism/Re-Reading Booker T*. Durham, N.C.: Duke University Press, 2001.

Baker, Houston A., Jr., and Patricia Redmond, eds. *Afro-American Literary Study in the 1990s*, Chicago: University of Chicago Press, 1989.

Baker, Lee D. "Research, Reform, and Racial Uplift: The Mission of the Hampton Folk-Lore Society, 1893–1899." In *Excluded Ancestors, Inventible Traditions: Essays Toward a More Inclusive History of Anthropology*, edited by Richard Handler, 42–80. Madison: University of Wisconsin Press, 2000.

"The Bakuba." *Missionary* 26, no. 5 (May 1893): 168–72.

Baldwin, James. "A Negro Assays the Negro Mood." *New York Times Magazine*, March 12, 1961, 25.

Baldwin, Kate. *Beyond the Color Line and Iron Curtain: Reading Encounters between Black and Red, 1922–1963*. Durham, N.C.: Duke University Press, 2002.

Banning, Émile. *Mémoires politiques et diplomatiques: Comment fut fondé le Congo belge*. Paris-Brussels: Renaissance du Livre, 1927.

Baraka, Amiri. *The Autobiography of LeRoi Jones*. Chicago: Lawrence Hill Books, 1997.

———. "The Black Arts Movement." In Baraka, *LeRoi Jones/Amiri Baraka Reader*, 495–506.

———. "Black Dada Nihilismus." 1964. In Baraka, *LeRoi Jones/Amiri Baraka Reader*, 71–73.

———. "[Conakry, Guinea, February 4, 1973 after Amilcar Cabral's funeral]." *Black World* 22, no. 7 (May 1973): 44–48.

———. *Conversations with Amiri Baraka*, edited by Charlie Reilly. Jackson: University Press of Mississippi, 1994.

———. "Cuba Libre." 1960. In LeRoi Jones, *Home: Social Essays*, 11–62. New York: Morrow, 1966.

———. *The LeRoi Jones/Amiri Baraka Reader*, edited by William J. Harris. 1991. New York: Basic Books, 2009.

———. "A Post-Racial Anthology?," review of *Angles of Ascent: A Norton Anthology of Contemporary African American Poetry*, edited Charles Henry Rowell. *Poetry* (May 2013), http://www.poetryfoundation.org/poetrymagazine/articles/detail/69990. May 16, 2016.

———. "Somebody Blew Up America." *African American Review* 37, no. 2–3 (Summer–Fall 2003): 198–203.

Baraka, Amiri [as LeRoi Jones] and Larry Neal eds. *Black Fire: An Anthology of Afro-American Writing*. New York: Morrow, 1968.

Barber, Jesse Belmont. *Climbing Jacob's Ladder: Story of the Work of the Presbyterian Church U.S.A. among the Negroes*. New York: Board of National Missions, Presbyterian Church (U.S.A.), 1952.

Barksdale, Richard K. *Langston Hughes: The Poet and His Critics*. Chicago: American Library Association, 1977.

Baylen, Joseph O. "Senator John Tyler Morgan, E.D. Morel, and the Congo Reform Association." *Alabama Review* 15, no. 2 (April 1962): 117–32.

Bearden, Romare, and Harry Henderson. *A History of African-American Artists: From 1792 to the Present*. New York: Pantheon, 1993.

Beardslee, Howard, Lois Edmund, James Evinger, Nancy Poling, Geoffrey Stearns, and Carolyn Whitfield. *Final Report of the Independent Committee of Inquiry, Presbyterian Church (U.S.A.)*. Louisville, Ky.: Presbyterian Church (U.S.A.), 2002.

Bedinger, Robert Dabney. "Althea Brown Edmiston: A Congo Crusader." In *Glorious Living: Informal Sketches of Seven Missionaries of the Presbyterian Church, U.S.*, edited by Sarah Lee Timmons, 261–86. Atlanta: Committee on Woman's Work, Presbyterian Church (U.S.), 1937.

———. *Triumphs of the Gospel in the Belgian Congo*. Richmond, Va.: Presbyterian Committee of Publication, 1920.

Beinin, Joel, and Zachary Lockman. *Workers on the Nile: Nationalism, Communism, Islam and the Egyptian Working Class, 1882–1954*. Princeton, N.J.: Princeton University Press, 1987.

"Bells Appealing." *The Bulletin* (Brussels), August 14, 2008, 14–16.

Benedetto, Robert. "The Presbyterian Mission Press in Central Africa, 1890–1922." *American Presbyterians* 68, no. 1 (Spring 1990): 55–69.

———, ed. *Presbyterian Reformers in Central Africa: A Documentary Account of the American Presbyterian Congo Mission and the Human Rights Struggle in the Congo, 1890–1918*. Translated by Winifred Kellersberger Vass. New York: Brill, 1996.

"Benefactions: Mrs. Valeria G. Stone." *American Missionary* 38, no. 3 (March 1884): 69–70.

Benson, Brian Joseph. "The *Southern Workman*." In *Black Journals of the United States*, edited by Walter C. Daniel, 350–58. Westport, Conn.: Greenwood, 1982.

Benston, Kimberly W. *Performing Blackness: Enactments of African-American Modernism*. New York: Routledge, 2000.

———. "Performing Blackness: Re/Placing Afro-American Poetry." In Baker and Redmond, *Afro-American Literary Study in the 1990s*, 164–85.

Berghahn, Marion. *The Image of Africa in Black American Literature*. London: Macmillan, 1977.

Bergman, Jill. *The Motherless Child in the Novels of Pauline Hopkins*. Baton Rouge: Louisiana State University Press, 2012.

Bernard, Catherine. "Patterns of Change: The Work of Loïs Mailou Jones." *Anyone Can Fly Foundation On-Line Journal* (June 2003), http://www.anyonecanflyfoundation.org/library/Bernard_on_Mailou_Jones_essay.html. August 26, 2015.

Bernstein, Jeremy. "The Dark Continent of Henry Stanley." *New Yorker*, December 31, 1990, 93–107.

Bernstein, Lee. *America Is the Prison: Arts and Politics in Prison in the 1970s*. Chapel Hill: University of North Carolina Press, 2010.

Berzock, Kathleen Bickford, and Christa Clarke, eds. *Representing Africa in American Art Museums: A Century of Collecting and Display*. Seattle: University of Washington Press, 2011.

Bethune, Mary McLeod. Interview by Charles S. Johnson. 1940. In Bethune, *Mary McLeod Bethune*, 35–51.

———. *Mary McLeod Bethune: Building a Better World: Essays and Selected Documents*, edited by Audrey Thomas McCluskey and Elaine M. Smith. Bloomington: Indiana University Press, 1999.

———. "Yes, I Went to Liberia." 1952. In Bethune, *Mary McLeod Bethune*, 274–77.

Beveridge, Lowell P., Jr. *Domestic Diversity and Other Subversive Activities*. Minneapolis: Mill City, 2009.

Bierman, John. *Dark Safari: The Life behind the Legend of Henry Morton Stanley*. New York: Knopf, 1990.

Biggers, John. *Ananse: The Web of Life in Africa*. Austin: University of Texas Press, 1962.

———. "Artists Series: An Interview with John Biggers," by Rebecca N. Felts and Marvin Moon. *Texas Trends in Art Education* 2, no. 8 (Fall 1983): 8–21.

———. Interview by David Courtwright. September 15, 1975. Houston Oral History Project, Houston Public Library Digital Archives, item no. OH 011B, http://digital.houstonlibrary.org/oral-history/john-biggers-1.php. June 25, 2015.

———. "Interview: John Biggers," by Christian Walker. *Art Papers* 14, no. 4 (July/August 1990): 8–11.

———. "Introduction." In Biggers, Mothershed, and Hudnall, *Traditional African Art Collection*, 10–11.

Biggers, John, Speasio W. Mothershed, and Earlie Hudnall Jr. *The Traditional African Art Collection: Texas Southern University Library*. Houston: Texas Southern University, 1980.

Biggers, John, and Carroll Simms with John Edward Weems. *Black Art in Houston: The Texas Southern University Experience*. College Station: Texas A&M University Press, 1978.

Biggers, Sanford. Interview by Terry Adkins. *Bomb* 117 (Fall 2011), http://bombmagazine.org/article/5987/sanford-biggers. August 15, 2015.

Bilotta, Lynn. "Royal Art of the Kuba." *African Arts* 12, no. 4 (August 1979): 77.

Binkley, David A., and Patricia Darish. "'Enlightened but in Darkness': Interpretations of Kuba Art and Culture at the Turn of the Twentieth Century." In Schildkrout and Keim, *Scramble for Art in Central Africa*, 37–62.

———. *Kuba*. Milan: Five Continents, 2009.

Black Panther Party (Northern California) and House of Umoja (Unity). "Editorial." *Black Power!* 1, no. 11 (1968): 20.

Black Panther Party, Southern California Chapter. "You Can Kill a Revolutionary but You Can't Kill a Revolution." *Black Panther* 4, no. 29 (January 16, 1971): 12.

Blumenthal, Ralph. *Stork Club: America's Most Famous Nightspot and the Lost World of Café Society*. Boston: Back Bay Books, 2001.

Blyden, Edward W. *The African Problem, and the Method of Its Solution*. Washington, D.C.: Gibson, 1890.

Boatner, Edward, and Willa A. Townsend. *Spirituals Triumphant, Old and New*. Nashville, Tenn.: Sunday School Publishing Board (National Baptist Convention), 1927.

Bobo, Nab Eddie. "Carlos Cooks: African Nationalism's Missing Link." In *The Harlem Cultural/Political Movements, 1960–1970: From Malcolm X to "Black is Beautiful,"* edited by Klytus Smith and Abiola Sinclair, 19–26. New York: Gumbs and Thomas, 1995.

Bolden, Tony. "All the Birds Sing Bass: The Revolutionary Blues of Jayne Cortez." *African American Review* 35, no. 1 (Spring 2001): 61–71.

Bontemps, Arna. "Marching Song." *Crisis* 70, no. 2 (February 1963): 121–22.

Bontinck, Francois. *Aux origines de l'État Indépendant du Congo: Documents tirés d'archives américaines*. Louvain, Belgium: Éditions Nauwelaerts, 1966.

Borstelmann, Thomas. *The Cold War and the Color Line: American Race Relations in the Global Arena*. Cambridge, Mass.: Harvard University Press, 2001.

Bostick, Herman F. "A Tribute to Albert H. Berrian (1925–1989)." *CLA Journal* 36, no. 2 (1992): 240–43.

Bote-Tsheik, Etienne, and Ntambue Kazadi, translators. *Shapeta, Tshilobo Tshia mu Kasayi*, by William Phipps. Kanaga, Democratic Republic of the Congo: Imprimerie Protestante du Kasai (IMPROKA), [2002].

Bourke, John Gregory. "The American Congo." *Scribner's Magazine* 15, no. 5 (May 1894): 590–610.

Bowser, Benjamin. "Studies of the African Diaspora: The Work and Reflections of St. Clair Drake." *Sage Race Relations Abstract* 3, no. 14 (August 1989): 3–29.

Boya, Loso K. *DR Congo: The Darkness of the Heart, How the Congolese Have Survived Five Hundred Years of History*. N.p.: Xlibris, 2010.

Boyd, Melba Joyce. "Sierra Maestra." In *Letters to Ché*, 11–13. Roseville, Mich.: Ridgeway Press, 1996.

Bradford, Phillips Verner, and Henry Blume. *Ota Benga: The Pygmy in the Zoo*. New York: St. Martin's, 1992.

Brantlinger, Patrick. *Rule of Darkness: British Literature and Imperialism, 1830–1914*. Ithaca, N.Y.: Cornell University Press, 1988.

Brawley, Benjamin. *Africa and the War*. New York: Duffield, 1918.

Breitman, George. "Foreword." In Malcolm X, *Malcolm X Speaks*, vii–viii.

Brimah, Najib Peregrino. "Nkrumah Never Dies." *Black World* 21, no. 9 (July 1972): 11.

Brooks, Daphne A. *Bodies in Dissent: Spectacular Performances of Race and Freedom, 1850–1910*. Durham, N.C.: Duke University Press, 2006.

Brown, Lois. *Pauline Elizabeth Hopkins: Black Daughter of the Revolution*. Chapel Hill: University of North Carolina Press, 2008.

Brown, Scot. *Fighting for US: Maulana Karenga, the US Organization, and Black Cultural Nationalism*. New York: New York University Press, 2003.

Bruce, Dickson D., Jr. "Booker T. Washington's *The Man Farthest Down* and the Transformation of Race." *Mississippi Quarterly* 48, no. 2 (Spring 1995): 239–53.

Bunyan, John. *Luendu lua muena Kilisto* [*Pilgrim's Progress*]. Translated by George McKee (Muambi Ntalasha). Luebo, Belgian Congo: Imprimerie APCM [J. Leighton Wilson Press], 1934.

Burgess, G. Thomas. "An Imagined Generation: Umma Youth in Nationalist Zanzibar." In *In Search of a Nation: Histories of Authority and Dissidence in Tanzania*, edited by Gregory H. Maddox and James L. Giblin, 216–49. Athens: Ohio University Press, 2005.

Burrell, Reuben V. *One Shot: A Selection of Photographs by Reuben V. Burrell, Hampton University (Institute) Campus Photographer, Griot and Mentor*. Hampton, Va.: Hampton University Museum and Archives, 2012.

Busch, Briton Cooper. *Britain, India, and the Arabs, 1914–1921*. Berkeley: University of California Press, 1971.

Calo, Mary Ann. "A Community Art Center for Harlem: The Cultural Politics of 'Negro Art' Initiatives in the Early 20th Century." *Prospects* 29 (January 2005): 155–83.

Cameron, Dan, ed. *Dancing at the Louvre: Faith Ringgold's French Collection and Other Story Quilts*. Berkeley: University of California Press, 1998.

Cameron, Elisabeth L. "Coming to Terms with Heritage: Kuba *Ndop* and the Art School of Nsheng." *African Arts* 45, no. 3 (Autumn 2012): 28–41.

Campbell, James T. *Middle Passages: African American Journeys to Africa, 1787–2005*. New York: Penguin, 2006.

———. *Songs of Zion: The African Methodist Episcopal Church in the United States and South Africa*. 1995. Chapel Hill: University of North Carolina Press, 1998.

Carby, Hazel V. *Reconstructing Womanhood: The Emergence of the Afro-American Woman Novelist*. New York: Oxford University Press, 1987.

Carew, Jan. *Ghosts in Our Blood: With Malcolm X in Africa, England, and the Caribbean*. Chicago: Lawrence Hill Books, 1994.

Carson, Clayborne. *Malcolm X: The FBI File*, edited by David Gallen. New York: Carroll and Graff, 1991.

Cash, Stephanie. "In the Studio: Sanford Biggers." *Art in America* 99, no. 3 (March 2011): 90–98.

Castro, Fidel. *Speech at the United Nations: General Assembly Session, September 26, 1960*. New York: Fair Play for Cuba Committee, 1960.

Cave, Nick. "On Kuba Cloths." *The Artist Project*, The Metropolitan Museum of Art, http://artistproject.metmuseum.org/1/nick-cave. November 29, 2015.

Chapman, Chris. "'Full Circle': An Interview with Dr. Chris Chapman, Executive Trustee, Loïs Mailou Jones Pierre-Noël Trust," by Philip C. Kolin. *Southern Quarterly* 49, no. 1 (Fall 2011): 95–103.

Cheatwood, Kiarri T-H. *Elegies for Patrice: A Lyrical Historical Remembrance*. Detroit: Lotus Press, 1984.

Chester, Samuel H. "Foreign Mission Committee Notes." *Missionary* 28, no. 10 (October 1895): 446.

———. "Foreign Mission Committee Notes." *Missionary* 28, no. 11 (November 1895): 491–92.

———. "Help Needed for Africa." *Missionary* 28, no. 9 (September 1895): 398.

———. "Introduction." In William Sheppard, *Presbyterian Pioneers in Congo*, 11–12.

———. Letter to APCM. January 9, 1900. In Benedetto, *Presbyterian Reformers in Central Africa*, 127–29.

———. "A Man Needed at Once for Our African Work." *Missionary* 28, no. 10 (October 1895): 446–47.

Chinitz, David. *T.S. Eliot and the Cultural Divide*. Chicago: University of Chicago Press, 2003.

Chrisman, Laura. "Du Bois in Transnational Perspective: The Loud Silencing of Black South Africa." *Current Writing: Text and Reception in Southern Africa* 16, no. 2 (2004): 18–30.

———. *Postcolonial Contraventions: Cultural Readings of Race, Imperialism, and Transnationalism*. Manchester, U.K.: Manchester University Press, 2003.

Clarke, John Henrik. "Cry Rape!," review of *Who Killed the Congo?*, by Philippa Schuyler. *Freedomways* 2, no. 3 (Summer 1962): 334–55.

———. "Martyr's Legacy," review of *Congo, My Country*, by Patrice Lumumba. *Freedomways* 3, no. 1 (Winter 1963): 119–20.

———. "The New Afro-American Nationalism." *Freedomways* 1, no. 3 (Fall 1961): 285–95.

———, ed. *Malcolm X: The Man and His Times*. New York: Collier, 1969.

Cleveland, Todd C. "A Reversing Current: The African American Arrival In Colonial Angola." *Contours: A Journal of the African Diaspora* 3, no. 2 (Fall 2005): 21–46.

Cohen, Robert Carl. *Black Crusader: A Biography of Robert Franklin Williams*. N.p.: Radical Books, 2008.

Coker, Gylbert. "A Textile Artist's Historical and Anthropological Mission." *International Review of African American Art Plus* (2015), http://iraaa.museum

.hamptonu.edu/page/A-Textile-Artist's-Historical-and-Anthropological-Mission. November 29, 2015.

Collins, Rodnell P., and A. Peter Bailey. *Seventh Child: A Family Memoir of Malcolm X*. New York: Dafina Books, 1998.

Collins, Thom, and Tracy Fitzpatrick, eds. *American People, Black Light: Faith Ringgold's Paintings of the 1960s*. Purchase, N.Y.: Neuberger Museum of Art, 2010.

Communauté Presbytérienne au Congo (31ᵉ). *Misambu Ya Kutumbisha Nayi Nzambi*. Kananga, Democratic Republic of the Congo: Imprimerie Protestante Du Kasai (IMPROKA), [n.d.].

Compagnie du Kasai. *Question congolaise: La Compagnie du Kasai à ses actionnaires, réponse à ses détracteurs*. Brussels: Imprimerie Tr. Rein for Compagnie du Kasai, 1906.

"The Congo Boat Company." *Missionary* 26, no. 3 (March 1893): 113–14.

"The Congo: Is Anyone in Control?" *Time*, June 26, 1964, 31–32.

"The Congo Massacre." *Time*, December 4, 1964, 28–32.

"The Congo Mission." *Missionary* 35, no. 1 (January 1902): 5.

"Congo Missionaries Acquitted." *Colored American Magazine* 17, no. 4 (October 1909): 248.

Conrad, Joseph. *Heart of Darkness*. Norton Critical Edition, 3rd ed., edited by Robert Kimbrough. New York: Norton, 1988.

———. *Heart of Darkness*. Norton Critical Edition, 4th ed., edited by Paul B. Armstrong. New York: Norton, 2006.

Cook, James W. "Finding Otira: On the Geopolitics of Black Celebrity." *Raritan* 34, no. 2 (Fall 2014): 84–111.

Cookey, S. J. S. *Britain and the Congo Question, 1885–1913*. New York: Humanities Press, 1968.

Cooks, Carlos A. "There Is Going to Be a New Day: Lumumba Foils Colonialist Plot to Partition the Congo." *Black Challenge*, 1960, 9, 17.

Cooksey, Susan, Robin Poynor, and Hein Vanhee, eds. *Kongo across the Waters*. Gainesville: University Press of Florida, 2013.

Coombes, Annie E. *Reinventing Africa: Museums, Material Culture and Popular Imagination*. 1994. New Haven, Conn.: Yale University Press, 1997.

Coombs, John Hartley, ed. *Dr. Livingstone's 17 Years' Explorations and Adventures in the Wilds of Africa*. Philadelphia: J. T. Lloyd, 1857.

Cortez, Jayne. "Festivals & Funerals." In Cortez, *Festivals and Funerals*, 9–11.

———. *Festivals and Funerals*. New York: Jayne Cortez, 1971.

———. "Initiation." In Cortez, *Festivals and Funerals*, 3.

Coupland, Reginald. *The Exploitation of East Africa, 1856–1890: The Slave Trade and the Scramble*. 1939. Evanston, Ill.: Northwestern University Press, 1967.

Crawford, John R. "Pioneer African Missionary: Samuel Phillips Verner." *Journal of Presbyterian History* 60, no. 1 (Spring 1982): 42–57.

Crawford, Malachi D. "Malcolm X and Human Rights: An Afrocentric Approach to Reparations." In *Malcolm X: A Historical Reader*, edited by James L. Conyers Jr. and Andrew Smallwood, 227–234. Durham, N.C.: Carolina Academic, 2008.

"*Crisis* School Directory." *Crisis* 40, no. 10 (October 1931): 328.

Crummell, Alexander. Letter. *Southern Workman* 23, no. 1 (January 1894): 5.
Cruz, Jon. *Culture on the Margins: The Black Spiritual and the Rise of American Cultural Interpretation*. Princeton, N.J.: Princeton University Press, 1999.
Cruz, Victor Hernandez. "third world." *The Floating Bear* 37 (March–July 1969): 144.
Culin, Stewart. *Primitive Negro Art, Chiefly from the Belgian Congo*. Brooklyn: Brooklyn Museum, Department of Ethnology, 1923.
Cullen, Countee. "Heritage." *Survey Graphic* 6, no. 6 (March 1925): 674–75.
Cunard, Nancy, ed. *Negro: Anthology Made by Nancy Cunard, 1931–1933*. London: Nancy Cunard at Wishart, 1934.
Cureau, Harold G. "The Art Gallery in the Negro College: Neglect, Half Measures and Progress." *Art Journal* 32, no. 2 (Winter 1972–73): 172–74.
———. "The Art Gallery, Museum: Their Availability as Educational Resources in the Historically Negro College." *Journal of Negro Education* 42, no. 4 (Autumn 1973): 452–61.
———. "The Visual Arts in Black Colleges: From Benign Neglect to Progress." *Negro Educational Review* 34, no. 1 (January 1983): 27–36.
———. "William H. Sheppard: Missionary to the Congo, and Collector of African Art." *Journal of Negro History* 67, no. 4 (Winter 1982): 340–52.
Daerden, Peter, and Maurits Wynants. "About the Stanley Archives." *Metafro Infosys Project*, Royal Museum for Central Africa, http://www.metafro.be/stanley/about_explorator_archive. August 3, 2012.
Daulatzai, Sohail. *Black Star, Crescent Moon: The Muslim International and Black Freedom beyond America*. Minneapolis: University of Minnesota Press, 2012.
Davis, Frank Marshall. "Chicago's Congo." 1935. In *Black Moods: Collected Poems*, edited by John Edgar Tidwell, 5–7. Urbana: University of Illinois Press, 2002.
Davis, R. Hunt. "John L. Dube: A South African Exponent of Booker T. Washington." *Journal of African Studies* 2, no. 4 (Winter 1975): 497–528.
Davis, Rebecca Harding. "In Proof of To-Morrow." *Harper's Bazaar*, September 17, 1898, 787.
Davis, Richard Harding. *The Congo and Coasts of Africa*. New York: Scribner's, 1907. London: Unwin, 1908.
Deacon, Deborah A. "The Arts and Artifacts Collection of the Schomburg Center for Research in Black Culture: A Preliminary Catalogue." *Bulletin of Research in the Humanities* 84, no. 2 (Summer 1981): 145–67.
"The Death of Lumumba." *Liberation* [*Liberator* 1] (March 1961): 1–5.
De Costa, Miriam. "Poetry for Afro-Americans." *Black World* 22, no. 11 (September 1973): 13–16.
Defoe, Daniel. *Lusumuinu lua Robinson Crusoe*. Translated by Virginia Allen (Mama Bitshhilualua). Luebo, Belgian Congo: APCM [J. Leighton Wilson Press], 1931.
de Jongh, James. "The Poet Speaks of Places: A Close Reading of Langston Hughes's Literary Use of Place." In *Historical Guide to Langston Hughes*, edited by Steven C. Tracy, 65–84. New York: Oxford University Press, 2004.
———. *Vicious Modernism: Black Harlem and the Literary Imagination*. New York: Cambridge University Press, 1990.

Delany, Martin Robison. *Principia of Ethnology: The Origin of Races and Color, with an Archeological Compendium of Ethiopian and Egyptian Civilization, from Years of Careful Examination and Enquiry.* 1879. Reprinted as *The Origin of Races and Color.* Baltimore: Black Classic Press, 1991.

Devlin, Larry. *Chief of Station, Congo: A Memoir of 1960-67.* New York: Public Affairs, 2007.

De Witte, Ludo. *The Assassination of Lumumba.* Translated by Ann Wright and Renée Fenby. New York: Verso, 2002.

Dickinson, Donald C. *A Bio-bibliography of Langston Hughes, 1902-1967.* Hamden, Conn.: Archon Books, 1967.

di Prima, Diane. "Goodbye Nkrumah." In *Revolutionary Letters*, 145-46. San Francisco: Last Gasp Books, 2007.

Djungu-Simba, Charles. "La figure de Patrice Lumumba: Lumumba dans les lettres du Congo-Zaire: Quelques observations." In Halen and Riesz, *Patrice Lumumba entre dieu et diable*, 81-91.

Donaldson, Jeff. "Africobra 1 (African Commune of Bad Relevant Artists): 10 in Search of a Nation." *Black World* 19, no. 12 (October 1970): 80-89.

Douglass, Frederick. *Address by Hon. Frederick Douglass, Delivered in the Congregational Church.* Washington, D.C., 1883.

———. *Autobiographies*, edited by Henry Louis Gates Jr. New York: Library of America, 1996.

———. *The Life and Times of Frederick Douglass.* 1893. In Douglass, *Autobiographies*, 453-1045.

———. *My Bondage and My Freedom.* 1855. In Douglass, *Autobiographies*, 103-452.

Doyle, A. Conan. *The Crime of the Congo.* New York: Doubleday, 1909.

Drake, St. Clair. "Introduction." In Washington, *Man Farthest Down*, v-lxiv.

———. "Mbiyu Koinange and the Pan-African Movement." In *Pan-African Biography*, edited by Robert A. Hill, 161-207. Los Angeles: African Studies Center, University of California, Los Angeles, and Crossroads Press, African Studies Association, 1987.

———. "The Negro's Stake in Africa: The Meaning of 'Negritude.'" *Negro Digest* 13, no. 8 (June 1964): 33-48.

———. *The Redemption of Africa and Black Religion.* Chicago: Third World Press, 1970.

———. Review of *Negro Thought in America, 1880-1915: Racial Ideologies in the Age of Booker T. Washington*, by August Meier. *American Sociological Review* 30, no. 2 (April 1965): 329-30.

———. "The Tuskegee Connection: Booker T. Washington and Robert E. Park." *Society* 20 (May/June 1983): 83-92.

Dreypondt [sic], Director [Dryepondt, Gustave]. Letter to the *Kassai Herald.* March 6, 1908. In Benedetto, *Presbyterian Reformers in Central Africa*, 284-85.

Driskell, David C. *African Art: The Fisk University Collection.* Nashville, Tenn.: The Art Gallery, Fisk University, 1970.

Driver, Felix. *Geography Militant: Cultures of Exploration and Empire.* Malden, Mass.: Blackwell, 2001.

Dryepondt, Gustave. *See* Dreypondt [*sic*], Director.
Dube, John. "Need of Industrial Education in Africa." *Southern Workman* 26, no. 7 (July 1897): 141–42.
Dubois, Laurent. "A Free Man." *Nation*, March 29, 2007, http://www.thenation.com/article/free-man. November 27, 2015.
Du Bois, W. E. B. "The African Roots of the War." *Atlantic Monthly* 115 (May 1915): 707–14. In *W. E. B. Du Bois: A Reader*, edited by David Levering Lewis, 642–51. New York: Holt, 1995.
———. *The Autobiography of W. E. B. Du Bois*. New York: International Publishers, 1968.
———. "The Colored Magazine in America." *Crisis* 5, no. 1 (November 1912): 33–35.
———. *Dark Princess: A Romance*. 1928. Jackson: Banner Books/University Press of Mississippi, 1995.
———. *Darkwater: Voices from within the Veil*. 1920. Mineola, N.Y.: Dover, 1999.
———. *Dusk of Dawn: An Essay toward an Autobiography of a Race Concept*. 1940. In Du Bois, *Writings*, 549–802.
———. "Eternal Africa." *Nation*, September 25, 1920, 350–52.
———. "Foreword." In *Charlotte Manye: "What an Educated African Girl Can Do,"* by Alfred Xuma, 8. Women's Parent Mite Missionary Society of the AME Church, 1930.
———. "A Logical Program for a Free Congo." 1961. In Du Bois, *World and Africa*, 320–25.
———. "The Looking Glass: Literature." *Crisis* 12, no. 4 (August 1916): 182–83.
———. *The Negro*. New York: Holt, 1915. Reprint in *Project Gutenberg*, http://www.gutenberg.org/files/15359/15359-h/15359-h.htm. September 15, 2010.
———. "On Migration to Africa." c. 1897. In *Against Racism: Unpublished Essays, Papers, Addresses, 1887–1961*, edited by Herbert Aptheker, 43–49. Amherst, Mass.: University of Massachusetts Press, 1985.
———. "A Poem on the Negro." *Crisis* 10, no. 1 (May 1915): 18–19.
———. *The Souls of Black Folk*. 1903. In Du Bois, *Writings*, 357–547.
———. "The Talented Tenth." 1903. In Du Bois, *Writings*, 842–61.
———. *The World and Africa*. New York: International Publishers, 1965.
———. "The World Must Soon Awake to Bar War in Congo." 1960. In Du Bois, *World and Africa*, 317–20.
———. *Writings*, edited by Nathan I. Huggins. New York: Library of America, 1996.
duCille, Ann. *Skin Trade*. Cambridge, Mass.: Harvard University Press, 1996.
Dudziak, Mary L. *Cold War Civil Rights: Race and the Image of American Democracy*. Princeton, N.J.: Princeton University Press, 2000.
Dunbar, Rudolph. "The Influence of Negro Art." *Crisis* 46, no. 1 (January 1939): 13.
Dunkley, Tina Maria. "Compendium of Atlanta University Art Annual Participants (1942–1970)." In Dunkley and Cullum, *In the Eye of the Muses: Selections from the Clark Atlanta University Art Collection*, CD-ROM.
Dunkley, Tina Maria, and Jerry Cullum. *In the Eye of the Muses: Selections from the Clark Atlanta University Art Collection*. Atlanta: Clark Atlanta University, 2012.

Dunn, Kevin C. *Imagining the Congo: The International Relations of Identity*. New York: Palgrave Macmillan, 2003.
DuPlessis, Rachel Blau. *Genders, Races, and Religious Cultures in Modern American Poetry, 1908–1934*. New York: Cambridge University Press, 2001.
Dworkin, Ira, ed. *Daughter of the Revolution: The Major Nonfiction Works of Pauline E. Hopkins*. New Brunswick, N.J.: Rutgers University Press, 2007.
"Editorial: The *Southern Workman*." *Southern Workman* 21, no. 1 (January 1892): 3–4.
"Editorial and Publishers' Announcements." *Colored American Magazine* 1, no. 1 (May 1900): 60–64.
Edmiston, Althea Brown. *The Development of the Native Church of Our Congo Mission*. Nashville, Tenn.: Educational Department, Executive Committee of Foreign Missions Presbyterian Church (U.S.), 1930.
———. *Grammar and Dictionary of the Bushonga or Bukuba Language as Spoken by the Bushonga or Bukuba Tribe Who Dwell in the Upper Kasai District, Belgian Congo, Central Africa*. Luebo, Belgian Congo: J. Leighton Wilson Press, [1932].
———. *Maria Fearing: A Mother to African Girls*. [Atlanta]: [Committee on Woman's Work, Presbyterian Church (U.S.)], [1937].
———. "Missions in Congo Free State, Africa." *American Missionary* 62, no. 10 (December 1908): 306–10.
———[Biwata]. *Nkana mu Ilonga. Bamamukalal a buola*. Luebo, État indépendant du Congo: J. Leighton Wilson Press, 1905.
Edwards, Brent Hayes. "Langston Hughes and the Futures of Diaspora." *American Literary History* 19, no. 3 (2007): 689–711.
———. *The Practice of Diaspora: Literatures, Translation, and the Rise of Black Internationalism*. Cambridge, Mass.: Harvard University Press, 2003.
———. "The Uses of Diaspora." *Social Text* 19, no. 1 (Spring 2001): 45–73.
Eglash, Ron. "A Geometric Bridge across the Middle Passage: Mathematics in the Art of John Biggers." *International Review of African American Art* 19, no. 3 (2004): 28–33.
"Egypt and India." *Crisis* 18, no. 2 (June 1919): 62.
Eisenberg, Bernard. "Only for the Bourgeois? James Weldon Johnson and the NAACP, 1916–1930." *Phylon* 43, no. 2 (1982): 110–24.
Elliott, R. S. "The Story of Our Magazine." *Colored American Magazine* 3, no. 1 (May 1901): 43–77.
Ellison, Ralph. *Invisible Man*. 1952. New York: Vintage, 1995.
Emanuel, James A. *Langston Hughes*. New York: Twayne, 1967.
Emblidge, David. "Rallying Point: Lewis Michaux's National Memorial African Bookstore." *Publishing Research Quarterly* 24, no. 4 (2008): 267–76.
Engel, Elisabeth. *Encountering Empire: African American Missionaries in Colonial Africa, 1900–1939*. Stuttgart, Germany: Franz Steiner, 2015.
Engs, Robert Francis. *Educating the Disfranchised and Disinherited: Samuel Chapman Armstrong and Hampton Institute, 1839–1893*. Knoxville: University of Tennessee Press, 1999.
Epps, Archie. *Malcolm X: Speeches at Harvard*. New York: Paragon House, 1991.

Equiano, Olaudah. *The Interesting Narrative of the Life of Olaudah Equiano, or Gustavus Vassa, the African, Written by Himself,* edited by Werner Sollors. New York: Norton, 2001.

Erlmann, Veit. "'A Feeling of Prejudice': Orpheus M. McAdoo and the Virginia Jubilee Singers in South Africa 1890–1898." *Journal of Southern African Studies* 14, no. 3 (April 1988): 331–50.

———. "'Spectatorial Lust': The African Choir in England, 1891–1893." In *Africans on Stage: Studies in Ethnological Show Business,* edited by Bernth Lindfors, 107–34. Bloomington: Indiana University Press, 1999.

Evanzz, Karl. *The Judas Factor: The Plot to Kill Malcolm X.* New York: Thunder's Mouth, 1992.

Evinger, James, Carolyn Whitfield, and Judith Wiley. *Final Report of the Independent Abuse Review Panel, Presbyterian Church (U.S.A.).* Louisville, Ky.: Presbyterian Church (U.S.A.), 2010.

Ewing, Adam. *The Age of Garvey: How a Jamaican Activist Created a Mass Movement and Changed Global Black Politics.* Princeton, N.J.: Princeton University Press, 2014.

Fabian, Johannes. *Anthropology with an Attitude: Critical Essays.* Stanford, Calif.: Stanford University Press, 2001.

———. *Language and Colonial Power: The Appropriation of Swahili in the Former Belgian Congo, 1880–1938.* Berkeley: University of California Press, 1986.

Fanon, Frantz. "Lumumba's Death: Could We Do Otherwise?" In *Toward the African Revolution,* translated by Haakon Chevalier, 191–97. New York: Grove, 1988.

Farrington, Lisa E. *Faith Ringgold.* San Francisco: Pomegranate, 2004.

Fauset, Jessie. "Impressions of the Second Pan-African Congress." *Crisis* 23, no. 1 (November 1921): 12–18.

———. "Nationalism and Egypt." *Crisis* 19, no. 6 (April 1920): 310–16.

Feinstein, Sascha. *A Bibliographic Guide to Jazz Poetry.* Westport, Conn.: Greenwood, 1998.

Fields, Barbara J. "Ideology and Race in American History." In *Region, Race, and Reconstruction: Essays in Honor of C. Vann Woodward,* edited by J. Morgan Kousser and James M. McPherson, 143–77. New York: Oxford University Press, 1982.

Fierce, Milfred C. *The Pan-African Idea in the United States, 1900–1919: African-American Interest in Africa and Interaction with West Africa.* New York: Garland, 1993.

Firchow, Peter Edgerly. *Envisioning Africa: Racism and Imperialism in Conrad's* Heart of Darkness. Lexington: University Press of Kentucky, 1999.

Fisk University. *Catalogue of the Officers and Students of Fisk University, Nashville, Tennessee, for the College Year, 1883–84.* Nashville, Tenn.: Marshall and Bruce, 1884.

———. *Catalogue of the Officers and Students of Fisk University, Nashville, Tennessee, for the Scholastic Year, 1892–93.* Nashville, Tenn.: Marshall and Bruce, 1893.

———. *Catalogue of the Officers and Students of Fisk University, Nashville, Tennessee, for 1897–1898.* Nashville, Tenn.: Marshall and Bruce, 1898.

---. *Fisk University. History, Building and Site, and Services of Dedication at Nashville, Tennessee, January 1st, 1876.* New York: Trustees of Fisk University, 1876.

---. *General Anniversary Program of Fisk University in the City of Nashville Tennessee* (April 8, 1921–June 1, 1921). Nashville, Tenn.: Fisk University, 1921.

Fleming, Robert E. *James Weldon Johnson.* Boston: Twayne, 1987.

"Folk-Lore and Ethnology." *Southern Workman* 22, no. 12 (December 1893): 180–81.

Folsom, Cora Mae. Review of *Songs and Tales from the Dark Continent*, by Natalie Curtis Burlin. *Southern Workman* 50, no. 3 (March 1921): 133–34.

Ford, James W. *The Communists and the Struggle for Negro Liberation.* New York: Harlem Division of the Communist Party, [1936].

Fox, Stephen. *The Guardian of Boston: William Monroe Trotter.* New York: Atheneum, 1970.

Francis, Jacqueline. "Modern Art, 'Racial Art': The Work of Malvin Gray Johnson and the Challenges of Painting, 1928–1934." PhD dissertation, Emory University, Atlanta, 2000.

Franck, Louis. "Recent Developments in the Belgian Congo." *Journal of the Royal Society of Arts* 72, no. 3745 (August 29, 1924): 711–24.

Franklin, John Hope. *George Washington Williams: A Biography.* Chicago: University of Chicago Press, 1985.

Freeman, Kenn M. "Did the United Nations Benefit Congo?" *Soulbook* 1, no. 2 (Spring 1965): 87–103.

Frissell, H[ollis] B[urke]. "Thirty-Second Annual Report of the Principal of Hampton Institute." *Southern Workman* 29, no. 5 (May 1900): 289–301.

---. "Twenty-Seventh Annual Report of the Principal." *Southern Workman* 24, no. 6 (June 1895): 87–92.

Fromkin, David. *A Peace to End All Peace: Creating the Modern Middle East, 1914–1922.* New York: Holt, 1989.

Fry, Joseph A. *Henry S. Sanford: Diplomacy and Business in Nineteenth-Century America.* Reno: University of Nevada Press, 1982.

---. *John Tyler Morgan and the Search for Southern Autonomy.* Knoxville: University of Tennessee Press, 1992.

Fuller, Hoyt W. "Editor's Notes." *Black World* 19, no. 7 (May 1970): 4.

---. Review of *The Negro*, by Saunders Redding. *Negro Digest* 17, no. 1 (November 1967): 86–87.

Fuller, Meta Vaux Warrick. "Helpful Suggestions to Young Artists." *New Era Magazine* 1, no. 1 (February 1916): 44–45.

---. "Helpful Suggestions to Young Artists." *New Era Magazine* 1, no. 2 (March 1916): 109–11.

Gaines, Kevin K. *American Africans in Ghana: Black Expatriates and the Civil Rights Movement.* Chapel Hill: University of North Carolina Press, 2006.

---. "Black Americans' Racial Uplift Ideology as 'Civilizing Mission': Pauline E. Hopkins on Race and Imperialism." In Kaplan and Pease, *Cultures of United States Imperialism*, 433–55.

---. "Malcolm X in Global Perspective." In *The Cambridge Companion to Malcolm X*, edited by Robert E. Terrill, 158–70. New York: Cambridge University Press, 2009.

Gaither, Edmund Barry. "John Biggers: A Perspective." In Wardlaw, *Art of John Biggers*, 76–95.

Gallen, David, ed. *Malcolm X: As They Knew Him*. New York: Carroll and Graf, 1992.

Gálvez, William. *Che in Africa: Che Guevara's Congo Diary*. Translated by Mary Todd. Melbourne, Australia: Ocean Press, 1999.

Garnet, Henry Highland. *The Past and the Present Condition, and the Destiny, of the Colored Race*. 1848. Miami: Mnemosyne, 1969.

Garza, Alicia. "A Q&A with Alicia Garza, Co-Founder of #BlackLivesMatter," by Mychal Denzel Smith. *Nation*, March 24, 2015, http://www.thenation.com/article/qa-alicia-garza-co-founder-blacklivesmatter. December 7, 2015.

Gates, Henry Louis, Jr. *Figures in Black: Words, Signs, and the "Racial" Self*. New York: Oxford University Press, 1987.

Gebrekidan, Fikru Negash. *Bond without Blood: A History of Ethiopian and New World Black Relations, 1896–1991*. Trenton, N.J.: Africa World, 2005.

———. "Ethiopia and Congo: A Tale of Two Medieval Kingdoms." *Callaloo* 33, no. 1 (Winter 2010): 223–38.

Geiss, Imanuel. *The Pan-African Movement: A History of Pan-Africanism in America, Europe, and Africa*. Translated by Ann Keep. New York: Africana Publishing, 1974.

Gerard, Emmanuel, and Bruce Kuklick. *Death in the Congo: Murdering Patrice Lumumba*. Cambridge, Mass.: Harvard University Press, 2015.

Gerdes, Paulus. "Interweaving Art and Mathematics in African Design." *International Review of African American Art* 19, no. 3 (2004): 45–51.

Gianpetri, Charles Louis. "Verdict of the Tribunal of the First Instance at Léopoldville." In Benedetto, *Presbyterian Reformers in Central Africa*, 411–16.

Gikandi, Simon. "W. E. B. Du Bois and the Identity of Africa." *GEFAME: Journal of African Studies* 2, no. 1 (2005), http://hdl.handle.net/2027/spo.4761563.0002.101. August 27, 2013.

Gillman, Susan. *Blood Talk: American Race Melodrama and the Culture of the Occult*. Chicago: University of Chicago Press, 2003.

Gilroy, Paul. *The Black Atlantic: Modernity and Double Consciousness*. Cambridge, Mass.: Harvard University Press, 1993.

Giovanni, Nikki. "Adulthood." In *Black Judgment*, 18. Detroit: Broadside Press, 1969.

Gish, Steven. *Alfred B. Xuma: African, American, South African*. New York: New York University Press, 2000.

Gizenga, Antoine. "Declaration of the Government of the Congo." *Freedomways* 1, no. 2 (Summer 1961): 173–84.

Gleijeses, Piero. *Conflicting Missions: Havana, Washington, and Africa, 1959–1976*. Chapel Hill: University of North Carolina Press, 2001.

Glover, Gisele. "The Life and Career of Edward Boatner and Inventory of the Boatner Papers at the Schomburg Center." *American Music Research Center Journal* 8–9 (1998/1999): 89–106.

Goldman, Peter. *The Death and Life of Malcolm X*. 2nd ed. Urbana: University of Illinois Press, 1979.

Gomez, Michael A. *Exchanging Our Country Marks: The Transformation of African Identities in the Colonial and Antebellum South*. Chapel Hill: University of North Carolina Press, 1998.

Gonzales, Babs. *I Paid My Dues: Good Times . . . No Bread*. East Orange, N.J.: Expubidence Publishing, 1967.
Gordon, Allan M. *Echoes of Our Past: The Narrative Artistry of Palmer C. Hayden*. Los Angeles: Museum of African American Art, 1988.
Gordon, Robert. "Black Man's Burden." *Evangelical Missions Quarterly* (Fall 1973). Reprint in *African-American Experience in World Mission: A Call Beyond Community*, edited by Vaughn J. Walston and Robert J. Stevens, 55–60. Pasadena, Calif.: William Carey Library, 2002.
Gosse, Van. *Where the Boys Are: Cuba, Cold War America, and the Making of the New Left*. New York: Verso, 1993.
Gott, Richard. "Introduction." In Guevara, *African Dream*, ix–xli.
"Graduates and Ex-Students." *Southern Workman* 44, no. 2 (February 1915): 125.
Graham [Du Bois], Shirley. "History as It Is Made," review of *To Katanga and Back: A UN Case History*, by Conor Cruise O'Brien. *Freedomways* 3, no. 2 (Spring 1963): 221–27.
Granger, Lester B. "Belgium." In *The Dunbar Speaker and Entertainer*, edited by Alice Moore Dunbar-Nelson, 183–84. 1920. New York: G. K. Hall, 1996.
Greene, Alison de Lima. "John Biggers: American Muralist." In Wardlaw, *Art of John Biggers*, 96–107.
Greene, J. Lee. *Time's Unfading Garden: Anne Spencer's Life and Poetry*. Baton Rouge: Louisiana State University Press, 1977.
Griffin, Farah Jasmine. "Pearl Primus and the Idea of a Black Radical Tradition." *Small Axe* 17, no. 1 (March 2013): 40–49.
———. "When Malindy Sings: A Meditation on Black Women's Vocality." In *Uptown Conversation: The New Jazz Studies*, edited by Robert G. O'Meally, Brent Hayes Edwards, and Farah Jasmine Griffin, 102–25. New York: Columbia University Press, 2004.
Grigsby, Jefferson Eugene, Jr. "African and Indian Masks: A Comparative Study of Masks Produced by the Bakuba Tribe of the Congo and Masks Produced by the Kwakiutl Indians of the Northwest Pacific Coast of America." PhD dissertation, New York University, New York, 1963.
———. "Ba Kuba Art at the Brussels International Exposition." In *Africa Seen by American Negroes*, edited by John A. Davis, 143–61. Dijon, France: Imprimerie Bourguignonne, 1958.
Grogan, Kevin. "The Fisk University Galleries and Collections." *International Review of African American Art* 11, no. 4 (1994): 41–45.
Gruesser, John Cullen. *Black on Black: Twentieth-Century African American Writing about Africa*. Lexington: University Press of Kentucky, 2000.
———. *The Empire Abroad and the Empire at Home: African American Literature and the Era of Overseas Expansion*. Athens: University of Georgia Press, 2012.
Guevara, Ernesto "Che." *The African Dream: The Diaries of the Revolutionary War in the Congo*. Translated by Patrick Camiller. London: Vintage, 2000.
———. "At the United Nations." December 11, 1964. In *Che Guevara Reader: Writings on Politics and Revolution*, edited by David Deutschmann, 325–39. Melbourne, Australia: Ocean Press, 2003.

Guridy, Frank Andre. *Forging Diaspora: Afro-Cubans and African Americans in a World of Empire and Jim Crow*. Chapel Hill: University of North Carolina Press, 2010.

Guterl, Matthew Pratt. *The Color of Race in America, 1900–1940*. Cambridge, Mass.: Harvard University Press, 2001.

Guy, Rosa. "Castro in New York." *Black Renaissance* 1, no. 1 (Fall 1996): 10–19.

Hairston, Loyle. "The Winds of Change." *Freedomways* 3, no. 1 (Winter 1963): 49–58.

Hakiza, Paul Serufuri. "Les États-Unis d'Amérique et l'enseignement en Afrique noire (1910–1945)." In Mantuba-Ngoma, *La nouvelle histoire du Congo*, 229–49.

Halen, Pierre, and Janos Riesz, eds. *Patrice Lumumba entre dieu et diable: Un héros africain dans ses Images*. Paris: Harmattan, 1997.

Hall, Stuart. "Cultural Identity and Diaspora." In *Identity: Community, Culture, Difference*, edited by Jonathan Rutherford, 222–37. London: Lawrence and Wishart, 1990.

Hamedoe, S. E. F. C. C. "The First Pan-African Conference of the World." *Colored American Magazine* 1, no. 4 (September 1900): 223–31.

Hamer, Fannie Lou. "I'm Sick and Tired of Being Sick and Tired." December 20, 1964. In *The Speeches of Fannie Lou Hamer: To Tell It Like It Is*, edited by Maegan Parker Brooks and Davis W. Houck, 57–64. Jackson: University Press of Mississippi, 2011.

Hamilton, Charles V. *Adam Clayton Powell, Jr.: The Political Biography of an American Dilemma*. New York: Cooper Square, 2001.

Hampton Normal and Agricultural Institute. *Catalogue of the Hampton Normal and Agricultural Institute, Hampton, Virginia, For the Academic Year 1889–90*. Hampton, Va.: Institute Steam Press, 1890.

———. *The Forty-Sixth Annual Catalogue: The Hampton Normal and Agricultural Institute*. Hampton, Va.: Press of the Hampton Normal and Agricultural Institute, 1914.

———. *Hampton Bulletin* 39, no. 6 (1943–44). Hampton, Va.: Press of the Hampton Normal and Agricultural Institute, 1943.

———. *The Seventy-Second Annual Catalogue: The Hampton Normal and Agricultural Institute*. Hampton, Va.: Press of the Hampton Normal and Agricultural Institute, 1940.

"Hampton's Collections and Connections: A Unity of Art and Life." *International Review of African American Art* 20, no. 1 (2005): 5–31.

*Hand-book for New Missionaries Going to the Belgian Congo, Africa: Suggestions for Outfit and Travel*. Nashville, Tenn.: Executive Committee of Foreign Missions, Presbyterian Church (U.S.), 1923.

Hanks, Eric. "Journey from the Crossroads: Palmer Hayden's Right Turn." *International Review of African American Art* 16, no. 1 (1999): 30–41.

Hansberry, Lorraine. "Congolese Patriot" (letter to the editor). *New York Times Magazine*, March 26, 1961, 4.

Hansberry, William Leo. "Africa: The World's Richest Continent." *Freedomways* 3, no. 1 (Winter 1963): 59–77.

Harlan, Lewis R. "Booker T. Washington and the White Man's Burden." *American Historical Review* 71, no. 2 (January 1966): 441–67.

———. *Booker T. Washington: The Making of a Black Leader, 1856–1901*. Vol. 1. New York: Oxford University Press, 1972.

———. *Booker T. Washington: The Wizard of Tuskegee, 1901–1915*. Vol. 2. New York: Oxford University Press, 1983.

Harlan, Louis R., and Raymond W. Smock, eds. *The Booker T. Washington Papers*. 14 vols. Urbana: University of Illinois Press, 1972–89.

Harleston, E. A. "Voice of Congo." *Crisis* 13, no. 5 (March 1917): 247, illustration.

Harper, Michael S. "Patrice Lumumba." In *Songlines in Michaeltree: New and Collected Poems*, 290–91. Urbana: University of Illinois Press, 2000.

Harris, Joseph E., ed. *Global Dimensions of the African Diaspora*. 2nd ed. Washington, D.C.: Howard University Press, 1993.

Harris, Leonard, and Charles Molesworth. *Alain Locke*. Chicago: University of Chicago Press, 2008.

Hawkins, Hunt. "Mark Twain's Involvement with the Congo Reform Movement: 'A Fury of Generous Indignation.'" *New England Quarterly* 51, no. 2 (June 1978): 147–75.

Hébert, Paul. "'Stronger in Death Than Alive': Reactions to the Assassination of Patrice Lumumba in Montreal," February 2, 2016. *African American Intellectual Society*, blog, http://www.aaihs.org/reactions-to-the-assassination-of-patrice-lumumba. February 9, 2016.

Heikal, Mohamed Hassanein. *The Cairo Documents: The Inside Story of Nasser and His Relationship with World Leaders, Rebels, and Statesmen*. Garden City, N.Y.: Doubleday, 1973.

Helmreich, Jonathan E. *United States Relations with Belgium and the Congo, 1940–1960*. Newark: University of Delaware Press, 1998.

Henderson, David. "They Are Killing All the Young Men." 1967. In Adoff, *Poetry of Black America*, 417.

Henderson, Lawrence W. *Galangue: The Unique Story of a Mission Station in Angola Proposed, Supported and Staffed by Black Americans*. New York: United Church Board for World Ministries, 1986.

Henderson, Louise C. "David Livingstone's *Missionary Travels* in Britain and America: Exploring the Wider Circulation of a Victorian Travel Narrative." *Scottish Geographical Journal* 129, no. 3–4 (September/December 2013): 179–93.

Henderson, Stephen E. "Response." In Baker and Redmond, *Afro-American Literary Study in the 1990s*, 190–93.

———. "'Survival Motion': A Study of the Black Writer and the Black American Revolution in America." In *The Militant Black Writer in Africa and the United States*, by Mercer Cook and Stephen E. Henderson, 65–129. Madison: University of Wisconsin Press, 1969.

———. *Understanding the New Black Poetry: Black Speech and Black Music as Poetic References*. New York: Morrow, 1973.

Herman, Beno von. Letter to Booker T. Washington. September 3, 1900. In Washington, *Booker T. Washington Papers*, 5:633–36.

Herzog, Melanie Anne. *Elizabeth Catlett: An American Artist in Mexico*. Seattle: University of Washington Press, 2000.

Heywood, Linda M., ed. *Central Africans and Cultural Transformations in the American Diaspora*. New York: Cambridge University Press, 2002.

Hickner, Jamie Elizabeth. "'History Will One Day Have Its Say': Patrice Lumumba and the Black Freedom Movement." PhD dissertation, Purdue University, West Lafayette, Ind., 2011.

Higashida, Cheryl. *Black Internationalist Feminism: Women Writers of the Black Left, 1955–1995*. Urbana: University of Illinois Press, 2011.

Hill, Kimberly. "Antislavery Work by the American Women of the Presbyterian Congo Mission," 205–30. In *Faith and Slavery in the Presbyterian Diaspora*, edited by William Harrison Taylor and Peter C. Messer. Bethlehem, Pa.: Lehigh University Press, 2016.

Himes, Chester. *My Life of Absurdity*. New York: Doubleday, 1976.

Hitti, Philip K. *The Syrians in America*. 1924. Piscataway, N.J.: Gorgias, 2005.

Hochschild, Adam. "In the Heart of Darkness." *New York Review of Books* 52, no. 15 (October 6, 2005).

———. *King Leopold's Ghost: A Story of Greed, Terror, and Heroism in Colonial Africa*. New York: Houghton Mifflin, 1999.

———. "Reply to Jean-Luc Vellut." *New York Review of Books* 53, no. 1 (January 12, 2006).

Hogan, Ernest, Theodore H. Northrup, and James O'Dea. *My Little Jungle Queen: A Congo Love Song*. New York: Stern, 1900.

Holloway, Karla F. C. *Passed On: African American Mourning Stories*. Durham, N.C.: Duke University Press, 2002.

Holt, Rackham. *Mary McLeod Bethune: A Biography*. Garden City, N.Y.: Doubleday, 1964.

Hopkins, Pauline E. "*The Dark Races of the Twentieth Century*, Part IV–Africa: Abyssinians, Egyptians, Nilotic Class, Berbers, Kaffirs, Hottentots, Africans of Northern Tropics (including Negroes of Central, Eastern, and Western Africa), Negroes of the United States." June 1905. In Hopkins, *Daughter of the Revolution*, 322–26.

———. "A Dash for Liberty." 1901. In *Short Fiction by Black Women, 1900–1920*, edited by Elizabeth Ammons, 89–98. New York: Oxford University Press, 1991.

———. *Daughter of the Revolution: The Major Nonfiction Works of Pauline E. Hopkins*, edited by Ira Dworkin. New Brunswick, N.J.: Rutgers University Press, 2007.

———. "*Famous Men of the Negro Race* III: William Wells Brown." January 1901. In Hopkins, *Daughter of the Revolution*, 34–39.

———. "*Famous Men of the Negro Race* VIII: Sergeant William H. Carney." June 1901. In Hopkins, *Daughter of the Revolution*, 70–76.

———. "*Famous Men of the Negro Race* XII: Booker T. Washington." October 1901. In Hopkins, *Daughter of the Revolution*, 103–10.

———. "*Heroes and Heroines in Black* 1: Neil Johnson, America Woodfolk, Robert Smalls, et al." January 1903. In Hopkins, *Daughter of the Revolution*, 285–90.

———. "How a New York Newspaper Man Entertained a Number of Colored Ladies and Gentlemen at Dinner in the Revere House, Boston, and How the Colored American League Was Started." March 1904. In Hopkins, *Daughter of the Revolution*, 226–37.

———. Letter to William Monroe Trotter. April 16, 1905. In Hopkins, *Daughter of the Revolution*, 238–48.

———. "Mrs. Jane E. Sharp's School for African Girls." *Colored American Magazine* 7, no. 3 (March 1904) 181–84.

———. *Of One Blood; Or, the Hidden Self*. 1902–3. In *The Magazine Novels of Pauline Hopkins*, edited by Hazel V. Carby, 439–621. New York: Oxford University Press, 1988.

———. *A Primer of Facts Pertaining to the Early Greatness of the African Race and the Possibility of Restoration by Its Descendants*. 1905. In Hopkins, *Daughter of the Revolution*, 334–52.

Horne, Gerald. *Mau Mau in Harlem? The U.S. and the Liberation of Kenya*. New York: Palgrave Macmillan, 2009.

———. "Toward a Transnational Research Agenda for African American History in the 21st Century." *Journal of African American History* 91, no. 3 (Summer 2006): 288–303.

Horner, Mrs. Norman A. "Last Chat with a Congo Pioneer." *Presbyterian Survey*, September 1955, 28+.

Howard, Charles P., Sr. "How the Press Defames Africa." *Freedomways* 2, no. 4 (Fall 1962): 361–70.

———. "Katanga and the Congo Betrayal." *Freedomways* 2, no. 2 (Spring 1962): 136–48.

———. "The Last Phase of the African Revolution." *Freedomways* 3, no. 2 (Spring 1963): 173–83.

Hoyet, Marie-José. "Quelques images de Patrice Lumumba dans la littérature du monde noir d'expression française. Un panorama." In Halen and Riesz, *Patrice Lumumba entre dieu et diable*, 49–80.

Hoyt, Michael P. E. *Captive in the Congo: A Consul's Return to the Heart of Darkness*. Annapolis, Md.: Naval Institute Press, 2000.

Hughes, Heather. *First President: A Life of John Dube, Founding President of the ANC*. Auckland Park, South Africa: Jacana, 2011.

Hughes, Langston. "Ask Your Mama." 1961. In Langston Hughes, *Collected Poems*, 510–14.

———. *The Big Sea*. 1940. New York: Hill and Wang, 1993.

———. "Bird in Orbit." 1961. In Langston Hughes, *Collected Poems*, 515–19.

———. "Blues in Stereo." 1961. In Langston Hughes, *Collected Poems*, 494–96.

———. "Bread Not Enough in Congo." *Chicago Defender* (national edition), September 5, 1959, 10.

———. *Collected Poems*, edited by Arnold Rampersad and David Roessel. New York: Vintage, 1995.

———. *The Collected Works of Langston Hughes, Vol. 10: Fight for Freedom and Other Writings on Civil Rights*, edited by Christopher C. De Santis. Columbia: University of Missouri Press, 2001.

———. *Fight for Freedom: The Story of the NAACP*. 1962. In Hughes, *Collected Works*, 10:23–205.

———. "Final Call." 1964. In Langston Hughes, *Collected Poems*, 545.

———. "Golden Anniversary of the NAACP." 1959. In Langston Hughes, *Collected Works*, 10:252–54.

———. "I, Too." 1925. In Langston Hughes, *Collected Poems*, 46.

———. *Langston Hughes and the* Chicago Defender: *Essays on Race, Politics, and Culture, 1942–62*, edited by Christopher C. De Santis. Urbana: University of Illinois Press, 1995.

———. "Letter from Spain." 1937. In Langston Hughes, *Collected Poems*, 201–2.

———. "Lumumba's Grave." 1961. In Langston Hughes, *Collected Poems*, 533.

———. "Memo to Non-White Peoples." 1957. In Langston Hughes, *Collected Poems*, 456–57.

———. "The Negro." *Crisis* 24, no. 3 (January 1922): 113.

———. "The Negro Speaks of Rivers." *Crisis* 22, no. 2 (June 1921): 71.

———. "Ode to Dinah." 1961. In Langston Hughes, *Collected Poems*, 488–93.

———. "Ride, Red, Ride." 1961. In Langston Hughes, *Collected Poems*, 482–84.

———. "Shades of Pigmeat." 1961. In Langston Hughes, *Collected Poems*, 485–87.

———. "Ships, Sea and Africa: Random Impressions of a Sailor on His First Trip Down the West Coast of the Motherland." *Crisis* 27, no. 2 (December 1923): 69–71.

———. "Simple at the U.N." *Chicago Defender* (national edition), October 29, 1960, 10.

———. *The Weary Blues*. 1926. New York: Knopf, 1947.

———. "Week by Week" ["Simple and the Congo"]. *Chicago Defender* (national edition), August 13, 1960, 10.

———. "We, Too." 1963. In Langston Hughes, *Collected Poems*, 538.

———, ed. *Poems from Black Africa: Ethiopia, South Rhodesia, Sierra Leone, Madagascar, Ivory Coast, Nigeria, Kenya, Gabon, Senegal, Nyasaland, Mozambique, South Africa, Congo, Ghana, Liberia*. Bloomington: Indiana University Press, 1963.

Hultgren, Mary Lou. "The African Art Collections: To Be a Great Soul's Inspiration." *International Review of African American Art* 20, no. 1 (2005): 32–43.

———. "Roots and Limbs: The African Art Collection at Hampton University Museum." In Berzock and Clarke, *Representing Africa in American Art Museums*, 44–61.

Hultgren, Mary Lou, and Jeanne Zeidler, eds. *A Taste for the Beautiful: Zairian Art from the Hampton University Museum*. Hampton, Va.: Hampton University Museum, 1993.

Hunt, Nancy Rose. *A Nervous State: Violence, Remedies, and Reverie in Colonial Congo*. Durham, N.C.: Duke University Press, 2016.

Hunter, Helen-Louise. *Zanzibar: The Hundred Days Revolution*. 1965. Santa Barbara, Calif.: ABC-CLIO, 2010.

"In the Heart of Africa." *Southern Workman* 29, no. 4 (April 1900): 220–21.

Isaacs, Harold R. *The New World of Negro Americans*. New York: John Day, 1963.

Ismael, Tareq Y. *The U.A.R. in Africa: Egypt's Policy under Nasser*. Evanston, Ill.: Northwestern University Press, 1971.

Ismaili, Rashidah. "Bajji." In *Onyibo and Other Poems*, 33–34. New York: Shamal Books, 1985.

Issa, Ali Sultan. *Walk on Two Legs: The Life Story of Ali Sultan Issa*. In *Race, Revolution, and the Struggle for Human Rights in Zanzibar: The Memoirs of Ali Sultan Issa and Seif Sharif Hamad*, edited by G. Thomas Burgess, 27–167. Athens: Ohio University Press, 2009.

"Items of Intelligence." *African Repository* 54, no. 2 (April 1878): 62.

Jabavu, Davidson D. T. *The Black Problem: Papers and Addresses on Various Native Problems*. Lovedale, South Africa: Lovedale Institution Press, 1920.

Jackson, Esther Cooper, ed. *Freedomways Reader: Prophets in Their Own Country*. Boulder, Colo.: Westview, 2000.

Jackson, Lawrence P. *The Indignant Generation: A Narrative History of African American Writers and Critics, 1934–1960*. Princeton, N.J.: Princeton University Press, 2011.

Jacobs, Sylvia M. *The African Nexus: Black American Perspectives on the European Partitioning of Africa, 1880–1920*. Westport, Conn.: Greenwood, 1981.

———. "Their 'Special Mission': Afro-American Women as Missionaries to the Congo, 1894–1937." In *Black Americans and the Missionary Movement in Africa*, edited by Sylvia M. Jacobs, 155–76. Westport, Conn.: Greenwood, 1982.

Jacobson, Matthew Frye. *Barbarian Virtues: The United States Encounters Foreign Peoples at Home and Abroad, 1876–1917*. New York: Hill and Wang, 2000.

Jacques, Geoffrey. *A Change in the Weather: Modernist Imagination, African American Imaginary*. Amherst: University of Massachusetts Press, 2009.

Jaji, Tsitsi Ella. *Africa in Stereo: Modernism, Music, and Pan-African Solidarity*. New York: Oxford University Press, 2014.

James, Winston. *Holding Aloft the Banner of Ethiopia: Caribbean Radicalism in Early Twentieth-Century America*. New York: Verso, 1998.

Jeal, Tim. *Stanley: The Impossible Life of Africa's Greatest Explorer*. New Haven, Conn.: Yale University Press, 2007.

Jewsiewicki, Bogumil, ed. *A Congo Chronicle: Patrice Lumumba in Urban Art*. New York: Museum for African Art, 1999.

———. "Congolese Memories of Lumumba: Between Cultural Hero and Humanity's Redeemer." In Jewsiewicki, *Congo Chronicle*, 73–91.

Joans, Ted. "Afrique Accidentale." *City Lights Journal* 1 (1963): 72–78.

———. *Afrodisia*. New York: Hill and Wang, 1970.

———. *All of Ted Joans and No More*. New York: Excelsior Press-Publishers, 1961.

———. "Bird and the Beats." *Coda*, December 1981, 14–15.

———. "Bird Lives!" *Jazz Magazine* 216 (1973): 44–45.

———. "Black February Blood Letting." In Joans, *Black Pow-Wow*, 65.

———. *A Black Manifesto in Jazz Poetry and Prose*. London: Calder and Boyars, 1971.

———. *Black Pow-Wow: Jazz Poems*. New York: Hill and Wang, 1969.

———. "Him the Bird." 1958. *Gargoyle* 35 (1988): 219.

———. *In Thursday Sane*, edited by Sandra McPherson. Davis, Calif.: Swan Scythe Press, 2001.

———. "The Langston Hughes I Knew: A Memoir." *Black World* 21, no. 11 (September 1972): 14–18.

———. "LUMUMBA LIVES!" In Joans, *All of Ted Joans*, 12.

———. *Our Thang*. Victoria, B.C.: Ekstasis Editions, 2001.

———. "Passed On Blues: Homage to a Poet." *Black Dialogue* 4, no. 1 (Spring 1969): 26–27.

———. "The Sax Bit." In Joans, *Black Manifesto*, 73.

———. *Teducation: Selected Poems, 1949–1999*. Minneapolis: Coffee House, 1999.

———. "Who Shook." 1985. In Joans, *Our Thang*, 66–70.

Johnson, Abby Arthur, and Ronald Maberry Johnson. *Propaganda and Aesthetics: The Literary Politics of Afro-American Magazines in the Twentieth Century*. Amherst: University of Massachusetts Press, 1979.

Johnson, Cedric. *Revolutionaries to Race Leaders: Black Power and the Making of African American Politics*. Minneapolis: University of Minnesota Press, 2007.

Johnson, Charles S. "The Creative Art of Negroes." *Opportunity* 1, no. 8 (August 1923): 240–45.

———. "Introduction." In Charles S. Johnson, *Ebony and Topaz*, 11–14.

———, ed. *Ebony and Topaz: A Collectanea*. New York: National Urban League, 1927.

Johnson, Harvey. Interview by Danielle Burns. January 10, 2013. Houston Oral History Project, Houston Public Library Digital Archives, item no. OH GS 0051, http://digital.houstonlibrary.net/oral-history/harvey-johnson_OHGS0051.php. November 1, 2015.

Johnson, James Weldon. "Africa at the Peace Table and the Descendant of Africans in Our American Democracy." In Kallen and Johnson, *Africa in the World Democracy*, 13–23.

———. *Along This Way*. 1933. In *Writings*, edited by William L. Andrews, 129–604. New York: Library of America, 2004.

———. "Lynching—America's National Disgrace." 1924. In *The Selected Writings of James Weldon Johnson: Social, Political, and Literary Essays*, edited by Sondra Kathryn Wilson, 71–78. New York: Oxford University Press, 1995.

———. *Native African Races and Culture*. Charlottesville, Va.: Trustees of the John F. Slater Fund and the Michie Company, 1927.

———. "Preface." In Johnson, Johnson, and Brown, *Book of American Negro Spirituals*, 11–50.

Johnson, James Weldon, J. Rosamond Johnson, and Lawrence Brown. *The Book of American Negro Spirituals*. New York: Viking Press, 1925.

Johnson, Maggie Pogue. *Virginia Dreams; Lyrics for the Idle Hour. Tales of the Time Told in Rhyme*. 1910. In *Collected Black Women's Poetry*, edited by Joan R. Sherman. Vol. 4. New York: Oxford University Press, 1988.

Johnston, James, ed. *Report of the Centenary Conference on the Protestant Missions of the World, Held in Exeter Hall (June 9th–19th)*. 2 vols. London: James Nisbet, 1888–89.

Johnston, Percy. "Variation on a Theme by Johnston." In *Burning Spear: An Anthology of Afro-Saxon Poetry*, 46. Washington, D.C.: Jupiter Hammon, 1963.

Jones, Jeanette Eileen. *In Search of Brightest Africa: Reimagining the Dark Continent in American Culture, 1884–1936*. Athens: University of Georgia Press, 2010.

Jones, LeRoi. See Baraka, Amiri.

Jones, Matthew. "Oginga Odinga." In *Sing for Freedom: The Story of the Civil Rights Movement through Its Songs*, edited by Guy Carawan and Candie Carawan, 124–27. Montgomery, Ala.: NewSouth Books, 2007.

Jones, Meta DuEwa. *The Muse Is Music: Jazz Poetry from the Harlem Renaissance to Spoken Word*. Urbana: University of Illinois Press, 2011.

Jones, Thomas Jesse. "L'éducation des nègres: Rapport de la mission d'études du 'Phelps–Stokes Fund.'" *Congo: Revue générale de la Colonie belge/Algemeen Tijdschrift van de Belgische Kolonie* 2 (1921): 162–75.

Jordan, June. "On Record." *Black World* 26, no. 5 (March 1975): 53, 63.

———. "Poem about My Rights." In *Passion: New Poems, 1977–1980*, 86–89. Boston: Beacon, 1980.

Joseph, Peniel. "Dashikis and Democracy: Black Studies, Student Activism, and the Black Power Movement." *Journal of African American History* 88, no. 2 (Spring 2003): 182–203.

Joyce, Donald Franklin. *Black Book Publishers in the United States: A Historical Dictionary of the Presses, 1817–1990*. Westport, Conn.: Greenwood, 1991.

———. *Gatekeepers of Black Culture: Black-Owned Book Publishing in the United States, 1817–1981*. Westport, Conn.: Greenwood, 1983.

Kabamba, Patience. "'Heart of Darkness': Current Images of the DRC and Their Theoretical Underpinning." *Anthropological Theory* 10, no. 3 (2010): 265–301.

Kallen, Horace, and James Weldon Johnson. *Africa in the World Democracy*. New York: National Association for the Advancement of Colored People, 1919.

Kalumvueziko, Ngimbi. *Le Pygmée congolais exposé dans un zoo américain: Sur les traces d'Ota Benga*. Paris: l'Harmattan, 2011.

Kanza, Thomas. *Conflict in the Congo: The Rise and Fall of Lumumba*. Harmondsworth, England: Penguin, 1972.

Kaplan, Amy. *The Anarchy of Empire in the Making of U.S. Culture*. Cambridge, Mass.: Harvard University Press, 2002.

———. "'Left Alone with America': The Absence of Empire in the Study of American Culture." In Kaplan and Pease, *Cultures of United States Imperialism*, 3–21.

Kaplan, Amy, and Donald E. Pease, eds. *Cultures of United States Imperialism*. Durham, N.C.: Duke University Press, 1993.

Kebede, Alitash. "A Visit with Collector Extraordinaire Samella Lewis." *International Review of Africa American Art* 21, no. 1 (2007): 5–41.

Kellersberger, Julia Lake. *A Life for the Congo: The Story of Althea Brown Edmiston*. New York: Fleming H. Revell, 1947.

———. *Lucy Gantt Sheppard: Shepherdess of His Sheep on Two Continents*. [Atlanta]: Committee on Woman's Work, Presbyterian Church (U.S.), [1938].

Kelley, Robin D. G. *Freedom Dreams: The Black Radical Imagination*. Boston: Beacon, 2002.

Kennedy, Adrienne. *People Who Led to My Plays*. New York: Theatre Communications Group, 1987.

Kennedy, Pagan. *Black Livingstone: A True Tale of Adventure in the Nineteenth-Century Congo*. New York: Viking, 2002.

Kgositsile, Keorapetse. "Lumumba Section." *Negro Digest* 17, no. 9 (July 1968): 46.

———. *My Name Is Afrika*. Garden City, N.Y.: Doubleday, 1971.

Khalidi, Rashid. "Fallujah 101." *In These Times*, November 12, 2004, http://www.inthesetimes.com/article/1683. May 14, 2011.

———. *Resurrecting Empire: Western Footprints and America's Perilous Path in the Middle East*. Boston: Beacon, 2005.

Kilbride, Daniel. "The Old South Confronts the Dilemma of David Livingstone." *Journal of Southern History* 82, no. 4 (November 2016): 789–822.

Killens, John Oliver. *The Cotillion, or, One Good Bull Is Half the Herd*. 1971. Minneapolis: Coffee House, 2002.

Kim, Daniel Won-gu. "'We, Too, Rise with You': Recovering Langston Hughes's African (Re)Turn 1954–1960 in *An African Treasury*, the *Chicago Defender*, and *Black Orpheus*." *African American Review* 41, no. 3 (2007): 419–41.

King, Martin Luther, Jr. "Press Release and Interview from Radio Norway." December 9, 1964. The King Center Archive, http://www.thekingcenter.org/archive/document/press-release-and-interview-radio-norway. January 20, 2013.

Kirschke, Amy Helene. *Art in Crisis: W. E. B. Du Bois and the Struggle for African American Identity and Memory*. Bloomington: Indiana University Press, 2007.

Kitt, Eartha. *Confessions of a Sex Kitten*. New York: Barricade Books, 1991.

Kiwara-Wilson, Salome. "Restituting Colonial Plunder: The Case for the Benin Bronzes and Ivories." *Journal of Art, Technology and Intellectual Property Law* 23, no. 2 (Spring 2013): 375–425.

Knight, Alisha R. *Pauline Hopkins and the American Dream: An African American Writer's (Re)Visionary Gospel of Success*. Knoxville: University of Tennessee Press, 2012.

Kodi, M. W. "The 1921 Pan-African Congress at Brussels: A Background to Belgian Pressures." In Harris, *Global Dimensions of the African Diaspora*, 263–88.

Kondo, Baba Zak A. *Conspiracys: Unravelling the Assassination of Malcolm X*. Washington, D.C.: Nubia Press, 1993.

Krosney, Herbert. "America's Black Supremacists." *Nation*, May 6, 1961, 390–92.

Lane, Sara. "African Textile Craftsmanship." *Southern Workman* 57, no. 7 (July 1928): 262–67.

———. "African Weapons and Tools." *Southern Workman* 58, no. 8 (August 1929): 353–60.

———. "Some Musical Instruments of the Primitive African." *Southern Workman* 56, no. 12 (December 1927): 552–56.

Langhorne, Orra. "The Mother of a Famous Missionary." *Southern Workman* 29, no. 4 (April 1900): 218–19.

Lapsley, Samuel N. "Letters from the Missions" (October 2, 1890). *Missionary* 24, no. 1 (January 1891): 33–34.

———. "Letters from the Missions" (October 5, 1892 [sic]). *Missionary* 25, no. 4 (April 1892): 151–57.

———. *Life and Letters of Samuel Norvell Lapsley: Missionary to the Congo Valley, West Africa*. Richmond, Va.: Whittet and Shepperson, 1893.

Leach, Laurie F. *Langston Hughes: A Biography.* Westport, Conn.: Greenwood, 2004.
Lee, Chana Kai. *For Freedom's Sake: The Life of Fannie Lou Hamer.* Urbana: University of Illinois Press, 2000.
Lee, Don L. "Rise Vision Comin: May 27, 1972." *Black World* 21, no. 9 (July 1972): 26–28.
LeFalle-Collins, Lizzetta. "*Contribution of the American Negro to Democracy*: A History Painting by Charles White." *International Review of African American Art* 12, no. 4 (1995): 38–41.
Legum, Colin. "Foreword: The Life and Death of Patrice Lumumba." In Lumumba, *Congo, My Country,* vii–xxix.
Leighten, Patricia. "The White Peril and *l'art nègre*: Picasso, Primitivism, and Anticolonialism." *Art Bulletin* 72, no. 4 (December 1990): 609–30.
Leon, Eli. *Accidentally on Purpose: The Aesthetic Management of Irregularities in African Textiles and African-American Quilts.* Davenport, Ia.: Figge Art Museum, 2006.
———. *Who'd A Thought It: Improvisation in African-American Quiltmaking.* San Francisco: San Francisco Craft and Folk Art Museum, 1987.
Leonard, John W., ed. *Who's Who in New York City and State.* New York: L. R. Hamersly, 1907.
Levy, Eugene. *James Weldon Johnson: Black Leader, Black Voice.* Chicago: University of Chicago Press, 1976.
Lewis, David Levering. *W. E. B. Du Bois.* 2 vols. New York: Holt, 1993–2000.
Lewis, John. *Walking with the Wind: A Memoir of the Movement,* with Michael D'Orso. New York: Harvest Books, 1999.
Lewis, Todd E. "Mob Justice in the 'American Congo': 'Judge Lynch' in Arkansas during the Decade after World War I." *Arkansas Historical Quarterly* 52, no. 2 (Summer 1993): 156–84.
Likaka, Osumaka. *Naming Colonialism: History and Collective Memory in the Congo, 1870–1960.* Madison: University of Wisconsin Press, 2009.
Lindberg, Kathryne V. "Mister Joans, to You: Readerly Surreality and Writerly Affiliation in Ted Joans, Tri-Continental Ex-Beatnik." *Discourse* 20, no. 1–2 (Winter–Spring 1998): 198–227.
Lindfors, Bernth. "Heroes and Hero-Worship in Nigerian Chapbooks." *Journal of Popular Culture* 1, no. 1 (Summer 1967): 1–22.
Lindsay, Vachel. *The Congo and Other Poems.* 1914. New York: Dover, 1992.
Livingston, Jane. *The Quilts of Gee's Bend.* Atlanta: Tinwood Books, 2002.
Lock, Graham. "Wadsworth Jarrell and AFRICOBRA: Sheets of Color, Sheets of Sound." In *The Hearing Eye: Jazz and Blues Influences in African American Visual Art,* edited by Graham Lock and David Murray, 150–70. New York: Oxford University Press, 2009.
Locke, Alain L. "The American Negro as Artist." In Locke, *Works of Alain Locke,* 129–35.
———. "Art Lessons from the Congo." *Survey* 57, no. 9 (February 1927): 587–89.
———. "The Blondiau-Theatre Arts Collection." In Locke, *Works of Alain Locke,* 127–28.
———. *The Works of Alain Locke,* edited by Charles Molesworth. New York: Oxford University Press, 2012.

Logan, Rayford W. *The Negro in American Life and Thought: The Nadir, 1877–1901*. 1954. Revised as *The Betrayal of the Negro: From Rutherford B. Hayes to Woodrow Wilson*. New York: Collier, 1965.

Lomax, Louis. *When the Word Is Given: A Report on Elijah Muhammad, Malcolm X, and the Black Muslim World*. New York: Signet, 1964.

Long, Richard A. "Major Art Collections in Historically African American Institutions: An Interview with Richard A. Long," by M. J. Hewitt. *International Review of African American Art* 11, no. 4 (1994): 9–13.

———. "Perspectives on African Art: A Strategy for Investigation." *African Forum: A Quarterly Journal of Contemporary Affairs* 3, no. 4 (Spring 1968); 4, no. 1 (Summer 1968): 5–11.

Lowenfels, Walter. "Patrice Lumumba Speaks—A Poem." *Freedomways* 2, no. 1 (Winter 1962): 32.

Lumumba, Patrice. *Congo, My Country*. Translated by Graham Heath. London: Pall Mall, 1962.

———. "Dawn in the Heart of Africa." In Langston Hughes, *Poems from Black Africa*, 135–36.

———. "Lest We Forget: Lumumba's Last Letter to His Wife." *Liberator* 3, no. 2 (February 1963): 15.

———. "Letter to Pauline Lumumba." In Van Lierde, *Lumumba Speaks*, 421–23.

"Lumumba's Murderers Exposed: UN Demonstrations Justified." *Liberator* 1 (November 1961): 1.

Lyman, Stanford M. *Militarism, Imperialism, and Racial Accommodation: An Analysis of the Early Writing of Robert E. Park*. Fayetteville: University of Arkansas Press, 1992.

Lynch, Hollis R. *Edward Wilmot Blyden: Pan-Negro Patriot, 1832–1912*. New York: Oxford University Press, 1967.

Lyon, Ernest. Letter to Booker T. Washington. September 19, 1908. In Washington, *Booker T. Washington Papers*, 9:625–27.

Mabintch, Belepe Bope. "La statuaire royale kuba." In Mantuba-Ngoma, *La nouvelle histoire du Congo*, 73–90.

Mack, John. "Bakuba Embroidery Patterns: A Commentary on Their Social and Political Implications." In *Textiles of Africa*, edited by Dale Idiens and K. G. Ponting, 163–74. Bath, U.K.: Pasold Research Fund, 1980.

———. *Emil Torday and the Art of the Congo, 1900–1909*. Seattle: University of Washington Press, [1990].

Mahaniah, Kimpianga. "The Presence of Black Americans in the Lower Congo." In Harris, *Global Dimensions of the African Diaspora*, 405–20.

Malcolm X. See X, Malcolm.

Malval, Fritz J. *A Guide to the Archives of Hampton Institute*. Westport, Conn.: Greenwood, 1985.

Mann, Michael, and Valerie Sanders. *A Bibliography of African Language Texts in the Collections of the School of Oriental and African Studies, University of London, to 1963*. London: Hans Zell, 1994.

Mantuba-Ngoma, Pamphile Mabiala, ed. *La nouvelle histoire du Congo: Mélanges eurafricain offerts à Frans Bontinck, c.i.c.m.* Paris: Harmattan, 2004.

Marable, Manning. "Booker T. Washington and African Nationalism." *Phylon* 35, no. 4 (December 1974): 398–406.

———. *Malcolm X: A Life of Reinvention*. New York: Viking, 2011.

———. "The Pan-Africanism of Booker T. Washington: A Reappraisal." *Claflin College Review* 2 (May 1978): 1–14.

Marchal, Jules. *Lord Leverhulme's Ghosts: Colonial Exploitation in the Congo*. 2001. Translated by Martin Thom. New York: Verso, 2008.

Markle, Seth M. "'We Are Not Tourists': The Black Power Movement and the Making of Socialist Tanzania, 1960–1974." PhD dissertation, New York University, New York, 2011.

Marsh, J. B. T. *The Story of the Jubilee Singers*. New edition. Cleveland: Cleveland Printing and Publishing, 1892.

Martin, John Franklin. "Gloucester Caliman Coxe." In *The Encyclopedia of Louisville*, edited by John E. Kleber, 228–29. Lexington: University Press of Kentucky, 2001.

Mathews, Basil Joseph. *Booker T. Washington: Educator and Interracial Interpreter*. Cambridge, Mass.: Harvard University Press, 1948.

Matthews, Fred H. *Quest for an American Sociology: Robert E. Park and the Chicago School*. Montreal: McGill-Queen's University Press, 1977.

McAlister, Melani. "Guess Who's Coming to Dinner: American Missionaries, Racism, and Decolonization in the Congo." *OAH Magazine of History* 26, no. 4 (October 2012): 33–37.

McCray, Carrie Allen. *Ota Benga under My Mother's Roof*. Columbia: University of South Carolina Press, 2012.

McHenry, Elizabeth. *Forgotten Readers: Recovering the Lost History of African American Literary Societies*. Durham, N.C.: Duke University Press, 2002.

McKay, Claude. *The Negroes in America*, edited by Alan L. McLeod. Translated by Robert J. Winter. Port Washington, N.Y.: Kennikat, 1979.

McKoy, Sheila Smith. See Smith McKoy, Sheila.

McStallworth, Paul. "The United States and the Congo Question, 1884–1914." PhD dissertation, Ohio State University, Columbus, 1954.

Mealy, Rosemari. *Fidel and Malcolm X: Memories of a Meeting*. Melbourne, Australia: Ocean Press, 1993.

Meeuwis, Michael. "The Origins of Belgian Colonial Language Policies in the Congo." *Language Matters* 42, no. 2 (2011): 190–206.

Meier, August. "Booker T. Washington and the Negro Press, with Special Reference to the *Colored American Magazine*." *Journal of Negro History* 38, no. 1 (January 1953): 67–90.

———. *Negro Thought in America, 1880–1915*. Ann Arbor: University of Michigan Press, 1966.

Melhem, D. H. *Heroism in the New Black Poetry: Introductions and Interviews*. Lexington: University Press of Kentucky, 1990.

"Men of the Month." *Crisis* 22, no. 2 (June 1921): 72–73, 87.

"Men of the Month: A Missionary." *Crisis* 10, no. 1 (May 1915): 15.

Meriwether, James H. *Proudly We Can Be Africans: Black Americans and Africa, 1935–1961*. Chapel Hill: University of North Carolina Press, 2002.

Meyerowitz, Lisa. "The *Negro in Art Week*: Defining the 'New Negro' through Art Exhibition." *African American Review* 31, no. 1 (Spring 1997): 75–89.

Michaels, Jeffrey H. "Breaking the Rules: The CIA and Counterinsurgency in the Congo 1964–1965." *International Journal of Intelligence and CounterIntelligence* 25, no. 1 (2012): 130–59.

Miller, Ivor. "Introduction." *Contours* 2, no. 2 (Fall 2004): 141–56.

Minter, William. "The Limits of Liberal Africa Policy: Lessons from the Congo Crisis." *TransAfrica Forum: A Quarterly Journal of Opinion on Africa and the Caribbean* 2, no. 3 (Fall 1984): 27–47.

*A Mission to Africa: Althea Brown Edmiston, 1874–1937.* Nashville, Tenn.: Office of Alumni Affairs and Student Support Services Program of Fisk University, [n.d.].

Mitchell, David Fontaine. "The Monumental Plot: An Overview of the 1965 Conspiracy to Destroy the Statue of Liberty, Liberty Bell, and Washington Monument." *Journal of Counterterrorism and Homeland Security International* 16, no. 4 (Winter 2010): Online Lexis Nexis.

Monson, Ingrid. *Freedom Sounds: Civil Rights Call Out to Jazz and Africa*. New York: Oxford University Press, 2007.

Moody-Turner, Shirley. *Black Folklore and the Politics of Racial Representation*. Jackson: University Press of Mississippi, 2013.

Moore, Carlos. *Castro, the Blacks, and Africa*. Los Angeles: Center for Afro-American Studies, University of California, Los Angeles, 1988.

———. *Pichón, a Memoir: Race and Revolution in Castro's Cuba*. Chicago: Lawrence Hill Books, 2008.

Moore, Dennis D., Vincent Carretta, Ugo Nwokeji, Betsy Erkkila, and Marion Rust. "Colloquy with the Author: Vincent Carretta and 'Equiano, the African.'" *Studies in Eighteenth-Century Culture* 38, no. 1 (2009): 1–14.

Moore, Fred R. "Retrospection of a Year." *Colored American Magazine* 8, no. 6 (June 1905): 342–43.

Morgan, John Tyler. "The Future of the American Negro." *North American Review* 139, no. 332 (July 1884): 81–84.

Morgan, Stacy I. *Rethinking Social Realism: African American Art and Literature, 1930–1953*. Athens: University of Georgia Press, 2004.

Morrin, Peter. "Cutting a Swath." *Kentucky Humanities* (October 2007): 8–14.

Morrison, William McCutchan. "Address of Rev. W. H. [sic] Morrison." In Rose, *Official Report of the Thirteenth Universal Peace Congress*, 235–39.

———. "Africa between the Upper and Nether Millstones." *Missionary* 33, no. 2 (February 1900): 64–67.

———. *Grammar and Dictionary of the Buluba-Lulua Language as Spoken in the Upper Kasai and the Congo Basin*. New York: American Tract Society, 1906.

———. "Late War as Reported on the Congo." *Missionary* 32, no. 1 (January 1899): 29–30.

———. Letter to Director Dreypondt [Gustave Dryepondt]. April 27, 1908. In Benedetto, *Presbyterian Reformers in Central Africa*, 287.

———. Letter to E. D. Morel. October 11, 1909. In Benedetto, *Presbyterian Reformers in Central Africa*, 417–20.

———. Letter to Lachlan Cumming Vass II. April 3, 1909. In Benedetto, *Presbyterian Reformers in Central Africa*, 357–58.
———. Letter to Samuel Clemens [Mark Twain]. October 28, 1904. In Benedetto, *Presbyterian Reformers in Central Africa*, 217–22.
———. Letter to "Whom It May Concern." July 1, 1907. In Benedetto, *Presbyterian Reformers in Central Africa*, 244–48.
———. Letter, June 5, 1897. In Benedetto, *Presbyterian Reformers in Central Africa*, 109–11.
———. Letter, December 7, 1897. In Benedetto, *Presbyterian Reformers in Central Africa*, 112–14.
———. "Treatment of the Native People by the Government of the Congo Independent State." In *William McCutchan Morrison: Twenty Years in Central Africa*, by T. C. Vinson, 179–91. Richmond, Va.: Presbyterian Committee of Publication, 1921.
Morrissette, Noelle. *James Weldon Johnson's Modern Soundscapes*. Iowa City: University of Iowa Press, 2013.
Morsell, John A. "The Meaning of Black Nationalism." *Crisis* 69, no. 2 (February 1962): 69–74.
Moses, Wilson Jeremiah. *Afrotopia: The Roots of African American Popular History*. New York: Cambridge University Press, 1998.
———. *Creative Conflict in African American Thought: Frederick Douglass, Alexander Crummell, Booker T. Washington, W. E. B. Du Bois, and Marcus Garvey*. New York: Cambridge University Press, 2004.
———. *The Golden Age of Black Nationalism, 1850–1925*. 1978. Rev. ed. New York: Oxford University Press, 1988.
Moten, Fred. *In the Break: The Aesthetics of the Black Radical Tradition*. Minneapolis: University of Minnesota Press, 2003.
Mputubwele, Makim M. "The Zairian Language Policy and Its Effect on the Literatures in National Languages." *Journal of Black Studies* 34, no. 2 (November 2003): 272–92.
"Mr. B. T. Washington on the Emigration Question." *Southern Workman* 19, no. 3 (March 1890): 25.
Mudimbe, V. Y. *The Idea of Africa*. Bloomington: Indiana University Press, 1994.
———. *The Invention of Africa: Gnosis, Philosophy and the Order of Knowledge*. Bloomington: Indiana University Press, 1988.
Murphy, Gretchen. *Shadowing the White Man's Burden: U.S. Imperialism and the Problem of the Color Line*. New York: New York University Press, 2010.
Murray, Albert. *The Omni-Americans: Black Experience and American Culture*. New York: Da Capo, 1990.
Murray, Andrew E. *Presbyterians and the Negro—A History*. Philadelphia: Presbyterian Historical Society, 1966.
"Museum Additions." *Southern Workman* 40, no. 7 (July 1911): 448.
Museum of Modern Art. "Biographical Notes of Exhibiting Artists—*Young Negro Art: Work of Students at Hampton Institute*." September 30, 1943. Museum of Modern Art, https://www.moma.org/momaorg/shared/pdfs/docs/press_archives/904/releases/MOMA_1943_0056_1943-10-04_431004-53.pdf. September 21, 2015.

Mwissa, Camille Kuyu. *Les Haitiens au Congo*. Paris: Harmattan, 2006.

Nabaroui, Céza. "African Women Seek Independence and Peace." *Freedomways* 1, no. 1 (Spring 1961): 102–6.

Naff, Alixa. "The Arabic-Language Press." In *The Ethnic Press in the United States: A Historical Analysis and Handbook*, edited by Sally M. Miller, 1–14. Westport, Conn.: Greenwood, 1987.

Ndaywel è Nziem, Isidore. *Nouvelle histoire du Congo: Des origines á la République Démocratique*. Brussels: Cri Édition, 2009.

Neal, Larry. "Any Day Now: Black Art and Black Liberation." *Ebony*, August 1969, 54–62.

———. "Black Boogaloo." In *Black Boogaloo: Notes on Black Liberation*, 44. San Francisco: Journal of Black Poetry Press, 1969.

"Needs of the Congo Mission." *Missionary* 31, no. 8 (August 1898): 339.

Nelson, Cary. *Repression and Recovery: Modern American Poetry and the Politics of Cultural Memory, 1910–1945*. Madison: University of Wisconsin Press, 1989.

———. *Revolutionary Memory: Recovering the Poetry of the American Left*. New York: Routledge, 2003.

Nemiroff, Robert, ed. *Les Blancs: The Collected Last Plays of Lorraine Hansberry*. New York: Vintage, 1973.

Newkirk, Pamela. *Spectacle: The Astonishing Life of Ota Benga*. New York: Amistad, 2015.

"*New Names in American Art*: Recent Contributions to Painting and Sculpture by Negro Artists, October 6–October 31, 1944." The Renaissance Society at the University of Chicago, http://archive.renaissancesociety.org/site/Exhibitions/Works.New-Names-in-American-Art-Recent-Contributions-to-Painting-and-Sculpture-by-Negro-Artists.429.html. November 29, 2015.

Ngoma, Florian Alphonse. "Tom-Tom." Translated by Mary Beach. *City Lights Journal* 1 (1963): 104–9.

Nielsen, Aldon Lynn. *Black Chant: Languages of African-American Postmodernism*. New York: Cambridge University Press, 1997.

———. *Integral Music: Languages of African American Innovation*. Tuscaloosa: University of Alabama Press, 2004.

Nielsen, Aldon Lynn, and Lauri Ramey, eds. *Every Goodbye Ain't Gone: An Anthology of Innovative Poetry by African Americans*. Tuscaloosa: University of Alabama Press, 2006.

"1961: Lumumba Rally Clashes with UK Police." *BBC*, http://news.bbc.co.uk/onthisday/hi/dates/stories/february/19/newsid_2748000/2748931.stm. July 9, 2011.

Nkrumah, Kwame. "Address to the United Nations." *Freedomways* 1, no. 1 (Spring 1961): 45–72.

———. "Africa's Liberation and Unity." *Freedomways* 2, no. 4 (Fall 1962): 409–35.

Norden, Hermann. *Fresh Tracks in the Belgian Congo: From the Uganda Border to the Mouth of the Congo*. Boston: Small, Maynard, 1924.

Norrell, Robert J. *Up from History: The Life of Booker T. Washington*. Cambridge, Mass.: Harvard University Press, 2009.

North, Michael. *Dialect of Modernism: Race, Language, and Twentieth-Century Literature*. New York: Oxford University Press, 1994.

Nottage, Lynn. *Ruined*. New York: Theatre Communications Group, 2009.
Nurse, Derek, and Gérard Philippson, eds. *The Bantu Languages*. New York: Routledge, 2003.
Nwankwo, Ifeoma Kiddoe. *Black Cosmopolitanism: Racial Consciousness and Transnational Identity in the Nineteenth-Century Americas*. Philadelphia: University of Pennsylvania Press, 2005.
Nzongola-Ntalaja, Georges. *The Congo from Leopold to Kabila: A People's History*. London: Zed Books, 2002.
Obiechina, Emmanuel. *An African Popular Literature: A Study of Onitsha Market Pamphlets*. Cambridge, Mass.: Cambridge University Press, 1973.
O'Brien, Colleen C. "'Blacks in All Quarters of the Globe': Anti-Imperialism, Insurgent Cosmopolitanism, and International Labor in Pauline Hopkins's Literary Journalism." *American Quarterly* 61, no. 2 (June 2009): 245–70.
Ogali, Ogali A. *The Ghost of Patrice Lumumba*. In *Veronica, My Daughter, and Other Onitsha Market Plays and Stories*, edited by Reinhard Sander and Peter K. Ayers, 245–71. Washington, D.C.: Three Continents Press, 1980.
Okihiro, Gary Y. "Toward a Black Pacific." In *AfroAsian Encounters: Culture, History, Politics*, edited by Heike Raphael-Hernandez and Shannon Steen, 313–30. New York: New York University Press, 2006.
Oliver, Lawrence J. "'Jim Crowed' in Their Own Countries: James Weldon Johnson's *New York Age* Essays on Colonialism during the Wilson Years." In *Critical Essays on James Weldon Johnson*, edited by Kenneth M. Price and Lawrence J. Oliver, 209–22. New York: G. K. Hall, 1997.
Ott, John. "Labored Stereotypes: Palmer Hayden's *The Janitor Who Paints*." *American Art* 22, no. 1 (Spring 2008): 102–15.
Otten, Thomas J. "Pauline Hopkins and the Hidden Self of Race." *ELH* 59, no. 1 (Spring 1992): 227–56.
Owen, Thomas McAdory, and Marie Bankhead Owen. *History of Alabama and Dictionary of Alabama Biography*. Vol. 4. Chicago: Clarke, 1921.
Pakenham, Thomas. *The Scramble for Africa: White Man's Conquest of the Dark Continent from 1876 to 1912*. New York: Avon Books, 1991.
Parezo, Nancy J., and Don D. Fowler. *Anthropology Goes to the Fair: The 1904 Louisiana Purchase Exposition*. Lincoln: University of Nebraska, 2007.
Park, Robert Ezra. "The Blood-Money of the Congo." 1907. In Lyman, *Militarism, Imperialism, and Racial Accommodation*, 234–45.
———. Letter to Booker T. Washington. April 26, 1911. In Washington, *Booker T. Washington Papers*, 11:116–17.
———. "Methods of Teaching: Impressions and a Verdict." 1941. In Lyman, *Militarism, Imperialism, and Racial Accommodation*, 306–18.
———. "Recent Atrocities in the Congo State." 1904. In Lyman, *Militarism, Imperialism, and Racial Accommodation*, 205–9.
———. "The Terrible Story of the Congo." 1906. In Lyman, *Militarism, Imperialism, and Racial Accommodation*, 221–33.
Patterson, Martha H. "'Kin o' Rough Jestice fer a Parson': Pauline Hopkins's *Winona* and the Politics of Reconstructing History." *African American Review* 32, no. 3 (Fall 1998): 445–60.

Patterson, Raymond R. *Elemental Blues: Poems 1981–1982*. Merrick, N.Y.: Cross-Cultural Communications, 1989.

———. "Lumumba Blues." In Patterson, *Elemental Blues: Poems 1981–1982*, 36.

"Pauline E. Hopkins." *Colored American Magazine* 2, no. 3 (January 1901): 218–19.

Peck, Raoul. *Stolen Images: Lumumba and the Early Films of Raoul Peck*. New York: Seven Stories, 2012.

Perpener, John O., III. *African-American Concert Dance: The Harlem Renaissance and Beyond*. Urbana: University of Illinois Press, 2001.

Perry, Regenia A. *Art of the Kuba: Selected Works from the William H. Sheppard Collection, Hampton Institute, Hampton, Virginia*. Richmond, Va.: Anderson Gallery, Virginia Commonwealth University, 1979.

———. *Free within Ourselves: African-American Artists in the Collection of the National Museum of American Art*. Washington, D.C.: National Museum of American Art, Smithsonian Institution, 1992.

Perry, Rufus L. *The Cushite; or, The Children of Ham (the Negro Race), as Seen by the Ancient Historians and Poets*. Brooklyn: Brooklyn Literary Union, 1887.

Petridis, Constantine. "'A World of Great Art for Everyone': African Art at the Cleveland Museum of Art." In Berzock and Clarke, *Representing Africa in American Art Museums*, 104–21.

Philip, Marlene NoubeSe. *Looking for Livingstone: An Odyssey of Silence*. Stratford, Ont.: Mercury, 1991.

Phipps, William E. *William Sheppard: Congo's African American Livingstone*. Louisville, Ky.: Geneva, 2002.

Pickens, William. "The American Congo: Burning of Henry Lowry." *Nation*, March 23, 1921, 426–28. Reprinted as William Pickens. "The American Congo—Burning of Henry Lowry." *Chicago Defender* (national edition), April 23, 1921, 9.

———. *Lynching and Debt-Slavery*. New York: American Civil Liberties Union, 1921.

Pierre, Jemima. *The Predicament of Blackness: Postcolonial Ghana and the Politics of Race*. Chicago: University of Chicago Press, 2013.

Pike, Gustavus D. *The Jubilee Singers, and Their Campaign for Twenty Thousand Dollars*. Boston: Lee and Shepard, 1873.

———. "The Possibilities of African Civilization." In Fisk University, *Fisk University. History, Building and Site*, 48–63.

Pleck, Elizabeth Hafkin. *Black Migration and Poverty in Boston, 1865–1900*. New York: Academic (Harcourt Brace Jovanovich), 1979.

Plummer, Brenda Gayle. *Rising Wind: Black Americans and U.S. Foreign Affairs, 1935–1960*. Chapel Hill: University of North Carolina Press, 1996.

Plumpp, Sterling. "Half Black Half Blacker." 1970. In Adoff, *Poetry of Black America*, 386.

Polsgrove, Carol. *Divided Minds: Intellectuals and the Civil Rights Movement*. New York: Norton, 2001.

Porra, Véronique. "L'Afrique du Che: Du mythe de Lumumba à la réalité de la guérilla." In Halen and Riesz, *Patrice Lumumba entre dieu et diable*, 277–94.

Posnock, Ross. *Color and Culture: Black Writers and the Making of the Modern Intellectual*. Cambridge, Mass.: Harvard University Press, 1998.
Post, K. W. J. "Nigerian Pamphleteers and the Congo." *Journal of Modern African Studies* 2, no. 3 (November 1964): 405–18.
Powell, Adam Clayton, Jr. *Adam by Adam: The Autobiography of Adam Clayton Powell, Jr.* New York: Dafina Books, 2001.
Power-Greene, Ousmane K. *Against Wind and Tide: The African American Struggle against the Colonization Movement*. New York: New York University Press, 2014.
Pratt, Mary Louise. *Imperial Eyes: Travel Writing and Transculturation*. New York: Routledge, 1992.
Primus, Pearl. "People and Ideas: In Africa." *Vogue*, October 15, 1950, 98–99+.
Pruitt, Virginia Gray, and Winifred Kellersberger Vass, eds. *A Textbook of the Tshiluba Language*. Rev. ed. Luebo, Democratic Republic of the Congo: J. Leighton Wilson Press, 1965.
"Publishers' Announcements." *Colored American Magazine* 7, no. 11 (November 1904): 700.
Radano, Ronald. *Lying Up a Nation: Race and Black Music*. Chicago: University of Chicago Press, 2003.
Rahier, Jean Muteba. "The Ghost of Leopold II: The Belgian Royal Museum of Central Africa and Its Dusty Colonialist Exhibition." *Research in African Literatures* 34, no. 1 (Spring 2003): 58–84.
Rahman, Aishah. "Living in the Black Arts Movement." *Konch Magazine*, January 2015, http://ishmaelreedpub.com/Living-in-the-Black-Arts-Movement-by-Aishah-Rahman. May 3, 2016.
Rambsy, Howard, II. *The Black Arts Enterprise and the Production of African American Poetry*. Ann Arbor: University of Michigan Press, 2011.
Rampersad, Arnold. "Introduction." In Langston Hughes, *Big Sea*, xiii–xxvi.
———. *The Life of Langston Hughes*. 2 vols. New York: Oxford University Press, 1986–88.
Randall, Roslyn Walker. "Selected Bibliography." In Sieber, *African Textiles and Decorative Arts*, 228–38.
Ratcliff, Anthony James. "Liberation at the End of a Pen: Writing Pan-African Politics of Cultural Struggle." PhD dissertation, University of Massachusetts, Amherst, 2009.
Raushenbush, Winifred. *Robert E. Park: Biography of a Sociologist*. Durham, N.C.: Duke University Press, 1979.
Reaves, William. *Walk Together Children: The Poetry of Harvey Johnson with Tribute to John Biggers*. Houston: William Reaves Fine Art, 2009.
Redmond, Eugene B. *Drumvoices: The Mission of Afro-American Poetry: A Critical History*. New York: Anchor Books, 1976.
Reed, Ishmael. "Patrice." *Umbra* 2 (December 1963): 36.
Reisner, Robert George. *Bird: The Legend of Charlie Parker*. 1962. New York: Da Capo, 1975.
Reitan, Ruth. *The Rise and Decline of an Alliance: Cuba and African American Leaders in the 1960s*. East Lansing: Michigan State University Press, 1999.

"A Remarkable Missionary." *Missionary* 27, no. 7 (July 1894): 272–73.

Revolutionary Action Movement. "Why Malcolm X Died: An Analysis by RAM." *Liberator* 5, no. 4 (April 1965): 9–11.

Reynolds, David S. *John Brown, Abolitionist: The Man Who Killed Slavery, Sparked the Civil War, and Seeded Civil Rights*. New York: Knopf, 2005.

———. *Mightier Than the Sword:* Uncle Tom's Cabin *and the Battle for America*. New York: Norton, 2011.

Richardson, Joe M. *A History of Fisk University, 1865–1946*. Tuscaloosa: University of Alabama Press, 1980.

Rickford, Russell J. *Betty Shabazz, Surviving Malcolm X*. Napierville, Ill.: Sourcebooks, 2003.

Ringgold, Faith. *We Flew over the Bridge: The Memoirs of Faith Ringgold*. Boston: Bulfinch, 1995.

Ritter, Rebecca E. *Five Decades: John Biggers and the Hampton Art Tradition*. Hampton, Va.: Hampton University Museum, 1990.

Rivera, Pedro R. "Carlos Cooks and Garveyism: Bridging Two Eras of Black Nationalism." PhD dissertation, Howard University, Washington, D.C., 2012.

Roberts, Mary Nooter, and Alison Saar. *Body Politics: The Female Image in Luba Art and the Sculpture of Alison Saar*. Los Angeles: UCLA Fowler Museum of Cultural History, 2000.

Roessel, David. "Process of Revision and Hughes." In *A Langston Hughes Encyclopedia*, by Hans Ostrom, 327–32. Westport, Conn.: Greenwood, 2002.

Rogers, Donna Coates. *Royal Art of the Kuba*. Austin: University of Texas, 1979.

Rojo, Ricardo. *My Friend Che*. Translated by Julian Casart. New York: Dial Press, 1968.

Rosa, Andrew J. "New Negroes on Campus: St. Clair Drake and the Culture of Education, Reform, and Rebellion at Hampton Institute." *History of Education Quarterly* 53, no. 3 (August 2013): 203–32.

———. "The Roots and Routes of 'Imperium in Imperio': St. Clair Drake, the Formative Years." *American Studies* 52, no. 1 (2012): 49–75.

Rose, William J. *Official Report of the Thirteenth Universal Peace Congress, Held at Boston, Massachusetts, U.S.A., October Third to Eighth, 1904*. Boston: Peace Congress Committee, 1904.

Rossen, Susan F., ed. *African Americans in Art: Selections from the Art Institute of Chicago*. Seattle: Art Institute of Chicago/University of Washington Press, 1999.

Rowbotham, Arthur. "Letters from the Missions" (February 17, 1893). *Missionary* 26, no. 6 (June 1893): 230–32.

Rubango, Nyunda ya. "Patrice Lumumba at the Crossroads of History and Myth." In Jewsiewicki, *Congo Chronicle*, 43–57.

Ryan, Jennifer D. *Post-Jazz Poetics: A Social History*. New York: Palgrave Macmillan, 2010.

Said, Edward. *Culture and Imperialism*. 1993. New York: Vintage, 1994.

Sales, William W., Jr. *From Civil Rights to Black Liberation: Malcolm X and the Organization of Afro-American Unity*. Boston: South End, 1999.

Sanborn, Geoffrey. "The Wind of Words: Plagiarism and Intertextuality in *Of One Blood*." *J19: The Journal of Nineteenth-Century Americanists* 3, no. 1 (Spring 2015): 67–87.

Sanders, Mark A. "Brief Reflections on the Discourse of Transnationalism and African American Studies." *PMLA* 122, no. 3 (May 2007): 812–14.

Sanford, Henry S. "Report of Hon. Henry Shelton Sanford, U.S. Delegate from the American Branch to the Annual Meeting of the African International Association, in Brussels, in June, 1877." *Bulletin of the American Geographical Society* 4 (1877): 86–93.

Sartre, Jean-Paul. "Introduction." In Van Lierde, *Lumumba Speaks*, 1–52.

Sawyer, Granville. "Preface." In Biggers, Mothershed, and Hudnall, *Traditional African Art Collection*, 6.

Scarborough, Dorothy. "New Lights on an Old Song." In Charles S. Johnson, *Ebony and Topaz*, 59.

———. *On the Trail of Negro Folk-Songs*, assisted by Ola Lee Gulledge. Cambridge, Mass.: Harvard University Press, 1925.

Schachter, Harry. "Barebreasted in Leopoldville—A Poem." *Freedomways* 2, no. 2 (Spring 1962): 149.

Schatt, Stanley. "Langston Hughes: The Minstrel as Artificer." *Journal of Modern Literature* 4, no. 1 (September 1974): 115–20.

Schildkrout, Enid. "Personal Styles and Disciplinary Paradigms: Frederick Starr and Herbert Lang." In Schildkrout and Keim, *Scramble for Art in Central Africa*, 169–92.

Schildkrout, Enid, and Curtis A. Keim. "Objects and Agendas: Re-Collecting the Congo." In Schildkrout and Keim, *Scramble for Art in Central Africa*, 1–36.

———, eds. *The Scramble for Art in Central Africa*. New York: Cambridge University Press, 1998.

Schraeder, Peter J. *United States Foreign Policy toward Africa: Incrementalism, Crisis, and Change*. New York: Cambridge University Press, 1994.

Schrager, Cynthia D. "Pauline Hopkins and William James: The New Psychology and the Politics of Race." In *The Unruly Voice: Rediscovering Pauline Elizabeth Hopkins*, edited by John Cullen Gruesser, 182–209. Urbana: University of Illinois Press, 1996.

Schuyler, Philippa. *Who Killed the Congo?* New York: Devin-Adair, 1962.

Schwartz, Peggy, and Murray Schwartz. *The Dance Claimed Me: A Biography of Pearl Primus*. New Haven, Conn.: Yale University Press, 2011.

"The Secretary General and the Congo." *Liberator* 1 (October 1961): 1.

Seghers, Maud. "Phelps-Stokes in Congo: Transferring Educational Policy Discourse to Govern Metropole and Colony." *Paedagogica Historica* 40, no. 4 (August 2004): 455–77.

Seligmann, Herbert J. *The Negro Faces America*. New York: Clarence S. Nathan, 1920.

Semmes, Clovis E. *Roots of Afrocentric Thought: A Reference Guide to* Negro Digest/Black World, *1961–1976*. Westport, Conn.: Greenwood, 1998.

Senate Permanent Subcommittee on Investigations of the Committee on Government Operations. *State Department Information Program—Information*

Centers, March 24. 83rd Congress, 1st session, 1953, vol. 2, s. prt. 107–84. Washington, D.C.: Government Printing Office, 2003.

Seniors, Paula Marie. *Beyond Lift Every Voice and Sing: The Culture of Uplift, Identity, and Politics in Black Musical Theater.* Columbus: Ohio State University Press, 2009.

Seon, Yvonne. "Alphabet Name Game." In Seon, *Totem Games*, 26–28.

———. *Totem Games: Poems in Search of African Identity.* Yellow Springs, Ohio: Bunches of Thyme, 2007.

———. "Uhuru Hop Scotch." In Seon, *Totem Games*, 29–30.

Seraile, William. "Black American Missionaries in Africa, 1821–1925." *Social Studies* 63 (October 1972): 198–202.

Shaloff, Stanley. "William Henry Sheppard: Congo Pioneer." *African Forum: A Quarterly Journal of Contemporary Affairs* 3, no. 4 (Spring 1968); 4, no. 1 (Summer 1968): 51–62.

Shannon, Helen Marie. "From 'African Savages' to 'Ancestral Legacy': Race and Cultural Nationalism in the American Modernist Reception of Africa Art." PhD dissertation, Columbia University, New York, 1999.

Sheppard, Lucy Gantt. "Progress at Ibanj." *Kassai Herald* 1, no. 2 (July 1901): 16–17.

———. "Sunshine in Congo-Land." *Kassai Herald* 3, no. 4 (October 1903): 41–42.

Sheppard, William Henry. *An African Daniel: True African Stories.* Hampton, Va.: Hampton Institute Press, [1915].

———. "African Handicrafts and Superstitions." *Southern Workman* 50, no. 9 (September 1921): 401–8.

———. "From the Bakuba Country." *Kassai Herald* 8, no. 1 (January 1908): 12–14. In Benedetto, *Presbyterian Reformers in Central Africa*, 281–83.

———. "Interview with Chief M'lumba N'kusa Concerning the Zappo Zap Raid" (September 14, 1899). In Benedetto, *Presbyterian Reformers in Central Africa*, 121–26.

———. "Into the Heart of Africa." November 14, 1893. *Southern Workman* 22, no. 12 (December 1893): 182–87.

———. Letter, May 17, 1890. *Missionary* 23, no. 9 (September 1890): 352–55.

———. Letter, September 1, 1890. *Southern Workman* 20, no. 3 (March 1891): 168.

———. "Light in Darkest Africa." *Southern Workman* 34, no. 4 (April 1905): 218–27.

———. *A Little Robber Who Found a Great Treasure: True African Stories.* Hampton, Va.: Hampton Institute Press, [1915].

———. *Presbyterian Pioneers in Congo.* Richmond, Va.: Presbyterian Committee of Publication, 1917.

———. "A Semi-civilization in Africa," November 14, 1893. *Southern Workman* 24, no. 5 (May 1895): 82.

———. *The Story of a Girl Who Ate Her Mother: True African Stories.* Hampton, Va.: Hampton Institute Press, [1915].

———. *A Young Hunter: True African Stories.* Hampton, Va.: Hampton Institute Press, [1915].

Shepperson, George. "The Centennial of the West African Conference of Berlin, 1884–1885." *Phylon* 46, no. 1 (March 1985): 37–48.

Sherwood, Marika. *Malcolm X Visits Abroad: April 1964 to February 1965.* Hollywood: Tsehai Publishers, 2011.

Short, Wallace V. "William Henry Sheppard: Pioneer African-American Presbyterian Missionary, Human Rights Defender, and Collector of African Art, 1865–1927." PhD dissertation, Howard University, Washington, D.C., 2006.

Sieber, Roy. *African Textiles and Decorative Arts.* New York: Museum of Modern Art, 1972.

Siegmann, William. "A Collection Grows in Brooklyn." In Berzock and Clarke, *Representing Africa in American Art Museums,* 62–80.

Sikes, William Marion. "The Historical Development of Stillman Institute." MA thesis, University of Alabama, Birmingham, 1930.

Simmons, Roscoe Conkling. "Europe's Reception to Negro Talent." *Colored American Magazine* 9, no. 5 (November 1905): 635–42.

Sims, Lowery S. "Race Riots, Cocktail Parties, Black Panthers, Moon Shots and Feminists: Faith Ringgold's Observations of the 1960's in America." In *Faith Ringgold: A 25 Year Survey,* curated by Eleanor Flomenhaft, 17–21. Hempstead, N.Y.: Fine Arts Museum of Long Island, 1990.

Singletary, Richard A. "The William H. Sheppard African Art Collection at Hampton Institute." MA thesis, Old Dominion University, Norfolk, Va., 1982.

"Six Months Later: No Investigation of Lumumba's Death." *Liberator* 1 (August 1961): 1.

Skinner, Elliot P. *African Americans and U.S. Policy toward Africa, 1850–1924.* Washington, D.C.: Howard University Press, 1992.

Slaughter, Joseph. "Pathetic Fallacies: Human Rights, the Humanities, and the Human." *Human Rights and the Humanities: An International Conference,* American University of Beirut, Lebanon, May 10, 2012, featured address.

Sliwinski, Sharon. "The Childhood of Human Rights: The Kodak on the Congo." *Journal of Visual Culture* 5, no. 3 (2006): 333–63.

Smallwood, Stephanie E. *Saltwater Slavery: A Middle Passage from Africa to American Diaspora.* Cambridge, Mass.: Harvard University Press, 2007.

Smethurst, James Edward. *The Black Arts Movement: Literary Nationalism in the 1960s and 1970s.* Chapel Hill: University of North Carolina Press, 2005.

———. "'Don't Say Goodbye to the Porkpie Hat': Langston Hughes, the Left, and the Black Arts Movement." *Callaloo* 25, no. 4 (Fall 2002): 1225–36.

———. *The New Red Negro: The Literary Left and African American Poetry, 1930–1946.* New York: Oxford University Press, 1999.

Smiley, Tavis. *My Journey with Maya,* with David Ritz. New York: Little, Brown, 2015.

(Smith), Hurley X. *Poem for Patrice Lumumba.* Broadside Series no. 87. Detroit: Broadside Press, 1974.

Smith, Charles Spencer. *Glimpses of Africa: West and Southwest Coast.* Nashville, Tenn.: AME. Church Sunday School Union, 1895.

Smith, Peter. "The Hampton Years: Lowenfeld's Forgotten Legacy." *Art Education* 41, no. 6 (November 1988): 38–43.

Smith, Shawn Michelle. *Photography on the Color Line: W. E. B. Du Bois, Race, and Visual Culture.* Durham, N.C.: Duke University Press, 2004.

Smith McKoy, Sheila. "'This Unity of Spilt Blood': Tracing Remnant Consciousness in Kofi Awoonor's *Comes the Voyager at Last.*" *Research in African Literatures* 33, no. 2 (Summer 2002): 194–209.

Snyder, De Witt C. "Letters from the Field" (April 20, 1895). *Missionary* 28, no. 9 (September 1895): 410–11.

———. Letter to Brother Phillips. January 13, 1894. In Benedetto, *Presbyterian Reformers in Central Africa*, 97–99.

Snyder, May Heginbotham Thompson. "Letter from Luebo" (October 18, 1895). *Missionary* 29, no. 2 (February 1896): 78.

Sotiropoulos, Karen. "'Town of God': Ota Benga, the Batetela Boys, and the Promise of Black America." *Journal of World History* 26.1 (March 2015): 41–76.

*Soulbook* editors. "To the Peoples of Afroamerica, Africa, and to All the Peoples of the World." *Soulbook* 1, no. 1 (Winter 1964): 2–3.

"The *Southern Workman.*" *Southern Workman* 27, no. 12 (December 1898): 234.

"*Southern Workman* Prospectus 1898." *Southern Workman* 27, no. 1 (January 1898): 2.

Speer, Robert Elliott. Letter to Booker T. Washington. September 19, 1902. In Washington, *Booker T. Washington Papers*, 6:524–25.

Spellman, A. B. "James Phillips." *International Review of African American Art* 7, no. 4 (1987): 4–8.

Spencer, Chauncey. *Who Is Chauncey Spencer?* Detroit: Broadside Press, 1975.

Spriggs, Edward S. "Every Harlem Face Is AFROMANISM Surviving." In Baraka (Jones) and Neal, *Black Fire*, 341.

Sprunt, James. "Augusta County's Pioneer Missionary to the Dark Continent." *Augusta Historical Bulletin* 6, no. 2 (Fall 1970): 20–28.

Spurgeon, James Robert. "New York and Liberia Steamship Company." *Colored American Magazine* 7, no. 12 (December 1904): 734–42.

Stanard, Matthew G. *Selling the Congo: A History of European Pro-Empire Propaganda and the Making of Belgian Imperialism.* Lincoln: University of Nebraska Press, 2012.

Stanford, Maxwell, Jr. See Ahmad, Muhammad.

Stanley, Henry Morton. *The Autobiography of Sir Henry Morton Stanley*, edited by Dorothy Tennant Stanley. New York: Houghton Mifflin, 1909.

———. *The Congo and the Founding of Its Free State: A Story of Work and Exploration.* 1885. 2 vols. Detroit: Negro History Press, 1971.

———. *The Exploration Diaries of H. M. Stanley*, edited by Richard Stanley and Alan Neame. New York: Vanguard, 1961.

———. *Stanley's Despatches to the New York Herald, 1871–1872, 1874–1877*, edited by Norman R. Bennett. Boston: Boston University Press, 1970.

———. *Through the Dark Continent.* 1878. 2 vols. New York: Greenwood, 1969.

Starr, Frederick. *A Bibliography of Congo Languages.* Chicago: University of Chicago Press, 1908.

Stearns, Jason K. *Dancing in the Glory of Monsters: The Collapse of the Congo and the Great War of Africa.* New York: Public Affairs, 2011.

Stengers, Jean, and Jan Vansina. "King Leopold's Congo, 1886–1908." In *The Cambridge History of Africa*, edited by Roland Oliver and G. N. Sanderson, 315–58. Vol. 6. New York: Cambridge University Press, 1985.

Stepto, Robert B. *From behind the Veil: A Study of Afro-American Narrative*. Urbana: University of Illinois Press, 1979.
Stiles, T. J. *Jesse James: Last Rebel of the Civil War*. New York: Knopf, 2003.
Streitmatter, Rodger. "*Black Panther* Newspaper: A Militant Voice, a Salient Vision." In *The Black Press: New Literary and Historical Essays*, edited by Todd Vogel, 228–43. New Brunswick, N.J.: Rutgers University Press, 2001.
Strickland, William, and Cheryl Y. Greene. *Malcolm X: Make It Plain*. New York: Penguin, 1994.
Sublette, Ned. *The World That Made New Orleans: From Spanish Silver to Congo Square*. Chicago: Chicago Review Press, 2008.
Sundquist, Eric J. *To Wake the Nations: Race in the Making of American Literature*. Cambridge, Mass.: Belknap, 1993.
Sweeney, James Johnson, ed. *African Negro Art*. New York: Museum of Modern Art, 1935.
Tabor, Connie Matthews. "In Memoriam—Patrice Lumumba." *Black Panther* 4, no. 29 (January 16, 1971): 13–15.
Temkin, Moshik. "From Black Revolution to 'Radical Humanism': Malcolm X between Biography and International History." *Humanity: An International Journal of Human Rights, Humanitarianism, and Development* 3, no. 2 (Summer 2012): 267–88.
Terry, William E. *Origin and Development of Texas Southern University, Houston, Texas*. Houston: Dr. William Terry, 1968.
Theisen, Olive Jensen. *A Life on Paper: The Drawings and Lithographs of John Thomas Biggers*. Denton: University of North Texas Press, 2006.
———. *Walls That Speak: The Murals of John Thomas Biggers*. Updated ed. Denton: University of North Texas Press, 2010.
Thelwell, Chinua Akimaro. "Toward a 'Modernizing' Hybridity: McAdoo's Jubilee Singers, McAdoo's Minstrels, and Racial Uplift Politics in South Africa, 1890–1898." *Safundi: The Journal of South African and American Studies* 15, no. 1 (2014): 3–28.
Thomas, Lorenzo. "A Tale of Two Cities." *Umbra* 1 (Winter 1963): 36–37.
Thompson, Robert Farris. *Flash of the Spirit: African and Afro-American Art and Philosophy*. New York: Vintage, 1984.
———. "John Biggers's *Shotguns* of 1987: An American Classic." In Wardlaw, *Art of John Biggers*, 108–11.
———. "The Song That Named the Land: The Visionary Presence of African-American Art." In Wardlaw, *Black Art, Ancestral Legacy: The African Impulse in African-American Art*, 97–141.
Thornton, John. "The African Experience of the '20. And Odd Negroes' Arriving in Virginia in 1619." *William and Mary Quarterly* 55, no. 3 (1998): 421–34.
Thurston, Michael. *Making Something Happen: American Political Poetry between the World Wars*. Chapel Hill: University of North Carolina Press, 2001.
Tillery, Alvin B. *Between Homeland and Motherland: Africa, U.S. Foreign Policy, and Black Leadership in America*. Ithaca, N.Y.: Cornell University Press, 2011.
Tinson, Christopher M. "'The Voice of the Black Protest Movement': Notes on the *Liberator* Magazine and Black Radicalism in the Early 1960s." *Black Scholar* 37, no. 4 (Winter 2008): 3–15.

Tolliver, Cedric R. "The Racial Ends of History: Melancholic Historical Practice in Pauline Hopkins's *Of One Blood*." *Arizona Quarterly* 71, no. 1 (Spring 2015): 25–52.

Torday, Emil. *Causeries congolaises*. Brussels: Vromany, 1925.

———. *On the Trail of the Bushongo*. Philadelphia: Lippincott, 1925.

Totten, Gary. "Southernizing Travel in the Black Atlantic: Booker T. Washington's *The Man Farthest Down*." *MELUS* 32, no. 2 (Summer 2007): 107–31.

Trafton, Scott. *Egypt Land: Race and Nineteenth-Century American Egyptomania*. Durham, N.C.: Duke University Press, 2004.

Tuck, Stephen G. *The Night Malcolm X Spoke at the Oxford Union: A Transatlantic Story of Antiracist Protest*. Berkeley: University of California Press, 2014.

Twain, Mark. *King Leopold's Soliloquy: A Defense of His Congo Rule*. Boston: P. R. Warren, 1905. New York: International Publishers, 1961.

Tyson, Timothy. *Radio Free Dixie: Robert F. Williams and the Roots of Black Power*. Chapel Hill: University of North Carolina, 1999.

Van Beurden, Sarah. "Authentically African: African Arts and Postcolonial Cultural Politics in Transnational Perspective [Congo (DRC), Belgium and the USA, 1955–1980]." PhD dissertation, University of Pennsylvania, Philadelphia, 2009.

Vandervelde, Émile. *La Belgique et le Congo. Le passé, le présent, l'avenir*, edited by Felix Alcan. Paris: Librairies Félix Alcan and Guillaumin Réunies, 1911.

———. *Souvenirs d'un militant socialiste*. Paris: Éditions Denoël, 1939.

———. "Speech for the Defense." In Benedetto, *Presbyterian Reformers in Central Africa*, 387–404.

Van Lierde, Jean, ed. *Lumumba Speaks: The Speeches and Writings of Patrice Lumumba, 1958–1961*. Translated by Helen R. Lane. Boston: Little, Brown, 1972.

Vansina, Jan. *Being Colonized: The Kuba Experience in Rural Congo, 1880–1960*. Madison: University of Wisconsin Press, 2010.

———. *The Children of Woot: A History of the Kuba Peoples*. Madison: University of Wisconsin Press, 1978.

———. *Living with Africa*. Madison: University of Wisconsin Press, 1994.

Vellut, Jean-Luc. "Letter." *New York Review of Books* 53, no. 1 (January 12, 2006).

Verner, Samuel Phillips. *Pioneering in Central Africa*. Richmond, Va.: Presbyterian Committee of Publication, 1903.

Victor, Desmond. "Star of the Congo." *Freedomways* 2, no. 4 (Fall 1962): 407.

Villafana, Frank. *Cold War in the Congo: The Confrontation of Cuban Military Forces, 1960–1967*. New Brunswick, N.J.: Transaction, 2009.

Vinson, Robert Trent. "'Sea Kaffirs': 'American Negroes' and the Gospel of Garveyism in Early Twentieth-Century Cape Town." *Journal of African History* 47, no. 2 (July 2006): 281–303.

Vitalis, Robert. *White World Order, Black Power Politics: The Birth of American International Relations*. Ithaca, N.Y.: Cornell University Press, 2015.

Vlach, John Michael. *By the Work of Their Hands: Studies in Afro-American Folklife*. Charlottesville: University Press of Virginia, 1991.

Vogel, Susan, ed. *Art/Artifact: African Art in Anthropology Collections*. 2nd ed. New York: Center for African Art, 1989.

———. "Introduction." In Vogel, *Art/Artifact*, 11–17.

"The *Voice of the Negro* for July 1905." *Voice of the Negro* 2, no. 6 (June 1905): 364.

Von Eschen, Penny M. *Satchmo Blows Up the World: Jazz Ambassadors Play the Cold War*. Cambridge, Mass.: Harvard University Press, 2004.

Wagner, Jean. *Black Poets of the United States: From Paul Laurence Dunbar to Langston Hughes*. Translated by Kenneth Douglas. Urbana: University of Illinois Press, 1973.

Wahlman, Maude Southwell. *Signs and Symbols: African Images in African American Quilts*. Rev. ed. Atlanta: Tinwood Books, 2001.

Walker, Alice. *Overcoming Speechlessness: A Poet Encounters the Horror in Rwanda, Eastern Congo, and Palestine/Israel*. New York: Seven Stories, 2010.

Walker, Roslyn. See Randall, Roslyn Walker.

Wallace, Michele. "Faith Ringgold's Political Posters: Power to the People," May 26, 2010. *The 1960s*, blog, http://ringgoldinthe1960s.blogspot.com/2010/05/blog-post.html. November 29, 2015.

Wallinger, Hanna. *Pauline E. Hopkins: A Literary Biography*. Athens: University of Georgia Press, 2005.

Wamba, Philippe. *Kinship: A Family's Journey in Africa and America*. New York: Plume, 1999.

"Wanted—Another White Missionary for Africa." *Missionary* 35, no. 10 (October 1902): 461.

Ward, Andrew. *Dark Midnight When I Rise: The Story of the Jubilee Singers Who Introduced the World to the Music of Black America*. New York: Farrar, Straus and Giroux, 2000.

Wardlaw, Alvia J. *The Art of John Biggers: View from the Upper Room*. New York: Harry N. Abrams and Museum of Fine Arts, Houston, 1995.

———. "An Interview with Alvia Wardlaw," by Charles Henry Rowell. *Callaloo* 32, no. 1 (2009): 261–76.

———. "A Spiritual Libation: Promoting an African Heritage in the Black College." In Wardlaw, *Black Art, Ancestral Legacy: The African Impulse in African-American Art*, 53–74.

———, curator. *Black Art, Ancestral Legacy: The African Impulse in African-American Art*. Dallas: Dallas Museum of Art, 1989.

Washburn, Dorothy K. "Style, Classification and Ethnicity: Design Categories on Bakuba Raffia Cloth." *Transactions of the American Philosophical Society* (New Series) 80, no. 3 (1990): i–157.

Washburn, Hezekiahm M. *A Knight in the Congo: God's Ambassador in Three Continents*. Bassett, Va.: Bassett Printing, 1972.

Washington, Booker T. "Address of Dr. Booker T. Washington." In Rose, *Official Report of the Thirteenth Universal Peace Congress*, 258–60.

———. "The African at Home." *Outlook* 93, no. 1 (September 4, 1909): 19–26. Reprint in *Colored American Magazine* 17, no. 4 (October 1909): 261–73.

———. *The Booker T. Washington Papers*, edited by Louis R. Harlan and Raymond W. Smock. 14 vols. Urbana: University of Illinois Press, 1972–89.

———. "Christianizing Africa." 1896. In Washington, *Booker T. Washington Papers*, 4:251–52.

———. "Cruelty in the Congo Country." *Outlook* 78 (October 8, 1904). In Washington, *Booker T. Washington Papers*, 8:85–90.

———. *The Future of the American Negro*. Boston: Small, Maynard, 1899.
———. "A Helpful Life." 1890. In Washington, *Booker T. Washington Papers*, 3:24–25.
———. "Industrial Education in Africa." 1906. In Washington, *Booker T. Washington Papers*, 8:548–52.
———. "Industrial Schools as an Aid to Missions." *Missionary Review of the World* 29 (March 1906): 197–99. Reprint in *Kassai Herald* 6, no. 3 (July 1906): 30–31.
———. "Internation[al] Conference on the Negro." *Tuskegee Student* 24, no. 6 (February 10, 1912): 3.
———. Letter to Cain Washington Triplett and Others. December 12, 1904. In Washington, *Booker T. Washington Papers*, 8:153–54.
———. Letter to *Colored American* (Washington, D.C.). 1899. In Washington, *Booker T. Washington Papers*, 5:164–66.
———. Letter to James Jenkins Dossen, August 29, 1908. In Washington, *Booker T. Washington Papers*, 9:617–18.
———. Letter to Marcus Mosiah Garvey. September 17, 1914. In Washington, *Booker T. Washington Papers*, 13:133–34.
———. Letter to Robert Curtis Ogden. October 14, 1904. In Washington, *Booker T. Washington Papers*, 8:94.
———. "The Man Farthest Down." *Outlook* 98 (May 6, 1911). In Washington, *Booker T. Washington Papers*, 11:131–40.
———. *The Man Farthest Down: A Record of Observation and Study in Europe*. 1912. New Brunswick, N.J.: Transaction, 1984.
———. *My Larger Education*. Garden City, N.Y.: Doubleday, 1911.
———. "The Opening Address of the International Conference on the Negro." 1912. In Washington, *Booker T. Washington Papers*, 11:520–22.
———. *Some European Observations and Experiences*. Tuskegee, Ala.: Tuskegee Institute Press, 1899.
———. "The Storm before the Calm," *Colored American Magazine* 1, no. 4 (September 1900): 203–4.
———. *The Story of the Negro: The Rise of the Race from Slavery*. 2 vols. New York: Negro Universities Press, 1969.
———. *Up from Slavery*. 1901. In Washington, *Booker T. Washington Papers*, 1:211–388.
Watson, Zhinia. "The Case of the Missing Bells." *VUU Informer* (Virginia Union University) 108, no. 2 (January 2010): 1, 4–5.
Watts, Jerry Gafio. *Amiri Baraka: The Politics and Art of a Black Intellectual*. New York: New York University Press, 2001.
Webb, Virginia-Lee. *Perfect Documents: Walker Evans and African Art, 1935*. New York: Metropolitan Museum of Art, 2000.
Weissman, Stephen R. *American Foreign Policy in the Congo, 1960–1964*. Ithaca, N.Y.: Cornell University Press, 1974.
Wells, Ida B. *A Red Record*. 1895. In *Southern Horrors and Other Writings: The Anti-Lynching Campaign of Ida B. Wells, 1892–1900*, edited by Jacqueline Jones Royster, 73–157. New York: Bedford St. Martin's, 1997.
Wenzel, Jennifer. "Intertextual Africa: Chinua Achebe on the Congo, Patrice Lumumba on the Niger." In *African Writers and Their Readers: Essays in Honor of*

*Bernth Lindfors, Volume II*, edited by Toyin Falola and Barbara Harlow, 219–53. Trenton, N.J.: Africa World, 2002.

———. "Remembering the Past's Future: Anti-Imperialist Nostalgia and Some Versions of the Third World." *Cultural Critique* 62, no. 1 (Winter 2006): 1–32.

Wharton, Annabel Jane. *Building the Cold War: Hilton International Hotels and Modern Architecture*. Chicago: University of Chicago Press, 2001.

Wharton, Ethel Taylor. *Led in Triumph*. Nashville, Tenn.: Board of World Missions, Presbyterian Church (U.S.), 1952.

"Where God Is Black." *Time*, September 6, 1963, 22–23.

Whitburn, Joel. *The Billboard Book of Top 40 R&B and Hip-Hop Hits*. New York: Billboard Books, 2006.

White, Luise. *Speaking with Vampires: Rumor and History in Colonial Africa*. Berkeley: University of California Press, 2000.

Whoriskey, Kate. "Introduction." In Nottage, *Ruined*, ix–xiii.

Wilentz, Gay. "'What Is Africa to Me?': Reading the African Cultural Base of (African) American Literary History." *American Literary History* 15, no. 3 (Fall 2003): 639–53.

Wilkins, Fanon Che. "The Making of Black Internationalists: SNCC and Africa before the Launching of Black Power, 1960–1965." *Journal of African American History* 92, no. 4 (Autumn 2007): 467–90.

Willard, Carla. "Timing Impossible Subjects: The Marketing Style of Booker T. Washington." *American Quarterly* 53, no. 4 (December 2001): 624–69.

Williams, George Washington. *Centennial: The American Negro, from 1776 to 1876*. Cincinnati: Robert Clarke, 1876.

———. *History of the Negro Race in America, from 1619 to 1880: Negroes as Slaves, as Soldiers, and as Citizens*. 1882–1883. 2 vols. New York: Arno, 1968.

———. *A History of the Negro Troops in the War of Rebellion*. 1887. New York: Kraus Reprint, 1969.

———. *Memorial Day. The Ethics of the War*. Newton, Mass.: Office of the Graphic, 1884. Louisville, Ky.: Lost Cause Press, 1976.

———. *The Negro as a Political Problem*. Boston: Alfred Mudge, 1884.

———. "The New South: The Measures Which Will Result in the Solution of the Negro Problem and the Regeneration of Africa." *New York Globe*, May 24, 1884, 2.

[———.] "On the Congo. First Impressions of the Great African State." *New York Tribune*, June 8, 1890, 19.

[———.] "The Opening of Africa." *New York Tribune*, November. 24, 1889, 15.

———. *An Open Letter to His Serene Majesty Leopold II, King of the Belgians and Sovereign of the Independent State of Congo*. In Franklin, *George Washington Williams*, 243–54.

———. *A Report on the Proposed Congo Railway*. In Franklin, *George Washington Williams*, 255–63.

———. *A Report upon the Congo-State and Country to the President of the Republic of the United States of America*. In Franklin, *George Washington Williams*, 264–79.

Williams, R. Waldo. "The Awakening Call." *Black Challenge*, 1960, 16.

Williams, Vernon. *Rethinking Race: Franz Boas and His Contemporaries.* Lexington: University Press of Kentucky, 1996.

Williams, Walter L. *Black Americans and the Evangelization of Africa.* Madison: University of Wisconsin Press, 1982.

Willis, Jack. "A Harlem Education." *Ducts* 27 (Summer 2011), http://www.ducts.org/content/a-harlem-education. June 28, 2011.

Wilson, Amrit. "Abdul Rahman Mohamed Babu: Politician, Scholar and Revolutionary." *Journal of Pan African Studies* 1, no. 9 (August 2007): 8–25.

Wilson, Ivy G. "On Native Ground: Transnationalism, Frederick Douglass, and 'The Heroic Slave.'" *PMLA* 121, no. 2 (March 2006): 453–68.

Wilson, Judith. "Hagar's Daughters: Social History, Cultural Heritage, and Afro-U.S. Women's Art." In *Bearing Witness: Contemporary Works by African American Women Artists*, curated by Jontyle Theresa Robinson, 95–112. New York: Spelman College and Rizzoli International, 1996.

Wolfskill, Phoebe. "Caricature and the New Negro in the Work of Archibald Motley Jr. and Palmer Hayden." *Art Bulletin* 91, no. 3 (Sept. 2009): 343–65.

Woodard, Komozi. *A Nation within a Nation: Amiri Baraka (LeRoi Jones) and Black Power Politics.* Chapel Hill: University of North Carolina Press, 1999.

Woodson, Carter G. "Thomas Jesse Jones." *Journal of Negro History* 35, no. 1 (January 1950): 107–9.

Woodward, C. Vann. *Origins of the New South, 1877–1913.* Baton Rouge: Louisiana State University Press, 1971.

Wright, George C. *Life behind a Veil: Blacks in Louisville, Kentucky, 1865–1930.* Baton Rouge: Louisiana State University Press, 1985.

Wright, Sarah. "The Lower East Side: A Rebirth of World Vision." *African American Review* 27, no. 4 (Winter 1993): 593–96.

X, Hurley. See (Smith), Hurley X.

X, Malcolm. "After the Bombing." February 14, 1965. In Malcolm X, *Malcolm X Speaks*, 157–77.

———. "After the Bombing/Speech at Ford Auditorium." February 14, 1965. In *Malcolm-x.org*, edited by Noaman Ali, http://www.malcolm-x.org/speeches/spc_021465.htm. August 1, 2012.

———. "After the Firebombing (February 14, 1965)." In Malcolm X, *Malcolm X: Collected Speeches, Debates and Interviews (1960–1965)*, http://malcolmxfiles.blogspot.ca/2013/07/after-firebombing-feb-14-1965.html. May 30, 2016.

———. "Answers to Questions at the Militant Labor Forum." April 8, 1964. In Malcolm X, *By Any Means Necessary*, 37–56.

———. "At the Audubon." December 13, 1964. In Malcolm X, *Malcolm X Speaks*, 88–104.

———. "At the Audubon." December 20, 1964. In Malcolm X, *Malcolm X Speaks*, 115–36.

———. *The Autobiography of Malcolm X*, with Alex Haley. 1965. New York: Ballantine Books, 1973.

———. "The Black Revolution." June 1963. In Malcolm X, *End of White World Supremacy*, 67–80.

———. *By Any Means Necessary*, edited by George Breitman, 1970. New York: Pathfinder, 1992.

———. "Communication and Reality." December 12, 1964. In Clarke, *Malcolm X*, 307–20.

———. "The Congo, Cuba and Law." January 7, 1965. In Malcolm X, *Malcolm X Speaks*, 219–20.

———. *The Diary of Malcolm X (El Hajj Malik El-Shabazz) 1964*, edited by Herb Boyd and Ilyasah Al-Shabazz. Chicago: Third World Press, 2014.

———. "Educate Our People in the Science of Politics." February 14, 1965. In Malcolm X, *February 1965*, 75–105.

———. "Elijah Is Willing to Sit and Wait—I'm Not." February 3, 1965. In Malcolm X, *February 1965*, 20–22.

———. *The End of White World Supremacy: Four Speeches*, edited by Imam Benjamin Karim. New York: Arcade, 2011.

———. "An Exchange on Casualties in the Congo." November 28, 1964. In Malcolm X, *By Any Means Necessary*, 157–62. New York: Pathfinder, 1992.

———. *February 1965: The Final Speeches*, edited by Steve Clark. New York: Pathfinder, 1992.

———. "The Founding Rally of the OAAU." June 28, 1964. In Malcolm X, *By Any Means Necessary*, 57–96.

———. "God's Judgment of White America (The Chickens Are Coming Home to Roost)." December 4, 1963. In Malcolm X, *End of White World Supremacy*, 121–48.

———. "The Harvard Law School Forum of December 16, 1964." In Epps, *Malcolm X: Speeches at Harvard*, 161–82.

———. "The Homecoming Rally of the OAAU." November 29, 1964. In Malcolm X, *By Any Means Necessary*, 164–88.

———. "La communauté noire américaine et la révolution africaine." November 23, 1964. *Présence Africaine* 54 (2nd trimester 1965): 37–53.

———. *The Last Speeches*, edited by Bruce Perry. New York: Pathfinder, 1989.

———. "Linking the Problem." January 28, 1965. In Malcolm X, *Malcolm X Speaks*, 217–18.

———. "Louis Lomax Interviews Malcolm X." December 1963. In Lomax, *When the Word Is Given*, 169–80.

———. "Malcolm X at Yale." October 20, 1962. In Lomax, *When the Word Is Given*, 153–67.

———. *Malcolm X: Collected Speeches, Debates and Interviews (1960–1965)*, edited by Sandeep S. Atwal. http://malcolmxfiles.blogspot.ca. May 30, 2016.

———. "Malcolm X on Afro-American History." January 24, 1965. In Malcolm X, *Malcolm X on Afro-American History*, 11–57.

———. *Malcolm X on Afro-American History*, edited by Steve Clark. 3rd ed. New York: Pathfinder, 1990.

———. "Malcolm X on 'Unity.'" Spring 1960. In Lomax, *When the Word Is Given*, 128–35.

———. *Malcolm X Speaks: Selected Speeches and Statements*, edited by George Breitman. New York: Grove Press, 1965.

———. *Malcolm X Talks to Young People: Speeches in the U.S., Britain, and Africa*, edited by Steve Clark. New York: Pathfinder, 1991.

———. "Moise Tshombe and Jesse James." December 31, 1964. In Malcolm X, *Malcolm X Speaks*, 218.

———. "Not Just an American Problem, but a World Problem." February 16, 1965. In Malcolm X, *Last Speeches*, 151–81.

———. "The Old Negro and the New Negro." 1963. In Malcolm X, *End of White World Supremacy*, 81–120.

———. "On Politics." November 23, 1964. In Malcolm X, *Malcolm X Speaks*, 201–2.

———. "The Oppressed Masses of the World Cry Out for Action against the Common Oppressor." February 11, 1965. In Malcolm X, *February 1965*, 46–64.

———. "Our People Identify with Africa." December 27, 1964. In Malcolm X, *Last Speeches*, 91–107.

———. "The Oxford Address at the Oxford Union Debate." December 3, 1964. In Ambar, *Malcolm X at Oxford Union*, 169–80.

———. "Oxford University Debate (December 3, 1964)." In Malcolm X, *Malcolm X: Collected Speeches, Debates and Interviews (1960–1965)*, http://malcolmxfiles.blogspot.ca/2013/07/oxford-union-debate-december-3-1964.html. June 14, 2016.

———. "Prospects for Freedom in 1965." January 7, 1965. In Malcolm X, *Malcolm X Speaks*, 147–56.

———. "The Second Rally of the OAAU." July 5, 1964. In Malcolm X, *By Any Means Necessary*, 103–36.

———. "See for Yourself, Listen for Yourself, Think for Yourself." January 1, 1965. In Malcolm X, *Malcolm X Talks to Young People*, 48–82.

———. "Telephone Conversation." February 9, 1965. In Clarke, *Malcolm X*, 205–11.

———. "There's a Worldwide Revolution Going On." February 15, 1965, In Malcolm X, *Last Speeches*, 111–49.

———. "Twenty Million Black People in a Political, Economic, and Mental Prison." January 23, 1963. In Malcolm X, *Last Speeches*, 25–57.

———. "Whatever Is Necessary: The Last Television Interview, with Pierre Berton." January 19, 1965. In Gallen, *Malcolm X: As They Knew Him*, 179–87.

———. "With Mrs. Fannie Lou Hamer." December 20, 1964. In Malcolm X, *Malcolm X Speaks*, 105–14.

———. "The 'Young Socialist' Interview." January 18, 1965. In Malcolm X, *By Any Means Necessary*, 189–99.

Yates, Barbara A. "The Origins of Language Policy in Zaire." *Journal of Modern African Studies* 18, no. 2 (June 1980): 257–79.

Young, Bernard, ed. *The Eye of Shamba: The Art of Eugene Grigsby, Jr., A 65-Year Retrospective Exhibition*. Phoenix, Ariz.: Phoenix Art Museum, 2001.

Young, Cynthia. *Soul Power: Culture, Radicalism, and the Making of a U.S. Third World Left*. Durham, N.C.: Duke University Press, 2006.

Young, Jason R. *Rituals of Resistance: African Atlantic Religion in Kongo and the Lowcountry South in the Era of Slavery*. Baton Rouge: Louisiana State University Press, 2007.

Youngs, Tim. *Travellers in Africa: British Travelogues, 1850–1900*. New York: Manchester University Press, 1994.

Zangana, Haifa. *City of Widows: An Iraqi Woman's Account of War and Resistance*. New York: Seven Stories, 2007.

Zeidler, Jeanne. "The Hampton University Museum Collections." *International Review of African American Art* 11, no. 4 (1994): 46–54.

———. "John Biggers' Hampton Murals." *International Review of African American Art* 12, no. 4 (1995): 51–57.

Zeidler, Jeanne, and Mary Lou Hultgren. "'Things African Prove to Be the Favorite Theme': The African Collection at Hampton University." In Vogel, *Art/Artifact*, 97–111.

Zeilig, Leo. *Patrice Lumumba: Africa's Lost Leader.* London: Haus, 2008.

Zimmerman, Andrew. *Alabama in Africa: Booker T. Washington, the German Empire, and the Globalization of the New South.* Princeton, N.J.: Princeton University Press, 2010.

# Credits

Jayne Cortez, "Festivals & Funerals." © Estate of Jayne Cortez, courtesy of Melvin Edwards.

Jayne Cortez, "Initiation." © Estate of Jayne Cortez, courtesy of Melvin Edwards.

Frank Marshall Davis, "Chicago's Congo," from *Black Moods: Collected Poems*. © 2002 by the Board of Trustees of the University of Illinois. Used with permission of the University of Illinois Press.

Michael S. Harper, "Patrice Lumumba," from *Songlines in Michaeltree: New and Collected Poems*. © 2000 by Michael S. Harper. Used with permission of the University of Illinois Press.

Langston Hughes, "Bird in Orbit," from *The Collected Poems of Langston Hughes*, edited by Arnold Rampersad with David Roessel, associate editor. © 1994 by the Estate of Langston Hughes. Used by permission of Alfred A. Knopf, an imprint of the Knopf Doubleday Publishing Group, a division of Penguin Random House LLC. All rights reserved.

Langston Hughes, "Lumumba's Grave," from *The Collected Poems of Langston Hughes*, edited by Arnold Rampersad with David Roessel, associate editor. © 1994 by the Estate of Langston Hughes. Used by permission of Alfred A. Knopf, an imprint of the Knopf Doubleday Publishing Group, a division of Penguin Random House LLC. All rights reserved.

Langston Hughes, "Memo to Non-White Peoples," from *The Collected Poems of Langston Hughes*, edited by Arnold Rampersad with David Roessel, associate editor. © 1994 by the Estate of Langston Hughes. Used by permission of Alfred A. Knopf, an imprint of the Knopf Doubleday Publishing Group, a division of Penguin Random House LLC. All rights reserved.

Langston Hughes, "We, Too," from *The Collected Poems of Langston Hughes*, edited by Arnold Rampersad with David Roessel, associate editor. © 1994 by the Estate of Langston Hughes. Used by permission of Alfred A. Knopf, an imprint of the Knopf Doubleday Publishing Group, a division of Penguin Random House LLC. All rights reserved.

Ted Joans, "Black February Blood Letting." © Estate of Ted Joans, courtesy of Laura Corsiglia.

Ted Joans, "Him the Bird." © Estate of Ted Joans, courtesy of Laura Corsiglia.

Ted Joans, "Lumumba Lives." © Estate of Ted Joans, courtesy of Laura Corsiglia.

Ted Joans, "The Sax Bit." © Estate of Ted Joans, courtesy of Laura Corsiglia.

Ted Joans, "Who Shook." © Estate of Ted Joans, courtesy of Laura Corsiglia.

## Index

Page numbers and plate numbers in italics refer to illustrations.

Abbott, Robert S., 132, 177
Achebe, Chinua, 47
Adorno, Theodor, 257
*Africa* (J. Biggers), *188*
*Africa and the Wa*r (Brawley), 205
*Africa in the World Democracy* pamphlet, 342n45
African American art and artists: Catlett, 183–84, 190; M. Fuller, 163, 166, 185; Harlem Museum of Art, 180; Hayden, *plate 3*, 181–82, 336n122; at HBCUs, 183–84, 185; M. G. Johnson, *plate 4*, 182; L. M. Jones, 185; S. Lewis, 186–87, 199, 337n140; J. Phillips, *plate 9*, 198; political aspects, 164–65; resistance of, 126–27; Ringgold, *plate 10*, 198–99, 340nn230–31; C. White, 183–84, 187, 190, 199; *Young Negro Artists*, 184. *See also* Biggers, John; *and individual artists*
African American missionaries: on American Baptist Foreign Mission, 10; in Angola, 186; attitudes toward, 134, 136–37, 146; educational model of, 97; Garvey and, 134; home designs of, 192; marital status of, 115, 307n7, 309n47; politics of, 132–33; racism and, 66, 109, 115–16, 325n167; recruitment of, 19–22; in Sierra Leone, 109, 122, 167; significance of, 145. *See also* American Presbyterian Congo Mission; Edmiston, Althea Brown; Sheppard, Lucy Gantt; Sheppard, William Henry; *and individual missionaries*

African American print culture: Hopkins and, 142, 147–50, 157; Lumumba and, 231–34, 235–36, 348n52; significance of, 224. *See also individual periodicals*
African art. *See* Kuba art; Sheppard art collection
"African at Home, The" (Washington), 91–92, 95, 100, 154
African Choir, 94, 121
African Commune of Bad Relevant Artists (AFRICOBRA), 198, 340n226
African diasporic networks. *See* networks, African diaspora
African National Congress (ANC), 93
African Nationalist Pioneer Movement, 228–29
"African Roots of the War, The" (Du Bois), 11, 213, 300n37
African students at HBCUs, 92–95, 121–22, 175, 195, 315n65, 333n70
*African Textiles and Decorative Arts* exhibition, 174
AFRICOBRA (African Commune of Bad Relevant Artists), 198, 340n226
Afro-modernity, 105
AIA (International African Association), 7, 27
Alabama State Normal School, 78
Algeria, 264, 281, 284–85, 360n144
*All of Ted Joans and No More* (Joans), 238, *239*, 240
AMA (American Missionary Association), 109, 306n129
Ambar, Saladin, 278–79, 281

American Baptist Foreign Mission Society, 10
American Colonization Society (ACS), 21, 80–81
"American Congo" rhetoric, 214–15, 218–19
American Folklore Society, 311n102, 328n55
American Missionary Association (AMA), 109, 306n129
American Presbyterian Congo Mission (APCM): colonial state and, 54–55, 111–12, 134–38, 326n170; conflicts within, 127–29, 309n46, 323n113; ECFM of, 49, 54, 115–16; establishment of, 9, 49; Fisk University and, 324n129; *Kassai Herald*, 55, 77, 97, 308n31, 310n66; language policies of, 111–12, 130, 131, 134; Lapsley and, 49, 52–53, 66, 70, 143; music and, 116–17; J. Phipps and, 73–74; racial policies of, 60–66, 109, 115–16, 325n167; recruitment of blacks, 50–52; Verner appointment, 62–64; women in, 307n7. *See also* Edmiston, Althea Brown; language and linguistics; Sheppard, William Henry; *and individual missionaries*
Amoo-Gottfried, Kojo, 281
*Ananse: The Web of Life in Africa* (J. Biggers), 191, 192
ANC (African National Congress), 93
Anderson, James D., 97
Anderson, Jon Lee, 359n142
Angelou, Maya, 227, 231, 258, 284, 346n20, 347n47
Angola, 20, 186, 274, 278, 287, 337n155
anticolonialism: in *The Big Sea*, 207; of Du Bois, 11, 213–14; of Malcolm X, 264, 272, 280–87; in "The Negro," 213–14
"Any Day Now" (Neal), 250
APCM. *See* American Presbyterian Congo Mission
Appiah, Kwame Anthony, 120, 328n65
Arabic newspapers, 207, 342n22

Armstrong, Jack Proby, 57, 59
Armstrong, Louis, 220–21, 243
Armstrong, Mary Alice Ford, *196*
Armstrong, Samuel Chapman: background of, 97; on Hampton alumni in Africa, 22–23; "Invitation to Congo," 301n14; sculpture of, *196*; W. Sheppard and, 50; G. W. Williams and, 19, 21. *See also* Hampton Normal and Agricultural Institute
art, Kuba. *See* Kuba art; Sheppard art collection
Art Ensemble of Chicago, 343n64
Arthur, Chester A., 27
Art Institute of Chicago, 200
"Art Lessons from the Congo" (Locke), 181
*Ascent of Ethiopia, The* (L. M. Jones), 185
Ashcroft, Bill, 206
*Ask Your Mama* (L. Hughes), 220–21
Associated Literary Press, 30
Ater, Renée, 163
Atlanta Cotton States Exposition, 80–82, 166
*Atlanta Daily World*, 348n52
*Atlantic Monthly*, 11, 213
Attwood, William, 355n51
Auer, Bernard M., 356n72
"Awakening Call, The" (R. W. Williams), 228
*Awakening of Ethiopia, The* (M. Fuller), 163
Awoonor, Kofi, 291
Azikiwe, Nnamdi, 279, 349n63

Babu, Mohamed Abdul Rahman, 266, 285–86, 360n157
Bacon, Alice, 311n102
Baker, Houston A., Jr., 14, 91, 97, 101–2, 105, 150, 206
Baker, Josephine, 217
Bakuba people. *See* Kuba people and culture
Baldwin, James, 228
Baldwin, Kate, 215
Ballantine, Anna Thankful, 318n7

Banner, David, 212–13
Baraka, Amiri, 222, 227, 228, 242, 244, 255, 286
Barbour, Thomas Seymour, 89–90
"Barebreasted in Leopoldville" (Schachter), 231–32
Barnes, Jack, 272
Barnett Aden Gallery, 185, 337n140
Barry Gray Show, 257, 259–60
Barthes, Roland, 142
Bedinger, Robert Dabney, 65, 128, 138
Belgian Commercial Companies, 19, 20–21
Belgian government. *See* colonial state
"Belgium" (Granger), 211–12
Benga, Ota, 63, 65, 310n62, 310n68
Benston, Kimberly, 234, 236–38, 242–44, 246, 251
Bergman, Jill, 146
Berlin Conference and Act, 20, 27, 29, 89, 90, 303n55
Bethune, Lebert, 263, 281
Bethune, Mary McLeod, 109
Bhabha, Homi, 206
*Bibliography of the Congo Language* (Starr), 319n21
Biggers, John: African travel and interest of, 185–87, 191–92, 195; Hampton commission, 196; influences on, 193–94; Locke and, 184, 186, 337n140; McDowell and, 186, 337n155; quilting and, 187–89; "sacred geometry" of, 195; at TSU, 194–95; C. White and, 183–84
Biggers, John, works: *Africa*, 188; *Ananse*, 191, 192; *Country Preacher*, 187, 188; *The Dying Soldier*, 338n166; *House of the Turtle*, plate 7, 197; *Nubia*, 197; *Quilting Party*, plate 5, 193–94, 199; *Salt Marsh*, 197; *Starry Crown*, plate 6, 195; *Three Quilters*, 189–91, 190, 195; *Tree House*, plate 8, 197
Biggers, Sanford, 199
*Big Sea, The* (L. Hughes), 204–6, 215–17
Binkley, David A., 169
"Bird Lives" graffiti (Joans), 236–37, 244

*Black America*, 286
Black Arts movement: Baraka, 227, 242, 255; Cortez, 236, 245–50, 291; L. Hughes and, 222; Lumumba and, 234, 248, 255; organizations, 230–31; transnational aspects, 235–36; U.N. protest and, 226–28
*Black Atlantic, The* (Gilroy), 7, 104
*Black Challenge*, 228–29
*Black Cosmopolitanism* (Nwankwo), 13
"Black Dada Nihilismus" (Baraka), 242
"Black February Blood Letting" (Joans), 243–44
*Blacklash*, 286
Black Lives Matter, 288, 292
*Black Man's Verse* (F. Davis), 215
black nationalism, 225–31, 235–36, 258–60, 261–62, 353n6
*Black Panther, The*, 232–33, 233
*Black Pow-Wow* (Joans), 240
*Black World*, 233–34
Blondiau, Raoul, 180–81
"Blues in Stereo" (L. Hughes), 220
Blume, Harvey, 63
Blyden, Edward Wilmot, 21, 41, 95, 301n12, 307n144
Boatner, Edward, 125, 126, 322n97
*Body Politics* exhibition, 199
Bolden, Tony, 250
*Book of American Negro Spirituals, The* (Johnson, Johnson, and Brown), 122–23, 140
Borchgrave, Paul de, Count, 29
Boston *Guardian*, 152–53
Boston Literary and Historical Association, 151
Boya, Loso K., 8
Boykin, Cloyd, 181, 336n122
Bradford, Phillips Verner, 63
Brandford, Edward J., 181
Brantlinger, Patrick, 158
Brawley, Benjamin, 205
"Bread Not Enough in Congo" (L. Hughes), 218
*Breakfast in Bed, Windows of the Wedding Series* (Ringgold), plate 10, 198

Breitman, George, 279
British Cotton Growing Association, 96
British government: colonialism of, 206–7, 208–9; support for W. Sheppard, 59; Thesiger, 59
British Museum, 169–70
Brooklyn Museum, 180
Brooks, Daphne, 140
Brown, Althea Maria. *See* Edmiston, Althea Brown
Brown, Lois, 149, 151, 154
Brown, William Wells, 156, 326n6
Bryce, James, Lord, 101
Bulape station, 127–28, 323n113
Bunche, Ralph, 218–19, 226–27, 231, 232, 259
Bunseki, Fu-Kiau, 119–20
Bushong language: dialects of, 127–29; *Grammar and Dictionary*, 111, 127–32; hymnal, 112, 124; Tshiluba in relation to, 111, 130; value of, 131. *See also* Edmiston, Althea Brown; Kuba people and culture

Cahill, Marie, 6
Caluza, Reuben Tholakele, 333n70
Campbell, James T., 12, 67, 133, 145
CAO (Committee of African Organizations), 277, 281, 290
Carby, Hazel, 141
Carew, Jan, 282
Carlson, Paul, 267, 270, 356n60
Carretta, Vincent, 144
Carter, Alprentice "Bunchy," 233
Castro, Fidel, 230, 283–86
Catholic missionaries, 131, 319n19
Catlett, Elizabeth, 183–84, 190
*Celebrations and Solitudes* (Cortez), 250
*Centennial: The American Negro, from 1776 to 1876* (G. W. Williams), 24
Césaire, Aimé, 235
Cheatwood, Kiarri T-H., 236, 254
Chester, Samuel H., 54, 61–63, 66, 113–16
*Chicago Defender*: Abbott at, 177; "American Congo" (Pickens), 214; "An American Lynching" (Pickens),

343n63; "Bread Not Enough in Congo" (L. Hughes), 218; Congo Square in, 343n58; A. B. Edmiston and, 132; Leopold regime and, 334n83; on Lumumba assassination, 259, 348n52; "Simple and the Congo" (L. Hughes), 218; on Tshombe, 259
"Chicago's Congo (Sonata for an Orchestra)" (F. Davis), 215
Chicago Woman's Club, 182
"chickens coming home to roost," 260–61, 267–68, 272, 286
*Chi-Congo* (Art Ensemble of Chicago), 343n64
Chrisman, Laura, 94, 104
"Civilization (Bongo Bongo Bongo)," 220–21
C. K. (Compagnie du Kasai), 56, 57
Clark, Steve, 278–79
Clarke, John Henrik, 222, 225–26, 230, 231
Cleveland, Grover, 29
*Cleveland Advocate*, 214
*Cleveland Gazette*, 42
Cohen, Robert Carl, 286
Cold War, 271, 277–78
Collier, Robert Steele, 359n141
colonialism and imperialism: British, 206–7, 208–9; HBCUs and, 22–23; Hopkins and, 155–56, 160; U.S., 264–65, 267–68, 270–73, 276–78
colonial state: APCM and, 134–35, 326n170; art exhibitions of, 168–69; attitudes toward African Americans, 136–37; attitude toward Garvey, 133; Belgian government and, 211; cabinet members, 29; *Chicago Defender* and, 334n83; criticism of, 30–32, 54–56; Du Bois on, 11, 213; establishment of, 29; Hopkins on, 160; L. Hughes on, 218; language policies of, 111, 318n18; Lumumba assassination and, 225; military, 9; racial policies of, 134–38; resistance to, 291–92; transportation and, 322n89; U.S. government and, 137–38; Washington and, 86–87;

G. W. Williams and, 19, 20, 27, 33–34. *See also* hand-severing; Leopold II of Belgium
*Colored American Magazine*: *Crisis* compared to, 204; Hopkins at, 148–49; management of, 153–54; "Mrs. Jane E. Sharp's School," 143; *Of One Blood* in, 139–41; W. Sheppard in, 139–47, 154; *Southern Workman* compared to, 148–49; Washington in, 103–4. *See also* Hopkins, Pauline E.
Colored Co-operative Publishing Company, 148, 328n62
Colored National League, 150–51
Coltrane, John, 234, 243
Columbian Exposition, 166
*Comes the Voyager at Last* (Awoonor), 291
Committee of African Organizations (CAO), 277, 281, 290
Compagnie du Kasai (C. K.), 56, *57*
"Congo (A Study of the Negro Race), The" (Lindsay), 10–11
*Congo, My Country* (Lumumba), 232, 252
*Congo and the Founding of Its Free State, The* (Stanley), 21, 34, 36, 37
Congolese art. *See* Kuba art
"Congo Love Song" (J. W. and R. Johnson), 1–5, *6*
Congo Reform Association (CRA), 55, 83–87, 89–90, 208
Congo Square, 214, 343n58
Conrad, Joseph: CRA and, 46; Harper on, 254; *Heart of Darkness*, 5, 7, 37, 46, 47, 291; Lindsay on, 10–11; W. Sheppard compared to, 70; Washington compared to, 86
"Conservation of Races, The" (Du Bois), 121
contact zones, 96, 98
*Contending Forces* (Hopkins), 148, 151, 157
*Continents, Les*, 210–11
*Contribution of the Negro to Democracy, The* (C. White), 184
Cooks, Carlos A., 227, 228–29

Coombs, John Hartley, 145–47
Coppedge, Llewellyn, *50*
Cortez, Jayne, 236, 245–50, 291
*Cotillion, or One Good Bull Is Half the Herd, The* (Killens), 224
*Country Preacher* (J. Biggers), 187, *188*, 191, 196, 338n166
Coxe, Gloucester Caliman, 200
CRA (Congo Reform Association), 55, 83–87, 89–90, 208
*Crime of the Congo, The* (Doyle), 60
*Crisis: Africa in the World Democracy*, 342n45; *Colored American Magazine* in relation to, 154–55; Egyptian art in, 163; hand-severing in, 212–13; on Hopkins, 153; "The Negro," 210; "The Negro Speaks of Rivers" in, 203–4, 206, 209–10; on W. Sheppard, 10, *75*; on U.N. protest, 226–27. *See also* National Association for the Advancement of Colored People
"Cruelty in the Congo Country" (Washington), 84–85, 88–89
Crummell, Alexander, 72, 122, 147–48
Cruz, Jon, 126, 127
Cruz, Victor Hernandez, 235
Cuba: Algeria and, 360n144; anti-Castro Cubans, 264–65, 271, 277–78; Congo support, 282–87
Culin, Stuart, 180
Cullen, Countee, 105, 120
Cultural Association for Women of African Heritage, 230, 262
*Culture and Imperialism* (Said), 45
*Cultures of the United States Imperialism* (Kaplan and Pease), 14
Cunard, Nancy, 136, 179
Curiosity room (Hampton), 167–71, *168*
Curtis, Natalie, 178

*Daily Express*, 269–70, 271
Darish, Patricia J., 169
*Dark Races of the Twentieth Century, The* (Hopkins), 154, 159
*Darkwater* (Du Bois), 3, 120, 213
Davis, Benjamin J., Jr., 227

Davis, Frank Marshall, 215
Davis, Rebecca Harding, 69
Davis, Richard Harding, 311n80
"Dawn in the Heart of Africa" (Lumumba), 222
"Dedicated to Dr. W. H. Sheppard" (M. P. Johnson), 160–61
de Jongh, James, 205
Delany, Martin Robison, 156, 158
DeYampert, Lillian Thomas, *51*, 112, 114
DeYampert, Lucius, *50*, 112, 114, 118
di Prima, Diane, 241
"Do bana coba," 118–22, *119*, 321n61
Donaldson, Jeff, 340n226
Dorsey, Hugh M., 5
Douglass, Frederick, 81–82, 148, 166, 302n38, 313n19
Doyle, Arthur Conan, 60, 87, 103
Drake, St. Clair: on Africa, 145, 213; Koinange and, 175; W. Sheppard and, 10, 75; on Washington, 80, 88
Driver, Felix, 37, 47
*Dr. Livingstone's 17 Years' Exploration and Adventure in the Wilds of Africa* (Coombs), 145–47
*Drumvoices* (Redmond), 246
Dryepondt, Gustave, 56
Dube, John L., 93
Du Bois, David. *See* Graham Du Bois, David
Du Bois, Shirley. *See* Graham Du Bois, Shirley
Du Bois, W. E. B.: African interests of, 165, 207–8; "The African Roots of the War," 11–12, 213; anticolonialism of, 213–14; "The Conservation of Races," 121; *Crisis* and, 204; *Darkwater*, 3, 120; A. B. Edmiston linked to, 117–18; on Lumumba, 230; Malcolm X compared to, 258–59; Manye and, 93–94, 121–22, 316n79; *The Souls of Black Folk*, 117, 118–19, 196; Washington and, 81; at Wilberforce University, 121–22
duCille, Ann, 48
Dunbar, Paul Laurence, 161

*Dunbar Speaker and Entertainer, The*, 211
Dunn, Kevin, 47
DuPlessis, Rachel Blau, 203
*Dying Soldier, The* (J. Biggers), 338n166

*Ebony and Topaz* (C. Johnson), 123
Edmiston, Alonzo Lmore: APCM appointment and service, 63–64, 112–13, 319n28; art collection of, 165–66; on colonial state, 133; photo of, *50*, *114*; retirement of, 138. *See also* American Presbyterian Congo Mission; Edmiston, Althea Brown
Edmiston, Althea Brown: Bakuba name, 110; death of, 138; Du Bois linked to, 117–18; family of, 109; Fisk and, 109–10, 129, 130, 318n6; *Grammar and Dictionary*, 111, 127–32, 135; hymn and spiritual translations of, 112, 116–17, 124–27; linguistic method of, 131–32; marriage of, 112–16; *Nkana mu Ilonga, Bamamukalal a buola*, 111; photo of, *50*, *110*, *114*; politics of, 132, 135; resistance of, 126–27, 137; L. Sheppard compared to, 126; "Swing Low, Sweet Chariot" translation, 124–25; Verner and, 319n25; H. Washburn and, 128–29, 323n113; C. T. Wharton and, 128–29, 323n113; "What Missionaries Have Done for the World," 110. *See also* American Presbyterian Congo Mission; Edmiston, Alonzo Lmore
Edmiston, Sherman Kuetu, *50*, 113, *114*, 129
Edwards, Brent Hayes, 94, 124, 147, 205–6
Egyptian revolution (1919), 208–9
Egyptian revolution (1952), 217, 342n27
El-Din, Nasir, 268
Ellerson, Nannie J., 148
emigration to Africa, African American, 21–22, 44, 78–81, 102–4, 158
Engel, Elisabeth, 146–47, 150
Engs, Robert, 92

Equiano, Olaudah, 144
*Errand into the Wilderness* (Miller), 14
Essie Green Gallery, 200
Ethiopia: Congo and, 160; Egypt and, 156, 159; Malcolm X in, 281; as Meroe, 158–59
*Ethiopia* (M. Fuller), 163
Euphrates River and valley, 206–8
Europe, Booker T. Washington on, 100–104
Evers, Medgar, 245, 260, 351n111
"Evil Knievel" (Banner), 212
Ewing, Adam, 134
Ewing, Quincy, 152
Executive Committee of Foreign Missions (ECFM), 49, 54, 115–16. *See also* Presbyterian Church (U.S.)
*Exhibition of Bakuba Art*, 174
expatriates, African American, 266, 273, 279–80, 281–82, 284–85

Fabian, Johannes, 168, 171
Fabo, M. Paul, 230
*Famous Men of the Negro Race* (Hopkins), 152, 153
Farnana, Paul Panda, 210, 342n36
Farrington, Lisa, 198
Fauset, Jessie, 208–9, 210
FBI (Federal Bureau of Investigation), 358n125
Fearing, Maria, *51*, 51–52, 110, 138, 311n80
*February 1965: The Final Speeches* (Malcolm X), 278–79
Federal Bureau of Investigation (FBI), 358n125
"Festivals & Funerals" (Cortez), 236, 248–50, 291
*Festivals and Funerals* (Cortez), 245–47
*Fétiche et Fleurs* (Hayden), *plate 3*, 181, 182
Fields, Barbara J., 64
*Fight for Freedom* (L. Hughes), 211
*Figures in Black* (Gates), 45
"Final Call" (L. Hughes), 222
Firchow, Peter Edgerly, 47

Fisk Jubilee Singers, 94, 117, 121–22, 139–40, 144–45, 307n6
Fisk University: APCM and, 324n129; art collection of, 165; Ballantine at, 318n7; Chester on, 114–15; Du Bois and, 117; A. B. Edmiston and, 129, 130–31, 318n6; Jubilee Hall, 122; Locke and, 182; missionaries from, 109
*Flash of the Spirit* (Thompson), 118
Florida Land and Colonization Committee, 289
Folsom, Cora Mae, 168, 177–78
Forbes, George Washington, 152, 329n79
Force Publique, 9, 10, 65, 136
Ford, James W., 353n2
*For the Women's House* (Ringgold), 198
Fox, Francis W., 41, 165–66, 305n116
Francis, Jacqueline, 182
Franck, Louis, 128, 133. *See also* colonial state
Franklin, John Hope, 34, 38, 40–41, 45–46, 302n32, 303n61
Frederick Loudin's Original Fisk Jubilee Singers, 51, 116, 121, 307n6
*Freedomways*, 225–26, 231–32, 355n51
Freeman, Kenn M. (Mamadou Lumumba), 232
Frelinghuysen, Frederic T., 27–28
Freund, John C., 152, 153
Frissell, Hollis Burke, 71–72, 75, 93. *See also* Hampton Normal and Agricultural Institute
"From the Bakuba Country" (W. Sheppard), 55–56
Fryer, Alice, 306n120
Fuller, Hoyt, 233–34
Fuller, Meta Vaux Warrick, 163, 166, 185
*Funnyhouse of the Negro* (Kennedy), 235
"Future of Africa, The," 211

Gaines, Kevin K., 151, 160, 261, 273
Gaither, Edmund Barry, 193
Garon, Paul, 250
Garvey, Marcus, 106, 133, 134, 136, 149
Gates, Henry Louis, Jr., 45, 313–14n19

General Federation of Labour Unions in the Nile Valley, 342n27
*Geography Militant* (Driver), 47
German government, Tuskegee and, 95–96
*Ghost of Patrice Lumumba, The* (Ogali), 235, 245
Gianpetri, Charles Louis, 60
Gikandi, Simon, 121
Gilliard, Joseph, 183
Gillman, Susan, 156–57
Gilroy, Paul: on the African past, 105, 155; *The Black Atlantic*, 7, 104; on diaspora, 94, 206; on Du Bois and Africa, 94, 165; on Europe, 104; identity, 12–13, 205–6; routes and roots, 7, 147, 155–56, 162
*Glimpses of Africa* (C. S. Smith), 47–48, 49, 146–47, 311n80
"Go Down, Moses," 140–41, 142, 150
*Golden Age of Black Nationalism, The* (Moses), 149
Goldman, Peter, 258, 280
Gomez, Michael A., 149, 159
Gonzales, Babs, 237–38
Gonzalez, Armando Entralgo, 284
Graham Du Bois, David, 268
Graham Du Bois, Shirley, 231, 232
*Grammar and Dictionary of Buluba-Lulua Language* (Morrison), 111, 130–31, 324n125
*Grammar and Dictionary of the Bushonga or Bukuba Language as Spoken by Bushonga or Bukuba Tribe Who Dwell in the Upper Kasai District, Belgian Congo* (A. B. Edmiston), 111, 127–32, 135
Granger, Lester B., 211–12, 226
Greener, Richard, 28
Gregg, James Edward, 176
Gregory, Dick, 270
Griffin, Farah Jasmine, 119
Griffith, Sanford, 257
Gruesser, John Cullen, 139, 145
*Guardian* (Boston), 152–53
Guevara, Ernesto "Che," 282–87
Guridy, Frank, 79

Guthrie, Malcolm, 131–32
Guy, Rosa, 227, 248, 258, 349n67

Hairston, Loyle, 232
Haiti, 24, 30, 104, 152, 347n31
Hale, Edward Everett, 143
Hall, Stuart, 13, 142, 155
Hamer, Fannie Lou, 273–74
Hampton, Karen, 199
*Hampton and Its Students*, 118
Hampton Normal and Agricultural Institute: administration of, 339n202; AMA and, 306n129; artists at, 183–85; art program, 182; Curiosity room, 167–71, *168*; domestic science students at, *178*; donors, 333n70; Folklore Society, 147, 150, 311n102; founding of, 97; Lowenfeld and, 182–84; museums, 168–69, 174–78, 196–98, 200, 333n70, 334n85; music, 118, 197; Press, 312n121; TSU and, 194–95; Tuskegee and, 92; G. W. Williams and, 19–22, 44. *See also* Armstrong, Samuel Chapman; Sheppard, William Henry; Sheppard art collection; *Southern Workman*
hand-severing: Baraka on, 255; Cortez on, 246; Granger on, 211; Harleston on, 212–13; L. Hughes on, 210–11; Malcolm X on, 257–58; Nottage on, 255–56; W. Sheppard on, 9, 12, 54–55; trope of, 55, 255; A. Walker on, 255
Hansberry, Lorraine, 228, 231, 235
Hansberry, William Leo, 232
Harlan, Louis R., 79, 87–88, 92
Harlem Museum of Art, 180
Harlem Writers Guild, 228, 230
Harleston, E. A., 212–13
Harper, Frances Ellen Watkins, 156
Harper, Michael S., 236, 254–55
Harris, Donald, 357n86
Harris, John, 88, 103–4
Harrison, Benjamin, 8, 20, 31
Harvey, William R., 195–96, 339n210
Hawkins, Coleman, 244–45
Hawkins, Henry: as APCM officer, 64; as editor of *Kassai Herald*, 55, 97;

family of, 309n47; photo of, *50, 51*;
translation work of, 111, 130
Hayden, Palmer, *plate 3*, 181–82, 336n122
Haynes, George E., 129
HBCUs. *See* Historically Black Colleges and Universities
*Heart of Darkness* (Conrad), 5, 7, 37, 46, 47, 291
"Helpful Suggestions for Young Artists" (M. Fuller), 163
Hemenway, Mary, 328n55
Henderson, Stephen, 236–37, 241–42, 250, 254
"Heritage" (Cullen), 105, 120
*Heroic Slave, The* (Douglass), 148
Herring, James Vincent, 185
Herskovitz, Melville, 164
"Hidden Self, The" (James), 139, 142
Higashida, Cheryl, 231
"Him the Bird" (Joans), 237–38
Historically Black Colleges and Universities (HBCUs): African students at, 92–94, 121–22, 333n70; Alabama State, 78; alumni role in Africa, 23; art at, 183–84; built environments of, 173–74; as a contact zone, 96; Howard, 185, 229, 340n225; Stillman, 63, 76, 112; Talladega College, 51, 115; Texas Southern University (TSU), 194, 269, 339n202; in Togo, 95–96; Virginia Union University, 331n23; Wilberforce, 93–94, 121–22. *See also* Fisk University; Hampton Normal and Agricultural Institute; Tuskegee Institute
*History of the Negro Troops in the War of Rebellion, A* (G. W. Williams), 25
*History of the Negro Race in America, from 1619–1880* (G. W. Williams), 28, 35, 156–57
Hochschild, Adam, 7–8, 12, 30–32, 291, 307n144
Hogan, Ernest, 2–3, 140
Hopkins, Pauline E.: Africa of, 156; colonialism and, 155–56, 160; Colored National League and, 150–51; cosmopolitanism of, 13–14; Equiano compared to, 144; local and international interests of, 154; network of, 163; politics of, 157–58; W. Sheppard compared to, 155–56, 159; significance of, 161–62; transatlantic networks of, 142; transnational interests of, 143, 148, 153. *See also Colored American Magazine*
Hopkins, Pauline E., works: *Colored American Magazine*, 148–49, 153–54; *Contending Forces*, 151, 156; *The Dark Races of the Twentieth Century*, 159; *Famous Men of the Negro Race*, 152; "Mrs. Jane E. Sharp's School," 143; *New Era Magazine*, 163; *Primer of Facts, A*, 153, 158–59, 163. *See also Of One Blood; Or, the Hidden Self*
Horne, Gerald, 24, 175
*House of the Turtle* (J. Biggers), *plate 7,* 197
Howard, Charles P., Sr., 231, 348n51
Howard University, 185, 229, 340n225
Howe, Mary Armstrong, *196*
"How Long Has Trane Been Gone" (Cortez), 251
Huggins, John, *233*
Hughes, Langston: Africa trips, 343n57; Congo and, 203, 218–22; *Crisis* and, 204, 208–10; Jess B. Simple, 218–19, 259; Lumumba and, 245; politics of, 214–16, 217
Hughes, Langston, works: *Ask Your Mama*, 220–21; *The Big Sea*, 204–6, 215–17; "Blues in Stereo," 220; "Bread Not Enough in Congo," 218; "Drums," 343n58; *Fight for Freedom*, 211; "Final Call," 222; "Letter from Spain," 216–17; "Lumumba's Grave," 221–22; "Memo to Non-White Peoples," 217–18; "The Negro," 210–11; "Negro Artist and the Racial Mountain, The," 207; *Poems from Black Africa*, 222; *Selected Poems*, 216; "Simple and the Congo," 218; *The Weary Blues*, 210, 213; "We Too," 219–20. *See also* "Negro Speaks of Rivers, The"

Hultgren, Mary Lou, 167
Huntington, Collis P., 19, 23, 39, 42, 44, 165
hymnal translations, 112, 116–17, 124–27, 138, 319nn21–22

Ibanche station, *110*, 112–13, 127–28, 323nn113–14, 324n139
"Image of Africa, An" (Achebe), 47
"Industrial Education in Africa" (Washington), 85–86
"Industrial Schools as an Aid to Missions" (Washington), 97
"Initiation" (Cortez), 245–46, 255
*Interesting Narrative of the Life of Olaudah Equiano*, 144
International African Association (AIA), 7, 27
International Conference on the Negro (1912), 79, 86, 95, 314n65
Iraq, 12, 205–8
Ismaili, Rashidah, 236
"I Too" (L. Hughes), 219, 220

Jabavu, John Tengo, 93
Jacobson, Matthew Frye, 68
James, William, 139, 142
*Janitor Who Paints, The* (Hayden), 182
Janssen, Camille, 40, 41
jazz and poetry, 220–21, 234, 236–38, 241–45, 350n76
Jefferson School, 238
Jennings, Persis, 184
Jewsiewicki, Bogumil, 248
J. Leighton Wilson Press, 111, 125, 129
Joans, Ted, 234, 237–45, *239*, 253–54, 351n106
Joans, Ted, works: "Afrique Accidentale," 241; *All of Ted Joans and No More*, 238–40; "Bird Lives" graffiti, 236–37, 244; "Black February Blood Letting," 243–44; *Black Pow-Wow*, 240; "Him the Bird," 237–38, 350n81; "LUMUMBA LIVES!," 234, 236, 238–42, *239*; "The

Sax Bit," 244–45, 249; *Teducation*, 237, 240; "Who Shook," 243
Johnson, Charles S., 123, 184, 185, 321n82
Johnson, Harvey, 187
Johnson, James Weldon: "Africa in the World Democracy," 12; *Book of American Negro Spirituals*, 122–23, 140; "Congo Love Song," 1–5, *6*; network of, 163; scholarship on, 7; on spirituals, 116
Johnson, Lyndon B., 265, 267
Johnson, Maggie Pogue, 160–61
Johnson, Malvin Gray, *plate 4*, 182
Johnson, Rosamond, 4, 6
Johnston, Harry, 101
Jones, LeRoi. *See* Baraka, Amiri
Jones, Löis Mailou, 185
Jones, Meta DuEwa, 241
Jones, Thomas Jesse, 86, 133–34, 325n145
Jordan, June, 236, 250
Joseph, Peniel, 230
Jubilee Hall (Fisk University), 122, 173

Kabamba, Patrice, 13
Kanza, Thomas, 228, 266, 355n51
Kaplan, Amy, 3, 14, 15, 92
"Kasai velvets," 172–73. *See also* textiles, Kuba
Kasavubu, Joseph, 261
*Kassai Herald*, 55, 77, 97, 308n31, 310n66. *See also* American Presbyterian Congo Mission
Kasson, John A., 8, 29
Keim, Curtis A., 169
Keith, Arthur Berriedale, 208
Kellersberger, Julia Lake, 136
Kelley, Robin D. G., 250
Kennedy, Adrienne, 235
Kennedy, Pagan, 64–65, 76
Kennedy assassination, 260–61, 272–73, 286
Kgositsile, Keorapetse, 234, 235, 236
Khalidi, Rashid, 207
Killens, John Oliver, 224, 230
Kim, Daniel Won-gu, 217–18
Kimbrough, Robert, 46

King, Martin Luther, Jr., 267–68
*King Leopold's Ghost* (Hochschild), 12, 291
*King Leopold's Soliloquy* (Twain), 55, 257–58, 353n6
Kisangani. *See* Stanleyville
Koinange, Mbiyu, 175
Kondo, Zak A., Baba, 284–85, 354n35
Kot aMbweeky II, 66, 69, 170, 174
Kowalsky, Henry I., 86
Kuba art: appreciation of, 180–81; collecting, 164–66; design, 193; at expositions, 166–67; Leopold II and, 168–69; *ndop* statues, 169–72; objects, 173; patterns in, 173; political aspects, 165. *See also* Sheppard art collection; textiles, Kuba
Kuba people and culture: capitol, 66, 169, 170, 171; catechism of, 111; characteristics of, 69–70, 71–72; Chief Niakai, 59; Kot aMbweeky II, 66, 69, 170, 174; poetry on, 160–61; reincarnation, 144. *See also* Kuba art; language and linguistics; Sheppard art collection; textiles, Kuba
Kupcinet, Irv, 356n63
Kwete Mbuek III, 200

Lalaing, Charles, Count, 29
Lane, Sarah, 177, 178
language and linguistics: APCM experts, 53, 109, 131–32; Bushong, 111, 130–31; dialects, 128–29, 130; *Grammar and Dictionary of Buluba-Lulua Language*, 111, 130–31, 324n125; hymnal translations, 116–17, 125–27, 138; spiritual translations, 117–18, 124–27; Swahili, 318n18. *See also* Bushong language; Edmiston, Althea Brown; Tshiluba translation
Lanier, Raphael O'Hare, 194–95, 339n202
Lapsley, Samuel Norvell, 49, 52–53, 66, 70, 143. *See also* Sheppard, William Henry
Lawrence, Olatunde, 234–35

LCA (Liberation Committee for Africa), 225–26, 230, 231. *See also Liberator*
Leighten, Patricia, 7, 164–65
Leon, Eli, 173
Leopold II of Belgium: art policy of, 168–69; founding of Congo state, 7–11; W. Sheppard and, 75, 211; U.S. lobby of, 27, 288–89; Verner and, 64; A. Walker and, 255–56; Washington and, 85–87, 89; G. W. Williams and, 19–21, 26–34, 36–39, 40–43, 46–47. *See also* colonial state
*Les Blancs* (L. Hansberry), 235
*Les Demoiselles d'Avignon* (Picasso), 164
*Les Fétiches* (L. M. Jones), 185
"Letter from Spain" (L. Hughes), 216–17
Lewis, David Levering, 11
Lewis, John, 357n86
Lewis, Samella Sanders, 184, 186–87, 199, 337n140, 339n201, 341n234
Liberation Committee for Africa (LCA), 225–26, 230, 231. *See also Liberator*
*Liberator*, 231, 232, 290, 348n53. *See also* Liberation Committee for Africa
Liberia, 22, 25–26, 109, 143, 158, 301n12
*Life and Letters of Samuel Norvell Lapsley*, 53
"Lift Every Voice and Sing" (J. W. Johnson and R. Johnson), 4
Lincoln, Abbey, 227, 230
Lincoln, Abraham, 241, 302n38
Lindberg, Kathryn, 247
Lindo, Nashormeh, 340n230
Lindsay, Vachel, 10–11, 71, 203
linguistics and language. *See* language and linguistics
Lippens, Maurice, 134–35
Livingstone, David, 35–36, 145–47, 304n86
Locke, Alain, 179, 180–81, 182, 336n128, 337n140
Logan, Rayford, 5, 100
London School of Economics, 277, 278
Long, Richard, 174
*Looking for Livingstone* (Philip), 147
Loudin, Frederick, 51, 116, 121, 307n6

Index   429

L'Ouverture, Touissaint, 104, 152
Lovedale school, 87
Low, Sidney, 37
Lowenfeld, Viktor, 182–87, 194, 337n140, 339n201
Lowenfels, Walter, 231
Lowry, Henry, 214, 343n63
Luce, Henry, 356n60
Lucy Sheppard Art Club, 77, 313n132
Lumumba, Patrice: in *Ask Your Mama*, 220–21; assassination and martyrdom of, 224–31; in *The Black Panther*, 232–33, *233*; *Congo, My Country*, 232, 252; Cuban support for, 282–84; "Dawn in the Heart of Africa," 222; inauguration and government of, 224–25, 228–29, 252; Kennedy assassination in relation to, 260–61; Malcolm X compared to, 290–91, 361n12; in Nigerian chapbooks, 349n66; photo of, *263*; plays about, 235, 245; Soviets and, 348n52; *Time* on, 270; U.S. visit of, 228–29, 347n31; "We Too" in relation to, 219; writings of, 222, 232–33. *See also* African American print culture; Lumumba poems
Lumumba, Pauline, 225
"Lumumba Blues" (Patterson), 250–56
"LUMUMBA LIVES!" (Joans), 236, 238–42, *239*, 243
Lumumba poems: by African American poets, 228, 236; by African poets, 234–35; and black journals, 224, 228–29, 234–35; by Cortez, 245–50, 291; by diasporic black poets, 235–36; emergence and significance of, 234–36; by L. Hughes, 221–22; by Joans, 238–42, 243, 351n106; by R. Patterson, 250–56; by white poets, 349n73
"Lumumba's Death" (Lawrence), 234
"Lumumba's Grave" (L. Hughes), 221–22
lynching, 5, 84, 214, 244–45, 252–53, 343n63

Mack, John, 169
Mack, Joseph, 183
Mackinnon, William, 38–40, 41, 289, 305n109
Malcolm X. *See* X, Malcolm
*Malcolm X at Oxford Union* (Ambar), 278–79
*Malcolm X Speaks*, 279, 287
*Malcolm X Talks to Young People*, 278
*Man Farthest Down, The* (Washington), 88, 102, 104–5
Manye, Charlotte, 93–94, 121–22, 316n79
Marable, Manning, 92, 284, 285
Markle, Seth, 229
Martin, Bessie, *50*
Martin, Motte, *50*
Martin, Trayvon, 288
Mason, Charlotte Osgood, 180–81
Matthews, Fred, 87
Mayfield, Julian, 273
Mbop Mabinc maMbeky, 185
McBroom, Marie, 228
McClure, S. S., 30
McCray, Carrie Allen, 310n62
McDowell, Henry Curtis, 186, 337n155
McHenry, Elizabeth, 7, 151
McKay, Claude, 177
Meeuwis, Michael, 133
Meier, August, 152
Melhem, D. H., 247
"Memo to Non-White Peoples" (L. Hughes), 217–18
Menelik II, 159
Meroe, 158–59, 163
Michaux, Lewis, 248, *249*, 257–58
Middle Passage, 20, 74, 144, 155, 215, 245–46
Miller, Ivor, 119
Miller, Perry, 14
*Misambu ya Kutumbisha n'ai Nzambi*, 125
*Missionary*, 52, 53, 54, 67–68
*Missionary Survey*, 74
missions and missionaries. *See* African American missionaries; American Presbyterian Congo Mission

430   Index

Mississippi: compared to Congo, 214, 219, 259, 271–72; Mississippi Freedom Democratic Party, 273, 277
Mitchell, Bettye Jean, 229–30
MMI (Muslim Mosque Inc.), 268
MNC (Mouvement National Congolais), 224
mobility, black, 100–106, 150
Monroe Doctrine, 303n55
Moore, Carlos: conflict with African American activists, 359n127; Congo and, 258, 353n6, 355n51; Malcolm X and, 263, 281–82, 359n130, 359n142; U.N. protest and, 227
Moore, Fred R., 153. *See also Colored American Magazine*
Morel, E. D., 55, 208. *See also* Congo Reform Association
Morgan, John Tyler, 8, 49, 78, 81
Morgan, Stacy I., 183–84
Morrison, Bertha, *50*
Morrison, William M.: African American missionaries and, 309n47; Edmistons and, 113–15; *Grammar and Dictionary of Buluba-Lulua Language*, 111, 130–31, 324n125; Kot aMbweeky II and, 172; on Leopold regime, 54–55; photo of, *50, 51, 57*; W. Sheppard and, 61, 84, 309n46; W. Sheppard trial, 56–60, 65; Torday and, 171–72; translations of, 111, 319n22; at Universal Peace Congress, 83–84, 308n29, 314n23; Washington and, 84–85
Morrissette, Noelle, 5–6
Moses, Wilson Jeremiah, 25, 80, 86, 149, 328n65
*Moses: A Story of the Nile* (Harper), 156
Moten, Fred, 237, 242
Moton, Robert Russa, 74–75, 93, 180. *See also* Tuskegee Institute
Mouvement National Congolais (MNC), 224
Mputubwele, Makim M., 125
"Mrs. Jane E. Sharp's School" (Hopkins), 143

Mudimbe, V. Y., 36, 112, 164
Muhammad, Elijah, 260
*Muhammad Speaks*, 273, 275, 355n46
*Mukanda wa Malu a Kukema* (Hawkins), 111
Murphy, Gretchen, 13–14
Murray, Albert, 357n81
Museum of Modern Art (MoMA), 174, 184
Mushenge, 66, 71–72, 127–29, 169–72, 184–85
music: *The Book of American Negro Spirituals*, 122–23, 140; "Congo Love Song," 1–5, *6*; "Do bana coba," 118–22, 321n61; Fisk Jubilee Singers, 121, 139, 144, 307n6; hymns, 111–12, 116–17, 124–27, 138, 319nn21–22; jazz, poetry and, 220–21, 234, 236–38, 241–45, 350n76; L. Sheppard interest in, 50–52; slave songs, 126; "Swing Low, Sweet Chariot," 117–18, 122–27; transatlantic circulation of, 116–17
Muslim Mosque Inc. (MMI), 268
*My Larger Education* (Washington), 82, 103–4
"My Little Jungle Queen" (Hogan), 2–3, 140

NAACP. *See* National Association for the Advancement of Colored People
NAHV (Nieuwe Afrikaansche Handels Vennootschap), 32
Nasser, Gamal Abdel, 265, 355n46
*Nation, The*, 207, 214
National Association for the Advancement of Colored People (NAACP): "African in the World Democracy," 12; on "American Congo," 214, 343n63; "The Future of Africa," 211; L. Hughes and, 203–4, 211, 215; W. Sheppard and, 10, 74, 75, 211, 342n45; U.N. protest and, 226–27, 346n16. *See also Crisis*
National Memorial African Bookstore, 248, *249*, 257–58

Nation of Islam (NoI), 258, 260–61, 272–73, 286, 291
Ndaywel é Nziem, Isidore, 9
*ndop* statues, 169–72, *170*, 332n38
Neal, Larry, 242, 250, 253
"Negro, The" (L. Hughes), 210–11
*Negro: Anthology Made by Nancy Cunard, 1931–1933*, 136, 179, 214–15
"Negro Artist and the Racial Mountain, The" (L. Hughes), 207
*Negro Digest*, 233–34
*Negro Faces America, The* (Seligmann), 214
*Negro in Art Week* exhibition, 182
*Negro in the American Rebellion, The* (W. W. Brown), 326n6
*Negro Masks* (M. G. Johnson), *plate 4*, 182
"Negro Speaks of Rivers, The" (L. Hughes): anticolonial aspects, 207–8; composition of, 214–16; debut of, 209–10; Du Bois and, 213; genealogy of, 204–6; internationalism of, 206–10, 216–17; "Memo to Non-White Peoples" compared to, 218; politics and, 214–16; significance of, 203–4, 222–23
*Negro World*, 133, 136
networks, African diaspora: art and, 163–64, 174, 184, 200; Hampton and, 21–23; Hopkins and, 141–43; "The Negro Speaks of Rivers" and, 222–23; Sheppards and, 52, 55, 64, 77; Washington and, 79–80
*New Era Magazine*, 157, 163
Newkirk, Pamela, 112
New Orleans, Congo Square in, 214, 343n58
*New York Age*, 4, 302n44, 314n30
*New York Amsterdam News*, 261, 348n52
New York and Liberia Steamship Company, 302n30
*New York Globe*, 28, 302n44
*New York Herald*, 35, 36, 38
*New York Times*: on Congo, 230, 264–65; on Malcolm X, 260, 267, 275, 361n6; on U.N. protest, 225, 228, 353n7; on G. W. Williams, 20–21

*New York Tribune*, 21, 30, 31, 42, 303n61
Ngoloshang Mbeky, 200
Ngoma, Florian Alphonso, 235–36
Niakai (Kuba chief), *59*
Nielsen, Aldon Lynn, 242, 350n75
Nieuwe Afrikaansche Handels Vennootschap (NAHV), 32
Nile River and valley, 159, 205, 207–8, 209–10, 215, 342n27
*nkala*, 144
*Nkana mu Ilonga, Bamamukalal a buola* (A. B. Edmiston), 109
*Nkana mu Ncema* (APCM), 112
Nkrumah, Kwame, 231–32, 243, 265, 279, 284–85
Norden, Hermann, 136
Nottage, Lynn, 255–56
Nwankwo, Ifeoma Kiddoe, 13
Nyerere, Julius, 266, 279, 284
Nzongola-Ntalaja, Georges, 264

OAAU (Organization of Afro-American Unity), 257, 261–62, 264, 268–70, 280–86
OAU. *See* Organization of African Unity
O'Brien, Colleen, 148
*Of One Blood; Or, the Hidden Self* (Hopkins): Africa in, 149, 156–60; geography of, 145–46; plot, 139–41; Sheppards linked to, 141–45, 147; significance of, 150–51
Ogali, Ogali A., 235, 245
Ogden, Robert Curtis, 84, 168
"Oginga Odinga," 273–74
Okihiro, Gary, 97
On Guard, 232
*Open Letter to His Serene Majesty Leopold II, King of the Belgians and Sovereign of the Independent State of Congo, An* (G. W. Williams), 32, 33
Organization of African Unity (OAU): Cairo conference (1964), 262, 266, 358–59n125; King and, 268, 356n62; Malcolm X and, 264, 266, 281, 354n35, 358–59n125; OAAU and,

432  Index

261–62; Stanleyville negotiations, 265, 355n49
Organization of Afro-American Unity (OAAU), 257, 261–62, 264, 268–70, 280–86
Osadebay, Dennis, 234
*Outlook*, 84–86, 90

Page, Patti, 221, 345n103
*Palm-Wine Drinkard, The* (Tutuola), 238–39
Pan-African Conference (1900), 151–52, 159
Pan-African Congress (1921), 179, 210
Pan-African thought: Du Bois and, 94, 120–21; Ethiopianism and, 156; Hopkins and, 147, 149, 154; L. Hughes and, 217; Lumumba and, 226, 230
Park, Robert E., 79–80, 86–90, 314n45
Parker, Charlie "Bird," 236–37, 244
Patrice Lumumba Friendship University, 351n106
"Patrice Lumumba Speaks" (Lowenfels), 231
Patterson, Raymond R., 250–56
Peabody, George Foster, 181
Pease, Donald, 14
Peck, Raoul, 347n31
*Performing Blackness* (Benston), 234, 242–44, 246, 251
Perry, Rufus, 156–57
Phelps-Stokes Fund, 133–34, 229, 325n145
Philip, NoubeSe, 147
Phillips, James, *plate 9*, 198
Phipps, Joseph, *51*, 73–74, 109–10, *110*, 112, 309n47, 312n111
Phipps, William, 64–65, 76
*Photographs of African Negro Art* exhibition, 182
Picasso, Pablo, 164
Pickens, William, 214–15
Pierre, Jemima, 14–15, 164
Pike, Gustavus D., 122
*Pittsburgh Courier*, 75, 331n23, 348n52
*Poems from Black Africa* (L. Hughes), 222

poetry and poets: Baraka, 227, 228, 242, 244, 255, 286; Coltrane poems, 234, 242; Cortez, 236, 245–50, 291; V. H. Cruz, 235; F. Davis, 215; Di Prima, 241; P. L. Dunbar, 161; F. Harper, 156; M. Harper, 254–55; S. Henderson on, 236–37, 241–42, 250, 254; M. P. Johnson, 160–61; Jordan, 250; Kgositsile, 234, 235, 236; Lindsay, 10–11, 203; Lowenfels, 231; Neal on, 242, 250–53; R. Patterson, 250–56; N. Philip, 147; *Poetry*, 222; A. Spencer, 63, 310n62; surrealism in, 245–46, 247; Lorenzo Thomas, 248. *See also* Hughes, Langston; Joans, Ted; Lumumba poems; *and specific poets*
Powell, Adam Clayton, Jr., 280–81
Pratt, May Louise, 96
*Predicament of Blackness, The* (Pierre), 14–15, 164
Presbyterian Church (U.S.) (PCUS, Southern): colonial politics and, 115; *Missionary*, 52, 53, 54, 67–68, 74; racial policies of, 61–66, 73, 307n3, 309n47; W. Sheppard and, 49, 68. *See also* American Presbyterian Congo Mission
Presbyterian Church (U.S.A.) (PCUSA, Northern), 49, 73–74, 97, 109, 307n3
*Presbyterian Pioneers in Congo* (W. Sheppard), 65–70, *173*
*Primer of Facts Pertaining to the Early Greatness of the African Race and the Possibility of Restoration by the Its Descendants, A* (Hopkins), 153, 157, 158–59, 163
Primitive African Art Center, 181
*Primitive Negro Art* exhibition, 180
Primus, Pearl, 184–85
*Principia of Ethnology* (Delany), 158
print culture, African American. *See* African American print culture
Prophet, Nancy Elizabeth, 185
Pruitt, William, 137, 325n167
Psalm 68, 156, 159, 164

*Quilting Party* (J. Biggers), *plate 5*, 193–94
quiltmaking, 187–91, 193–94

racial uplift, 44, 74–75, 91, 106, 151, 160
Radano, Ronald, 126
raffia textiles. *See* textiles, Kuba
Rahman, Aishah, 225
RAM (Revolutionary Action Movement), 232, 286, 290
Rampersad, Arnold, 215, 217
Ratcliff, Anthony James, 232
Raushenbush, Winifred, 79
*Reason Why the Colored American Is Not in the World's Columbian Exposition, The*, 166
*Reconstructing Womanhood* (Carby), 141
recruitment of African Americans to Congo: Lumumba and, 228–29; Malcolm X and, 266–69, 277, 281–84, 354n35, 358–59n125, 359n130; Sheppards and, 50–52; G. W. Williams, 19–23; R. F. Williams, 286–87
Redmond, Eugene B., 246
Reed, Ishmael, 236
*Report on the Proposed Congo Railway, A* (G. W. Williams), 32, 43–44
*Report upon the Congo-State and Country to the President of the Republic of the United States of America, A* (G. W. Williams), 33, 42–43
return narratives: Awoonor, 291; Garvey, 136; Hopkins, 141–44, 147, 149–50; W. Sheppard, 67–68, 73–74, 149–50
Revolutionary Action Movement (RAM), 232, 286, 290
Ringgold, Faith, *plate 10*, 198–99, 340nn230–31
Rivalta, Pablo, 285
Roberts, Mary Nooter, 199
Robinson, John Winfrey, 95
Rochester, Adolphus, 50, 309n47

Rochester, Annie Katherine Taylor, 309n47
Rochester, Edna Atkinson, 309n47
Roessel, David, 216
Roosevelt, Theodore, 69
Root, Elihu, 101
Rowan, Carl, 232, 265
Rowbotham, Arthur, 53, 73
*Ruined* (Nottage), 255–56
*Rural Preacher* (J. Biggers). See *Country Preacher*
Russia, 215–16, 244
Ryan, Jennifer, 247

Saar, Alison, 199
Said, Edward, 45
Sales, William W., Jr., 262
Sanborn, Geoffrey, 142, 147
Sanchez, Sonia, 242
Sanders, Samella. *See* Lewis, Samella Sanders
Sanford, Henry Shelton, 8, 29, 288–90, 292, 293
"Sax Bit, The" (Joans), 244–45, 249
Scarborough, Dorothy, 123–24, 321n82
Schachter, Harry, 231–32
Schildkrout, Enid, 169
Schuyler, Philippa, 232
Scott, William, 50, 115
sculpture, African, 168–72, 174, 191–92, 194, 332n38, 332n48. *See also* Kuba art
Selassie, Haile, 281
*Selected Poems* (L. Hughes), 216
Seligmann, Herbert J., 214
Seme, Pixley ka Isaka, 93
Seon, Yvonne, 229, 236
September 11, 2001, 255, 291
Serguera, Jorge, 285
Shadrach, J. Shirley, 143, 327n20
Shepheard's Hotel, 217
Sheppard, Barry, 272
Sheppard, Lucy Gantt: career and legacy, 50–52, 76–77, 320n49; Locke and, 182, 336n128; musical work and interests, 50–51, 116, 144, 320n49; *Of*

*One Blood* and, 141–42; photo of, *50*, *57*, *110*
Sheppard, Maxamalinge "Max" William Lapsley, 68–69, *69*, 75–76, *110*, 200
Sheppard, Sarah Frances Martin, 97
Sheppard, William Henry: APCM reputation and impact, 52–55; arrival in the Congo, 49–50; attitudes toward, 73; in *Colored American Magazine*, 154; in *Crisis*, 10, 210–11; Hopkins compared to, 155–56, 159; Kuba and, 66–69; legacy and influence of, 3, 75–76; on Leopold regime, 54; S. Lewis linked to, 341n234; in Louisville, 74–75; Malcolm X and, 257–58; music and, 116–17, *117*; *Of One Blood* and, 143–44; photo of, *50*, *57*, *59*, *110*; removal from the APCM, 60; in *Southern Workman*, 10, 55, 75, 158–59, 170, 175–79; as transnational subject, 64–65; trial, 56–60; U.S. activities of, 73–75, 77; Verner and, 63; Washington and, 83; G. W. Williams and, 49
Sheppard, William Henry, works of: "From the Bakuba Country," 55–56; "The Future of Africa," 211; "Into the Heart of Africa," 71–73; "Light in Darkest Africa," 158, 175; *Presbyterian Pioneers in Congo*, 65–70; "True African Stories," 312n121
Sheppard art collection: acquisition of, 168, 169; in the classroom, 177, *178*; exhibition of, 174–75; at Hampton, 175–76; impact of, 186–87, 199; Lowenfeld and, 186; political aspects, 176–77; provenance and nature of, 170–71; role of, 183; sale of, 331n36; significance and impact of, 178–79; significance of, 164–65; textiles in, *plates 1–2*, 172–73
Sherman, John, 20, 289
Short, Wallace, 76, 336n128
shotgun house architecture, 191–92
Shyaam aMbul aNgoong, 169–70 332n38
Sieber, Roy, 174

Sieg, James McClung, *50*
"Simple and the Congo" (L. Hughes), 218–19
Sims, Lowry, 340n231
Slaughter, Henry, 302n32, 305n116
Slaughter, Joseph, 238–39
slavery: abolition in U.S., 81, 302n38; in Africa, 19, 23, 30; in "Chicago's Congo," 215; in "The Negro Speaks of Rivers," 214; songs of, 118, 122, 126; transatlantic slave trade, 74; Washington on Congo compared to U.S., 90–91
Smallwood, Stephanie, 74
(Smith), Hurley X, 236, 254
Smith, Charles Spencer, 47–48, 49, 146–47, 311n80
Smith, Shawn Michelle, 166
Smith, William Gardner, 285
Snyder, DeWitt, 53, 62, 73
"Somebody Blew Up America" (Baraka), 255
*Some European Observations and Experiences* (Washington), 102, 317n114
*Songs and Tales from the Dark Continent* (Curtis), 178
*Songs of Zion* (Campbell), 12
sorrow songs. *See* spirituals
*Soul and Spirit of John Biggers, The* (Phillips), *plate 9*, 198
*Soulbook*, 232
*Souls of Black Folk, The* (Du Bois), 117, 118–19, 196
South, the, Washington on, 98–99, 105–6
South Africa: Congo mercenaries from, 264–65, 270, 272, 274; HBCU students from, 93–94, 333n70; Malcolm X and, 261, 290; music and, 118–19, 121, 126; Washington and, 90, 93–94, 98, 101
*Southern Workman*: on African Americans in Africa, 23; *Colored American Magazine* compared to, 147–49; financing of, 328n55; Gregg and, 176; Hopkins and, 147; "Into the

*Southern Workman* (cont.)
Heart of Africa," 71–72; on Leopold II regime, 55; "Light in Darkest Africa," 158, 175; on recruitment of Hampton students, 21, 22–23; Sheppard art collection in, 170, 175–79, *179*; W. Sheppard in, 10, 55, 75, 158–59; transatlantic aspects, 74; Washington in, 78, 93; G. W. Williams in, 21–23. *See also* Hampton Normal and Agricultural Institute
Speer, Robert Eliott, 97
Spencer, Anne, 63, 310n62
Spencer, George, 183
"Spirit of Patrice Lumumba Lives, The" (Osadebay), 234
spirituals, 116–18, 121, 122–23, 125, 127
*Spirituals Triumphant* (Townsend), 126
Spurgeon, James Robert, 21, 26, 302n30
Stanley, Dorothy Tennant, 36, 37
Stanley, Henry Morton: *Autobiography of Sir Henry Morton Stanley*, 36; background of, 304n96; *The Congo and the Founding of Its Free State*, 21, 34, 36, 37; criticism of, 33–35; Du Bois on, 213; *In Darkest Africa*, 158; in *Of One Blood*, 145–46, 158; representations of, 35–38; Sanford and, 8, 29–30, 288–89; W. Sheppard and, 70–71; *Through the Dark Continent*, 35, 304n95; on U.S. involvement in the Congo, 29; G. W. Williams and, 31
Stanleyville (Kisangani), 220, 267, 269–71, 272–73, 353n1
"Star of the Congo" (Victor), 232
Starr, Frederick, 64, 167, 319n21
*Starry Crown* (J. Biggers), *plate 6*, 195
Stepto, Robert, 88
Stillman College, 63, 76, 112
Stiner, Larry "Watani," 233
St. Louis World's Fair, 62–64, 112, 166–67, 310n68
Stork Club, 217
*Story of the Congo State, The* (Wack), 86–87

*Story of the Jubilee Singers, The* (Marsh), 118
*Story of the Negro, The* (Washington), 91–92, 95, 98–99
Sumner, Doyle, 333n70
Sundquist, Eric J., 6, 118, 120, 122, 316n79
surrealism, 245–46, 247, 250
*Survey Graphic*, 181, 219
"Swing Low, Sweet Chariot," 117–18, 122–27
"Symposium on Traditional African Art," 174

Taft, William Howard, 101
Talladega College, 51, 115
Taylor, Katie Ann, 115
*Teducation* (Joans), 237, 240
Telli, Diallo, 230, 262, 264
Tervuren Exposition (1897), 166, 169
Texas Southern University (TSU), 192, 194–95, 339n202
textiles, Kuba: in African American art, 187–89, 195, 197–99; influence of, 199–200; patterns in, 173; photo of, *plates 1–2*, *173*, *178*; W. Sheppard and, 169; *Southern Workman* cover, *179*; use of, 172–74
*Theatre Arts Monthly*, 180
Theisen, Olive Jensen, 188, 191
Thesiger, Wilfred G., 56, *57*, 59–60
Thomas, Lillian. *See* DeYampert, Lillian Thomas
Thomas, Lorenzo, 248
Thompson, Robert Farris, 118, 164, 191–92
Thrasher, Max B., 87
*Three Quilters* (J. Biggers), 189–91, *190*, 195
*Through the Dark Continent* (Stanley), 35, 304n95
Thys, Albert, 20–21, 289
Tillery, Alvin, 348n52
*Time*, 222, 264, 270, 356n60
Tinson, Christopher, 230
*To Katanga and Back* (Conor Cruise O'Brien), 232

436  Index

Tolliver, Cedric R., 155
"Tom-Tom" (Ngoma), 235–36
Torday, Emil, 169–70, 171–72
Townsend, Willa, 126
*Tree House* (J. Biggers), *plate 8*, 197
Trotter, Geraldine Pindell, 150, 152–53
Trotter, William Monroe, 151–53
Tshiluba translation: dictionary, 130; of hymns and spirituals, 112, 116–17, 124–27, 138, 319nn21–22; of scripture, 111; "Swing Low, Sweet Chariot" in, 124–25
Tshombe, Moise, 219, 258–59, 264–65, 276
TSU (Texas Southern University), 192, 194–95, 339n202
Tuck, Stephen, 269
Turner, Henry McNeal, 81
*Turning South Again* (Baker), 14, 91, 97, 101–2, 105
Tuskegee Institute: African efforts, 85–86; attitudes toward, 329n79; Hampton compared to, 96–97; International Conference of the Negro at, 79, 86, 95, 314n65; international students at, 92–93; Malcolm X at, 277; role and purpose of, 95–96; significance of, 106; transnational aspects of, 78–79. *See also* Washington, Booker T.
Tutuola, Amos, 238–39
Twain, Mark, 55, 87, 89–90, 98, 141, 257–58, 353n6

*Umbra*, 248
*Une Saison au Congo* (Césaire), 235
UNIA (Universal Negro Improvement Association), 106
United Nations: African delegates, 228, 262, 271–72, 275, 285; Castro at, 283–84; Congo troops, 264; Freeman on, 232; Guevara at, 282–84; Hammarskjold death, 235, 349n67; L. Hughes on, 218–19, 222; Lumumba assassination protest, 222, 225–28, 231, 258–59; Malcolm X on, 275–76, 280

United States government: anti-Castro Cubans and, 264–65, 271, 277–78; Belgian collaboration, 133; Berlin Act ratified by, 20; Congo and, 27–28, 43, 137–38, 267–68; FBI, 358n125; Lumumba assassination and, 260–61; neocolonial activities of, 264–65, 272–73, 276; W. Sheppard and, 59–60; support for Congo emigration, 78; Tshombe and, 264–65; Vietnam and, 276–77, 354n40
United Transport Service Employees, 338n166
Universal Negro Improvement Association (UNIA), 106
Universal Peace Congress (1904), 83–84
Université Presbytérienne Sheppard et Lapsley du Congo (UPRECO), 76, 77
*Up From Slavery* (Washington), 80, 82, 83, 96
uplift ideology, 44, 74–75, 91, 106, 151, 160
UPRECO (Université Presbytérienne Sheppard et Lapsley du Congo), 76, 77

Vandermeeren, Gaston, 59–60
Vandervelde, Émile, 58–59
Van Eetvelde, Edmond, 40
Vann, Robert, 331n23
Vass, Lachlan Cumming, II, *50, 51*
Vass, Winifred Kellersberger, 118
Verner, Samuel Phillips, 62–64, 112, 310n59, 319n25
Victor, Desmond, 232
Vietnam, 276–77, 354n40
*Virginia Dreams* (M. P. Johnson), 160–61
Virginia Jubilee Singers, 121
Virginia Union University, 331n23
Vitalis, Robert, 180
"Voice of Congo" (Harleston), 212–13
*Voice of the Negro*, 154–55
von Herman, Beno, Baron, 95

Wack, Wellington, 86–87
Wafd Party, 209, 342n27

Wagner, Jean, 217
Walker (Randall), Roslyn, 174
Walker, Alice, 255
Wallace, Walter W., 148, 157
Wamba, Philippe, 292
Wardlaw, Alvia, 186, 193
Washburn, Hezekiah, 127–28, 135–36, 323n113
Washington, Booker T.: African interests, 78–80, 104–5; colonists and, 101; *Colored American Magazine* and, 151–52; "country districts," 98–99, 101–2; CRA and, 83–87; death and significance of, 106; on Douglass, 313–14n19; European travels of, 100–104; Garvey and, 106; localism of, 81–82; mobility of, 105; in poetry, 161; pragmatism of, 105; W. Sheppard and, 74; significance of, 90–91, 96–97, 106, 292; on the South, 98–99, 105–6; transnational aspects of, 82, 85, 89–91; Twain and, 89–90
Washington, Booker T., works: Atlanta Cotton States Exposition address, 80–82; "Cruelty in the Congo Country," 84–86, 88–89; "Industrial Education in Africa," 85–86; "Industrial Schools as an Aid to Missions," 97; *The Man Farthest Down*, 88; *My Larger Education*, 82, 103–4; *Some European Observations and Experiences*, 102, 317n114; *The Story of the Negro*, 91–92, 98–99; *Up From Slavery*, 80, 82, 83
*Washington Post*, 291
Watts, Daniel, 225–26, 227–28, 231
*Weary Blues, The* (L. Hughes), 210, 213
Welbeck, N. A., 265
Wells, Ida B., 5, 104
Wenzel, Jennifer, 235, 253, 291
*West African Pilot*, 349n63
*West Indian Gazette*, 277
"We Too" (L. Hughes), 219–20
Wharton, Catherine, 123
Wharton, Conway T., 123–24, 127–29, 323n113

"What Missionaries Have Done for the World" (A. B. Edmiston), 110
White, Ackrel E., 19, 167
White, Charles, 183–84, 187, 190, 199
White, Luise, 245
White, Walter, 12, 180
*Who Killed the Congo?* (Schuyler), 232
"Who Shook" (Joans), 243
Wilberforce University, 93–94, 121–22
Wilentz, Gay, 156–57
Willard, Carla, 106
Williams, George Washington: art collection, 165–66; career, 24, 25, 26, 30, 36; death, 41–42, 293, 305n116; Harrison and, 8–9; ideology, 44; influence, 3, 32–33, 38–39, 156; Leopold II and, 27, 30, 38; Mackinnon and, 39–40, 305n109; Malcolm X compared to, 287; recruitment drive of, 19–22, 44; response to works, 40–41, 46; Sanford and, 289–90; W. Sheppard and, 52; significance of, 37–38, 45, 46–48; Stanley and, 33–35, 38–39, 305n104
Williams, George Washington, works: *Centennial*, 24; *A History of the Negro Troops in the War of Rebellion*, 25; *History of the Negro Race in America*, 24–26, 28, 35; *New York Tribune* articles, 303n61; "The Opening of Africa," 31; *An Open Letter to His Serene Majesty Leopold II, King of the Belgians and Sovereign of the Independent State of Congo*, 32, 33, 38–39; *A Report on the Proposed Congo Railway*, 43–44; *A Report upon the Congo-State and Country*, 42–43
Williams, Robert F., 227, 228, 286–87, 351n150
Williams, R. Waldo, 228
Williams, Vernon, 81
Williams, Walter L., 100
Wilson, Ivy, 148
Wilson, Judith, 163–64
Wilson, Leonard, 38

Woman's Era Club, 151
Woodruff, Hale, 184, 185, 200, 333n64
Woodward, C. Vann, 106
Work, Monroe, 87
Works Project Administration (WPA), 149–50
Wright, Richard, 230
Wright, Sarah, 228

X, Hurley, 236, 254
X, Malcolm: African project, 280–87; Africa trips, 260–61; on anti-Castro Cubans, 264–65, 271, 277–78; "chickens coming home to roost," 260–61, 267–68, 272, 286; Congo readings of, 257–58; Cuban allies of, 282–86; in Detroit, 278–79; on expatriates, 279–80; Lumumba and, 230, 263, 361n12; on media, 269–70, 288; on Mississippi and Congo, 271–75; on neocolonialism, 264, 272; organizing diaspora Africans, 281–82, 284–85; recruitment of blacks to Congo, 264, 277–78, 287, 358n125; in Selma, 277; Telli and, 264, 266; G. W. Williams compared to, 290
Xuma, Alfred, 93–94

Yates, Barbara, 134
Young, Cynthia, 226
Young, Jason, 20
*Young Negro Artists* exhibition, 184
*Young Socialist*, 272

Zaghloul, Saad, 208, 209
Zanzibar Nationalist Party (ZNP), 285, 360n157
Zappo Zaps, 53–54
Zeidler, Jeanne, 197
Zimmerman, Andrew, 86, 106
ZNP (Zanzibar Nationalist Party), 285, 360n157

www.ingramcontent.com/pod-product-compliance
Lightning Source LLC
Chambersburg PA
CBHW051202300426
44116CB00006B/409